TERRORISM, 2002–2004

TERRORISM, 2002–2004

A CHRONOLOGY

VOLUME 1

Edward F. Mickolus and Susan L. Simmons

PRAEGER SECURITY INTERNATIONAL
Westport, Connecti

For the men and women of the Central Intelligence Agency
and all others around the world engaged in the battle against terrorism

Library of Congress Cataloging-in-Publication Data is available at www.loc.gov

British Library Cataloguing in Publication Data is available.

Copyright © 2006 by Edward F. Mickolus and Susan L. Simmons

ISBN: 0–313–33474–9 (set)
        0–313–33475–7 (vol. 1)
        0–313–33476–5 (vol. 2)
        0–313–33757–8 (vol. 3)

First published in 2006

Praeger Security International, 88 Post Road West, Westport, CT 06881
An imprint of Greenwood Publishing Group, Inc.
www.praeger.com

Printed in the United States of America

The paper used in this book complies with the
Permanent Paper Standard issued by the National
Information Standards Organization (Z39.48–1984).

10 9 8 7 6 5 4 3 2 1

CONTENTS

INTRODUCTION vii

2002–2004 INCIDENTS 1

UPDATES OF 1935–2001 INCIDENTS 389

1969–2004 BIBLIOGRAPHY 463

  General Topics 463

  Regional Approaches 542

    United States and Canada 542

    Latin America 567

    Europe 573

    Middle East 600

    Asia 623

    Africa 629

  Special Topics 632

    Nuclear, Mass Destruction, and High-Tech Terrorism 632

    Hostage-Taking and Hijacking 649

    Narcoterrorism 666

    State-Supported and -Conducted Terrorism 668

    Media 681

    Economic Terrorism and Economic Effects 693

Special Topics *(cont.)*

Internet Sites 694

    Terrorist Groups 694

    U.S. Government and Organization Home Pages 694

    University Affiliated Sites 696

    Additional Noteworthy Sites 696

Responses and Approaches 697

    Responses 697

    Legal Approaches 727

    Philosophical Approaches 748

    Psychological Approaches 754

Terrorism Topics in Fiction 773

Bibliographies on Terrorism Topics 788

COUNTRY AND DATE INDEX 793

NAME INDEX 805

SUBJECT INDEX 827

INTRODUCTION

Since 1974, my colleagues and I have written seven chronologies on international terrorism. This is the first volume that covers post-September 11, 2001, years and chronicles several major developments in the evolution of international terrorism as a threat to world public order and safety. Developments included sophisticated, multitarget attacks modeled after al Qaeda; the end of Saddam Hussein's regime; and the dispersal, imprisonment, or death of much of 's leadership. Sadly, increased international attention and revised approaches to the war on terrorism have yet to result in decreased incidence or impact.

To ensure comparability across volumes, we have continued to use the same definitions and criteria for inclusion. Our definition of terrorism is the use or threat of use of anxiety-inducing, extranormal violence by any individual or group for political purposes. The perpetrators may be acting for or in opposition to established governmental authority. Two key components of terrorism are influence and ramification. A terrorist action is intended to influence the attitudes and behavior of a target group wider than the immediate victims, and its ramifications transcend national boundaries through the nationality or foreign ties of its perpetrators, its location, the nature of its institutional or human victims, or the mechanics of its resolution. We thus do not include thousands of domestic terrorist events, such as when citizen of country X is attacked by citizen of country X in country X. Nor do we include attacks by insurgents on combatants. For example, attacks in Iraq on coalition forces in uniform are considered part of an ongoing military campaign, rather than terrorism. Attacks against civilians, however, constitute terrorism.

Although most 2002–2004 terrorist events showed little innovation and consisted of time-worn and, unfortunately, time-tested methods—simple pipe bombs, shootings, arson, threats—many incidents pressed the boundaries of what terrorists had earlier been willing to attempt. Al Qaeda, previously the leader in bloodthirstiness and daring, continued to shift its methods to deal with the new environment brought on by governments unwilling to face a September 11 sequel on their watch. While pre-September 11 al Qaeda attacks had taken several years to develop and rarely entailed claims of credit for al Qaeda by that name, post-September 11 attacks in the name of al Qaeda were taken by what appears to be a loosely affiliated set of organizations inspired by, but not necessarily controlled by, Osama bin Laden, Ayman Zawahiri, and the older generation of al Qaeda leaders. Their attacks ranged from fairly sophisticated, multitarget approaches as seen perpetrated by earlier al Qaeda terrorists to surprisingly amateurish attacks.

The post-September 11 global war on terrorism led by the United States put the original leadership of al Qaeda on the run. As of this writing, the Bush administration had reported that fully three-quarters of the group's leadership was in detention or in graves. Thousands of members and supporters of the organization and its affiliates had been detained for questioning throughout the world. Various coalitions of the willing rooted out al Qaeda and their Taliban associates from caves in Afghanistan and brought a fragile peace to a new administration in Kabul. A second military front of the war on terrorism ended the Iraq regime of Saddam Hussein, whose record of support to terrorists throughout his tenure was undeniable, even though many questioned his specific links to al Qaeda. Unfortunately, Islamic terrorists used the porous borders of the new Iraqi state to slip into what has become a shooting gallery against their perceived enemies—Americans and other members of the coalition.

The terrorist laboratory in Iraq has seen numerous groups of varying nationalities, motivations, and capabilities vying for recognition as the most callous. Terrorist Internet use, already favored by several leftist and irredentist groups around the world, was furthered by several Iraqi and visiting groups in Iraq to publish gory details of their actions. Through its September 11 attack, al Qaeda had established that it was looking to have a lot of people dead while a lot of people watched. In Iraq, terrorists ensured that their ability to bring eyeballs to their message would not be undermined by the unwillingness of several news organizations to broadcast videos of their atrocities. Rather, they resorted to populating Web sites with the same videos, showing screaming hostages begging for their lives before masked cowards beheaded them.

The shift to frequent beheadings in Iraq marked a new phase in terrorist violence as well. Begun initially as a headline-grabbing threat against American hostages, the tactic soon proliferated to threats against Kenyans, Turks, Somalis, Egyptians, Filipinos, Iraqis, and the gruesome murders of Nepalese. A shocked public feared to ask the question, "What could the terrorists devise that is even worse than *this*?"

Sadly, we may have seen an example of what's worse with the September 2004 takeover by Chechen rebels and their associates of the Beslan School Number 1. Twelve hundred hostages, including hundreds of children aged 6 to 16, were held, then brutally murdered by the hundreds. Shooting fleeing children in the back can hardly promote a political agenda to those who might otherwise be willing to listen, making any rationale behind this carnage incomprehensible.

Hostage cases in general shifted somewhat from their classical patterns. While they remained a major source of income for terrorists in Latin America, in Iraq they became a method of intimidating a wide range of governments, corporations, and individuals simply trying to feed their families. In any given month following the fall of Saddam Hussein, one could count up to 100 hostages from more than a dozen countries being held by a variety of shadowy groups. These groups called for their governments and corporations to leave Iraq to the tender mercies of various crazies. Negotiation rules shifted as hostage-takers —be they barricade-and-hostage, conveyance, or hidden victims (kidnappings) perpetrators—ended episodes far quicker than their terrorist forebears. The terrorist objective appeared to be to make a quick point and kill the hostage, rather than patiently negotiating for tangible rewards, such as freed colleagues or ransom demands. Gone appear to be the trend of the 1980s, when Hizballah would patiently wait out negotiators in Lebanon for months and years.

While al Qaeda, its affiliates, and its sympathizers get most of the media coverage concerning terrorism, al Qaeda has not cornered the market on the use of terrorism. Various leftists, rightists, environmentalists, animal rightists, separatists, irredentists, and other religious/cultists who employ terrorism to intimidate audiences and publicize their causes remain active. Despite a global concern about the spread of terrorism and an increased willingness by governments to cooperate, terrorism by all sorts of groups has continued apace.

Government responses to terrorism came under increased scrutiny around the world, but particularly so in the United States where various congressional commissions, pundits, news media, and the September 11 Commission made recommendations for sweeping government change based upon a snapshot in time. As of this writing, the ramifications and end-game of these recommendations are not in sight.

Official chronologies themselves became subject to intense scrutiny by the media, private research groups, and pundits. The U.S. State Department's widely disseminated *Patterns of Global Terrorism* series came in for criticism in 2004 when errors were found in the coverage of its 2003 chronology. Some observers attributed grave ulterior motives to the Bush administration based on scant evidence. Others who have worked in government suggested that it was probably simple human error. *Patterns* uses a different, congressionally mandated definition of terrorism and has different coverage criteria than these volumes. Data from *Patterns* and these chronologies (ITERATE numbers) are not comparable.

Where does the world go from here? Fear of terrorist use of weapons of mass destruction (WMD)—not just jetliners, but chemical, biological, radiological, and nuclear weapons—appears justified and remains on the front burner for many law enforcement and intelligence officials. Al Qaeda and its far-flung affiliates have already shown a willingness to take thousands of lives and sacrifice their own. Crossing these two barriers to using WMD causes many observers to believe that it is only a matter of time, acquisition, and planning before terrorists implement attacks that were once only the province of imaginative thriller writers.

And where this chronology goes from here is probably already decided in the caves and underground hideouts of numerous terrorists. Despite the best efforts of law enforcement, defense, homeland security, and intelligence services, the good guys still have to secure thousands of potential targets, whereas the terrorists can pick and choose. In baseball, a .998 fielding percentage sends you to the Hall of Fame. In combating terrorism, a .998 success ratio means failure in .002 cases and a lot of lives lost. A lot of lives will continue to be lost to terrorism in the years to come.

Readers of this series of chronologies will recognize its organization. The volumes are divided into three sections: Incidents, Updates, and Bibliography plus Indexes. The Incidents section provides a chronology and description of international terrorist activity from January 2002 to December 2004. The Updates section provides follow-up material to incidents first reported in previous chronologies. Updates are identified by the original incident date and include enough prefatory material to give some context to the events that succeeded the incident. The Bibliography section gives citations on key events and terrorist-related topics. It may be referenced for more detail on specific incidents described in the Incidents section. For the first time, bibliographies from the previous chronologies have been combined and included in this section.

Sources remain the same—major Western news print media (such as the *Washington Post, New York Times, Los Angeles Times, Washington Times*, and various local papers), news networks (such as CNN, MSNBC, CBS, ABC, NBC, Fox, National Public Radio), news services (such as Reuters, AFP, and AP), some foreign services (such as al-Jazeera), and scholarly articles, books, government reports, and conference presentations. We maintained consistent spelling of names and entities where we could, but translation, transliteration, changes of common usage over time, and the number of sources made absolute consistency impossible. Any differences can be traced back to differences in the source documents. We tried to rectify inconsistencies in dates or dead and injured counts, referencing variants to assist clarity. Again differences are due to differences in source documents. The many source documents led to gathering duplicate information and cross references about incidents. Any duplicate information present was kept in the interest of clarity and readability.

As in earlier volumes, the international terrorist incidents are identified by an 8-digit unique identification number or ITERATE (International Terrorism: Attributes of Terrorist Events) number. The first six digits identify the date on which the incident became known as a terrorist attack to someone other than the terrorists themselves (for example, the time bomb finally detonated even though set in place a week earlier; responsibility for an ambiguous event was later claimed by a terrorist group). The final two digits rachet the number of attacks that took place on that date. If the day or month is unknown, "99" is used in that field.

Events which do not have an ITERATE number have been included to give an idea of other types of episodes the world experienced. In some cases, they have been included to examine the types of threats and security environments in which the terrorists operate. In others, they offer incidents which the terrorists might watch and mimic, such as the Washington, D.C., area sniper attacks in October 2002. For further discussions of these conventions, please consult:

Mickolus, Edward F. *Transnational Terrorism: A Chronology of Events, 1968–1979.* Westport, CT: Greenwood Press, 1980. 967 pp.

Mickolus, Edward F., Todd Sandler, and Jean M. Murdock. *International Terrorism in the 1980s: A Chronology of Events, Volume I: 1980–1983.* Ames, IA: Iowa State University Press, 1989. 541 pp.

Mickolus, Edward F., Todd Sandler, and Jean M. Murdock. *International Terrorism in the 1980s: A Chronology of Events, Volume II: 1984–1987.* Ames, IA: Iowa State University Press, 1989. 776 pp.

Mickolus, Edward F. *Terrorism, 1988–1991: A Chronology of Events and A Selectively Annotated Bibliography.* Westport, CT: Greenwood Press, 1993. 917 pp.

Mickolus, Edward F., with Susan L. Simmons. *Terrorism, 1992–1995: A Chronology of Events and A Selectively Annotated Bibliography.* Westport, CT: Greenwood Press, 1997. 963 pp.

Mickolus, Edward F., with Susan L. Simmons. *Terrorism, 1996–2001: A Chronology, Volume 1 and Volume 2.* Westport, CT: Greenwood Press, 2002. 850 pp.

Events coded with an 8-digit number appear in Vinyard Software's ITERATE (International Terrorism: Attributes of Terrorist Events) numeric and textual databases. For those interested in running textual searches for specific groups, individuals, or incidents, computer versions of this and previous chronologies and bibliographies are available from Vinyard Software, Inc., 2305 Sandburg Street, Dunn Loring, Virginia 22027-1124. A numeric version offers circa 150 numeric variables describing the international attacks. Greenwood's online version of this material, including monthly additions of new incidents, will be available in 2006.

As always, many people have contributed to this research effort. My family again endured my disappearing act on nights and weekends with good grace, but just enough eye-rolling to remind me that I'm valued and missed. Susan's family suffered enigmatic, rhetorical queries like "a horse bomb?" and "who changed the spelling of fatwa?" along with her growing somberness as she worked her way through the manuscript. Thanks goes to Marie Sobolewski for her work verifying Web sites and helping to combine the bibliographies. Special thanks goes to Greenwood's Michael Hermann for shepherding this book to press.

Appreciation is also extended to all who sent comments and suggestions about the previous edition or publication citations for this one. Please continue to forward terrorism citations to me at Vinyardsoftware@hotmail.com to ensure inclusion in the next volume of the bibliography. Unfortunately, there will be a next volume in this series of chronologies.

2002–2004 INCIDENTS

2002. *Worldwide/Burma.* During the year, several Burmese embassies abroad received letters containing blasting caps and electric batteries. None of the devices exploded. 02999901

2002. *Egypt.* During the year, the government prosecuted 94 members (7 *in absentia*) of The Promise (al-Wa'ad) accused of having supplied arms and financial support to Hamas and Chechen rebels.

2002. *Paraguay.* Authorities arrested Hizballah fund-raiser Sobhi Fayad after he violated the terms of his conditional release from detention while awaiting charges. He had been in prison for nearly ten months on charges of tax evasion and criminal association before being tried. He subsequently was convicted and sentenced to six and one-half years in prison. Fayad was an associate of Assad Ahmad Barakat, who was himself arrested in June in Brazil on terrorism funding charges.

2002. *Brazil.* A Sao Paulo judge sentenced three Chileans, two Colombians, and an Argentine to 16 years in prison for kidnapping a Brazilian advertising executive. Among them was Mauricio Hernandez Norambuena, former senior member of the Manuel Rodriquez Patriotic Front (Chile).

January 2002. *Spain.* Police arrested Najib Chaib Mohamed, a Moroccan, for his alleged involvement in a suspected al Qaeda recruiting and logistics cell led by Imad Eddin Barakat Yarkas. Spanish authorities had arrested Yarkas in November 2001.

January 1, 2002. *Indonesia.* A hand grenade exploded in front of a restaurant at a busy Jakarta shopping center, killing one person.

January 2, 2002. *United States.* The Federal Bureau of Investigation (FBI) alerted eighteen thousand domestic law enforcement agencies that it had extended its nationwide warning of possible terrorist attacks until March 11.

January 3, 2002. *United States.* Talcum powder was found in an envelope postmarked from London and containing a threatening message addressed to Senate Majority Leader Thomas A. Daschle. The incident was ruled an anthrax hoax. Daschle had received an envelope with anthrax on October 15, 2001. The writer of the new envelope had attempted to mimic the handwriting. A staffer opened the letter at 11:40 a.m. and called Capitol Police. Daschle told reporters that the letter said that "this was , death to America … and stop the bombing." Police dismissed the claim of responsibility by Elijah Wallace, 18, who had been arrested on burglary charges in Fremont, New Hampshire. Wallace also claimed to have sent anthrax to the New Hampshire Department of Motor Vehicles in Concord and two businesses. His father said his son is a compulsive liar who had been treated in a psychiatric hospital.

January 3, 2002. *Red Sea.* Israeli navy commandos boarded the *Karine*, a cargo ship, some 300 miles off Eilat and found 50 tons of weapons—including Katyusha rockets, antitank missiles, mortars, mines, and sniper rifles—believed originating in Iran and destined for the Palestinian Authority. Israeli Army Chief of Staff Lt. Gen. Shaul Mofaz said the Palestinian Authority ship was captained by Omar Akawi (variant Akkawi), 44, a lieutenant colonel in the Palestinian Naval Police (part of the Palestinian Transportation Ministry). Yasir Arafat denied knowledge of the ship. The weapons were in quantities banned by the 1993 Oslo peace agreement. Israel said interrogation of the 13 crewmen determined that the arms smuggling was coordinated by Lebanese Hizballah. Israel said the ship was purchased for $400,000 in Greece or Bulgaria in October 2000 by Adil Mughrabi, who handles weapons purchases for the Palestinian Authority. The ship went on to Sudan, where a crew with five Palestinians boarded, including Omar Akawi. From there, the ship went to Iran, where it loaded eight boxes of weapons at or near the island of Qeshm. The cargo transfer was handled by Hizballah member Haj Muhammed. Akawi said he got his orders from someone in the Palestinian Authority and that the operation was overseen by Adel Awadallah. He said he joined Fatah in 1976. He claimed that a crewman recognized a Hizballah member when the tens of millions of dollars worth of weapons were loaded.

The Palestinian Authority arrested three men on January 11. They included Fuad Shubaki, a major general in Arafat's security forces whom Israel claims is the Palestinians' main weapons buyer. The trio also included Adel Mughrabi. In mid-February, Israeli Defense Minister Binyamin Ben-Eliezer said that Hizballah leader Imad Mughniyah had purchased the arms.

On May 1, as part of a deal between Israel and the Palestinian Authority that led to Yasir Arafat's release from his besieged headquarters, the Palestinian Authority turned over Fuad Shubaki, Arafat's chief accountant, to U.K. and U.S. guards.

On October 18, 2004, the Erez Military Court in Israel convicted Akawi of trafficking in weapons and sentenced him to 25 years in prison. Two other Palestinian crew members received 17-year sentences.

January 5, 2002. *United States.* Student pilot Charles J. Bishop, 15, of Palm Harbor, Florida, took off in a four-seat 2000 Cessna 172R without flight clearance at 5:00 p.m. and crashed it into the 28th floor of the 42-story Bank of America building in Tampa, killing himself but causing no other injuries. A few hours earlier, an attorney had been present in the office of Shumaker, Loop and Kendrick, where the plane hit. Bishop's grandmother had driven him to the airport for his National Aviation Academy flying lesson. The air traffic control center of the St. Petersburg–Clearwater Airport alerted the Coast Guard of the flight. Bishop ignored a Coast Guard helicopter's direction to land at a nearby airport. Two F-15s were scrambled from Homestead Air Reserve Base after the crash. The military didn't hear about the plane until it crashed into the building, even though it flew into restricted air space over MacDill Air Force Base. Bishop flew just a few feet over the MacDill control tower and 75 to 100 feet over two loaded tanker planes on the flight line. He also buzzed three base hangars. Police later found a suicide note in which he expressed support for bin Laden and the September 11 attacks. Police found that he had a prescription for Accutane, used to treat severe acne, which was the subject of a congressional investigation for possible links to suicide and depression. However, no drugs were found in his system.

On April 15, 2002, Bishop's family sued Hoffmann-La Roche, Inc., the maker of Accutane, for $70 million, alleging that the drug spurred his psychotic episode.

On January 17, 2003, the National Transportation Safety Board declared the crash a suicide.

The FBI released documents on June 19, 2003, suggesting that Bishop's original target might have been MacDill Air Force Base.

January 8, 2002. *United States.* Police arrested David Reza, 43, who had recently been fired from the San Onofre Nuclear Generating Station in north San Diego County, for threatening to kill his former coworkers. Police raided his

Laguna Niguel home and storage unit and discovered a cache of unregistered firearms. He had at his home 61 firearms—shotguns, pistols, rifles, and assault rifles. The Capistrano Properties Self Storage unit had another 200 firearms, about 5,000 rounds of ammunition, an expended anti-tank weapon similar to a rocket launcher, gunpowder, and 4 inert grenades. Only two weapons were registered. Two deputies were overcome by a cloud of yellow vapor when they opened an ammunition canister; the fumes were identified as military-grade tear gas. Reza was held without bail for making terrorist threats and possession of illegal firearms and narcotics. Reza had worked there since 1984 as a maintenance mechanic, but his access to the nuclear reactor area was permanently revoked in 1995 for undisclosed reasons.

January 9, 2002. *Israel.* At 4:20 a.m., two Hamas gunmen used grenades and assault rifles to kill four Israeli soldiers and injure two more during a predawn raid on a remote Israeli army outpost a few yards inside Israel beyond the gates of the southern Gaza Strip. The terrorists died in the gun battle. The dead soldiers were part of an Israeli Arab Bedouin infantry battalion. Israel said the terrorists were aided by six others who created a diversion by touching a security fence in several locations to set off numerous sensors.

January 9, 2002. *United States.* The Treasury Department blocked the assets of the Afghan Support Committee (set up by Osama bin Laden in Jalalabad, Afghanistan) and the Pakistan branch of the Kuwait-based Revival of Islamic Heritage Society, which allegedly diverted charitable contributions to al Qaeda. Treasury officials said that since September 23, it had blocked $34 million in the United States and arranged for the blocking of another $34 million in other countries of the assets of 168 entities. Treasury also banned Abu Bakr Jaziri, bin Laden's head of organized fund-raising, who served as the Committee's financial chief. Jaziri moved to Pakistan in 2000. Treasury also banned Abd Muhsin Libi,

manager of the Committee's office in Peshawar, Pakistan, and office director for the Revival of Islamic Heritage Society.

January 9, 2002. *Afghanistan.* Clark Bowers, 37, a political consultant from Harvest, Alabama, was kidnapped by a tribal warlord who demanded a $25,000 ransom. Bowers had been attempting to distribute medical and other supplies. His wife, Amanda, said he phoned on January 9, then called again on January 14 with details on how to pay the ransom. She said Bowers and an Afghan interpreter were on a chartered plane that left Istanbul for Kabul. The plane landed safely, but the duo was kidnapped and were driven blindfolded for several hours. Bowers had been to Afghanistan twice since September 11, according to his wife.

January 9, 2002. *Indonesia.* Local intelligence agents arrested Muhammad Saad Iqbal Madni, 24, an al Qaeda operative who had worked with would-be shoe bomber, Richard C. Reid. The *Washington Post* reported on March 11, 2002, that the Central Intelligence Agency (CIA) had provided information about his whereabouts to the State Intelligence Agency, and Egypt requested extradition. Iqbal held Egyptian and Pakistani passports. The stocky, bearded Iqbal was wanted on terrorism charges in Egypt. The *Post* reported that Indonesia sent him quietly to Egypt on January 11 without a court hearing or lawyer. He was put on an unmarked, United States-registered Gulfstream V parked at a Jakarta military airport and flown to Egypt. His name appeared on al Qaeda documents found in Afghanistan. Indonesian officials told the media that he had been sent to Egypt because of visa violations—failing to identify a sponsor for his visit. He had arrived in Jakarta on November 17, 2001. He had visited Solo located in central Java, which is believed to be a base for the al Qaeda affiliated Jemaah Islamiah, a military Muslim group with bases in Indonesia, Singapore, and Malaysia.

January 10, 2002. *United States.* Law enforcement authorities were investigating a plot to kill Florida Governor Jeb Bush with a truck bomb in Tallahassee.

January 12, 2002. *Spain.* Some 44 pounds of dynamite hidden in a stolen red Renault exploded during the afternoon in downtown Bilbao, wounding two people with flying glass. The Basque Nation and Liberty (ETA) claimed credit. A caller phoned a warning to a newspaper, but authorities could not find the bomb soon enough.

January 12, 2002. *Venezuela.* In El Amparo, armed militants kidnapped an Italian and a Venezuelan. On May 17, a defector from the Revolutionary Armed Forces of Colombia (FARC) released the hostages. 02011201

January 13, 2002. *India.* Two knife-wielding Muslim militants attacked two Indian military officers in Srinagar, the summer capital of Indian Kashmir. The duo, carrying Dutch passports, were shot dead. 02011301

January 14, 2002. *Yemen.* The United States suspended consular services in San'a and warned that Americans could be terrorist targets. A caller had warned the previous day that the mission and American citizens would be attacked. The *Washington Post* reported on January 22 that the tipoff came from Ibn al-Shaykh al-Libi, the former head of al Qaeda training in Afghanistan, during interrogation at a U.S. military base in Qandahar. Al-Libi mentioned a plan to set off a truck bomb at the U.S. Embassy in Yemen. U.S. officials said information from interrogations of al Qaeda prisoners helped thwart attacks in Singapore and Bosnia as well. 02011401

January 14, 2002. *Israel.* Raed Karmi, 27, a Palestinian militant, died when a bomb exploded outside his hideout in Tulkarm, West Bank. He had lost an eye via shrapnel in a bombing on September 6, 2001, and was on Israel's most-wanted list. Israel neither confirmed nor denied

Palestinian charges of culpability. Prime Minister Ariel Sharon's office said Karmi was responsible for numerous shootings and the deaths of nine Israelis. The al-Aqsa Martyrs Brigades said it would resume attacks against Israel after a month-long stand-down.

Israeli officials said on January 23, 2001, Karmi was among four Palestinian gunmen who kidnapped two Israeli restaurateurs from a Tulkarm sandwich shop while they were lunching with an Arab friend. The Israelis were bound, gagged, and shot in the head near the shop. Karmi said it was in revenge for the assassination three weeks earlier of Thabet, a local Palestinian leader. The four were jailed by the Palestinian Authority but escaped after a few months in custody. They later often appeared in public. Israel also accused Karmi of several drive-by shootings, snipings, and bombings that injured more than a dozen people and killed nine.

January 15, 2002. *Israel.* Palestinian gunmen shot to death two carriers of U.S. passports in Bayt Sahur, West Bank, near Jerusalem. The dead included American Avi Boaz, 72, an architect who moved to Israel from New York 40 years earlier but had never obtained U.S. citizenship. (The U.S. State Department's *Patterns of Global Terrorism 2002* said he had dual U.S.–Israeli citizenship.) He had Jewish blood relatives close by in Israel—a daughter and baby grandson. He also had close Arab friends. He was pulled from his car, taken to a field, and shot to death. The other victim was a 45-year-old motorist who was shot as she entered a gas station. According to Prime Minister Ariel Sharon, she also held a U.S. passport. The al-Aqsa Martyrs Brigades said the attack was in revenge for the killing of Raed Karmi and deemed Boaz "a filthy Israeli agent." Boaz was born in Israel and lived in Maale Adumim, a West Bank settlement. He was driving to buy materials at midday when the gunmen grabbed him at a Palestinian police post near Bethlehem. They pulled out a Palestinian passenger, Bashir Arjas, pistol-whipped him, then drove the car to Beit Sahour, where they fired 13 bullets into him. In the second attack, the female driver, Yoela Chen, 45, was killed and her passenger, a 70-year-old aunt or mother of Chen, was hit in the chest and injured. Chen was a resident of the West Bank settlement of Givat Zeev. The gunmen ran toward the village of Jib.

The Palestinian Authority announced the arrest of Ahmed Saadat, leader of the Popular Front for the Liberation of Palestine (PFLP) that had killed Israel Tourism Minister Rehavam Zeevi in October 2001. 02011501

January 16, 2002. *United States.* The FBI warned law enforcement agencies that terrorists could use government Web sites to learn about vulnerabilities of the U.S. infrastructure, such as water plants, reservoirs, dams, storage sites for highly enriched uranium, nuclear and gas facilities, and other installations.

January 17, 2002. *United Kingdom.* British police charged Algerians Baghdad Meziane, 37, and Brahim Benmerzouga, 30, with planning and financing terrorist acts for al Qaeda in Leicester. Local police also detained 11 other men on charges of terrorism and immigration fraud. Prosecutors said Meziane had raised money to finance terrorist acts and had planned an attack overseas. Benmerzouga was charged with similar offenses and "possessing racially inflammatory materials." French media said the Leicester cell planned and financed an aborted al Qaeda effort in 2001 to bomb the U.S. Embassy in Paris. The duo was to appear in court the next week for a bail hearing. 02011701

January 17, 2002. *Afghanistan.* U.S. authorities announced that videotapes found in an al Qaeda compound indicated that five terrorists, including a September 11 accomplice, could be on the loose and planning suicide attacks against Western targets. The tapes were found near Kabul in the bombed house of the late al Qaeda commander Muhammad Atef and appeared to be the final words of the terrorists before they went off on planned operations. Four of the men were identified as Ramzi Binalshibh (an

Atta colleague), Abd al-Rahim, Muhammad Sa'id Ali Hasan, and Khalid Ibn Muhammad al-Juhani. Binalshibh, a Yemeni wanted by Germany, who had helped to organize and finance the September 11 attacks from Hamburg. He had attempted to enter the United States several times to join the hijackers. He was an unindicted coconspirator in the case against Zacarias Moussaoui. Al-Juhani kissed a Kalashnikov rifle on camera. Hasan read something in his hands. Al-Rahim gestured at the camera.

On January 25, authorities said two Tunisian-born Canadian citizens were al Qaeda terrorists who vanished with four others and may be planning suicide attacks on Americans. Al Rauf bin Al Habib bin Yousef al-Jiddi, 36, was identified as the fifth man in the videos. U.S. military forces also found a suicide note written by al-Jiddi in August 1999. U.S. authorities said he could be traveling with Tunisian-born Canadian Faker Boussora, 37. They were believed to have left Montreal with Canadian passports in November. The United States said that the terrorists might have been killed in a U.S. bombing in Afghanistan. Al-Jiddi used six aliases and arrived in Canada in 1991. He obtained Canadian citizenship in 1995 and a local passport in 1999 using the name Abderraouf Jdey. Boussora obtained his passport in October 2000. Al-Jiddi was seen conducting surveillance in Canada several times before the September 11 attacks. He generally dressed in Western clothes.

January 17, 2002. *Israel.* A Palestinian gunman fired an M-16 assault rifle into a bat mitzvah celebration in Hadera in northern Israel, killing 6 and wounding 30 before the crowd beat him unconscious and police shot him to death. Couples were videotaped on the dance floor when the terrorist entered the David's Palace wedding hall at 10:45 p.m. Most of the guests were Russian-speaking immigrants, who reported that the terrorist was carrying grenades in his belt. The terrorist was Abed Hassouneh of the al-Aqsa Martyrs Brigades, Fatah's military wing. He made a video pledging to avenge the death of

Raed Karmi. The group claimed credit in a call to the Associated Press.

January 19, 2002. *Bosnia.* U.S. forces detained five Algerians and a Yemeni and flew them to a detention camp in Guantanamo Bay after they were ordered released by the Bosnian Supreme Court for lack of evidence.

January 20, 2002. *United Kingdom.* A bomb threat scrawled in soap on a restroom mirror diverted a Virgin Atlantic Airways B-747 flight to Keflavik, Iceland. The flight was en route from London to Orlando with 322 passengers and 18 crew. The crew found anti-American messages and asked passengers for handwriting samples. Police found no explosives on board. On March 28, federal authorities arrested Michael Philippe, 25, a flight attendant, for falsely reporting that he had found the note stating, "Bin Laden is the best Americans must die there is a bomb on board Al Quaida" written on an air sickness bag in the plane's restroom. No bomb was found. Philippe faced 20 years for interference with and intimidating a flight crew. On May 16, a federal grand jury indicted him; he could face life in prison on the new charges of threatening to use a weapon of mass destruction against U.S. citizens, communicating false information and so endangering the safety of a flight, intimidating flight crew members, and lying to an FBI agent. The charges carried maximum respective sentences of life in prison, 20 years, 20 years, and 5 years. 02012001

January 21, 2002. *Somalia.* Somalia's transitional government announced that in December it had arrested 20 people, including 8 Iraqis, for possible links to terrorism. Not all of the Iraqis were still held.

January 22, 2002. *India.* At 6:30 a.m., four gunmen on two motorcycles fired AK-47 automatic weapons at the guard post of the American Center, a U.S. cultural center on Jawaharlal Nehru Road in downtown Calcutta, killing 5 policemen and wounding 20 people, including police

officers, pedestrians, and a private security guard hired by the U.S. government. No one was in the building, which houses a two-story library, the U.S. Embassy's public affairs office, and a wing for cultural programs. The U.S. Consulate is located nearby. Some 54 shell casings were found at the scene. Authorities questioned 55 people, detaining 3. Somen Mitra, a senior police official, said many were "associated with the underworld in Calcutta." Other police officials announced the arrest of six people at an Islamic school—three Bangladeshis and three Indians. Various sources blamed Pakistan, al Qaeda, and local criminals aiming at police. A group of Indian criminals and an Islamic militant group based in Pakistan separately claimed credit. Farhan Malik, leader of the criminal Reza Commando Force (variant Asif Raza Commandoes), phoned Calcutta police to claim credit. Police said the group's leaders are based in Dubai, United Arab Emirates, and have ties to Pakistani intelligence and Kashmiri separatists. Harkat-e-Jihad-e-Islami (variant Harakat ul-Jihad-I-Islami), a Kashmiri separatist group with bases in Bangladesh, also claimed responsibility, although leader Mohammed Rizwan Kashmiri denied it.

A fifth Indian policeman died of his injuries on January 31.

On February 9, 2002, Indian police said that Indian national Aftab Ansari phoned them from the United Arab Emirates to take credit. He was extradited on February 9 after he was arrested attempting to travel out of the United Arab Emirates with Pakistani travel documents. The United Arab Emirates also deported his accomplice, Raju Sharma, who is wanted in India on weapons charges. The Indian Foreign Ministry said Ansari was in contact with Omar Saeed, chief suspect in the January 23 kidnapping of *Wall Street Journal* reporter Daniel Pearl. Ansari and Saeed met in an Indian prison. Ansari was serving time in the 1990s for criminal operations; Saeed was sentenced for kidnapping Western tourists. In 1999, Saeed was one of the prisoners freed during the hijacking to

Afghanistan of an Indian Airlines flight carrying 168 passengers.

By March 4, the Pakistani prosecution was worried that they had slim evidence against the four men charged with the kidnap/murder and terrorist activities—Saeed, Salman Saqib, Sheik Adil, and Fahah Naseem. The latter trio were believed to have sent the e-mail. Seven other suspects remained at large. 02012201

January 22, 2002. *United States.* The Department of the Treasury announced that foreign governments had frozen another $10 million belonging to the Taliban and al Qaeda terrorists, bringing the total since September 11 to $80 million.

January 22, 2002. *Israel.* During the afternoon, Said Ramadan, a Palestinian gunman, fired at people on busy Jaffa Street near Zion Square in West Jerusalem, shooting an M-16 assault rifle into a crowded bus stop. Ramadan fatally wounded 2 women and injured 14 other Israelis before being shot to death by policeman Sgt. Hanan Ben Naim. The al-Aqsa Martyrs Brigades claimed credit. One woman was in critical condition and six others were in serious to moderate condition. Among those injured was a bus driver, Chaim Salah.

January 22, 2002. *India.* In Jammu, Kashmir, a bomb exploded in a crowded retail district, killing one and injuring nine. No one claimed credit.

January 22, 2002. *Pakistan.* Ghulam Hasnain, a Pakistani reporter for *Time* magazine, was kidnapped and held for more than 30 hours by unknown individuals. He had been investigating local Islamic militant groups.

January 23, 2002. *Pakistan.* American Daniel Pearl, 38, a *Wall Street Journal* reporter based in Bombay since 1990, disappeared in Karachi after a taxi dropped him off at the Village Restaurant for an evening meeting with a representative of Harkat ul-Mujaheddin. He met with two members of the group at the restaurant, then was told a meeting with a more senior member would be held elsewhere. He phoned his wife at 7:00 p.m. to say he would be home late for dinner, but did not show up. Police detained the cabbie and a Pakistani journalist who helped arrange the interview, and were searching for a Pakistani representative of the group that corresponded with Pearl via e-mail from Rawalpindi. The United States had earlier declared the group a terrorist organization.

Pearl had been investigating the ties between the December 22, 2001, would-be al Qaeda shoe bomber Richard Reid and Pakistani Islamic groups. Pearl was also attempting to trace Reid's Karachi-based cyber café e-mail.

Pearl's freelance journalist wife, Mariane, is six-months pregnant and had lived with him in Karachi following the September 11 attacks.

On January 26, the previously unknown National Movement for the Restoration of Pakistani Sovereignty sent an e-mail with four photographs of Pearl. In one, Pearl was seated in front of a blue curtain with his head bowed and his wrists in chains. A white-robed terrorist was holding a gun to his head and yanking on his hair. Another photo had Pearl holding a current copy of *Dawn*, a local newspaper. The e-mail noted, "The National Movement for the Restoration of Pakistani Sovereignty has captured CIA officer Daniel Pearl, who [was posing] as a journalist of the *Wall Street Journal*." The Pakistani group demanded the release of Pakistanis detained on Guantanamo on suspicion of helping al Qaeda. The e-mail said that "they will be tried in a Pakistani court." Pearl's freedom would be obtained if "all Pakistanis being illegally detained by the FBI inside America merely on suspicion" were given legal counsel and allowed to see family members. The group also demanded the delivery of U.S. F-16 fighters that Pakistan had purchased in the 1980s but not received because of congressional sanctions imposed in 1990. The e-mail was sent to 31 addresses, including six *Washington Post* individuals, nine departments of the *New York Times*, and one department of the *Los Angeles Times*, plus media and government agencies in Pakistan, the United Kingdom, and the United Arab Emirates. The *Wall Street Journal* was not on the dissemination list. The *Post* addresses appeared to have been taken alphabetically from an employee list, starting with National Editor Michael Abramowitz. All of their last names began with the letters A, B, or C. A CIA spokeswoman and a *Journal* spokesman denied that Pearl worked for the CIA. The e-mail, from "kidnapperguy," said Pearl was being kept in "inhumane" conditions to protest U.S. treatment of prisoners in Cuba.

Investigators determined that the kidnappers used false identities, cell phones purchased using faked names, and e-mail from cyber cafés.

On January 29, *Wall Street Journal* managing editor Paul Steiger told the kidnappers via e-mail that the *Journal* was willing to work with them and underscored that the hostage "has never worked for the CIA or the U.S. Government in any capacity." He added, "You should know that Danny has a wife. I would like to you know that she is greatly distressed over Danny's situation. She hopes that you will come to understand that keeping Danny will not alter U.S. Government policy or accomplish your goals.... He has no ability to change the policies of the U.S. Government or the Government of Pakistan. Nor do I. Therefore, I would ask that you release Danny so that he may return home safe to his wife and soon-to-be-born child." Steiger issued a similar open letter on February 4, while Pearl's wife said she was willing to die in his place.

Pakistani police said a man calling himself Bashir told Pearl he represented Harkat. They met via two Pakistani journalists. Pearl and the two journalists met Bashir and a man named Arif (true name Hashim) two weeks earlier in a Rawalpindi hotel room. Bashir offered an interview with Sheik Mubarik Ali Gilani, head of Jamaat ul -Fuqra, which had earlier been on the U.S. terrorist list. Pearl was looking into links between Reid and Gilani. The two kept in touch via phone and e-mail; Bashir used the address "nobadmashi" (Urdu for "not a crook"). Bashir

offered a meeting at the restaurant with a Harkat leader named Amir Siddiqi (police later determined this was faked). Witnesses said Pearl met two bearded men. The cell phone the kidnappers used to call Pearl before the meeting was purchased under a fake name and address. It was also used to call New Delhi twice after the kidnapping. Police suggested it was an attempt to finger Indian intelligence.

Police detained Gilani's son and raided his offices in Lahore and a Northwest Frontier Province site, but said that the group probably was not involved. Gilani turned himself in to Rawalpindi police, claiming no knowledge of the kidnapping.

Hashim (alias Arif), a known Harkat member, was wanted on seven murder charges. Police visited Hashim's father in Bahawalpur, where they were told that he had been killed in Afghanistan. Police said, "We will not buy the story unless we can get an independent confirmation."

Kidnapperguy e-wrote again to news organizations on January 30, threatening to kill Pearl within 24 hours if the demands were not met. Two more photographs were attached to the rambling, frequently misspelled note. One photograph showed a man holding a revolver in both hands, aimed at Pearl's head. This time, the kidnappers decided that Pearl was not working for the CIA, but for Mossad. "Therefore, we will execute him within 24 hours unless amreeka flfils our demands. We apologise to his family for the worry cause and we will send them food packages just as amreeka apologised for collateral damage and dropped food packets on the thousands of people ... it had killed [sic]." The group also warned that U.S. journalists should leave Pakistan within three days unless the demands were met. "Anyone remaining after that will be targetted."

Another e-mail showed up on January 31, saying the execution had been delayed 24 hours. The group made the same demands, noting, "We will give you one more day. If America will not meet our demand we will kill Daniel. Then this cycle will continue and no American journalist could enter Pakistan." The group also demanded the release of Abdul Salam Zaeef, former Taliban ambassador to Pakistan. U.S. Secretary of State Colin Powell said that these "are not demands that we can either deal with or enter into a negotiation about."

Pakistan suggested that India could be involved because six phone calls were made to two New Delhi numbers via a cell phone used by a suspect.

A BBC reporter in Islamabad said he had received a message from the group several weeks after the September 11 attacks. The message included a photo of a photo of a man with a gun to his head. He was identified as Joshua Weinstein, of unknown nationality. U.S. law enforcement had deemed it a hoax, as no one by that name had lived in Pakistan.

Things became more complicated on February 1, when one group sent an e-mail to CNN and Fox News claiming to have killed Pearl, while the U.S. Consulate in Karachi was phoned by an individual demanding $2 million and the Taliban diplomat's freedom for his release. Police searched Karachi's 400 cemeteries after an e-mail said the body had been dumped in a graveyard. The all-night search as of February 2 had turned up nothing. The e-mail said, "We have killed Mr. Danny. Now Mr. Bush can find his body in the graveyards of Karachi. We have thrown him there. The reason why we killed him is because United States killed so many people in Afghanistan and other parts of the world and said ... the people who are killed are collateral damage." Police believed the ransom demand was a hoax.

Police also raided a middle class suburb in east Karachi and seized a computer used to send two of the four e-mail. Neighbors said it was recently rented but used only sporadically. Authorities had said that the first two e-mail were sent from a public cyber café. The second two e-mail differed from the first in the type of language used and in not including photos.

Other messages claiming to be from the kidnappers and saying that other messages were hoaxes, propaganda, or otherwise not to be trusted pelted the news media.

The body of a light-skinned man in his late 30s was found in Pakistan on February 3; some believed it was Pearl's. Police said it was that of an Iranian.

On February 5, police arrested three youths in a Karachi suburb and accused them of sending the e-mail. They had been handed the texts by Sheik Omar Saeed, believed by police to be one of the two men who met Pearl in the restaurant. The trio were linked to Jaish-i-Muhammad. Two of the youths admitted fighting alongside the Taliban in Afghanistan. One of the three, Adeel, was a member of the Pakistani police force serving in the Sindh Province's police intelligence department.

On February 6, Pakistani police said Sheik Omar Saeed, 27, who was freed from an Indian prison in 1999 during the hijacking of an Indian Airlines flight to Afghanistan, was a key suspect after he was fingered by several people who were arrested in connection with the kidnapping. Several Saeed family members were detained. Saeed was born in London and has U.K. citizenship. He attended the London School of Economics and Politics. He went to Bosnia on a charity mission in 1993. He then received military training in Khost, Afghanistan, and has ties to the banned Islamic radical groups Harkat ul-Mujaheddin and Jaish-i-Muhammad. In 1994, he kidnapped four Western tourists in Indian Kashmir, then was captured after being wounded in a shootout. Saeed spoke with his aunt over a cell phone on February 5, during which she told him she was in police custody and asked him to turn himself in. She and one of her three sons were later released.

The next day, police said e-mail recovered on the hard drive seized with the trio was linked to Saeed. The e-mail was traced to an Internet service provider in a Karachi apartment complex. The laptop computer belonged to Farhad Naseem. Naseem admitted receiving the e-mail from Saeed, who remained at large.

On February 8, Pakistani President General Pervez Musharraf said that Indian intelligence agencies could have been involved in the kidnapping. Investigators privately said they doubted that the phone calls from the kidnappers' cell phone to two members of the Indian Parliament and an Indian cabinet minister were legitimate, and had been placed to throw off the investigation.

Police asked for assistance from Masood Azhar, the jailed leader of Jaish-i-Muhammad, who called Saeed from his cell asking for Pearl's release. Saeed took the call on his cell phone, but denied involvement.

Saeed surrendered to Lahore police just before dawn on February 12 (although later reports said February 5). He said that Pearl was alive and admitted to involvement in the kidnapping. He insisted he did not know the victim's whereabouts. On February 14, a judge ordered him held for two more weeks on kidnapping charges. There were no plans to extradite him to the United States.

Police also quizzed two former members of the Inter-Services Intelligence (ISI) Agency. Khalid Khawaja, a former mid-level ISI official and friend of Gilani, was detained after the English-language the *News* said he was a Pearl contact. Khawaja had written to the newspaper saying he had not introduced Pearl to the abductors. Police also detained ISI alumnus Aslam Khan Sherani. The two had been close to Islamic guerrillas, including Osama bin Laden.

Saeed told his interrogators that while he was involved in planning the kidnapping, another group provided the safe house. He also backed off from saying that Pearl was alive and soon told a Karachi court that he was dead, shot while trying to escape around January 31. He had called his accomplices to tell them to release Pearl on February 5, saying "shift the patient to the doctor," but was told "Dad has expired." Saeed said his partner was Hyder, known to Pearl as Imtiaz Siddique, whom police identified as Mansur Hasnain, who was involved in the Indian air hijacking. Police raided the Hasnain residence in Punjab's Toba Tek Singh town and detained some of his relatives.

Meanwhile, Pakistani President General Pervez Musharraf, during his visit to the Oval Office, said that Pearl was alive.

Saeed further endeared himself to local authorities on February 17 when he said that the kidnapping was a "warning shot" to Musharraf for his crackdown on Islamic militants. He said three recent attacks in India—against the U.S. cultural center in Calcutta, the Indian Parliament, and a Kashmir legislative assembly—were aimed at provoking India against Pakistan. He claimed he visited Afghanistan a few days after September 11 to meet with bin Laden and then met with Aftab Ansari, chief suspect in the U.S. cultural center shooting, while the duo was jailed in New Delhi's Tihar prison. He also identified the attackers against the Indian Parliament.

As of February 18, Pakistani authorities were searching for Haider Ali Faruqi (alias Hyder), who was believed to have carried out the kidnapping, Mansur Hasnain, Mansur Hussain, and Imtiaz Siddiqi.

On February 20, a three and one-half minute (some reports say three and one-half hours) digital videotape of the terrorists slitting Pearl's throat and mutilating his body was delivered to authorities in Pakistan and relayed to the U.S. Consulate in Karachi on February 21. Pearl's body was not found. Some news media reported that Pearl's last words on the tape were "I am a Jew and my father was a Jew." (Other reports claimed he said, "My mother was a Jew.") He also read scripted lines about Pakistani prisoners at Guantanamo Bay. However, other news services said that the tape did not have an audio track. The tape jumps from scene to scene, ending with the knife sitting on Pearl's chest and a terrorist holding Pearl's severed head. The man who delivered the videotape claimed to be a journalist and was held for questioning. The video was interpreted by many as suggesting that the kidnappers never intended to free him alive. Analysts said that Pearl had been cut in the chest and was probably already dead when his throat was slit. The "I am a Jew" angle suggested an Arab accomplice.

Saeed said that a parallel attack against the U.S. Consulate was also planned. A phoned threat was made against the consulate in early February.

The United States requested that Pakistan turn over Saeed to the United States and offered a $5 million reward for information leading to the arrest or conviction of the kidnappers and murderers. Saeed had been indicted in the United States for the 1994 kidnapping of four Westerners, including a U.S. citizen, in India. Mrs. Saeed on March 2 asked a Pakistani court to block extradition.

On March 14, 2002, a federal grand jury in U.S. District Court in Trenton, New Jersey, indicted Saeed with conspiracy to commit hostage-taking that resulted in Pearl's death, and hostage-taking that resulted in his death; both are capital crimes. The indictment said he used the alias Chaudrey Bashir to send the e-mail to Pearl offering the meeting with the cleric. Prosecutors also unsealed a secret indictment filed in November 2001 in a Washington, D.C., federal court that said he had participated in the 1994 kidnapping of U.S. tourist Bela J. Nuss in India for 11 days.

On March 15, 2002, George Washington University President Stephen Tractenberg told a memorial service on campus that he had set up a full four-year scholarship for Pearl's unborn son.

On March 22, Pakistan charged 11 men with the kidnap/murder of Pearl. Chief among them was Sheik Omar Saeed (alias Ahmad Omar Saeed Sheik) and an accomplice, Sheik Adil, who were brought into an antiterrorism court on capital charges of murder, kidnapping for ransom, and terrorism. A March 29 trial date was set. Several other defendants remained at large. The defendants included veteran policeman Sheik Adil, Faha Naseem, and Salman Saqib, who were accused of purchasing the scanner and digital camera used for the e-mail. Prosecutor Raja

Quereshi said he would call 31 witnesses, including taxi driver Nasir Abbas who drove Pearl to the restaurant, where he saw Pearl meet Saeed. The accomplices were represented by attorney Khawaja Naveed Ahmed. The State Department ordered dependents and nonessential workers out of its diplomatic facilities in Islamabad, Lahore, Karachi, and Peshawar.

Pearl's trial was delayed on April 5 when the judge ordered prosecutors to share basic evidence with the defense. The defense also requested that Judge Arshad Noor Khan be disqualified because he heard Saeed's confession, which was not under oath. The trial was again delayed on April 12 to enable the court to try conspirators still at large. The trial was to be reconvened on April 22.

On April 19, 2002, Judge Arshad Noor Khan was removed from the case because he was present during a February 14 hearing at which Saeed had admitted his role in the kidnapping; Saeed later recanted. Judge Abdul Ghafoor Memon replaced him.

During the trial on April 22, the four defendants pleaded not guilty at the courtroom in the Karachi city jail. Each faced the death penalty in the nonjury trial on charges of kidnapping for ransom, conspiracy, murder, and acts of terrorism. Seven other suspects still at large would not be tried *in absentia*. Initial witness taxi driver Nasir Abbas said he saw Pearl shake hands with Saeed and join him in the backseat of a white Toyota Corolla the day Pearl was kidnapped. On April 23, two Pakistani police officers testified that they heard Saeed admit involvement in the kidnapping. That same day, defendant Salman Saquib said witness Jameel Yusuf was a Jewish agent.

The next day, Chief Prosecutor Raja Quereshi said defendants Sheik Adil and Salman Saquib had made threatening gestures in the courtroom. Four law enforcement agencies uncovered plans by the Jaish-i-Muhammad to blow up the Karachi city jail where the trial was being held. The trial was moved to Hyderabad on May 2 despite defense protests. A third judge, Ali Ashraf Shah, headed the hearings. In early May, defense attorney Rai Bashir told the judge that unfit jurists would be condemned to hell. Outside the courtroom, he accused Prosecutor Raja Qureshi of blasphemy. Bashir accused witness Asif Farooqui, a Pakistani journalist Pearl had hired to help track down Islamic militants, of working for the CIA. By May 11, only nine witnesses had testified because of continuing interruptions over security concerns. An FBI agent testified on May 11 that the decapitation video was genuine. The video was shown in court on May 14. The video also appeared on some Internet sites in the Arab world; a portion of it ran on CBS News that evening.

Pakistani President General Pervez Musharraf said on May 4 that he turned down extradition so that he could make a domestic example of the terrorists by punishing them as part of his crackdown.

An expert witness, Gulam Akbar Jafri, testified on May 13 that the written English-language drafts of an e-mail sent by the kidnappers matched the writing of Saeed. The Urdu drafts matched Adil's writing.

On May 15, Laura Bush, wife of President Bush, met with Mariane Pearl in Paris. Mrs. Pearl denounced CBS News for airing part of the video of the murder, saying she was worried about it being exploited as propaganda. Prosecutors sought to block its showing on May 28, saying it would only "generate terrorism." Although the judge had granted the defense request to show it, Quereshi got a 72-hour stay so he could appeal to the Sindh provincial high court.

On May 16, police arrested three new suspects. Later that day, the remains of Pearl's body were unearthed in a secluded compound of a Karachi suburb. Police were brought to the shallow grave by a suspected member of Lashkar-e-Jhangvi, who said he had killed Pearl five or six days after abducting him in a red Suzuki Alto sedan outside a restaurant. Pakistani police doctors gave U.S. officials hair samples for DNA tests. A U.S. official confirmed on July 19 that the tests had confirmed that the body was Pearl's. Defense attorneys said that a new trial should

start. The suspect told investigators that Naeem Bukhari (alias Ata-ur-Rahman) was the leader of the kidnappers. He was wanted for the killings of ten prominent Pakistani Shias and was believed to be operations chief of a group that included three Pakistanis of Yemeni descent who had guarded Pearl and participated in the murder.

On May 21, prosecutors dropped 13 witnesses, saying the 20 already called, plus an upcoming 5, would be sufficient to establish the case.

On May 28, six-pound Adam D. Pearl was born to widow Mariane Pearl in Paris.

Pakistani authorities said that al Qaeda members who had fled Afghanistan were involved in the Pearl kidnap/murder.

On June 21, Saeed told the court that the evidence had been fabricated, he had been illegally detained, and two defendants had been tortured, according to defense attorney Rai Bashir.

On July 10, the prosecution rested its case and requested the death penalty.

Pearl's 278-page book, *At Home in the World: Collected Writings from the Wall Street Journal*, edited by Helene Cooper, was made available posthumously by Simon and Schuster.

The four were convicted and sentenced on July 15. Saeed was sentenced to hang; the three e-mailers, Sheik Adil, Salman Saqib, and Fahad Naseem, received 25-year sentences. The trio's lawyers appealed the verdict. Rai Bashir, Saeed's attorney, said he would also appeal. Various observers said that the new arrests and repressed evidence of the involvement of others in the case could spur a new trial. For example, Karim admitted to holding Pearl's head while three Yemenis decapitated Pearl. Karim also led the police to Pearl's likely gravesite.

On September 25, 2003, Justices Ghulam Nabi Soomro and Afzal Soomro heard the appeal and said they might appoint a state lawyer if Rai Bashir, the attorney for three of the men, continued to miss proceedings. Five appeal hearings had been postponed since December 2002. They said they might appoint new counsel if he missed the October 21 hearing. British citizen Ahmed Omar Saeed Sheikh was represented by a different attorney.

Pearl's body returned to the United States on a Cathay Pacific Airways flight from Pakistan to Los Angeles International Airport on August 8. The family planned a private funeral service.

On January 30, 2003, Secretary of State Colin Powell designated Lashkar-e-Jhangvi a terrorist group.

On October 12, 2003, Mariane Pearl, who was promoting *A Mighty Heart: The Brave Life and Death of My Husband, Danny Pearl*, her book about the kidnap/murder, charged that *Washington Post* freelancer stringer Kamran Khan had put her husband in extreme jeopardy by quoting a Pakistani official in the English-language Pakistani newspaper the *News* as saying a "Jewish reporter serving a largely Jewish media organization should have known the hazards of exposing himself to radical Islamic groups." Her book was optioned by Warner Brothers as a potential movie.

On October 21, 2003, U.S. investigators concluded that al Qaeda operations chief Khalid Sheikh Muhammad killed Pearl. The killer was captured in March 2003 at a safe house in Rawalpindi, Pakistan.

On April 16, 2004, Pakistani police arrested two suspected Islamic militants in two raids, picking up a man wanted for the Pearl killing. Seven suspects, including those who slit his throat, remained at large.

On September 25, 2004, following a two-hour gun battle in Nawabshah, a town in the southern province of Sindh, Pakistani security forces killed Amjad Hussain Farooqi, a fugitive wanted for organizing Pearl's kidnap/murder and carrying out two unsuccessful assassination attempts against President Pervez Musharraf in December 2003. Three other al Qaeda associates, including an Islamic cleric, were arrested in the raid. Pakistani authorities said Farooqi worked with Abu Faraj Libbi, a Libyan al Qaeda lieutenant closely linked to Ayman Zawahiri. Farooqi was one of the hijackers of an Indian Airlines plane in December 1999. On September 27, 2004, Pakistani police arrested four more suspected extremists. On October 5, 2004, DNA tests confirmed that the dead Pakistani was Farooqi.

On November 17, 2004, Pakistani authorities shot to death Asim Ghafoor while they tried to arrest him at a hideout in Karachi. Ghafoor was wanted in the Pearl murder. 02012301

January 23, 2002. *United States.* The U.S. Nuclear Regulatory Commission warned 103 nuclear power plants that according to an al Qaeda terrorist being questioned by U.S. forces in Afghanistan, three terrorists in the United States were attempting to recruit non-Arabs to fly a plane into a nuclear power plant. If they were intercepted, the plane would be crashed into the nearest tall building.

January 24, 2002. *Lebanon.* Former Christian militia commander Elie Hobeika, 45, and three bodyguards were killed when a bomb in a parked car went off as they drove from his east Beirut home. Six others were wounded. Palestinians claimed he led the militia that killed hundreds of Palestinians in the Sabra and Shatila refugee camps in Beirut in 1982. Police questioned George Massoud Hanna, 40, the former owner of the car, and his cousin, Charbel Hanna, in Ein el-Mir in southern Lebanon. The previously unknown Lebanese for a Free and Independent Lebanon claimed credit, saying he was a Syrian agent. Lebanese Interior Minister Michel Murr blamed Israel.

January 24, 2002. *Algeria.* Militants set up an illegal roadblock on Larbaa-Tablat Road, killing three people, including a Syrian. No one claimed credit. 02012401

January 25, 2002. *Colombia.* A bicycle bomb exploded in a Bogota restaurant frequented by police, killing 4 officers and a child and wounding 26 other people. Police deactivated a second bomb in northern Bogota. No one claimed credit.

January 25, 2002. *Israel.* At 11:15 a.m., a Palestinian suicide bomber set off a bomb in the Tel Aviv neighborhood of Neve Shaanan (Tranquil Oasis), wounding at least 25 people, principally immigrants and foreign laborers from Romania, Thailand, the Philippines, and the former Soviet Union. The wounded included a four-year-old boy and an Ethiopian immigrant, 65, who was coming home after attending a wedding. Meir Chen, 32, a convenience store owner, was hit by shrapnel in his left temple. One man in his 40s had shrapnel lodged in his brain. Islamic Jihad told Hizballah's Al Manar radio station in Beirut that the terrorist was Safwat Abdurrahman Khalil of the Jerusalem Brigades. Yasir Arafat's Palestinian Authority condemned the bombing.

Meir Setone told the press, "The terrorist had asked my friend, 'Is this Neve Shaanan Street?' My friend said yes and a few minutes later [it] exploded alongside a motor scooter" in front of the Pub Maestro, a beer garden. The bomber wore a belt packed with explosives and cylindrical metal shrapnel.

After the bombing, survivors beat the remains with sticks; nothing remained intact except his legs. 02012501

January 26, 2002. *Philippines.* A kidnapping gang raided a Dole Food Company plantation, apparently intending to grab a U.S. executive. Acting on a tip, police ambushed the group.

January 27, 2002. *Israel.* Wafa Idriss, 28, a Palestinian emergency medical technician, set off a bomb on central Jerusalem's Jaffa and King George Streets, killing herself and Pinhas Tokatli, 81, and injuring more than 150 people, 2 in serious condition. Tokatli was a male tour guide, seventh-generation Jerusalem resident, and grandfather of 13. The attack occurred a half block from the attack two days earlier. Jerusalem Police Chief Mickey Levy, 50, suffered a heart attack as he was directing his officers at the scene and was hospitalized in stable condition. Hizballah radio said the attacker was a woman. Some reports named her as Shahinaz Amari, an al-Najah University student in her early 20s and a Hamas member. Her head lay in the street.

Among the injured was Mark Sokolow, 43, a New York lawyer with Thacher Proffitt and Wood, who had fled from his 38th floor law office at the World Trade Center's South Tower on September 11. He was injured along with his daughter Lauren, 16, his wife, Rena, and daughter Jamie, 12. They had been scheduled to fly home that evening after a ten-day vacation in Israel where eldest daughter Ilana studies. The family was hospitalized with burns and injuries from shrapnel and flying glass. Sokolow had a perforated eardrum; Rena had a broken leg. Lauren lost some hearing in one ear and had cuts on her face. Jamie's right eye was damaged from flying glass. Sokolow's stepmother survived World War II as a young Jewish girl in Nazi Germany.

Also injured was Police Sgt. Maj. Vladimir Fishman, 39, who was hit in the ankle by shrapnel. He emigrated from Moscow in 1991.

Terrorist Wafa Idriss had worked as a volunteer assisting ambulance medics for the Palestinian Red Crescent Society since 1999. Supporters painted "the militia of the al-Aqsa Martyrs Brigades announces with all pride and honor the martyrdom of Wafa" at her home in the Al-Amari refugee camp near Ramallah. She apparently was the first female suicide bomber in Israel. She was a childless divorcee and ninth-grade dropout. Iraqi President Saddam Hussein ordered a memorial to her built in one of Baghdad's main squares. 02012701

January 28, 2002. *United States.* The Illinois-based Global Relief Foundation, which claims to be the second-largest U.S. Islamic relief group, sued the U.S. Treasury in U.S. Federal Court in Chicago to lift a freeze on its assets. The freeze had been imposed after the September 11 attacks.

January 29, 2002. *Nepal.* During the evening, a small bomb exploded at the Coca-Cola factory in

Bharatpur, southwest of Kathmandu, causing slight damage and no injuries. No Americans are employed at the plant. 02012901

January 30, 2002. *United States.* At 6:50 a.m., Argenbright Security personnel detected explosive residue on the shoes of a passenger in San Francisco International Airport's United Airlines domestic terminal, but failed to detain him. The error caused the evacuation of 3,000 individuals from the terminal for two and one-half hours and the delay of 27 flights while police searched for the explosives and the man, who was white and in his 40s. Police said the residue might also have been from fertilizer, fireworks, or heart medication.

January 30, 2002. *Israel.* A Palestinian suicide bomber, Murad Abu Asal, 23, threw himself on an Israeli vehicle parked near Taibe on the West Bank border, wounding two Shin Bet members sitting inside. Police checked the terrorist's body for booby traps. Radio reports said Asal had been an Israeli collaborator.

January 30, 2002. *Philippines.* The New People's Army shot to death Brian Thomas Smith, an American, while he was hiking with a German friend in Pampanga Province near the Mount Pinatubo volcano. Sigfried Whitman was found injured the next day. Police found Smith's body near a waterfall in a deep ravine, but were unable to retrieve it by sundown on January 31. 02013001

January 31, 2002. *Qatar.* CNN aired a video in which Osama bin Laden told a Qatar-based al-Jazeera reporter in October that "freedom and human rights in America are doomed" and that the U.S. government was leading its people and the West "into an unbearable hell and a choking life." Bin Laden initially said United States claims that "we are carrying out acts of terrorism is unwarranted." Rethinking the statement, he quickly said, "If inciting people to do that is terrorism, and if killing those who kill our sons is terrorism, then let history be

witness that we are terrorists." He was vague on being responsible for the anthrax attacks, observing, "These diseases are a punishment from God and a response to oppressed mothers' prayers in Lebanon, Iraq, Palestine, and everywhere." Bin Laden said, "We kill the kings of the infidels, kings of the crusaders and civilian infidels in exchange for those of our children they kill. This is permissible in Islamic law and logically." Speaking of the U.S. government, he said, "They made hilarious claims. They said that Osama's messages have codes in them to the terrorists. It's as if we were living in the time of mail by carrier pigeon, when there are no phones, no travelers, no Internet, no regular mail, no express mail, and no electronic mail." The video was made before the U.S. defeat of the Taliban in Afghanistan and bin Laden had high hopes, saying that "we believe that the defeat of America is possible, with the help of God, and is even easier for us—God permitting—than the defeat of the Soviet Union was before." Al-Jazeera suspended its relationship with CNN, saying that it had decided not to broadcast the tape—the only post-September 11 news interview with bin Laden—and that the tape had been stolen.

February 2002. *Macedonia.* Two Jordanians and two Bosnians were arrested near the U.S. ambassador's residence in late February. Macedonian officials claimed that the foursome was turned over to U.S. officials on March 6, but reversed that claim the next day. The foursome reportedly talked of plans to "destroy the devil." The government also reportedly gave the United States diskettes with thousands of pages of documents, including references to "we should destroy the devil and axis," apparently the United States, United Kingdom, and Germany. The Macedonian officials said that the group appeared to be students carrying Belgian passports. They reportedly cased U.S., U.K., and German embassies. The Macedonians later said that they were expelled from the country, but did not specify to where. 02029901

February 2002. *Italy.* Eight Pakistani men jumped off the freighter *Twillinger* at Trieste after traveling from Cairo. The men had lied about being crewmen. They carried false ID and large amounts of money, and had been sent by al Qaeda. According to the Romanian newspaper *Ziua*, Romanian and U.S. intelligence investigated the shipping firm Nova and its ships. Nova is incorporated in Delaware and Romania. 02029902

February 2002. *Turkey.* The Great East Islamic Raiders-Front (IBDA-C) claimed credit for setting off four bombs in Istanbul. The Sunni Salafist group supports Islamic rule in Turkey and believes that the secular leadership is "illegal."

February 2002. *United Kingdom.* Authorities arrested Shaykh Abdullah Ibrahim el-Faisal on charges of inciting racial hatred for remarks he made calling for the murder of nonbelievers, Jews, Americans, and Hindus. He was charged under the Public Order Act and the Offences Against the Person Act.

February 1, 2002. *United States/Sweden.* Lawyers for three Swedish citizens identified as Abdirisak Aden, Abdi Abdulaziz Ali, and Yusaf Ahmed asked that their clients' names be removed from the U.S. terrorism financial sanctions list. The United States denied the request.

February 2, 2002. *Colombia.* The Revolutionary Armed Forces of Colombia (FARC) hijacked Aires flight 1891. 02020201

February 4, 2002. *France.* Local intelligence agents in Paris arrested three Islamic militants wanted for plotting to attack a Strasbourg cathedral. Among them was Yacine Akhnouche, 27, a French citizen of Algerian origin, who said he visited al Qaeda camps during three trips to Afghanistan. In 2000, he met Zacarias Moussaoui and Richard C. Reid in Afghanistan. In his 1998 Afghan visit, he met Ahmed Ressam. He implicated Abu Doha, jailed in the United Kingdom for the Strasbourg cathedral plot. He also

mentioned Abu Zubaydah, military operations chief of al Qaeda, and Abu Jafar, possibly referring to Abu Jafar al-Jaziri, the late al Qaeda financier and logistics chief.

February 5, 2002. *Italy.* Judge Giovanna Verga presided in the Milan trial of Essid Ben Khemais (alias The Saber), the head of Osama bin Laden's European operations, and three other Tunisian men charged with providing false passports for al Qaeda members in Europe, breaking immigration laws, and criminal association with the intent to obtain and transport arms, explosives, and chemicals. Wiretaps indicated the intention to obtain the arms, although none were found. Ben Khemais was suspected of supervising a plan to attack the U.S. Embassy in Rome in January 2001, although he was not charged. Spanish authorities believed he met with hijack leader Mohamed Atta in Spain in 2001. The four were arrested between April and October 2001 in a joint German–Italian investigation.

On February 18, the government began the trial in Milan against the three Tunisians. The trio was convicted on May 17. (The State Department said four members of the Tunisian Combatant Group were sentenced in February to up to five years for providing false documentation and planning to acquire and transport arms and other illegal goods.) Judge Ambrogio Moccia said they would be expelled from Italy after serving their sentences. They had been cleared of several charges of supplying false documents and smuggling arms. Mehdi Kammoun received five years and ten months. Riadh Jelassi and Adel Ben Soltane received four years and six months.

February 6, 2002. *Israel.* A Palestinian gunman raided a Jewish settlement in the Jordan Valley and killed three Israelis, including a 50-year-old mother, her 11-year-old daughter, and a soldier.

February 7, 2002. *United States.* Salt Lake City police blew up a plastic grocery bag with fuses and electric wire inside. Construction workers found the package in a downtown parking garage the day before the Winter Olympics opening ceremony. No explosives were found.

February 7, 2002. *United States.* Five hours into the flight, Pablo Moreira Mosca, 29, a bank employee from Uruguay, kicked in the bottom of the cockpit door on United Airlines flight 855, flying from Miami after midnight with 142 passengers and 15 crew members bound for Buenos Aires, Argentina. Three passengers subdued him from the passenger cabin while the copilot hit him in the head with a small fire ax, leaving a two-inch gash. The plane landed safely and on time in Buenos Aires. There was no evidence that Moreira was linked to terrorists. Passenger Jan Boyer said that Moreira was kicking the door "kung fu style." Boyer sat on Moreira while the captain shackled him with plastic arm and leg restraints. Other passengers said that he was behaving erratically in the waiting area before the flight began, demanding to smoke in the nonsmoking area. Moreira was put on a flight for the United States that evening and faced charges of interfering with a flight crew. He told the FBI, "I wanted to destroy everything." He was held without bail and faced up to 20 years in prison. 02020701

February 8, 2002. *Israel.* Arab youths stabbed to death a 24-year-old woman in the Forest of Peace in south Jerusalem. Police shot at the attackers, killing one at the scene. Family members said he was a 14-year-old Arab from Jerusalem. A second suspect sustained slight wounds. No one claimed credit.

February 8, 2002. *Israel.* A bomb went off in a car on a road in the north, killing two Palestinians who apparently planned to set it off in a city.

February 8, 2002. *Algeria.* In a two and one-half hour gun battle, authorities killed Antar Zouabri, the country's most wanted man, who had led the Armed Islamic Group since 1996.

February 9, 2002. *Israel.* Palestinian gunmen ambushed and shot to death a 79-year-old Israeli settler at a crossroads in the West Bank.

February 9, 2002. *France.* Unidentified individuals threw gasoline bombs at a police headquarters in Saint-Jean-De-Luz, causing material damage to police barracks and three parked vehicles, but harming no one. No one claimed responsibility, but the Basque Nation and Liberty (ETA) was suspected. 02020901

February 10, 2002. *Israel.* At 1:30 p.m., two Palestinian gunmen belonging to Hamas jumped from their car and fired assault rifles near the gates of a Beersheba Israeli military base—one of three main regional command bases—killing two female soldiers and wounding four other people. They were killed in the ensuing gun battle with Israel's Southern Command. The dead soldiers were identified as Lt. Karen Rothstein, 20, and Cpl. Aya Malachi, 18. The attack took place at a popular café while soldiers were on their lunch break. Capt. Guy Shaham said he shot to death one of the terrorists. One of the gunmen was wearing an explosives belt. Reports of a third gunman were incorrect.

February 10, 2002. *Israel.* Palestinians fired two homemade 120-mm Qassam 2 rockets developed by Hamas into Israeli farming communities. The rocket has a range of over five miles and can carry 20 pounds of explosives. This was apparently the first use of the weapon.

February 11, 2002. *United States.* Two northern Virginia men drove a tow truck through a security checkpoint near the Pentagon. Police were unsure whether they were terrorists casing the area or merely lost. The driver was charged in U.S. District Court in Alexandria under the name Imad Abdel-Fattah Hamed, 26, with ID fraud for having Virginia driver's licenses in two names. U.S. Magistrate Judge Theresa C. Buchanan had him held without bond. He claimed to be a dual U.S. and Jordanian citizen who did not see the signs prohibiting commercial truck traffic. His passenger had ID in several names, including a U.A.E. passport for Sultan Rashed Sultan Jasmon Alzaabi, 22. He was detained by the Immigration and Naturalization Service (INS). He panicked because his license was suspended and his visa had expired, according to the affidavit. The duo failed to stop at a checkpoint along Route 110 in Arlington. State troops stopped them at a second checkpoint at 10:30 p.m. No weapons or explosives were found. The duo told the FBI they were taking the truck to be serviced in Maryland. The truck, which had a Virginia inspection sticker and temporary Maryland plates, allegedly belonged to Hamed's brother, Basel, who runs a towing company from his family's Manassas home.

The FBI had questioned Hamed, a copier repairman, in October, when he gave a different social security number to them. He faced up to 15 years in prison if convicted. Police found a separate driver's license in his wallet for Imad Nimer with an Arlington address. He said he paid someone $100 to get the license. He was released on $5,000 bond on February 15. His family paid the bond. He was not permitted to leave the region. He surrendered two passports. Michael Hadeed, his attorney, said the Arlington license was issued in Hamed's Jordanian name.

On March 4, Imad Abdel-Fattah Hamed pleaded guilty to using a legal loophole to obtain a second Virginia driver's license, using a variant of his real name (Imad Nimer) and a fake Arlington address. Sentencing was set for May 24, when he was expected to get less than a year because of a plea agreement.

February 11, 2002. *United States.* The FBI issued a nationwide terrorist alert based upon interrogation of detained al Qaeda terrorists in Afghanistan and Guantanamo Bay, Cuba, and a document found in an al Qaeda site in Afghanistan. Fawaz Yahya Al-Rabeei (alias Furqan the Chechen), a Yemeni believed born in Saudi Arabia in 1979, and perhaps 16 others from Saudi Arabia, Yemen, and Tunisia were believed to be planning a terrorist attack in the United States

or on U.S. interests in Yemen. The alert, which ran on the FBI's Web site, said the terrorists could attack the next day. The alert gave the suspects' names, places of birth, dates of birth, and nationalities as:

- Fawaz Yahya Al-Rabeei, Saudi Arabia, 1979, Yemeni
- Issam Ahmad Dibwan Al-Makhlafi, Saudi Arabia, 1977, Yemeni
- Ahmad Al-Akhader Nasser Albidani, Yemen, 1977, Yemeni
- Alyan Muhammad Ali Al-Wa'eli, Yemen, 1970, Yemeni
- Bashir Ali Nasser Al-Sharari, Yemen, 1970, Yemeni
- Bassam Abdullah Bin Bushar Al-Nahdi, Saudi Arabia, 1976, Yemeni
- Abdulaziz Muhammad Saleh Bin Otash, Saudi Arabia, 1975, Yemeni
- Mustafa Abdulkader Aabed Al-Ansari, Saudi Arabia, DOB unknown, Saudi
- Omar Ahmad Omar Al-Hubishi, Saudi Arabia, 1969, Yemeni
- Ammar Abadah Nasser Al-Wa'eli, Yemen, 1977, Yemeni
- Shuhour Abdullah Mukbil Al-Sabri, Saudi Arabia, 1976, Yemeni
- Samir Abduh Sa'id Al-Maktawi, Saudi Arabia, 1968, Yemeni
- Abdulrab Muhammad Muhammad Ali Al-Sayfi, a Yemeni
- Abu Nasr Al-Tunisi, possibly a Tunisian
- Abu Mu'Az Al-Jeddawi, possibly a Saudi
- Riyadh Shikawi, possibly a Yemeni
- Amin Saad Muhammad Al-Zumari, Saudi Arabia or Yemen, 1968, Yemeni

On February 14, the FBI removed six names from the list; they were being held in Yemeni jails. Five whose photographs were issued were identified as Issam Ahmad Dibwan Al-Makhlafi, Ahmad al-Akhader Nasser Albidani, Bashir Ali Nasser al-Sharari, Abdulaziz Muhammad Saleh bin Otash, and Shuhour Abdullah Mukbil al-Sabri. An unphotographed man was Riyadh Shikawi.

In early April 2003, Yemeni authorities arrested Fawaz al-Rabeei. He apparently escaped an explosion on August 9, 2002, that killed two accomplices in a San'a warehouse, where terrorists had hidden 650 pounds of Semtex in pomegranate crates. Yemeni officials also seized weapons, including rocket-propelled grenades.

February 13, 2002. *United States.* The FBI issued a tristate alert after the driver of an empty fuel truck called 911 to say that two Middle Eastern men tried to force him off U.S. 264 in Nash County, North Carolina at 6:40 a.m. 40 miles east of Raleigh. The duo was driving a bronze Dodge Neon with New Jersey license plates. An APB went out in the Carolinas and Virginia.

February 13, 2002. *Yemen.* Sameer Mohammed Ahmed al-Hada, 25, a suspected al Qaeda courier, blew himself up with a grenade after trying to flee Yemeni authorities who had surrounded him at his San'a home. He was threatening police with the grenade when it went off in his hand. He was the son of Ahmad Mohammad Ali al-Hada, an al Qaeda operative. Al-Hada's sister was married to September 11 American Airlines flight 77 hijacker Khalid Almihdhar. Flight 77 hit the Pentagon. Al-Hada was also a brother-in-law of Mustafa Abdulkader, one of the 17 men named by the FBI on February 11 planning terrorist attacks. Police arrested a man sitting in a car outside al-Hada's house. The al-Hada clan had been linked to the August 7, 1998, bombings of the U.S. embassies in Tanzania and Kenya, the October 2000 bombing of the USS *Cole*, and the September 11 hijackings. A cell phone (number 011-967-1-200-578) traced to the al-Hada clan was used in all three attacks.

During the embassy bombing trial, Mohamed Rashed Daoud Owhali said he visited Yemen in the months before the bombings and was given the al-Hada phone number to reach Ahmed al Hazza (another way to spell al-Hada's name). Owhali called the number before and after the Nairobi attack, and attempted to get money and a passport to leave Kenya. The same number was called by bin Laden's cell phone during Owhali's attempts.

Ahmad was at large and being sought by authorities. Another of his sons, Najeeb, may have died in Afghanistan during al Qaeda explosives training in 1999.

February 14, 2002. *Israel.* A bomb exploded under a tank in the Gaza Strip near the Netzarim intersection southeast of Gaza City, killing three Israelis and wounding two in the tank. The Palestinians fired on a civilian convoy guarded by soldiers, then set off a bomb. When the tank responded to the firefight, the terrorists set off the bomb under the tank. Police arrested 18 Palestinians; all but two were released.

February 15, 2002. *Israel.* Sgt. Lee Nachman Akunis was shot to death at close range by armed Fatah gunmen at a military checkpoint north of Ramallah.

February 15, 2002. *Turkey.* Turkish police in Van Province arrested two Palestinians and a Jordanian suspected of coming from Iran and attempting to enter Israel to carry out a suicide bombing at the behest of an Islamic cleric with al Qaeda ties. One confessed to plans to attack a crowded area of Ramat Gan, a Tel Aviv suburb. They were members of the Union of Imams, a Jordanian group with links to al Qaeda. Turkish police later arrested Ahmet Abdullah, a courier from northern Iraq, for providing assistance to the Union of Imams. 02021501

February 16, 2002. *Israel.* Just before 8:00 p.m., a Popular Front for the Liberation of Palestine (PFLP) suicide bomber blew himself up at a pizzeria in an outdoor food court in Karnei Shomron, a Jewish settlement in the West Bank between Qalqilyah and Nablus, killing himself, 2 Israelis—a girl, 14, and a boy, 16—and 2 Americans—Keren Shatsky and Rachel Donna

Thaler—and injuring 27 others, including 2 U.S. citizens. 02021601

February 16, 2002. *Israel.* A car bomb exploded in Jenin in the West Bank, killing Nazih Al Sibaa, a local Hamas leader who helped plan suicide bombings. Palestinians said the car was booby-trapped and set off by an overhead drone.

February 17, 2002. *Israel.* Police foiled a suicide bombing when they killed a Palestinian in a gun battle. His aide fled in a car that exploded, killing him and injuring three policemen. While driving to an army base near Hadera, the duo was stopped by traffic police on suspicion of having a stolen car. The passenger got out of the car and fired on the police outside the base. He was shot to death by police, who said he had a bomb strapped to his body. The al-Aqsa Martyrs Brigades claimed credit.

February 17, 2002. *Nepal.* Maoist rebels killed 129 police, soldiers, and civilians in a series of attacks on government offices and an airport in the northwest. They torched buildings and shot at police in Mangalsen in Achham District, killing 49 police officers. They attacked a small airport in neighboring Sanphebagar, killing 27 policemen and 48 Royal Nepalese Army soldiers stationed in Mangalsen. They also attacked the district's chief administrator, Mohan Singh Khadka, a central intelligence bureau official and his wife, a postal worker, and a civilian. They also burned down the CARE International building in Mangalsen.

February 18, 2002. *United Kingdom.* Scotland Yard's antiterrorist branch conducted a dawn raid in East London and arrested Abdullah Faisal, 38, a Jamaican Muslim cleric who had called for Muslims to kill Jews and other nonbelievers. Members of Parliament demanded his arrest after videotapes with his message went on sale in London Islamic bookstores. His audiocassettes instructed men to train for battle and called on boys to learn how to use Kalashnikovs. He was charged with incitement to murder two weeks

after the *Times* of London had reported his statement. He was detained pending a hearing on February 21 at Bow Street Magistrates Court. 02021801

February 18, 2002. *Pakistan.* A Karachi police bomb squad defused four 107-mm rockets with a timer aimed at Karachi airport facilities used by the international coalition for operations in Afghanistan. Islamic radicals were blamed. Two rockets were aimed at a terminal; the other two at an airport hotel used as a barracks for troops. A passerby spotted the rockets and alerted police.

February 18, 2002. *Israel.* Two Palestinian gunmen tried to infiltrate a Jewish settlement in Gaza, but soldiers fired on them, killing a gunman.

Palestinians fired on an Israeli vehicle near Gaza's Kissufim crossing into Israel; a suicide bomber then blew himself up, killing three Israelis and wounding four. The al-Aqsa Martyrs Brigades said the suicide bomber was Mohammed Kasser, 22, of Gaza City.

Police stopped a suspicious car on the highway between Jerusalem and the West Bank's Jordan Valley. The driver got out of the car, and as police raised their guns, he set off a car bomb by remote control, killing himself and a policeman and slightly injuring another policeman.

February 20, 2002. *Italy.* Italian police arrested four Moroccans at a Rome apartment and seized a powder containing small amounts of cyanide and maps highlighting the U.S. Embassy and the city's underground water system. Police confiscated ten pounds of white powder—identified as potassium ferrocyanide—from the apartment of one suspect. Government officials said the material would have been filtered out of the city's water supply. The Moroccans were held on suspicion of receiving stolen property. They all carried false working papers, marked maps, and radical Islamic videotapes. An Italian news agency said they were members of the Salafist Group for Preaching (Call) and Combat, an Algerian organization under the al Qaeda umbrella.

By February 22, police had detained two other Moroccans and were searching for another.

Police found holes in the walls of a utility tunnel near the U.S. Embassy and were attempting to determine if they were part of the terrorists' plans. The holes were large enough for a person to crawl through.

In a February 24 court hearing, the Moroccans denied belonging to a terrorist group and did not know how the cyanide made its way into the apartment.

The court refused on March 9 to release the eight Moroccans; the defense counsel said the evidence was flimsy.

On April 28, 2004, the court acquitted nine Moroccans of plotting to attack the U.S. Embassy by poisoning its water supply and of charges of association aimed at international terrorism. 02022001

February 20, 2002. *Colombia.* The government ended peace talks with the Revolutionary Armed Forces of Colombia (FARC) and ordered the military into the 16,000-square-mile rebel haven in the south just hours after rebels hijacked a Dash-8 twin-propelled commercial airliner carrying 35 passengers and crew and kidnapped a prominent senator.

Four FARC gunmen hijacked the plane scheduled to fly from Neiva to Bogota and forced it to land at Hobo, where they were met by 50 other rebels. The hijackers fled to the rebel-controlled area after kidnapping two or three passengers, one of whom was Senator Jorge Eduardo Gechem Turbay, whose cousin was killed by the FARC in December 2000. The government said the hijackers were members of FARC's Teofilo Forero Column, a mobile unit based in the haven.

The Colombian military struck back the next day with 200 sorties by A-37 jet fighters, AC-47 gunships, and armed helicopters firing on 80 FARC installations, including landing strips, drug labs, and training camps. 02022002

February 21, 2002. *United States.* Federal authorities stepped up local security after receiving a threat against the Liberty Bell in Philadelphia. It was not closed to tourists.

February 21, 2002. *Spain.* Police arrested six members of the Basque Nation and Liberty and seized arms and explosives.

February 21, 2002. *Nepal.* Soldiers killed at least 48 Maoist rebels. Meanwhile, Parliament approved a three-month extension of the national emergency imposed on November 26 after the rebels ended peace talks.

February 21, 2002. *Sri Lanka.* The government and the Liberation Tigers of Tamil Eelam (LTTE) agreed in principle to a long-term cease-fire, perhaps ending the 18-year civil war, thanks to Norwegian mediators. The parties signed a cease-fire agreement on February 22.

February 21, 2002. *Thailand.* Malaysia, Indonesia, and the Philippines announced an antiterrorism cooperation agreement during a meeting of foreign ministers of the ten-member Association of Southeast Asian Nations in Phuket. Police could make arrests in any of the three countries. Thailand said it would probably join the agreement; Singapore said it was not ready. Philippine Foreign Minister Teofisto Guingona, Jr., said, "A terrorist leader fleeing to one of our three countries can be detained in the country where he flees." The agreement permitted exchange of information.

February 22, 2002. *United States.* A suspicious plastic sandwich bag-type container was found at U.S. Army Reserve Command Headquarters in Atlanta, Georgia, at 4:00 p.m. Initial tests suggested anthrax, although more sensitive CDC tests ruled it out. Seven civilians exposed to the package were sent to a hospital for observation. The package apparently did not arrive via the mail.

February 22, 2002. *Italy.* A Milan court convicted four Tunisians on terrorist charges, including criminal association with intent to transport arms, explosives, and chemicals, and falsifying

235 work permits, 130 driver's licenses, several foreign passports, and various blank documents. They were acquitted of charges of possession of arms and chemicals. The guilty verdicts were the first in Europe against al Qaeda operatives since the September 11, 2001, attacks. The four belonged to the Salafist Group for Preaching (Call) and Combat, an Algerian wing of al Qaeda.

Two of the men, senior al Qaeda operative Essid Sami Ben Khemais and Bouchoucha Moktar, received five-year sentences. Charaabi Tarek and Belgacem Mohamed Ben Aouadi received four-year sentences. Ben Khemais had trained in Afghan camps for two years before arriving in Italy in 1998. He was suspected in an aborted plot to attack the U.S. Embassy in Rome in January 2001.

Italian investigators had used wiretaps and hidden microphones to bug the al Qaeda cell in Milan. The group had discussed using explosives and a deadly chemical in attacks as well as a bombing of a marketplace in Strasbourg, France.

Earlier in 2002, a Tunisian military court had sentenced three of the defendants to 20-year prison terms for belonging to a terrorist group.

The defense attorneys, Maris and Antonio Nebuloni, requested Italian political asylum for their clients.

February 23, 2002. *Colombia.* The jeep of Colombian presidential candidate Ingrid Betancourt, 40, and her campaign manager, Clara Rojas, another campaign staffer, a French journalist writing for *Marie Claire*, and a Colombian journalist was stopped by two buses packed with explosives and manned by ten members of the Revolutionary Armed Forces of Colombia (FARC), 15th Front, at a roadblock between Paujil and La Montanita, 55 miles south of San Vicente del Daguan. She was traveling from the provincial capital Florencia toward San Vicente del Caguan, the largest town inside the former rebel haven. The rebels released driver Adair Lamprea and the two journalists. The candidate of the small Green Oxygen Party had ignored

military advice to avoid the area. Betancourt had earlier served as a senator and representative and had condemned official corruption. She was the daughter of a prominent UN diplomat and a fierce critic of the right-wing vigilantes. On February 27, FARC gave the government a year to swap rebel prisoners for its hostages, including Betancourt, according to senior rebel commander Fabian Ramirez in a talk with CNN. Ramirez said FARC was also holding five members of Congress and senators. The government said it would not bow to the demands.

Although the government believed it knew the location where she was held, it called off a rescue attempt after her family publicly pleaded for restraint. Betancourt's book was recently released in the United States, after appearing in Spanish and French. Its U.S. title was *Until Death Do Us Part: My Struggle to Reclaim Colombia*, translated by Steven Rendall and published by Ecco Press (228 pages). It was reviewed in a March 3, 2002, *Washington Post Book World* article entitled "Hostage to History," by Karen DeYoung (pages 4–5).

In July 2002, the rebels released a tape of Betancourt.

On August 30, 2003, *Noticias Uno* television ran a video of Betancourt urging the government to rescue her. She said, "A rescue, yes, definitely, but not just any rescue. It's important that it be the President who directly makes this decision."

In October 2003, U.S. pay cable ran a documentary, "The Kidnapping of Ingrid Betancourt," produced by filmmakers Victoria Bruce and Karin Hayes, who also produced a video on the kidnapping on February 13, 2003, of three Americans. The video included a plea by Betancourt in captivity, who calls for an end to political violence. 02022301

February 24, 2002. *United States.* The FBI announced on February 28 that an electrical outage in Salt Lake City, Utah, on the last day of the Olympics was caused by a powerful explosive device.

February 25, 2002. *Israel.* At 3:00 a.m., Israeli troops in Nablus without warning shot to death Mohammed Hayek, a Palestinian house painter, 22, and critically injured his wife, Maysoun Hayek, and father, Abdullah Hayek, 64. Mohammed and Abdullah were taking Maysoun, who was in labor, to the hospital. Maysoun was the second Palestinian woman in labor to be shot within the previous two days. The previous day, at roughly the same location, Israeli troops shot at Shadyah Shehadeh, 27, hitting her in the chest, as husband Issam drove her to the hospital. She gave birth to a baby girl named Heba. Maysoun gave birth to a girl after being shot in the back twice. Abdullah was hit by four shots and was critically injured and partially paralyzed.

Twelve hours later and 80 miles away, a pregnant Israeli woman's father was killed as was another man in her car during an ambush by Palestinian gunmen in Bethlehem. She was shot in the stomach and gave birth by Caesarean section.

A Palestinian gunman shot at bystanders and police on a residential street in Neve Yaacov, a northern Jerusalem suburb, wounding eight people, including three policemen. The gunman was wounded by return fire. Some believed that a second gunman escaped.

Noura Shalhoub, 15, was shot to death after the Palestinian girl pulled out a knife and ran at an Israeli army checkpoint near Tulkarm in the West Bank. Her suicide note said, "I have decided to send a message to the occupation that there is no safety on our soil for Jews."

February 26, 2002. *Pakistan.* Terrorists shot to death nine people and wounded ten others in a Shi'ite mosque in Rawalpindi.

February 26, 2002. *United States.* The U.S. Treasury added 21 individuals to the list of terrorist financiers at the request of the Spanish government. All had aided the Basque Nation and Liberty (ETA). They were identified as:

- Javier Abaunza Martinez
- Itziar Alberdi Uranga

- Angel Alcalde Linares
- Miguel Albisu Iriarte
- Eusebio Arzallus Tapia
- Paulo Elcoro Ayastuy
- Antonio Agustin Figal Arranz
- Eneko Gogeascoechea Arronategui
- Cristina Goiricelaya Gonzalez
- Maria Soledad Iparraguirre Guenechea
- Gracia Morcillo Torres
- Ainhoa Mugica Goni
- Alona Munoa Ordozgoiti
- Juan Jesus Narvaez Goni
- Juan Antonio Olarra Guridi
- Zigor Orbe Sevillano
- Mikel Otegui Unanue
- Jon Inaki Perez Aramburu
- Carlos Saez de Eguilaz Murguiondo
- Kemen Uranga Artola

February 26, 2002. *Italy.* A bomb hidden in a motor scooter on a side street exploded outside the Interior Ministry in Rome at 4:00 a.m., causing no injuries but breaking windows and damaging vehicles. No one claimed credit.

February 27, 2002. *India.* A Muslim mob threw firebombs and acid at the Sabarmati Express train as it was pulling away from a rail station in the Muslim neighborhood of Godhra in western India, killing 57 people and injuring another 43. Those killed included 25 women and 15 children. The Vishwa Hindu Parishad (World Hindu Council) activists on the train were shouting provocative slogans while the train was in the rail station. They were returning from Ayodhya, where they hope to construct a temple at the site of the 16th-century Babri Mosque destroyed in 1992 by a Hindu mob. Many Hindus believe the site was the birthplace of Lord Ram, a Hindu god.

India sent troops to Gujarat after two days of rioting that killed nearly 300 people. Some 1,200 people were arrested statewide. Police killed 17 rioters after receiving a shoot-on-sight order. At least 27 Muslims were burned alive in their homes in Ahmadabad.

The attacks continued into March 2, when a mob of 500 Hindus torched a Muslim residence in Sardarpura, killing another 29 Muslims and seriously burning 20 others. The nationwide death toll passed 350.

By mid-March, the nationwide death toll passed 700. The toll ultimately reached 1,000 people.

On March 17, Gujarat police announced the arrest of a Muslim man who was the prime suspect in the attack.

On February 19, 2003, Indian authorities charged 131 suspects in the arson attack; 65 of them were in custody, including Maulana Mussain Umarji, a Muslim cleric from Godhra accused of organizing the attack. The suspects were charged under the Prevention of Terrorism Act. No Hindus have been charged under the Act.

February 27, 2002. *Israel.* Dareen Abu Aisheh, 21, rode in a car to a military checkpoint near the West Bank settlement of Modiin and set off explosives wrapped around her body, killing two Palestinians, two Israelis, and herself. She had approached two Islamic groups to serve as a suicide bomber, but was turned down, once because she was a woman. The secular al-Aqsa Martyrs Brigades gave her the explosives. She was an English major at al-Najah University in Nablus, near her home of Beit Wazan. She was active on the student council and in Hamas (which turned down her suicide offer). She was depressed and angry over the death of her cousin, Safwad, who blew himself up at a Tel Aviv bus station in January. Her parents believed she snapped at the news of the wounding of a pregnant woman at an Israeli military checkpoint on February 25. She left behind a suicide note that mentioned the death 17 months earlier of Mohammed Dura, a boy shot dead by Israeli soldiers while walking with his father in Gaza.

February 28, 2002. *Jordan.* A primitive car bomb exploded in Amman's Jebal Amman section, killing an Iraqi and an Egyptian—apparently bystanders—and destroying the car of the wife of Lt. Col. Ali Burjak, Jordan's key terrorism investigator and head of the Jordanian Anti-Terrorism Unit. He had brought the case in 2001 against 28 al Qaeda terrorists plotting attacks against the U.S. and Israeli tourists in December 1999. The Iraqi had worked at a nearby food shop. The car was parked near the Burjaks' home. In May 2002, the State Security Court indicted six unnamed suspects in the case. 02022801

February 28, 2002. *Colombia.* Armed rebels kidnapped an Italian tourist at an illegal checkpoint in Antioquia. He was released on March 17 in San Francisco. 02022802

March 2002. *Russia.* The late March death in Chechnya of Arab guerrilla leader Khattab was announced by the Federal Security Service on April 25. Khattab had ties to bin Laden. Khattab claimed in November that he and the Taliban were fighting "infidels" on Muslim territory. He had fought against Russian troops in Chechnya since 1991, having fought in the 1980s against the Russian invasion of Afghanistan. He was blamed for a 1996 attack that killed 53 soldiers and wounded 52 others. He was believed to be from either Saudi Arabia or Jordan. A Chechen Web site and Moscow newspapers suggested that he was killed by a fast-acting poison hidden in a letter.

March 2002. *Bosnia.* A U.S. military task force helped raid the Sarajevo offices of the Benevolence International Foundation, a Muslim charity with ties to al Qaeda. Authorities grabbed computer disks and documents that they used the next month to indict Enaam Arnaout, the foundation's executive director in Chicago. He was charged with perjury for claiming that the group had never provided money to al Qaeda.

March 2002. *Lebanon.* Hizballah, Hamas, and al Qaeda representatives met.

March 1, 2002. *United Kingdom.* Scotland Yard intercepted packages containing a caustic substance that had been mailed to Prime Minister Tony Blair's wife, Cherie, and Scottish Member of Parliament Mike Rumbles. An anonymous caller from the Scottish National Liberation Army said that 16 packages had been mailed that week. Police found a vial of liquid falsely labeled as a free sample of a new eucalyptus oil-based aromatic skin lotion. The substance might be sodium hydroxide and could cause serious injury. The group had been credited with sending hoax anthrax letters in the summer of 2001 to St. Andrews University in Scotland, where Prince William is a student. Blair was in Australia at the time the package was discovered.

The next day, two other prominent Britons received similar parcels, but threw them out unopened and before police could examine them.

March 1, 2002. *Italy.* Police announced the arrest of six men on suspicion of al Qaeda ties. Pakistani citizen Ahmad Naseer was taken into custody at Fiumicino Airport after arriving from Saudi Arabia via Egypt. Police believed he heads an Islamic terrorist cell in Rome. On March 2, Naseer was released when police said they did not have enough evidence to hold him. His traveling companion was detained but not arrested. The others were picked up at the airport or in early morning raids on Rome apartments and in a garage used as a mosque. The other five, aged 22 to 39, were identified as Chibab Ghoumri, an Algerian; Ben Khalifa Mansour, a Tunisian; and Iraqis Faysal Salah Muhamed, Ahmad Isa Muhamed, and Ali Hemin Kadir. They were held on suspicion of association with a "criminal organization with terrorist intentions" and intent to obtain and transfer arms and weapons. Wiretaps of their conversations included discussions of killing President Bush, a cyanide compound, and weapons needed for terrorist training camps

in Afghanistan. Police seized videotapes, address books, and a plane ticket to Phoenix. They also found a letter with the address of Lotfi Raissi, an Algerian accused in the United Kingdom of giving pilot training to the September 11 hijackers. 02030101

March 2, 2002. *Macedonia.* Police killed seven men who they said were plotting terrorist attacks at the U.S., German, and U.K. embassies in Skopje. Five of the dead were Pakistani or Middle Eastern; the others could be ethnic Albanians. Police had been following them since detaining two Jordanians and two Bosnians in February and seizing computer disks with information on embassies and government installations. The police fired warning shots when attempting to detain the terrorists, who reportedly fired back. Police suffered no casualties in the shoot-out on a dirt road leading to Ljuboten. Police said they had seized eight Chinese-designed hand grenades (probably from Albania), a rocket-propelled grenade launcher with ammunition, an antitank weapon, four automatic weapons, two pistols, a bazooka, flares, and more than a dozen new uniforms of the Albanian National Liberation Army. The terrorists were in civilian clothing. Some carried Turkish bank notes and two plastic cards with Arabic writing.

Police later said all seven were Pakistanis and identified one as Ahmet Ikaz, 24, listed by Interpol as a criminal.

On April 30, 2004, Macedonian police spokeswoman Mirjana Konteska told the media that police had ambushed and killed seven innocent South Asian (six Pakistanis and one Indian) illegal immigrants to show that police were participating in the War on Terrorism. Three former police commanders, two special police officers, and a businessman were charged with murder and faced life sentences. The immigrants were smuggled into Macedonia from Bulgaria by a special Macedonian police group who told the victims that they would be transferred to Western Europe. The next day, police accused former Interior Minister Ljube Boskovski of ordering the killings. He reportedly skipped to Croatia, where, police said, they could not arrest and extradite him because of his Croatian citizenship. 02030201

March 2, 2002. *Israel.* Mohamed Ahmed Durarme (variant Darameh), 18, a resident of the Daheisha refugee camp near Bethlehem, became an al-Aqsa Martyrs Brigades Palestinian suicide bomber when he set off an explosives belt in Beit Israel, an ultra-Orthodox neighborhood of Jerusalem, as worshipers left synagogues at the end of the Jewish Sabbath. Durarme killed 9 people, including 3 children, wounding 40 others, 5 of them seriously, and setting four cars on fire. The bomber was standing near a group of women waiting with baby carriages for their husbands to finish their prayers. Seven of the dead, including five children, were from the same family. They were attending the coming-of-age party for a cousin.

Shortly after the attack, an al-Aqsa Martyrs Brigades gunman shot to death an Israeli motorcycle policeman outside Jerusalem.

March 3, 2002. *Colombia.* The Revolutionary Armed Forces of Colombia (FARC) tortured and killed Senator Martha Catalina Daniels, a member of the opposition Liberal Party who was attempting to obtain the release of hostages Ricardo Tafur Gonzales and Cristhian Mauricio Rodriguez. She sustained two bullets to the head shot from close range; she was also tortured. An assistant and a friend accompanying her in her bulletproof Mercedes truck were also killed. She was found in a ravine off a country road 25 miles west of Bogota.

March 3, 2002. *Israel.* A Palestinian sniper using a single-shot carbine fired on an Israeli military checkpoint in the West Bank, killing seven soldiers and three Jewish settlers, and injuring another six Israelis, several critically. He fired from a ridge 75 yards above the checkpoint next to an old British colonial police station in the Valley of the Thieves, north of Ramallah and near the Jewish settlement of Ofra. He escaped

after 25 minutes, leaving his rifle and 25 spent casings. The al-Aqsa Martyrs Brigades claimed credit.

March 3, 2002. *Israel.* A Palestinian gunman shot to death an Israeli soldier near the Gaza Strip. The al-Aqsa Martyrs Brigades claimed credit.

March 3, 2002. *Belgium.* Molotov cocktails were thrown at a synagogue in Antwerp.

March 4, 2002. *Afghanistan.* In Zurmat, a group of Western journalists overheard two Afghan gunmen plotting to kidnap them. The journalists retreated quickly.

Their convoy was attacked when an individual threw an explosive at one of the cars, injuring *Toronto Star* correspondent Kathleen Kenna. Also in the convoy were journalists from the *Washington Post, Newsweek,* and *Agence France-Presse.* 02030401

March 4, 2002. *United States.* A Texas lab worker examining specimens from the October and November anthrax attacks himself became infected with cutaneous anthrax on his neck. Going against procedure, his doctor permitted him to take the swab with him for processing in his own lab.

March 5, 2002. *Israel.* Just before 8:00 a.m., Jewish vigilantes were suspected of setting off a bomb in a triangular package in the courtyard of a Palestinian school in East Jerusalem's Sur Bakhar village as hundreds of students were arriving. Seven children and a teacher were injured. The Revenge of the Innocent Babes claimed credit. School officials said they had called the bomb in 30 minutes earlier; police claimed they were on the way, and had been called only 15 minutes beforehand.

March 5, 2002. *Israel.* At 2:00 a.m., a Palestinian gunman fired his M-16 assault rifle from an overpass outside, killing three Israelis in a trendy Tel Aviv seafood restaurant. The al-Aqsa Martyrs Brigades member then ran into the restaurant, where a soccer team and a bride-to-be were having dinner, and stabbed several Israelis. Ibrahim Hassouna, 20, a resident of the Balata refugee camp near Nablus, injured 31 people before being shot to death by police and customers.

March 5, 2002. *Israel.* A Palestinian suicide bomber boarded a bus in the morning in Afula and set off a bomb, killing an Israeli and himself.

March 5, 2002. *Israel.* Palestinians fired three rockets from Gaza into an apartment building in Sderot, wounding two children.

March 5, 2002. *Israel.* A sniper killed a Jewish settler on a road in the West Bank.

March 7, 2002. *Israel.* Palestinian gunmen on a roadside in the West Bank ambushed an Israeli settler, seriously injuring him.

March 7, 2002. *Israel.* A Palestinian gunman opened fire on a Jewish settlement in Gaza, killing 5 Israelis and wounding 20.

March 7, 2002. *Israel.* A Palestinian suicide bomber set off an explosive in a hotel lobby collocated with a supermarket in the Jewish settlement of Ariel in the West Bank, wounding ten people, including a U.S. citizen. The Popular Front for the Liberation of Palestine (PFLP) claimed responsibility. 02030701

March 7, 2002. *Israel.* A Palestinian carried a large bomb in a backpack into a popular café in Jerusalem's German Colony neighborhood, but was detained before he could set it off. Customers noticed wires sticking out of the bag and into the pocket of a heavy coat he was wearing on a hot day.

March 7, 2002. *United States.* A federal grand jury in Washington, D.C., indicted three members of the Revolutionary Armed Forces of Colombia (FARC) and four other South Americans on charges of conspiracy to import cocaine into the United States. The indictment, which was unsealed on March 18, was the first time

the United States had brought charges against the FARC. The defendants included Tomas Molina Caracas, commander of the FARC's 16th Front in eastern Colombia, near the Venezuelan and Brazilian borders; and Luis Fernando da Costa, alleged to be a Brazilian arms smuggler and drug trafficker who was arrested in April 2001 in Barrancominas, the center of Molina's operations. He was deported to Brazil to face murder and drug charges. Three Brazilians were among the indicted.

March 8, 2002. *Israel.* A Palestinian gunman killed five Israeli teenagers in Atzmona, an Israeli military training academy. On March 11, an Israeli military armored bulldozer demolished the gunman's home in the Gaza Strip's Jabalya camp.

March 9, 2002. *Israel.* Shortly after 8:00 p.m., two Palestinian gunmen threw grenades and fired assault rifles on people in the lobbies of two hotels near the Netanya beach, killing 2 Israelis—a woman and a baby—and injuring more than 40 people, 5 of them seriously, before being shot to death by Israeli police. One of the gunmen was dressed as an Israeli police officer. The al-Aqsa Martyrs Brigades claimed credit.

March 9, 2002. *Israel.* At 10:30 p.m., a Palestinian suicide bomber set off explosives in the courtyard entry of Moment, a popular Jerusalem café, killing 11 Israelis and injuring 52, including a U.S. citizen. The dead were between the ages of 22 and 31. Blood was visible 12 feet high on the eaves of the entranceway. The café is a block from the Prime Minister's residence. Hamas claimed credit, saying the attack was carried out by Fuad Ismail Hourani, 20, a student at a teachers' college in Ramallah. Hourani's father said he was proud of his son, saying that his other sons were available for similar attacks. "One is gone but another five are left. I'm willing to sacrifice them all for the homeland." The al-Aqsa Martyrs Brigades also claimed credit.

Café owner Ilan Gordon had recently hired a security guard.

Among the dead were Uri Felix, 28, a security guard, and his fiancee, Danit Dagan, 25, a student. They were engaged to be married in May. They were buried side by side in a Jerusalem cemetery; her mother laid the bridal bouquet on the graves.

On November 5, four Palestinian residents of East Jerusalem pleaded guilty to involvement in a series of bombings, including the March 9 attack that killed 35 people. House painter Mohammed Oudeh admitted planting the bomb in Hebrew University's cafeteria that killed nine people in the summer of 2001. 02030901

March 9, 2002. *United States.* University of Illinois at Chicago police arrested Joseph Konopka, 25, and a 15-year-old on suspicion of trespassing in a steam tunnel under the school's education building during the night. On March 11, Konopka was charged with storing powdered cyanide in an underground passage that is part of the Chicago Transit Authority's facilities. He apparently broke into the storage room, where he hid sodium cyanide and potassium cyanide. He was charged with possession of a chemical weapon and held pending a hearing on March 13. He faced a maximum fine of $250,000 and a jail sentence. The unemployed Konopka, formerly of De Pere, Wisconsin, had lived in the Chicago subway system for several weeks. The former systems administrator was wanted in Wisconsin for skipping out on charges of vandalizing power stations in Door County. He had attacked a television station transmitter, electric power stations, and a natural gas pipeline. In June, he failed to appear in court to face charges of burglary, theft, and criminal damage to communications towers. The Door County district attorney said he was a self-described anarchist, involved in the group The Realm of Chaos.

On December 20, 2002, Konopka (alias Dr. Chaos) pleaded guilty to causing power outages in Wisconsin. On March 13, 2003, he was sentenced to 13 years in prison. On April 12, 2003, Konopka said he wanted to withdraw his guilty plea and separate federal charges that he conspired to knock out power lines, burn buildings, and damage computers in Wisconsin. Sentencing had been scheduled for April 17. His attorney filed a motion to withdraw the guilty plea.

March 10, 2002. *United States.* Minneapolis police shot to death Abu Kassim Jeilani, 28, a mentally ill Somali who was carrying a machete and a crowbar. Police had trailed him for several blocks, and people who knew him tried to get him to drop the weapons. Police then fired on him and were accused by critics of using excessive force. Five officers were put on routine administrative leave. Jeilani came to the United States in 1997.

March 10, 2002. *Israel.* Two Palestinians were killed inside a car that exploded in Jerusalem.

March 10, 2002. *Israel.* A Palestinian gunman fired an M-16 rifle, wounding a 13-year-old Israeli boy.

March 10, 2002. *Israel.* Soldiers shot to death a Palestinian who was entering Jerusalem with a rifle and grenades stashed in a backpack.

March 10, 2002. *Israel.* A Palestinian gunman shot and killed an Israeli soldier guarding the Jewish settlement of Netzarim in Gaza. An Israeli security guard shot the terrorist to death.

March 11, 2002. *United States.* Bassam Youseff Hammoud, Mohammed Atef Darwiche, Ali Hussein Darwiche, and Mehdi Hachem Moussaoui pleaded guilty to racketeering conspiracy in a Charlotte court. They faced 20 years in prison for funneling profits from cigarette smuggling to Hizballah.

On February 27, 2003, the Darwiche cousins were sentenced to more than three years in prison. U.S. District Judge Graham Mullen sentenced Samuel Chahrour, a Dearborn, Michigan, man who bought large quantities of the cigarettes, to two years in prison. On March 19, 2003, Said Harb, the key government witness against Hammoud, who was convicted of aiding

Hizballah, was sentenced to 41 months in prison. In a separate sentence, Mohamad Hammoud received 155 years. On April 2, 2003, his wife, Angela Tsioumas, was sentenced to four months of house arrest.

March 11–12, 2002. *United States.* Some 40 envelopes containing hate letters and a white powder falsely alleged to be anthrax were sent to the offices of the National Association of Latino Elected and Appointed Officials, the League of United Latin American Citizens, the Aspira Association, Inc., and the National Association of Hispanic Journalists, all in Washington, D.C. Five offices of the National Council of La Raza in the Southwest United States in Texas and the American Legal Defense Fund in Sacramento also received letters. Attorney General John D. Ashcroft said that such hoaxes were "serious violations of federal law." The powder tested negative for anthrax. Most of the letters were postmarked in Oakland, California.

March 12, 2002. *Israel.* Two Arab gunmen believed to belong to Hizballah shot to death seven Israelis. The duo wore Israeli army uniforms and apparently tunneled under or jumped over the border fence with Lebanon.

March 12, 2002. *Philippines.* Authorities in Zamboanga arrested Munib Assa, an Abu Sayyaf terrorist accused of kidnapping students and beheading two teachers in 1999.

March 12, 2002. *United States.* Homeland Security Director Tom Ridge announced a five-tier system of color-coded terrorist alerts that would constitute the Homeland Security Advisory System (HSAS).

- Green indicates low risk of terrorist attacks and permits refining and exercising planned protective measures; training personnel on HSAS, departmental, and agency-specific protective measures; and regularly assessing facilities for vulnerabilities and taking preventive measures.

- Blue indicates a general risk of terrorist attacks and adds checking on communications with designated emergency response/command locations; reviewing and updating emergency response procedures; and disseminating information to the public.

- Yellow indicates significant risk of terrorist attacks and adds increased surveillance of key locations; coordinating with local jurisdictions; further refining protective measures; and implementing contingency/emergency response plans.

- Orange indicates a high risk of terrorist attacks and adds permitting coordination of necessary security efforts with armed forces/law enforcement; additional precautions at public events; preparing to work at an alternate site and/or with a dispersed workforce; and restricting access.

- Red indicates a severe risk of terrorist attacks and adds assigning emergency response personnel/specially trained teams; monitoring/redirecting/constraining transportation systems; closing public/government facilities; and increasing/redirecting personnel to address critical emergency needs.

Attorney General John D. Ashcroft will set the alert levels, which are modeled after the armed forces' Defense Condition (DefCon) threat scale. Tom Ridge said the United States was currently experiencing Yellow risk level.

March 13, 2002. *Philippines.* Police at Manila International Airport arrested three Indonesians believed to belong to a group with al Qaeda ties. They were held for possession of components for explosives. They were attempting to board a plane for Bangkok during the night. Police said their luggage held "components for improvised explosives."

By May 8, Western and Philippine intelligence services were saying that one of them, Agus Dwikarna, 36, was a commander of the Laskar Jundullah militia that helped train al Qaeda operatives. The group wanted to evict Christians from several central Indonesian islands. It had set up a secret paramilitary training camp on Sulawesi Island in central Indonesia in late 2000. The camp was in a dense jungle near the port city of Poso. Its trainees included two dozen Filipino members of the Moro Islamic Liberation Front, several members of the Malaysian Mujaheddin Group (which is affiliated with Jemaah Islamiah, an al Qaeda linked group that planned to bomb several Western embassies in Singapore), and scores from the Middle East, Europe, and North Africa. It apparently was dismantled soon after the September 11 attacks.

Dwikarna was a businessman active in several radical groups, such as the Indonesian Mujaheddin Council. The Council is led by Abubakar Baasyir, a cleric accused by Malaysia and Singapore of being the ideological leader of the Jemaah Islamiah. Police had found plastic explosives and detonation cable in Dwikarna's suitcase. He claimed he was set up by Indonesian intelligence. He claimed he and his two arrested traveling companions were on a business trip. Authorities said Dwikarna provided alibis to several hundred foreigners traveling in the area by giving them documents with the letterhead of the Muslim charity for which he worked—the Committee to Overcome Crisis. Police believed he worked with Parlindungan Siregar, an Indonesian living in Spain who helped arrange for several hundred al Qaeda operatives from Europe to travel to Indonesia for training, according to Spanish authorities.

Dwikarna's colleagues, Abdul Jamal Balfas and Tamsil Linrung, were released in April because Philippine prosecutors did not have enough evidence to charge them. Tamsil Linrung had been the treasurer of one of Indonesia's largest Muslim political parties, which said the government had orchestrated the arrests as a political attack.

On July 12, a Philippine regional trial court sentenced Dwikarna to 17 years. (The U.S. State Department's *Patterns in Global Terrorism 2002* reports it was ten years.) Police found the name of Omar al-Farouq, another al Qaeda operative, in Dwirkarna's computer. Indonesian police tracked him down in June and handed him over to U.S. authorities, who interrogated him in Afghanistan. 02031301

March 13, 2002. *Israel.* Mohammed Farahat, 17 (some reports say 19), attacked a school for army-bound religious Israelis at the Gush Katif settlement, killing 7 (some reports say 5) young cadets and wounding 23 others. Farahat used an automatic rifle and grenades. He was a longtime follower of Imad Aql, a Hamas activist in the Gaza Strip who was killed by Israeli troops. Farahat was killed by Israeli soldiers who returned fire.

Farahat's mother, Mariam, 52, told visitors "I don't want condolences. I want congratulations. I encouraged my son to sacrifice himself. It is a victory." She appeared in a video with him and took the name Um Nidal–Mother of Struggle. She said he joined the Izzedine al Qassam Brigades, the military branch of Hamas, as a teen. His father, Fathi, 57, belonged to the political wing of Hamas. Two other sons belonged to the brigades; Wusam Farahat lost three fingers on his right hand when tossing a grenade at an Israeli army patrol. Mariam recalled, "He was filled with hate for the Jews. He told me he wanted to carry out an operation against the Israelis. I told him it was a good idea and wished him luck. I knew that almost no one comes back alive from such operations. But I kept those thoughts to myself." Fathi was later fired from the Palestinian police department.

March 14, 2002. *Israel.* Palestinians set off a bomb during an ambush of Israeli soldiers, killing three soldiers and destroying a tank in Gaza.

March 14, 2002. *Israel.* Two Palestinians believed to be driving to a terrorist attack in Jerusalem died when their car bomb exploded east of Ramallah. Palestinians blamed Israel, saying the car was booby-trapped.

March 14, 2002. *Colombia.* Motorcycle-riding gunmen shot to death two U.S. citizens, brothers Jaime Raul and Jorge Alberto Orjuela, who had arrived in Cali the day before to negotiate the release of their father, who had been kidnapped by the Revolutionary Armed Forces of Colombia (FARC). No one claimed credit. 02031401

March 15, 2002. *Yemen.* Samir Yahya Awadh, 25, an unemployed Yemeni male, threw one or two sound grenades at the U.S. Embassy, hitting a wall but causing no injuries. The incident came the day after U.S. Vice President Richard Cheney had visited the country. Yemeni security guards fired on him and then grabbed him as he was pulling a grenade out of his pocket. Witnesses saw a car speeding away from the site. 02031501

March 16, 2002. *Germany.* An explosive device was thrown into a Jewish cemetery in Berlin.

March 17, 2002. *Nepal.* In a clash at a Maoist rebel training camp in the hills, Nepalese soldiers killed 62 rebels.

March 17, 2002. *Israel.* A Palestinian, 26, fired a pistol at pedestrians at an intersection near restaurants and shops during lunchtime in Kfar Saba, killing Noa Orbach, 18, a high school senior walking down the street with her friends, and injuring eight others before being shot to death by police and security guards. The Nablus resident emptied two clips of ammunition before he died.

Two hours later, an Arab male suicide bomber in Jerusalem's French Hill neighborhood set off an explosives belt full of screws and nails between a municipal bus and a taxi van near the line between the Jewish western area and the Arab eastern section, slightly injuring nine people on the bus with flying glass and killing himself. The terrorist ran at a bus and set off the bomb just as he reached it. Islamic Jihad claimed credit.

March 17, 2002. *Pakistan.* One or two men (witnesses differed) broke into the Protestant International Church in Islamabad's diplomatic district at 10:50 a.m., just after the pastor began his sermon to the 70 worshipers. They threw hand grenades, killing an Afghan, a Pakistani, Barbara Green—an American who worked for the U.S. Embassy, Kristen Wormsley, 17— Green's daughter who was a senior at the American School in Islamabad, and an unidentified person (possibly an assailant), and wounding 46

others. Green worked in the administrative section of the embassy; husband Milton worked as an engineer in the computer division. Milton and son Zachary, 10, suffered abdominal wounds in the attack. The family had lived in Howard County, Maryland, returning to Pakistan in February. Kristen had been a senior at Howard High School in Ellicott City. They had been evacuated from Pakistan after the September 11, 2001, attacks. The injured included 10 Americans (including Pakistan-American Naseem Christopher), 12 Pakistani Christians— including the church's director, Pakistani doctor Christy Munir—and the Sri Lankan ambassador and his family. Among the injured was Elizabeth Mundhenk, who sustained shrapnel wounds in her leg. Mundhenk was an English teacher from Germany who had lived in the country for a dozen years and plays piano for the congregation. Pakistani Georgina Dabassum sustained a gaping wound on her face and was hit by shrapnel in her side. Blood was found on the 30-foot-high ceiling. No one immediately claimed credit.

Police suggested that only one attacker, possibly a suicide attacker, was involved, and that the witnesses who saw two attackers merely saw him entering the church twice. The body was so disfigured that it was difficult to even determine its race. Some believe he may have been of African descent; others said Pakistani. Police said they had made no arrests, but questioned several people.

Pakistani officials said that members of al Qaeda who had fled Afghanistan were involved in the attack.

Police also worried that five banned militant groups were planning follow-up attacks. They identified them as Jaish-i-Muhammad, Lashkar-i-Taiba, Sipah-i-Sahaba, the Tehrik-i-Jafria party, and the Tehrik Nifaz-i-Shariat Mohammedi.

Islamabad's chief of police and four other senior police officials were fired in the case. Pakistan said that they would send the United States DNA samples from the body of the suspected terrorist.

On November 17, 2004, Pakistani authorities arrested Osama Nazir, deputy chief of Jaish-e-

Muhammad, who was wanted for the attacks on the church. Nazir was found at a *madrassa* in Faisalabad, the city where al Qaeda leader Abu Zubayda was captured in 2002. Nazir was also believed to be involved in the failed assassination attempts on Pakistani President General Pervez Musharraf in December 2003 and on Prime Minister Shaukat Aziz. Authorities confiscated cell phones, computer disks, documents, and other materials related to the organization. The Pakistani daily *Dawn* said Nazir had direct links with bin Laden. 02031701

March 18, 2002. *Georgia.* In Abkhazia, Georgian guerrillas kidnapped four Russian peacekeepers and demanded the release of two Georgian gunmen held by Russian authorities. On March 21, the four Russian peacekeepers and their weapons were exchanged for the two Georgians. Georgian guerrillas claimed credit. 02031801

March 20, 2002. *Israel.* At 7:00 a.m., a bearded Islamic Jihad suicide bomber wearing a green jacket and chewing gum, paid his $2.60 fare and then set off an explosive on the Number 823 commuter bus as it was going from Tel Aviv to Nazareth, killing himself and 7 others, and wounding 27 people. Among the dead was Meir Pachima. Four of the dead were Israeli soldiers; two others were Jewish Israeli citizens. The third dead civilian was unidentified. Jewish and Arab citizens of Israel were wounded. Soldier Evran Ashkenazi, 18, lost hearing in his right ear and was hit with shrapnel. Arab college student Salam Daif suffered first- and second-degree burns. Terrorist Rafat Abu Diyak, 24, who was from Jenin on the West Bank, said he was going to Afula. The bomb went off near Umm el-Fahm, an Arab town in the Galilee region. Bus 823 had been hit by terrorists in November 2001 and earlier in March 2002.

March 20, 2002. *France.* Police raided the Rivera villa of Osama bin Laden's half brother in a money-laundering investigation.

March 20, 2002. *Philippines.* Police defused six bombs in Manila during an alert against the possible entry of al Qaeda members from Afghanistan.

March 20, 2002. *Peru.* At 10:45 p.m., a 100-pound package bomb placed under a car exploded at the upscale El Polo Shopping Center in Lima's Monterrico district, across the street from the U.S. Embassy in Lima, killing 10 people—including 2 police officers and a teenager—and wounding 32. No Americans were hurt. Two local guards died when they went to examine what they believed to be a car fire. The bomb had a long fuse that drew the attention of police. The bomb contained ammonium nitrate and fuel oil—a staple of Shining Path bombings. The uncle of Carlos Rodriguez died in the attack. Several buildings were badly damaged and three cars were on fire. Police believed remnants of the Shining Path or Tupac Amaru Revolutionary Movement (MRTA) were responsible. The attack came two days before President Bush visited Peru to meet with Peruvian President Alejandro Toledo, who offered a $1 million reward for the capture of the bombers. President Toledo announced in early June that three suspected Shining Path rebels had been arrested for the bombing. 02032001

March 20, 2002. *Italy.* A renascent Red Brigades–Communist Combatant Party (BR-PCC) appeared responsible for the shooting death in front of his home in Bologna of Marco Biagi, 52, an academic who was working with the government on changing labor laws. Forensic tests indicated that the gun was used in a murder three years earlier credited to the Red Brigades. On March 23, in the largest post–World War II demonstration in the country, Italy's largest trade union led hundreds of thousands (organizers said 3 million) of people who marched in Rome to protest the proposed labor law changes and the return of political violence. A person claiming Red Brigades membership claimed credit for killing Biagi, who was shot twice in the back of the head as he parked his bicycle at his front door at 8:00 p.m. A witness said two killers wore helmets and rode a motor scooter. Biagi was a professor of labor law at the University of Modena and an adjunct professor at a Bologna center of Pennsylvania's Dickinson College. He left behind a wife and two sons.

In late June, someone leaked letters Biagi had sent to police asking for bodyguards in the weeks before his death.

On July 3, Interior Minister Claudio Scajola resigned after telling reporters that Biagi was "a pain in the neck" (his choice of language was stronger) who just wanted to get his consulting contract renewed. Scajola had defended the police refusal to provide a bodyguard, saying it was too costly to protect everyone associated with the government.

March 20, 2002. *Peru.* A small bomb exploded during the night in front of a Spanish-owned telephone company in Lima, causing no injuries. The Shining Path was suspected. 02032002

March 20, 2002. *United States.* At 10:30 a.m., federal agents from ten agencies raided 14 sites (and 2 others later in the week) across northern Virginia, including Herndon, Falls Church, and Leesburg, seizing boxes of documents in Operation Green Quest, an investigation of terrorist funding led by the Treasury Department. Most of the sites had links to the Middle East, and numerous Arab and Islamic groups complained of discrimination. No arrests were made, and none of the businesses were closed down.

Among the sites were the Herndon offices of the International Institute for Islamic Thought and MarJac Investments, both on Grove Street. The Institute had made large contributions to World Islamic Studies Enterprise in Tampa. In November, the Justice Department had deemed World Islamic Studies Enterprise a "front organization that raised funds for militant Islamic-Palestinian groups such as the Palestine Islamic Jihad and Hamas."

A raid was also conducted at the Graduate School of Islamic and Social Science on Miller Drive in Leesburg, which had opened in 1996. It was the first facility in the country approved by the Pentagon to train Muslim chaplains. Nine of the Department of Defense's 13 Islamic chaplains are alumni.

Also raided was the SAAR Foundation in Herndon, led by M. Yaqub Mirza, a financier with a doctorate in physics from the University of Texas.

Also raided was the Safa Trust, Muslim World League, and the Fiqh Council of North America. The companies and charities raided were tied to the al-Rajhis, Saudi Arabia's leading banking family, and had moved $1.7 billion amongst them.

On May 3, Nancy Luque, attorney for the International Institute of Islamic Thought, the Graduate School of Islamic and Social Sciences, Sterling Management Group, Inc., and ten U.S. citizens, asked a judge in U.S. District Court in Alexandria to return their property and 500 boxes of records, and unseal the secret evidence. Not yet, said U.S. Magistrate Judge Theresa C. Buchanan.

On October 9, 2003, Soliman S. Biheiri, 51, was convicted on two federal immigration charges in U.S. District Court in Alexandria, Virginia. Prosecutors said they would seek a longer term, up to ten years, because he did business with a leader of the Islamic Resistance Movement (Hamas) and served as personal banker to a nephew of Osama bin Laden. Biheiri would normally have served less than six months in prison and revocation of citizenship for lying under oath on his 1999 application for citizenship. Sentencing was set for January 9, 2004. He was sentenced to a year in prison. Biheiri founded BMI, Inc., an investment firm that adhered to Islamic principles, in New Jersey in 1986. Islamic charities based in northern Virginia and sponsored by the Saudi government invested nearly $4 million in BMI, which may have passed the money to terrorist groups. On October 12, 2004, a federal jury convicted Biheiri of lying about his ties to Mousa Abu Marzook, a leader of Hamas. He had been indicted in May 2004 on the charge as well as on separate counts of passport fraud and hiding his dealings with University of Florida Prof. Sami al-Arian, charged with being a leader of Palestine Islamic Jihad. A judge dismissed the al-Arian count. In early October 2004, Biheiri pleaded guilty to illegally possessing and using a U.S. passport to enter the United States. Prosecutors requested a "terrorism enhancement" to stiffen the sentence, saying he obstructed a federal terrorism probe. A hearing was scheduled for October 29, 2004, to explore whether he should receive 15 years or merely a year and deportation to Egypt.

March 21, 2002. *Bosnia.* Bosnian officials said they had discovered that al Qaeda terrorists had met in Bulgaria to identify European targets and to attack Americans in Sarajevo. The next day, the U.S. Embassy in Sarajevo shut down all operations after closing to the public two days earlier.

March 21, 2002. *Israel.* At 4:15 p.m., Mohammed Hashaikeh, 22, a Palestinian policeman from a West Bank village near Nablus, set off a nail-packed bomb in downtown Jerusalem, killing himself and three others, and injuring 86 people, including two Americans. Blood was seen on the third floor facade of an office tower. The al-Aqsa Martyrs Brigades and the Palestine Islamic Jihad took credit. U.S. Secretary of State declared al-Aqsa a terrorist group and ordered its assets frozen. Hashaikeh was arrested in mid-February by Palestinian Authority police on suspicion of planning a suicide bombing at an Israeli mall. He was soon released. Among the dead were Sgt. Maj. Gadi Shemesh and his pregnant wife, Tsipi, who were leaving a medical office. 02032101

March 22, 2002. *Pakistan.* The government quietly permitted terrorist leader Maulana Masood Azhar to go home as a form of house arrest. His group, Jaish-i-Muhammad, is on the State Department list of terrorists and was banned by Pakistan in January. Pakistan had recently freed 1,300 militants who had not been charged with any crimes.

March 22, 2002. *India.* Terrorists threw four or five grenades at an Anantnag bus stop and in a Shopiyan, Srinagar marketplace filled with Muslims going to Friday prayers, causing 52 injuries. Some 35 people were hurt in the marketplace; another 15 civilians and 2 paramilitary troops were injured five hours later when two grenades went off in the Anantnag bus stop. Among the injured in Shopiyan was Mohammed Shaban, 55, who said civilians apparently were targeted. No one claimed credit. In Rajouri, Kashmir, a bomb exploded in a sweet shop, injuring five people.

March 22, 2002. *Israel.* A Palestinian suicide bomber set off an explosive at a military checkpoint outside Jenin in the West Bank, killing himself and injuring a soldier.

March 22, 2002. *Uganda.* In Kalosaric, gunmen stopped a vehicle traveling on the Moroto–Kotido Road, killing an Irish Catholic priest, his driver, and his cook. Karamojong gunmen were suspected. 02032201

March 23, 2002. *India.* In Kadal, Kashmir, a grenade thrown at a police installation missed its target and landed in a group of civilians, killing 2 people and injuring 20, including 9 police officers. No one claimed credit.

March 26, 2002. *Israel.* Two Palestinian men were killed when their car bomb exploded near Jerusalem's main shopping mall and the Biblical Zoo. Police stopped them from entering a Jerusalem shopping area. The al-Aqsa Martyrs Brigades claimed credit.

March 26, 2002. *Israel.* A Swiss woman and a Turkish man from the Temporary International Presence in Hebron were shot to death in a roadside ambush of their car. An injured survivor—a Turkish army officer—said the killer was a Palestinian in military garb. On September 21, 2003, an Israeli military court sentenced Sufuwan

Mahmoud Yousri, the getaway driver, to two consecutive life sentences. 02032601

March 26, 2002. *France.* Richard Durn, 33, fired two Glock semi-automatic pistols in a Nanterre city council meeting, killing eight people and wounding ten. The council had just finished a six-hour budget meeting. More than 100 ambulances and a visiting contingent of New York City Fire Department firefighters responded to the scene. Durn, who also carried a .357 Magnum, was taken into custody. Most of the victims were council members. No motive was given. On March 28, the shooter killed himself by jumping out of a fifth-floor window at police headquarters while he was being questioned. Durn held a master's degree in political science, but was unemployed. He had done volunteer work at the local Human Rights League and belonged to a recreational shooting club. Police found a 13-page confessor letter in his home and said he wanted police to kill him. He had yelled, "Kill me, kill me" when struggling with police in the council chamber.

March 26, 2002. *Senegal.* In Kadountine, Casamance Province, rebels attacked the coastal resort, killing five people and wounding four, including a French citizen. The Casamance Movement of Democratic Forces was suspected. 02032602

March 27, 2002. *Israel.* Two Palestinian gunmen attacked Israeli soldiers guarding a kibbutz. The gunmen died but injured two soldiers.

March 27, 2002. *Israel.* At 7:30 p.m., a Hamas suicide bomber killed 28 people, including an American, Hannah Rogen, and injured 172 people, 48 of them seriously, at the seaside Park Hotel in Netanya during a Seder dinner at the start of Passover. Terrorist Abdel Basset Odeh, 24, a Palestinian who lived in Tulkarm, had worked in hotels in Netanya and elsewhere in Israel, and had been on Israel's wanted list. The hotel's guards did not spot him. When a reception clerk asked what he was doing, he ran into

the dining room and set off the 20-pound bomb strapped to his waist and hidden by an overcoat. He had disappeared several months before the bombing after being told to report for questioning to the . He was one of eight children. He was to be married to a Palestinian woman he had met in Baghdad, but was refused entry to the Allenby Bridge to Jordan at the beginning of his return visit. Iraqi President Saddam Hussein had pledged to send $25,000 to each suicide bomber's family. Posters of Odeh named him "The Lion of the Holy Revenge."

The dead included a 68-year-old woman and her 78-year-old husband, a 70-year-old Swedish female tourist, a 25-year-old soldier, a couple in their late 40s, and a 20-year-old woman. Six of the dead were Holocaust survivors. Ami Hamami, the hotel's manager, was killed.

Among the injured was Isaac Atsits, 73, a veteran of four Arab-Israeli wars, who suffered a punctured eardrum and serious bruising to his left eye.

Andre Landerlok, a Jewish man from Sweden celebrating Passover and visiting his son, Yoel, 20, studying at a Tel Aviv–area seminary, spotted the bomber, who looked to be wearing a long-haired wig. Everyone in the family was injured.

The attack led Prime Minister Ariel Sharon to invade the West Bank in an effort to shut down the bombers. 02032701

March 27, 2002. *United States.* The Treasury Department's Office of Foreign Assets Control implemented Secretary of State Colin Powell's earlier announcement that the United States would block the financial assets of the al-Aqsa Martyrs Brigades, Asbat al-Ansar (a Sunni Muslim group based in Palestinian refugee camps in Lebanon), and the Algerian Salafist Group for Preaching (Call) and Combat.

March 27, 2002. *Italy.* The U.S. Embassy announced that it had received "credible reports" of possible Middle Eastern terrorist attacks against U.S. citizens in Milan, Florence, Venice, and Verona in the coming month. Easter Sunday was a particularly dangerous time for Americans in restaurants, open-air cafés, tourist spots, places of worship, and other public locations. The next day, an Italian official called the warning "inopportune."

March 27, 2002. *United Kingdom.* Abdel-Bari Atwan, editor of the London-based Arabic language newspaper *al-Quds al-Arabi* said that he had received an e-mail from Osama bin Laden, whom he had met in 1996, that attacked that day's Saudi peace plan for the Middle East. Bin Laden called for Muslims to revolt against their leaders. The e-mail was entitled "Statement from Sheikh Osama bin Laden on the initiative of Prince Abdullah," which it deemed "a Zionist-American one in Saudi clothes…. The initiative of Prince Abdullah … is a conspiracy and another display of repeated betrayals." The e-mail praised recent Palestinian suicide bombers.

March 27–28, 2002. *Pakistan.* Eight teams of Pakistani police assisted by FBI officials raided Islamic radical sites in Lahore and Faisalabad, arresting more than 60 Islamic militants, including al Qaeda members, 25 Arabs, and 4 Afghans. One suspect was killed when he pulled a knife after being arrested. A policeman and four suspects were wounded in a shoot-out in Faisalabad. Two of the injured terrorists were foreigners; one was from Syria. Detainees included citizens of Egypt and Yemen, along with 40 Pakistanis. Police said some of those arrested may have been involved in the March 17 grenade attack on an Islamabad church. Another was Prof. Hameedullah Khan Niazi, Faisalabad leader of the banned Lashkar-i-Taiba (Holy Army)

U.S. and Pakistani authorities said that one of the detainees may be Abu Zubaida, al Qaeda's senior field commander who joined the group in the 1990s. The Saudi-born Palestinian, whose full name is Zayn Abidin Muhammed Hussein abu Zubaida, was the chief recruiter for the group in the House of Martyrs in Peshawar, Pakistan. He was sentenced by a Jordanian court to death *in absentia* for his role in plotting to bomb

hotels in Jordan during millennium celebrations. His satellite phone number was found in the memory of a cell phone of a man accused of plotting to bomb the U.S. Embassy in Sarajevo. Another man involved in an al Qaeda plot against the U.S. Embassy in Paris told a French judge that Abu Zubaida had briefed him in bin Laden's residence. Convicted millennium bomber Ahmed Ressam testified in July 2001 in a U.S. court that "he is the person in charge of the camps. He receives young men from all countries. He accepts you or rejects you. And he takes care of the expenses of the camps. He made arrangements for you when you travel, coming in or leaving."

Following the raids, the *Washington Post* offered the following breakdown of the status of the most wanted al Qaeda leaders:

Dead

- Muhammad Atef
- Mafouz Ould Walid (alias Abu Hafs al-Mauritania), counselor
- Assadullah (alias Mohammad Omar Abd-al-Rahman), son of Omar Abd-al-Rahman, the blind Egyptian sheik serving time in the United States for the 1993 World Trade Center bombing
- Mohammad Salah, Egyptian Islamic Jihad leader
- Tariq Anwar Fathy, Egyptian Islamic Jihad aide
- Abu Saleh al-Yemeni, operational facilitator
- Abu Jafar Jaziri, logistician
- Abu Ubaida, trainer
- Hamza al-Qatari, financial aide

Detained

- Sharqaqi Abdu Ali al-Hajj, operational facilitator
- Ibn Shayk al-Libi, training camp commander

At large

- Osama bin Laden
- Ayman Zawahiri
- Abu Gaith Sulaiman, spokesman
- Saif Al-Adel Almasari (alias Muhammad Al-Makkawi), senior aide

- Shaykh Said Al-Sharif, financial aide
- Abu Mohammad Al-Masri, chief of training
- Abu Musab Zarqawi, operational planner
- Abu Zubaida, operational coordinator (and possibly in detention)
- Abu Khalid al-Masri, senior aide
- Tawfiq Attash Khallad, senior aide
- Fazul Abdullah, operational coordinator
- Saleh Abdullah, operational coordinator
- Abdu Nashri, operational coordinator
- Zaid Khayr, trainer
- Abu-Bashir al-Yemeni, training camp commander

Some of them could be dead but not yet identified.

Pakistan turned 20 of the Arabs over to the United States on March 31. They were to be flown to Guantanamo Bay. Abu Zubaida was in serious condition, having been hit in the stomach and groin by three bullets, and was kept in an undisclosed location.

March 28, 2002. *Israel.* A Palestinian gunman broke into a home in the Elon Moreh settlement near Nablus during the night, killing four members of a family.

March 29, 2002. *Israel.* Just before 2:00 p.m., Ayat Akhras, an 18-year-old female al-Aqsa Martyrs Brigades suicide bomber from the Deheishe refugee camp near Bethlehem, set off an explosive in a Jerusalem supermarket in Kiryat Hayovel, killing 2 Israelis and injuring 31. Ghazi Algosaibi, Saudi ambassador to the United Kingdom, wrote a poem praising her and other Palestinian suicide bombers.

March 29, 2002. *Israel.* A Palestinian man stabbed to death two elderly men who were on their way to a synagogue in a Jewish settlement in the central Gaza Strip. Israeli soldiers shot to death the killer.

March 29, 2002. *Ukraine.* Unidentified gunmen broke into an Ivano-Frankivsk apartment in the west during the night and shot to death Mykola Shkriblyak, 42, deputy governor of the region. Members of his political party said the killing was aimed at intimidating them before the March 31 election.

March 30, 2002. *Israel.* In a gun battle, Israeli border police killed two al-Aqsa Martyrs Brigades Palestinians coming into Israel with grenades and explosives. One policeman died in the firefight that started when the terrorists' car was stopped for questioning in Baka Al-Gharbiya on the West Bank–Israel border. One of the Palestinians set off an explosives belt.

March 30, 2002. *Israel.* An al-Aqsa Martyrs Brigades suicide bomber injured 32 people in Tel Aviv's My Coffee Shop café on Allenby Street during the evening. There was no security guard at the door. Six were in serious condition. The blast destroyed the shop and a neighboring café was heavily damaged. The terrorist group said the bomber was a 23-year-old Palestinian from Nablus.

March 30, 2002. *India.* The Islamic Front set off a bomb at a Hindu temple in Jammu, Kashmir, killing ten people.

March 30, 2002. *France.* Vandals torched a Strasbourg synagogue during the night. Earlier that day, hooded thugs crashed two cars into the La Duchere synagogue in Lyon, setting fire to one of the vehicles inside the temple's prayer hall. Someone fired a machine gun into a Kosher butcher shop in Toulouse, but caused no injuries. A Jewish couple was attacked in Villeurbanne.

March 31, 2002. *Israel.* At 2:30 p.m., a Palestinian Hamas suicide bomber wearing a black jacket set off several pounds of explosives wrapped around his torso at Haifa's Matza restaurant, killing 15 people, both Jews and Israeli Arabs, and injuring at least 36 others. Eight were in serious condition; one in critical condition. The Jewish-owned restaurant (Miki Matza owns it) is managed by an Israeli-Arab family. Five Arab employees of the restaurant, including Ali Adawi, were injured. There was no security guard. One of the people in the restaurant, Shimon Sabag, said, "I tried to put out the fire. Even the moderately injured were on fire." The building collapsed on the 40 people inside. Hamas said the terrorist was Israeli citizen Shadi Abu Tubasi, 22, of Jenin, son of a Palestinian father and an Israeli-Arab mother.

March 31, 2002. *Israel.* A Palestinian suicide bomber set off explosives next to an ambulance station at a small medical center in Efrat, a Jewish settlement on the West Bank, wounding four people, including an American. A paramedic was critically injured. Another person had serious wounds. The other two had minor injuries. The terrorist walked up to volunteer medics and blew himself up. The al-Aqsa Martyrs Brigades claimed credit.

Prime Minister Ariel Sharon told a national television audience, "Citizens of Israel: the State of Israel is at war, a war against terror. We must fight this terrorism, in an uncompromising war to uproot these savages, to dismantle their infrastructure, because there is no compromise with terrorists." Sharon charged that Yasir Arafat, whose complex was under attack by the Israeli armed forces after a Saudi peace initiative at an Arab summit was rejected by Israel, "activated, coordinated, and directed" the recent attacks. 02033101

April 2002. *People's Republic of China.* A bomb exploded in Chengdu, capital of Sichuan Province. Police arrested Lobsang Dhondup, 28, near the site of the explosion. The Chinese executed Lobsang on January 26, 2003, in Ganzi near the Tibetan border in Sichuan Province. He was convicted of carrying out a string of bombings to protest Chinese rule in Tibet. The Sichuan Provincial High People's Court rejected an appeal by his teacher, Tenzin Deleg Rinpoche, 52, a senior Buddhist monk, and affirmed his suspended death sentence, which usually means life in prison. Tenzin was held incommunicado for eight months until the day of his trial. Human rights organizations said that attorneys Zhang Sizhi and Li Huigeng were not permitted to represent him in his appeal and that the two defendants were tortured into confessing. Ten other Tibetans were detained in connection with the series of bombings, which killed at least one person.

April 2002. *Mexico.* The government closed the offices of the Revolutionary Armed Forces of Colombia after a presence of a decade.

April 2002. *Turkey.* Police in Bursas arrested four people linked to al Qaeda.

April 2002. *Azerbaijan.* The government sentenced six members of Hizb ut-Tahrir, an extremist movement that wants to establish a borderless, theocratic caliphate throughout the entire Muslim world (also a goal of Osama bin Laden), to up to seven years in prison for attempted terrorist activities.

April 2002. *Nepal.* Maoist rebels bombed a locally operated Coca-Cola bottling plant. 02049901

April 2002. *Netherlands.* In April and August, Dutch authorities arrested two dozen extremists —ten of whom remained in custody as of April 2003—and accused them of supporting terrorists and recruiting combatants for jihad.

April 1, 2002. *Israel.* An al-Aqsa Martyrs Brigades Palestinian suicide bomber set off a car bomb when approached by a patrolman at a police checkpoint near the Old City of Jerusalem, killing himself and seriously injuring the police officer.

April 1, 2002. *Israel.* A terrorist sniper shot to death a 22-year-old Israeli in Har Homa, a Jewish housing project in an area occupied in the 1967 Middle East war and later annexed to Jerusalem.

April 1, 2002. *France.* Marseille's Or Aviv synagogue was destroyed by firebombs during the night. Torah scrolls were burned. No one claimed credit.

A Jewish school in Sarcelles was attacked.

April 1, 2002. *Belgium.* A fire caused minor damage to the Anderlecht synagogue in Brussels.

April 1, 2002. *Russia.* Thugs scrawled a black swastika across a synagogue in Kostroma during the night.

April 1, 2002. *Germany.* Two Orthodox Jews from New York were attacked on a Berlin street.

April 1, 2002. *Nigeria.* Ten oil workers contracted to the Royal Shell Oil Group were kidnapped by militant youths. The hostages included an American, a Filipino, and four Ghanaians. 02040101

April 2, 2002. *France.* A prayer pavilion in a Jewish cemetery in Strasbourg was burned to the ground.

April 3, 2002. *France.* Thugs threw a firebomb at a Marseille synagogue.

April 3, 2002. *France.* Paris police arrested five people for throwing gasoline-filled bottles at a synagogue during the night. No damage was reported.

April 4, 2002. *France.* Jewish school vehicles were burned in Aubervilliers.

A synagogue in Montpellier was firebombed. Two of three male detainees in the attack were Muslims of North African descent.

April 5, 2002. *Singapore.* Singaporean Prime Minister Goh Chok Tong told Parliament that Mas Selemat Kastari, who was believed to have fled Thailand in January, was a member of Jemaah Islamiah, which is linked to al Qaeda. He was suspected of planning to hijack a plane from Indonesia, Malaysia, or Thailand and fly it into Singapore's Changi Airport.

April 5, 2002. *France.* A suspected home-made bomb was found in a Jewish cemetery in Strasbourg.

April 6, 2002. *France.* A Jewish sports association storefront in Toulouse was firebombed.

April 7, 2002. *France.* Gas bombs were thrown into two synagogues.

April 9, 2002. *Israel.* At 7:00 a.m., a suicide bomber and snipers killed 13 Israeli soldiers in the Burqin refugee camp in Jenin. Several soldiers were injured by falling rubble and sniper fire.

April 9, 2002. *United States.* Attorney General John Ashcroft announced the indictment of attorney Lynne Stewart, 62, and three others for helping to pass unlawful messages between an Egyptian terrorist organization and Sheik Omar Abd-al-Rahman, who was serving a life sentence for plotting to blow up the World Trade Center and United Nations buildings in 1993. The other defendants were Yasser Sirri, who was held in the United Kingdom for links to the assassins of Afghan leader Ahmed Shah Massoud on September 9, 2001; paralegal Ahmed Abd-al Sattar, 42, who worked for Abd-al-Rahman's legal team; and translator Mohammed Yousry, 46. The foursome were also charged with providing "material support and resources" to the Egyptian Islamic Group. Stewart pleaded not guilty and was released on $500,000 bond with the stipulation that she not contact Abd-al-Rahman. Yousry was released on $750,000 bond with the same stipulation. Sattar pleaded not guilty and was held without bail. Investigators had tapped Abd-al-Rahman's conversations in prison in Minnesota under the Foreign Intelligence Surveillance Act. Yousry and Sattar were also accused of relaying a 2000 fatwa in which the blind sheik called on Muslims everywhere "to fight the Jews and kill them wherever they are." Sirri was in frequent contact with Sattar and provided financial support for the terrorists, according to the indictment. Two other attorneys who worked for

Abd-al-Rahman—Ramsey Clark and Abdeen Jabara—were not indicted. Stewart, represented by attorney Susan Tipograph, faced a 40-year sentence.

April 10, 2002. *Israel.* A suicide bomber killed 8 Israelis and wounded 14 others on the Number 960 bus near Haifa at Yagur kibbutz. The bus had made its second stop of the morning. Passengers included four Israeli soldiers, three policemen, and a Jerusalem nursing student. Bus driver Yeshoshua Akst, 55, said in a hospital that the terrorist might have been wearing an Israeli army uniform that was hiding a belt packed with nails, screws, and 18 pounds of explosives. Among the injured was Omri Saleh, 29. Among those dead was Noa Shlomo, 18, the teen niece of Yehuda Lancr, Israel's ambassador to the United Nations. Hamas said the bomber was Ayman Abu Haija, 22, a resident of Jenin. Police said he may have come from Tulkarm.

April 10, 2002. *India.* Armed militants killed five people and injured four in their residence in Gando, Kashmir. No one claimed credit.

April 11, 2002. *Israel.* A Palestinian died when his explosive blew up at a taxi stand in Hebron near an Israeli military checkpoint, injuring several people. Investigators believed his main bomb went off prematurely and that he had intended to kill the Israeli soldiers.

April 11, 2002. *Tunisia.* A truck transporting natural gas exploded outside the outer wall of North Africa's oldest synagogue on the island of Djerba, killing 17 people, including 11 German tourists, 5 Tunisians, and a French citizen. Several German tourists were injured and evacuated to a hospital in Berlin. The government said the explosion at the Ghriba synagogue was not a suicide bombing, but said on April 22 that it was a terrorist attack. The driver had ignored a security guard's order to stop and had sped up to hit the synagogue. No Jews were injured and the building was not damaged.

On April 16, the Islamic Army for the Liberation of the Holy Sites, which has links to bin Laden, claimed credit. The same name was used in claiming credit for the bombing of the U.S. embassies in Kenya and Tanzania on August 7, 1998. The newspaper *Al Hayat* received an Arabic-language fax at its Islamabad office; the stationery had al Qaeda's logo. The fax said, "The martyrdom operation is a response to Israeli crimes against the sons of the Palestinian people. The martyrdom operation is a retaliation to the [Arab] governments' refusal to allow their peoples to join jihad against the Jews." *Al-Quds Al-Arabi* newspaper received a will, dated July 5, 2000, left by one of the men in the truck, identifying him as Nizar bin Mohammed Nawar, 25 (alias Sword of the Faith), a Tunisian who had lived in Lyon. Nawar called on his family to contribute to a holy war "with their souls and money." The fax included Nawar's name before the police released the name.

The same day, German police arrested and released a Muslim radical in Duisburg on suspicion of acting as a contact for one of the two men in the truck. German police also raided five apartments. The man was a German citizen convert to Islam. The truck driver was a former resident of Lyon, France. Before the bombing, the German Embassy in Tunisia had received a letter from al Qaeda Tunis that warned that German goods would "be burned and poisoned" if Germany did not "uncouple itself from the club of colonialism" and cut ties with the "Zionist entity." Police identified one of the detainees as Karim M., a Moroccan who had the phone number of Ramzi Binalshibh, who was believed to have been initially scheduled as the 20th hijacker for the September 11 attacks. Binalshibh was wanted on an international arrest warrant.

On April 22, Tunisia blamed the attack on Tunisian citizen Nizar Nawar and a relative living in the country. Police had discovered a phone call to Germany by Nawar shortly before the blast. Nawar phoned Christian Ganczarski, 35, a Polish-born German convert to Islam. He was asked if he needed anything, and replied, "I only need the command." Ganczarski, active in radical Muslim circles in Duisburg, was released without charge after being questioned. Ganczarski said he had met Nawar in August 2001 in Pakistan. He also admitted knowing Mouhamedou Ould Slahi, who was extradited by Mauritania to the United States on suspicion of involvement in the December 1999 plot to bomb the Los Angeles airport. The duo apparently attended the same Duisburg mosque. Police also found in Ganczarski's apartment the bank account number of the wife of a Mounir Motassadeq, who had witnessed the will of September 11 hijacker Mohamed Atta. A witness at Motassadeq's terrorism trial, Jordanian citizen Shadi Abdallah (variant Abdellah), 27, said Ganczarski had trained in Afghan camps. Ganczarski and his family quietly left Germany for Saudi Arabia via Frankfurt and Amsterdam in November; police learned of his departure post facto. On June 2, 2003, police at Charles de Gaulle Airport arrested Christian Ganczarski.

The duo's alleged accomplices appeared to have links to the Hamburg al Qaeda cell that was involved in the September 11, 2001, attacks.

On April 27, Tunisian President Zine Abidine Ben Ali fired Interior Minister Abdallah Kaabi and Chief of National Security Mohamed Ali Ganzoui.

On April 29, hundreds of Jews visited the synagogue on an annual pilgrimage that usually brings thousands.

Another German burn victim died on May 2, bringing the total to 14 dead German tourists and 19 people overall.

On November 5, French police arrested eight suspects in the case, including the parents and brother, Walid Naouar, 22, of the suspected bomber, Nizar Nawar (variant Naouar). Three people close to the family were also arrested. Documents seized near Lyon appeared to be directly related to the bombing.

In March 2003, Tunis issued a warrant for the arrest of Khalid Sheikh Mohammed for his role in the bombing. By April 2004, Belgacem Nawar, an uncle of suicide bomber Nizar Nawar,

remained in Tunisian custody, charged with complicity in the attack.

On March 7, 2003, Spanish national police in Valencia arrested four Spaniards and a Pakistani who were accused of belonging to a financial network involved in laundering money that was then sent to al Qaeda operatives. The Ministry of the Interior linked them to the Yerba attack. On March 12, 2003, a Spanish judge ordered two of them remanded to prison pending further investigation of the case. The other three were released.

On March 11, 2003, French intelligence agents in Lyon detained Slah Saadaoui, 25, who allegedly supplied the main suspect in the blast with fake ID papers.

On November 26, 2003, a Duesseldorf state court found Shadi Abdallah guilty of membership in a terrorist organization and of falsifying passports, which normally carries a ten-year term. The court found that he had helped plan terrorist attacks in Germany. He was sentenced to four years in prison because he had given valuable testimony about al Qaeda during his five-month trial. He said al-Tawhid terrorists were planning to attack Berlin's Jewish Museum. He claimed he had been a bin Laden bodyguard.

On January 13, 2004, a Spanish judge formally charged Enrique Cerda, a tile shop owner in Valencia, Ahmed Rukhar, a convenience store owner from La Rioja region, and Essa Ismail Muhamad with helping to finance the synagogue bombing. Muhammad remained at large; the other two were arrested in March 2003 and held on $127,000 bond on suspicion of helping to finance the bombing by sending money to al Qaeda contacts. 02041101

April 11–12, 2002. *Nepal.* Maoist rebels attacked two towns in the west, killing at least 160 police. During an attack on the home of Interior Security Minister Khum Bahadur Khadka, rebels killed 60 police officers in the gun battle. They beheaded another 27 police who had surrendered and burned alive two other police.

Some 30 police officers survived. Rebels also attacked neighboring Lamahi, killing 11 police. Overnight gun battles left hundreds of rebels dead. By April 14, the death toll had passed 300, including dozens of police officers forced to strip before being executed.

April 12, 2002. *Israel.* At 4:00 p.m., at the same time that U.S. Secretary of State Colin Powell was meeting with Israeli Prime Minister Ariel Sharon, Andaleeb Takafka, 20, a female Palestinian suicide bomber, set off an explosives belt at Jerusalem's Mahane Yehuda market's bus stop, killing 6 people, including 2 Chinese citizens, wounding 90 people, 6 of them seriously, and destroying the bus. The blast left body parts and torn metal strewn across Jaffa Road. The al-Aqsa Martyrs Brigades claimed credit. Among the injured was Majdi Alian, 29, a taxi driver, whose brother, Amir Alian, 28, is a first-responder ambulance driver. The Number 6 bus driver was Hussein Awadallah, who helped passengers escape.

Also injured was Jennifer (Gila) Weiss, 31, who had left Rockville, Maryland, the previous year to live in Israel. She was in intensive care at the Hadassah Hospital Ein Kerem, being treated for shrapnel to the chest and face. Her prognosis included the possibility of permanent blindness. She was at the market to buy cake for a Sabbath dinner with friends. She was studying to take the Israeli equivalent of a CPA exam. She had worked as an accountant for McGladrey and Pullen in Bethesda, Maryland, and had grown up in Gaithersburg, Maryland. She was working at a Jerusalem accounting firm. She intends to stay in Israel.

Takafka, whose name means *nightingale* in Arabic, lived in Beit Fajar, an isolated town south of Bethlehem, and sewed in a clothes factory. She never talked of politics. Her parents remembered that she woke up before 6:00 a.m., made them tea, and left the house without saying a word. At her wake, her father, Khalil, said, "I am happy. All the girls should do it."

April 12, 2002. *Belgium.* Antwerp police arrested Samih Osailly on charges of diamond smuggling and illegal weapons sales. He is an associate of ASA Diam, which served as a key facilitator for al Qaeda diamond purchase operations in Liberia and Sierra Leone. His cousin, Aziz Nassour, is a Lebanese diamond merchant associated with ASA Diam. Nassour pressed Sierra Leonean Revolutionary United Front (RUF) rebels to step up diamond production. Osailly pleaded not guilty. Belgian investigators said bank records showed ASA turned over almost $1 billion in the year before September 11. They also found phone records of calls to Afghanistan, Pakistan, Iraq, and Iran.

April 13, 2002. *Spain.* Police arrested Ahmed Brahim, 57, an Algerian suspected of financing the al Qaeda bombings of the U.S. embassies in Kenya and Tanzania in August 1998. He had a close relationship with Mamdouh Mahmud Salim, one of al Qaeda's founders, who was in a U.S. prison awaiting trial on conspiracy in the case. Brahim was arrested at his home in Sant Joan Despie, near Barcelona. Police also seized bank accounts, documents, and computer material. Police were also investigating his links to September 11 hijack leader Mohamed Atta.

April 13, 2002. *Ukraine.* Synagogue worshipers in Kiev were attacked.

April 14, 2002. *Colombia.* A bomb exploded in a parked bus as the motorcade of Colombian Presidential candidate Alvaro Uribe was driving by, killing three people and injuring several others, including three police officers. The leading candidate was unharmed. He had left a Barranquilla market. He said his armored vehicle was destroyed. He had campaigned against the violence of the Revolutionary Armed Forces of Colombia (FARC), which was the prime suspect. Uribe canceled further campaign trips.

April 14, 2002. *India.* A grenade fired at a police vehicle missed its target and landed in a crowded bus stop in Pulwama, Kashmir, killing

1 person and injuring 13 others. No one claimed credit.

April 15, 2002. *United States.* The issued an advisory warning of a bomb to be set off at noon at a national bank in Washington, D.C. Some 150 bank branches—including those of Riggs National Corporation, Bank of America Corporation, Wachovia Corporation, SunTrust Banks, Inc., Citibank, Branch Bank and Trust Company, Allfirst Bank, and Chevy Chase Bank—closed after receiving permission from the Office of the Comptroller of the Currency. A 13-year-old boy in the Netherlands confessed to local police that he had made the call the evening of April 14. The threat came on a major payday, a day that many people hoped to make Individual Retirement Account deposits that would generate tax benefits for 2001, as well as the day federal tax returns were due.

April 15, 2002. *United States.* Immigration and Naturalization Service (INS) officials detained Issaya Nombo, 44, a Tanzanian whose name was found in a computer printout in a cave in Afghanistan. He was charged with an immigration violation after U.S. intelligence reported the discovery. He was living in North Carolina on an expired visa. His name was on a public Web site for Voyager Aviation of Titusville, Florida, where he received a commercial pilot's license. The home page said, "Congratulations Issaya Nombo on completing your ATP" (airline transport pilot license).

April 15, 2002. *Israel.* Israeli forces arrested Marwan Barghouti, 42, who was hiding in a Ramallah house with another Palestinian activist. He was believed to be behind the suicide bombing campaign. Barghouti is the West Bank secretary of Fatah and the head of the Tanzim, the Fatah militia. Israel said it had documents indicating he had financed al-Aqsa Martyrs Brigades attacks.

On July 11, Israel's Justice Ministry announced Barghouti would be tried in civilian court in connection with suicide bombings that killed dozens of Israelis and injured hundreds of others. Four other Palestinians, including those charged in the March 27 Passover bombing at Netanya's Park Hotel that killed 30, were also to be tried soon. Barghouti was represented by attorney Jawad (variant Jawal) Boulos, who said his client had begun a hunger strike. While international human rights groups complained about his jailing, Amnesty International on July 11 also condemned the suicide bombings as "crimes against humanity."

On August 14, Israel charged him with seven counts of murder in a criminal trial in Tel Aviv District Court. He was charged with murder, attempted murder, conspiracy, and involvement with terrorist organizations responsible for the killings of 26 people in 37 attacks. The indictment said he was an "arch-terrorist whose hands are bloodied by dozens of terrorist attacks." He faced life in prison.

On May 20, 2004, a Tel Aviv tribunal convicted him of five counts of murder in three terrorist attacks: ordering the attacks that killed a Greek Orthodox monk in the West Bank in 2001, an Israeli at the Givat Zeev settlement in 2002, and three people at the Seafood Market restaurant in Tel Aviv in 2002. He was also convicted of individual counts of attempted murder and membership in a terrorist organization. He said in Hebrew, "This is a court of occupation that I do not recognize…. A day will come when you will be ashamed of these accusations. I have no more connection to these charges than you, the judges, do. The judges cannot judge on their own. They get their order from above." The three judges said there was insufficient evidence to prove guilt in another 21 deaths that were part of the original indictment. Sentencing was set for June 6. The prosecution requested five life terms plus 40 years for attempted murder. His attorney said he would not appeal because Barghouti did not recognize the court's jurisdiction.

April 15, 2002. *Qatar.* Al-Jazeera satellite broadcast another bin Laden tape, this one with

Ayman Zawahiri kneeling with him and praising the September 11 attacks. The hour-long tape had arrived a week earlier. The tape included a "will" by Saudi hijacker Ibrahim A. al Haznawi, who was wearing a black checked Palestinian *kaffiyeh* and was sitting in front of a photo of the World Trade Center in flames. The video was titled, "The Wills of the New York and Washington Battle Martyrs." Haznawi said, "Lord, I regard myself as a martyr for you, so accept me as such. It is high time that we killed Americans in their home." The will was dated March 2001. Zawahiri said the attacks were "a gift from God.... Those 19 brothers who went out and worked and sacrificed their lives for God, God granted this conquest that we enjoy today.... The great victory that was achieved was because of God's help and not because of our efficiency or power." The narrator also mentioned an Arab League summit in Beirut two weeks previously. Bin Laden did not speak in the tape. Some analysts suggested that the tape had been doctored, and that the duo was not sitting in a field shown on the tape. Al-Jazeera said it would air some, but not all of the tape, which it deemed "propaganda." Al-Jazeera editor in chief Ibrahim Hilal said, "This tape closes the door of suspicion. It is the final say that al Qaeda is behind it."

April 15, 2002. *Germany.* A woman was attacked for wearing a Star of David necklace in the Berlin subway.

April 16, 2002. *India.* Armed militants in Balhama-Rafiabad killed five people and injured two others. The Ikhwan were suspected.

April 17, 2002. *Germany.* "Six Million is Not Enough. PLO" was spray-painted on a Berlin synagogue.

April 17, 2002. *Israel.* Haitham Abu Hawgha, 14, and Ahmed Abu Selmiah, 16, charged the Dugit settlement north of Gaza City, but were killed by Israeli troops. Three boys—two 16-year-olds and a 15-year-old—had charged the

same settlement on December 30, 2001, also dying.

April 18, 2002. *Italy.* A single-engine Piper Commander 114TC crashed into the 32-floor Pirelli Building, Milan's largest skyscraper, killing the 68-year-old pilot and 2 female municipal attorneys who were in the building, and injuring 29 people with falling debris. Many initially thought it was a terrorist attack, then later an accident. Police moved to the theory that pilot Luigi Fasulo was suicidal after being swindled out of $1.54 million by an associate. The flight originated in Locarno, Switzerland, where Fasulo lived, and was scheduled to land at Milan's Linate Airport. Fasulo told ground control that he was having trouble with the landing gear. Ground control notified Fasulo twice that he was flying in the wrong direction, toward the city and away from the airport, but he did not reply. Some witnesses said the plane was on fire before it hit the 417-foot tower's 25th floor at 5:45 p.m. The building houses the offices of the Lombardy regional government.

April 18, 2002. *Malaysia.* Police conducted several raids across the country, arrested 14 suspected members of a group linked to al Qaeda, and confiscated military training notes, computers, and a map of Port Klang, the country's largest port. One of those arrested was the wife of a man accused of helping two of the September 11 hijackers. Police said about 100 suspects were still at large.

April 18, 2002. *Switzerland.* Prosecutors announced that police had seized documents from several firms and the homes of three suspects with terrorist connections in Graubuenden and southern Ticino regions.

April 19, 2002. *Northern Ireland.* Police announced that three weeks earlier they had discovered an Irish Republican Army (IRA) list of targets, including U.K. lawmakers and army bases.

April 19, 2002. *United States.* The Bush administration ordered U.S. banks to freeze assets of a Pakistan-based group and nine individuals as part of the war on terrorism. The al Rashid Trust had changed its name to the Aid Organization of the Ulema, based in Pakistan, and had been raising funds for the Taliban. The list also included Ahmed Idris Nasreddin, an Ethiopian who provided direct support for Youssef Nada and Bank al Taqwa, which gave financial aid to bin Laden. Also named were:

- Abdelkader Mahmoud Es Sayed, an Egyptian organizer of al Qaeda's Milan cell. He was convicted in Egypt for killing 58 foreign tourists.

- Khalid al-Fawaz, who was indicted in the United States on conspiracy to bomb the U.S. embassies in Kenya and Tanzania. The United States had requested extradition from the United Kingdom.

- Abu Hamza al-Masri, a London resident and member of the Islamic Army of Aden, which claimed credit for the USS *Cole* bombing.

- Tunisians Aouadi Mohamed Ben Belgacem, Bouchoucha Mokhtar, Charaabi Tarek, and Essid Sami Ben Khemais, member of an al Qaeda cell in Italy, who were serving prison terms in Italy for trafficking in arms and explosives.

- Libyan Lased Ben Heni, who was the liaison between an al Qaeda cell in Italy and a cell in Frankfurt that was wrapped up in December 2000. He was arrested in Germany and extradited to Italy. He was indicted for trafficking in arms, explosives, and chemical weapons.

April 19, 2002. *Israel.* Israeli soldiers stopped a suicide bomber's car at a checkpoint in Gaza near the Kissufim crossing. He killed himself when he set off the explosives, slightly wounding two soldiers.

April 19, 2002. *Israel.* Three Palestinian terrorists died in a gun battle with Israeli troops at the southern border with Egypt.

April 19, 2002. *Israel.* Two armed Palestinians died when they tried to sneak into the Netzarim Jewish settlement in Gaza.

April 19, 2002. *United States.* After detained al Qaeda Operations Chief Abu Zubaida, 31, told U.S. investigators of planned attacks against the U.S. banking system, the FBI issued a warning to 7,600 financial institutions in the northeast and mid-Atlantic to be on the alert. The alert went to banks, savings and loans, credit unions, and brokerage houses. Authorities believed it would be a physical attack at a building rather than hacking at computer systems. The nation was on the Yellow alert, denoting a significant risk of terrorist attack.

Two days later, Abu Zubaida claimed that al Qaeda personnel know how to build a radiation bomb.

April 20, 2002. *Spain.* A Basque Nation and Liberty (ETA) car bomb exploded.

April 20, 2002. *Israel.* A Palestinian gunman killed an Israeli border policeman at the Erez crossing from the Gaza Strip into Israel. An Israeli tank shot the terrorist to death.

April 21, 2002. *Philippines.* Three bombs went off in General Santos after an Abu Sayyaf phone call to a local radio station warned of the explosions. A bomb outside a department store killed at least 15 people, 4 of them children. Less than 40 minutes later, bombs went off near a radio station and a bus terminal. Some 71 people were injured in the bombings. A separate cell phone text message warning said that 18 bombs would start exploding after lunch. Police also received an Abu Sayyaf confessor phone call.

Police were put on high alert. President Gloria Macapagal Arroyo offered a $100,000 reward for information on the bombers.

On April 23, two men arrested in the case said that they were trained abroad and that more attacks were planned. Witnesses said they saw the duo put a bag in a motorcycle taxi that blew up in front of the department store.

On September 14, police arrested an Indonesian man, Uskar Mukawata, in the case.

On September 18, officials said that he would be charged with planning the bomb attacks.

Police suggested that Jemaah Islamiah had established a beachhead in Mindanao. 02042101

April 21, 2002. *Colombia.* Revolutionary Armed Forces of Colombia (FARC) rebels kidnapped Antioquia Province Guillermo Gaviria, a Roman Catholic priest, and a former defense minister at a peace march that brought 1,000 activists to a rural area 175 miles northwest of Bogota. The kidnappers dragged them into the mountains.

April 23, 2002. *Spain.* Madrid police arrested Muhammed Galeb Kalaje Zouaydi, a Syrian-born businessman accused of helping finance bin Laden's operations. He was arraigned, charged with "multiple crimes of terrorism," and ordered held indefinitely without bail by antiterrorism judge Baltasar Garzon. He was represented by attorney Maria Angeles Ruiz Martinez. The judge said there was evidence that he had sent money to suspects in Germany linked with September 11 hijack leader Mohamed Atta.

On July 16, 2002, Spanish Interior Minister Angel Acebes announced that Ghasoub Abrash Ghalyoun (alias Abu Musab), who was born in Syria, was "directly implicated in the financial activities of the al Qaeda cell, which has already been dismantled." Ghalyoun shot extensive videos of the World Trade Center towers and other U.S. landmarks during a 1997 visit to the United States. Spanish police had seized the tapes in April and found scenes of the Brooklyn Bridge, the Statue of Liberty, a New York airport, the Sears Towers in Chicago, San Francisco's Golden Gate Bridge, Disneyland, and Universal Studios in California. The statement noted that "the form and type of recording go beyond touristic curiosity as shown by two of the tapes, which are entirely of different angles from different distances of the twin towers in New York." Ghalyoun was detained at his Madrid home with two other Syrian al Qaeda suspects, but later released. He was rearrested with the two others on July 16.

April 23, 2002. *Germany.* Police detained 11 Muslim radicals in apartments in several cities. They were members of the Palestinian group Al Tawhid and were planning attacks in Germany. The Federal Prosecutor's Office said, "The cell in Germany was until now predominantly involved in falsifying passports and travel documents, collecting money, and smuggling 'fighters.'"

On August 9, the Federal Court of Justice in Karlsruhe lifted the arrest warrant against Mouhammed A., 28, who was living in Leipzig, because according to the Federal Prosecutor's Office there was no compelling evidence that he would commit a crime if released. He remained under investigation on suspicion that he assisted a radical Islamic group planning terrorist attacks in Germany. Four of the dozen other men detained at the same time were freed for lack of evidence shortly after they were picked up. The court had ordered the release of an Iraqi in the case on August 6. As of August 9, none of those who remained in custody had been charged.

On June 24, 2003, Shadi Abdellah, 26, a Jordanian arrested with the group, told judges at the Duesseldorf state court that while he was on welfare, he became a trusted aide of Abu Musab Zarqawi, an al Qaeda operational leader. Abdellah said he served as bin Laden's bodyguard at an al Qaeda camp in Afghanistan. He faced ten years in prison if convicted of membership in a terrorist group and forging passports. Prosecutors said the defendants plotted to shoot people in a German city square and set off a hand grenade near a Jewish or Israeli target in another city. Prosecutors said Zarqawi told Abdellah in May 2001 to go to Germany to help Mohammed Abu Dhess, another Jordanian, who headed the cell. In September 2001 in Iran, Zarqawi told Abu Dhess to attack Jewish or Israeli targets in Germany. 02042301

April 23, 2002. *Israel.* Palestinian 15-year-old boys Yusef Zaqout, Ismail Abu Nadi, and Anwar Hamdounah were shot to death near the Netzarim settlement by Israeli soldiers firing a .50 caliber machine gun. The trio had planned to set off a crude pipe bomb and were armed with knives. The trio had competed for top honors at Salahuddin School in Gaza City. They left confessor letters to their families, saying they were seeking to be heroes. Hamas condemned the boys' gesture and forbade adolescent attacks.

April 24, 2002. *United States.* During interrogations, al Qaeda operations chief Abu Zubayda claimed that U.S. shopping malls and supermarkets were also on the terrorist target list.

April 25, 2002. *Pakistan.* A bomb exploded in a Shi'ite Muslim mosque in Bhakkar District in eastern Punjab Province, killing 12 women and wounding several others. The bomb was planted in the section where only women pray.

April 26, 2002. *India.* In Gharat, Kashmir, a bomb exploded by remote control under a bus, killing 1 person and injuring 21 others, including 9 security personnel and a dozen civilians. No one claimed credit.

April 27, 2002. *Colombia.* The army blamed the FARC when explosives in an abandoned van went off inside a tunnel in northwestern Colombia, killing two and injuring four others.

April 27, 2002. *Pakistan.* On September 9, 2002, police announced the arrest of five Islamic militants, including a naval employee, for plotting to kill Pakistani President General Pervez Musharraf at a public ceremony. The five belonged to the same outlawed group as the trio on trial for the bombing of the U.S. Consulate in Karachi. The trio was accused in a separate assassination plot. The assassinations were planned for two consecutive April days. The five were suspected of smuggling assault rifles and hand grenades to the April 27 ceremony to lay the foundation stone for the Lyari Expressway outside a naval base in Karachi. An investigator said it was to be a suicide mission. President Musharraf showed up three hours late, foiling the carefully timed terrorist plans.

April 27, 2002. *Israel.* At 9:00 a.m., Palestinian gunmen disguised as Israeli soldiers attacked the Adora Jewish settlement in the West Bank, killing four Israelis before fleeing into the hills. Dead were Danielle Shefi, 5; Katya Greenberg, 45, shot in bed; Yakov Katz, shot in front of his home; and Arieh Becker, 25, who was giving chase to the killers. Danielle was the daughter of Jakov (variant Yaacov), 31, and Shiri Shefi, 29, whose two sons, aged 4 and 2, were wounded, as was Shiri. Katya Greenberg's son Nathan, 14, and husband Vladimir, 51, were wounded; Vladimir took five AK-47 bullets in his arms and head. The Popular Front for the Liberation of Palestine (PFLP) terrorists also wounded seven people, three of them younger than age 15. Men in a synagogue who raced home to grab their weapons were joined by four Israeli soldiers to fend off the attackers. Israeli troops tracked down and killed a Palestinian gunman in the nearby Palestinian village of Tufah. Other assailants remained at large.

Vladimir and Katya Greenberg had emigrated to Israel from Moldova 11 years earlier, fearing local anti-Semitism. Shiri Sheffi was born in Kiryat Arba.

April 27, 2002. *United Kingdom.* Vandals broke into a synagogue in Finsbury Park in north London during the night and painted a swastika, smashed windows, and defiled holy books.

April 28, 2002. *Russia.* A pipe bomb containing 18 ounces of TNT went off in a Vladikavkaz market, killing 7 people and injuring 45. Most of the shoppers were buying flowers to put on relatives' graves.

April 28, 2002. *Colombia.* In Bogota, a car packed with 88 pounds of explosives was discovered adjacent to the World Business Port commercial building that houses the U.S. Agency for International Development and other international organizations. A police officer identified the vehicle as suspicious and called the bomb squad, who disarmed the device. No one claimed credit. 02042801

April 30, 2002. *United States.* A 35-page FBI indictment in Chicago charged the $4 million per year Illinois-based Benevolence International Foundation and its executive director, Syria-born Enaam Arnaout, 39, with perjury regarding his denial that he and his group had provided aid to bin Laden or any other terrorists. The indictment said the group was financing terrorists and helping al Qaeda obtain weapons of mass destruction. The affidavit said Mamdouh Salim, a bin Laden aide, traveled to Bosnia using documents signed by Arnaout saying Salim was a Benevolence director. Salim was awaiting trial in New York on charges of conspiracy to kill Americans in the 1998 bombings of the U.S. embassies in Tanzania and Kenya. Arnaout was ordered held without bond after a hearing. Arnaout had said in a January lawsuit that the group "never provided aid or support to people or organizations known to be engaged in violence, terrorist activities, or military operations of any nature." He had challenged the U.S. Treasury's December 2001 seizure of the group's assets. An unnamed source said that in 1989 while living in Pakistan, Arnaout picked up a bin Laden wife at the airport and took her to his home. Bin Laden and his bodyguards picked her up a week later. The FBI claimed Arnaout transferred money, equipment, and weapons for Muslim movements in Afghanistan, Bosnia, and Chechnya, some with al Qaeda ties. Mohamed Bayazid, who tried to obtain uranium for al Qaeda, listed Benevolence's Illinois address as his residence in obtaining a driver's license.

Benevolence was founded in the 1980s by Sheik Adil Abdul Galil Batargy, a Saudi bin Laden associate. They opened an office in Palos Hills, a Chicago suburb, in 1993, when Batargy handed the reins over to Arnaout.

A federal judge denied bond to Arnaout on May 28, saying he was a flight risk.

On September 13, 2002, U.S. District Judge Joan Gottschall threw out the perjury charges against the charity and Arnaout on technical grounds, citing a 1979 Supreme Court decision limiting the filing of perjury charges for false statements made in civil litigation. The Chicago-based judge said perjury could not be charged in the type of declaration Arnaout had made. Patrick J. Fitzgerald, U.S. attorney in Chicago, said he would file new charges of obstruction of justice and making false statements. Arnaout was to stay in a Chicago jail until September 16, when a hearing in the case was scheduled.

On October 9, Arnaout was charged with using donations to fund bin Laden and conspiring to defraud his group's donors. Arnaout faced 90 years for wire and mail fraud, money laundering, conspiring to provide material support to terrorists, and conspiracy to engage in racketeering. Defense attorneys admitted that Arnaout dealt with bin Laden in the 1980s. The foundation was represented by Matthew Piers. The seven-count indictment said Benevolence funded terrorist activities and commingled dollars from altruistic donors with money from Saudis who knew of its terrorist ties. The indictment noted that in the late 1990s, Said al Islam el Masry, an al Qaeda military instructor, served as an officer of the Chechen branch of Benevolence. In the late 1980s, Arnaout was a top official of an Afghan camp run by bin Laden, distributing weapons and other gear. In a March 2002 search of Benevolence's eight Bosnian offices, investigators found notes on al Qaeda's founding in August 1988 in Afghanistan and other papers linking the group to bin Laden. Arnaout's attorneys complained that the government was holding him responsible for the activities of an unrelated group formed in 1987, the Lajnat al-Birr al-Islamiah, which U.S. officials said was a precursor to Benevolence. Arnaout was represented by attorney Joseph Duffy, who said the government was trying to criminalize his dealings with Afghan Hezb e Islami leader Gulbuddin Hekmatyar, who had called for an anti-U.S. jihad.

On October 10, perjury charges against Benevolence and Arnaout were dismissed at the prosecution's request.

On November 5, a federal judge set a February 3, 2003, trial date for Arnarout, who was charged with racketeering and other offenses. Arnaout pleaded not guilty. U.S. District Judge Suzanne Conlon on February 5, 2003, rejected the prosecution's request for permission to offer hearsay evidence at the trial.

On February 10, 2003, a day before the trial was to begin, Arnaout pleaded guilty to one count of racketeering for his illegal diversion of charitable contributions to armed fighters in Bosnia and Chechnya. As part of a plea agreement, prosecutors dropped all terrorism-related charges and agreed to reduce his potential 20-year sentence if he cooperates in future terrorism investigations. The six dropped counts included money laundering, wire fraud, and conspiracy to provide material support to terrorists.

On July 17, 2003, a judge refused to add 12 years to Arnaout's racketeering sentence, saying it was not a terrorism-related offense.

On August 18, 2003, U.S. District Judge Conlon sentenced Arnaout to more than 11 years in prison for defrauding donors. Judge Conlon said that the prosecutors had not established that he supported terrorism.

April 30, 2002. *United States.* Mohammed Hussein was convicted on two charges of illegally transferring money. He worked for Barakaat North America, a franchise of the international Al Barakaat network that on November 7, 2002, was placed on a U.S. list of groups whose assets were frozen because of financial facilitation of terrorism.

On June 4, Canada's Justice Department halted extradition of his Somali-born Canadian brother, Liban Hussein, 31, who was charged in the United States with operating an unlawful money-transfer business. He is the president of Barakaat North America and had been arrested in Ottawa in November, when his assets were frozen. He was freed on bail a week later. Canada said that the United States was not able to present enough information to support an extradition request. Liban Hussein, an Ottawa resident, had been on U.S., Canadian, and UN lists as a suspected al Qaeda associate. He was represented by attorney Michael Edelson.

May 2002. *United States.* Christopher B. Jones, 45, armed with a scissors, walked through an open fence gate in a small Chesapeake, Virginia, airfield and tried to take control of a private plane from a pilot who had just landed with his family. Pilot Steven S. Warden escaped and the would-be hijacker tried to drive away from the airport. But Jones' father had disabled the car because his son had been drinking that day.

On November 1, 2002, Circuit Court Judge Bruce H. Kushner sentenced Jones to ten years in prison, with all but eight months suspended, for attempted robbery. Jones had already spent three of the months in jail. Jones blamed alcohol and painkillers for his actions and said that he had been sober since his arrest. Kushner said the suspended sentence could be revived if Jones drank again. 02059901

May 2002. *Italy.* Milan police arrested five individuals who were suspected of providing funds to al Qaeda.

May 2002. *Nepal.* Maoist rebels destroyed a Pepsi-Cola truck and its contents. 02059902

May 2002. *Pakistan.* Three men were arrested late in the month for firing rockets at an air base used by U.S. troops outside Jacobabad. They were members of Sipah Sahaba Pakistan, a banned Sunni Muslim group that had specialized in Pakistani Shi'ite targets, not Westerners.

May 2002. *Cabinda.* Cabindan separatists were suspected in a grenade attack on a convoy of U.S. oil workers. No one claimed credit. 02059903

May 2002. *Morocco.* Police arrested three Saudi members of al Qaeda who were planning to attack U.S. and British warships in the Strait of Gibraltar. The trio planned to sail a dinghy loaded with explosives from Morocco into the strait. The trio were aged between 25 and 35. They were not wanted in any other country and remained in Moroccan hands as of June 10, 2002. They told investigators that senior al Qaeda leaders in Gardez had sent them. They said Mullah Bilal (probably Abd al-Rahim al-Nashiri), a senior Saudi al Qaeda leader, gave them instructions to attack ships. Two of the Saudis were married to Moroccans. They arrived in Morocco in late January via Lahore, Pakistan, and either Qatar or Abu Dhabi. One of them was seen in Melilla, a Spanish enclave in northern Morocco, and was identified as Zuher Hilal Mohamed al Tbaiti, who married a Moroccan. He was under surveillance for a month, visiting Melilla and Ceuta, another Spanish enclave opposite Gibraltar. He was inquiring about buying Zodiac speedboats. In April, he was directed via phone call to return to Saudi Arabia. He was arrested at the Casablanca airport with fellow Saudi Hilal Jaber Alassiri and two Moroccan women. The detainees had $10,000 in case they found the boats. They led authorities to Abdallah M'Sefer Ali al Ghamdi in another Moroccan city. The trio told authorities that after they had obtained the boats, a logistics team would bring in explosives and weapons, and then a suicide team would conduct the operations. While in Afghanistan, Tbaiti and Alassiri had committed themselves eventually to conduct suicide operations. Moroccan authorities said the terrorists also planned, but later aborted, a local attack as well. They were arraigned in a Moroccan court on June 17, 2002, during which prosecutors said that the trio tried to recruit locals to al Qaeda, considered blowing up a café in central Marrakech, and plotted a suicide attack against the local bus company. Alassiri argued against killing fellow Muslims, but Tbaiti said it was "justified by the nobleness of the operation."

On June 25, 2002, Morocco announced the arrests of three more men—including a policeman and a court clerk—who were held at Casablanca's Oukacha prison with three Saudis and four other Moroccans in the case. An investigator said the group was led by three Saudis.

On February 21, 2003, a Morocco court sentenced three Saudi men to ten-year sentences for criminal conspiracy, use of false documents, and illegal stay in Morocco. They were acquitted of attempted sabotage and attempted homicide, according to defense attorney Khalil Idrissi. The court sentenced several Moroccan accomplices to lesser terms.

May 2002. *United States.* The Puget Sound Joint Terrorist Task Force arrested Semi Osman, 32, a Lebanese imam, at Seattle's Dar-us-Salaam (Taqwa) mosque and charged him with immigration fraud and illegal possession of a semiautomatic .40 caliber handgun with its serial numbers removed. Police seized from his residence additional firearms, military field manuals, instructions on poisoning water supplies, a visa application to Yemen, various items associated with Islamic radicalism, and papers by London-based Muslim radical Sheik Abu Hamzi al-Masri, who had publicly supported the September 11 attacks. British citizen Osman is an active duty U.S. Navy reservist and a former army enlistee who lives in Tacoma. He was represented by attorney Robert M. Leen. Osman lived for a time on a ranch in Blye, Oregon, which was raided in June 2002 by FBI agents investigating reports of a 1999 "jihad training camp," conducted by al-Masri. Others who visited Osman's mosque included Zacarias Moussaoui, the "September 11–20th hijacker," and Richard Reid, the "would-be shoe bomber."

Police were also investigating mosque members James and Mustafa Ujaama, brothers who grew up in Seattle and converted to Islam. Police believed James posted radical Islamic teachings on a Web site for al-Masri's London mosque and escorted two representatives from the mosque to the Oregon ranch.

On August 2, 2002, Semi Osman, 32, of Tacoma, pleaded guilty to a weapons violation in exchange for immigration charges being dropped. Prosecutors had stated that Osman "was committed to facilitate an act of international terrorism," which defense attorney Robert Leen denied.

May 2002. *Azerbaijan.* The government convicted seven Azerbaijanis who had received military and other training in Georgia's Pankisi Gorge and who had intended to fight in Chechnya. Four received suspended sentences. The others were sentenced to four to five years.

May 2002. *France.* The Corsican National Liberation Front claimed credit for a series of nonlethal bombings in Paris and Marseilles in early May.

May 1, 2002. *Algeria.* The Armed Islamic Movement attacked two locations in the Tiaret region, killing 31 and injuring 5.

May 1, 2002. *Spain.* A car bomb went off near Madrid's Santiago Bernabeu Stadium hours before a European Champions League semifinal soccer match between Real Madrid and Barcelona, injuring 17 people. Basque Nation and Liberty (ETA) separatists were blamed. A second bomb went off on the other side of the city, destroying the possible getaway car.

May 1–2, 2002. *Colombia.* The Revolutionary Armed Forces of Colombia (FARC) attacked paramilitary troops in Vigia del Fuerte, chasing them across the river and to a basketball court in the center of Bellavista (or Bojaya, according to some reports). Other paramilitaries fled to the nearby St. Paul the Apostle Church and health clinic. Their leader, Commander Camilo, was shot in the face. The next day, a FARC bomb landed on top of the church's ceramic roof, where 300 people were hiding in the town's only concrete building. The bomb was made from spent propane gas cylinders. Two others hit the health clinic and two wooden homes near the basketball court. At least 117 people, one-third of them children, perished in the attack. Farmer Heiler Martinez lost his 5 daughters, pregnant wife, and 16 other relatives in the church. The killings were the single largest massacre of civilians in decades.

May 2, 2002. *United Kingdom.* Three accused Irish Republican Army terrorists admitted in court to trying to buy weapons and bomb-making equipment in Slovakia, and taking part in a bomb plot.

May 2, 2002. *Philippines.* Police arrested Salip Abdullah Mundar, a key aide of Abu Sayyaf leader Khadaffy Janjalani.

May 2–3, 2002. *Nepal.* Security forces claimed to have killed 350 Maoist guerrillas in gun battles in the Rolpa District, 220 miles west of Kathmandu. Two soldiers and a policeman also died. Rebel leader Pushpa Kamal Dahal (alias Prachanda) offered to resume peace talks; the offer was rejected by Prime Minister Sher Bahadur Deuba.

May 3, 2002. *Philippines.* Police arrested Satar Yacub, the fourth-ranking leader of Abu Sayyaf on Basilan Island, during the night.

May 3, 2002. *United States/Europe.* The U.S. and European Union froze the assets of seven people and one group—Askatasuna—involved with the Basque Nation and Liberty (ETA).

May 3, 2002. *United States.* Seven pipe bombs exploded in rural mailboxes along the Mississippi River in Iowa and Illinois, injuring five mail carriers and two residents. None of the injuries was critical. Authorities found two other unexploded bombs with typewritten antigovernment notes attached. The notes were signed, "Someone Who Cares." They promised that "more attention getters are on the way." The bombs were made of three-quarter-inch pipe and nine-volt batteries. Investigators said the bombs were placed in the mailboxes, not mailed, a view backed by one of the notes, which observed, "Mailboxes are exploding! Why, you ask? Attention people…. If the government controls what you want to do, they control what you do…. PS. More info. will be delivered to various locations around the country."

The first bomb went off at 11:00 a.m. when a rural letter carrier opened a mailbox near Mount Carroll, Illinois.

One mail carrier suffered lacerations on her arm and face when she opened a mailbox at a rural residence in Morrison, Illinois. A plastic bag containing a note was eight feet away.

The other bombs went off in Elizabeth and Morrison, Illinois, and Asbury and Tipton, Iowa.

The next day, five more pipe bombs were found in Nebraska; none exploded. Two were found in mailboxes. Bomb specialists investigated the south central counties of Howard, Platte, Fillmore, Thayer, and Valley. A least one note was identical to an earlier one. Another bomb was found in Salida, Colorado.

By May 6, authorities had reported finding bombs in the Nebraska towns of Albion, Scotia, Columbus, Dannebrog, Seward, Ohiowa, Davenport, and Hastings. Bombs exploded in the Iowa towns of Asbury, Farley, Anamosa, and Tipton; one did not explode in Eldridge. All of the Nebraska bombs were detonated by police. Other bombs exploded in the Illinois towns of Elizabeth, Mount Carroll, and Morrison. Authorities believed that the 17 bombs came from the same source. Another bomb was later found in Amarillo, Texas, by Roberto Martinez, 42, who tossed the bomb in a trash can when he found it in his mailbox.

Hundreds of thousands of local mail customers left their mailboxes open or removed the doors entirely. Postal authorities sent out a warning to district managers in Colorado, Wyoming, Montana, the Dakotas, Minnesota, Kansas, and Missouri.

A college student warned police that roommate Luke Helder had made several threatening statements before leaving Menomonie, Wisconsin. Helder had sent a seven-page letter to the *Badger Herald* student newspaper, which turned it over to the FBI. Helder said he was willing to die and threatened to hurt others. It was headed, "Explosions! A Bit of Evidence for You!" and said, "I will die/change in the end for this, but that's ok, hahaha paradise awaits!" The letter

was postmarked in Omaha on May 3. Helder also sent a letter to his parents.

On May 7 at 7:55 p.m. Eastern time, undercover police arrested Lucas John Helder, 21, a junior art major in industrial design from Pine Island, Minnesota, after a 40-mile chase on Interstate 80 outside Fernley, Nevada. Helder drove a 1992 four-door Honda Accord with Minnesota license plates. A motorist had spotted the car and alerted police, who chased Helder at 100 mph before the FBI contacted Helder on a cell phone. Helder had a handgun and was arrested after an FBI hostage negotiator intervened. He admitted to the FBI of planting 24 bombs. He had called two friends in Minnesota on May 7 to claim credit for the bombings and had left bomb-making materials under his bed in his apartment. The FBI found six pipe bombs in his car. He said he made many of the bombs in an Omaha motel room. Helder had been pulled over twice for speeding and once for not wearing a seat belt during his odyssey.

Helder faced federal charges in Illinois, Nebraska, and Iowa. He was arraigned in Reno on May 8. His initial court appearance in Cedar Rapids, Iowa, was on May 10. He was charged with using a destructive device in a crime of violence and destroying property (a mailbox) used in interstate commerce. He was called responsible for injuring Delores Werling, 70, of Tipton, Iowa, who was wounded in the face, arms, and hands. He was held without bail in the Linn County Jail. Jane Kelly, a federal public defender, was named his attorney. A preliminary hearing was set for May 22. Helder faced a life sentence.

Helder said that he chose the locations where he had planted the bombs to make a "smiley face" on a U.S. map. The Nebraska bombs made one eye; another eye could be seen in the Iowa and Illinois pattern. The Texas and Colorado bombs made the start of a smile.

Helder's friends and teachers at the University of Wisconsin at Stout were surprised that he was the suspect. He sang and played guitar for Apathy, a Rochester, Minnesota, rock trio. He was preoccupied with Nirvana's suicidal lead singer Kurt Cobain.

On June 7, an attorney entered a not guilty plea for Helder on federal charges. Helder was ordered held for trial in September.

May 4, 2002. *Indonesia.* Police arrested Jafar Umar Thalib, commander of Laskar Jihad, in the East Java capital of Surabaya. He was wanted for questioning regarding the previous weekend's violence in Ambon that killed a dozen people. Laskar Jihad wants to evict Christians and establish *sharia* Islamic law in the Moluccas, formerly the Spice Islands. He had acknowledged meeting Osama bin Laden. On July 25, he was released from custody to await trial on charges of inciting religious violence by calling on his followers to ignore a February peace deal between Muslims and Christians. Two days after a March speech, masked men attacked a Christian village in Ambon, killing 13 people. While in prison, he was visited by Vice President Hamzah Haz and other senior officials.

May 4, 2002. *Turkey.* A gunman took 13 people, including a Bulgarian, hostage at a luxury hotel in Istanbul to protest Russia's military campaign in Chechnya. He freed them unharmed and surrendered to police after an hour. No group claimed credit. 02050401

May 6, 2002. *Netherlands.* During the night, a gunman shot to death Pim Fortuyn, 54, a leader of a right-wing, anti-immigrant Dutch opposition party, as he was walking to his car outside a radio station in Hilversum, near Amsterdam. Fortuyn was hit by six bullets. He said he had received numerous death threats, including one the day of his death.

Police arrested a native Dutchman, 32, and charged him with the first murder of a political leader in recent Dutch history. The accused killer was a vegetarian and animal rights activist who opposed "factory farming." He was arrested with the gun still in his hands. Police raided his apartment, where they found literature from radical leftist groups and environmental causes.

Tens of thousands came to see his body lying in state; thousands of people attended Fortuyn's May 10 funeral. He had created a party called List Pim Fortuyn, which remained leaderless during the runup to the election; parties suspended campaigning. He had also been a member of Livable Netherlands. He had criticized immigrants who did not assimilate and deemed Islam to be biased against gays and women. Fortuyn's party finished second in parliamentary elections on May 15.

On August 9, 2002, prosecutors laid out their case against the accused killer, noting that the suspect was captured with gunpowder on his gloves and cell tissue matching Fortuyn's on his pants.

On March 27, 2003, Volkert van der Graaf, 33, who had confessed, told a panel of judges that he acted out of concern for the country's Muslim minority. He pleaded guilty to illegally possessing firearms and sending threats to Fortuyn before the assassination. He was arrested minutes after the killing. On April 15, 2003, Presiding Judge Frans Bauduin sentenced van der Graaf to 18 years in prison. On April 22, the defense counsel said he would appeal the sentence.

May 7, 2002. *Denmark.* Threatening messages were found in a restroom at Seattle-Tacoma International Airport and a Jack in the Box restaurant south of the airport. Authorities diverted SAS flight 937 from its Copenhagen to Seattle route, landing it safely in Greenland. Passengers were taken to a nearby hotel and put on a flight to Seattle the following day.

May 7, 2002. *Colombia.* A section of the Cano Limon–Covenas pipeline was bombed in Quebradas, killing two people, wounding four others, and causing millions of dollars in damage. The Revolutionary Armed Forces of Colombia (FARC) and the National Liberation Army (ELN) were the main suspects. 02050701

May 7, 2002. *India.* A bomb exploded on a bus in Lunavada, injuring ten people.

May 7, 2002. *Israel.* At 11:00 p.m., a Palestinian suicide bomber set off a satchel explosive in the crowded third-floor Sheffield's pool hall in Rishon Letzion, south of Tel Aviv, killing 15 people and injuring 57. The club had no license and no guard. A policeman said the bomber "entered all of a sudden into the hall and then he exploded." The attack came as Prime Minister Ariel Sharon was in Washington, D.C., meeting with President George Bush. Sharon cut short his trip. The Islamic Resistance Movement (Hamas) claimed responsibility and told Al-Manar Television in Lebanon that it would continue attacks and "the strength of the Palestinian resistance is greater than that of Israel's ability to resist." Mahmoud Zahar, a Gaza City Hamas spokesman, could not confirm the claim.

Daniel Termeforoosh, 35, an auto air-conditioning parts salesman, was wounded and his wife Annette, 35, was killed. They spent most nights at home, but had finally decided to venture out. Annette's mother, Hana Almassi, was slightly wounded; Annette's sister had more serious injuries. A 27-year-old man was made a paraplegic with a severed spine. A woman lost a kidney when a bolt went through her. Other victims included Miarm Mussa, 47, and Eli Ninio, 52.

May 8, 2002. *Israel.* A would-be suicide bomber injured himself and no one else in Haifa.

May 8, 2002. *France/United States.* The West Coast chapter of the American Jewish Congress called on Hollywood figures to boycott the Cannes Film Festival, citing at least 440 anti-Semitic attacks in France in April.

May 8, 2002. *Pakistan.* At 7:52 a.m., a car bomb exploded next to a pink and white 46-seat Pakistani navy Mercedes Marco Polo bus outside the upscale Karachi Sheraton Hotel and Towers on Club Road. Dead were 16 people, including 11 French citizens working for a technical company on a submarine project, 2 Pakistani beggars, and the bus driver of unidentified nationality. Wounded were 22 people, including 12 French citizens and 8 Pakistanis. One of the Pakistani victims was Razia Begum, who had walked out of a nearby drugstore with cookies for a street person. The driver of the car was killed in the blast. The Frenchmen were working for France's state-owned maritime construction company Direction des Constructions Navales. They were helping Pakistan build subs capable of delivering nuclear weapons. They had been in Karachi for months.

Singapore Airlines, whose flight crew were eating breakfast in the Sheraton restaurant, canceled its Pakistan routes.

The Karachi stock exchange lost three percent.

The New Zealand cricket team, which had been staying in the hotel across the street, canceled its final match and returned home.

Police traced the car bomb's engine's serial number to a red 1974 Toyota Corolla sedan that was purchased 17 hours earlier by three men who appeared to be Pakistanis. The buyers spoke Urdu and Punjabi, two local languages. They gave the car a push start rather than waiting for a new battery to be installed and overpaid, handing over 100,000 rupees ($1,666), about a third more than what Majeed Motors expected for the vehicle. They avoided providing identification to make it a legal transaction by promising to bring $100 more for the vehicle, but never returned to the lot in Nasirabad, a lower middle-class Karachi neighborhood. The lot's owner said the trio's leader was a heavyset man with a long beard and a tattoo of piety—a dark spot worn into a forehead that touches the ground five times a day for Muslim prayer.

The TNT was packed into a pipe running the length of the car.

Observers said this was a very sophisticated suicide bombing, unlike attacks by locals, but typical of the sophistication of al Qaeda. Authorities later said that al Qaeda members fleeing Afghanistan had been involved in the bombing.

Police were also questioning Saeed, one of the defendants in the Daniel Pearl killing, who had said that suicide bombers were not only Palestinians, but could also be Pakistanis.

By May 10, Pakistan had arrested 300 suspected militants in connection with the case.

On December 28, 2002, Asif Zaheer, 24, who was detained for planning an attack on U.S. diplomats, told police that he prepared the car bomb. A judge ordered him held for a fortnight so that police could investigate his claim. He was one of three men arrested in December for planning an attack on U.S. diplomats in Karachi; authorities seized 250 sacks of ammonium nitrate—which can be used in explosives—in the case. Zaheer was also a suspect in the murder of a television producer in Islamabad in 2002. Police arrested, but did not immediately charge two other people on January 7 as a result of Zaheer's information. In a January 8, 2003, update of his confession, Zaheer said that after packing the car with explosives, he turned the car over to Bashir Ahmed and Mohammed Rashid shortly before the attack. Ahmed was at large; Rashid was believed to be the suicide bomber.

On June 30, 2003, the Pakistani Anti-Terrorism Court sentenced three Islamic militants to death for the bombing. 02050801

May 8, 2002. *Nepal.* Some 500 Maoist rebels retook a key mountain stronghold in the remote village of Gam, killing all 40 government soldiers and 60 police officers guarding the base. The government had seized the base two months earlier after six years in rebel hands. The next day, the rebels announced a one-month cease-fire, which was rejected by the government.

May 8, 2002. *United States.* Authorities arrested Jose Padilla (variant Abdullah al Muhajir), 31, a U.S. citizen, as he was entering the United States at Chicago's O'Hare International Airport on a flight from Pakistan, where he had been under FBI and CIA surveillance, according to the *Washington Post.* The al Qaeda associate was accused of conspiracy to build and detonate a "dirty bomb"—a bomb consisting of normal explosives plus radioactive material. The explosion would be conventional, but would disperse radioactive

debris. The U.S. government had concluded that al Qaeda controlled enough cesium, strontium, or cobalt to conduct such an attack, but also speculated that bin Laden might be considering acquiring the material in the United States. Padilla's arrest was announced on June 10. He had studied how to build such a bomb while in Afghanistan and was scouting possible targets in the United States. At the Chicago airport, Customs officers discovered that he was carrying $10,526 in undeclared currency. He was transferred to a brig in the Charleston Naval Weapons Station in South Carolina on June 9 after President Bush designated him an "enemy combatant," not subject to civil trial. The announcement came two days before he was to appear at a secret hearing before a New York civilian judge. During questioning, Padilla showed some knowledge of the Washington, D.C., area. He had made a stop in Switzerland, possibly to avoid surveillance, before coming to Chicago. Authorities wanted him to testify before a New York grand jury investigating terrorism, but he refused to cooperate. Prosecutors withdrew a material witness warrant and subpoena ordering him to testify. He was turned over to the military. On June 13, Bush administration officials said he would not be tried by a military tribunal, but could be held until the President declared the war over. He was represented by attorney Donna R. Newman, who petitioned for a writ of habeas corpus by Federal Judge Michael B. Mukasey, saying Padilla's constitutional rights had been violated.

Benjamin Ahmed Mohammed, an associate in the plot, was arrested in Pakistan. Padilla and his friend in Pakistan had been fingered in April by al Qaeda detainee Abu Zubayda, who gave vague references to an individual involved in such a plot. Authorities quizzed other al Qaeda detainees and developed enough clues to identify the duo. Prisoners saw Abu Zubayda meet Padilla after the September 11 attacks in Afghanistan and Pakistan. After digging through travel records and criminal records, authorities identified the duo. Padilla had been arrested in Pakistan for failure to have proper travel documents, but was released. He traveled in Europe and the Middle East in April. Authorities showed photographs of Padilla and the other individual to Abu Zubayda, who confirmed their identities.

Padilla had been a Latin Kings street gang member in Brooklyn and was well known to the local jail system. He was involved in a killing as a 13-year-old (other sources say he was 15). He also joined the Maniac Latin Disciples gang. He was arrested five times in Chicago for assault and other crimes between 1985 and 1991. He worked in a hotel in Florida and was sent to prison following a road-rage shooting on October 8, 1991. He drew a gun on police who attempted to arrest him at his girlfriend's apartment, but thought better of it. He assaulted a sheriff's deputy while in jail. After his release, he was arrested nearly a dozen more times until 1997 on traffic offenses, such as speeding and driving with a revoked license. In one arrest, he produced a driver's license for Jose Alicea. The Puerto Rican had been born a Catholic and may have converted to Islam in or following prison and a substance abuse course. He married an Egyptian and left the United States. He visited Lahore and Karachi, Pakistan, discussing the dirty bomb plan. He met with senior al Qaeda officials in March regarding the plot. Authorities believed he intended to return to Pakistan with the results of his reconnaissance. He traveled to Zurich then Cairo, where he spent a month with his wife and two children.

On June 12, the South Florida Joint Terrorism Task Force arrested Adham Hassoun, 40, one of the leaders of the al-Iman Mosque in Broward County that Padilla attended in the early and mid-1990s. Hassoun was the founder of the Florida chapter of the Benevolence International Foundation, which has funded al Qaeda. Hassoun was held on an immigration violation.

In an affidavit filed on August 27 in a federal court in New York, the government said that while in Afghanistan and Pakistan in 2001 and 2002, Padilla met several times with al Qaeda leaders and discussed "detonation of explosive devices in hotel rooms and gas stations."

On October 24, the Associated Press reported that the defense lawyers Donna Newman and Andrew Patel complained that prosecutors refused to show them evidence which prosecutors said would harm ongoing investigations and national security.

On December 4, Chief Judge Michael B. Mukasey of New York's Southern District stated in a 102-page decision that Padilla could have access to an attorney to challenge his detention as an enemy combatant. He rejected the Bush administration's claim that access to an attorney would impede intelligence gathering and jeopardize national security, but did uphold the government's right to designate enemy combatants, including U.S. citizens, in the war on terrorism. On January 15, 2003, Judge Mukasey criticized the government's request to reverse the decision, saying "this conference ... was supposed to be for the purpose of discussing what steps had been taken voluntarily by the parties to arrange for counsel to see Mr. Padilla. It appears ... that the government has no intention of allowing that to happen." The government was given until January 22 to respond; Padilla's lawyers could respond by January 29.

On March 11, 2003, Judge Mukasey ruled that Padilla must be allowed access to his lawyers, rejecting a government plea to reverse his December decision.

On April 9, 2003, Judge Mukasey asked the U.S. Court of Appeals of the Second Circuit to determine whether President Bush can hold Padilla as an enemy combatant until the conflict with al Qaeda ends.

On July 30, 2003, the Cato Institute, the People For the American Way, and four other groups filed a brief challenging Padilla's detention.

On November 17, 2003, a three-judge federal U.S. Court of Appeals of the Second Circuit considered whether the President has sole authority to declare a U.S. citizen an enemy combatant. As of the hearing, Padilla had not been charged for 18 months and had been held in a naval brig in South Carolina sans access to family, friends, or an attorney. The panel included Judges

Rosemary S. Pooler, Richard C. Wesley, and Barrington D. Parker. Padilla was represented by Donna Newman and Jenny S. Martinez, a law professor at Stanford.

On December 18, 2003, the U.S. Court of Appeals of the Second Circuit, in a 2 to 1 ruling, said that the President does not have the power to declare a U.S. citizen seized on U.S. soil an "enemy combatant" to be held indefinitely in military custody and gave the United States 30 days to release Padilla, declare him a material witness, or charge him. Judges Barrington D. Parker and Rosemary S. Pooler held that "the President's inherent constitutional powers do not extend to the detention as an enemy combatant of American citizens without express congressional authorization. Padilla will be entitled to the constitutional protections extended to other citizens." Dissenting Judge Richard C. Wesley agreed that the President had such authority, but could not prevent Padilla's access to counsel.

On January 22, 2004, the U.S. Court of Appeals of the Second Circuit granted the Bush administration's request for a stay of the order to free Padilla.

On February 11, 2004, the Pentagon said that Padilla would be permitted to consult with an attorney but that this access "is not required by domestic or international law and should not be treated as a precedent." He met with attorney Donna Newman on March 3, 2004.

On February 20, 2004, the U.S. Supreme Court said it would rule on *Rumsfeld v. Padilla, No. 03-1027*, regarding the President's assertion of authority to declare U.S. citizens captured on U.S. soil "enemy combatants" who could be detained indefinitely without charges or access to counsel. The case was to be heard by the last week of April and decided by July. The Court heard oral arguments on April 28, 2004.

On June 1, 2004, the government announced in its seven-page summary of its case against Padilla that he had met with Khalid Shaykh Muhammad, mastermind of the September 11 attacks, as well as al Qaeda leaders Muhammad Atef, Abu Zubayda, and Ramzi Binalshibh.

Padilla was told to try to blow up 20 apartment buildings by sealing them, letting them fill with natural gas, and setting off timed explosions. Targets were to be in New York, Washington, Florida, and Chicago. A Padilla accomplice was in custody. Padilla was to conduct attacks with Adnan G. El Shukrijumah, but they clashed, and the project was scrapped.

On June 28, 2004, the Supreme Court ruled 5 to 4 that Padilla's attorney filed his habeas corpus request in the wrong court—a New York court—whereas Padilla was held in South Carolina. The majority included Justices Rehnquist, O'Connor, Scalia, Kennedy, and Thomas; dissenters were Justices Sevens, Souter, Ginsburg, and Breyer.

Chief Justice William H. Rehnquist, writing the opinion of the Supreme Court, stated, "We confront two questions: First, did Padilla properly file his habeas petition in the Southern District of New York; and second, did the President possess authority to detain Padilla militarily. We answer the threshold question in the negative and thus do not reach the second question presented.... The federal habeas statute straightforwardly provides that the proper respondent to a habeas petition is 'the person who has custody over [the petitioner].' ... We have never intimated that a habeas petitioner could name someone other than his immediate physical custodian as respondent simply because the challenged physical custody does not arise out of a criminal conviction. Nor can we do so here just because Padilla's physical confinement stems from a military order by the President.... We turn now to the second subquestion. District courts are limited to granting habeas relief 'within their respective jurisdictions.' 28 U.S.C. @2241(a). We have interpreted this language to require 'nothing more than that the court issuing the writ have jurisdiction over the custodian.' ... Thus, jurisdiction over Padilla's habeas petition lies in the Southern District only if it has jurisdiction over Commander Marr. We conclude it does not."

Justice Anthony M. Kennedy concurred, saying, "I would not decide today whether these habeas rules function more like rules of personal jurisdiction or rules of venue. It is difficult to describe the precise nature of these restrictions on the filing of habeas petitions, as an examination of the Court's own opinions in this area makes clear.... Here there has been no waiver by the Government; there is no established exception to the immediate-custodian rule or to the rule that the action must be brought in the district court with authority over the territory in question; and there is no need to consider some further exception to protect the integrity of the writ or the rights of the persons detained. For the purposes of this case, it is enough to note that, even under the most permissive interpretation of the habeas statute as a venue provision, the Southern District of New York was not the proper place for this petition."

Justice John Paul Stevens dissented, saying, "All Members of this Court agree that the immediate custodian rule should control in the ordinary case and that habeas petitioners should not be permitted to engage in forum shopping. But we also all agree to Judge Bork that 'special circumstances' can justify exceptions from the general rule.... Executive detention of subversive citizens, like detention of enemy soldiers to keep them off the battlefield, may sometimes be justified to prevent persons from launching or becoming missiles of destruction. It may not, however, be justified by the naked interest in using unlawful procedures to extract information. Incommunicado detention for months on end is such a procedure."

May 9, 2002. *Lebanon.* Bombs were found at a Kentucky Fried Chicken and another U.S. fast food restaurant in Tripoli. Other reports said the bomb at KFC exploded, wounding an employee. No one claimed credit. 02050901-02

May 9, 2002. *Thailand.* A bomb exploded at a hotel in Tachilek, killing a Burmese and injuring three others. No one claimed credit. 02050903

May 9, 2002. *Saudi Arabia.* Saudi soldiers found an empty tube from a Soviet-made SA-7 shoulder-fired antiaircraft missile a half mile away from Prince Sultan Air Base south of Riyadh, from which the United States runs its bombing campaign in Afghanistan. The tube was found inside the outer perimeter fence. The cover on the front of the tube was intact but the back of it was scorched. Observers suggested that someone had attempted to shoot down a plane.

In early June, at Washington's request, Sudan captured Abu Huzifa, a Sudanese and suspected al Qaeda terrorist in connection with the case. He was brought out of the country for interrogation, during which he said that he had gone into Saudi Arabia to survey U.S. bases. He breached the outer perimeter of the base, carrying two SA-7 surface-to-air missiles. He tried to fire one at a departing U.S. plane. He panicked, buried the SA-7 in the sand, and ran. 02050903

May 9, 2002. *Russia.* At 9:30 a.m. during a Victory Day military parade, some 42 people, including 13 children, 18 servicemen, most of them musicians, and 5 adult bystanders, were killed and another 150 injured, one-third of them servicemen, when a radio-controlled mine exploded in Kaspiisk, Dagestan, 100 miles west of Chechnya. Islamic extremists linked to al Qaeda were blamed. The World War II celebration draws veterans and soldiers. The bomb consisted of 6 to 11 pounds of TNT, along with metal balls, plates, and screws. Russian President Vladimir Putin condemned "scum who hold nothing sacred." The town ran out of ambulances for the wounded; some were driven in private cars.

Other mines in other Chechen towns had been defused.

May 9, 2002. *United States.* The Federal Reserve announced a positive test for anthrax in its mail room; it was later determined to be a false positive.

May 10, 2002. *Mexico.* A truck carrying 7.6 tons of sodium cyanide in 76 containers was hijacked in Hidalgo State, 100 miles north of Mexico City. The material is used in silver mining and gas chamber executions. The hijacking raised fears of terrorist attacks. The truck was found in mid-May. On May 23, two fishermen near Mazatlan found a container of cyanide that officials said probably was not part of the truck's cargo. Seventy of the drums were found in Puebla on May 29, dumped off a dirt road 50 miles from the scene of the crime. All of the containers had been accounted for by May 30. The material, owned by Degussa AG, a mining company, was worth only $15,000, so the truck did not have an armed guard.

May 10, 2002. *United Kingdom.* A timer-detonated bomb exploded at the Armenian Embassy, causing no casualties. No one claimed credit. 02051001

May 13, 2002. *United States.* A package bomb found in a Postal Service mailbox in Philadelphia was attached to a note that mentioned al Qaeda and said, "Free Palestine Now." A police bomb squad detonated the bomb with a water cannon. Preston Lit, 53, was arrested at his Philadelphia home and turned over to the FBI, who charged him with threatening to use explosive devices. He had no known link to terrorist groups.

May 13, 2002. *United States.* The press reported that U.S. intelligence and law enforcement officials discounted information suggesting that terrorists would attack a nuclear power plant on July 4. Apparently the information did not come from interrogations of detained bin Laden lieutenant Abu Zubayda.

May 14, 2002. *Spain.* Police arrested two suspected members of the Basque Nation and Liberty (ETA) who had hidden 440 pounds of explosives, detonators, automatic weapons, and false license plates in a Madrid apartment. They apparently were planning a major attack against the May 17 summit of European and Latin American leaders. 02051401

May 14, 2002. *India.* At dawn, three male Islamic militants in combat uniforms fired AK-47s at an interstate bus. After boarding, they forced the driver to stop at an Indian army camp outside Jammu in Kashmir. As the passengers got off the bus, the terrorists fired on them and threw a grenade, killing seven people. They then attacked the camp, throwing more grenades and shooting at soldiers in their residential quarters. The terrorist attack killed 31 and injured 47. Among the dead were 11 women, including many wives of soldiers, and 10 children, most of them between ages 4 and 10. Soldiers fired back, killing the trio after a three-hour gun battle. Al Mansooren and Jamiat ul-Mujaheddin individually claimed credit for the attack. Home Minister L. K. Advani told Parliament that Al Mansooren is a "new outfit floated by the Lashkar-i-Taibi," an Islamic group that Pakistan had banned in January.

India said that the terrorists were Pakistanis and ordered the expulsion of Pakistani Ambassador Ashraf Jehangir Qazi. The Indian Foreign Ministry said this was the first time a Pakistani ambassador had been expelled. A senior Indian intelligence official said that "we found chocolate wrappers that were made in Pakistan on one of the bodies. And on the second man, a recently used cinema ticket from the Pakistani city of Sialkot. Obviously, they had crossed over very recently into Indian territory." 02051402

May 14, 2002. *Liberia.* Rebels were believed to have kidnapped a British Reverend Garry Jenkins and 60 blind people in Bomi County, 38 miles north of Monrovia. 02051403

May 17, 2002. *Yemen.* Yemeni tribes near the Saudi border warned the United States not to launch attacks on their territory, observing it would be "a strategic mistake."

May 17, 2002. *India.* A bomb exploded outside the high-security civil secretariat area in Srinagar, Kashmir, injuring six people. In Jammu, Kashmir, a bomb exploded at a fire services headquarters, killing 2 and injuring 16 others. No one claimed credit for either attack.

May 17, 2002. *United States.* The *Washington Post* and *New York Times* quoted senior U.S.

officials as saying that an increase in intercepted al Qaeda messages appeared to presage a planned, albeit unspecified, strike in the United States.

Meanwhile, a rash of finger-pointing continued, with politicized calls for investigations into how President Bush responded to analysis in his August 6, 2001, President's Daily Briefing that mentioned possible al Qaeda hijackings.

May 18, 2002. *Honduras.* Gunmen kidnapped former Honduran Economy Minister Reginaldo Panting, 72, a lawmaker from the opposition Liberal Party, as he drove his car in San Pedro Sula. Late in the month, the family paid a $122,000 ransom. His body was found late on June 1 in the town with his hands tied behind his back and a rope around his neck. He had interests in banking and oil. The town was hard hit by a nationwide campaign of kidnappings and crime.

May 19, 2002. *United States.* Vice President Richard Cheney warned of a "real possibility" that suicide bombers would carry out attacks in the United States. He said that "the prospects of a future attack against the U.S. are almost certain" and "could happen tomorrow, it could happen next week, it could happen next year, but they will keep trying." It is "not a matter of if, but when."

May 19, 2002. *Israel.* A Palestinian suicide bomber wearing an olive-drab Israeli army uniform walked into a fruit and vegetable market in Netanya and killed 3 Israelis plus himself and injured more than 50 people. The powerful bomb ripped open steel shutters in front of the vendors' stalls and severed the bomber in two. Among the dead was Russian immigrant Arkady Wieselman, father of two and a chef at the Park Hotel, who had survived the March 27 Passover bombing in Netanya that killed 29 people. He had cared for the surviving family members of Ami Hamamy, who was killed in the earlier attack. Among those injured was Moti Holder, 21, who was helping out at a fruit stand, and

Amos Gilam, 29, who was sleeping in his apartment when glass shards cut his left elbow. Israel said the terrorist came from Tulkarm, nine miles to the east.

Credit was claimed by the Islamic Resistance Movement (Hamas) and the Popular Front for the Liberation of Palestine (PFLP) led by Ahmed Saadat.

May 20, 2002. *Lebanon.* A car bomb in Beirut's Mar Elias neighborhood killed Mohammed Jibril, the son of Ahmed Jibril, the head of the Popular Front for the Liberation of Palestine-General Command (PFLP-GC). The bomb was connected to wires hidden in his Peugeot. The PFLP-GC blamed Israel, which denied the charge. PFLP-GC officials in Damascus said Mohammed Jibril was coordinator of military operations in the Palestinian territories. The senior Jibril had earlier claimed credit for gunrunning to Palestinian terrorists.

May 20, 2002. *Israel.* A Palestinian suicide bomber injured a policeman and killed himself near Jenin.

May 20, 2002. *United States.* FBI Director Robert S. Mueller, III, warned that walk-in suicide attacks similar to those in Israel were "inevitable" in the United States. Earlier in the week, the FBI warned that al Qaeda terrorists might rent apartments and set off bombs in them.

May 20, 2002. *United States.* Families of seven Americans killed or injured in terrorist attacks in Israel brought suit against the Islamic Resistance Movement (Hamas) for millions of dollars in damages for attacks by gunfire and explosives on December 1, 1993, and April 17, 2001. The suits were assigned to U.S. District Judge James Robertson and Judge Ricardo M. Urbina. Yitzhak Weinstock was killed in the 1993 attack.

May 20–21, 2002. *United States.* At 4:00 p.m., the 1,200 employees in the Africa and Training Divisions of the World Bank's J Building at 18th Street and Pennsylvania Avenue in

Washington, D.C., were sent home after a batch of mail tested positive for anthrax in a preliminary check. Four employees were put on antibiotics. A second test at another facility was negative. The International Monetary Fund (IMF) closed its mail room and prescribed doxycycline antibiotics to 100 employees after a positive test result the next day. Washington, D.C., health officials complained that the World Bank and International Monetary Fund did not notify them before taking action.

Meanwhile, the FBI announced plans to administer polygraph examinations to more than 200 current and former employees at the U.S. Army Medical Research Institute of Infectious Diseases (USAMRIID) at Fort Detrick, Maryland, Dugway Proving Ground in Utah, and other U.S. facilities that have anthrax stores. Genetic studies indicated that the anthrax unleashed against the American public was descended from Fort Detrick stocks.

May 21, 2002. *Thailand.* A man dressed in Buddhist monk robes and armed with an assault rifle took 30 hostages at the parliament building and demanded to speak to Prime Minister Thaksin Shinawatra. He fired into the air, but no one was injured in the one-hour standoff. Sayan Chitasuro yelled through a megaphone, "I am demanding to talk with Prime Minister Thaksin to lodge a complaint about my unjust treatment when I was arrested by local police." He talked to reporters via a mobile phone, saying that he was arrested in 1996 for trespassing in a national park. He claimed he had come to the 500-member lower House to hand a petition to the president of the Parliament and to see the prime minister. The attack came just before the House was to debate a no-confidence motion against 15 cabinet members. Police took Chitasuro into custody.

May 21, 2002. *India.* Two masked gunmen wearing police uniforms shot to death Abdul Ghani Lone, 70, a nonviolent Muslim separatist leader of the All Parties Hurriyet Conference,

who favored dialogue with India over Kashmir. He had just finished participating in a rally in Srinagar for another assassinated Kashmir independence leader. He had left a wooden stage and was walking toward a row of white sedans when he was shot in the chest at close range by pistols. His son blamed Pakistani's Inter-Services Intelligence agency and a conservative Hurriyet leader, Syed Ali Shah Geelani. One of Lone's police guards was killed, and another was wounded.

May 21, 2002. *United States.* Defense Secretary Donald H. Rumsfeld told the Senate Appropriations Committee's Defense Subcommittee, "In just facing the facts, we have to recognize that terrorist networks have relationships with terrorist states that have weapons of mass destruction, and that they inevitably are going to get their hands on them, and they would not hesitate one minute in using them. That's the world we live in." Homeland Security Director Tom Ridge said additional attacks are "not a question of if, but a question of when."

May 21, 2002. *United States.* The FBI warned that terrorists had threatened New York landmarks, including the Statue of Liberty and the Brooklyn Bridge. Security personnel used facial recognition cameras to compare photos of tourists with those of known terrorists and suspects. The technology was provided by Visionics of Jersey City.

May 22, 2002. *United States.* A man firing a shotgun wounded two people at the New Orleans airport. He told police that he was angry that people had made fun of his turban.

May 22, 2002. *Israel.* During the evening, a Palestinian suicide bomber with dyed blond hair and dressed like an Israeli—in jeans and a T-shirt—walked into a pedestrian mall frequented by elderly chess players in Rishon Letzion, a southern suburb of Tel Aviv. He set off an explosives belt at a pavilion covered by a blue awning, killing 2 Israelis and injuring more than 25 people, several of them seriously. The dead included a 15-year-old and a 51-year-old man. Police speculated that the terrorist had been turned away from entering a nearby shopping mall. Al-Aqsa said the killer was Issa Bdeir (variant Badir), 16, of Al Doha outside Bethlehem. Bdeir left a videotaped message that said he was "going to carry out my operation to avenge the continuous Israeli aggression that is still committed against our people."

Hours earlier, Israeli tank gunners killed Mahmoud Titi, a commander of the al-Aqsa Martyrs Brigades, in Nablus. The Brigades claimed credit, saying it was in revenge for Palestinian "martyrs" killed by Israel.

On May 30, Israeli police said a Palestinian man, Ibraham Sarachne, a Muslim from Bethlehem's Deheisheh refugee camp, drove Bdeir to the scene of the crime. Sarachne and his wife, Medina Pinsky, a Russian immigrant initially thought to be Jewish, had also driven to the town a Palestinian woman, Arin Ahmed, 20, who intended to set off a suicide bomb against the rescuers, but she apparently had second thoughts. The duo drove her back to Bethlehem after hiding her explosives belt in a car. She was arrested in Beit Sahour. The next day police said that the wife was Irena Plitzik, 26, a Ukrainian Christian, not an Israeli Jew. She was carrying a forged ID card for Marina Pinsky, who saw her name in the Israeli papers and alerted authorities to the error. Police also arrested a young man who dyed the bomber's hair blond. Soldiers detained Ahmed Mugrabi, who was believed to be behind the attack and prepared explosives for other missions.

May 22, 2002. *Israel.* Israeli soldiers killed Moussa Daraghmeh, a Palestinian, as he made "suspicious movements" near a checkpoint on the road between Bethlehem and Jerusalem. He was with a group of 20 people who were trying to get around the checkpoint on their way to work.

May 22, 2002. *Israel.* A Palestine Islamic Jihad activist died when explosives he was carrying blew up in Jenin.

May 23, 2002. *Colombia.* Four Venezuelan members of the Revolutionary Armed Forces of Colombia (FARC) were killed in a shoot-out with the army.

May 23, 2002. *Spain.* The Basque Nation and Liberty (ETA) was suspected of setting off a car bomb in a parking lot near a building at the University of Navarra in Pamplona. Two people were injured and several university buildings were damaged. A Basque newspaper received a warning phone call half an hour earlier. The caller gave the vehicle's location and license plate number.

May 23, 2002. *Israel.* A remotely detonated bomb went off in a diesel tank truck parked at a major fuel depot near Tel Aviv. The bomb was set off via a cell phone at the Pi-Glilot facility. The terrorists had attempted to create a chain-reaction explosion, but workers with hand-held extinguishers quickly put out the fire. A truck driver standing on top of the cab when the bomb went off was not injured. Nearby trucks were also undamaged.

May 24, 2002. *Israel.* At 1:00 a.m., a Palestinian tried to ram his car filled with explosives into a crowded Tel Aviv Studio 49 dance club. Eli Federman, a quick-thinking security guard, fired through the windshield. The driver fell from the car, which blew up before impact, injuring three passersby. Federman said, "Then I fired the rest of the bullets into his head," killing the terrorist. The al-Aqsa Martyrs Brigades said the terrorist was Amer Shkokani of El Bireh in the West Bank.

May 24, 2002. *Israel.* Officials said they had thwarted terrorist plans to set off a ton of explosives beneath Tel Aviv's twin Azrieli Towers, the country's tallest office building complex.

May 24, 2002. *Somalia.* Hundreds of opposition gunmen led by militia leader Mohamed Dhereh attacked the Mogadishu home of the transitional government's Interior Minister Dahir Dayah, killing 8 people and injuring 20.

May 24, 2002. *United States.* The FBI and U.S. Department of Transportation warned of possible terrorist attacks on the nation's transportation system, including airports and subways. Airports and pilots were warned that "terrorists may still be interested in the use of small aircraft for suicide attacks in the United States.

May 24, 2002. *United States.* The Nuclear Regulatory Commission put the country's 103 nuclear power plants on a higher state of alert.

May 27, 2002. *Israel.* A Palestinian suicide bomber walked into a crowd of after-work shoppers at the sidewalk Village Café in a suburban strip mall in Petah Tikva (seven miles east of Tel Aviv) and set off an explosion that killed an elderly Israeli woman, Ruth Peled, and her 18-month-old granddaughter, Sinai Kanaan, and injured more than 50 others. The girl's parents were wounded. The bomber, Jihad Titi, 18, wore blue jeans and a gray shirt, and used a bomb packed with nails and shrapnel to spray the Em Hamoshavot strip mall and supermarket. Also injured was Violet Maslush, 53, a waitress at the café. The al-Aqsa Martyrs Brigades claimed credit in a statement released in Beirut, saying it was retaliating for Israel's killing three Palestinian militants in a refugee camp near Nablus the previous week. The killer was a cousin of Mahmoud Titi, a militant in Nablus killed by an Israeli tank shell the previous week. Jihad's brother, Munir, was paralyzed from shrapnel wounds during an April invasion of the Balata refugee camp. Munir's 14-year-old son lost two fingers in that attack. Jihad recorded a videotape in which he said he would get revenge against the "pig government." Haleema, his mother, praised his act, saying that when he said goodbye to her, "I realized he was going to carry out a suicide attack. I

said, 'Oh, son, I hope your operation will succeed.' "

May 27, 2002. *Israel.* A gardener found a large explosive device at an apartment building in French Hill, a Jewish neighborhood of East Jerusalem. Police defused the device.

May 27, 2002. *Russia.* Tatyana Sapunova stopped her car when she saw a sign that said "Death to Jews" on the side of a Moscow highway. She sustained severe burns and eye injuries when she tried to remove it and a booby trap exploded. Russia's Jewish community paid to send her to Israel for plastic surgery for her injuries.

May 28, 2002. *Israel.* During the evening, Palestinian gunmen ambushed a car that had left the Jewish settlement of Ofra, north of Ramallah, killing Albert Maloul, 50, the Israeli driver, and wounding a passenger. The terrorists were not captured.

May 28, 2002. *Israel.* Later in the evening, a Palestinian gunman cut through a fence at the Jewish settlement of Itamar, near Nablus, and killed three Jewish religious students at a religious high school. Two of the students were killed on a basketball court; another was killed in the school. A security guard shot to death the terrorist.

May 28, 2002. *Nepal.* One hundred Maoist rebels died in an attack on a Nepalese army camp hours after the king renewed emergency rule.

May 29, 2002. *Afghanistan.* Kyrgyz secret police announced that Sheraly Akbotoyev had been captured in Afghanistan and brought to Kyrgyzstan to face trial on terrorism charges. He was a member of the pro-Taliban Islamic Movement of Uzbekistan (IMU). Police hoped to question him about the fate of IMU leader Juma Namagani, who was reported killed in Afghanistan in late 2001; many doubted the report regarding this associate of Osama bin Laden.

May 30, 2002. *Algeria.* Islamic gunmen killed 25 civilians in Sendjas in Chlef Province, 125 miles west of Algiers, hours after voting began in nationwide parliamentary elections. The victims included a 2-month-old. Most were nomads living in tents. The terrorists slit 21 throats. Two other victims were set on fire, and two were shot dead.

May 30, 2002. *Pakistan.* The FBI and local authorities conducted a nighttime raid on a *madrassa* (religious school) operated by Bangladeshis with suspected al Qaeda ties. Police seized CD ROMs and documents containing al Qaeda information.

May 30, 2002. *United States.* The government warned that al Qaeda might be considering using scuba divers to attack ships at anchor, power plants, bridges, depots, or other waterfront targets. The FBI contacted hundreds of dive shops across the country. In early June, the Professional Association of Diving Instructors gave the FBI a list of 2 million people certified to dive in the past three years. The Coast Guard sent out a follow-up warning in early June. Security around ports and ships was tightened.

May 30, 2002. *India.* Armed militants shot and injured a subeditor of the local English language newspaper *Kashmir Images*. No one claimed credit.

June 2002. *Italy.* Palermo police raided an Islamic social center, seizing documents and videotapes and briefly detaining 12 individuals. Police later said that six Italian converts to Islam were involved in attempts to set off small homemade bombs at an ancient Greek theater in Agrigento, Sicily, and in Milan's subway. No arrests were made.

June 2002. *Jordan.* Jordan rendered to Lebanese authorities three Lebanese Hizballah members arrested after trying to smuggle weapons destined for the West Bank into Jordan.

Jordanian authorities also arrested three Jordanian youths suspected of planning to infiltrate into Israel to conduct terrorist attacks.

June 2002. *Brazil.* Brazil arrested Assad Ahmad Barakat, a Brazil-based Lebanese businessman suspected of opening two businesses in Chile as cover to move money clandestinely to Lebanese Hizballah. The arrest was made in Foz do Iguacu, Parana, in the Triborder Area. Paraguay had requested extradition on criminal charges. Barakat was a naturalized Paraguayan who had lived in the Triborder Area for seven years. The Supreme Court ordered his extradition to Paraguay in December 2002. His lawyers applied for refugee status in Brazil; he was to remain in detention in Brazil while his refugee case was considered. The Chilean government opened an investigation in the northern port city of Iquique. He no longer has significant holdings in Chile, and his partners in Saleh Trading, Ltd., located in Iquique, severed ties with him in 2002. Assad and his brother still owned an import-export firm in Iquique, but the Chilean government reported that it had been inactive. He was extradited to Paraguay in November 2003.

June 2002. *Morocco.* In mid-June, authorities arrested Abu Zubair Haili, a senior al Qaeda lieutenant who worked for Abu Zubayda, the group's deputy, handling logistics in and out of training camps. He also recruited Islamic fighters for the camps and placed them in cells around the world. The Saudi was nicknamed "the bear" because he weighed 300 pounds.

June 2002. *United States.* Two Middle Eastern looking men tried to pay cash for a used ambulance in Lyndhurst, New Jersey. The dealer refused, took down the license plate of one of the men, and called police. Authorities were attempting to locate the owner of the vehicle for questioning.

June 2002. *Ethiopia.* The government blamed the indigenous Oromo Liberation

Front for an attack on a railway station in Dire Dawa.

June 2002. *United States.* Authorities arrested Adham Amin Hassoun, a Palestinian, who was indicted on eight charges, including unlawful possession of a firearm and perjury.

On September 16, 2004, Hassoun and Mohamed Hesham Youssef, who was serving a sentence in Egypt on terrorism charges, were indicted in Florida for providing financial support and recruitment for al Qaeda and other terrorist groups fighting in Afghanistan, Chechnya, Kosovo, and Somalia, and for helping Jose Padilla (arrested on May 8, 2002, in the "dirty bomb" case) to attend Afghan terrorist training camps. The U.S. District Court in Miami charged them each with two counts of providing material support to terrorists. The indictment said that between 1994 and 2001, Hassoun wrote more than two dozen checks totaling $53,000 to support terrorists. Many were written to the Holy Land Foundation and Global Relief Foundation charities, which funneled money to terrorists.

June 1, 2002. *Worldwide.* Al Hayat's Web site www.alneda.com reported that Sulaiman Abu Gaith, Osama bin Laden's spokesman, warned that "we confirm our continuation in working to attack Americans and Jews, and targeting them, both people and buildings. What will come to the Americans, God willing, won't be less than what has come. America should be ready and on high alert and fasten the seat belts, as with the will of God, we will come to them, from where they didn't expect."

June 1, 2002. *India.* In Kulgam, Kashmir, a grenade thrown into a crowd killed one person and injured seven. In Srinagar, armed militants tossed a grenade into a paramilitary foot patrol, killing one person and injuring 13 others. In Anantnag, armed militants threw a grenade into a police station, injuring 18 people. No one claimed credit for any of these attacks.

June 3, 2002. *United States.* Molotov cocktails exploded at the Miami buildings housing the Cuban American National Foundation and Alpha 66 before employees of the anti-Castro exile organizations arrived. No one was injured, but slight damage was reported. 02060301-02

June 3, 2002. *Latin America.* Foreign ministers throughout the Americas signed a treaty in Barbados to prevent and punish terrorism.

June 4, 2002. *Thailand.* Three masked, hooded gunmen wearing fatigues fired M-16s at a Thai school bus carrying 20 junior high school students as it was climbing a steep road in the mountainous jungle district of Suan Phung in Ratchaburi Province, 12 miles from the Burmese border. The gunmen killed 2 teens—a boy and a girl—and wounded 15 others, aged between 14 and 17. Nine of those injured were in critical condition. Authorities blamed Burmese ethnic guerrilla groups, suggesting Karen militants. A Karen rebel group denied responsibility. The terrorists apparently escaped back to Burma. 02060401

June 5, 2002. *Russia.* Three more "Death to Jews" posters showed up in Voronezh, 300 miles south of Moscow. The posters had packages attached to them that police believed could contain bombs. Police fired water cannons at the packages, which contained bricks. The posters were pulled down.

June 5, 2002. *Indonesia.* A bomb exploded on a bus in remote Sulawesi, killing 4 people and injuring 17 in an afternoon attack. The bus was carrying 25 people toward Poso, the district capital of Sulawesi. Police were looking for three unidentified passengers who got off before the blast and questioned six others, including the driver.

June 5, 2002. *Northern Ireland.* Alex Maskey, a former Irish Republican Army (IRA) prisoner who nearly died in an assassination attempt in 1987, was elected Sinn Fein's first mayor of

Belfast. He was the city's second Roman Catholic mayor in recent years, following two centuries of Protestants.

June 5, 2002. *Israel.* At 7:15 a.m., an Islamic Jihad car bomb exploded next to a Number 80 Egged bus in Megiddo, killing 17 people, including Hamza Samudi, 16, the Jenin-based terrorist, and 13 soldiers, and wounding 45 people. Many of those injured were trapped on the burning bus, parts of which flew over the fencing of the local prison. Islamic Jihad said it timed the bombing to coincide with the 35th anniversary of the Arab-Israeli war of 1967. Among the injured was bus driver Mickey Harel, 60, who had seen three other bus bombings during the past six months. He had helped rescue other injured passengers, who were going from Tel Aviv to Tiberias. He fought in the 1967 and 1973 wars and has three sons in the army. Also wounded were Haim Tubul, 20, and Sgt. Zvi Avraham.

Police said the car was stolen inside Israel in February and driven to the scene from the West Bank.

The Israeli army retaliated with tank and helicopter attacks on Jenin and bombing Yasir Arafat's headquarters in Ramallah.

Megiddo (Hebrew for Armageddon) Junction lies near the area the Book of Revelation identifies as the location of the final battle between good and evil before the end of the world.

Netanya residents buried four soldiers and a civilian victim on June 6. One of the soldiers was Avraham Barzilai, 20. Another was SFC David Stanislavski, 22, who came to Israel from the Ukraine four and a half years earlier and settled in Netanya with his mother. He had planned to go back to the Ukraine in July to celebrate his engagement to his childhood sweetheart, who would return to Israel with him. He was on the bus to visit his mother.

June 6, 2002. *United States.* In a speech from the Oval Office, President George W. Bush proposed the creation of the Cabinet-level Department of Homeland Security, which would absorb agencies with 169,154 employees and a budget of $37,450,000,000. The department would have four main functions. Its border and transportation security group would include the Immigration and Naturalization Service, the Customs Service, the Agriculture Department's Animal and Plant Health Inspection Service, the Coast Guard, General Services Administration's (GSA) Federal Protective Service, and the Transportation Security Administration. Its emergency preparedness and response group would include the Federal Emergency Management Agency, Department of Health and Human Services' (HHS) Chemical, Biological, Radiological, and Nuclear Response Assets, an interagency Domestic Emergency Support Team, the Department of Energy's Nuclear Incident Response team, the Justice Department's Office of Domestic Preparedness, and the FBI's National Domestic Preparedness Office. Leading the federal government's efforts to prepare for and respond to attacks involving weapons of mass destruction/disruption would be the HHS Civilian Biodefense Research Programs, Energy's Lawrence Livermore National Laboratory, a new National Biological Weapons Defense Analysis Center, and Agriculture's Plum Island Animal Disease Center. To provide information analysis and infrastructure protection, the department would include the Department of Commerce's Critical Infrastructure Assurance Office, GSA's Federal Computer Incident Response Center, The Department of Defense National Communications System, the FBI's National Infrastructure Protection Center, and Energy's National Infrastructure Simulation and Analysis Center. The Secret Service would also join the new department. Cabinet-level organizations can be created only by an act of Congress, which had 88 committees with some jurisdiction over the proposed department's functions.

June 7, 2002. *India.* Armed militants killed one person, injured three others, and damaged several houses in Pindi. No one claimed credit.

June 8, 2002. *Greece.* A man fired a shotgun at the residence of Prime Minister Costas Simitis. The gunman was arrested following a gun battle with police.

June 8, 2002. *Israel.* At 2:00 a.m., two Palestinian gunmen snuck from Halhoul into Karmei Tsur, a Jewish settlement of 13 trailer homes near Hebron, and killed two Israelis—Eyal Sorek, 23, a young soldier, and his eight-months-pregnant wife, Yael, 24—and wounded six Israeli army patrol members whose unit fired on the assailants. The Israeli couple came out of their trailer when they heard the shots. A terrorist shot him, then stabbed and hit him with an ax. They also shot Yael to death. The terrorists were armed with an M-16 and a Kalashnikov, and fired 300 rounds. One terrorist was killed, the other escaped into a nearby Palestinian village. A patrolman later died of his wounds. The Popular Front for the Liberation of Palestine (PFLP) was suspected.

June 8, 2002. *Israel.* Authorities said at least six more Palestinians were killed while attempting attacks. Two men were spotted swimming toward the Jewish settlement in Dugit in the Gaza Strip. They were carrying grenades and firearms. One of them was killed.

Another three Palestinians died when a large bomb they were carrying went off accidentally near Rafah in the southern Gaza Strip. One of the terrorists was a member of Yasir Arafat's Preventive Security Force. The others were members of Hamas and Islamic Jihad.

Four Israelis were injured, two seriously, when three gunmen fired on homes in the Yizhak settlement in the northern West Bank. Soldiers shot and killed two of the gunmen.

June 9, 2002. *India.* Police arrested Syed Ali Shah Geelani, 73, a prominent Kashmiri separatist leader, at his Srinagar home, on charges of funneling money to Islamic radicals who wanted to unite Kashmir with Pakistan. Police seized large amounts of cash, financial records, and a diamond-studded watch with an inscription from the Pakistani government. Geelani had led the All Parties Hurriyet Conference, an alliance of Kashmiri separatist groups.

June 9, 2002. *United States.* Rabbi Yakove Lloyd, founder and president of the Jewish Defense Group, said that citizens armed with shotguns would patrol the Jewish Brooklyn neighborhoods of New York City after Abdul Rahman Yasin told CBS's *60 Minutes* on June 2 that he and his accomplices originally targeted those neighborhoods. Yasin, speaking from Iraq, was wanted by the FBI for the 1993 bombing of the World Trade Center. Yasin said the group decided to bomb the towers because they believed most of the occupants were Jewish.

Lloyd announced that the first neighborhood watch by a dozen armed colleagues would begin on June 23, after the FBI warned that terrorists could be planning to use fuel tanker trucks in attacks.

June 9, 2002. *Ethiopia.* At 5:15 p.m., two men armed with knives attempted to hijack an Ethiopian Airlines Fokker-50 plane carrying 42 passengers from Bahir Dar to Addis Ababa. Sky marshals shot the hijackers to death. A crew member sustained a minor injury. No passengers were hurt. 02060901

June 9, 2002. *India.* In Rajouri, Kashmir, armed militants wounded six people, including three security personnel, and damaged a television tower building. No one claimed credit.

June 11, 2002. *United States.* John Walsh of *America's Most Wanted* told *Elliott in the Morning* on WWDC-101 in Washington that Customs agents in Florida had discovered a cargo container with scraps of food, water, and Islamic literature. The Customs agents worried that this was an indication that 15 al Qaeda terrorists had been smuggled into the United States.

June 11, 2002. *El Salvador.* CNN reported that an American citizen was kidnapped. A $500,000 ransom was demanded. 02061101

June 11, 2002. *Israel.* At 7:50 p.m., a suicide bomber killed himself and a teenage Israeli girl and injured eight others at a restaurant in Herzliya, north of Tel Aviv.

June 11, 2002. *Israel.* The al-Aqsa Martyrs Brigades said it had killed two Palestinians in Hebron who were suspected of collaborating with Israel. The Brigades left a leaflet saying that the duo helped Israel spot Marwan Zalloum, a local Brigades leader who was killed on April 22 by an Israeli helicopter attack on his car. Palestinians had killed at least 42 suspected collaborators in the past 20 months.

June 11, 2002. *Israel.* Three Israeli 15-year-olds from a Jewish settlement were injured, one seriously, when a bomb exploded after they picked cherries in a field near Hebron, south of Jerusalem. The trio were helping with the harvest, which many Israeli teens do during the summer. No one claimed credit.

June 11, 2002. *Israel.* A Palestinian stabbed and seriously wounded an Israeli policeman at Herod's Gate, an entrance to the Old City of Jerusalem. The assailant escaped.

June 11, 2002. *Israel.* A Palestinian died when a bomb he was planting went off near the fence between Gaza and Israel.

June 12, 2002. *Russia.* Another "Death to Jews" sign—red with black letters—showed up on a Moscow highway. An explosives team using a robot and sniffer dog dismantled a package attached to the sign. No bomb was found. Russian skinheads had threatened a "war against foreigners."

June 12, 2002. *Spain.* Police found a large cache of explosives, including 288 pounds of dynamite, other explosive material, and detonators, in the woods near Valencia. Two days earlier, they had detained a suspected Basque Nation and Liberty (ETA) member in the area. Authorities said the ETA planned to attack tourist targets during a

European Union summit scheduled for the next week in Seville.

June 12, 2002. *India.* Local officials reported receiving evidence of an imminent al Qaeda attack on Bombay financial institutions.

June 12, 2002. *Germany.* Authorities reported receiving intelligence of an al Qaeda plan to shoot down civilian airliners. A civilian had intercepted radio traffic in the Middle East in which someone was talking about an attack on airliners in Germany.

June 14, 2002. *Kyrgyzstan.* CNN reported that three Chinese nationals were arrested in connection with a plot against the U.S. Embassy. 02061401

June 14, 2002. *Pakistan.* At 11:09 a.m., a car bomb carrying 40 pounds of explosives (later the FBI said it was 500 pounds of fertilizer bomb) exploded outside the U.S. Consulate on Abdullah Haroon Road in Karachi, killing 14 Pakistanis, including 2 policemen, and injuring 51 others, including a Japanese citizen. No Americans were killed, but a U.S. Marine was slightly injured. The Khanum Driving School's Toyota Corolla sedan went off as the female driver steered into a row of barricades outside the Consulate's ten-foot-high concrete wall. The car carried four female passengers. A white van hit by the blast was thrown across the street into a park; inside were a Karachi man and his niece, a physician who was to be married the next day. A Pakistani employee in the Consulate's canteen was in critical condition. Most of the Consulate's windows and those of the nearby Marriott Hotel and shopping arcade were blown out. A dozen cars were burned; one Suzuki had been flipped into the air. The previously unknown Tarjuman-al-Qanoon (Spokesman for the Law; or al Qanoon–the Law, variant al-Qa'nun) warned that it would continue to attack Americans and "officials of the puppet regime" if President General Pervez Musharraf did not resign. Connections with al Qaeda were being investigated.

Washington Post writer Kamran Khan said that two minutes before the bomb went off, a young man in traditional Pakistani dress speaking in Punjab-accented Urdu asked, "Brother, this is the American Embassy? Do you know, are the offices on the right or left side of the building?" The individual may have been holding a telephone.

Karachi Mayor Naimat Ullah said, "The terrorists have no religion. They are not Muslim. They are not human. They are just terrorists."

A "duck and cover" drill had been scheduled for the Consulate for 11:30 a.m.

The next day, Pakistani police were considering whether the bomb was set off by remote control and that the passengers were unaware that they were driving a vehicle bomb. Police were searching for Lashkar-e-Jhangvi leader Naeem Bukhari, also suspected in Daniel Pearl's murder, and Asif Ramzi, a militant who named himself after noted terrorist Ramzi Yousef, who was convicted for the 1993 World Trade Center bombing.

On June 17, police questioned Mohammed Umer, a religious student with ties to Lashkar-e-Jhangvi, who was already in custody and had provided information about a militant group trained in explosives. He had been arrested after the May 8 suicide bombing that killed 11 French engineers. He had yet to be charged.

On June 20, Pakistani police arrested seven more Arabs suspected of having al Qaeda ties and detained another seven Pakistanis in connection with the bombing and the May 8 hotel bombing. None were charged. The Arabs were arrested over the previous two days and included Saudis, Yemenis, and others of undisclosed nationalities.

By June 22, Pakistani police held 45 Muslim militants for questioning in the case. They belonged to the two banned Sunni groups Lashkar-e-Jhangvi and Sipah-i-Sahaba. Another eight suspects, including three Palestinians and two Sudanese, were arrested in two raids on June 26

in Karachi. The raid also netted satellite telephones, laptop computers, computer disks, and other items.

The FBI said on June 22 that the 500 pound fertilizer bomb was hidden in a Suzuki pickup truck driven by a suicide bomber and that the driver's education Toyota Corolla was merely one of the vehicles hit in the blast. The FBI was back to the suicide bomber theory.

Pakistan issued a wanted poster on June 29 that listed 12 individuals wanted for the Daniel Pearl murder, the May 8 bombing that killed 11 French engineers and 3 Pakistanis, and the U.S. Consulate truck bombing. The poster included five photos of Asif Ramzi, whose arrest would include a $50,000 bounty. Two other men were worth $25,000 each. Another three were associates of Saud Memon, who owned the property where Daniel Pearl was held, killed, and buried. One of them, Abdul Rehman Sindhi, was named. Another bearded youth was identified as Sharib and wanted for the two bombings. Naveed Ul Hassan was wanted in the consulate case. (Hassan was arrested on November 17, 2004, near Pakistan's main border checkpoint with India at Wagah, near Lahore, for the consulate bombing and a small New Year's 2003 blast that wounded nine people in Karachi.) Also worth $50,000 was Naeem Bukhari, who earlier was reported in custody.

On July 8, Pakistani authorities announced at a press conference that on July 7 they had arrested three members of the Harkat ul-Mujaheddin al-Almi, a branch of Harkat ul-Mujaheddin, in connection with the bombing. They also seized a large quantity of explosives and weapons. At the press conference, two men publicly admitted their guilt and said that the bomb had originally been prepared to kill Pakistani President General Pervez Musharraf. The duo, identified as Mohammed Imran, the group's leader, and Mohammed Hanif, his deputy, said they tried to set off the bomb near the president's motorcade in Karachi in April, but the remote control failed. Hanif, heavily bearded and wearing a *shalar kameez*, said, "I, along with my other friends, were involved in the U.S. bombing. We acted in consultation. One of our friends, who was willing to be a suicide bomber, carried out the attack." Police differed as to whether the arrests occurred on July 7 or two weeks earlier. The trio—Imran, Hanif, and Mohammed Ashraf—were arraigned in the case on August 3 in the Anti-Terrorism Court on charges of conspiracy, terrorism, attempted murder, and use of a lethal explosive. The terrorism charge carries the death penalty. The trio and Waseem Akhtar, a member of the Pakistan Rangers paramilitary police, were also arraigned on charges of plotting to kill Musharraf.

On September 17, local police and intelligence officers arrested Sharib Ahmad, 30, the country's most-wanted Islamic militant, and five other men in a house in the middle-class residential district of Dhoraji, a suburb of Karachi. He was named the leader of the attack on the consulate by three other suspects. They were captured less than a mile from the site of a military equipment exhibition that was attended the previous day by President Musharraf. Police seized a large cache of weapons, ammunition, and explosives, including an antitank rifle. A police official said, "In their sole aim to kill President Musharraf, these militants had collected 70 hand grenades, 40 rocket-propelled grenades and rockets, and about [2,000 pounds] of bomb-making chemicals at their hideout in Karachi. This is the largest seizure of arms and ammunition from any terrorist group in Pakistan since September 11." All six were affiliated with Harkat ul-Mujaheddin al-Almi, which was also involved in an attempt to assassinate President Musharraf in April by setting off a car bomb which failed to detonate. Police said the arms cache had been moved from Afghanistan in the previous months and that "each one of them had received guerrilla training in camps inside Afghanistan before the U.S. attacks began in October."

On November 8, a Pakistani court indicted five Islamic militants in the case. They pleaded not guilty to charges of murder, attempted murder, terrorism, conspiracy, and the use of explosives.

On April 14, 2003, an antiterrorist court inside the Karachi central jail sentenced to death Mohammed Hanif and Mohammed Imran for the bombing. Two others received life sentences; a fifth was acquitted. The defense said it would appeal. 02061402

June 15, 2002. *Israel.* Shortly after soldiers foiled a car bomb attack, Palestinian gunmen killed two Israeli soldiers and wounded four others in a gun battle near Dugit in the northern Gaza Strip. The car bomb contained mortar rounds and launchers and more than 330 pounds of explosives. Authorities said the terrorists would lure soldiers to the booby-trapped car by firing the mortars from the vehicle and then setting off the explosives when the car was searched. Hamas claimed credit.

June 17, 2002. *Philippines.* At 6:00 p.m., gunmen fired on U.S. troops in Kumalarang, on Basilan Island, but caused no injuries. The Abu Sayyaf, which has strong popular support in the area, was suspected. 02061701

June 17, 2002. *Democratic Republic of the Congo.* Rwandan-backed rebels from the Congolese Rally for Democracy kidnapped and beat two UN peacekeepers at the compound of the UN mission in Kisangani. The duo was held at a rebel base where they were assaulted, interrogated, and sustained injuries to the face before being released. One of the hostages was a Moroccan. 02061702

June 17, 2002. *Israel.* Soldiers shot and killed Walid Sbeh, an al-Aqsa Martyrs Brigades activist, in his car as he was leaving al-Khader, a village near Bethlehem. Military sources said he was responsible for sending suicide bombers into Israel and had been fingered by three would-be bombers who had been arrested.

June 17, 2002. *Israel.* A Palestinian suicide bomber killed only himself in an attack near a border patrol north of Tulkarm in the Gaza Strip.

June 18, 2002. *Israel.* Just before 8:00 a.m., a Palestinian Hamas member who wore a red shirt boarded Number 32A Egged commuter bus and set off a bomb, killing himself and 19 other people, primarily commuters and school children, and injuring 55 people at the Patt Junction in Jerusalem. The bomb was packed with nuts, bolts, and nails. The Palestinian Authority condemned the attack. Israel announced that it would seize West Bank Palestinian land every time Palestinians conducted such attacks.

Hamas said the terrorist was Mohammed Ghoul, 22, a stocky student working on his Master's degree in Islamic studies at Al-Najah University in Nablus. He lived in the Fara refugee camp near Nablus. He boarded the bus in the suburb just south of Jerusalem. He did not stop to pay and set off his 22 pounds of explosives hidden in his backpack after taking two steps behind the driver. His suicide note said that he had twice before tried to conduct attacks.

Among the dead was Rahamim Zidkiyahu, 51, who had driven a city bus for 27 years. He was the father of a daughter and three sons; one son was to have his bar mitzvah in two months. Bus drivers said he was the first driver to die in the recent bus bombings. He had volunteered to take an earlier shift when the regular driver decided to watch the World Cup on television.

Among the injured was passenger Michael Lasri, 15.

On June 30, Israeli military forces killed Muhanad Taher (alias the Engineer-4), 26, who was believed to be one of the top bomb makers for Hamas. He was implicated in this bombing, the bombing in the summer of 2001 at a Tel Aviv disco that killed 21 people and wounded 120 others, and the Passover Seder attack on March 27, that killed 29 people and injured 140. The university graduate had become a regional leader of the Izzedine al Qassam Brigade. A second Hamas operative was killed and a third critically wounded when Israeli troops fired on them in a

Nablus house. Israeli authorities said he prepared numerous suicide bombers for their attacks.

June 18, 2002. *United States.* CNN reported that the U.S. Coast Guard was chasing a container ship believed to be carrying al Qaeda terrorists attempting to enter the United States.

June 18, 2002. *Saudi Arabia.* The government announced the arrests during the previous several months of 13 al Qaeda members believed to have attempted unsuccessfully to fire a ground-to-air missile at a U.S. war plane taking off from Prince Sultan Air Base, 60 miles southeast of Riyadh in May. They were also alleged to be planning attacks on "vital sites" in the kingdom. The 13 veterans of Afghan terrorist camp training came from two separate al Qaeda cells that regrouped in Saudi Arabia. One was led by a Sudanese; the other by an Iraqi. Their 11 followers were Saudis, who had smuggled munitions, including two SAM-7 surface-to-air missiles brought in from Yemen by a Sudanese with local assistance, and had hidden supplies in several caches. One empty missile tube was found at the outskirts of the base in May; another was found buried in the desert near Riyadh. Some had entered Saudi Arabia since September 11; others had returned within the previous two years after fighting in Chechnya. They were ordered—by individuals now hiding in Pakistan—to attack any targets in Saudi Arabia, particularly the Defense and Interior Ministries, and Western targets. The 13 decided against attacking fellow Muslims and wanted to concentrate on American soldiers.

On May 18, the Saudis asked Khartoum to apprehend and deport to Saudi Arabia the Sudanese SAM smuggler. He was later arrested in Khartoum and admitted to a role in attempting to fire the missile.

June 18, 2002. *Suriname.* The government extradited Eugenio Vargas Perdomo (alias Carlos Bolas) to the United States. Perdomo was a member of the Revolutionary Armed Forces of Colombia (FARC) who had been arrested for immigration violations for using a fake Peruvian passport. After being turned over to the U.S. Drug Enforcement Administration (DEA), he faced federal drug trafficking charges, including conspiracy to import more than five kilograms of cocaine into the United States. On July 9, defense attorney Joseph Virgilio asked a federal judge to force his trial within three months, instead of permitting the government to have time to build a case of international terrorism against him. The Drug Enforcement Administration (DEA) said FARC had murdered 13 Americans and kidnapped more than 100 since 1980. U.S. District Court Chief Judge Thomas F. Hogan scheduled a July 18 hearing to set a trial date.

June 19, 2002. *Israel.* At 7:10 p.m., an al-Aqsa Martyrs Brigades suicide bomber was let out of a car and ran toward commuters in northeastern Jerusalem. As a border policeman tried to intercept him, he set off an explosive near a bus stop and hitchhiking spot, killing himself and 6 other people, and injuring 43, including two Americans. Among the injured was Efrat Goren, 41, a sixth-grade teacher, who was treated for shock at a local hospital. 02061901

June 20, 2002. *Norway.* Authorities indicted on money laundering, tax, and accounting charges a Somali-born man who ran a banking system that may have helped al Qaeda. A second Somali faced the same charges. Both faced nine years if convicted. One of the duo ran the Norwegian branch of Al Barakaat, the international money transferring company. The duo sent $7.5 million per year out of Norway.

June 20, 2002. *Saudi Arabia.* At 9:00 a.m., Simon Veness, 35, a British executive at the Saudi French Bank, was killed when a bomb destroyed his vehicle outside his home in the Al Nakheel compound in Riyadh. No one else was injured. 02062001

June 20, 2002. *Israel.* At 9:00 p.m., at least two Palestinian gunmen snuck into Itamar, an Israeli settlement, during the night and fired automatic weapons in a street. They then ran into a nearby settler family's house, taking hostages. One of the gunmen died in a clash with civilian settlement guards and Israeli border police who surrounded the house. Another five people, including Boaz Shabo's wife Rachel and their three sons (Neria, 15, Zvi, 12, and Avishai, 5), and a civilian security guard, were killed and another four, including two border policemen, a woman, and a boy, were wounded in the gun battle. Among the wounded were a Shabo daughter and son. Yossi Twito, Shabo's neighbor, was shot as he tried to enter her house and fight the terrorists. Media accounts differed as to whether the second terrorist was killed or escaped through a window. The house caught fire. The Abu Ali Mustafa Brigades of the Popular Front for the Liberation of Palestine (PFLP) claimed credit, saying it was retaliating for Israel's arrest on June 11 of the PFLP's deputy secretary general, Abdul Rahim Mallouh. Israeli forces killed Mustafa, former PFLP chief, in August 2001.

June 20, 2002. *Pakistan.* Armed militants fired on a passenger bus, sending it over a cliff in the Neelum Valley, killing the driver and nine passengers and injuring a dozen others. No one claimed credit.

June 21, 2002. *United States.* A Lebanese-born U.S. citizen told authorities that he overheard a cell phone conversation between people who said that there was to be a terrorist attack on "the American day of freedom" and that they were in the land of corruption, which he took to mean an attack on Las Vegas on July 4.

June 21, 2002. *United States.* A federal jury in Charlotte, North Carolina, found Mohamad Youssef Hammoud, 28, and his brother, Chawki Hammoud, 37, guilty of running a multimillion dollar cigarette smuggling operation to raise funds for Hizballah. Mohamad Hammoud was caught on phone taps chatting with Sheik Abbas Harake, Hizballah's military leader in Lebanon, and Sheik Muhammed Hussein Fadlallah, the group's spiritual leader. Mohamad Hammoud was guilty of violating a ban on material support of groups designated as terrorist organizations by the United States. The two Lebanese natives were convicted of cigarette smuggling, racketeering, and money laundering. Deke Falls, Mohamad's attorney, said he would appeal. The brothers and 16 others were arrested in the summer of 2000 and were accused of smuggling at least $7.9 million of cigarettes from North Carolina into Michigan. At least $3,500 of the profits were sent to senior Hizballah leaders. Mohamad faced up to 155 years in prison, which could be increased if the judge decided he had also committed perjury. Chawki faced 70 years. On February 28, 2003, Mohamad Hammoud was sentenced to 155 years. He planned to appeal.

Seven defendants had pleaded guilty to other smuggling charges. Angie Tsioumas, Hammoud's wife, was among them.

On November 10, federal authorities announced the discovery of a plot to kill the prosecutor—First Assistant U.S. Attorney Kenneth Bell—or blow up the evidence against the brothers. FBI agents believed Mohamad had written a letter to an informant suggesting someone be brought in to the plot. The letter said, "His assignment is to put bullets into the skull of the arrogant ... prosecutor or to annihilate with massive explosives the evidence against us." Prosecutors intended to introduce the evidence of the plot in the sentencing hearing expected in the upcoming months. Mohamad's attorney said the FBI had illegally obtained the evidence and that the informant had fabricated the letter because he was facing deportation.

On February 27, 2003, U.S. District Judge Graham Mullen in Charlotte sentenced cousins Mohamad Atef Darwiche and Ali Hussein Darwiche to more than three years in prison for their roles in smuggling cigarettes and sending the profits to Lebanese Hizballah. He also sentenced Samuel Chahrour to two years in prison. Chahrour was a Dearborn, Michigan, man who bought large quantities of the cigarettes.

June 21, 2002. *Canada.* The Integrated National Security Enforcement Team arrested Algerian citizen Adel Tobbichi, 34, in Montreal following a Dutch extradition request on charges of altering passports and other documents and providing them to terrorists who planned to bomb the U.S. Embassy in Paris. Dutch authorities had earlier arrested two French citizens in the plot. Rotterdam prosecutors said that wiretaps linked Jerome Courtailler and Mohammed Berkous, both 27, to Nizar Trabelsi, the would-be suicide bomber who was under arrest in Belgium.

June 21, 2002. *Spain.* In Fuengirola, a vehicle bomb exploded in a parking lot adjacent to a beach hotel/apartment building, injuring six people, including four Britons, a Moroccan, and a Spaniard. The Basque Nation and Liberty was suspected. 02062101

June 23, 2002. *Italy.* *Corriere della Sera* said that Islamic militants were planning to attack the San Petronio basilica in Bologna because it contains a 15th-century fresco that depicts the prophet Muhammad in Hell, being devoured by demons. In 2001, a group of Italian Muslims asked the Vatican to have Giovanni da Modena's fresco removed or have parts of it covered, claiming that it offended Muslims. The Union of Muslims in Italy denied any link to terrorist plots.

June 23, 2002. *Qatar.* Al Qaeda spokesman Sulaiman Abu Ghaith, a Kuwaiti, said in an audiotape broadcast on al-Jazeera television that bin Laden was alive and would soon appear in a television broadcast and that the group was ready to conduct more attacks against the United States. He said the April bombing of a Tunisian synagogue was an al Qaeda operation by an individual who was angry that Jews were practicing their religion in his country while Palestinians were besieged in Israel. "Our martyrs are ready for operations against American and Jewish targets inside and outside. America should be prepared. It should be ready. They should fasten the seat belts. We are coming to them where they never expected. The current American administration every once in a while releases terrorist attack warnings. I say yes, yes, yes, we are going to launch attacks against America." He added, "I really want to assure the Muslims that Sheik Osama bin Laden, with the mercy of Allah, is in good and prosperous health and all that is rumored about Sheik Osama's sickness and injuries in Tora Bora is completely inaccurate news." As for whether the coalition's attacks on al Qaeda in Afghanistan had harmed the group, "The system is still there. And it is operating at full power. Al Qaeda is not a fragile organization as some might think. [The next attacks will happen] in the time we choose and the place we choose and the method we choose. Not Dick Cheney, not the American secretary of defense, not the America president can determine the place, the method, and the means that we will use." Kuwait had revoked his citizenship when he turned up as a bin Laden spokesman after the September 11 attacks.

Government analysts announced three days later that it was "highly probable" that the tape was genuine.

June 24, 2002. *India.* In Kupwara, Kashmir, a bomb exploded at the state law and parliamentary minister's residence, injuring five police guards. No one claimed credit.

June 27, 2002. *United States.* The Bush administration listed as specially designated global terrorist entities two Sikh separatist groups: Babbar Khalsa and the International Sikh Youth Federation.

June 27, 2002. *Saudi Arabia.* A bomb was found under the bottom of a car belonging to an American hospital worker of the King Faisal Specialist Hospital in Riyadh. It was removed safely. 02062701.

June 27, 2002. *Paraguay.* SEPRINTE, the counterterrorism secretariat, arrested suspected Sunni extremist Ali Nizar Dahroug, nephew of former Triborder shopkeeper and suspected al Qaeda associated Muhammad Dahroug Dahroug. Police seized counterfeit goods and wire transfers of large sums of money to people in the United States and the Middle East, some payable to Muhammad Dahroug Dahroug in Lebanon.

June 28, 2002. *Algeria.* Islamic rebels killed 13 bus passengers and wounded 9 on the outskirts of Algiers's Les Eucalyptus district. The attackers shot and killed the driver and then fired automatic weapons at the passengers for ten minutes, said Said Bahlouli, one of the passengers.

June 29, 2002. *Greece.* Savas Xiros (or Xyros), 40 (or 44), a church icon painter and the son of a Greek Orthodox priest, lost a hand when a bomb he was carrying exploded as he walked past a busy dock in Piraeus. He was arrested by police, who suspected he was a member of 17 November. He was charged with possession of explosives. He was being guarded at an Athens hospital. His fingerprints matched those found in a car used by the group in the 1997 murder of Greek shipowner Costis Peratikos. The pistol found on the street beside Xiros had been used to shoot at a police officer during a 1984 robbery. ID documents and keys on Xiros led police to two apartment hideouts. In one of the apartments, police found a .45 caliber pistol used in 6 of 23 killings by 17 November. Two of his brothers were arrested. Christodoulos Xiros confessed to taking part in the murders of publisher Nikos Momferratos in 1985; a police officer in 1985; industrialist Dimitris Angelopoulos in 1986; U.S. Navy Attaché William Nordeen in 1988; and the fatal car bombing of U.S. Air Force Sgt. Ronald O. Stewart in 1991. Vassilis Xiros confessed to the Peratikos killing and the assassination of British military attaché Stephen Saunders in 2000. Dionissis Georgiadis, who was also arrested, confessed to robberies and bombings in which no one was injured. Police found bombs, mortars, antitank rockets, and police uniforms among the Xiros family possessions.

On August 11, Savas Xiros told investigators that he fired the four killing shots at British military attaché Saunders after his accomplice's gun jammed. He offered ten hours of testimony from his hospital bed, confessing to involvement in nine killing and dozens of bomb and rocket attacks. He apologized to the families of the victims, including a Turkish diplomat and U.S. Captain Nordeen. Xiros was charged with killing Saunders and other offenses.

June 30, 2002. *Saudi Arabia.* A suspicious object was stuck to the underside of a British citizen's vehicle in the same neighborhood in Riyadh in which British banker Simon Veness was killed on June 20. The device was safely removed. 02063001

June 30, 2002. *Israel.* A 12-pound bomb exploded on a train track in Lod, wounding four people during the morning rush hour.

June 30, 2002. *India.* In Nishat, Kashmir, armed militants killed a National Conference leader. No one claimed credit.

July 2002. *Jordan.* Four Syrians were sentenced to prison for illegal possession of explosives they intended to carry to the West Bank.

July 1, 2002. *Indonesia.* A bomb exploded at a Jakarta supermarket near a large army housing complex, killing one and injuring six.

July 3, 2002. *Greece.* Dozens of police raided 17 November's main hideout and seized antitank rockets, missiles, declarations, stamps, wigs, disguises, and the group's flag. They detained one suspected member of the group. The apartment was rented eight years earlier under a false name by a suspected member of the group; he was injured in a botched bomb attack at Piraeus on June 29. On July 6, Greece police, aided by U.S. and U.K. agents, raided an Athens apartment and seized dozens of antitank rockets believed stolen from the army in the late 1980s by 17 November.

July 3, 2002. *Yemen.* Walid, suspected of al Qaeda membership, escaped from prison. He had been arrested earlier in the year in the desert near the Oman-Yemen border and handed over to Yemeni authorities on charges of trying to enter the country illegally. He was in his thirties and had fled Afghanistan after fighting U.S. forces in the Tora Bora region in December. He had been transferred in June from a prison in San'a to Aden, where several other al Qaeda suspects were being held.

July 3, 2002. *Germany.* In an early morning raid, Hamburg police arrested seven Islamic radicals, including Abdelghani Mzoudi, 29, a United Arab Emirates citizen, who had roomed with September 11 hijacking leader Mohamed Atta in a Marien Street apartment in August 1999. Mzoudi had witnessed Atta's last will and testament. One of the suspects who had worked as an archivist for the state police in Hamburg fell under suspicion for credit card fraud. Surveillance of him led to the others. The seven were questioned, photographed, and fingerprinted. By the end of the evening, five were back on the streets for lack of evidence. The suspects included Moroccans, Egyptians, Afghans, and a German citizen. All of the men were between ages 28 and 51. They met regularly at the Attawhid bookshop near the al Quds mosque in Hamburg that had been frequented by Atta. They had been overheard saying that they wanted to "give their lives for Islam." They also used "secret knocks" to enter meetings at the bookstore.

Mzoudi had replaced fugitive Said Bahaji, who left Hamburg shortly before September 11, as Atta's roommate.

Another suspect linked to the group was questioned in Italy following a tip from the German police.

July 3, 2002. *Pakistan.* Three Pakistanis died in a shoot-out at a remote checkpoint on the Afghan border with Chechen al Qaeda members, four of whom died. The al Qaeda members threw grenades at security personnel when ordered to stop their vehicle at the Jarma bridge, six miles from Kohat in northwestern Pakistan. A police officer and a soldier died in the ensuing gun battle. Another Pakistani died when a grenade exploded as he was searching the car following the shoot-out. A witness told Reuters that "the vehicle was full of explosives, sophisticated weapons, and grenades." The vehicle was coming from the direction of Miranshah in North Waziristan.

The previous week, ten soldiers died in a raid on a house in Wana, 120 miles southwest of Kohat, where al Qaeda members were hiding.

July 4, 2002. *United States.* Egyptian-born limousine driver Heshem Mohamed Hadayet, 41, shot to death Victoria Hen, 25, who provided ground services to El Al (some reports said she worked at the ticket counter) and jewelry shop owner Yaakov Aminov, 46, and wounded four other people at the El Al ticket counter at Los Angeles International Airport (LAX). He fired 10 or 11 bullets. He stabbed an El Al security guard, who in turn shot the killer to death. The FBI was not sure whether it was a terrorist case or a lone nut, but Israeli authorities said it was a terrorist attack.

Police reported that his wife, Hala, and two sons (some reports said a daughter) had returned to Cairo the previous week and that there had been three reports of domestic disturbances at his residence in Irvine, California, about 45 miles from the airport. He had no criminal history or known ties to terrorists, but he apparently planned the attack in advance. He carried no identification and was armed with two Glock pistols and a six-inch hunting knife. Abdul Zahev, a former employee, said Hadayet often expressed hatred for Israel and said the United States was biased against Arabs. He had taken exception to his upstairs neighbors hanging American and Marine Corps flags from their balcony, which was above his door, after the September 11 attacks. He said it was a challenge to him as a Muslim immigrant. He entered the United States via LAX as a visitor in December 1992 and was granted a green card in March 1993. (Other reports said that he left an upper-class family in Egypt and moved to the United States on a six-month tourist visa, which he overstayed.) One of his California driver's licenses listed his birthday as July 4, 1961. He worked as a bank accountant in Egypt before immigrating to the United States. The government had initiated deportation proceedings against him in 1996, but he gained U.S. residency in August 1997 after his wife obtained that status in a lottery. His uncle said that he had only about a year to go before qualifying for U.S. citizenship. He had purchased the limo before he knew how to drive it. He had trouble keeping up with liability insurance costs, and his wife began babysitting for neighbors.

The Tom Bradley International Terminal was shut down for four hours and 6,000 were forced to evacuate the terminal. Two dozen outbound international flights were delayed.

Aminov's brother-in-law, Mark Ezerzer, said that Aminov has eight children and a pregnant wife. Aminov had taken a friend, Michael Shabtay, to the airport. He collapsed in Shabtay's arms.

The injured included a 61-year-old woman who was hit in the ankle, a 40-year-old man who was knifed, and a 20-something man who was pistol-whipped. Two other people were treated for heart problems.

The Transportation Security Administration said it did not have direct responsibility for security at ticket counter areas.

In a March 30, 1993, interview for asylum, Hadayet had told the Immigration and Naturalization Service (INS) that Egyptian authorities had arrested him for involvement with Al-Gama'at al-Islamiyya. INS denied his asylum request, but he did not show up for a 1995 removal hearing. His wife said he was falsely accused. Al-Gama'at al-Islamiyya is now on the State Department's list of terrorist organizations, which was created in 1997.

On May 12, 2003, the Department of Justice said that the attack was an act of terrorism, although Hadayet acted alone and did not have any terrorist organization affiliation. FBI spokesman Matthew McLaughlin said, "The investigation developed information that he openly supported the killings of civilians in order to advance the Palestinian cause." 02070401

July 4, 2002. *Israel.* A bomb went off during the night in Gaza City, killing Jihad Amerin, 38, the Gaza leader of the al-Aqsa Martyrs Brigades, and Nael Namera, 27, a lieutenant in the Palestinian security forces, and destroying a white Mercedes. Israeli agents were blamed.

July 5, 2002. *Nepal.* Maoist terrorists conducted a fatal bombing against the Kathmandu office of the Prime Minister.

July 5, 2002. *Algeria.* At 9:15 a.m., a bomb hidden in a sewer exploded in an open-air market in Larba, 15 miles southwest of Algiers, killing at least 35 people, including 2 Nigerians, and injuring 80 on Algeria's independence day. The area is infested with Armed Islamic Group terrorists.

During a ceremony honoring independence war veterans, a second bomb exploded at a cemetery near Jijel, 150 miles east of Algiers, injuring one person.

A third bomb exploded at Azur Plage, a Mediterranean beach 20 miles west of Algiers, slightly injuring a five-year-old boy. 02070501

July 5, 2002. *United States.* The Transportation Security Administration warned owners of smaller airports and aircraft that terrorists might be considering using private planes for attacks, noting "terrorists who are no longer able to hijack commercial airliners because of increased security at commercial airports may turn to 'general aviation' airports and aircraft to conduct operations."

July 8, 2002. *United States.* Federal jury selection began in the trial of white supremacists Leo Felton, 31, and Erica Chase, 22, who planned to bomb Jewish and Black landmarks in Boston, such as the U.S. Holocaust Memorial Museum

in Washington or a Holocaust memorial in Boston, to set off a "racial holy war." They were charged with conspiracy, making counterfeit bills, obstruction, and firearms and explosives violations. Chase faced 35 years in prison; Felton faced life. Felton had mused about killing movie director Steven Spielberg, Jesse Jackson, and others. On July 26, after deliberating for seven hours over two days, the jury found the duo guilty of plotting to blow up the landmarks.

July 8, 2002. *United States.* The FBI and Immigration and Naturalization Service (INS) announced that in June, they had raided 75 jewelry stores and kiosks, most of them called Intrigue Jewelers, in shopping malls in eight states as part of an investigation into al Qaeda money laundering. A dozen men, mostly Pakistanis, were taken into custody on immigration charges. Authorities also seized documents, computer records, and other evidence against the Orlando, Florida-based company Gold Concept, Inc., owned by naturalized U.S. citizen Arif Rajan of Ocoee, Florida. He was represented by attorney Philip K. Calandrino.

The press had reported that in the weeks after September 11, authorities had raided an Intrigue Jewelers in Allentown, Pennsylvania. The operators had come under suspicion after developing World Trade Center photographs; one fled the United States, another was charged with immigration violations.

July 8, 2002. *India.* In Indh, Kashmir, armed militants attacked a village, killing 27 people. The Lashar-e-Tayyiba was suspected.

July 9, 2002. *Israel.* A Palestinian gunman killed a passerby and injured a police officer at Jerusalem's Old City.

July 9, 2002. *Algeria.* The Algerian daily *El Youm* ran an interview with Sulaiman Abu Ghaith, al Qaeda's spokesman, who said that "al Qaeda still maintains its military, security, economic, and informational structures," and "functions according to a rigorous, secret logic…. Al Qaeda will organize more attacks against American and Jewish targets, inside and outside American territory, at the moment we choose, at the place we choose, and with the methods we want." He said the U.S. campaign against his group was a "Hollywood script."

July 11, 2002. *United States.* FBI officials said that a week earlier, they had received information that oil refineries in Pasadena, California, could be targeted. Pasadena has no refineries. They also shared the information to authorities in Texas, where oil refineries were placed at a high level of alert.

July 11, 2002. *Italy.* Police seized false documents from suspected al Qaeda terrorist sympathizers in Milan and other northern cities and arrested nine Arab suspects. Two Moroccan men, Muhammad and Said Kazdari, had been arrested, sentenced, and jailed for several months earlier in the year but were paroled. They had also made false papers for stolen cars. Police were investigating whether this was a counterfeiting operation that assisted al Qaeda worldwide. Police said some of the detainees had contacts with Abdelkader es-Sayed (alias Abu Saleh), an Egyptian al Qaeda operative who fled Italy in July 2001 and apparently was killed in the allied bombing campaign in Afghanistan. He reportedly had organized the 1997 massacre of 58 tourists in Luxor, Egypt; nonetheless, Italy gave him political asylum. A January 2001 wiretap revealed him talking to a Tunisian about false documents easing entry to the United States, saying at one point, "If you have to speak to me about these things, you should come to me and speak in my ear. This subject is secret, secret, secret." Abu Saleh was also linked to Essid Sami Ben Khemais, a major Algerian al Qaeda organizer in Europe who was sentenced to five years in prison in February for arms trafficking, manufacturing false papers, and arranging illegal immigration.

July 13, 2002. *India.* Local authorities suspected Pakistani involvement when four or five gunmen in Hindu holy garb threw grenades and fired in a crowded Jammu City slum in Indian Kashmir, killing 28 and injuring more than 30 people, including several children. The terrorists escaped into neighboring hills. Lashkar-i-Taiba was suspected.

July 13, 2002. *Pakistan.* Grenades were thrown at a group of European tourists at an archaeological site in Mansehra in the north. Injuring 12 people, including 7 Germans, an Austrian, a Slovak, and 3 Pakistanis. No one claimed credit. 02071301

July 14, 2002. *France.* Maxime Brunerie, 25, a neo-Nazi with a history of mental problems, fired a .22 caliber rifle at President Jacques Chirac, 69, near the Arc de Triomphe during the annual Bastille Day parade. Brunerie pulled the rifle from a guitar case and fired as President Chirac passed in an open-top jeep about 50 yards away at the beginning of the parade on the Champs-Elysees. No one was injured. Brunerie had acquired the gun only eight days earlier. He rented a car three days after obtaining the gun and traveled to Burgundy to take target practice. He was held in a psychiatric hospital. Police said Brunerie was a member of "neo-Nazi and hooligan" groups. They seized his computer. The President telephoned four bystanders to thank them for helping to save him. Among them was Algerian born Canadian tourist Mohamed Chelali, who grabbed the rifle. Brunerie tried to shoot himself after the failed attempt.

July 16, 2002. *Israel.* At 3:00 p.m., Palestinian gunmen disguised as soldiers electronically detonated a bomb on a light pole near the bulletproof Number 189 Israeli Dan bus as it was 400 yards from the gates of the Emmanuel settlement on the West Bank. The gunmen then opened fire with M-16s and threw hand grenades through the small, broken ventilation windows, killing 7 and wounding 16. (The death toll reached ten on July 19 when a woman died of her wounds.) The passengers could not escape because the driver was shot and the door was jammed shut.

The bus was carrying 30 passengers between Bnei Brak on the eastern edge of Tel Aviv to the settlement. Believing the trio to be soldiers, the gate security guard rushed to the site and asked the gunmen if they needed help. They did not. The gunmen fired at him, forcing him to drive away. The terrorists also fired on a truck behind the bus. Among the dead was an 8-month-old girl, her father, and her grandmother. A pregnant woman lost her baby. A 15-year-old boy had chest wounds. An 8-month-pregnant woman was also hospitalized. The six injured victims at Tel Aviv's Tel Hashomer Hospital were children aged between 6 and 12. Siton Tehilla, 12, was hospitalized in severe condition. She had been injured in a similar attack on December 12 only yards away that led to the deaths of 11 people and injuries to 30 others. In that incident, Avi Yokobov, 40, a plumber, was so gravely injured in the attack on his car that he was hauled away in a body bag before medics realized he was alive.

Three groups claimed credit: the Izzedine al-Qassam Brigades, which is the military wing of the Islamic Resistance Movement (Hamas); the al-Aqsa Martyrs Brigades; and the Syrian-based Democratic Front for the Liberation of Palestine. The Palestinian Authority condemned the attack.

The attackers escaped.

The next day, a one-month premature infant died after an emergency Caesarean section on her injured mother. Later that day, Israeli Lt. Elad Grenadier, 21, died, as did a Palestinian identified as one of the three gunmen. The attackers were found in a rugged valley near Emmanuel. Three other soldiers were wounded in the 150 minute shoot-out. The surviving duo escaped.

Israel announced on July 31 that it would deport to the Gaza Strip a relative of a Palestinian who ambushed the bus.

Authorities announced on August 2 that some of the attackers came from Nablus.

July 16, 2002. *United Kingdom.* The Irish Republican Army (IRA) publicly expressed on a Web site and in an IRA-affiliated newspaper "sincere apologies and condolences" for all of the people it killed during the three decades of *Troubles.* The statement, signed by the mythical "P. O'Neill" said, "There have been fatalities amongst combatants on all sides. We also acknowledge the grief and pain of their relatives. The process of conflict resolution requires the equal acknowledgment of the grief and loss of others. We are endeavoring to fulfill this responsibility to those we have hurt.... The future will not be found in denying collective failures and mistakes, or closing minds and hearts to the plight of those who have been hurt. That includes all the victims of the conflict, combatants and noncombatants. It will not be achieved by creating a hierarchy of victims in which some are deemed more or less worthy." The group said that the peace process required "acceptance of past mistakes and of the hurt and pain we have caused to others." The IRA noted the upcoming 30th anniversary of the July 21, 1972, "Bloody Friday" bombing that killed nine people in Belfast, and said it was appropriate to issue apologies.

July 16, 2002. *United States.* California State Police doubled patrols near San Francisco's Golden Gate Bridge after Spanish authorities seized videotapes of the bridge and other California sites from al Qaeda terrorists.

July 17, 2002. *Greece.* An antiterrorism squad helicoptered to the island of Lipsoi, 160 miles from Athens, and arrested Paris-born Alexandros Giotopoulos (alias Michael Oikonomous), 58 (or 60), at his pink holiday home. Police believed he was the ideological leader and possibly a founder of 17 November. He was questioned in Athens about items seized from his Athens residence, including a typewriter that might have been used for 17 November propaganda statements. Police had set a fire as a ruse, permitting the helicopter team to swoop in.

On July 19, police charged Giotopoulos with the premeditated murder of 13 people, including

2 U.S. military officials and a U.K. military attaché, back to 1984. Also charged with murder was Vassilis Tzortzatos, 48, an electrician accused of killing eight Greeks, including businessmen, politicians, and police officers.

July 17, 2002. *Spain.* Police arrested Kamal Hadid Chaar, a Syrian-born Spanish citizen and al Qaeda suspect, at his Madrid home. Police confiscated numerous documents. Police said he belonged to the al Qaeda cell led by Imad Eddin Bakarat Yarkas, who had been arrested in November on charges of recruiting and fund-raising for the group. Police believed the group played a key role in the preparation of the September 11 attacks in the United States.

The State Department reported in 2003 that Spain had arrested three Syrians in July because of their suspected al Qaeda links. One of the detainees made suspicious videotape recordings while on a trip to the United States in 1997. The videos included the World Trade Center. The trio were released on bail because of weak evidence in the case.

July 17, 2002. *India.* A bomb exploded in a government building in Anantnag, Kashmir, killing three and injuring nine. No one claimed credit.

July 17, 2002. *Israel.* On the Jewish holiday of Tisha B'Av, which marks the destruction of ancient Jewish temples, two Palestinian suicide bombers set off explosives outside the 24-hour Sunflower Seed Center convenience store on a busy walkway in a working-class Tel Aviv immigrant neighborhood. The bombers killed 5 people, including a Romanian and 2 Chinese, and injured 40, including a Romanian. One terrorist wore a red shirt; the other, blue. Their bodies were found 30 yards apart. At 10:20 p.m., the first killer set off his bomb near tables where customers, mostly Romanians and Russians, were eating and drinking. The panicked victims then ran toward the accomplice, who set off his bomb. Among the injured was Benita Ustaris, 24, a housekeeper and Bolivian immigrant who had been in the country for four years. She and her daughter were hit by flying glass. Police found an Arabic note on the body of one of the terrorists, whose actions were claimed by Islamic Jihad. The Palestinian Authority condemned the attack.

The bombs went off 200 yards from where another suicide bomber injured 23 people on January 25.

On July 19, Israeli troops set off explosives and bulldozed the homes of two men linked to the two recent incidents and arrested 21 members of the duo's families. They were not able to find Ali Ajouri, 23, an al-Aqsa leader who had dispatched the two suicide bombers, nor could they locate Nasser Assid, 26, in the village of Tel south of Nablus. He was accused of organizing the bus ambush. Israeli authorities ordered Ajouri's brother Kifah and sister Intizar, 26, banished to the Gaza Strip because they provided him refuge and food. (There was some question in press reporting as to whether Kifah was banished. His wife is pregnant with the couple's third child. He had been ordered banished, but appealed.) On August 6, after a three-hour gunfight involving tanks and AH-64 Apache helicopter gunships, Israeli forces shot Ali Ajouri dead. Later that day, the Israeli Supreme Court upheld the military's right to demolish homes of Palestinians accused of terrorist attacks without giving family members warning, throwing out the appeals of 44 Palestinian families. On September 3, the Israeli High Court of Justice ruled that in "extreme cases" the government can banish to the Gaza Strip relatives of West Bank Palestinians involved in attacks. It refused to give the government blanket approval, but upheld a military court's decision to banish Intizar and Kifah Ajouri. Israel said Ali had dispatched two suicide bombers to a pedestrian mall in Tel Aviv. It held that Intizar sewed explosives belts and Kifah hid Ali from the authorities and served as a lookout while Ali moved explosives. The government banished the duo to the Gaza Strip the next day.

July 17, 2002. *Italy.* Anti-Semitic vandals destroyed marble columns and statues, overturned flower vases, and dug down to the coffins of 40 graves in the Verano cemetery east of central Rome. Some metal Stars of David were pried from tombs and then used to deface the marble. No one claimed credit.

July 17, 2002. *United States.* U.S. Customs agents arrested Omar Shishani, 47, a Jordan-born man carrying $12 million in false cashiers checks as he arrived at Detroit Metropolitan Airport from Indonesia. He appeared on a watch list of people trained in Afghanistan by al Qaeda; his name had turned up in captured documents in Afghanistan. Shishani was carrying a U.S. passport and claimed to be a naturalized citizen. Investigators searching his bags found nine cashier's checks—two for $5 million each, two for $500,000 each, and five for $200,000 each. Six checks were posted for June; one for September 2002. The faked checks were supposedly issued by the Pomona, California, branch of West America bank (which does not have a Pomona branch). The checks had the words "cashier's check" on them; the bank uses the term "official check." On July 23, a federal grand jury indicted Shishani on charges of possession of counterfeit security and smuggling merchandise into the United States. On July 24, U.S. District Court Magistrate Judge Donald A. Scheer ordered Shishani held without bond after prosecutors said he had acknowledged that Baharuddin Masse, who was listed on six of the checks, could be part of al Qaeda and that he had made "pro al Qaeda statements" and had named his daughter "al Qaeda." Shishani was carrying a photocopy of Masse's passport. Judge Scheer called Shishani a flight risk who faced 15 years in prison. The maximum penalty for the counterfeiting charge is ten years and a $250,000 fine, and, on the other charge, five years and a $250,000 fine.

Shishani had previously lived in San Francisco and Napa, California. He claimed to be a salesman who had earned no commissions this year. He said his wife was a resident alien from Japan who works for Northwest Airlines. His family is from Chechnya. One source said he had served with the Jordanian army. He had claimed to come from a powerful Jordanian family with close relations to the king and the military. He claimed to have served in the Jordanian intelligence service from 1974 to 1976, and that his brother was commander of the Jordanian Special Forces. He had lived in the United States since 1979 and had become a U.S. citizen in 1989, according to his lawyer. His attorney said he was merely a broker, carrying the checks for a client. Shishani had filed for Chapter 7 bankruptcy while living in San Francisco in 1991. He incorporated Shojoma Trading and Consulting Company, Inc., in Michigan in 1993, and dissolved it in 1996. He had no apparent source of income; his Northwest Airlines flight attendant wife was temporarily unemployed.

Members of the U.S. Joint Terrorism Task Force in Detroit searched Shishani's Dearborn, Michigan, apartment the next day. Authorities found several financial documents, including a December 2000 net worth statement indicating $38.5 million in assets. His lawyer said he didn't even own his home, and authorities said the document could be a fake to be used in a scam.

A U.S. Secret Service agent was later suspended for writing an anti-Islam epithet ("Islam is Evil, Christ is King") on a Muslim prayer calendar in the Shishani home.

Shishani was represented by court-appointed federal defender Andrew Wise and by Nabih Ayad.

July 18, 2002. *Pakistan.* Pakistani police arrested seven Somalis and Sudanese individuals suspected of al Qaeda membership in several predawn raids at the University Town area of Peshawar. The targets were two senior al Qaeda figures, who remained at large.

July 21, 2002. *Greece.* Authorities charged Iraklis Kostaris, 36, a real estate agent, with participating in four 17 November murders, including that of U.S. Air Force Sgt. Ronald O. Stewart in March 1991 and U.K. Defense Attaché Brigadier Stephen Saunders in June 2000. The defendant's close friend, Costas Karatsolis, was charged with carrying out three armed robberies and participating in the theft of dozens of antitank rockets from an army base in central Greece in 1989. The duo was arrested in the north over the weekend.

Police arrested a tenth 17 November suspect later that day, identifying him as Thomas Serifis, 36, who worked for the Athens public bus company.

The arrests derailed a plot to attack a convoy of NATO peacekeepers driving from Thessaloniki to Macedonia and Kosovo.

July 22, 2002. *United States.* Attorney General John D. Ashcroft asked the U.S. Department of State to add nine groups and companies to the list of terrorist organizations, thereby prohibiting any noncitizen members from entering the United States. The 39-item list would be expanded to include:

- Afghan Support Committee
- Al Taqwa Trade, Property, and Industry Co., Ltd. (also known as Himmat Establishment)
- Bank Al Taqwa, Ltd.
- Loyalist Volunteer Force
- Nada Management Organization
- Revival of Islamic Heritage Society
- Ulster Defence Association/Ulster Freedom Fighters
- Ummah Tameer E-nau
- Youssef M. Nada and Co. Gesellschaft

A separate list is kept of terrorist groups/supporters whose assets are to be frozen.

July 22, 2002. *United States.* Authorities in Denver arrested James Ujaama, 36, of Seattle, as a material witness to terrorist activities. Authorities believe the American Muslim activist trained at an al Qaeda terrorist camp in Afghanistan. He was flown to Virginia. The terrorist activity was not related to September 11. A federal official said he may have supplied terrorists in Afghanistan with computer equipment.

July 22, 2002. *India.* In Sumber, Kashmir, armed militants killed three members of the Village Defense Committee. No one claimed credit.

July 23, 2002. *Russia.* Gunmen firing Kalashnikovs kidnapped Nina Davidovich, head of the Druzhba ("friendship" in Russian) nongovernmental aid group, from her car on the road between Crozny and Nazran, the region base for many Ingushetia humanitarian groups. Her three traveling companions were not taken. The United Nations suspended humanitarian assistance in Chechnya on July 29. UN officials said the suspension would last for two days in Ingushetia, but indefinitely in Chechnya.

July 24, 2002. *Colombia.* The secret police said it had derailed a plot by the Revolutionary Armed Forces of Colombia (FARC) to crash a plane into the Congress building or the presidential palace. The plot was ended on July 18, when police in Bogota arrested mastermind Jorge Enrique Carvajalino, who had recruited a pilot to fly a plane into the Congress building during Independence Day ceremonies on July 20 or into the presidential palace on August 7, during the inauguration of the next president. Carvajalino is the brother of a top FARC leader also known as Andres Paris. Col. Gustavo Jaramillo, secret police director, said the suicide police had worked with drug traffickers and agreed to fly the plane for $2 million.

July 24, 2002. *Greece.* Police arrested Pavlos Serifis, 46, who is related to two other suspected 17 November detainees. They believed he was the second-in-command of the group and had used the alias Nikitas. He may have carried instructions from the group's leader, Alexandros Giotopoulos, to the group's hit squad. Serifis, a telephone operator at an Athens children's hospital, was arrested in Karditsa.

July 24, 2002. *India.* In Rajouri, Kashmir, a grenade exploded in a crowded marketplace, killing 1 and injuring 27. No one claimed credit.

July 25, 2002. *United States.* Shueyb Mossa Jokhan, 24, of Hollywood, Florida, pleaded guilty to a federal indictment that carried a sentence of 5 to 20 years. He had hoped to destroy power stations, a National Guard armory, Jewish businesses, and Mount Rushmore. He told Judge William Dimitrouleas in Fort Lauderdale that he and a Pakistani immigrant, Imran Mandhai, 19, of Hollywood, scouted targets in Broward and Miami-Dade counties in pursuit of their jihad. Jokhan agreed to turn state's evidence in the August 12 trial of Mandhai. On August 8, Mandhai pleaded guilty to conspiring to bomb power stations, a National Guard armory, and Jewish-owned businesses. He faced a sentence of 5 to 20 years and a $250,000 fine. Shueyb received four years and ten months on October 4. Mandhai was scheduled for sentencing on October 17.

July 25, 2002. *Israel.* Gunmen shot to death Rabbi Elimelech Shapira, 40, principal of a religious military prep school in a Jewish settlement in the West Bank and wounded his companion in their car, then fired on an ambulance and rescue team trying to aid the victims. The attack occurred near the Alei Zahav settlement inside the north-central area of the West Bank. The al-Aqsa Martyrs Brigades claimed credit, as did the Popular Army Front Return Battalion, who said it was to avenge the death of 15 people killed in an Israeli F-16 airstrike on July 22 that killed Salah Shehada, a leader of the Izzedine al-Qassam Brigades of Hamas. The air strike also killed nine children, including Shehada's wife and 14-year-old daughter, two other women, and two other men. Another 150 people were wounded.

July 25, 2002. *Worldwide.* After several phone calls during the week threatened the destruction of all U.S. embassies in Islamic countries, the State Department issued an alert to all overseas diplomatic posts. A self-described spokesman/interpreter for Osama bin Laden phoned AP, CNN, and other news organizations during a several hour period, then called AP the next day. He told AP that he was with bin Laden on the Afghan-Pakistan border, and observed, "Muslims don't lie."

July 25, 2002. *India.* In Batmaloo, Kashmir, militants threw a grenade into a crowded marketplace, injuring 15. No one claimed credit.

July 25, 2002. *Paraguay.* SEPRINTE, the counterterrorism secretariat, raided the Ciudad del Este office and apartment of alleged money launderer Fajkumar Naraindas Sabnani, who is allegedly connected to Hizballah. Police found letters detailing the sale of military assault rifles and other military weapons, receipts for large wire transfers, and what appeared to be bomb-making materials. Although police arrested three of his employees, he remained in Hong Kong.

July 26, 2002. *Greece.* Police in Athens arrested Nikos Papanastasio, 50, who ran a souvenir shop. They believed that he and Alexandros Giotopouloso, 58, already in custody, were the ideological founders of 17 November.

July 26, 2002. *Israel.* Palestinians fired an antitank grenade at an armored bus carrying five Israelis to the Netzarim settlement in the Gaza Strip, damaging the bus but causing no injuries.

July 26, 2002. *Israel.* At 6:30 p.m., Palestinian gunmen ambushed a car near the Zif Junction southeast of Hebron in the West Bank, killing an Israeli couple—Ya-acov and Hannah Dickstein—and their nine-year-old son. The Dicksteins were the parents of ten children. A few minutes later, the gunmen fired on a second car; the driver drove a short distance before dying. A passenger was wounded. The al-Aqsa Martyrs Brigades phoned Abu Dhabi Television to claim credit. Israeli soldiers searched for suspects in the nearby Yatta village.

During the July 28 funeral of Elazar Leibovitz, 21, one of those killed, Jewish settlers opened fire in Hebron, killing Niveen Jamjoum, 14, a Palestinian girl who was the youngest of nine children in her family, and wounding 15 Palestinians, including Niveen's brother. Some 15 police officers suffered minor injuries in the rioting.

July 27, 2002. *Austria.* Someone threw a hand grenade onto the dance floor of the X-Large disco in Linz, 100 miles west of Vienna, wounding 27 people. The disco was popular with Balkan immigrants. The device was packed with hundreds of metal ball bearings. Among the wounded was Robert Akalovic, a young man who had arm and thigh injuries.

July 29, 2002. *Italy.* A rudimentary bomb was discovered outside Fiat's Milan headquarters. Another was discovered outside a labor union building near Milan.

July 29, 2002. *India.* Soldiers killed four rebels attempting to cross the Line of Control into Indian Kashmir from Pakistani Kashmir.

The fifth separatist grenade attack since July 24 injured 13 people.

July 29, 2002. *Afghanistan.* Two would-be car bombers were arrested by police when their explosives-laden yellow Toyota Corolla station wagon was in a traffic accident in Kabul. Police determined that the would-be assassins, one of whom was injured, intended to set off the bomb by ramming it into a convoy of the country's national leaders; others had believed they were on the way to the nearby U.S. Embassy or to kill international peacekeepers. An Afghan and a "foreigner" of undetermined nationality who speaks English, Dari, Pashto, and Uzbek were taken to an Afghan intelligence service's offices for questioning. A senior security official described the foreigner as Arab or Chechen. A second passenger escaped.

Deputy Interior Minister General Din Mohammed Jurat said that the car "was filled with C-4 and dynamite and packed with small pieces of iron. If you explode this car in a crowded place, it would kill 600 or 700 people." Jurat said that the government had received a tip

of a planned attack a week earlier and that the car was stopped at a roadblock at one of the four major entrances to Kabul. An Afghan intelligence official said that the driver had taken delivery of the Toyota near the Pakistani border and "admitted he worked for al Qaeda."

July 30, 2002. *Israel.* At 10:30 a.m., masked gunmen shot to death two Israeli brothers, Sholomo Odesar, 60, and Mordachi Odesar, 52, who had come to the Palestinian West Bank town of Jamain from their settlement of Kfar Tapuah to sell diesel fuel. The terrorists escaped with the bodies, which they dumped into a nearby quarry. Police found two damaged cars without license plates that might have been used by the terrorists. The al-Aqsa Martyrs Brigades claimed credit. At least one attacker was arrested.

July 30, 2002. *United Kingdom.* A London tribunal ruled in favor of nine Muslim detainees who had challenged the country's new antiterrorist law, finding that it discriminated against foreigners. The group was held pending further appeal.

July 30, 2002. *Israel.* At 1:00 p.m., Majed Atta, 17, a Palestinian suicide bomber with a black bag, black shirt, and black greased-back hair killed himself and wounded five Israelis in a Jerusalem sandwich shop popular with police officers. He had been hailed by a police officer, but ran into the Yemenite Felafel Stand, a Jerusalem landmark. The bomb had been packed with nails and other sharp objects. Atta had lived in Beit Jala, south of Bethlehem, and was a member of the al-Aqsa Martyrs Brigades.

July 30, 2002. *Israel.* A knife-wielding Palestinian snuck into a home in the Jewish settlement of Itamar and injured a sleeping couple in their bedroom in the early morning. The terrorist was killed by soldiers.

July 31, 2002. *Israel.* In retaliation for Israel's killing of terrorist leader Salah Shehada on July 22, Hamas set off a 22-pound bomb hidden in a bag on a tabletop at Hebrew University's Frank Sinatra International Student Center in the Nancy Reagan Square on Mount Scopus outside Jerusalem. Nine people died, including 5 Americans, and 87 were wounded, including 5 Americans, 2 Japanese, and 3 South Koreans. One of the dead Americans had arrived in Israel for study the previous day. Many of the victims were exchange students from overseas, studying at the university for the summer. Among the injured were a French tourist, an Italian man, two people from East Asia, and several Arabs. Many were treated for burns.

Israeli police detained numerous Palestinians. Several thousand Palestinians marched through Gaza streets to celebrate the bombing by Hamas's Izzedine al-Qassam Brigades.

Among the dead Americans were:

- Janis Ruth Coulter, 36, who had worked as assistant director of academic affairs in New York for Hebrew University's Rothberg International School. She had left the United States on July 29 to accompany a group of U.S. students who were enrolling at the university. She had been expected to return to New York at the end of the week. A convert to Judaism, her Hebrew name, Yonit, means "little dove." The Boston-born former Episcopalian had moved to Brooklyn in August 1999 to work for American Friends. She had graduated from the University of Massachusetts in 1991 and did doctoral work at the University of Denver. Her unfinished thesis was on early Christianity and the development of anti-Jewish attitudes. Her grandmother was also a convert to Judaism. Janis would have turned 37 on August 5.

- Dina Carter (variant Diane Leslie Carter), 37, of Greensboro, North Carolina, a U.S.–Israeli citizen who worked as a librarian at the Hebrew University. She had earned a bachelor of arts from Duke University in Anthropology in 1986 and a master's degree in Social Work from the University of North Carolina in 1989. She had immigrated to Israel in 1990.

- David Gritz, 24, of Peru, Massachusetts, a U.S.–French citizen taking a course in Jewish thought. He was the only child of an American Jewish father and a Croatian gentile mother. He grew up in Paris on the Rue Mouffetard. He had studied at McGill University in Montreal and at the Sorbonne in Paris. He had turned down a University of Berlin grant to study Hebrew at Hebrew University. He played the piano and violin.

- Benjamin Blutstein, 25, of Harrisburg, Pennsylvania, who was in a two-year program to be a Jewish Studies teacher. He and his former girlfriend Rebecca Spilke started a hip-hop Jewish band known as Women, Slaves and Minors (the name is derived from the Torah). His father is a pediatrician; his mother is a Penn State microbiologist. He had worked as a DJ in Jerusalem clubs. He graduated from Dickinson College in 2000. He had been the master of ceremonies at the July 30 graduation ceremonies.

- Maria (or Marla) Bennett, 24, of San Diego, California, who was completing master's degree work in Judaic Studies. She was a 2000 graduate of the University of California at Berkeley. She had lived in Jerusalem for a year. She wanted to be a teacher. She had been scheduled to fly home on August 1.

The dead Israelis were Lavina Shapira, 53, and David Ludovsiky, 29.

President Bush said he was "furious" over their deaths and vowed to track down those responsible.

On August 2, in retaliation, Israeli tanks moved into Nablus where investigators said the bomb was made. Soldiers searching buildings in the Old City found two explosives labs that contained pipe bombs, gas containers, gunpowder, ammunition, electronic activation mechanisms, four barrels of acid, sacks of fertilizer, a grenade, and a homemade Qassam missile.

On August 17, Israeli police broke up the terrorist cell responsible for this and seven other bombings in the previous six months (including the March 9 suicide bombing of the Moment Café and the May 7 attack at the Rishon Letzion pool hall), arresting 15 men. Five of the men were identified as Palestinians, four of whom lived in East Jerusalem and held Jerusalem identity cards that facilitated movement throughout the country. The Israelis said they had learned that the Hamas cell was about to set off another bomb in central Israel. A senior security official reported, "The brains, the explosive charges, almost everything moved from Ramallah to East Jerusalem." The suspects were identified as Wael Kassem, 31, Wissam Abassi, 25, Alah Abassi, 30, and Mohammed Odeh, 29, all of East Jerusalem, and Mohammed Arman, 27, who lives outside Ramallah. Kassem was commander of the Jerusalem cell. Arman ran the Ramallah cell. Odeh worked at Hebrew University as a contract painter and used his university ID card to carry out the bombing. He hid the bomb the night before the attack in some shrubs, then placed it on a table in the cafeteria the next day. He set it off with a cell phone. Officials said the site was chosen because "they were looking for a place with no Arabs."

On September 12, 2002, an Israeli court charged four Arab residents of East Jerusalem with murder, attempted murder, and conspiracy to murder. They faced life in prison. They were also accused of having chosen the targets and transporting the suicide bombers to attacks on Café Moment in Jerusalem that killed 11 and at the Rishon Letzion pool hall that killed 16. 02073101

August 2002. *United States.* Mohammed Budeir, 20, a U.S. citizen of Syrian descent, was arrested taking photos of police cars in Paoli, Pennsylvania. The college student was charged with criminal trespassing and disorderly conduct while he was found photographing Willistown Township police vehicles. He said that the photos are a hobby.

August 2002. *Singapore.* Internal Security Department authorities arrested 18 Jemaah Islamiah (JI) and Moro Islamic Liberation Front (MILF) suspects. They included Mahfuh bin Haji Halimi, Azman bin Jalani, and Zukifli bin Mohamed Jaffar. According to the U.S. State Department's *Patterns of Global Terrorism 2002*, the groups were accused of:

... activities in support of the planned attacks on the Ministry of Defense, a U.S. ship, water pipelines, a bar frequented by U.S. service personnel, and other targets. Seventeen of these suspects were JI members; the other was a Moro Islamic Liberation Front (MILF) member.... According to reports released by the Singaporean authorities, several of those arrested ... had attended al Qaeda training camps in Afghanistan and MILF training camps in Mindanao. Before leaving for camps, JI leaders would conduct ideological and physical training sessions to prepare members for their trips. Singapore officials said that members conducted reconnaissance of selected targets in Singapore, acting on orders from the JI leaders arrested in December (2001). Some of the arrested members were found with evidence of their surveillance activities, including maps, drawings, reconnaissance reports, photographs, and videotaped recordings. The members had devised elaborate schemes to conduct surveillance. For instance, Ab Wahab bin Ahamd (Wahab) was a magazine deliveryman whose route included the Singapore Ministry of Defense. He allowed Mohd Aslam bin Yar Ali Khan (Aslam), a more senior JI operative, to deliver magazines on his behalf so that Aslam could personally conduct surveillance of the facility. This gave Aslam the opportunity to videotape the perimeter and entrances to the building. Notes and written summaries of the videotapes were later recovered in a raid on Wahab's home. The Singapore Government reported that JI members also cased other targets for possible attack, including water pipelines, the Changi Airport, an air traffic control radar site, petrochemical facilities, and various Western and other interests in Singapore.

Of the 18 men detained ... most were employed in everyday jobs as deliverymen, dispatch clerks, drivers, butchers, and used car salesmen. Only two were unemployed. About half had served full time in the National Service and were on reserve duty at the time they were arrested. According to the Singapore Government, most of the JI members in custody saw no contradiction between living in a peaceful multiracial society and pledging their allegiance to militant groups that could potentially harm other Singaporeans, including fellow Muslims whom they claimed to represent. During interviews by the ISD, the members revealed that they were so committed to pursuing jihad that they were willing to put fellow Muslims at risk to accomplish their goals.

The JI cell in Singapore was an important fund-raiser for regional JI groups. It would impose a tax on its members to raise funds. In the early 1990s, members were required to give two percent of their monthly salaries; this was later increased to five percent. According to Singapore authorities, half of the funds raised went to the Singapore cell, which used the money to fund its members' expenditures and provide for needy JI families. Money also was sent to members abroad for military training. The other hand of the money raised was split between the Indonesian and Malaysian branches of JI.

Home Affairs Minister Wong Kan Seng emphasized the complex organizational structure of JI and noted the need for continued regional cooperation to counter the terrorism threat from the group. Referring to the second roundup of suspects, Mr. Wong said, 'This particular group in JI is not confined to Singapore but is connected to the JI organization in Malaysia and Indonesia and some in the Philippines. We also found that some Singaporeans were involved or into training in the Moro Islamic Liberation Front training camps. That is a concern that this network is not found only in Singapore but also in the region.' Some members of the Singapore organization are believed to be hiding out in neighboring countries, and it is possible that they may yet carry out their bombing plans.

02089901

August 1, 2002. *Northern Ireland.* Police blamed dissident Irish republicans for setting off a bomb at the Territorial Army Camp in Londonderry, killing David Caldwell, 51, a civilian worker.

August 2, 2002. *Greece.* Authorities discovered that thieves had tunneled through a wall and stolen a cache of weapons, including 15 .45-caliber pistols, 3 automatic rifles, and 3 machine guns from a military armory on the island of Kos in the Aegean Sea. The 17 November terrorist group and ordinary criminals were suspected.

August 4, 2002. *Greece.* Antiterrorist police found a hand grenade, detonators, and a small quantity of dynamite buried in a shallow pit on a hill overlooking the 19th-century marble stadium scheduled for use in the 2004 Olympics. The stadium had been used in the 1896 Olympics—the first "modern" Olympics.

August 4, 2002. *Spain.* A car bomb outside a police barracks at the Santa Pola resort near Alicante killed Cecilio Gallego, 50, and the six-year-old daughter of a Civil Guard police officer. She was the youngest fatality since the Basque Nation and Liberty resumed its terrorist campaign in January 2000 after a 14-month ceasefire. She was killed when shock waves from the blast toppled furniture on top of her while she was in her home.

August 4, 2002. *Israel.* A Hamas suicide bomber set off a bomb in the center of Number 361 Egged commuter bus filled with soldiers returning from weekend leaves at the Meron Junction, killing himself and 9 others, including 3 soldiers, and injuring 50 people, including 23 soldiers. Hamas said it was retaliating for the July 22 killing of a terrorist leader. The attack came near a remote bus stop five miles from the Lebanese border near the Israeli town of Safed. The dead soldiers, all sergeants, were Roni Ganm, 28, Omri Goldin, 20, and Yfat Gabrieli, 19. Other people killed included two Philippine workers, two Israeli women, and a 24-year-old Israeli man. A young woman believed to be Palestinian also died. In a new policy, Hamas said it would not release the bomber's name to prevent Israeli military forces from punishing family members. 02080401

August 4, 2002. *Israel.* Three men died in a shoot-out between a 19-year-old Palestinian gunman and Israeli police at an Israeli telephone company truck parked across the street from the Damascus Gate entrance to the Old City of Jerusalem. The terrorist leaned into the passenger window of the truck and shot dead a 32-year-old security guard sitting inside. After pulling the guard out, he shot the driver. The gunman ran to the front of a nearby restaurant, the Al Omal Café, to change the clip in his pistol. Police fired on him and detained the wounded Palestinian. Israeli fire also killed a 50-year-old Arab from East Jerusalem and wounded four other men inside the café. Some 17 people were reported injured; it was unclear whether any of the terrorist's bullets had harmed anyone besides the telephone company employees. The al-Aqsa Martyrs Brigades claimed credit.

August 4, 2002. *Israel.* Soldiers shot and killed a Palestinian man in a scuba diving suit after he came out of the Mediterranean Sea near the settlement of Elei Sinai. Authorities found a Kalashnikov with four magazines of bullets and eight grenades on the body.

August 4, 2002. *Israel.* Three Israeli soldiers were injured, one seriously, when a booby trap exploded near them in Nablus.

August 4, 2002. *Israel.* During the early evening, three Israelis were injured when their bus was fired on near the settlement of Avnei Khefets by members of the al-Aqsa Martyrs Brigades.

August 4, 2002. *Israel.* During the night, al-Aqsa Martyrs Brigades gunmen set off a bomb alongside the road north of Ramallah as two cars passed. They then fired on the vehicles, injuring three Israelis.

August 5, 2002. *Israel.* In the morning, terrorists ambushed a car in Nablus, killing two Israelis.

August 5, 2002. *Pakistan.* The U.S. Consulate in Karachi was closed after local authorities reopened Abdullah Haroon Road, a street in front that U.S. officials said was a security risk. Pakistani authorities removed large concrete blocks in front of the building.

August 5, 2002. *Pakistan.* Four clean shaven, masked gunmen attacked the Murree Christian School, killing six Pakistanis (two security guards, a receptionist, a cook, a carpenter, and a bystander) and injuring three others with Kalashnikov fire. One of the injured was a Filipina who has two children in the school; she was shot in the hand. None of the 150 students, including 30 Americans, along with Australians, Europeans, and New Zealanders, or the principally British teaching staff were harmed in the attack in the Himalayan foothills 35 miles from Islamabad.

The district police commander said, "Their goal was to hit foreigners." The gunmen were believed to be in their mid-twenties. They attacked a guard post set up three months earlier at the school's entrance. They pulled their guns out of duffel bags and fired, killing a guard and a pedestrian. They then ran through the gates, killing another guard and a receptionist and destroying the windows of a dorm. Staff members locked the door to the kindergarten, preventing the terrorists from entering. Another guard returned fire, apparently wounding an attacker (police found a blood trail along the escape route) and the gunmen disappeared over a back fence and into the woods. While escaping, they shot the cook and the carpenter, who were hiding away from where the attack began. Police said a note found at the scene expressed "resentment against world powers," and the "unjust" killings of Muslims, Palestinians, and Kashmiri fighters. The note said that the group would "do more in the future to avenge what is being done by infidels with Muslims all over the world."

The school's director is Russell Morton, an Australian.

Police later found grenades, knives, and ammunition, and suggested that the terrorists had planned to kill the students or take them hostage.

On August 7, Pakistani authorities reported that three of the gunmen may have been individuals who blew themselves up with grenades after fleeing a checkpoint near Dherkot, 25 miles northeast of Murree, in Pakistani Kashmir. Police overpowered a man who resisted efforts to search him. A companion pulled out a grenade and said, "We are not your enemy. We are the ones who killed the nonbelievers in Murree." Police freed the trio, who ran toward the Jhelum River. The grenade went off, throwing two of the men into the river; a third body was found on the riverbank. Police recovered an exploded grenade similar to that used in Murree.

The al-Intigami al-Pakistani claimed credit. 02080501

August 5, 2002. *Israel.* A car bomb injured 40 people.

August 5, 2002. *Uganda.* At dawn, Lord's Resistance Army gunmen attacked a camp for Sudanese refugees in the north, driving away 100 Ugandan soldiers, killing 14, looting the camp, setting fire to anything they could not carry, and forcing 24,000 people to flee during the two-hour raid. The terrorists kidnapped two Ugandan aide workers, stole an armored vehicle, and turned its guns on the refugees before setting the vehicle alight. The group is led by Joseph Kony. 02080502

August 5, 2002. *India.* At 5:00 a.m., four or five gunmen came down from the forested mountains to throw grenades and fire automatic weapons at sleeping Hindu pilgrims, killing 9 and wounding 32 (including 4 Kashmiri Muslim porters who assisted the pilgrims) at the Nunwan camp in Pahalgam in southern Kashmir. Islamic militants were suspected. The Hindus were on an annual, month-long pilgrimage called the Amarnath Yatra to a cave containing an ice formation they believe represents the Hindu god Siva. Security officers returned fire in an hour-long gun battle, killing a terrorist armed with an AK-47 assault rifle and three grenades. Deputy Prime Minister L. K. Advani said Al Mansoorian

claimed credit. He said it was a front for Lashkar-i-Taiba, a Pakistan-based Islamic group fighting to end Indian rule in divided Kashmir.

August 5, 2002. *Italy.* On September 11, Sicilian police announced the arrest by Servizo per le informazione e la sicurezza militare (the Italian military Intelligence agency known as SISMI) officers on a Tonga-flagged ship of 15 Pakistanis with al Qaeda ties. The August 5 arrests were based on a tip from U.S. naval intelligence. SISMI also found seven Romanian crew. SISMI confiscated phone numbers, encoded messages, and Karachi-Casablanca airline tickets. Some of the phone numbers were linked to al Qaeda operatives in France and Spain. The ship is owned by a Greek who lives in Romania. It had left Casablanca in mid-July and was scheduled to visit Tunisia, Malta, and Tripoli.

The group, who ranged in age from 24 to 38, were charged on September 12 with "association" to commit terrorist acts. Investigators found a coded notation on the ship to someone "united in matrimony." They were to be arraigned in a court in Gela, a Sicilian port. Prosecutor Francesco Messineo told the press, "It's a conventional reference to indicate membership in a terrorist organization." The term had been used in the 1993 World Trade Center attack. Santi Giuffre, police chief at Caltanissetta where the detainees were held, said, "We are certain that these people are part of a terrorist organization and we are almost certain that the organization is al Qaeda." Messineo ruled out a terrorist attack in Italy, but said they might have been "trying to reach other branches of the network." Pakistan denied that they were Pakistanis, saying their documents were counterfeit.

August 5, 2002. *India.* In Malik, Kashmir, a grenade was thrown into a crowded marketplace, injuring ten. No one claimed credit.

August 6, 2002. *Colombia.* The Revolutionary Armed Forces of Colombia (FARC) set off a bomb on a segment of the Canadian-owned Ocensa oil pipeline in Cuanata, causing oil spillage and environmental damage. The explosion forced the suspension of crude oil transport to the Port of Covensa. 02080601

August 7, 2002. *Colombia.* Leftist rebels fired a dozen 120-mm homemade mortars at the presidential palace and surrounding streets, killing 14, as President Alvaro Uribe was being inaugurated two blocks away at the parliament building. None of the presidential party or foreign dignitaries were injured. Four officers were injured when a mortar round landed on the grounds of Casa de Narino, the presidential palace. Another round landed near a restaurant outside the palace grounds, causing no injuries. Four blocks from the palace, 19 people died, including 3 children, and 69 were injured when two other homemade mortars exploded. Most of the injured were destitute residents of Bogota. Police blamed the Revolutionary Army Forces of Colombia (FARC), which did not immediately take credit.

August 9, 2002. *Pakistan.* Three Pakistani nurses were killed in a grenade attack as they were leaving a Presbyterian hospital chapel in Taxila, 25 miles west of Islamabad, during the morning. Three men, one carrying a pistol, ran through the front gate, locked two watchmen into a guard booth, and threw grenades at women leaving the chapel. Another 25 people were injured, half of them seriously. Witnesses said that the attack's leader was killed by his two accomplices as they were fleeing. Security aides to President Musharraf said that the banned Islamic groups Harkat ul-Mujaheddin and Jaish-i-Muhammad had joined forces to attack Westerners and may have ties to al Qaeda and the Taliban.

August 9, 2002. *United States.* The U.S. Department of State designated the Communist Party of the Philippines (also known as New People's Army) as a terrorist group, making it illegal for Americans to provide financial support. Financial institutions must block the group's assets. Party representatives cannot enter the United States and are subject to expulsion if already in the United States.

August 9, 2002. *Yemen.* Authorities in San'a found a 650-pound cache of Semtex plastic explosives and rocket-propelled grenades hidden in pomegranate crates in a warehouse. They were investigating an explosion that killed two al Qaeda terrorists identified as Abd-al-Karim al-Jabiri and Abdallah Muhammad Fari, who died when a wire-guided missile blew up. The Web site of Dubai newspaper *al-Bayan* said that the duo had a large cache of C-4 and planned to attack U.S. naval interests.

August 10, 2002. *Israel.* At 10:00 p.m., a Palestinian broke through a security fence and fired on a couple in their car in the settlement of Mehora in the Jordan Valley southeast of Nablus in the West Bank, killing an Israeli woman and seriously injuring her husband. Israeli soldiers shot and killed him. Two other people were injured in the shoot-out.

August 10, 2002. *Israel.* Israeli soldiers shot an armed Palestinian who was crossing into Israel through a fence on the Gaza Strip border near the Niram kibbutz. He was carrying hand grenades and died when one went off. Soldiers found an AK-47 near his body. Hamas said the attacker was Maher Masri, 20, from the village of Beit Hanun in the northern Gaza Strip.

August 11, 2002. *Israel.* Soldiers shot and killed a Palestinian who fired on Israeli road workers near the Jewish settlement of Dugit. A wounded worker was hit five times in the arms and legs, but was in stable condition. The gunman ran into a house in the nearby Palestinian area of Beit Lahiya. After he shot at soldiers, they shot back, killing him. The soldiers also found a bomb hidden on a trail leading to the house where the gunman fled. Hamas said the gunman was Basil Naji, 22.

August 12, 2002. *Russia.* Gunmen kidnapped Arjan Erkel, 32, the Dutch head of the Doctors Without Borders mission in Dagestan, on the outskirts of Makhachkala. Makhachkala is the Dagestan capital and borders Chechnya. The

Washington Post reported that two Russian law enforcement officers watched the kidnapping, doing nothing to stop it. It was the second abduction of an aide worker in the area since July. Erkel is an employee of the group's Swiss branch. He was driving home when his car was intercepted by three men—two armed—in a vehicle. He was forced into their vehicle. As of August 11, 2003, he was still being held, according to videotapes released by the kidnappers.

In December 2003, the head of the Dagestani police department who was in charge of investigating this case was arrested on suspicion of involvement in abductions. Meanwhile, negotiations between Doctors Without Borders and the kidnappers broke down.

Erkel was freed by police and Federal Security Service rescuers on April 18, 2004, after 607 days in captivity. He was in good health. Initial reports said that no ransom was paid. Reports differed as to whether he was released on April 11 or 18. However, on July 27, 2004, the Dutch government filed suit in Switzerland to compel Doctors Without Borders to recompense the Dutch government the $936,000 it paid in ransom. 02081201

August 13, 2002. *India.* In Anantnag, Kashmir, a bomb exploded at a bus stop, killing 1 and injuring 21 others. No one claimed credit.

August 16, 2002. *Algeria.* Islamic terrorists killed 26 people, including women and children, from three families in a hamlet in Chlef, 155 miles west of Algiers.

August 16, 2002. *Germany.* Police in Solingen and Braunschweig raided an al-Aqsa charity organization suspected of sending money to Hamas. Police seized numerous documents and computers at apartments and offices. Earlier in the month, police seized more than 150 crates of documents at the group's Aachen offices.

August 17, 2002. *Iraq.* The Palestinian newspaper *al-Ayyam* reported that Sabri al-Banna (alias Abu Nidal), 65, had been found dead from gunshot wounds to the head in Baghdad. (The Western press had the story two days later. Iraq did not release the date he was found.) Fatah Revolutionary Council sources said he was suffering from cancer and had become addicted to painkillers, but later said that he was assassinated by an Iraqi intelligence agency. Iraqi government sources later said it was a suicide. Iraqi intelligence chief Tahir Jalil Haboush said that he killed himself rather than face a trial for communicating with a foreign country. (The suicide theory was difficult to support as there was no explanation of how he could shoot himself several times in the head.) Police searching Abu Nidal's apartment found automatic weapons and false passports. In the 1970s and 1980s, his group was responsible for the deaths of 900 people in attacks in 20 countries.

August 19, 2002. *Italy.* Bologna police arrested five people—four Moroccans and an Italian—on suspicion of planning to attack the 14th-century Basilica of San Petronio, which contains a fresco depicting Muhammad in hell. The police grabbed the group as they were videotaping the church in the morning. They were overheard discussing an attack. The Moroccans said they were tourists; police said they belonged to al Qaeda.

On August 21, Judge Diego Di Marco ordered the group released for lack of evidence.

August 20, 2002. *Afghanistan.* CNN ran some of the 64 tapes (out of a cache of 251) found in al Qaeda safe houses of terrorist training and chemical warfare experiments that showed dogs dying in clouds of toxic gases.

August 20, 2002. *Philippines.* The Abu Sayyaf group was suspected in the kidnapping of eight people, initially identified as five female and three male door-to-door cosmetics salespeople. They were later identified as four male and four female Jehovah's Witnesses.

On August 22, the group beheaded two male Christian preachers. The heads of Lemuel Bantolo and Leonel Mantic were found in a Jolo Island jungle. Mantic's wife was among the hostages. Two hostages—both Muslim men—were freed.

August 20, 2002. *India.* The army said it had killed 14 Muslim rebels trying to enter Indian Kashmir from Pakistan.

August 20, 2002. *United States.* The FBI issued a worldwide alert for the arrest of Saud Abdulaziz Saud Al-Rasheed, 21, who was believed to have ties with the September 11 hijackers and was considered "armed and dangerous." The information on him came from material recovered overseas. The material included an image of a Saudi passport issued to him in May 2000 in Riyadh which was found on a CD-ROM that also included pictures of some of the hijackers. He surrendered to Saudi Interior Ministry officials in Riyadh on August 22 and was being questioned. His family doubted that he had connections to the attackers, claiming that he spent a year working in Afghanistan on humanitarian projects, returning to Saudi Arabia four months before the attacks. Al-Rasheed was on vacation in Egypt when he saw his photo on CNN.

August 20, 2002. *Germany.* At 2:26 p.m., using mace or pepper spray, Iraqi dissidents peacefully took over the Iraqi Embassy in Berlin, taking six Iraqis hostage. The previously unknown Democratic Iraqi Opposition of Germany called for the ouster of Saddam Hussein. At 7:40 p.m., German police stormed the building, arrested five hostage-takers, and freed two remaining hostages without firing a shot. Among the hostages was the senior-most Iraqi diplomat in Germany, First Secretary Shamil A. Mohammed. Two people were slightly injured. Other Iraqi dissident groups said that the new group had only 20 members, including expatriate Iraqi army officers.

August 23, 2002. *United States.* Tashala Hayman, 22, of Vaughn, Montana, was charged with one count of mailing poison with intent to kill and one count of identity theft in a plot to mail poisoned soft drinks to Senator Edward M. Kennedy (Democrat–Massachusetts) and U.K. Prince William. Arraignment was scheduled for August 26.

August 23, 2002. *United States.* Podiatrist Robert J. Goldstein, 37, of St. Petersburg, Florida, was charged with possession of a nonregistered destructive device, and attempting to use an explosive to damage and destroy Islamic centers. Police searching his suburban home found 40 weapons, 30 explosive devices—including a 5-gallon gasoline bomb with a timer attached—a list of 50 Islamic mosques in Florida, and detailed plans to bomb an Islamic education center. One of the discovered notes read, "set timers for approximately 15–20 minutes to allow for enough time to get out of area, but to confirm explosions have been successful.... The amount of explosives should be ample to take down the building." He was detained when his mother phoned police after his spouse, Kristi, called her to talk about marital problems.

On October 18, a federal judge ruled that Goldstein was competent to stand trial. On October 24, Kristi was charged with being an accomplice, because she knew about his plans, according to federal prosecutors. Kristi turned state's evidence in a plea bargain on February 24, 2003. Robert Goldstein pleaded guilty to plotting the bomb attack on April 3, 2003. Goldstein received 12 years in prison on June 19, 2003.

August 23, 2002. *Israel.* Israeli soldiers shot to death two al-Aqsa Martyrs Brigades gunmen attempting to infiltrate a Jewish settlement in the West Bank. The gunmen were carrying assault rifles and hand grenades, and died in a gun battle near the security fence at the Kfar Darom settlement. One died near the fence; the second escaped to an abandoned house before being shot to death. Police were searching for a third terrorist who might have been wounded.

August 23, 2002. *Israel.* The al-Aqsa Martyrs Brigades kidnapped and killed Ikhlas Khouli, 35, believed to be the first Palestinian woman murdered for alleged aid to Israel. Dozens of male "collaborators" had been murdered previously. Khouli's bullet-riddled corpse was left in a public square in Tulkarm. The Brigades said she helped Israeli services find the hiding place of a Brigades leader killed by Israeli troops. The Brigades kidnapped Ikhlas Khouli and her eldest son, Bakir Khouli, from their home and took them to an abandoned building. Bakir said he was tortured by the terrorists, who "accused me of helping Israeli intelligence. When they started beating me with this wire, I confessed and invented a story." The terrorists videotaped Ikhlas admitting spying for Israel, then killed her the next day, firing several bullets into her head and chest. A 30-second tape shown on Israel's Channel 2 television news showed her claiming to have phoned Israeli security services with information about Ziad Daas, 27, a regional commander for the group. Daas was shot by a sniper while on the roof of his house on August 7 in Tulkarm. Daas was wanted for planning the killing of two Israelis in a Tulkarm restaurant in January 2001 and for involvement in a January 2002 killing of six Israelis in Hadera.

August 23, 2002. *Iran/United States.* The U.S. Department of State warned USA Wrestling of an unspecified threat against the team that was to compete in the September 5–7 world freestyle championships in Iran. The seven wrestlers went home on August 26.

August 25, 2002. *Afghanistan.* At 9:00 p.m., a small package bomb went off in a trash bin next to the outside wall of a guarded and gated UN staff house, injuring two Afghans and shattering windows. There were 50 people living at the guesthouse. No one claimed credit.

Three rockets were fired at a U.S. Special Forces outpost in Konar Province. 02082501

August 26, 2002. *United States.* Deputy Secretary of State Richard L. Armitage announced the addition of the East Turkestan Islamic Movement (ETIM) to the terrorist group list earlier in the week. ETIM seeks independence for China's Xinjiang Province. Listing triggers financial sanctions and immigration controls. Armitage noted that "after careful study, we judged … that it committed acts of violence against unarmed civilians without any regard for who was hurt." Beijing said the Uighur terrorists were behind several bombings and assassinations. It claimed that al Qaeda had provided weapons, money, and training in Afghanistan to ETIM members who then created secret cells across the country to produce more weapons. The *Washington Post* reported that terrorists captured in Afghanistan said the group was responsible for the murder of a Chinese diplomat in Central Asia. In a January *Radio Free Asia* interview, Hasan Mahsum, the group's leader, denied ties with al Qaeda.

August 27, 2002. *United States.* The Bush administration removed three groups and three people from the list of entities whose assets were frozen because of support to al Qaeda. Somali-born Swedish citizens Abdi Abdulaziz Ali and Abdirisak Aden, who worked with the Swedish chapter of the Somalia-based Al-Barakaat, and Grand Jama, owner of the Aaran Money Wire Service, Inc., of Minneapolis, Minnesota, were dropped from the list, as were Barakaat Enterprise of Columbus, Ohio, and Global Service International of Minneapolis.

August 28, 2002. *Iran.* The Bush administration condemned Iran for providing safe haven to al Qaeda functionaries a day after the *Washington Post* reported that dozens of al Qaeda fighters were hiding near the border with Pakistan. Among them were Saif al-Adel, an Egyptian, and Mahfouz Ould Walid, whom the Pentagon had claimed was killed in January.

August 28, 2002. *Pakistan.* Local and U.S. law enforcement officers arrested 12 men and seized explosives and weapons in a Peshawar office of a group believed working with the Taliban and al Qaeda fugitives to conduct terrorist attacks in Pakistan.

August 28, 2002. *People's Republic of China.* The U.S. Embassy in Beijing reported that there was evidence that the East Turkestan Islamic Movement (ETIM) was planning a terrorist attack against the U.S. Embassy in Bishkek, Kyrgyzstan. One suspect was found with a map showing embassies in Bishkek. A U.S. spokesman said the ETIM was responsible for more than 200 terrorist attacks in China, including bombings, assassinations, and arsons, which killed 162 and injured 440. He noted that in May, two suspected ETIM members—Mamet Yasyn and Mamet Sadyk—were deported by Kyrgyzstan to China for planning terrorist attacks against embassies, markets, and public gathering places in Bishkek.

August 28, 2002. *Ecuador.* In Guayaquil, a Revolutionary Armed Forces of Ecuador pamphlet bomb exploded at a McDonald's restaurant, injuring three and causing major property damage. 02082801

August 29, 2002. *Sweden.* Police arrested Kerim Chatty, a Tunisian-born Swedish man, 29, as he prepared to board a plane bound for London's Stansted Airport with 185 passengers. Chatty was accused of planning to hijack a plane after an x-ray detected a handgun in a toiletries bag in his carry-on luggage. He was in a group of 20 people going to an Islamic conference in Birmingham, United Kingdom, according to police in Vaesteraas, 60 miles northwest of Stockholm. The suspect had prior convictions for theft and assault, including a 1999 (or 1997, according to other sources) attack on a U.S. embassy marine guard in a gym. The other members of the group included 17 adults and 2 children. Several passengers were evacuated from the Ryanair plane.

Chatty initially told police that the gun had been planted, but later said he was carrying it because he feared for his safety in the United Kingdom. His father said his son might have forgotten that the gun was in the bag.

Reuters reported that Chatty had planned to crash the plane into a U.S. embassy in Europe.

Four accomplices, including an explosives expert, remained at large, and were deemed wannabes, not al Qaeda members. Police initially denied the story. Others said it might have been a dry run for a terrorist attack. Nils Uggla, Chatty's attorney, said that this was not terrorism nor religiously inspired, but that he was not at liberty to discuss why his client was carrying the weapon. Chatty had studied at the North American Institute of Aviation in Conway, South Carolina, from September 1996 to April 1997, but he had been "terminated" for substandard performance and lack of progress in the course. Friends said that he had studied Islam and visited Saudi Arabia in September 2001 and February 2002. He had been questioned by local police shortly after the September 11 attacks. One newspaper said he had been a regional Swedish gold medalist in Thai boxing. Others said he was a bodybuilder, martial arts fan, and a bodyguard/enforcer for Yugoslav gangsters. He was convicted in 1993 for possession of an unregistered shotgun. He was later arrested with a Glock machine pistol. His father is Tunisian; his mother, Swedish. She claimed her son became interested in Islam during his flight school training.

Prosecutors were given a deadline of September 2 to persuade a court to remand him to custody for two more weeks. Police said he would probably be charged with planning a hijack or illegal possession of firearms. He could face life in prison. Police raided his apartment in a town between Stockholm and Vaesteraas and carted away documents.

On September 2, Chatty was charged with attempted hijacking; the judge agreed to the two-week extension of his detention. Chatty pleaded guilty to illegal possession of a firearm and not guilty to attempted hijacking. His attorney said he would appeal the detention decision.

Chatty had befriended Oussama Kassir, Lebanese Palestinian and Stockholm resident, who allegedly participated in a plot to create a terrorist training camp in Oregon and had made threats against police. Kassir said the two met in Sweden's Osteraker prison in 1998, where Kassir taught him Islamic lessons and prayers. He said Chatty followed the ultraorthodox Salafi fundamentalist ideology, which does not advocate violence.

Chatty was freed on September 30 when prosecutors said that they did not have evidence that he intended a hijacking. The prosecutor imposed a travel ban on him and ordered him to report to police daily for the month of October. 02082901

August 30, 2002. *Netherlands.* Police arrested 12 suspected al Qaeda recruiters; 4 were held only briefly. One was freed by a judge on September 2. Wim de Bruin, spokesman for the National Prosecutor's Office, said, "We think they are providing financial and logistical support to al Qaeda and also recruiting young male persons for the jihad.... We are convinced that this network was preparing young people to be sent out to fight as jihad warriors.... They all claim to have nationalities not European.... We are still investigating the identities of the suspects. We are not quite sure of their real identities." The detainees apparently used faked passports and aliases, and were between 25 and 35 years old.

Meanwhile, prosecutors in Rotterdam charged a separate foursome—two Algerians, a French citizen, and a Dutch citizen—with plotting to attack Belgium's Kleine Brogel Air Force Base. They had earlier been charged with plotting to attack the U.S. Embassy in Paris.

August 31, 2002. *Indonesia.* About 15 gunmen carrying M-16 rifles shot to death 3 people (2 Americans and an Indonesian) and wounded 14 others, including 9 foreigners (among them 6 Americans, 4 of whom were seriously injured), in an attack on a convoy near a gold and copper mine in Papua Province operated by Freeport Indonesia, a subsidiary of U.S.–owned Freeport-McMoran Copper and Gold, Inc. of New Orleans. The dead were identified as Americans Ted Burcon of Sunriver, Oregon, and Rickey Lynn Spear of Colorado, both teachers at a school at the mine, and Indonesian Bambang Riwanto. The firm had been criticized by human rights activists for cooperating with local security forces in suppressing independence groups in Irian Jaya (Papua). After setting up a roadblock, the terrorists opened fire. The wounded were flown to Townsville, Australia, for emergency medical treatment. Many of the people in the convoy taught at an international school in Tembagapura, a local town two miles from the attack. No one claimed credit, but the Free Papua Movement was suspected. They denied involvement on September 2.

Among those who escaped harm were Saundra Hopkins and her daughter Taia, 6.

On the morning of September 1, government forces shot to death Danianus Waker, 25, a man suspected in the attack. Local media said that he was an informer for the authorities and suggested that the military was behind the attacks. A soldier was wounded in the gun battle, which occurred near the scene of the original attack. Troops conducted a search in jungles for separatist insurgents. By September 26, police were continuing their investigation of possible Indonesian Army Special Forces involvement in the attack. Many observers pointed out that the weapons used were more typically found in the hands of the army than the rebels, who tended to use spears and clubs in previous attacks. A 23-year-old Papua man said he was with the Special Forces when they set out to ambush teachers. He claimed that the soldiers had drained many bottles of alcohol before the attack. By October 26, police and intelligence officers believed that army soldiers were behind the attack. Police had questioned 30 soldiers and 44 civilians.

On June 16, 2004, Anthonius Wamang, 32, an Indonesian member of the National Freedom Force, the military branch of the Free Papua Movement, was indicted in the killings. A federal grand jury in Washington, whose indictment was unsealed on June 24, 2004, charged the commander of the separatists' military wing with two counts of murder, eight counts of attempted murder, and nine other charges. He faced the death penalty on two of the charges. He was not in custody. 02083101

August 31, 2002. *Israel.* A Popular Front for the Liberation of Palestine (PFLP) gunman fired at a school near Nablus, seriously injuring a man and a woman from Jerusalem who were on a weekend visit to the Jewish settlement of Har Bracha. Settlement guards shot the gunman while he was trying to escape. The PFLP called a Lebanese television station to claim credit.

August 31, 2002. *India.* At Mahore, armed militants entered the private residence of a Revenue Department official who had been deployed on election duty. The militants killed three people. No one claimed credit.

August/September 2002. *Chile.* Chilean authorities discovered several small arms caches throughout Santiago and other cities as well as the remnants of explosive material at two communications transmission towers outside Santiago. The weapons and explosives are believed to belong to the Manual Rodriguez Patriotic Front (FPMR). Law enforcement agents believe the weapons were smuggled into Chile in the 1980s, at the height of the FPMR's activities, but some believed the caches signified an FPMR comeback.

September 2002. *Ethiopia.* The government blamed the indigenous Oromo Liberation Front (OLF) for the bombing of an Addis Ababa hotel. OLF denied responsibility.

September 2002. *Indonesia.* The State Department's *Patterns in Global Terrorism 2002* mentioned a "botched grenade attack on a U.S. diplomatic residence in Jakarta." 02099901

September 1, 2002. *Colombia.* Authorities arrested 13 members of the National Liberation Army (ELN) in Bogota, Cali, and Medellin, breaking up a kidnapping ring that had abducted people in Argentina, Ecuador, Venezuela, and Central American nations. The Bogota-based group communicated with victims' families over the Internet and had ties to leftist groups in Chile, Ecuador, Mexico, and Peru. The

kidnappings usually netted between $3 million and $10 million. In the previous year, Colombia saw 3,700 kidnappings.

September 3, 2002. *India.* In Langet, Kashmir, armed militants attacked a political rally, killing three people and injuring four others. No one claimed credit.

September 3, 2002. *India.* The Hizb ul-Mujahedin was suspected when a bomb exploded near the downtown area of Kishtwar, injuring 19 people.

September 4, 2002. *United States.* At 12:30 p.m., police and a uniformed officer of the Secret Service arrested Jeffrey Cloutier, 35, of Newport, New Hampshire, at 17th and Euclid Streets, NW, in the Adams Morgan section of Washington, D.C., when they found six pistols, ten rifles, and ammunition in his rental car. He had made threats against government officials, saying he was "headed to Washington to straighten out the President." A woman was also in the car. She said they had been married a week earlier and were trying to get a "fresh start" in life.

September 4, 2002. *South Africa.* The *Sunday Times* reported on September 8 that police had stopped a plan by right-wing white extremists to detonate 120 booby-trapped canisters planted in and around the main summit venue in the Sandton suburb of Johannesburg during the ten-day Earth Summit, which ended without incident on September 4.

September 5, 2002. *Greece.* Dimitris Koufodinas (alias Poison Hand), the 17 November's main hit man, got out of a taxi at Athens police headquarters and surrendered.

September 5, 2002. *Afghanistan.* A car bomb in a parked taxi exploded in central Kabul, killing at least 26 people and hospitalizing 100 others, including several children. The bomb exploded moments after a small device went off on a bicycle nearby, luring onlookers to the area.

Three hours later at 6:30 p.m., U.S. troops guarding Afghan President Hamid Karzai, 44, in town for a family wedding, shot to death Abdur Rehman, a soldier and would-be assassin from Helmand, and two other people in Kandahar. An Afghan guard was also killed. Karzai had just stepped into a car outside the provincial governor's office when Rehman, still in uniform, fired on the vehicle. Karzai was unhurt. Governor Gul Agha Shirzai, a passenger in the vehicle, was hit in the neck. A U.S. Special Operations soldier suffered minor injuries and was in stable condition. Rehman had joined Gul Agha Shirzai's security force less than three weeks earlier.

No one claimed credit. Local officials blamed al Qaeda and the Taliban. Others suggested the work of Gulbuddin Hekmatyar, former Afghan prime minister and now a fugitive who had called for jihad against the Americans and the government.

September 5, 2002. *Israel.* Israeli civilian guards at a checkpoint near Pardes Hana, 30 miles north of Tel Aviv, chased a Volkswagen Golf and Isuzu 4 × 4 as they sped past. The two drivers jumped from the vehicles and escaped. The Isuzu was carrying 1,300 pounds of explosives, two barrels of gasoline and metal shards, and a cell phone detonator. Foreign Minister Shimon Peres said that the "mega-bomb ... would have cost such loss of life that it would have changed almost the entire political situation in one moment." Police detonated the bomb in a field near Hadera.

In the past four months, Israeli authorities had stopped six efforts to carry out large-scale attacks designed to kill hundreds or thousands of Israelis. In one instance, commandos found a pickup truck with 1.5 tons of explosives intended to destroy the Azrieli Towers in downtown Tel Aviv.

September 5, 2002. *Israel.* An Israeli tank drove over a 220-pound bomb, killing the driver and trapping two soldiers underneath.

Meanwhile, a Palestinian gunman fired on a jeep, killing an officer and wounding a soldier. Israeli forces chased the terrorist and

shot him to death. An umbrella group claimed credit.

September 6, 2002. *Germany.* German police arrested Osman Petmezci, 25, a Turkish al Qaeda sympathizer, and his dual citizen German American fiancee, Astrid Eyzaguirre, 23, who were planning to bomb the U.S. Army's European headquarters and other targets in Heidelberg on September 11. Police found 290 pounds of chemicals, five pipe bombs, gunpowder, and marijuana plants in their apartment in Walldorf, six miles south of Heidelberg. Police also found a picture of bin Laden, Islamic literature, and a book about bomb making. The chief law enforcement officer for Baden-Wuerttemberg state said the man is a Muslim "who hates Americans and Jews."

Petmezci worked at a chemical warehouse in Karlsruhe. Petmezci was born in Germany to Turkish parents and is a Turkish national; Germany does not offer citizenship to people born in the country to foreigners. He had a criminal record involving theft and drugs.

Eyzaguirre was an assistant manager at the post exchange store (PX) at the U.S. military facility in Heidelberg, which gave her access to many post facilities. The facility hosts the army headquarters (called Campbell Barracks), the army's Fifth Corps headquarters, a small NATO facility, and hundreds of U.S. service members and their families. She had worked at the base for several years. She was initially identified as of Turkish origin, but her neighbors said she was Hispanic, with a Peruvian father and a Dominican Republic mother. Her father, Marcos Eyzaguirre, 55, is a retired army officer who had worked for the U.S. military in Germany and had returned to the United States five years earlier. He now works as a civilian for the navy in Newport News, Virginia. He said his daughter was born and raised in Germany, where he was stationed for 23 years.

A Turkish man living below the duo had complained about a strange liquid leaking into his apartment from theirs. He had broken into a red rash on one side of his face. The neighbors also said Petmezci hated Jews.

Police had a tip on the couple in mid-July, but the arrest was delayed for two months. A judge put off questioning of a witness, originally scheduled for August 13, because a summons could not be delivered on time. Prosecutors obtained a search warrant on August 30.

Prosecutors said on September 18 that they had not found a link to international terrorists.

As the trial opened on April 11, 2003, Petmezci denied plotting an attack, and said the chemicals were intended for making firecrackers. On May 6, he was convicted of illegal possession of explosives, drug violations, stealing gunpowder and chemicals to make liquid potassium nitrate, and other lesser charges. He was sentenced to 18 months in prison. He had been represented by attorney Andrea Combe. Prosecutors withdrew the terrorism counts, saying there was not "sufficient specificity" to prove the plot against the base. Eyzaguirre was acquitted of the explosives charge but convicted of a drug offense and sentenced to six months. The eight months she had already served would be counted against the sentence. 02090601

September 6, 2002. *Macedonia.* A bomb exploded in a Skopje restaurant, injuring two people, including a Turk. No one claimed credit. 02090601

September 7–8, 2002. *Colombia.* Police discovered documents relating to the U.S. Embassy during weekend raids on rebel safe houses, suggesting an imminent attack.

September 8, 2002. *Nepal.* Maoist rebels attacked a police post in eastern Nepal, killing 49 policemen.

September 8, 2002. *India.* In Dodasanpal, Kashmir, armed militants killed five people and injured another. No one claimed credit.

September 9, 2002. *Nepal.* Just after midnight, thousands of Maoist rebels attacked Sandhikharka, a remote valley town 185 miles west of Katmandu, killing 40 policemen, 17 soldiers, and 1 civilian, and injuring 29 people, 10 critically. Three government officials were missing and believed kidnapped. The rebels used civilians as human shields, set fire to government buildings, and looted a bank.

September 9, 2002. *India.* A construction worker armed with a knife was subdued after attempting to hijack an Air Seychelles B-737 bound from Bombay to Male, Maldives, with 70 passengers. A crewman was injured when Harji Wasani tried to get into the cockpit. An Indian police official said the individual was apparently drunk and became angry when a stewardess deflected his pass. The hijacker, who carried an Indian passport, was turned over to Maldives police. 02090901

September 9, 2002. *Indonesia.* The U.S. Embassy in Jakarta and Consulate in Surabaya were closed until further notice after receipt of credible information about a specific terrorist threat.

September 9, 2002. *Egypt.* An Egyptian military court convicted 51 Muslim militants, sentencing them to 2 to 15 years in prison. The key defendants were charged with forming an illegal group that planned to assassinate President Hosni Mubarak and other public figures and attack government institutions. The court acquitted 43 others. They were members of all-Wa'ad (The Promise) and accused of supplying arms and financial support to Hamas and Chechen rebels.

September 9, 2002. *India.* At 10:40 p.m., the Rajdhani Express train from Calcutta to New Delhi was derailed—apparently intentionally—and crashed into a river about 40 miles south of Patna in the Dhawasimar Rathi Ganj area of Bihar, killing at least 105 passengers and injuring 180 in 11 cars. The engine and two cars were dangling from the bridge as the dead were pulled from the river. The People's War Group and other Maoist rebel groups were among the suspected saboteurs.

September 9–10, 2002. *Egypt.* Al-Jazeera broadcast a video that included a male voice believed to be Osama bin Laden's, naming all 19 September 11 hijackers and their places of birth. The voice said, "Those men have realized that the only course to achieve justice and defeat injustice is through jihad for the cause of God." The broadcast of September 9 had listed the four hijack leaders' names—Mohamed Atta, Marwan Al-Shehhi, Ziad Samir Jarrah, and Hani Hanjour. The tape included old footage from Afghanistan of several of the hijackers who were looking at Washington maps and manuals of cockpits.

September 10, 2002. *United States.* The Bush administration increased the national terrorist threat level to Orange (high). The Pentagon moved live antiaircraft missile launchers to the Washington area for the first time in 40 years. The State Department closed more than a dozen embassies and consulates, including the embassies in Pakistan, Indonesia, Vietnam, and Bahrain, and diplomatic missions in Malaysia, Cambodia, the United Arab Emirates, Tajikistan, and Malawi.

The administration was acting on information from Omar al-Farouq, an Arab in his mid-30s who is an al Qaeda detainee in Afghanistan. Al-Farouq said that the group wanted to conduct multiple attacks in South Asia around the first anniversary of September 11. He was picked up by Indonesian authorities in June after his phone number was found in the computer files of another al Qaeda member, Agus Dwirkarna. Al-Farouq was believed to be a native of Kuwait or Iraq who trained in al Qaeda camps in Afghanistan. Al Qaeda operations chief Abu Zubayda had sent him to Indonesia four years ago to build contacts with local Muslim radicals. He was a recruiter and top financier for Indonesian extremists.

September 11, 2002. *United States.* A flight from Memphis was grounded when three Arabs went into the plane's lavatory, apparently intending to shave off their body hair, as recommended by September 11, 2001, hijack leader Mohamed Atta.

September 11, 2002. *India.* Islamic militants assassinated State Law Minister Mushtaq Ahmad Lone, 44, who was a candidate in the September 16 legislative elections. He was machine gunned to death addressing a campaign rally in a high school courtyard in Tikipora/Lalpora, 70 miles north of Srinagar. Five policemen and another person were killed, and eight people were injured. The gunmen escaped. Lashkar-i-Taiba, Jamiat ul-Mujahedin, Hizb ul-Mujahedin, and the previously unknown Al-Arifeen Squad claimed credit.

Islamic gunmen killed another 15 people in Srinagar.

Insurgents fired at a bus station in Surankot, 125 miles northwest of Jammu, killing nine people, including four Border Security Force soldiers and a 12-year-old boy.

In Dhamhal Hanjipora, Kashmir, militants threw a grenade at the residence of the Minister of Tourism, injuring four people. No one claimed credit.

September 11, 2002. *United States.* American Airlines flight 1702, a Fokker 100 with 50 passengers going to Dallas, returned to Houston International Airport shortly after takeoff after passengers said they thought they saw a person with a weapon on board. Two F-16s escorted the plane to the airport. Two suspects were taken into custody. No weapons were found on the plane. Two sky marshals were on the flight.

September 11, 2002. *United States.* U.S. District Judge James C. Cacheris sentenced to prison Abdirahman Sheikh-Ali Isse, 49, who headed the Al Barakaat branch on Beauregard Street in Alexandria, Virginia, and his nephew Abdillah S. Abdi, 36, who were charged with wiring more than $7 million from their Raage Associates branch to Al Barakaat's headquarters in the United Arab Emirates over three and a half years.

The amounts were always for less than $10,000, the Internal Revenue Service reporting trigger on money laundering. They were permitted to remain free on bond while they appealed the length of their prison terms. In November 2001, the government had declared that Al Barakaat was helping to fund al Qaeda through the *hawalla* system. The duo had pleaded guilty in June to one count of conspiring to structure transactions to avoid reporting requirements. Isse sent more than $4.2 million; Abdi more than $3.4 million. Isse was represented by attorney Kevin Byrnes. Judge Cacheris sentenced Isse to 18 months; Abdi to 5 months in prison and 5 months of home detention.

September 12, 2002. *Algeria.* Islamic rebels killed 25 civilians and government troops in two attacks.

September 12, 2002. *Algeria.* Authorities shot and killed Emad Abdelwahid Ahmed Alwan (alias Abu Mohammed) in a raid in the eastern Batna region, 270 miles east of Algiers. On November 25, authorities identified him as a top al Qaeda operative in Africa.

September 12, 2002. *United States.* Eunice Stone, a nurse eating in a Shoney's restaurant in northern Georgia, overheard three men of Middle Eastern descent laughing about the September 11 morning and discussing plans to launch an attack in Miami. She told Tampa ratio station WFLZ they said, "If people thought September 11 was something, wait till September 13." One said, "Do you think that will bring it down?" Another replied, "If that doesn't bring it down, I have contacts. I'll get enough to bring it down." They spoke unaccented English. She gave police license numbers and descriptions of the individuals' two vehicles. Miami high-rises and government buildings tightened security.

The media reported that shortly after midnight, one of the vehicles sped through a toll booth outside Naples, Florida. (The media later reported that the second car apparently paid the 75 cent toll for both cars; a videotape later showed that both cars had stopped to pay the toll.) Police gave chase and stopped the scofflaw vehicle; the second vehicle pulled up behind. Police closed Alligator Alley—Interstate 75—a major east-west artery through the Everglades, for 16 hours after a bomb-sniffing dog reacted to one of the vehicles. Live national television coverage showed police robots and explosives ordnance teams in bombproof suits examining the vehicles. A package in one of the cars was detonated. The trio were detained in a police van and were described as very uncooperative.

The trio were later freed without charge, claiming that it was all a practical joke that they concocted when a Shoney's patron gave them a dirty look. They were medical students going to Miami's Larkin Hospital for a practical studies course. They had studied at Ross University in the island of Dominica. Two were U.S. citizens; the other was in the country on a student visa. Kambiz Butt, 25, Ayman Gheith, 27, and Omer Choudhary, 23, said they harbored no resentment toward her. However, the head of Larkin Community Hospital said he had received more than 2,000 e-mail after the incident, and the trio were no longer welcome. Ross University agreed to transfer them. Butt said, "Not once did we mention September 11. Not once did we mention anything about September 13, nor did we joke about anything of that sort. She was probably just eavesdropping on our conversation and might have heard a few key words that she misconstrued. The eavesdropper stood by her report.

September 13, 2002. *Netherlands.* Dutch police arrested Najmuddin Faraj Ahmad (alias Mullah Krekar), a Kurd suspected by the United States of leading the militant Islamic Ansar al-Islam in northern Iraq that had close ties to the Taliban. The group is suspected of hiding al Qaeda fugitives. Police grabbed him at Amsterdam's Schiphol Airport as he was on a stopover from Tehran to Oslo, Norway, where his relatives live as refugees. He came to Norway in 1991. Jordan requested extradition. In January 2003, the Dutch Justice Minister unexpectedly released and deported Krekar to Norway despite the Jordanian request.

On June 15, 2004, the Norwegian prosecutor dropped all changes against Krekar, now 47, citing lack of evidence and fears that witness testimony in Iraq was coerced. Police had believed that he financed terrorism and plotted to kill rivals in northern Iraq in 2000 and 2001.

September 13–14, 2002. *United States.* In late evening and early morning raids at residences and a social club, U.S. officials arrested five U.S. citizens of Yemeni descent residing in Lackawanna, a suburb of Buffalo, New York, who were identified as an al Qaeda trained terrorist cell on American soil. The five had attended an al Qaeda training camp in Afghanistan, learning how to use assault rifles, handguns, and other weapons, in June 2001, and left the camp before the September 11 attacks. They were charged with providing, attempting to provide, and conspiring to provide material support and resources to a foreign terrorist group (al Qaeda), which entail a maximum 15-year prison sentence. The recruits at the al-Farooq camp, which is located near Kandahar, were addressed by bin Laden. The camp was also attended by American Taliban John Walker Lindh.

The defendants were identified as Faysal Galab, 26, Sahim Alwan, 29, Yahya Goba, 25, Shafal Mosed, 24, and Hasein Taher (variant Ther), 24, who lived within a few blocks of one another. Two associates were believed to be in Yemen; another was out of the country. The associates, identified only as A, B, and C, included two U.S. citizens from Lackawanna. Prosecutors later identified the ringleader as unindicted coconspirator Kamal Derwish, 29, believed to be living in Yemen. The defendants were later joined by Mukhtar al-Bakri, 22, who, with Alwan, admitted attending the camp. Al-Bakri was arrested in Bahrain a day after he was married earlier in the month. He was accused of sending an e-mail warning of a "very big meal" to come, code words for an al Qaeda attack. "No one will be able to withstand it, except those with faith," said

the e-mail. His lawyer said he was merely referring to a third-hand warning at a dinner in Saudi Arabia. Al-Bakri had cocaptained the championship Lackawanna High School soccer team. His presence in Bahrain so concerned U.S. officials that they closed the U.S. Embassy there and had him arrested.

At the September 19 bail hearing, Alwan was represented by court-appointed attorney James Harrington, who said his client was seeking religious training at the Tablighi Jamaat religious school in Pakistan and naively visited the camp. Alwan said, "I was scared and missed my family, and on Day Six I pleaded to let me go. I faked an ankle injury to get them to let me go." Prosecutors said al-Bakri may have gone on to Bahrain in the summer of 2002 to plot a "very huge" attack. Alwan had worked as a security guard at the Iroquois Job Corps Center in Medina, New York. He had told the *Buffalo News* in September 2001 that he had been attacked by seven men during the Persian Gulf War in 1991. Attorney Patrick J. Brown, representing Mosed, said, "If Mr. Alwan is the head of a sleeper cell, he is not to be trusted. There was no proof that Mosed was there." Taher was represented by Rodney Persnius (variant Personius), who said that there was no proof his client was at the camp, but anyway, he didn't stay long. Alwan was represented by James Harrington.

The defendants were well-known in the local community. One was voted the high school's friendliest senior. Four are married; three have children.

Prosecutors noted that Mosed had spent $89,000 at the Casino Niagara in Canada within the year.

The FBI had begun an investigation when the men came to Lackawanna in June 2001. The Bureau said there was no evidence that they were planning a specific attack in the United States.

Federal prosecutors noted on September 27 that some of the accused had tapes and documents in their homes that called for suicide operations against Islam's "enemies." On September 25, authorities searching Yasein Tahein's

Hamburg, New York, apartment found a document that said, "Martyrdom or self-sacrifice operations are those performed by one or more people against enemies far outstripping them in numbers and equipment. The form this usually takes nowadays is to wire up one's body, or a vehicle or suitcase with explosives, and then to enter into a conglomeration of the enemy, or in their vital facilities, and to detonate in an appropriate place there in order to cause the maximum losses in enemy ranks." Sahim Alwan and Yahya Goba had audiotapes in their apartments that called for jihad and martyrdom. One of Alwan's tapes included a lecture by a radical Islamic cleric who called for "fighting the West and invading Europe and America with Islam." Mukhtar al-Bakri, still in Bahrain, told the FBI that bin Laden told them in the training camp that there "is going to be a fight against Americans," and that he was trained to fight Americans. Authorities found a registered pistol and rifle from a New York residence used by al-Bakri. Shafal Mosed had two different social security cards in his possession and 11 credit cards for six different names.

U.S. Magistrate H. Kennedy Schroeder, Jr., said he would rule on bail on October 3.

During the bail hearing, the defense claimed that prosecutors had used misleading evidence. The bail decision was expected to be rendered on October 8. Goba was represented by Buffalo public defender Marianne Mariano.

On October 8, Judge Schroeder released on $600,000 bond Sahim Alwan, but ordered the other five held without bail. Alwan had assisted the FBI after returning from Afghanistan. The judge said he must remain in his home most of the day and must pay for a Global Positioning (GPS) device that would track his every movement. He must also allow the FBI to search him or his home at any time. One of his phone lines would be tapped.

On October 21, a federal grand jury indicted the six on charges of providing and attempting to provide support to al Qaeda and with conspiring to provide material support to the terrorists.

They pleaded not guilty the next day to charges that they trained at an al Qaeda camp. They faced 15 years in prison.

On November 3, 2002, a U.S. Predator—reported by the press to be a CIA unmanned aerial vehicle—fired a Hellfire missile in Yemen at a car carrying a group of suspected al Qaeda terrorists, killing six of them, including Qaed Salim Sunian al-Harithi, wanted for the USS *Cole* bombing of October 12, 2000. With him in the car was Kamal Derwish (alias Ahmed Hijazi), one of two unindicted coconspirators in the Lackawanna case. The *Washington Post* noted that he appeared to have U.S. citizenship and was also a citizen of an unidentified Middle Eastern country. He was not born in the United States but had resided in the United States for an unknown period. He traveled often between the United States and Saudi Arabia. Prosecutors believed he had recruited the defendants for al Qaeda. Documents, weapons, and satellite telephones were found in the burned-out car.

On January 10, 2003, Faysal Galab pleaded guilty in the Western District of New York to a reduced charge of providing "funds and services" to bin Laden and al Qaeda, by attending the al Farooq terrorism training camp in spring 2001 in Afghanistan. The plea bargain included him agreeing to testify against the other defendants in exchange for a seven year sentencing recommendation from prosecutors. The defendants faced 15-year sentences.

On March 24, 2003, Shafal Mosed, 24, the college student and marketer, pleaded guilty in federal court in Buffalo to providing "material support" to al Qaeda by attending the al Farooq camp, a stronger charge than Galab's "funds and services." His attorney, Patrick Brown, said, "He is ashamed that he went. He absolutely does not buy into that, the al Qaeda party line." This was the first time an individual had been convicted of providing material support to al Qaeda. The conviction carries a ten-year sentence, but his cooperation was expected to shorten it to eight years. Sentencing was scheduled for July 16. Brown said Mosed agreed to the plea because he feared the government would tack on more serious charges, including treason and serving as an enemy combatant.

On March 25, 2003, Yahya Goba, 26, pleaded guilty, saying he attended the al Qaeda training camp and allowed a terrorist recruiter to stay in his home through September 11, 2001. He pleaded guilty to one count of providing material support to bin Laden and al Qaeda. The other three were discussing their own plea agreements.

On April 8, 2003, Sahim Alwan acknowledged that he had met bin Laden in Afghanistan in 2001 and pleaded guilty to charges of support to al Qaeda by attending the al Farooq camp and receiving weapons training there.

On May 12, Yasein Taher pleaded guilty to supporting terrorism, admitting to learning to fire guns and grenade launchers at the camp. He acted against his attorney's advice. He was expected to receive an eight year prison term when sentenced in September. Prosecutors said he was a member of a sleeper cell. The other men had been offered sentences of seven to ten years, contingent upon their cooperation in terrorism investigations. A conviction could entail a 15-year sentence.

On May 19, 2003, Mukhtar al-Bakri became the final member of the Lackawanna Six to plead guilty to supporting the group by attending the camp.

On May 21, an FBI criminal complaint charged a seventh man, Jaber Elbaneh, 36, with conspiring to provide support to al Qaeda. He was believed to be abroad. Prosecutors said other arrests were possible.

On December 3, 2003, a federal court in New York gave a ten-year sentence and a fine of $2,000 to Mukhtar al-Bakri, 23, the first of the six defendants. He was the last to accept a plea bargain and was one of only two who completed the training program. He could have received 15 years at trial.

On December 4, Yasein Taher, 25, was sentenced to eight years. He said, "I'd just like to apologize to the court, my family, the community, and most important my country. I know I've let a lot of people down."

On December 9, Shafal Mosed, 25, received eight years.

On December 10, Yahya Goba, 26, received ten years.

On December 17, Sahim Alwan, 31, became the last member of the group to be sentenced, receiving nine years.

September 14, 2002. *Afghanistan.* A fuel tanker truck carrying aviation fuel and with sticks of dynamite attached to it was found by Afghan soldiers and international peacekeepers at a checkpoint in the south on its way to Bagram Air Base, headquarters of the U.S. military in the country. Two men in the truck were arrested.

September 14, 2002. *People's Republic of China.* Du Shu Qiang, made with nerve agent tetramine—a rat poison banned in 1991—was deliberately placed in breakfast snacks at a small eatery in Tangshan on the outskirts of Nanjing, killing 100 people, many of them schoolchildren, and making 1,000 ill. Customers became ill after eating fried dough sticks, sesame cakes, and sticky rice buns. Blood poured from victims' mouths, ears, and noses as they collapsed.

On September 17, police arrested Chen Zhengping in Zhengzhou, a railroad junction hundreds of miles to the northwest. Chen said he was driven by jealousy and a hatred for a cousin, the owner of a competing snack shop.

September 15, 2002. *India.* In Dhamhal Hanijpora, Kashmir, armed militants fired on and then threw an improvised explosive device at the motorcade of the Minister of Tourism. Although he was unharmed, a police officer died and two others were injured. No one claimed credit.

September 16, 2002. *Israel.* On Yom Kippur, Abdelfatah Abudo, 25, threw several grenades at Israeli soldiers near an Israeli-controlled road intersection near the Jewish settlement of Gush Katif in the Gaza Strip. Soldiers shot and killed him. Abudo was an Egyptian who was visiting Gaza. 02091601

September 16, 2002. *France.* At 6:00 p.m., 50 French and Spanish police arrested Juan Antonio Olarra Guridi (alias Otsagi), 35, who heads the military wing of the Basque Nation and Liberty (ETA) and Ainhoa Mugica Goni (alias Olga the Viper), 32, as the duo returned from grocery shopping and approached a safe house in the Bourdeaux suburb of Talence. They were believed responsible for assassinating 20 people, including police officers and judges. Spanish Interior Minister Angel Acebes said the duo "were the ones who gave the orders, provided all the material for the attacks ... and most importantly, they were the ones who selected the targets." Mugica was accused of involvement in the 1995 car bombing against Jose Maria Aznar, then the opposition leader and now Prime Minister. Guridi was accused in the 1996 murder of former chief justice of the constitutional court Francisco Tomas y Valiente, who was shot in the head three times in his office at a Madrid law school. A neighbor had tipped off gendarmes two months earlier; police soon set up surveillance. Police seized a gun from Guridi. The duo surrendered without a fight. Police also grabbed Saroia Gallarada, 21, a Frenchwoman who had leased the two-bedroom apartment for two months, raising suspicions when she paid in cash. She is the daughter of a man who joined ETA in 1992. She had also lent the duo her car. Police believed Guridi succeeded Francisco Xabier Garcia Gaztelu, who was arrested in January 2001.

Police said they were using the apartment as a base for attacks into Spain. Guridi, born in Donostia, Spain, was linked to several murders in Spain, going back to 1991. Goni was born in San Sebastian and joined the ETA in 1994.

Their trial in Paris ended on January 10, 2003, when prosecutors demanded an eight-year prison term. Guridi said, "We tried several times to make peace proposals, and the solution will not come from a process like this one." Sentencing was set for February 2003. 02091602

September 16, 2002. *Singapore.* Police announced the arrests in August of 21 Islamic militants, disrupting an al Qaeda network planning to bomb the U.S., U.K., Australian, and Israeli embassies. Some 19 of the detainees belonged to Jemaah Islamiah (JI). The group had conducted reconnaissance of the intended targets at the direction of JI leaders, 15 of whom were arrested in December when the bomb plot was foiled. Two terrorists were linked to the Philippine Moro Islamic Liberation Front. All 21 were Singapore citizens, and held for "terrorism-related activities" under a law permitting indefinite detention without trial. Some of the militants had trained at al Qaeda camps in Afghanistan and at the Moro Islamic Liberation Front's Camp Abu Bakar in Mindanao. They included a butcher, taxi driver, used car salesman, and part-time foot reflexologist. 02091603

September 16, 2002. *Russia.* A land mine hidden at a busy intersection in Grozny, Chechnya, exploded as a passenger bus drove by, killing 8 and wounding 20.

September 17, 2002. *Israel.* At 9:50 a.m., a bomb exploded in the courtyard of the Ziff school, a Palestinian school in Yatta, a Hebron suburb, slightly injuring eight children. Palestinians blamed Jewish settlers. Police found and detonated a second bomb at the school. The first bomb was placed near the water taps. It shattered windows and heavily damaged walls, water pipes, and toilets. The injured included four boys aged 6 to 8 and four girls aged 11 to 13.

September 17, 2002. *Indonesia.* Jakarta police arrested Seyam Reda, a German of Afghan ancestry who worked for a German television network and who some news sources said had been rejected as a cameraman for al-Jazeera. He was held on suspicion of involvement in terrorism and misusing his tourist visa by working as a journalist. Police thought he could be Abu Daud, wanted in Singapore and Malaysia for links to international terrorism. Police believed he was involved with Omar al-Farouq, an al Qaeda operative from Kuwait who was arrested in June. Al-Farouq claimed he was to be the triggerman for a failed 1999 assassination attempt against President Megawati Sukarnoputri; his wife served as translator for the plot. Al-Farouq said he was part of a second assassination plot in 2002; the bomb exploded prematurely at a mall, blowing off the assassin's leg. The burly Reda speaks Arabic and German but little Indonesian. He was arrested in a $4,000 a month South Jakarta home with a swimming pool and internal camera system. In a search of the home, police found videotapes of al-Farouq giving weapons and military instruction to Islamic militants in eastern Indonesia. German police arrived the next week to assist in the investigation.

September 17, 2002. *Indonesia.* The U.S. Embassy warned American tourists visiting Yogyakarta in central Java of information that Westerners could be terrorist targets.

September 17, 2002. *India.* In Srinagar, Kashmir, armed militants shot and injured the leading editor of the *Urdu Daily Srinagar Times* at his residence. Elsewhere, militants threw a grenade at the office of a local political party, injuring a security guard. No one claimed credit for either attack.

September 18, 2002. *Sri Lanka.* In talks with the government, the Liberation Tigers of Tamil Eelam (LTTE) said they would accept self-determination, not independence, for the Tamil minority to end the 19-year civil war, a major concession. LTTE was led by chief negotiator Anton Balasingham.

September 18, 2002. *Israel.* At 4:50 p.m., one policeman was killed, one policeman lightly wounded, and a local resident seriously injured when a Palestinian strapped with explosives set them off at a busy intersection in Umm el-Fahm, an Israeli-Arab town near the West Bank in the north. Police said the bomber was a member of Islamic Jihad, although no group claimed credit. The terrorist was seen loitering near a bus stop.

When police came to investigate, the terrorist walked over to a police van and talked to the officers inside before setting off the bomb.

September 18, 2002. *Israel.* An Israeli was killed in a road ambush in Yahad. The al-Aqsa Martyrs Brigades gunmen overturned the vehicle on the Mevo Dotan-Hermesh Road, killing the Israeli and wounding a Romanian worker. 02091801

September 18, 2002. *Israel.* An Israeli was found dead and burned in a garbage dump.

September 18, 2002. *United States.* The FBI warned law enforcement agencies that al Qaeda had discussed using non-Arabic hijackers on commercial flights. Observers said that 10 to 20 al Qaeda affiliated Chechen Muslims already in the United States could overwhelm the crew after taking first class seats. The FBI warned that terrorists were searching for new ways to bring explosives onto planes, such as bringing liquid explosives mixed with coffee and hidden in carry-on bags.

September 19, 2002. *Israel.* At 1:00 p.m., a Palestinian man set off a bomb in a crowded Number 4 bus at Tel Aviv's Allenby Street, killing 5, including the driver and a U.K. citizen, and injuring 52. The bomber boarded near Rothschild Street and set off the bomb at the front of the bus a few seconds later. The bomb was packed with metal shards. The shopping strip includes outdoor cafés, restaurants, and shops. The bus was outside a major synagogue and across the street from a Starbucks. The explosion shattered the door of the Lotus bookshop of Yaakov Chen, 87. Salesclerk Carmit Ovadia, 24, who was on the bus, suffered shrapnel wounds in her feet. Islamic Jihad claimed credit, as did Hamas.

Hours later, Israeli tanks laid siege again to Yasir Arafat's compound in Ramallah, holding 300 plus people. Israel demanded the surrender of 20 to 25 wanted terrorists inside the compound. 02091901

September 19, 2002. *Germany.* Police raided 100 homes and offices and froze bank accounts in several communities after outlawing another 16 groups connected to jailed Turkish militant Mohammed Metin Kaplan. Kaplan was serving time for his role in the killing of a rival cleric in 1997 and plotting an airplane attack in Turkey. The groups were part of the Cologne-based Caliphate State. The Caliphate State called for the overthrow of Turkey's secular government and its replacement with an Islamic state. Banned in December, the Interior Minister called it "a breeding ground for terrorists." The group was also banned because of its anti-Semitic and anti-Israel statements and for its attempts to develop its own tax and legal systems.

September 20, 2002. *United States.* Mekki Hamed Mekki, 30, a Sudanese pilot, was held in North Carolina for making false statements while applying for a U.S. visa. Investigators were attempting to determine whether he was an al Qaeda terrorist planning to fly a plane into a U.S. target. Several other Sudanese were held elsewhere while federal authorities tried to determine if they had ties to Mekki. A court date was set for September 23.

September 20, 2002. *Hong Kong.* On November 5, local authorities announced the arrests of three men attempting to buy four Stinger missiles from undercover FBI agents during a September 20 meeting in a Hong Kong hotel. On November 6, the U.S. Justice Department announced that a naturalized U.S. citizen living in Minneapolis and two Pakistanis were indicted on October 30 for offering to trade 5 metric tons of hashish and 600 kilograms of heroin for four Stingers they would then sell to the Taliban and al Qaeda. Syed Mustajab Shah, 54, and Muhammed Abid Afridi, 29, were from Peshawar, Pakistan; Ilyas Ali, 55, of Minneapolis, was a naturalized U.S. citizen from India. They fought extradition to the United States. Hong Kong Magistrate Ariana Ching scheduled extradition proceedings for January 12, 2003. They were represented by attorney Jonathan Acton-Bond. An indictment in the U.S. District Court in Southern California said that Ali met in April with undercover FBI agents in San Diego to discuss drug deals. The drug charges each carried life sentences and fines of $4 million; supporting terrorists carries a sentence of 15 years and a $250,000 fine. On March 8, 2003, the trio pleaded guilty in a San Diego court to the charges. They were held without bond pending a detention hearing in federal court scheduled for March 12. They had arrived from Hong Kong on March 6 after having given up their extradition battle.

September 20, 2002. *India.* In Jammu, Kashmir, armed militants killed a senior National Conference Party worker in his home. No one claimed credit.

September 20, 2002. *India.* In Srinagar, Kashmir, armed militants opposed to Indian-held elections killed a political activist of the ruling National Conference Party. The Hizb ul-Mujahedin was suspected.

September 22, 2002. *Indonesia.* At 3:30 a.m., a low-explosive Toyota car bomb went off outside a U.S. embassy warehouse in Jakarta, killing one of four Indonesian passengers. The property had once been used as temporary housing on a residential street in the Menteng neighborhood. Police detained the driver; the other two fled. The car struck an electrical transformer and caught fire before exploding. National Police Chief Da'i Bachtiar told the press that the passengers intended to throw the grenade at the embassy warehouse, but the police shifted their story.

On October 10, the Bush administration warned Indonesia that it would withdraw some diplomats unless police stepped up the investigation of the network of Islamic radicals believed responsible. Two of the suspects were tracked to a house in Purwakarta, 70 miles east of Jakarta, that was frequented by other militants. Police believed that the grenade went off prematurely and that the men were about to collect a

$500,000 debt from Hasyim Setiono, the owner of a neighboring house. Police claimed that terrorism was ruled out, a claim that was disputed by the United States. 02092201

September 22, 2002. *India.* In Shopian, Kashmir, armed militants threw grenades and fired at the residence of the ruling National Conference legislator who was at his home at the time; he was not hurt. In Bandgam, Kashmir, armed militants shot to death the ruling Block president. No one claimed credit for either attack.

September 23, 2002. *India.* In Bijbiara, Kashmir, militants threw a grenade at a vehicle belonging to the Jammu and Kashmir People's Democratic Party. The grenade missed its target and exploded on the roadside, injuring eight people. In Sangam, Kashmir, armed militants attempted to throw a grenade at a political rally, but it missed the intended victims and exploded near a group of private citizens, injuring eight. In Srinagar, Kashmir, militants threw a grenade at an army vehicle but missed; the bomb exploded in a crowded marketplace, injuring 12 civilians and 2 police officers. No one claimed credit for any of the attacks.

September 25, 2002. *Pakistan.* Two bearded gunmen ran into the Karachi office of the Organization for Peace and Justice, a Catholic and Protestant-supported group that gives free legal advice to poor industrial workers and women, bound and gagged their victims, then shot seven Christians in the head at point-blank range. A Muslim eyewitness said the terrorists took 15 minutes to segregate the Christians, asking each worker to recite a well-known Islamic verse. Six victims were forced to sit together at a table in the library, where they were tied to chairs. A seventh was fatally shot in the bathroom. An eighth man was critically wounded with a gunshot to the head. The Muslim eyewitness was severely beaten by the terrorists, but alerted police after the attackers ran off. Police blamed Harkat ul-Mujaheddin al-Almi, a splinter of Harkat ul-Mujaheddin, for the attack at Rimpa Plaza, a

13-story building in Karachi's commercial district.

September 25, 2002. *India.* Gunmen took over a Hindu temple in Gandhinagar while 600 pilgrims were conducting evening prayers, killing 33 men, women, and children and holding dozens more in a 14-hour hostage siege. In a rescue operation, National Security Guard commandos killed two gunmen. A policeman died in the gun battle; ten more were wounded. More than 70 people were injured inside the Akshardham temple complex. The two dead terrorists appeared to be in their early 20s and were carrying dry fruits, dates, sweets, and Indian notes and coins in their pockets. They also had letters written in Urdu. Brigadier Sita Pathi, who headed the antiterrorist commandos, said, "They resemble Kashmiri militants, but I can say anything for certain because they are not carrying identity [documents]." Among those pilgrims who escaped during the attack were Vipul Soni, 15, and Gurumukh Palwani, 40, and his two children. The World Hindu Council's Gujarat unit called a demonstration to protest the attack on the temple, which is built with pink sandstone and visited by two million people annually. During the demonstrations, Hindu nationalist mobs stabbed two Muslim men in the west. Some officials suggested Pakistani complicity.

September 25, 2002. *France.* Customs agents found three and a half ounces of pentrite explosives—but no detonator—in the passenger section of a Royal Air Maroc plane after it landed in eastern France. The plane had taken off from Marseille for Marrakech before heading to Metz-Lorraine-Nancy Airport in eastern France.

On October 4, prosecutors said they believed that terrorists had tried to blow up the plane and were opening a formal criminal investigation for "attempted murder and attempt to destroy an aircraft in relation with a terrorist network." The explosives were wrapped in aluminum foil. No prints were found. Pentrite was used by Richard Reid, the would-be shoe bomber, in his failed

December 22, 2001, bomb attempt on an American Airlines flight from Paris to Miami. 02092501

September 27, 2002. *Jordan.* The U.S. Embassy alerted U.S. citizens that Washington had received information indicating that during the summer, an al Qaeda member was planning to kidnap U.S. citizens in Jordan.

September 27, 2002. *Malaysia.* Police arrested former university lecturer Wan Min Wan Mat in northern Kelantan state as a threat to national security. He was identified as one of the leaders of Jemaah Islamiah in Malaysia. The group is linked to al Qaeda and had planned to bomb United States and other targets.

September 27, 2002. *India.* In Pulwama, Kashmir, a grenade exploded on the road, injuring five soldiers and 17 civilians. The attack came just before the country's scheduled elections.

September 28, 2002. *Bangladesh.* Two bombs exploded inside the Roxie Cinema Hall, a movie theater in Satkhira, 100 miles southwest of Dhaka; two more went off a few blocks away in a crowded circus at a stadium in the town center. The bombs killed at least 10 people and injured 200. No one claimed credit.

September 28, 2002. *Afghanistan.* At 9:00 p.m., one or two bombs exploded, damaging a Defense Ministry apartment not far from the U.S. Embassy in Kabul. Reports differed as to whether it was two bombs or an echo that people heard.

September 28, 2002. *Turkey.* The media initially reported that paramilitary police in Sanliurfa in southeastern Turkey seized 35 pounds of refined fissionable (weapons-grade) uranium in a lead tube hidden in a taxicab and detained two men accused of smuggling the material across the Syrian border. International Atomic Energy Agency monitors were skeptical. The seized material was initially reported as nearly half as much as was used in the bomb on Hiroshima. It was later determined that police mistakenly had included the weight of the lead container—the radioactive material weighed three ounces. The duo was identified as Mehmet Demir and Saliah Yasar, who were arraigned that night on charges of trafficking. On September 30, Atomic Energy Institute Chief Guler Koksal said that the harmless material contained zinc, iron, zirconium, and manganese. The two Turks, who were trying to sell the material as uranium, were freed.

In 1998, local authorities seized ten pounds of unprocessed uranium and six grams of plutonium smuggled from the former Soviet Union. In November 2001, Istanbul police arrested two men who offered undercover agents two pounds of uranium wrapped in a newspaper.

September 28, 2002. *India.* In Devsar, Kashmir, a land mine exploded under a vehicle carrying a National Congress Party member and three other people. The explosion killed the three passengers and injured the National Congress Party member. No one claimed credit.

September 29, 2002. *Pakistan.* A small bomb exploded outside a remote village church hours after thousands demonstrated in Karachi to demand government protection of the minority Christian community.

September 29, 2002. *Saudi Arabia.* A car bomb killed a German man in Riyadh. A string of car bombings against foreigners was attributed to alcohol-smuggling gang battles.

September 29, 2002. *United States.* Nikolay Volodicv Dzhonev, 21, was charged with possession of a prohibited weapon when federal screeners at Atlantic City International Airport found a pair of scissors hidden in a bar of soap and two box cutters in a lotion bottle in the Bulgarian student's backpack. Egg Harbor Township police said he was held on $100,000 bail. He had a summer visa permitting him to work at a local convenience store. He was the last passenger to be screened for a flight to Myrtle Beach, South Carolina. Screeners spotted the scissors in the x-ray machine; a subsequent search found the box cutters. He had purchased his one-way Spirit Airlines ticket on the Internet in August. He claimed he packed those items to prevent them from damaging anything else in the backpack.

On October 1, prosecutors said that he had no apparent ties to terrorism and charged him with attempting to board an aircraft with a concealed weapon, a felony. On October 10, he struck a plea agreement. He pleaded guilty to knowingly and willfully violating airport rules. He was sentenced to a five-year probation and ordered to leave the country.

September 29, 2002. *India.* In Tral, Kashmir, militants threw a grenade at a bus station, killing 1 and injuring 12. In Ganderbal, Kashmir, armed militants killed a political activist of the ruling National Conference Party. No one claimed credit for either attack.

September 30, 2002. *Georgia.* The government announced that no more rebel groups were in the Pankisi Gorge and invited Russian observers to verify the statement.

September 30, 2002. *United States/Germany.* The U.S. and German governments blocked the financial assets of Ramzi Binalshibh, Mounir Motassadeq, Zakariya Essabar, and Said Bahaji, all of whom were implicated in the September 11 investigation.

September 30, 2002. *India.* In Manda Chowk, Kashmir, a time bomb exploded on a bus carrying Hindu pilgrims, killing 1 and injuring 18. No one claimed credit.

October 2002. *Colombia.* In the first week of October, leftist guerrillas attacked the 500-mile Occidental Petroleum/Ecopetrol oil pipeline near Arauquita, sending a dark plume of smoke into the sky. Two days earlier, rebels fired mortars into the Cano-Limon oil complex, damaging four wells. To date, guerrillas had attacked the pipeline 20 times, down from the 170 attacks in 2001. 02109901-02

October 2002. *Lebanon.* The judiciary arrested 2 Lebanese and 1 Saudi man, and indicted 18 others *in absentia* on charges of preparing to carry out terrorist attacks and forging documents and passports. Because of their al Qaeda connections, the group will be tried in a military tribunal.

October 2002. *Jordan.* The State Security Court sentenced four individuals to prison terms ranging from five to eight years after convicting them of possessing and attempting to transport machine guns and missiles into the West Bank.

October 2002. *Italy.* The captain of the *Sara*, a freighter belonging to the Nova firm, which is registered in Delaware and Romania, radioed to Italian maritime authorities that 15 Pakistani men were menacing the crew. The captain had been forced to take them on board in Casablanca, Morocco, by the ship's owner. U.S. and Italian naval officers questioned the 15, who claimed to be crewmen. The captain said they knew nothing about sailing. American authorities found tens of thousands of dollars, false documents, maps of Italian cities, and evidence that the 15 had ties to al Qaeda members in Europe. They were charged in Italy with conspiracy to engage in terrorist acts. 02109903

October 2002. *United Kingdom.* The government proscribed 4 terrorist groups associated with al Qaeda—Jemaah Islamiah, the Abu Sayyaf Group, the Islamic Movement of Uzbekistan, and Asbat al-Ansar—bringing to 25 the number of groups banned under the Terrorism Act of 2000.

October 2, 2002. *United States.* A sniper began a series of shootings in suburban Washington, D.C., killing ten and wounding three in the space of three weeks. Some speculated that terrorists were involved; others believed it was a lone nut or a gang-related shooting. Some witnesses said they saw more than one person in a series of getaway vehicles—a box truck and two white vans.

Thacher stepped down from the Muhammad case in Fairfax County. He was replaced by Fairfax County Circuit Court Judge M. Lanhorne Keith. On October 1, 2004, Judge Keith dismissed the capital murder charges, a ruling that could not be appealed. He said that the law required that a jail defendant must be brought to trial within five months and that the arrest occurred when Fairfax authorities sent notice to the Prince William County Jail on January 6, 2004, seeking Muhammad's detention.

On September 24, 2004, Malvo's lawyers said that a plea deal in Spotsylvania County would give him another life sentence but rule out the death penalty. He pleaded guilty on October 26 and received two more life terms in the death of Kenneth Bridges and wounding of Caroline Seawell.

October 2, 2002. *Philippines.* At 8:30 p.m., U.S. Army SFC Mark Wayne Jackson, a Special Forces soldier stationed at Camp Enrile, and two Filipinos were killed when a remotely detonated bomb exploded on a motorcycle on a street frequented by U.S. and local troops in Malagutay, near Zamboanga City. The explosion occurred outside a karaoke bar and outdoor food stand owned by a Philippine soldier. Twenty-three others, including a U.S. soldier assigned to the Green Berets, were injured. The blast also destroyed the roofs of several houses and nearby shops. The food stand belonged to Rodolfo and Natividad Enriquez. Rodolfo, a retired master sergeant, suffered a head injury. Darlene Enriquez sustained burns and bruises on her arms and face. A sister-in-law had eye injuries. Cherry Enriquez, 29, was knocked unconscious. No one claimed credit, although the previous week Khadaffy Abubakar Janjalani, an Abu Sayyaf leader, told Radio Mindanao Network that his group would attack U.S. civilian and military targets to retaliate for government offensives against the rebels. On October 7, Philippine immigration agents took into custody a Middle Eastern man, believed to be a Palestinian member of Hamas. Other authorities said he was

Mohammed Amin al Ghaffari, a Jordanian arrested in Zamboanga City (or Manila) for visa violations. Ghaffari ran the Islamic Worldwide Mission, a nongovernmental organization linked to al Qaeda. He was being questioned for financing the bombing. Authorities were also looking into links to Jemaah Islamiah. Investigators were surveilling four foreigners suspected of dealing with Abu Sayyaf. Two men seen in the vicinity of the bombing were known to have taken Abu Sayyaf urban guerrilla training on Mindanao Island. Police said the bomb was similar to one that exploded in September at a Zamboanga City bus terminal and an unexploded bomb found in August in Jolo.

Police announced on October 13 that they believed Abu Sayyaf was responsible. They noted that Janjalani phoned a close friend three days before the bombing to warn "you be careful, there will be a car bomb." After the bombing, he called to warn his friend of further bombings in the city. Investigators also said that they did not have enough evidence to charge al-Ghaffari in the case. He applied for voluntary deportation.

On February 12, 2003, the Philippines ordered the expulsion of Iraqi Embassy Second Secretary Husham Hussein, who had cell phone contact with two Abu Sayyaf rebels in Jakarta before the bombing. One rebel was in prison at the time of the bombing; the other was later arrested and linked to the bombing. 02100201

October 2, 2002. *India.* In Haihama, Kashmir, al-Arifeen terrorists killed three political activists working with India's ruling National Conference Party.

October 3, 2002. *United States.* At 1:10 p.m., Steve Kim, 57, a Korean American protesting against North Korea, fired seven shots from a .357 pistol in front of UN headquarters, hitting several offices but causing no injuries. The naturalized U.S. citizen who works at a U.S. post office in Des Plaines, Illinois, was born in 1945, apparently in Korea. At the time of the shooting, the UN Security Council was meeting on Iraq.

U.S. Secret Service agents, in the area to protect Cyprus President Glafcos Clerides, grabbed Kim just outside the building. Kim threw anti-North Korean leaflets in the area. He was expected to be arraigned in federal court in Manhattan for violation of the Protection of Foreign Officials Act. On April 3, 2003, he pleaded guilty to a single charge of making a violent attack on foreign officials. He said he did not intend to hurt anyone. He faced three years in prison. Sentencing was set for July 22, 2003. 02100301

October 4, 2002. *France.* A gunman driving an SUV shot at the window of a café in Dunkirk. He then fired at the fleeing customers, injuring three. Later, the gunman shot and killed Mohamed Maghara, 17, of Moroccan origin, outside Grande-Synthe café frequented by North Africans. Police officials deemed it an "obviously racist" attack. On October 6, a 45-year-old truck driver confessed. 02100401

October 4, 2002. *United States.* Federal authorities indicted six people from Portland, Oregon, including a former U.S. Army reservist, for conspiracy to join al Qaeda and the Taliban to wage war against the United States in Afghanistan after the September 11 attacks. None had arrived in Afghanistan, although two were still at large and believed to be overseas. The five men and one woman were charged with conspiracy to levy war against the United States, conspiracy to provide material support to a terrorist group, and conspiracy to contribute services to al Qaeda and the Taliban. The indictment said that in late 2001, five of the six tried to go through China, Bangladesh, or Indonesia to Afghanistan to fight American soldiers, but failed to enter Pakistan because of visa and financial problems.

The case began a fortnight after September 11, when Mark Mercer, a deputy sheriff in Skamania County, Washington, saw five men in Middle Eastern clothes take target practice with a shotgun, a Chinese assault rifle, and a semiautomatic pistol in a private quarry in Washougal, Washington. A few weeks later, he noticed one of them on television being arrested on weapons charges. He called the FBI about the suspect, Lebanese immigrant Ali Khaled Steitiye, a Hamas supporter who had received paramilitary training with pro-Palestinian militants in Lebanon. In October, FBI agents worked to find the four other shooters, but determined that they had left days earlier for Afghanistan.

Among those charged was Jeffrey Leon Battle, 32, who had served in the U.S. Army Reserves in 2000 in an Oregon military engineering unit. He failed to appear for drills and other reserve duties, so was discharged in 2002. The indictment said he had enlisted "in order to receive training in U.S. military tactics and weapons which he intended to use against the United States and in support of al Qaeda and the Taliban."

Another defendant was October Martinique Lewis (alias Khadijah), 25, Battle's ex-wife and the first woman charged in the indictments of 18 al Qaeda supporters in the United States. She wired money several times to the travelers. A neighbor reported that Battle's five-year-old son by another woman said, "Those people deserved to die," referring to the September 11 victims. Neighbors noticed Battle and Lewis meeting in their apartment building with nine or ten bearded men in Middle Eastern clothes.

At 6:00 a.m., federal agents scooped up Battle, Lewis, and Patrice Lumumba Ford, 31, in Portland. Police grabbed Muhammad Ibrahim Bilal, 22, in Dearborn, Michigan. Bilal's brother, Ahmed Ibrahim Bilal, 24, and Habis Abdulla al Saoub, 36, remained at large. al Saoub is a permanent U.S. resident born in Jordan. The others were U.S.–born American citizens.

Battle, Ford, al Saoub, and Ahmed Bilal were also indicted on charges of possessing and firing firearms in furtherance of a crime. Al Saoub left a "martyr's will" addressed to mujaheddin leaders.

Muhammad Bilal was extradited to Portland, where he once resided. Most of his family is in Saudi Arabia.

Ford's father, Kent, had been a member of the Black Panthers and named his son after the first Congolese president. Patrice Lumumba Ford spoke Mandarin Chinese, graduated from a local high school in 1989, and enrolled in Portland State University, studying international relations with a focus on East Asia. He had studied martial arts as a child. In the summer of 1998 and in September 1999, he was an international relations intern for Portland Mayor Vera Katz. He had also interned for previous Mayor Bud Clark in 1996. He had interned in the mayor's office of Kaohsiung, Portland's sister city in Taiwan. While there, he converted to Islam and met and married a Chinese woman. He taught physical education at the Islamic School of the Muslim Education Trust near Portland. In 2001, he sent threatening messages to members of the mayor's staff, who turned them over to police.

Battle and Lewis married in 1999 in Portland but divorced after five months. They apparently continued to cohabit. They had worked as nursing assistants at a retirement home. October Lewis was born in Vallejo, California. Battle was from Houston, where they met before moving to Portland. Battle obtained a license to work as an unarmed security guard in August 1998, then worked for the Portland-based security firm First Response. In September 2000, he created the as-Sabiqun Vanguard Security Corporation, which was dissolved by the state a year later after he failed to file an annual report. He joined the U.S. Army Reserves in fall 1999 and was assigned to the 671st Engineer Company in Portland; the group specializes in bridge construction. He underwent basic training in Fort Jackson, South Carolina, but failed to appear for advanced training at Fort Lee, Virginia, and was administratively dismissed.

Steitiye was named an unindicted coconspirator who lied in August 2001 to an Oregon gun dealer about a number of previous arrests and a felony conviction while purchasing an assault rifle. He was arrested in October 2001 with weapons and 1,000 rounds of ammunition. His house contained $20,000 in cash and photos of

him training in Lebanon with guerrillas. In September 2002, he was sentenced to two and a half years in prison on gun and fraud charges. Sheikh Mohamed Kariye, the imam of his mosque, the Islamic Center of Portland, had been indicted on charges of committing social security fraud from 1983 to 1995. Kariye had cofounded the Global Relief Foundation which is under investigation for al Qaeda ties.

On October 4, Ford pleaded not guilty to charges.

On October 7, Battle and Lewis pleaded not guilty in U.S. District Court in Portland to four federal counts, including one of conspiracy to "levy war against the U.S." Federal Magistrate Janice Stewart ordered October Lewis freed on bail on October 10; the decision was subject to a review by a federal judge the next day.

Federal prosecutors presented tape recordings of Battle speaking of attacking synagogues and schools, killing or injuring those inside. He considered but rejected a suicide attack, according to prosecutors. The FBI found articles and books in the couple's home and car that encouraged violent jihad.

On October 8, Ahmed Ibrahim Bilal surrendered to Malaysian authorities at the International Islamic School outside Kuala Lumpur, where he had been studying since early 2002. U.S. authorities revoked his passport, giving Malaysia grounds to hold him. He was extradited to the United States the next day. On October 15, he pleaded not guilty to being part of the sleeper cell.

On November 4, a federal judge in Portland set an October 1, 2003, trial date for the five.

On March 20, 2003, authorities arrested Maher "Mike" Hawash, 38, who had worked for Intel Corporation as a software engineer since 1992. He was held without charge under the federal material witness statute. On April 28, he was charged in Portland with conspiring to travel to Afghanistan to fight with al Qaeda and the Taliban against American troops. He had traveled in October 2001 with five members of the Portland Six to China. A neighbor identified him as a friend of Ahmed Bilal and Habis al Saoub.

Hawash was born in the West Bank and became a U.S. citizen in 1990. Hawash pleaded not guilty on May 5. On August 6, he pleaded guilty to a federal charge of conspiring to help the Taliban. According to his attorney, Stephen House, he agreed to testify against the Six at their trial, which was to begin in January 2004. Federal prosecutors agreed to drop terrorism charges, which carried a sentence of 20 plus years. He expected to serve seven to ten years in prison.

On September 18, 2003, Ahmed Bilal and Muhammad Bilal formally pleaded guilty to firearms charges and of conspiring to help al Qaeda and the Taliban. In turn, the prosecution dropped the charge of conspiring to levy war against the United States. Ahmed agreed to 10 to 14 years in prison; Muhammad agreed to 8 to 14 years. U.S. District Judge Robert E. Jones did not set a sentencing date. A pretrial hearing for those who had not pleaded was set for October 1.

On September 30, 2003, Abdurahman Alamoudi, 51, founder of the American Muslim Foundation and the American Muslim Council, was charged with illegally accepting money from Libya to influence U.S. policy and funding terrorists in the United States and abroad. Federal prosecutors said that the $340,000 he was carrying when arrested in August 2003 in London en route to Syria "was intended for delivery in Damascus to one or more of the terrorists or terrorist organizations active in Syria" such as al Qaeda, Hizballah, Islamic Resistance Movement (Hamas), and Palestine Islamic Jihad. The U.S. District Court in Alexandria, Virginia, was told that he had also given four checks for several hundred dollars each to pay the "salary" of Patrice Lumumba Ford. Two other checks paid the utilities of Ahmed Bilal. Alamoudi obtained his U.S. citizenship in 1996; prosecutors said it was fraudulently obtained, as he had lied on his immigration application. He was represented by attorney May Kheder.

On October 16, 2003, in a plea bargain, Jeffrey Leon Battle and Patrice Lumumba Ford admitted in federal court in Portland to one count of conspiracy to levy war against the United States. The deal required each to serve 18 years in prison. The duo had faced life if convicted on 14 other counts. Cell leader Habis Abdulla al Saoub remained at large, although some press reports said he had recently been killed in Pakistan.

On February 9, 2004, Hawash was sentenced to seven years; Ahmed Bilal to ten years; and Muhammad Bilal to eight years. 02100402

October 5, 2002. *Germany.* Prosecutors announced raids in three towns against Islamic militants believed planning attacks. Five people, most of them in Cottbus, were believed to be aiming at "committing attacks to defend and spread Islamic values."

October 6, 2002. *Yemen.* At 9:15 a.m. in al-Dhabbah (variant al-Dabah), al Qaeda set off an explosion against the *Limburg*, a French supertanker, in the Arabia Sea five miles off the coast. In the explosion, a Bulgarian crew member drowned and four people were injured. The explosion blasted a 26-foot-wide oval hole with jagged metal edges pointing inward, caused a huge fire, and released 50,000 barrels of oil into the Gulf of Aden. Initial theories of it being an accident gave way to the terrorism theory when fiberglass fragments and the outboard motor of a small boat apparently used in the attack were found in the area. Local police arrested 20 people as "a pre-emptive measure." The boat's owners, Euronav SA, said a small boat was seen speeding toward it as it waited for a tug to take it to Mina al-Dabah near Mukalla. The height and angle of the hole at the waterline was not consistent with an accidental explosion to one of the tanks. The vessel was crewed by 25 French and Bulgarian sailors, and carried 400,000 barrels of Saudi crude. The two-year-old, double-hulled ship was destined for Malaysia.

Among the crew were Dimov Kircho, 55, Radev Villagco, first engineer Renaud Humbert-Droz, Georgi Novakov, and Capt. Hubert Adrillon.

The Aden-Abyan Army, an Islamic group, claimed credit. Yemeni officials said the group was active since the late 1990s, but was defunct since its leader was hanged for his role in the 1998 kidnapping of 16 Western tourists, 4 of whom died in a rescue operation.

On October 16, police found a rented house in al Mukalla, 350 miles southeast of San'a, where they believed the explosives were prepared.

By October 30, Yemeni authorities had detained 20 people.

On August 28, 2004, following a three-month trial, a Yemeni court convicted 15 men accused in the *Limburg* attack, a November 2002 attack on a helicopter carrying U.S. workers, and plots to kill the U.S. ambassador and Yemeni security authorities. Yemeni citizen Hazam Majali was sentenced to death for killing a Yemeni policeman at a checkpoint in 2002. The others received three to ten years in jail. Yasser Ali Salem, tried *in absentia*, received ten years for being a key plotter in the *Limburg* case and buying and delivering the explosives used. One received three years for falsifying documents in the attacks. Defense attorney Fayez Hajoury said, "We never got a chance to get hold of the files of the case," and therefore would appeal. Six defendants were sentenced by Judge Ahmed Jarmouzi to ten years in the *Limburg* case. Six were sentenced to five years for setting off explosives at embassies, plotting to assassinate U.S. Ambassador Edmund Hull and security officials, and roles in the helicopter case. The defendants had said that Saudi-born Rahim Nashiri had obtained funds for the *Limburg* case. He was also believed to be the mastermind of the USS *Cole* attack. 02100601

October 6, 2002. *Middle East.* Al-Jazeera played an audiotape by Osama bin Laden, who called upon Americans to convert and vowed to attack "the vital sectors of your economy." The al Qaeda leader said, "By God, the youths of God are preparing for you things that would fill your hearts with terror and target your economic lifeline until you stop your oppression and aggression" against Muslims. The voice on the tape said that Americans should "understand the message of the New York and Washington attacks which came in response to some of your previous crimes." Reuters provided the following excerpts:

About a year has passed since the start of the U.S. crusade declared by the U.S. president in which he led an international coalition of more than 90 nations against Afghanistan.

America is now preparing a new stage in its crusade against the Islamic world, this time against the Muslim Iraqi people to complete its scheme to divide and rupture the [Muslim] nation, rob its riches and pave the way for a greater Israel after expelling the Palestinians....

Oh, nation of Islam ... whether this whole nation is targeted without distinguishing between allies or foes is no longer an issue because the enemy helped us unveil this fact. The issue now is how do we face this flagrant aggression.

If we want God to grant us victory ... we should arm ourselves with several tools, including:

- a return to God through repentance, honest work and true intentions.

- to united under God. If it is true that conflict and differences are the main reasons for failure, matters our nation is suffering from, it is true that unity, consensus and faith are the key to victory and the gate to domination.

- to stimulate the nation's capabilities, most important of which is the Muslim who is the fuel of battle.

- Our nation is one of the richest on Earth. Its resources have for ages been exploited to serve our enemies and conspire against our brethren. And its vast military capabilities are rusting in warehouses in Islamic nations.

- It is high time that these capabilities are freed to explode and defend the targeted faith, the violated sanctity, the tarnished honor, the raped land and the robbed riches....

- The priority in this war at this stage must be against the infidels, the Americans and the Jews, who will not stop infringing upon us except through jihad.

There are also merchants and capitalists who are not any less important than others in pushing this battle forward to its aim of spreading God's religion and teachings on Earth. Your money will stop a flooding that seeks our destruction....

We congratulate the Muslim nation for the daring and heroic jihad operations which our brave sons conducted in Yemen against the Christian oil tanker and in Kuwait against the American occupation and aggression forces.

By striking the oil tanker in Yemen with explosives, the attackers struck at the umbilical cord of the Christians, reminding the enemy of the bloody price they have to pay for their continued aggression on our nation and robbing our riches.

The heroic Kuwait operation also proves the level of danger that threatens U.S. forces in Islamic countries, and the political office will issue two separate statements on the two operations and their indications....

The timing of the attack against a military target of such importance as Marine forces in Kuwait and the bombing of an economic target the size of the oil tanker in Yemen, and issuing oral and written statements from Taliban and al Qaeda leaders who America thought it had killed....

The fact that all this coincided with the one-year anniversary of the start of the Christian crusade is not a coincidence but a clear and strong message to all our enemies and friends alike that the Mujaheddin, thanks be to God, have not been weakened or exhausted and that God repaid those who sinned with their mischief.

We are continuing our path ... and we renew our promise to God, and to the nation, and our promise to the Americans and Jews that they will not be at peace and should not dream of security until they let our nations be and stop their aggression and support for our enemies. The unjust know what awaits them."

On October 8, the network ran a follow-up tape by Ayman Zawahiri, his first communique since December's bombing of Tora Bora, that threatened attacks against "America and its allies." Zawahiri said that France and Germany were "deputies of America" and "we advise them to make a hasty retreat from Palestine, the Arabian Gulf, Afghanistan, and the rest of the Muslim states, before they lose everything." He noted, "America and its allies should know their crimes will not go unpunished." He told a reporter that the U.S. intends to go "far beyond Iraq to reach the Arab and Islamic world for its aims to destroy any effective military power next to Israel .... We've sent messages to the allies of the U.S. to stop their involvement in this American campaign .... We've sent a message to Germany and another to France. If those doses are not enough, we are ready to increase them." Zawahiri said that group "will continue.... Targeting the lifelines of the American economy."

October 8, 2002. *Kuwait.* At 11:30 a.m., U.S. Marine Lance Crp. Antonio J. Sledd, 20, of Hillsborough, Florida, was killed and U.S. Marine Lance Crp. George R. Simpson, 21, of Dayton, Ohio, was injured when two civilian-garbed al Qaeda gunmen fired assault rifles from a pickup truck on Failaka. Failaka is a small Kuwaiti island where the Marines were taking a break from urban warfare training in the Eager Mace annual exercise. The Marines were training with blank rounds, which could have hindered them returning fire. Marines killed the two Kuwaiti Islamic radicals when they attacked a second group of Marines. Sledd died during surgery at a military hospital. Simpson was hit in the arm. The Marines found three AK-47 assault rifles and ammunition inside the white truck.

Kuwaiti authorities arrested 31 Islamic extremists, including 15 suspected terrorists in a local al Qaeda cell. The cell members trained at al Qaeda camps in Afghanistan; some fought for the Taliban. The cell was led by Anas Ahmed Ibrahim Kandari, 21, one of the gunmen. Kandari had three relatives detained by the United States at Guantanamo Bay for al Qaeda involvement. Kandari had written a letter to his mother five days earlier, suggesting he would die soon.

The other gunman was his cousin, Jassem Mubarak Hajiri, 26. The duo had attended an al Qaeda Afghan training camp. One of the gunmen left a note in the vehicle saying he was angry over the massacres of Palestinians by Israeli authorities.

Kuwaiti authorities believed the terrorists planned other anti-U.S. attacks against military facilities, the embassy, and U.S.–owned businesses.

An October 14 fax to al-Jazeera that also appeared on www.islammemo.com was signed by bin Laden, praised the Kuwait and Yemen supertanker attacks, and repeated many of the same phrases from the October 6 audiotape. "We congratulate the Muslim nation for the daring and heroic jihad operations which our brave sons conducted in Yemen against the Christian oil tanker and in Kuwait against the American occupation and aggression forces. By striking the oil tanker in Yemen with explosives, the attackers struck at the umbilical cord of the Christians, reminding the enemy of the bloody price they have to pay for continuing their aggression against our nation.... We renew our promise to God, and to the nation, and our promise to the Americans and Jews that they will not be at peace.... The priority in this war at this stage must be against the infidels, the Americans and the Jews.... who will not stop infringing upon us except through jihad." The fax claimed that the one-year anniversary of the war in Afghanistan had not ended al Qaeda and the Taliban. "These attacks coincide with the anniversary of the crude and are a clear message to enemies and friends alike that the mujaheddin have not been weakened or exhausted."

On June 5, 2004, a Kuwaiti criminal court convicted seven Kuwaiti Islamic extremists of the attack. Three of the suspects received four or five years in prison for joining an illegal organization and weapons possession. They and three others were fined $680 to $17,000. One was given a two-year probation. Five were acquitted. 02100801

October 8, 2002. *India.* In Doda, Kashmir, armed militants threw grenades and fired into a polling station, causing no injuries. In Kashmir, militants threw a grenade at a security patrol but missed. The grenade exploded in a crowded marketplace, injuring 14. No one claimed credit for either attack.

October 9, 2002. *Kuwait.* A U.S. Marine fired at a civilian vehicle during the night after an individual pointed a gun at a Humvee carrying two U.S. soldiers on a highway west of Kuwait City. No Americans were injured. U.S. soldiers saw the vehicle veering off the roadway, but it was unclear what happened to the assailants. 02100901

October 9, 2002. *United States.* The FBI warned thousands of state and local law enforcement agencies that the release of audiotapes by Osama bin Laden and Ayman Zawahiri that called for attacks against the United States "suggest that an attack may have been approved, while the specific timing is left to operatives in the field." The Bureau said interrogations of detained al Qaeda leaders indicated that the terrorists "are independently interpreting these taped remarks as a sign of attack." The State and Defense Departments issued similar warnings. The U.S. State Department warned of possible terrorist attacks against travelers and other Americans abroad, based upon "the recent audiotape attributed to Osama bin Laden and other reports of threats to American interests."

October 10, 2002. *Philippines.* At 2:45 p.m., a bomb went off at a Kidapawan City bus terminal on Mindanao Island, killing 8 people, including a woman and child, and injuring 19. The improvised incendiary bomb was hidden under a seat in a ticket booth.

October 10, 2002. *Germany.* At dawn, Hamburg police arrested Abdelghani Mzoudi, an electrical engineering student from Karrakech, Morocco, on suspicion of providing logistical support to September 11 hijack leader Mohamed

Atta's al Qaeda cell in Hamburg. He had been questioned frequently in the investigation. Authorities seized a laptop, books, and other materials from his apartment; he had been arrested at the home of friends in Hamburg where he was staying overnight. Police had a witness statement that indicated the Mzoudi and the other members of the Hamburg cell had visited Afghan terrorist training camps in 2000. Mzoudi and Mounir Motassadeq, also from Marrakech, had signed Atta's will. Mzoudi had been briefly held in July with Abderrasak Labied, his roommate, along with five other men who had met in the back room of the Attawhid Islamic bookstore in Hamburg to plan suicide attacks. They were released for lack of evidence. A court ruled that the bookstore could reopen. Mzoudi had shared a Hamburg apartment with Ramzi Binalshibh and Zakariya Essabar, a Moroccan who remained at large. Mzoudi provided money to Essabar to attend a flight school in the United States; Essabar failed to obtain a U.S. visa. Mzoudi was in the wedding videotape of Said Bahaji, a German Moroccan fugitive who left Hamburg shortly before September 11. Atta appears in the video.

October 10, 2002. *Israel.* At 7:50 a.m., a man fell trying to board a crowded rush hour Dan bus at a stop near Bar Ilan University on a highway outside Tel Aviv. When the driver, Baruch Noyman, 50, and a passenger (who was a doctor) jumped out to administer first aid, they discovered a ten-pound explosives belt hidden under his shirt. They pinned him to the ground for five minutes while passengers and others fled. When the passengers were safe, the duo released the terrorist, who had been struggling and kicking his legs. The duo thought that the terrorist would be able to set off the bomb there and released him. The terrorist ran toward a group of people and set off the explosives, killing himself and a woman, Seada Aharon, 71. At least 50 people were treated at local hospitals; 6 had shrapnel wounds. The bomb was packed with nails and other objects. Noyman said, "Nails and other objects flew in every direction, and his body parts went 20 or 30 meters in the air. Some of his body parts hit me." Among the injured was Eli Dan, 38, an accountant for a security firm. Hamas claimed credit, saying it was avenging Israel's October 7 raid in the Gaza Strip that killed 16 and a July air strike that killed terrorist leader Salah Shehada, his aide, and 14 other Palestinians, including 9 children. The terrorist had tried to jump into the bus through a back door as it was pulling out of the station. But the door closed and the terrorist fell, hitting his head on the ground. The terrorist was identified as Rafik Hammad, 24, a construction worker who resided in Qalqilya in the West Bank.

October 10–11, 2002. *Italy.* Italian police arrested five North Africans in Milan, Naples, San Remo, and the island of Malta who were part of a Salafist Group for Preaching (Call) and Combat terrorist cell based in Milan. The cell was part of a European network with contacts in Iran, Malaysia, and Afghanistan that was suspected of plotting attacks on U.S. targets. A sixth suspect remained at large. A seventh, their leader, Farj Hassan, was already in a U.K. jail. The suspects had surveilled U.S. embassies in Belgium and the Netherlands. The FBI and Scotland Yard assisted in the investigation. Intercepted conversations showed the suspects talking about obtaining explosives in southern France. In September, they referred to an upcoming "soccer game," believed to be code for an attack. They also said they would take revenge against Italy for supporting U.S. antiterrorist efforts. A suspect named Nassim said, "You'll see what happens now in Italy. Now they are causing problems. Maybe you'll find 300 or 400 dead in the subway." Police had been investigating the cell for three years. The group is part of the al Qaeda network with ties to a group of seven Tunisians who had recently been convicted. The State Department reported that four Tunisians were arrested for document forgery, but may also have planned a terrorist attack in Europe, possibly in France. 02101001

October 11, 2002. *Israel.* Security guards fired shots into the air and overpowered a Palestinian wearing an explosives vest as he approached the U.S. Embassy in Tel Aviv. The guards held his hands to prevent him from setting off the charge. No injuries were reported. He was taken to a police station for questioning. The bomb squad disarmed the explosive. 02101101

October 11, 2002. *Finland.* A six-pound bomb collapsed part of a building at a suburban Vantaa shopping mall, killing 7 people and injuring 80, a dozen seriously. The mall was packed with 2,000 shoppers. The bomb went off near a spiral staircase between the second and third floors. Police were searching for a motive. The suspected bomber, Petri Gerdt, 19, a chemistry student with no criminal record, died in the blast. The bomb was packed with shotgun pellets. Gerdt was identified as a shy student from a middle-class Helsinki suburb who used the alias RC in a Finnish Internet chat room—Forum for Home Chemistry—where users exchanged tips on homemade explosives. Authorities shut down the chat room.

On October 15, police arrested a boy, 17, for providing information about explosives over the Internet to Gerdt. Police did not believe the youth was involved in placing the bomb. He was held on a preliminary charge of assisting in a grievous act of destruction; as a minor, he would face a maximum sentence of seven years. Police questioned three other men who apparently had Internet chats with Gerdt.

October 12, 2002. *Philippines.* At least 11 Philippine Marines on a hostage rescue mission were killed in two gun battles with Abu Sayyaf on Sulu Island. The Third Marine Battalion was looking for four Filipino Jehovah's Witnesses held since August. The first gun battle occurred at 7:20 a.m., when 9 soldiers were killed and 25 wounded. The guerrillas, led by Radulan Sahiron, battled the army again at 4:00 p.m., leaving two dead soldiers and one wounded. The Witnesses were taken hostage while selling Avon

cosmetics in a remote village on Sulu. Three Indonesian tugboat crew were also being held by the guerrillas.

October 12, 2002. *Indonesia.* Early in the morning, a small handmade bomb broke windows at the closed Philippine consulate in Manado on the island of Sulawesi. On October 24, police arrested two Indonesians in the case. 02101203

October 12, 2002. *Indonesia.* At 11:10 p.m., two bombs exploded within seconds of each other at the Sari Club and Paddy's, two Bali nightclubs popular with foreign tourists, on Legian Street near Bali's Kuta Beach strip. The first small bomb went off in front of Paddy's disco. The second larger bomb was in a Toyota Kijang SUV in front of the Sari Club. The second bomb set off a burst of flames from gas cylinders used for cooking in the open-air bar. The blasts shattered windows 400 yards away and set alight numerous cars. It left a hole 6 feet deep and 15 feet wide and destroyed 20 buildings.

The bombs killed at least 202 people, including 88 Australians, 4 French citizens, and 7 Americans, and injured more than 300 people, including 4 Americans, 7 French citizens, and at least 5 Britons. Among the dead were tourists celebrating the opening of a rugby tournament, including people from Canada, the United Kingdom, Germany, and Sweden. Also among the victims were New Zealanders, Norwegians, Italians, Swiss, and French. A total of 21 nationalities from six continents were represented among the victims. No one claimed credit. Jemaah Islamiah (JI) terrorists were suspected.

Tourists rushed to help rescue workers and volunteer at the overwhelmed hospitals. The State Department ordered all nonemergency U.S. government officials and their families to leave Indonesia. All Americans were urged to leave as well.

On October 14, Indonesian Defense Minister Matori Abdul Djalil said that "the Bali bomb blast is related to al Qaeda with the cooperation of local terrorists." Bali is 95 percent Hindu with a small Muslim population. Police detained 27 people for questioning. Ten Pakistanis were questioned but not detained.

On October 16, local police found traces of C-4 in the wreckage. They said they were "intensively" interrogating a guard who witnessed the attack and someone related to an individual whose ID card was found at the scene. They also detained a former military officer who might have fabricated the bomb.

On October 17, local authorities summoned Abubakar Baasyir, 64, a JI leader, to Jakarta for questioning. They wanted to discuss a series of church bombings by al Qaeda linked militants. He collapsed and was hospitalized after a press conference. Jailed al Qaeda operative Omar al-Farouq told local investigators that Baasyir was involved in the bombings.

On October 19, Baasyir was arrested for involvement in the church bombings. Police suspected that Baasyir knew ahead of time about the Bali attacks. Police said they were questioning eight people, including seven Indonesians (one of them a woman), who might know the occupants of the minivan that carried the bomb.

On October 21, police announced that the main bomb was made of ammonium nitrate, which is stockpiled by JI.

On October 21, a U.S. consular official said that at least seven Americans were believed dead, although only two bodies had been identified. The figure could rise because 45 Americans were believed to have been in Southeast Asia on the day of the bombing and remained unaccounted for by their families. The confirmed dead were Karri Jane Casner of Flower Mound, Texas, and Deborah Snodgrass, who had moved to Bali a year earlier to teach English.

The State Department ultimately listed seven dead Americans: Deborah Lea Snodgrass, Karri Casner, Jacob Young, Steven Brooks Webster, George "Joe" Milligan, Megan Heffrnan, and Robert McCormick. Webster of Huntington Beach, California, was originally listed as missing. He was an environmental consultant and avid surfer on the island to celebrate his 41st

birthday. Webster's friend, Steven Cabler, was treated for burns. Attorney Jake Young, 34, was also originally listed as missing. He was an Associated Press All-American football center for the University of Nebraska in 1988 and 1989, and was playing in the rugby tournament for his Hong Kong team. He worked in Hong Kong for a London-based law firm.

Dead Australians included Renae Anderson, who died at the scene, and sister Simone Hanley, who died 58 days later. Some 220 Australians were listed as missing. Among the injured Australians was Adam Nimmo, 20, who was burned. John Juniardi, one of 38 Indonesians who died at the scene, was married to Australian Natalie Juniardi.

On October 29, police said that they were searching for an Indonesian suspect and had made a composite sketch of him. Two days later, they released sketches of two others and were searching for another ten fugitives. The trio in the sketches were believed to be Indonesians aged 20, 27, and 30 and may have died in the explosions. One was believed to have links to al Qaeda.

On November 5, Indonesian authorities arrested two suspects. Two days later, police released composite sketches of four other suspects. Amrozi bin Nurhasyim, 30 (or 40), an East Javanese car repairman and the owner of the Mitsubishi L-300 minivan that exploded, said he was part of the group. He was arrested at Al Islam, an Islamic boarding school in Lamongan, where he had attended a lecture by Abubakar Baasyir, the head of JI. Amrozi—who has 12 brothers and sisters—said he was involved in the August 2000 remotely controlled bombing of Philippine Ambassador Leonides Caday's house in Jakarta. He said the Bali bombings were "revenge for what Americans have done to Muslims." He said he was trying to kill as many Americans as possible and that the terrorists were unhappy large numbers of Australians had died instead. Amrozi said he had met with Riduan Isamuddin (alias Hambali), the leader of JI and al Qaeda's leader in the region. He said he was also involved in the bombing of the Jakarta stock exchange in 2000 that killed 15 people and the October 12, 2002, bombing of the Philippine consulate in North Sulawesi. He said he also knew Fathur Rohman al-Ghozi, an Indonesian bombing expert arrested in January by Philippine authorities. Police were seeking six to ten other Amrozi associates.

Amrozi claimed to have purchased a ton of ammonium chlorate in Surabaya, East Java; police obtained the sales receipt. The seller was detained by police. Amrozi led police to a home in Denpasar, Bali, where explosive residue was found. Amrozi used Malaysian ringgit, Singapore dollars, and perhaps U.S. dollars to buy the minivan that carried the explosives.

Amrozi bin Nurhasyim's older brother, Mukhlas, is a JI operative wanted for the bombing. Police were seeking three other relatives, including two other brothers belonging to JI. Police believed Mukhlas was the Malaysia chief of JI and involved in a failed plot to blow up pipelines that supply Malaysian water to Singapore. Younger brother Ali Imron was believed to have helped detonate the car bomb. Brother Ghufron, 48, attended an Islamic boarding school founded by Baasyir. Brother Ali Fauzi was also wanted in connection with the bombing. Brother Khozin founded Al Islam, the Islamic boarding school.

On November 10, police detained Tafsir. They said that Tafsir had driven Amrozi in his Mitsubishi L-300 van to Bali.

On November 11, Indonesian police arrested a forest ranger in Tenggulun, Komarudin, on suspicion of storing weapons and explosives for his friend, Amrozi. Police found two canisters, one of which contained five weapons, including two M-16s and an AK-47.

On November 13, a smirking Amrozi appeared on television laughing and joking with Indonesian police as he told them that Imam Samudra (alias Hudama) asked him to buy the chemicals to make the bomb. Australians were outraged. Meanwhile, police named four new suspects, one (Samudra) in custody and three of

his brothers—Umar, Idris, and another Umar—who remained at large. (Police said later that Samudra was arrested on November 21.) Amrozi claimed that he, Samudra, and another man named Martin met more than once in Solo, Java, to discuss the bomb plan. Amrozi said Idris gave him more than $5,000 in U.S., Singaporean, and Malaysian currency.

On November 17, police said a computer engineer from West Java, Imam Samudra, 35, was the ringleader. The radical intellectual had received arms training in Afghanistan. The JI members had helped build the bomb. In a meeting in central Java on August 8, he decided to target the Sari Club in hopes of killing Americans. Police said the man suspected of setting off the car bomb was Amar Usman (alias Dulmatin), 32, an electronics expert from central Java.

On November 22, police reported that Samudra had confessed to the Bali bombings a day after his arrest (on November 21) and had also admitted involvement in the Christmas Eve 2000 church bombings. Police said two terrorist cells with a total of a dozen people were involved. One group of militants from Lamongan in eastern Java, including Amrozi, set off the remotely detonation bombing of the Sari Club. Another group from Serang in western Java set off the smaller Paddy's nightclub bomb, which involved a suicide bomber named Iqbal, who had an explosives-laden backpack. Samudra was following the directives of Mukhlas (alias Ali Ghufron), an Islamic teacher, JI strategist, and older brother of Amrozi.

On December 3, Mukhlas was arrested and confessed two days later to helping plan the Bali bombings.

On January 14, 2003, police arrested 2 more suspects on Berukan Island in eastern Kalimantan Province, including field coordinator Ali Imron, bringing the total to more than 20.

On January 28, 2003, Indonesian National Police Chief Da'i Bachtiar said that detained cleric Abubakar Baasyir had given a blessing to the "jihad operation" in Bali. Baasyir approved the plan developed by senior militants at a meeting in Bangkok in February to strike U.S. and other Western targets in Indonesia and Singapore. Chief Bachtiar also said Isamuddin provided $35,000 to finance the attacks, giving the money to Malaysian operative Wan Min Wan Mat, who forwarded the funds to Mukhlas. Mat was in Malaysian custody. Other Indonesian security officials believed the money came from Seyam Reda, a German held on immigration charges. As of January 28, police had detained 29 suspects and planned to try the first tranche of defendants in February. Indonesian authorities pointed to Chapter 39 of a JI terrorist handbook that said all armed operations must be approved by the group's emir, which they believed to be Baasyir.

On February 3, 2003, Indonesian police announced the arrest of two more JI members —Mas Selamat Kastari, a Singaporean wanted in Singapore for participating in a hijacking plot, and Malaysian citizen Noor Din, who was suspected of helping plan the Bali bombings. Kastari was picked up on February 2 on Bintan Island. He had fled Singapore in December 2001 and planned to hijack a U.S., U.K., or Singaporean jet flying out of Bangkok and crash it into Singapore's Changi Airport. Din was grabbed in Gresik on Java Island, where police seized an M-16 rifle and ammunition that belonged to Ali Imron.

On February 21, 2003, Silvester Tendean's trial began. Tendean was the store owner accused of selling the chemicals used in the bombing. He was the first suspect to face trial.

On March 11, 2003, the government announced that the August 1, 2000, car bombing of Philippine Ambassador Leonides Caday's home in Jakarta was carried out by the same JI terrorists accused in the Bali blasts. The government said the attack was ordered in July 2000 by Riduan Isamuddin (alias Hambali) during a meeting in Kuala Lumpur, Malaysia. One of the terrorists was Amrozi, who purchased the Sari Club van, and Mubarok, who distributed the money that financed the attacks and helped assemble the Jakarta bomb. Amrozi purchased the explosives for the two attacks at a shop in Surabaya, East Java. Ali Imron was also indirectly involved in the Jakarta bombing, according to police. Philippine investigators said JI was joined by the Moro Islamic Liberation Front (MILF) in the attack. MILF gave JI training.

On April 14, 2003, Indonesian prosecutors filed treason charges against Abubakar Baasyir for plotting to overthrow the government.

On April 23, 2003, the national police announced the arrests of 18 JI members, including Mohamad bin Abas (alias Nasir Abbas), Malaysian leader of the Mantiqi 3 cell that operates in the southern Philippines and northern Indonesia. Three of the 18 were linked to the Bali bombings. The Mantiqi 3 includes the Philippines, Brunei, eastern Malaysia, and Kalimantan and Sulawesi in Indonesia. It was based in Camp Abubakar and run by MILF of the Philippines before the Filipino military overran it in 2000. Police also arrested Abu Rusdan, who had been JI's temporary leader.

Baasyir's trial began on April 23. He was charged in a 25-page indictment with involvement in church bombings on Christmas Eve 2000 that killed 19 people, a failed plot to bomb U.S. interests in Singapore, and a plot to assassinate President Megawati Sukarnoputri in 2001 when she was vice president. The government said Baasyir is JI's leader. The charges carry a life sentence. He was not charged with the Bali bombings. On May 28, Ali Imron and Hutomo Pamungkas (alias Mubarok), both suspected of involvement in the Bali bombings, testified that they believe Baasyir is JI's leader. Other JI members Imam Samudra and Mukhlas did not implicate Baasyir; Samudra recanted, saying the government had beaten him.

On April 30, 2003, prosecutors charged Amrozi, the first suspect, with buying the explosives and driving the van that exploded. The charges carry the death penalty. His trial began on May 12.

On June 26, 2003, Faiz bin Abu Bakar Bafana, 41, a Malaysian and treasurer of JI, told the court via teleconference from a Singapore jail that bin Laden had set in motion a series of plots that JI pursued in Singapore and Indonesia in 2000. Bafana said Baasyir approved of the planned attacks and appointed Ali Ghufron as an operations chief of JI; Ghufron is charged with organizing the Bali bombings.

On June 30, 2003, police arrested Idris, one of the organizers of the Bali bombings. Idris had also helped in a bank robbery on Sumatra to fund terrorist operations. Meanwhile, prosecutors recommended the death sentence for Amrozi (alias The Smiling Bomber).

On August 7, 2003, Chief Judge I Made Karna Parna declared Amrozi, 41, guilty and sentenced him to death. Families of victims cheered in the courtroom. A smiling Amrozi turned to them and gave them a thumbs-up sign. Attorney Wirawan Adnan said, "The death penalty is speaking about revenge and that's not what justice is all about. We appeal not because we believe our client is innocent. We appeal because we believe we need to correct the applications of the law. We believe that our client … is not getting a fair trial."

On September 2, 2003, Chief Judge Muhammad Saleh announced that an Indonesian court had convicted Baasyir of treason for involvement in the JI and attempting to overthrow the government, sentencing him to four years in prison. The court ruled that the prosecution had not proven that he was JI's commander. The court also rejected the charge that he was involved in the series of church bombings on Christmas Eve 2000. He was also found guilty of an immigration violation for the 14 years he spent in exile in Malaysia. Prosecutors had requested 15 years; the maximum was life. Baasyir said he would appeal.

On September 8, 2003, prosecutors appealed Baasyir's verdict, hoping to win a ruling that he was the commander of JI. They also wanted a tougher sentence. On December 1, 2003, an Indonesian appeals court overturned the treason charges and reduced Baasyir's sentence from four to three years. He was cleared of charges of leading the JI. The court upheld his conviction of immigration violations. On March 9, 2004, the Indonesian Supreme Court further reduced Baasyir's sentence, permitting him to go free by April 4, 2004. The Court offered no explanation for halving his sentence.

Meanwhile, also on September 8, 2003, a Bali court sentenced three militants to 15 to 16 years for a robbery that funded the bombings.

On September 10, 2003, a court in Bali sentenced Imam Samudra to death by firing squad for masterminding the bombings. Samudra denied involvement during the trial, but after sentencing he said he wanted to die a martyr. Prosecutors said he chose the recruits and financed the attack. Samudra said the bombings were revenge for U.S. tyranny.

On September 17, 2003, a court upheld Amrozi's death sentence; he said he would appeal to the Supreme Court.

On September 18, 2003, a court sentenced Ali Imron to life in prison, finding that he had participated in making the bomb and driving the minivan to the area. The court also noted that he had asked his friends and family not to follow his example.

In 2003, Muhaimin, 42, an instructor of an April 2000 class of 17 Indonesians who took terrorist training in the Philippines, reported that one of the 17 graduates had been arrested for hiding a Bali bomber. By 2004, Muhaimin was an imam at a Jakarta mosque.

On April 16, 2004, Indonesian officials named Baasyir a terrorism suspect, which could permit them to keep him in prison after he finished serving his sentence on immigration charges two weeks later. As Baasyir (alias Sheik Abdush Shomad) was walking out of Jakarta's Salemba prison on April 28, he was rearrested on what the government said was solid evidence that he was the leader of JI, a terrorist group linked to al Qaeda. On July 23, 2004, the constitutional court ruled that Baasyir could not be tried by retroactive imposition of the antiterrorism laws. 02101201

October 12, 2002. *Indonesia.* At 11:30 p.m., another bomb exploded some 100 yards from a U.S. consular office in Denpasar, Bali's capital. The man apparently carrying the bomb was injured and taken into police custody. No other injuries were reported. 02101202

October 14, 2002. *Kuwait.* At 7:50 a.m., gunshots were fired in the vicinity of U.S. forces training in the desert near the Iraqi border. The Americans did not return fire. No one was injured. American authorities said the shots were fired deliberately at U.S. Army troops; some Kuwaiti officials said bird hunters were firing at passing flocks.

October 14, 2002. *Philippines.* Government prosecutors said they would file charges against a Jemaah Islamiah duo with ties to al Qaeda who purchased explosives in the Philippines. Riduan Isamuddin (alias Hambali) is an Indonesian cleric and suspected leader of the group. Faiz bin Abu Bakar Bafana is a Malaysian.

October 15, 2002. *Sudan.* A Saudi gunman was foiled on a Saudi Arabian Airlines plane that returned safely to Khartoum, where the would-be hijacker was questioned by local authorities. None of the 185 passengers and 19 crew were injured on the Airbus 300. Police said the hijacker was armed with a small gun and attempted to take over the jet 22 minutes after takeoff. His motives were unclear. 02101501

October 17, 2002. *Philippines.* Two bombs killed 7 people and wounded 152 in two department stores in Zamboanga City. Muslim militant members of Abu Sayyaf were suspected. Police blew up five other suspect packages, none of which contained explosives. The first bomb went off at 11:30 a.m. at the Shop-o-Rama. At noon, a bomb went off at the adjacent Shoppers Central store. The bombs were placed at counters where shoppers leave packages before entering.

On October 22, police arrested several Abu Sayyaf members in connection with the attacks.

On November 14, Manila police captured Abdulmukim Edris, alleged head of an Abu Sayyaf explosives team. Police said the group planned to use truck bombs against the U.S. Embassy, the Manila stock exchange, and other targets. Edris told police that the group planned to use cell phones to set off ammonium nitrate bombs in a series of attacks slated for November. Police said Edris's cohorts implicated him in the Zamboanga bombings and that he was trained by two Yemenis from al Qaeda to make car bombs at an Abu Sayyaf camp in Basilan Island in 2001.

October 17, 2002. *Kuwait.* Police arrested a Kuwaiti man with gasoline bombs in his car near a housing complex where scores of American military officers live. He said he had received orders over the Internet to use the Molotov cocktails. 02101701

October 18, 2002. *Pakistan.* Three parcel bombs exploded at three locations in Karachi, injuring nine people, including five policemen. One person lost a hand in the blast; the other hand was scheduled for amputation. Other victims were hit in the chest, neck, face, and hands. One of the bombs exploded in an office of terrorism investigators. A local news agency and major daily newspaper in Karachi received e-mail from the banned Lashkar-e-Jhangvi claiming credit. Five other parcel bombs were defused at police and investigation centers in the city. The parcels were sent by private courier services. One e-mail said the group was sending a warning to the police hunting members of banned Islamic groups, the Taliban, and al Qaeda. The e-mail was signed by Asif Ramzi, a notorious militant who claimed that 35 packages, each containing five ounces of explosives, had been mailed from three post offices. They threatened future attacks against "anti-Islam police officers and other infidels." All parcels included a tag that said "a gift from the MMA." MMA stands for Muttahida Majlis-i-Amal (United Action Front), a coalition of anti-U.S. religious parties that made major gains in the previous week's national elections. An MMA leader denied involvement.

October 18, 2002. *United States.* The Department of the Treasury designated the Illinois-based Global Relief Foundation, one of the country's largest Muslim charities, a terrorist organization because it had received more than $200,000 from Mohammed Zouaydi, a top al Qaeda financier. Zouaydi was arrested in Spain in April. The organization was represented by attorney Roger Simmons.

October 18, 2002. *Philippines.* A bomb went off on a bus on Quezon City's EDSA highway, killing 3 and injuring 23. The bomb carrier was among the dead. It was unclear whether the bomber intended a suicide attack.

October 18, 2002. *Russia.* At 9:14 a.m., Valentin Tsvetkov, 54, governor of Magadan region, was assassinated on a busy thoroughfare outside his Moscow office. The gunman fired a silenced pistol as traffic passed along New Arbat. In the previous few months, a member of Parliament, a vice governor, a deputy railways director, a deputy mayor, and a regional lawmaker had been assassinated and a senior executive of the country's largest oil company had been kidnapped. Police said it was a contract hit.

October 19, 2002. *Russia.* Shortly after 1:00 p.m., a car bomb stuffed with shrapnel exploded in front of a McDonald's in southwest Moscow, killing one person and injuring seven, including a five-year-old girl. Police said terrorists or criminals could be responsible. The red Russian-made car was parked near the drive-through window. Police were searching for the car's owner. 02101901

October 20, 2002. *Philippines.* A bomb exploded on a bike in front of a Catholic church in Zamboanga, killing a Philippine Marine and injuring 18 people. On October 22, police arrested several Abu Sayyaf members in connection with the case.

October 20, 2002. *India.* Armed militants killed three and injured two near a mosque in Onagam. No one claimed credit.

October 20, 2002. *Egypt.* The Supreme State Security Court began the trial of 26 members of the Islamic Liberation Party, including 3 Britons. The defendants were accused of joining a banned group, attempting to recruit members for that group, and spreading extremist ideology. The group was banned in Egypt in 1974, following an attempt to overthrow the government and establish an Islamic caliphate.

October 21, 2002. *Georgia.* Special Forces said they had captured 15 Arab militants linked to al Qaeda in the Pankisi Gorge and turned them over to the United States in recent weeks. Among those caught was Saif al Islam el Masry, an Egyptian member of the al Qaeda military committee. Masry had been trained by Hizballah in southern Lebanon and was among a group of al Qaeda members chosen to go to Somalia to fight the United States in the early 1990s. He had served as an officer of the Chechnya branch of the Benevolence International Foundation, which was cited in U.S. court as an al Qaeda financial conduit. The detainees had passports from Morocco, Egypt, and European countries. Georgian investigators reported that one team was attempting to obtain explosives to use against a U.S. or Western installation in Russia. Six other men were developing poisons to use against Western targets in Central Asia.

October 21, 2002. *United States.* The Bush administration asked the oil, gas, and transportation sectors to increase security against terrorist attacks.

October 21, 2002. *Israel.* At 4:30 p.m., a suicide bomber killed 14 people and injured 50 when he set off 175 pounds of explosives by ramming his four-wheel-drive vehicle into the rear of Number 841 Egged commuter bus at Karkur Junction in northern Israel. The bus was traveling from Kiryat Shemona to Tel Aviv when it was hit near

Pardes Hanna-Karkur. The resulting fireball set off the ammunition of some soldiers riding inside. The blast also destroyed six nearby cars, including that of Asi Dayan, 30. Islamic Jihad faxed a confessor letter to a news agency in Beirut stating that they were retaliating "for the series of massacres committed by the criminal enemy against our people." The group said it was also commemorating the assassination seven years earlier of its founder, Fathi Shiqaqi. Among those injured were Mark Fzezolayev, 18, a soldier who came to Israel two years earlier; Itzik Koren, 54, a banker from Tiberias; and Avi Fried, 43, an accountant from Gan Yavne, who saved several victims from the fire.

Three members of the six-member Border Police Monument Team were killed, including Sgt. Liat Ben-Ami, 20; Sgt. Ayman Sharuf, 20, who had joined the group two weeks earlier; and Sgt. Esther (Etti) Pesakhov, 19, whose cousin, Shoshana Reiss, 20, was killed on November 22, 2000, in a car bombing of a bus stop in Hadera.

October 23, 2002. *United States.* The Department of State listed Jemaah Islamiah as a terrorist organization.

October 23, 2002. *Thailand.* The Danish Foreign Ministry Web site said it had received information on possible terrorist attacks on Phuket Island, a popular Thai tourist resort. The ministry urged Danish citizens to use caution near religious shrines, restaurants, cafés, and bars and suggested avoiding areas not guarded by police, soldiers, or other security officials.

October 23, 2002. *United States.* At 1:45 p.m., Aeroflot flight 1357, carrying 176 passengers and 12 crew from Moscow to Washington, made an unscheduled stop at New York's JFK International Airport. Customs agents and Port Authority of New York and New Jersey police officers searched the flight for radioactive materials at the request of the Russians. Nothing was found. A male passenger was taken into custody; his luggage was filled with furs.

October 23, 2002. *Russia.* At 9:00 p.m., scores of masked Chechen gunmen and women armed with automatic weapons took over a Moscow theater on the corner of Dobrovskaya and Melnikova, holding nearly 900 people hostage. About 100 people escaped in the initial attack; another 46 were freed in stages. A doctor from the audience treated one of the wounded rebels. The House of Culture for the State Ball-Bearing Factory theater was showing *Nord-Ost* (Northeast), a popular musical. The terrorists demanded that Russian troops leave Chechnya within a week and end the war in the separatist region. They threatened to kill all the hostages if their demands were not met. At least one and perhaps two hostages were killed and two wounded in the initial assault by the gunmen, who had grenades strapped to their bodies. One of those wounded was the boyfriend of Tatyana Yefimova, 22, who was hit by shattered glass. The Chechens said they were holding 650 people after having released 150. They claimed to have placed land mines around the theater's perimeter.

Tatyana Solnishkina, an orchestra member, used her cell phone to inform authorities that the rebels were threatening to kill ten hostages if one of them was harmed. "Please don't start storming. There are a lot of explosives. Don't open fire on them. I am very scared. I ask you, please, do not start attacking."

Alevtina Popva, an actress, escaped from backstage and reported that "the most horrible thing is they were chanting, like kamikazes." She and some colleagues used curtains and scarves to climb out windows. Later, terrorists injured a Russian soldier when they fired rocket-propelled grenades at two teen girls who were attempting to run to safety.

A rebel named Hasmamat used Maria Shkolnikova's cell phone to contact Radio Echo Moskvy and say, "Our demands are of the very simplest: Stop the war and withdraw the troops." Another rebel who said his name was Abu Said claimed that the rebels were all *shahids* (Arabic for martyr). An *Interfax* reporter called from his cell phone to say that the rebels claimed membership in the Suicide Commandos of the 29th Division.

The rebels separated the men and women, and later separated out the foreign citizens into a third group. Some Muslim audience members were permitted to leave. The rebels also freed several children. One boy said that his mother and sister were still being held, as were dozens of other children.

The hostages included citizens of Australia, Austria, Azerbaijan, Belarus, Bulgaria, France, Georgia, Germany, Israel, the Netherlands, Switzerland, Ukraine, United Kingdom, and the United States. About 75 foreigners were being held, including at least 3 Americans and a Russian with a U.S. green card. Americans were identified as Sandy Alan Booker, 49, of Oklahoma City, Natalya Aleshnya, and Irina Shearel.

President Putin said that the attack was planned by foreign forces and was connected with the attacks in Bali and the Philippines. A police source said that the rebels were contacting accomplices in Turkey and the United Arab Emirates.

Aslan Maskhadov, former president of Chechnya, denied involvement with the hostage-takers, blaming a splinter faction with links to Muslim terrorists. Al-Jazeera played a tape that showed the hostage-takers in front of an Arabic-language banner. A Chechen Web site said the attackers were led by Movsar Barayev, 25, nephew of Arbi Barayev, a Chechen rebel leader who died in 2001. Movsar Barayev said he heads a group of Islamic radicals he calls the Islamic Special Purpose Regiment of the Chechen State Defense Committee (Majlis al-Shura) with 400 active fighters and as many again in reserve. His second in command was Abu Bakr. Al-Jazeera later said the group was the Sabotage and Military Surveillance Group of the Riyadh al-Salikhin Martyrs (variant the Riyadus-Salikhin Reconnaissance and Sabotage Battalion of the Chechen Martyrs). In a recorded statement, a group member said, "Our demands are stopping the war and withdrawal of Russian forces. We are implementing

the operation by order of the military commander of the Chechen Republic."

The State Department's *Patterns of International Terrorism 2003* said that the attack was by a trio of groups:

- The Islamic International Peacekeeping Brigade (IIPB), which was established in 1998 by Shamil Basayev. Basayev led the group with Saudi-born Ibn al-Khattab until the latter's death in March 2002. Arab mujaheddin leader Abu al-Walid had since taken over al-Khattab's position.

- The Riyadus-Salikhin Reconnaissance and Sabotage Battalion of Chechen Martyrs (RSRSBCM–Requirements for Getting into Paradise) also led by Shamil Basayev.

- The Special Purpose Islamic Regiment (SPIR) led by Movzar Barayev, who died in the attack. Leadership was picked up by a Chechen who used the alias Khamzat.

Yosif Kobzon, singer, politician, and Duma member from Chechnya, claimed he had established communications with the hostage-takers and was going to negotiate with the gunmen. On October 24 after 1:30 p.m., Kobzon and a Red Cross representative were permitted into the theater and obtained the release of five hostages, including a sick Briton in his 50s or 60s, a woman, and three children. During Kobzon's second visit, he was accompanied by Irina Khakamada, a parliamentarian. The rebels refused to free anyone else and said they did not want to deal with intermediaries, only with decision-makers. Mark Franchetti of the *Sunday Times of London* accompanied Kobzon on one visit and interviewed the rebels' leader. Parliamentarian Grigory Yavlinsky was permitted inside the theater later that day, as was another group of negotiators. Other negotiators included Sergei Govorukhin, a film director; Alexander Vershbow, U.S. ambassador; Aslanbek Aslakhanov, Duma member for Chechnya; Anna Politkovskaya, journalist; and Yevgeny Primakov, former prime minister. At 6:30 p.m., two more hostages fled.

On October 25 at 6:00 a.m., the Chechens freed seven more hostages. Early that morning, the terrorists reportedly killed two male hostages and wounded a man and woman during an escape attempt. Only two made it. At noon, eight children were freed. According to initial press reports, a Chechen woman shot a male hostage dead when he threw a bottle at her and then charged at her. She also killed a woman near him. That day, the Chechens called for antiwar demonstrations in Red Square and released 19 hostages, including children as young as 6 years. Four of the hostages were from Azerbaijan. The terrorists refused to improve the conditions of the hostages, who were starving and who had to use the orchestra pit as a toilet.

On October 26 at 3:30 a.m., the sound of gunfire and explosions was heard as Russian Special Forces raided the theater. The battle led to the deaths of 42 rebels, including rebel leader Barayev and 18 female suicide bombers with explosives strapped to their stomachs, and the deaths of 117 hostages, including one American, Sandy Booker. Most were killed by the incapacitating gas used by the rescue force. Some of the women were shot. A man with head wounds and a woman with stomach injuries were taken away by ambulance. Several rebels were captured. Most of the freed hostages were hospitalized due to the effects of the gas that was pumped into the ventilation system. Russian soldiers refused to identify the gas even to attending physicians. The gas came in so quickly that the terrorists did not have time to put on their gas masks. Pentagon sources suggested that the gas was opium-based. Other U.S. doctors suggested it was fentanyl, an opiate derivative. Still others said it was an aerosol form of carfentanil, a potent narcotic used to sedate big game animals, or halothane, an inhalational anesthetic used in surgery for 50 years. Tests on two surviving German hostages found no evidence of fentanyl. The derivative, carfentanil (trade name Wildnil), would not have shown up in such a test.

A total of 600 hostages were treated in hospitals; about 200 were released. Four dozen were in grave condition. At least 348 hostages were treated for bullet wounds and gas inhalation at City Hospital Number 13. It initially appeared that most of the foreign hostages survived. Among the dead hostages were 115 Russians, an American, an Azerbaijani, a Dutch citizen, two Ukrainians, an Armenian, an Austrian, a Kazakh, and a Belarussian.

Investigators later determined that none of the hostages were shot during the rescue. The only hostages killed were the berserk man and a woman killed at the start of the 58-hour standoff.

One of the ill Russians, Inna Belyantseva, worked as a researcher at the National Institute on Deafness and Other Communication Disorders at the National Institutes of Health in Bethesda and lived in Montgomery County with her husband and child. Her mother-in-law, who had given her tickets to the performance as a birthday present, died in the attack. Another ill hostage was American Natalya Aleshnya, 64, a retired piano teacher from Mountain View, California.

On October 28, the Russians arrested a pair of Chechens in connection with the attack.

On October 29, Denmark arrested Akhmed Zakayev, an aide to Chechen separatist leader Aslan Maskhadov, for possible involvement in the attack. He was held until November 12, pending investigation. He had been attending the final session of the World Chechen Congress in Copenhagen. Russian officials detained dozens of possible accomplices.

On January 25, 2003, the theater officially reopened after $2.5 million in renovations, including a new security system with metal detectors, a new audio system, and new orchestra pit. Elsewhere, 310 miles southeast of Moscow in Penza, Russian police detained three Chechens on suspicion of involvement in the attack. On February 8, 2003, *Nord-Ost* reopened.

In June 2003, Zaurbek Talkhigov was sentenced to eight and one half years for tipping off terrorists about police attempts to rescue the hostages.

On July 17, 2003, the *Washington Post* reported that the 793 former hostages and families of the 129 dead hostages were having a difficult time seeking redress in Russian courts. The 135 former hostages or family members who had agreed to sue were represented by attorney Igor Trunov. One of the hostages, Nikolai Lyubimov, reported that his left side was partially paralyzed from the gas. Antonina Titova, 46, had memory loss, pain in her right side, and nightmares. Others had severe headaches, temporary hearing loss, heart and liver troubles, and psychological distress. The wife of Oleg Zhirov, 39, died in the theater, as did Sandy Alan Booker, the American fiancé of Svetlana Gubareva, the son of Tatyana Karpova, and the son of Zoya Chernetsova. As of that date, Russian courts had rejected 35 of the 65 lawsuits filed against the state. On July 28, 2003, a Moscow court rejected appeals in 21 compensation cases; attorneys argued that the law applies only to material damages for loss of income.

As of April 2004, Parliament had yet to redraft the media law, prompted by Kremlin criticism of the role played by the media during the hostage crisis. 02102301

October 23, 2002. *United Kingdom.* Police arrested Omar Uthman Abu Omar (alias Abu Qatada), 42, a Jordan-born Palestinian Islamic cleric involved in the European operations of al Qaeda, in a raid on his hideout in a south London house. He had been underground since December. He was wanted for questioning in France, Spain, Italy, and Germany for recruiting for al Qaeda in Europe. He had been convicted and sentenced to life in prison *in absentia* by Jordan for a plot to bomb tourist sites and an American school. He also conducted prayer meetings attended by shoe bomber Richard Reid and Zacarias Moussaoui. France Judge Jean-Louis Bruguiere said Abu Omar laundered money and planned and financed attacks throughout Europe. Spanish Judge Baltasar Garzon said he was a contact between al Qaeda and a Spanish-based terrorist suspect and with terrorists in Germany, France, Italy, and Belgium. Hamburg authorities had found tapes by Abu Omar in Mohamad Atta's last known apartment. Abu Omar had been given asylum in the United Kingdom in 1994 after fleeing Jordan, but his travel documents were seized, assets frozen, and $600 weekly welfare payments suspended in October 2001 after it was determined that he had an unexplained $270,000 in his bank account. He had expressed admiration for Osama bin Laden in interviews.

October 24, 2002. *United States.* The FBI warned state and local law enforcement agencies that terrorists could soon attack transportation systems, particularly railroads. Interrogations of al Qaeda prisoners led to the warning. Prisoners suggested that targets could include bridges, sections of train tracks, or train engines, and attacks would be designed to cause derailments and major damage.

The Associated Press reported that intelligence authorities were warning that al Qaeda supporters could be planning attacks on commercial and military shipping in the Persian Gulf and neighboring seas.

October 25, 2002. *Russia.* A shrapnel-filled artillery shell equivalent to five kilograms of TNT exploded in an auto parked in a McDonald's parking lot in Moscow, killing one person, injuring eight others, and causing major damage. The device was similar to those commonly used in Chechnya. Russian police arrested a Chechen male. No one claimed credit. 02102501

October 26, 2002. *Bosnia.* U.S. troops from the NATO-led Stabilization Force (SFOR) peacekeepers based in Tuzla arrested Sabahudin Fijuljanin, 41, a Bosnian Muslim, on suspicion of spying on a U.S. base. Police found an antitank weapon and several passports in his home. On December 3, he was linked to al Qaeda. In late January 2003, he was turned over to Bosnian Federation authorities; they released him on bail. In February 2003, the Federation government charged him with illegal weapons possession. 02102601

October 26, 2002. *United Kingdom.* The London-based weekly magazine *al-Majallah* published what it claimed was a copy of Osama bin Laden's typewritten will, signed by bin Laden and dated December 14, 2001. The will accused Muslim leaders of betraying him and "the students of religion" (the Taliban). The will stated that "despite the setback the new battle will lead to the elimination of America and the infidel West even if decades later."

October 27, 2002. *Israel.* At 11:30 a.m., Mohammed Shqeir, 19, from Nablus and a Palestinian member of the al-Aqsa Martyrs Brigades, set off a suicide bomb at a gas station in Ariel, a Jewish settlement in the West Bank. He killed 3 soldiers and himself, and wounded 20 people. Two bystanders grabbed Shqeir and Israeli soldiers shot him in the head, but they were unable to stop him from setting off his explosives belt as he fell. The Brigades said the bombing was to "avenge the killing of Palestinian civilians by Israeli troops." Hamas separately claimed credit. Among the wounded was Eliezer Biton, a bus driver hit by shrapnel. The terrorist groups gave different names for the bomber. Hamas said he was Mohammad Bustami. The Brigades later said he was not a member.

October 27, 2002. *India.* Some 15 separatists shot to death 22 male villagers in Dadgiri in Assam State. Another dozen were wounded. Police blamed the National Democratic Front of Bodoland guerrillas, who called out the men from their homes near Bhutan.

October 28, 2002. *Jordan.* At 7:30 a.m., Laurence Foley, 60, a U.S. Agency for International Development employee, was hit by eight bullets fired by a masked gunman in front of his carport as he was getting ready to drive to work from his home in suburban Amman. The gunman ran away. Foley had been a federal employee for 37 years—14 for US AID—and had received

a service award the previous day. He had worked in the Peace Corps twice and had served his country in India, the Philippines, Peru, Bolivia, and Zimbabwe, as well as Jordan. Local authorities were not certain that it was a terrorist attack. The United States closed its embassy.

On October 29, a fundamentalist leader wanted for questioning in the case fired at police, wounding two policemen. The suspect, Mohammad Ahmad Chalabi (alias Abu Sayaff), was also wounded in the gun battle in Maan. Dozens of others were brought in for questioning across the country. Authorities doubted the claim of the obscure Honorables of Jordan to the London-based *Al-Quds al-Arabi* newspaper. The group said it was protesting U.S. support to Israel and "bloodshed in Iraq and Afghanistan." The group had earlier claimed credit for another shooting. Another group called the Honest People of Jordan claimed credit.

On December 14, Jordanian authorities announced that two members of al Qaeda were arrested "some while ago" at a home they shared in the Amman suburbs. Salem Saad bin Suweid, a Libyan, told police that he had surveilled Foley for several days, then hid with a silenced 7-mm pistol behind Foley's car. Suweid had worn a bulletproof vest and had covered his face. He said he shot Foley at least six times and then ran to a rented getaway car driven by Yasser Fatih Ibrahim, a Jordanian who was also arrested and admitted his role in the shooting. The duo said they were carrying out instructions by Ahmad Fadeel al-Khalaylah (alias Abu Musab Zarqawi), a Jordanian al Qaeda lieutenant they had met in Afghanistan when the trio were training in camps. Zarqawi was wanted for his role in a plot to bomb hotels in Amman and Europe in December 1999. The duo said they were to carry out other terrorist attacks against embassies, "Jordanian institutions and Jordanian personalities," and other foreign diplomats in Amman. Police found smuggled rockets intended for an unspecified attack, along with automatic weapons, tear gas, and hand grenades. They said Foley was a target of opportunity who kept a routine. Police recovered the murder weapon; ballistics tests matched it to bullets found in Foley's body. The duo was charged with the murder, and as of April 2003, remained in Jordanian custody awaiting trial.

On January 28, 2003, U.S. Secretary of State Colin Powell named former U.S. Ambassador to Jordan Wesley Egan to head an investigation into whether a security lapse contributed to the killing and report back in 60 days.

On May 11, 2003, a Jordanian military prosecutor charged 11 Arab men, some with al Qaeda links, with conspiracy to conduct terrorist attacks against U.S. and Israeli targets in Jordan and with Foley's assassination. Four of the men were in custody. The 11 men were scheduled to be tried at the State Security Court in May 2003. The men were of Libyan, Syrian, Palestinian, and Jordanian descent. They faced the death penalty.

On April 6, 2004, a Jordanian court convicted and sentenced to death eight terrorists for Foley's death. Six, including Jordanian terrorist leader Abu Musab Zarqawi, who is linked to al Qaeda in Iraq, remained at large. 02102801

October 29, 2002. *United States.* CNN reported that a UPS truck exploded on I-270 in Missouri. Observers initially suggested that a terrorist bomb had been hidden in a package, but police later said it was not terrorism.

October 29–30, 2002. *South Africa.* Nine bombs, possibly the work of right-wingers, exploded in Soweto during the night. At 11:55 p.m., a bomb exploded at a mosque. Shortly after midnight, four more bombs blew up near a rail station. Another two bombs exploded at a second station, and two more exploded at a third rail line. Claudina Mokane, 42, died in her sleep when hit by debris from a blast. Husband Simon Sikwati, 51, had head injuries.

October 30, 2002. *Denmark.* At Russia's request, the government detained Akhmed Zakayev, 43, on charges of armed insurrection, kidnapping, and execution of civilians in Chechnya. Zakayev is a leading representative of Chechnya rebel leader Aslan Maskhadov's government in exile. Russia accused him of involvement in the rebel seizure of a Moscow theater that left 128 hostages dead. On December 3, Denmark rejected extradition.

November 2002. *Australia.* Perth authorities charged an Australian citizen with conspiracy to bomb the Israeli Embassy in Canberra and the Israeli Consulate in Sydney.

November 2002. *Paraguay.* Immigration officials at Asuncion airport detained a self-proclaimed supporter of Osama bin Laden en route to the United States. Airline agents prevented three people claiming to be from Taiwan, but bearing false passports and U.S. visas, from boarding an aircraft bound for the United States.

November 2002. *Paraguay.* A court sentenced Sobhi Fayad, a prominent Hizballah fund-raiser, to a long prison term.

November 3, 2002. *Yemen.* A Hunt Oil Company helicopter was fired at by gunmen on the ground as it took off from San'a. One person in the helicopter was wounded. On August 28, 2004, following a three-month trial, a Yemeni court sentenced six people to five years in jail for the attack. 02110301

November 3, 2002. *India.* Indian police killed two Lashkar-i-Taiba gunmen in the basement parking lot of Ansal Plaza, an upscale New Delhi shopping mall. One policeman was wounded in the 15-minute gun battle. Police had been tipped off. They recovered two Chinese-made pistols, an AK-56 rifle, and ammunition clips. The attack was on the eve of Diwali, the Hindu festival of lights.

November 3, 2002. *Tajikistan.* The government extradited 12 members of the Islamic Movement of Uzbekistan, designated a Foreign Terrorist Organization by the United States, to Uzbekistan for prosecution. The Tajik Ministry of Security captured the suspects during a security sweep.

November 4, 2002. *Israel.* Nabil Sawalhe, an Islamic Jihad suicide bomber, set off an explosive outside a Shekem home electronics store in a Kfar Saba mall north of Tel Aviv, killing himself and two other people. Some reports indicated that the store's security guard died fighting with the terrorist. Sawalhe was a resident of the Balata refugee camp in Nablus.

November 4, 2002. *Kuwait.* Authorities arrested Mohsen al-Fadhli, 21, an alleged al Qaeda member suspected of plotting to car bomb a hotel in San'a, Yemen, housing 20 U.S. officials and 2 other men. Al-Fadhli was being investigated for involvement in the October 6 attack on the French oil tanker and the October 12, 2000, attack on the USS *Cole.* 02110401

November 5, 2002. *United States.* Authorities in Greensboro, North Carolina, arrested Abdel-llah Elmardoudi (alias Abdella), 36, of Minneapolis, at a bus stop. Elmardoudi is allegedly the leader of a "sleeper operational combat cell" centered in Detroit. He was believed to be from Morocco and lived primarily in the Chicago area in recent years. On November 14, he was transferred to Michigan to face federal terrorist charges. He was alleged to have provided direction to three others who sought to purchase weapons, obtain false ID documents, and identify security holes at Detroit Metropolitan Airport. A man with a similar name—Abdel-llah Elmardoudi—was arrested more than a year earlier and charged with stealing telephone calling card numbers by peering over people's shoulders at the Minneapolis–St. Paul airport. The foursome were members of Salafiyya and al-Takfir Wal Hijira, with ties to al Qaeda. They were planning "violent attacks against persons and buildings within the territory of Jordan, Turkey, and the U.S.," according to an August indictment. Karim Koubriti and Ahmed Hannan had been in federal custody since an FBI raid on their Dearborn, Michigan, apartment in September 2001. Farouk Ali-Haimoud was arrested with them, released, but rearrested in April. A trial for Koubriti,

Hannan, and Ali-Haimoud was scheduled for January 21, 2003.

November 6, 2002. *Israel.* Ismail Mashour, 25, a Palestinian, fired into a greenhouse in the Rafih Yam Jewish settlement in the southern Gaza Strip, killing two Israelis and injuring a third before he was shot to death by a guard. The Hamas terrorist killed Assaf Tsfira, 18, a member of the family that employed him as a farm laborer, then ran into a textile shop and shot to death Amos Saada, 51, the owner. He fought his war into a settlement guard's car, injuring the guard slightly before a second guard, Kobi Hadad, shot him as he threatened the guard with a hand grenade.

November 6, 2002. *United States.* The Justice Department announced that it had foiled two separate plots to use drug money to buy weapons for terrorists. Both groups of defendants were charged with providing material support to terrorist groups. One was the heroin-for-stingers September 20 case in Hong Kong.

Right-wing Colombian paramilitaries planned to buy $25 million worth of East European weapons with cocaine and cash. Operation White Terror began 13 months earlier with meetings with undercover FBI and Drug Enforcement Administration (DEA) agents in London, Panama City, and the Virgin Islands. The arms were to go to the Autodefensas Unidas de Colombia (AUC), a paramilitary umbrella group involved in hundreds of assassinations, kidnappings, and massacres. The group planned to buy 9,000 assault rifles, shoulder-fired antiaircraft missiles, grenade launchers, and nearly 300,000 grenades, 300 pistols, and 53 million rounds of ammunition. In April, a would-be buyer was shown samples in St. Croix. The four defendants were Carlos Ali Romero Varela and Uwe Jensen, both of Houston, and Colombian nationalists Cesar Lopez (alias Commandant Napo) and Commandant Emilio. They were charged in a Houston federal court with conspiracy to distribute cocaine and conspiracy to provide material support and resources to a foreign terrorist organization, which carry life sentences. Jensen was arrested on November 5 in Houston. He claimed he was Danish with U.S. citizenship. The others were grabbed the same day in San Jose, Costa Rica, and faced extradition to the United States.

November 6, 2002. *United States.* The United States added to the Terrorist Exclusion Designees List the following organizations:

- Al Taqwa Trade, Property and Industry Company, Ltd.
- Bank Al Taqwa, Ltd.
- Nada Management Organization
- Youssef M. Nada & Co., Gesellschaft MBH
- Ummah Tameer E-Nau (UTN)
- Loyalist Volunteer Force (LVF)
- Ulster Defense Association
- Afghan Support Committee
- Revival of Islamic Heritage Society (Pakistan and Afghanistan offices; Kuwait office was not designated)

November 7, 2002. *Israel.* Four Palestinian men kidnapped Nicolai Panke as colleagues watched from a balcony in broad daylight. Panke is a former official of the International Committee of the Red Cross (ICRC) in Khan Younis in the southern Gaza Strip. He was permitted to speak with the ICRC several times. He had worked for the Red Cross in Gaza since April, distributing supplies that included blankets and tents to Palestinians whose homes had been destroyed by Israeli military forces. Panke was released 11 hours later at 11:30 p.m. No reason for the abduction was given. 02110701

November 9, 2002. *Israel.* The Israeli army shot to death Iyad Sawalha, 28, head of Islamic Jihad's military wing in the northern West Bank, during a house-to-house hunt in Jenin. He had thrown grenades at the soldiers in an escape attempt.

He was behind suicide attacks that killed more than 30 people.

Islamic Jihad in Beirut claimed credit for setting off a bomb on a road Israeli troops were patrolling near Netzarim in the Gaza Strip, killing Israeli Army Sgt. Maj. Medin Gerifat, 23, in "an initial response to the assassination of the martyr Iyad Sawalha."

November 10, 2002. *Israel.* At 11:20 p.m., a Palestinian gunman killed five people when he fired an AK-47 at the Metzer kibbutz in northern Israel. After breaking through a fence, the al-Aqsa Martyrs Brigades terrorist fired on a couple walking nearby, killing Tirza Damari, 42, a counselor in a juvenile home in nearby Hadera. Her boyfriend, Uri Ronen, 49, said, "We tried to get away to the bushes, but he fired a burst at us and hit Tirza." While a neighbor fired a pistol at the terrorist, the gunman shot to death Yitzhak Dori, 44, a community official driving through the compound. He then broke into a home and shot a mother, Revital Ohayon, 34, and two of her children, Matan, 5, and son Noam, 4, in their beds.

On November 14, Israeli troops tracked down the ringleader of the terrorists, forced him to strip to his underwear, and made him surrender in Tulkarm, West Bank.

The kibbutz was begun in 1953 by Argentine Jewish settlers.

November 10, 2002. *Israel.* Two Palestinians planning a suicide bombing died when their car exploded after they were challenged by police a mile away from the Metzer kibbutz.

November 11, 2002. *Colombia.* Bishop Jorge Enrique Jimenez, head of the Latin American conference of bishops, and Reverend Desiderio Orejuela were kidnapped in an area where leftist rebels are active. Bishop Jimenez and Reverend Orejuela were on their way to perform a religious ceremony in Pacho, 35 miles north of Bogota. Their driver was captured but released. Colombian Army Comdr. Gen. Carlos Alberto Ospina offered a reward of $37,000 for help in finding the victims.

November 12, 2002. *Qatar.* Al-Jazeera broadcast an audiotape from Osama bin Laden that threatened Indonesia, Tunisia, Kuwait, Jordan, Pakistan, Russia, the United Kingdom, France, Italy, Germany, Canada, Australia, and the United States if a war began in Iraq. Bin Laden praised the recent attacks in Bali and Moscow, the fatal shooting of a U.S. Marine in Kuwait, the killing of a U.S. diplomat in Jordan, and the attempt to sink a French oil tanker near Yemen. The terrorist leader said that the attacks "were undertaken by the zealous sons of Islam in defense of their religion and in response to the call of their God and prophet, peace be upon him." Intelligence officials warned that they were seeing other indicators that terrorists were planning attacks.

November 13, 2002. *United States.* At 8:30 a.m., a man in a Budget Rent-A-Car truck stopped on Washington, D.C.'s Independence Avenue outside the Department of Agriculture and told police that there were explosives inside. The man said he wanted to see President Bush. Several downtown streets were closed, and 7,000 employees were evacuated from three buildings. Bomb technicians found no explosives, and the man, 38, from Woodbridge, was detained. At 10:30 a.m., he was strapped to a stretcher and loaded into an ambulance. He was taken to George Washington University Hospital for physical and psychological observation. At 10:45 a.m., the streets were reopened.

November 13, 2002. *Russia.* Masked Chechen gunmen abducted two Russian drivers for the Red Cross from their convoy of two trucks and an SUV between the villages of Pobedinskyoe and Goragorsky. The duo was returning to Ingushetia after delivering a humanitarian shipment to Grozny. Alexander Panov, 41, and Musa Satushev, 43, were released on November 17 without a ransom.

November 13, 2002. *United States.* The FBI backpedaled from an earlier warning that terrorists were planning to attack hospitals in Washington, D.C., Chicago, Houston, and San Francisco with explosives or anthrax. The White House said the advisory, apparently based upon a report from Pakistan, had "low credibility."

November 14, 2002. *United States.* The FBI warned law enforcement agencies that al Qaeda could be plotting "spectacular" attacks inside the United States "that meet several criteria: high symbolic value, mass casualties, severe damage to the U.S. economy, and maximum psychological trauma." The key targets were historic landmarks, the nuclear sector, aviation, and petroleum.

November 14, 2002. *Europe.* Intelligence and law enforcement officials throughout Europe warned that terrorists were planning major attacks using chemical weapons or other weapons of mass destruction. Hans-Joseph Beth, chief of Germany's international antiterrorism team, said that Abu Musab Zarqawi, a Jordanian al Qaeda leader and expert in toxins, could be planning an attack.

November 15, 2002. *Israel.* At 7:10 p.m., Palestinian gunmen with M-16 rifles ambushed an armored jeep convoy after the return of a group of Jewish settlers to their homes in Kiryat Arba, killing 12 and wounding 15 Israelis. The settlers were returning from Friday Sabbath at the Tomb of the Patriarchs shrine at the Gush Ezion Junction near Hebron. A night-long gun battle began; three Islamic Jihad terrorists, five border patrolmen, three armed settlement security officials, and four Israeli army soldiers, including Col. Dror Weinberg, 38, the commander of the Hebron region, were killed. No worshipers were injured. Ramadan Shallah, the leader of Islamic Jihad, claimed credit in a call to al-Jazeera, saying the attack was in retaliation for the killing of Iyad Sawalha the previous week. The next day, police arrested 40 Palestinians.

November 16, 2002. *United Kingdom.* Scotland Yard arrested three men and charged them under the Terrorism Act with possession of articles for the preparation, instigation, and commission of terrorism acts. Local press said that they had planned to release cyanide gas in the underground rail system. The unemployed trio were identified as Rabah Chekat-Bais, 21, Karim Kadouri, 33, and Rabah Kadris, mid-30s. 02111601

November 16–20, 2002. *Malaysia.* Police arrested four Islamic militants—three Malaysians and a Singaporean—in Johor State between November 16 and 20 who were planning to conduct a suicide attack against Western targets in Singapore, including the U.S. and other embassies. Police were investigating whether one of the suspects was involved in the Bali attack. The Indonesian was identified as Iqbal, who might have carried out the first of the two Bali bombings against Paddy's nightclub. Iqbal had left a note for his family apologizing for becoming a Muslim martyr. 02111602

November 17, 2002. *Israel.* Security guards overpowered Tawfiq Fukra, 23, an Israeli Arab, outside the cockpit of El Al flight 581, a B-757 going from Tel Aviv to Istanbul, 15 minutes before it was scheduled to land. Fukra hoped to take over the plane with a penknife hidden in his belt and crash it into a tall building in Tel Aviv. He was protesting Israeli actions against Palestinians in the Gaza Strip and West Bank. However, he lost his nerve. He pulled the knife on a flight attendant and demanded that the cockpit door be opened. She screamed, he tried to open the door himself, and two Israeli security agents and other passengers wrestled him to the floor. He told them, "Today is the day I die, and I do this because they killed my brothers." None of the 170 passengers were injured. The plane landed safely in Istanbul, where he appeared in court. He had collected piloting tips from Internet sites. He said he was a student with no affiliation to any organization. Fukra is of

Palestinian origin and holds an Israeli passport. He knew no one in Turkey, but booked a round-trip flight because the tickets were so cheap. 02111701

November 18, 2002. *Japan.* Two small bombs went off outside Camp Zama, a U.S. Army base near Tokyo, causing no damage or injuries. Police discovered a homemade projectile launcher 300 yards from the camp's logistical center. 02111801

November 18, 2002. *Germany.* The media reported that German authorities removed and studied the brains of four Red Army Faction (Baader-Meinhof Group) terrorists following their deaths in the 1970s. State prosecutors ordered the study of the brains of Ulrike Meinhof, Andreas Baader, Gudrun Ensslin, and Jan-Carl Raspe. Meinhof committed suicide in prison at age 41 in 1976. The other three killed themselves in prison in October 1977 after hearing that their colleagues had failed in the hijacking of a Lufthansa airliner. Their release was demanded in return for the 86 hostages, but German GSG-9 commandos stormed the plane on the ground.

November 18, 2002. *Indonesia.* Major international schools in Jakarta, including several with American students, were closed and requested extra security in light of reports of al Qaeda threats. Some of the al Qaeda terrorists making the threats were believed to have been behind the Bali bombings of October 12. One threat was made against the Jakarta International School. A third of the school's 2,500 students are Americans.

November 20, 2002. *Saudi Arabia.* A gunman broke into a McDonald's restaurant a few miles from a base used by U.S. forces and set it on fire during daylight hours, when Muslims fasting for Ramadan should not be there. 02112001

November 21, 2002. *Lebanon.* A gunman killed Bonnie Penner (later listed by the State

Department as Bonnie Denise Witherall), 31, an American missionary married to a Briton. She was killed by three shots to the head at the Unity Center, a Sidon clinic where she worked as a nurse. The center houses a Christian chapel and had received warnings from anti-American Lebanese Muslims demanding they leave the country. A colleague said, "About three to four months ago the frequency of the warnings increased and the language toughened. They came from Lebanese Sunni Muslim extremists asking them to stop their activities and leave." Muslim clerics claimed the evangelical group had attempted to convert Muslims. No group claimed credit, but the An' Asbat al-Ansar was suspected. 01112101

November 21, 2002. *Kuwait.* At 10:30 a.m., Khaled Shimmiri, 20, a deranged (according to the Kuwaiti government) Kuwaiti junior traffic policeman, shot and seriously wounded two American soldiers who were driving between bases. He fired on them after pulling them over on the highway between their headquarters at Camp Doha and Arifjan, a Kuwaiti base. The Americans, one injured in the face, the other in the shoulder, did not return fire. They were in a civilian vehicle and were not in uniform. Shimmiri was arrested in Saudi Arabia the next day. On November 23, he was extradited to Kuwait. On March 5, 2003, he was convicted and sentenced to 15 years in prison. His attorney said he would appeal. Judge Nayef Mutairat sentenced Shimmiri to ten years for attempted murder and five years for unlawful possession of a weapon, to be served consecutively. He also ordered Shimmiri to be dismissed from the Kuwaiti police force. 02112101

November 21, 2002. *Israel.* At 7:10 a.m., Nael Abu Hilayel, 22, a Hamas suicide terrorist from Bethlehem, set off a bomb in the Number 20 Egged bus in Jerusalem's working-class Kiryat Menachem neighborhood, killing 11 and injuring 47 passengers. The dead included Hodaya Asaraf, 13; Ella Sharshevsky, 44, and her son, Michael, 16; Kira Friedman, 67, and her grandson, Ilan Friedman, 8; Marina Bazarski, 46; Dakla Zino, 20; Slima Novak, 56; Yafit Ravivo, 13; and Vargas Mirsa, 25, a Romanian tourist. The injured included Maor Kimche, 15; Tova Itzhaki, 50; and Tami Ravivo, 40. Many students were on the bus. The terrorist was wearing an explosives vest packed with nails and screws. He boarded the bus two or three stops before the explosion, which broke windows on five nearby cars. Hamas said it was retaliating for the killing of its military commander, Salah Shehada, on July 23. Israel troops moved into Bethlehem the next day and arrested Hilayel's father. 02112102

November 22, 2002. *Colombia.* Leftist rebels were blamed when four 60-mm mortar shells were fired at the U.S. Embassy and the Bogota building housing the attorney general's office. Two people were slightly wounded when the shells fell on a grassy area outside the office a few blocks from the U.S. Embassy. Authorities found two unfired mortars at the National University after police raided the campus. President Alvaro Uribe offered an $18,000 reward for the attackers' arrest. 02112201

November 22, 2002. *Afghanistan.* Kabul authorities arrested Bokan Akram Khorani, 22, an Iraqi Kurd with 18 to 22 pounds of explosives taped under his vest. Intelligence police said he was plotting to assassinate either President Hamid Karzai or Defense Minister Mohammed Fahim. Police said he was a member of an international terrorist group that had tried to attack President Karzai in September. Amrullah Salihi, spokesman for the National Directorate of Security, told reporters, "He had been trained and assigned to carry out a suicide mission. He had very clear links with the Taliban and some extremist Pakistani groups." His assigned target was Karzai, but arrived too late to catch him from his return trip from the United States, so switched his target to Fahim. He was "casing" Fahim's upscale neighborhood when captured. Police had been watching him since he arrived from Pakistan several days earlier. Police claimed he had been trained in Pakistani Kashmir and had ties to three senior leaders of the former Taliban government who were hiding in Pakistan, plus to unnamed Pakistani extremist groups. Police showed reporters a table full of explosives and a detonator. 02112202

November 23, 2002. *Russia.* After taking credit for the Moscow theater hostage-taking of October, Chechen warlord Shamil Basayev warned of new strikes if Russian troops did not leave Chechnya.

November 24, 2002. *India.* Lashkar-i-Taiba attacked the Reghunath and Shiv temples in Jammu, Kashmir, killing 13 and wounding 50 people.

November 25, 2002. *Nepal.* The U.S. Embassy was threatened by communist rebels who warned that Americans faced a heightened risk. 02112501

November 25, 2002. *Turkmenistan.* Gunmen attempted to assassinate President Saparmurad Niyazov as he rode through the streets of Ashgabat. Leonid Komarovsky, 55, a former Russian journalist who became a U.S. businessman, was arrested and accused of driving one of the cars used in the failed attack. He had gone to Turkmenistan to set up a Czech liquor importing business. From his home in Newton, Massachusetts, he sold Russian alternative medicines from a Web site. Turkmen prosecutors called him "a mercenary from Moldova with an American passport." As of January 13, 2003, Komarovsky had admitted selling a cell phone to former Foreign Minister Boris Shikhmuradov, one of the accused plotters. Guvanch Dzhumayev, his long-time business partner, was also charged with plotting the assassination. Turkmen authorities arrested more than 100 people and blamed the plot on several opposition figures living in Russia. All of Dzhumayev's male relatives, including his ill father, 76, were arrested, according to www.freeturkmenistan.org.

Turkmenistan accused neighboring Uzbekistan's ambassador of aiding the plot and gave him 24 hours to leave the country. Turkmen troops went into the Uzbek ambassador's compound in Ashkhabad, claiming that the Uzbeks had given shelter and aid to Shikhmuradov.

On December 26, 2002, President Niyazov announced the arrest of former Foreign Minister Boris Shikhmuradov, one of his leading opponents, in the failed assassination attempt. Also arrested was Yklym Yklymov. Sapar Yklmov, a former deputy agriculture minister and now an opposition leader living in Sweden, denied involvement. On December 29, state television showed Shikhmuradov allegedly confessing while looking down, speaking haltingly, and claiming he was not tortured into the confession. On December 30, Turkmenistan's high court convicted Shikhmuradov and sentenced him to 25 years in prison for allegedly plotting to assassinate President Niyazov. Presidential loyalists comprising the People's Council then increased the sentence to life in prison.

On January 2, 2003, Turkmen Vice Premier and Defense Minister Rejepbay Arazov met with Russian Security Council Secretary Vladimir Rushailo to request assistance in investigating claims that the plot was organized and financed in Russia. He asked Russia to find and extradite Khudaiberdi Orazov, chief of Central Bank, and Nurmukhammed Khanamov, former ambassador to Turkey, for alleged involvement in the plot. President Niyazov said that 4 Russians from Chechnya were among the 51 people detained. On January 24, President Niyazov said that 46 people had been convicted.

November 26, 2002. *United Arab Emirates.* Police were investigating why a customs officer fired on a U.S. military helicopter.

November 26, 2002. *Northern Ireland.* Police arrested six people in a three-year plot to smuggle firearms from Florida to the Irish Republican Army. The suspects were believed to have financed the purchase of scores of firearms in 1999 and 2000.

November 27, 2002. *Italy.* Stefano Savorani, 29, a mentally ill ex-policeman, attempted to hijack an Alitalia flight from Bologna to Paris with 57 passengers (CNN said 74). He ran to the front of the plane, claimed to have a remotely controlled bomb, and ranted about belonging to bin Laden's al Qaeda. "I belong to al Qaeda and I want to make a declaration to the press." The plane landed safely in Lyons, France. He had tried another hijacking in 1999 against a domestic Air France flight; in 1998, he had hijacked an Italian train. His mother said he was being treated for schizophrenia. 02112701

November 28, 2002. *Israel.* At 3:20 p.m., two al-Aqsa Martyrs Brigades gunmen jumped out of a stolen white Mazda and fired hundreds of AK-47 bullets and threw a grenade at the Likud Party headquarters in Beit Shean. The gunmen killed 5 and wounded 20 Israelis before being shot to death in a five-minute gun battle with local guards. An explosives belt one of them was wearing failed to detonate. Voters were casting ballots in a nationwide primary that selected incumbent Ariel Sharon to run as prime minister in January. Among the injured were the three sons of former Israeli Foreign Minister David Levy. Uri Levy said, "I heard them release the pin of the hand grenade and they said, 'Lie down.' Then I saw one of them looking at me and he was going to shoot me, but he ran out of bullets. And I shouted at everyone to run away." Al-Aqsa said it was retaliating for the deaths of two militant commanders by Israelis forces in the Jenin refugee camp on November 26.

On November 29, Israeli troops blew up the Jalboun homes of the two Palestinian gunmen —cousins Omar and Yousef Abu Rub, both in their 20s.

November 28, 2002. *Kenya.* At 8:25 a.m., two Strela SA-7 MANPADS shoulder-fired missiles narrowly missed hitting an Arkia Israeli charter B-757-300 jet flying from Mombasa to Tel Aviv

with 261 passengers, most of them Israelis. Many of the passengers did not know they were fired on until pilot Rafi Marek informed them as the plane was landing in Israel. The attacks marked the anniversary of the November 29, 1947, partitioning of Palestine by the United Nations. The previously unknown Government of Universal Palestine in Exile, al Qaeda, and the Armed of Palestine claimed credit for the attack and for the Paradise Hotel bombing. The Al-Ittihad al-Islamai (AIAI) was believed linked to the attack.

Police found a launcher for an SA-7 Strela, a Soviet-designed antiaircraft missile, and two missile casings in the Changamwe area of Mombasa, a mile from Moi International Airport.

Radhi Idha, of Yemeni ancestry, along with his brother and cousin, were held for questioning. Idha was released after three days; the other two were still in custody as of December 9. The missiles were fired from near Idha's scrap metal yard. Police said the trio had been seen sitting in a car nearby, chewing khat leaves. 02112801

November 28, 2002. *Kenya.* At 8:30 a.m., three suicide terrorists drove a green 4-wheel-drive Mitsubishi Pajero bomb into the Israeli-owned Paradise Hotel resort in Mombasa, killing themselves, 3 Israelis, and 10 Kenyans, and injuring 80 others. Prior to the explosion, the terrorists had driven up and down the unpaved road that leads to the hotel. They sat 100 yards from the hotel for a few minutes, then gunned the engine and sped toward the entry gate. Security guard Justin Mundu, 57, who was at the booth at the gate, said, "It happened so fast. I heard this bang. Then I heard a loud bang, and then dust and smoke and people screaming. They came right through the gate." One of the terrorists got out and set off an explosives belt he was wearing. The two others then set off the car bomb. Al-Ittihad al-Islamiyah, a Somali group with al Qaeda ties, was suspected.

Eight dancers were among those killed, including Kafera Mukde, a dancer who sold seashells on the beach, and seven Giriama dancers, including Riziki Salim Yaa, Safari Yaa, Charo

Yaa, Agnes Tembo, and Kafedha Masha. The head of Shadrack Tindi Maina, the hotel's assistant manager, was still missing two weeks later. He left behind a wife pregnant with their seventh child. Also killed were brothers Dvir Anter, 14, and Noy Anter, 12. Their mother, Ora, was on a respirator. Father Rahamim and daughter Edva, 8, had minor injuries. Also killed was Albert de Havila, 60, a tour guide from the central Israeli town of Raanana. Asher Mkumbi was among the injured. Dozens of children were orphaned.

Police questioned a dozen suspects, including Abdullah Ahmed Abdullah. A man by that name had been indicted in the United States for the 1998 Nairobi embassy bombings. Police also questioned tourists Alicia Kalhammer, 31, who carried a U.S. passport and Jose Tena, her Spanish husband. They had checked out of the Le Soleil Beach Club at 10:00 a.m. Six Somalis and four Pakistanis were also questioned. Israeli observers said those ten had been arrested on November 25 when they arrived on a dhow with false passports, thereby making them unlikely bombers. On December 13, police said that they had no evidence that the Pakistanis and Somalis were involved in the attacks, but charged them with being in the country illegally. On November 30, Kalhammer and Tena were released.

The Government of Universal Palestine in Exile, al Qaeda, and the Armed of Palestine claimed credit. The Al-Ittihad al-Islamai (AIAI) was believed linked to the attack.

This appeared to be the first al Qaeda attack against Israeli interests. Authorities were unable to confirm an al Qaeda claim of responsibility on an Islamic Web site—rare for an al Qaeda attack. On an audiotape given to al-Jazeera, Sulaiman Abu Ghaith said, "I hereby confirm what has been issued by al Qaeda political office regarding our responsibility for the Mombasa attacks in Kenya. The Christian-Jewish alliance will not, God willing, be safe from attacks by the mujaheddin…. The alliance's installations and facilities everywhere will be subject to attacks." He called for Muslims to attack the United States with "focused and lightning

operations." He said the United States and its allies aim to "protect the Jewish occupiers and achieve their expansionist dream of setting up a [Jewish] state between the Nile and Euphrates," which runs from Turkey to Iraq through Syria.

On December 9, Kenyan police released computer-generated sketches of two "Arab-looking" men seen at the site of the attacks. They were between the ages of 30 and 40. One had a thick beard and eyebrows and a receding hairline. The other had thinning hair and no beard. Police offered a reward of $6,276, which is seven times the average annual Kenyan salary.

On December 10, police said that they were looking for Saleh Ali Saleh Nabhan, 23, who bought the Toyota sedan he traded in to buy the green Mitsubishi SUV used in the attack. They did not know if he was alive or one of the bombers. His relatives said that days before the attack, he told his parents he was going to South Africa. Police detained his wife, Fatuma Nabhan, 17, a Kenyan, for questioning in Lamu, an island north of Mombasa. Saleh had told her he was going to Somali. On December 16, police found bomb-making materials in his home. Police said the couple had lived in Mombasa for three years with their child and another young couple suspected in the attacks. They all left on November 27. Nabhan was seen in Lamu on November 26. Police were still holding Jelani Abu Sheikh, who sold the car to Nabhan and another man two weeks before the attack.

On March 21, 2003, investigators said they were looking for Fazul Abdullah Mohammed, a slight man in his late 20s or early 30s, in connection with these attacks and with the 1988 U.S. embassy bombings in Tanzania and Kenya. He was described as a computer expert who speaks many languages, including French, Arabic, and English. He was born in the Comoros Islands and also has a Kenyan passport. He trained with bin Laden in Afghanistan. His wife identified him from photos on the FBI's Most Wanted Terrorist list.

On June 23, 2003, the Kenyan government announced that it was charging four people with murder in the attacks. The four were connected with Fazul Abdullah Mohammed. Mohamed Kubwa, a trader, and his father, Kubwa Mohamed, a Lamu county councilman, own property in Siyu, a center of Islamic scholarship near the Somali border. Fazul is married to Mohamed Kubwa's half-sister, Amina, and taught at an Islamic school in Lamu under the alias Abdul Karim. Aboud Rogo Mohammed, a cousin of the first detainees, is a Kenyan Islamic preacher. The fourth suspect—not Fazul—was unnamed by authorities until the June 24 indictment on 13 counts of murder. The fourth suspect was Said Saggar Ahmed, a teacher. A court appearance was scheduled for July 8. Attorneys did not enter a plea. Among the attorneys was Maobe Mao.

On November 4, 2003, a UN report claimed that the al Qaeda terrorists responsible for the attack were trained and equipped in Mogadishu, Somalia, in November 2001. They then smuggled the missiles to Kenya in August 2002. They fled to Somalia after the attacks. 02118202

November 28, 2002. *Philippines.* Australia and Canada shut their Manila embassies, citing specific threats of attacks by Muslim extremists.

November 29, 2002. *Israel.* Two Hamas gunmen fired in the Gaza Strip Jewish settlement of Dolah, wounding two Thai workers and an Israeli. One gunman was killed. 02112901

November 30, 2002. *India.* A grenade exploded in Awantipora, injuring four people. A bomb exploded near a police vehicle in Srinagar, Kashmir, injuring seven. No one claimed credit for either attack.

December 2002. *Jordan.* Intelligence officers uncovered a plot by 13 militants to attack U.S. targets, including the U.S. embassy and Jordanian bases where the plotters believed U.S. troops were stationed. On August 14, 2003, militant prosecutors charged the group with conspiracy. Three Saudis and a Jordanian were at large and would be tried *in absentia*. The case

was to begin in the military State Security Court in September 2003. The indictment said funding came from two of the Saudi fugitives. The group received rockets, grenades, and detonators from Iraq via a Jordanian truck driver, who was in custody. No al Qaeda tie was found. 02129901

December 2002. *Canada.* Canadian intelligence arrested Mohamed Harkat, 34, an Algerian immigrant in Ottawa, shortly after he called suspected al Qaeda members in the United States. Harkat, born in Algeria, had lived in Canada since October 6, 1995, when he arrived in Toronto from Malaysia via the United Kingdom on a faked Saudi passport. He claimed he was fleeing persecution by the Algerians and was granted refugee status on February 24, 1997. He applied for permanent residence on March 18, 1997. He admitted membership in the Front Islamique du Salut (FIS), which Algeria outlawed in 1993. He had fled Algeria in April 1990, moved to Saudi Arabia on a visitor visa, then moved to Pakistan, living there until September 1995. He was linked to Abu Zubaida, a senior al Qaeda leader arrested in Pakistan in March 2002, who had fingered Harkat during interrogations.

On December 10, Canadian intelligence told a court that Harkat was from Taguine, Algeria, lived in Ottawa, was married, and worked as a gas station attendant and pizza delivery man. Harkat also claimed membership in the Armed Islamic Group. He was held without formal charge on a security certificate—a procedure deemed constitutional by an Ottawa federal appeals court on December 10, 2004.

Canadian officials earlier announced that they would hand over to the United States Mohammed Mansour Jabarah, a Canadian-Kuwaiti arrested in Oman earlier in the year on charges of organizing a plot to bomb the U.S. and Israeli embassies in Singapore. He was held in a secret location in the United States. Canada claimed that Jabarah volunteered to go to the United States for questioning.

December 2002. *Lebanon.* The media claimed that Iraqi intelligence killed Walid al-Mayahi, a Shi'a Iraqi refugee in Lebanon and member of the Iraqi National Congress.

December 2002. *Turkey.* Authorities arrested Ali Aslan Isik, reportedly one of the top leaders of Turkish Hizballah, a Kurdish Islamic (Sunni) extremist group unrelated to Lebanese Hizballah.

December 2002. *Nigeria.* The Haliburton company reported that a powerful radioactive device used for oil field surveys was stolen while being hauled through the Niger Delta between Warri and Port Harcourt. The driver became the prime suspect when police found holes in his story. The "well logger" device showed up in September 2003 in a private scrap yard in Germany.

December 4, 2002. *India.* Authorities in Srinagar, Kashmir, defused a bomb found at a bus station. No one claimed credit.

December 5, 2002. *Indonesia.* Explosions set off within an hour of each other damaged a McDonald's restaurant in Makassar and a car dealership in Ujungpandang, the South Sulawesi capital located 1,000 miles east of Jakarta. No one took credit. One of the bombers and 2 other people died; 11 people were seriously injured. The car dealership is owned by Indonesian Welfare Minister Yusuf Kalla. Police detained several suspects and believed the Laskar Jundullah was responsible.

In 2003, Indonesia arrested 63 terrorist suspects, including 17 wanted for the bombing of the McDonald's and the car dealership. 02120501

December 5, 2002. *Turkey.* The U.S. State Department warned Americans of a possible terrorist threat in southeast Turkey. The likely target would be official U.S. government facilities or personnel. It warned Americans to be cautious traveling in or out of the Gaziantep Airport.

December 5, 2002. *Pakistan.* A bomb exploded at Macedonia's consular offices in Karachi. Three

bodies—two men, one woman—were found inside. Their hands and feet were tied and their throats were slit. Police suspected revenge by al Qaeda for the killing of seven suspects in Macedonia on March 2. Police found graffiti on the wall referring to al Qaeda and warning "infidels." No one claimed credit. 02120501

December 5, 2002. *Worldwide.* The al Qaeda Web site www.mojahedoon.net said that the group had decided to launch suicide attacks against Israel and wanted to destroy the Jewish state. Al Qaeda formed a new branch—the Islamic al Qaeda Organization in Palestine—to undermine talks between Israel and the Palestinian Authority. The group took credit for the Mombasa bombing of November 28.

December 6, 2002. *United States.* Federal agents searched the Quincy, Massachusetts, headquarters of Ptech Inc., a computer software firm suspected of al Qaeda financial ties. The group does contracting work for the FBI, Federal Aviation Administration (FAA), NATO, and the Departments of Energy, Navy, and Air Force. Officials removed documents and were looking to see whether Ptech's information technology architecture work had compromised its federal clients. The U.S. Customs Service was examining links to Saudi businessman and philanthropist Yasin al-Qadi, listed by the United States as a terrorist financier in October 2001. His defunct Muwafaq (Blessed Relief) Foundation was listed as "an al Qaeda front that receives funding from wealthy Saudi businessmen" and was used for "transferring millions of dollars to bin Laden." Federal officials also said that his company Kadi International had sent $820,000 to Hamas. Ptech has some ties to al-Qadi's firms. Several Ptech officials or employees have worked for firms he owned or financed.

Another member of Ptech's board of directors was Yaqub Mirza, whose Herndon offices were searched by the U.S. Customs Service in March in another terrorist financing investigation.

December 6, 2002. *India.* A bomb exploded at a McDonald's restaurant in a busy Bombay rail station mall, injuring 23 people. The bomb consisted of gunpowder, nails, and iron balls. No one claimed credit. 02120601

December 6, 2002. *India.* The Lashkar-i-Taiba was suspected of throwing a grenade and firing shots at a residence of a former minister in Damhal Hanjipora, Kashmir.

December 6, 2002. *India.* Lashkar-i-Taiba claimed credit for killing the brother of the recently slain law minister outside his home in Pulwama, Kashmir. The terrorists threw a grenade and fired shots at him.

December 6, 2002. *India.* In Rajpora Chowk, Kashmir, militants threw a grenade toward a vehicle carrying several military officers, but missed. The bomb exploded near a group of civilians, injuring eight. No one claimed credit.

December 7, 2002. *Bangladesh.* Around 6:00 p.m., a series of nearly simultaneous bomb blasts went off in projection rooms of four movie theaters packed with families celebrating Eid al-Fitr, the end of Ramadan. The bombs killed 18 people and wounded nearly 200, many of whom lost limbs. No foreigners were injured in the attacks in Mymenshingh, 95 miles north of Dhaka. Police suggested al Qaeda or other terrorists were responsible, but later backed off from the al Qaeda theory. No one claimed credit. Police arrested five suspects in the area and questioned theater employees. An Indian newspaper had earlier suggested that Ayman al-Zawahiri was hiding in Bangladesh.

The army defused a fifth bomb during the night in a theater in nearby Gaibandh.

December 7, 2002. *United States.* The *New York Daily News* reported that a terrorism task force was investigating a report that the Revolutionary Armed Forces of Colombia (FARC) was plotting to kidnap former New York City Mayor Rudolph W. Giuliani for ransom. His

consulting firm had been hired to advise Mexico City police.

December 8, 2002. *Czech Republic.* Israel said it had received intelligence warning that al Qaeda planned to attack Jews and Israelis in Prague.

December 9, 2002. *Colombia.* During the lunch hour, a car bomb went off in a grocery store parking lot near a police command post in a residential neighborhood in western Bogota, injuring more than 60 people.

December 9, 2002. *Ecuador.* A group of criminals broke into a storage shed and stole five iridium-powered industrial devices from Interinspec, a private firm in Quininde, then demanded a "ransom" for their return. The company agreed to pay $5,000, but received only three "well-logger" devices. One of the thieves was a former employee who had recently been fired in a job dispute. The firm lost a sixth device in January 2003 when it fell from a boat into the Quininde River. A seventh device was accidentally left behind in a remote jungle location at the completion of a project. These two items were later recovered, but those in the hands of the bandits remained at large.

December 11, 2002. *Colombia.* Police defused five remotely controlled car bombs in Bogota. Each had 550 pounds of explosives and could be remotely driven to targets. Planned targets probably included a police barracks and a bus station. Police had arrested six people in raids during the previous two days. Some of the detainees had tipped police to the car bomb campaign planned by the Revolutionary Armed Forces of Colombia (FARC).

December 11, 2002. *Israel.* Around 8:00 p.m., two Palestinian gunmen shot to death two Israeli soldiers—one a woman—near a Hebron shrine The victims were at a small outpost. The gunmen escaped.

December 11, 2002. *Canada.* Canada banned Hizballah, including its political wing, after its leader, Sheik Hassan Hasrallah, called for additional suicide attacks against Israelis. Canada had banned Hizballah's military wing in late 2001. Canada also banned the Kurdistan Workers Party and the Aum Shin Rikyo cult.

December 12, 2002. *Iraq.* The *Washington Post* reported that in October or November 2002, al Qaeda-affiliated terrorists belonging to the Sunni Muslim extremist Asbat al-Ansar obtained a chemical weapon in Iraq. The paper said a courier for the Lebanese terrorists smuggled the likely nerve agent VX overland through Turkey.

December 13, 2002. *Kosovo.* A bomb exploded in the center of the capital city, injuring more than 20 people, 7 seriously.

December 13, 2002. *Greece.* A gunman fired into the car window of Athens Mayor-elect Dora Bakoyanni. She was bending over to pick up her purse when the shot was fired. She was treated for cuts to her hands and face. The gunman, 35, a former mental patient, was arrested nearby.

December 13–14, 2002. *Pakistan.* Karachi police foiled a suicide bomb plot by Islamic terrorists who planned to crash their Volkswagen car bomb into a car carrying American diplomats. Police arrested a trio over two days and confiscated 250 sacks each filled with 88 pounds of ammonium nitrate, a fertilizer also used in the manufacture of explosives. The trio were trained at an Afghan terrorist camp run by Islamic militants fighting Indian rule in Kashmir. The trio were surveilling a main road used by the diplomats. Detainee Asif Zaheer was tied to a suicide bombing outside a Karachi hotel in May that killed 14 people, including 11 French engineers. Provincial police chief Kamal Shah said that Zaheer was "an expert in explosives, and he was the man who prepared the car for suicide bombing at the Sheraton Hotel." Zaheer had told police, "Assessing the strength of the U.S. Consulate building [which had been attacked in June, killing a dozen Pakistanis but no Americans], we decided to target American diplomats as they

traveled on city roads." Six suspects remained at large. 02121301

December 16, 2002. *France.* French counterterrorism agents arrested three Algerians and a Moroccan in an apartment in a Paris suburb. The suspected Islamic militants had two vials of an unidentified liquid and an anticontamination suit that could protect "against biological, chemical, and nuclear risks." Police believed they were planning a terrorist attack on the Russian Embassy in Paris. The men were linked to Rabah Kadre, 35, an individual with al Qaeda ties, who was arrested with two others in November in the United Kingdom on terrorism-related charges. Kadre was accused of possessing materials for the "preparation, instigation or commission of terrorism." He had been to terrorist training camps in Afghanistan, according to French news reports. Police also seized faked ID papers, a video camera, and two empty gas canisters. They believed the group had trained in camps in Afghanistan and Chechnya.

Among those arrested was Menad Benchellali, 29, a suspected al Qaeda trained chemical weapons specialist who trained at camps in Afghanistan. He returned to France in 2001 and set up a lab in his parents' spare bedroom in Lyon to manufacture ricin, which he hid in Nivea skin cream containers. 02121601

December 17, 2002. *Afghanistan.* At 3:00 p.m., Amir Khan, an Afghan Islamic militant, 17, threw a hand grenade into a jeep in a crowded market in central Kabul, wounding two U.S. soldiers and their Afghan interpreter. A day later, they were in stable condition. One suffered injuries to the head and lower extremities; the second had shrapnel wounds in his lower right leg. The English-speaking Khan comes from Khost, a former Taliban stronghold. He recently trained at a Pakistani religious academy and was working on orders from an Islamic extremist group. He had earlier been seen praying at the Pul-i Khishti mosque. Khan said he had brought three grenades from Khost to use against Americans. He had earlier seen Turkish and German troops from the peacekeeping force, but waited until he could go up to the Americans' jeep. He regretted injuring the interpreter. 02121701

December 17, 2002. *United States.* Police arrested three people in Buffalo on allegations that they were involved in the unauthorized transfer of $50 million to Yemen via *hawalas* (informal financial houses) in violation of the USA Patriot Act. Mohammed Albanna, 51, owner of Queen City Cigarettes and Candy Company, was charged with sending $487,000 to Yemen since October without proper permits. He is a leader of the Yemeni community in Lackawanna, New York. He is the uncle of Jaber Elbaneh, an unindicted coconspirator in the case of the six men from Lackawanna who were indicted in October on charges of providing material support to al Qaeda. Also arrested were two members of his family, Ali A. Albanna, 29, and Ali Taher Elbaneh, 52, also of Lackawanna. Albanna faced five years in prison. The trio pleaded not guilty.

December 18, 2002. *United States.* A federal grand jury indicted five executives of Infocom, a suburban (Richardson) Dallas, Texas, computer firm, for conspiracy to conceal financial transactions with Mousa Abu Marzook, a leader of the Islamic Resistance Movement (Hamas). Marzook had been designated a terrorist by the U.S. government in 1995. He was also indicted by the Dallas federal grand jury. Infocom is tied to its next-door Richardson neighbor the Holy Land Foundation for Relief and Development, America's largest Islamic charity. The Holy Land Foundation for Relief and Development is believed to be a Hamas financier. One of those indicted, Infocom Vice President Ghassan Elashi, chairs Holy Land, which the government shut down in December 2001. Infocom had provided Internet services to Holy Land for years. The indictment charged Marzook, his wife Nadia Elashi, and five of Nadia's male cousins who run Infocom—Ghassan, Bayan, Basman,

Hazim, and Ihsan—with Marzook's investment of $250,000 in the firm from 1992 to 1993. Agents found that he initially gave the firm $150,000 in 1992; she made another $100,000 investment. In 1993, the firm agreed to repay her the entire amount, which the government said was a sham. The money was going to Marzook, thereby making it an illegal transaction. He had been deported in 1997, living in Jordan and then Syria. He is the deputy chief of the Political Bureau of Hamas. The five brothers were also charged with selling computers and computer parts to Libya and Syria in the late 1990s with a Commerce Department export license. They tried to hide the exports by claiming that one export was going to Malta.

December 18, 2002. *United States.* A federal task force announced the arrest of six men in the Detroit area and searches of ten local businesses and residences on allegations that they were involved in the unlicensed transfer of $50 million to Yemen via *hawalas*. Police seized five bank accounts in Detroit and Dearborn, Michigan.

On January 8, 2003, federal officials dropped the charges against Gamil Manea Ahmed Al-Najar, 26; David Nasser Ali, 40; Foiad Hussain Mohamed, 25; Mohammad Aidaros Abdulla, 62; Abdulla Hassan Mohamed, 31; and Hussein Ahmed Mohamed, 65. They were released on $10,000 unsecured bonds. Assistant Agent James Dinkins, in charge of the Customs Service investigation, said that new charges would be filed soon.

December 18, 2002. *India.* In Yaripora, Kashmir, terrorists threw a grenade at a parked military vehicle, but missed. The explosion injured 15 people, including 3 soldiers, and caused major damage to the vehicle. No one claimed credit.

December 19, 2002. *Afghanistan.* A man set off a grenade at an international peacekeeping headquarters in Kabul, killing the terrorist and injuring two French citizens and two Afghans.

Authorities arrested a second man carrying grenades. The French citizens worked for an aid organization. The locals worked as interpreters for the peacekeepers. The attacker approached the compound, pulled the pin, and was about to throw it when guards stopped him. He grounded the grenade, injuring Afghans nearby. Other compound guards opened fire. It was unclear whether he died from the gunfire or the explosion. 02121901

December 19, 2002. *Pakistan.* A blast in an underground bomb factory used by Islamic terrorists killed five suspected terrorists, including one linked to the murder of U.S. reporter Daniel Pearl and the bombing of a U.S. consulate. The explosion also destroyed the chemical storage warehouse in Karachi's eastern Korangi neighborhood. Police found high-grade explosives and a rocket-propelled grenade. They later found photos of a U.S.–owned gas station that might have been a terrorist target and a possible hit list of police officers and ethnic leaders. 02121902

December 19, 2002. *Pakistan.* Lahore police arrested nine family members suspected of being al Qaeda operatives. They included Jaded Ahmad, his two sons, two brothers, three nephews, and an uncle. Among the detainees was Canadian citizen Usman Ali Khawaja. Ahmad and sons Umar (variant Omar) Karar and Khyzer Ali are naturalized Americans and former Florida residents. Ahmad, a physician, had lived in the United States from 1972 to 1983. FBI agents seized four computers and CDs. The family's guards fired on the police during the raid, but no injuries were reported. Information Minister Rashid Ahmed said some of the detainees were suspected of having smuggled weapons for use in terrorist attacks.

On March 5, 2003, the Lahore High Court ordered the release of U.S. citizens Omar Karar Khawaja and Khyzar Ali, and the Canadian, Usman Ali Khawaja. The men's fathers—including Ahmad Javed Khawaja, a gastroenterologist, and his brother, Ahmad Naveed Khawaja, a Canadian—remained in jail awaiting trial.

On May 31, 2003, the three-judge panel of the Lahore bench of the Supreme Court ordered the release of Javed Khawaja and Ahmad Naveed Khawaja. The decision cannot be appealed. The decision came a few days after the duo was found not guilty of the last charges against them; prosecutors had sought to hold the two men despite their acquittal. 02121903

December 20, 2002. *India.* The Pakistan-based rebel group Save Kashmir Movement claimed credit for assassinating State Assembly Member Abdul Aziz Mir, 45, outside a mosque after prayers. This was the first shooting on a member of the new Jammu and Kashmir assembly since the fall elections, during which Islamic terrorists threatened to kill anyone who participated in the campaign.

Five other civilians were killed elsewhere in the Himalayan region.

Maoist Communist Center (MCC) rebels ambushed a police van in the east, killing 18 people, most of them police officers, and wounding another 20 policemen in the ambush and ensuing gun battle. The MCC was avenging the death of its leader, Ishwari Mahato, two days earlier.

December 21, 2002. *Pakistan.* A bomb exploded on a local passenger bus in Hyderabad, killing 2 people and injuring 18 others after police announced that they had arrested 4 Islamic terrorists armed with grenades. No one claimed credit.

December 21, 2002. *United Arab Emirates.* Sky marshals grabbed two Libyan men on a Royal Jordanian Airlines flight after they told a flight attendant that they were carrying a bomb. No bomb was found. The duo was questioned at Abu Dhabi airport by Jordanian and local authorities. 02122101

December 22, 2002. *Germany. Stern* magazine reported that the government was investigating a tip that a 50-member al Qaeda cell was planning attacks on embassies, banks, and multinational corporations in Germany and elsewhere in Europe. British, French, and U.S. consulates in Duesseldorf and Frankfurt were warned.

December 23, 2002. *United States.* The FBI announced it had intelligence that terrorists were planning to use shoe bombs against aircraft. Terrorists could also hide bombs in bulky winter coats or other garments.

December 24, 2002. *Kenya.* The U.S. Department of State warned Americans in East Africa that terrorists could strike and that Nairobi, Kenya, and Djibouti were under threat of a missile attack.

December 24, 2002. *Philippines.* The Moro Islamic Liberation Front was suspected of setting off a bomb that killed the mayor of Datu Piang and 16 others in Maguindanao Province on Mindanao.

December 24, 2002. *France.* Counterterrorist authorities arrested four suspected Islamic militants planning attacks in France. The agents discovered electronic components and an unidentified substance hidden in hair treatment bottles in a home in Romainville, a northern Paris suburb. They were believed linked to a group arrested the previous week in La Courneuve who had bomb-making materials.

Police later announced that the eight Islamic terrorists were planning attacks against Russian interests in France and abroad, including against the Russian Embassy in Paris. The group's leader was Menad Benchellali, the brother of an al Qaeda leader held by the United States at Quantanamo Bay. Menad was arrested on December 24. 02122401

December 24, 2002. *Russia.* Police arrested two Chechen men in their mid-20s who had entered a southwestern Moscow market armed with grenades and plastic cases packed with TNT and metal pellets. Each of the men had ten ounces

of TNT in a plastic case wrapped in material in their pants belts. They also had several grenades. The city prosecutor said the explosives had not been assembled as a working bomb. One man had a residence permit from Gudermes, Chechnya's third-largest city. The other had papers from Nadterechny in northern Chechnya. The duo had arrived in Moscow a month earlier. They were held for illegal possession of weapons and explosive substances. Police did not believe they were tied to the October theater incident.

December 24, 2002. *Pakistan.* Islamabad authorities dismantled several grenades and 30 rounds of ammunition that had been placed in a bag near a church where local and Western worshippers were to gather for Christmas services. An anonymous phone call to the local authorities had warned that a bomb had been placed near the church. No one claimed credit. 02122402

December 25, 2002. *India.* Twenty thugs armed with daggers, homemade pistols, and bombs attacked a church in Maliapota, West Bengal, injuring six people, including a priest. The thugs stole $3,000.

December 25, 2002. *Indonesia.* Police seized 550 pounds of ammonium nitrate, the same fertilizer used in the Bali bombings, from a car in Palu. As of December 31, police had arrested five people but were still searching for the owner.

December 25, 2002. *Pakistan.* Two terrorists wearing burqas (a woman's veil) threw a grenade into a small church during Christmas services for 40 people in Chianwala, 40 miles northwest of Lahore. They killed 3 people (aged 6, 10, and 15) and wounded 13 others. All three of the dead and most of those injured were women or girls. Police arrested six people, including an Islamic cleric who had called for the murder of Christians. Among those injured was Fazeelat James, 21, who recalled, "I was praying when these two youngsters threw a shopping bag into the congregation. Then something exploded and I fell down."

Islamabad police found 2 handmade grenades and 20 shell casings in a shopping bag in bushes about 100 yards from St. Thomas's Protestant Church.

December 26, 2002. *Philippines.* Rebels ambushed a vehicle owned by Toronto Ventures, Inc. Pacific, a Calgary, Canada-based mining company, killing 13 and injuring 10 Filipinos. The ambush took place in Baliguian in Zamboanga del Norte Province on Mindanao Island. Filipinos Moro Islamic Liberation Front rebels were blamed. Police said the rebels were extorting money from the firm. 02122601

December 27, 2002. *Russia.* At 2:30 p.m., suicide terrorists drove a Jeep SUV and a Kamaz heavy truck laden with more than a ton of explosives into the courtyard of the Russian government headquarters building in Grozny, Chechnya, killing more than 80 people, including a 14-year-old girl, and wounding 210 others. (The death toll could rise; several people took away relatives' bodies after the blast.) The jeep exploded after soldiers fired on it. The truck exploded 30 seconds later. The blasts left a huge crater less than 35 feet from the entrance and destroyed the four-story headquarters. The explosions shattered windows a third of a mile away. Rudnik Dudayev, chief of the Chechen Security Council, was hospitalized with a head injury. No one claimed credit. Akhmed Zakayev, a spokesman for the separatist government-in-exile, said on a rebel Web site that the attack "may be regarded as a terrorist act," but "there may be others who will assess today's event as a successful retribution act from Chechens." Moscow had sought his extradition from the United Kingdom on charges of armed insurrection.

Russian authorities said that the terrorists had worked with Arab terrorists in carrying out the attack. They said they had caught and killed an Arab mercenary in Stariye Atagi, 18 miles south of Grozny, on December 26. "We managed to

destroy ringleader Abu Tarik but did not manage to prevent the attack," Col. Ilya Shalbalkin told *Tass.* Russian officials claimed that Shamil Basayev, a rebel commander, met with Abu al-Walid, an Arab financier of the Chechens and member of the Muslim Brotherhood, just before the blast. The meeting took place in the Nozhai-Yurt region of Chechnya. Shabalkin blamed Aslan Maskhadov, ousted Chechen president, for planning the attack, saying he had issued orders to kill Chechens who cooperated with the Moscow-led government. Maskhadov condemned the attack.

Investigators said the terrorists had passed through three checkpoints on a highway and apparently had official government passes. They were dressed in the uniforms of a Russian major, lieutenant, and private. The truck had an armored cabin.

As of December 31, 15 people remained in critical condition.

December 27, 2002. *Kyrgyzstan.* Azizbek Karimov, 24, after finding the previous day that he could not get close enough to the U.S. Embassy, walked to a market in Bishkek and left his explosives-laden briefcase. When the bomb went off, 7 people died and 20 were injured.

On May 8, 2003, after being berated by his Islamic mentors for not bombing the U.S. Embassy, he brought a perfume box with a grenade and timer to a Bakai Bank wire transfer outlet in Osh. The grenade killed a cashier, Dilshat Aliyev, 27, whom he had met. He had used the alias Medetbek Taliyev, which was tracked down by police. He fled to Uzbekistan.

He was captured later in May 2003 in a shootout with Uzbekistan police in his basement hideout in Andijan. He unsuccessfully attempted to commit suicide with a spoonful of rat poison and by slicing his arm before capture.

After his capture, he told authorities that he was given explosives and thousands of dollars to kill Americans. If he could not attack the U.S. Embassy because it was too well protected, he was to bomb the Pinara-Bishkek Hotel, which attracts foreigners. He said his Islamic radical commanders told him in September 2002 in Istanbul that "Americans came to Afghanistan and killed our brothers. We have to pay them back."

Karimov was born in Andjian, Uzbekistan, 175 miles east of Tashkent. He underwent six months of training in guns and explosives at a Chechen camp near Khasavyurt, Dagestan. He linked up with the Islamic Movement of Uzbekistan terrorist group led by former Soviet paratrooper Juma Namangani. He claims he met bin Laden and went to Afghanistan for more training.

On February 16, 2004, the Uzbekistan Supreme Court convicted and sentenced to death Karimov, 25, who has ties to al Qaeda, for the December 2002 bombing of a market in Bishkek, Kyrgyzstan, and a May 2003, Western Union office in Osh, Kyrgyzstan. The attacks killed eight people. 02122701

December 27, 2002. *Israel.* At 7:45 p.m., Palestinian gunmen broke into a kitchen and dining hall of Otniel, a small Jewish settlement and religious community on the West Bank. They fired automatic weapons, killing four Israelis and wounding nine. During a 20-minute gunfight, Israeli soldiers shot and killed one gunman; two Israeli soldiers were injured. The troops chased a second gunman for 90 minutes through the countryside before shooting him to death a mile southwest of the settlement. He was wearing an Israeli army uniform and carried an M-16. Three Israeli soldiers were slightly injured in the pursuit. Otniel is 6 miles southwest of Hebron and 25 miles south of Jerusalem. Most of the victims were religious students. Islamic Jihad said it was avenging the death of Hamsa Abu Roub, 35, one of its leaders, in an Israeli raid in Qabatiya the previous day.

December 28, 2002. *Yemen.* Ali Jarallah, an opposition Islah Party member, shot to death Jarallah Omar, deputy secretary general of the Yemeni Socialist Party, minutes after he delivered a speech at the Annual Congress of the Islamic Reform Party in San'a. On September 14, 2003, a court sentenced Jarallah to death. Jarallah was also convicted of orchestrating the killings on December 30, 2002, of three Americans at a Southern Baptist missionary hospital and of forming a terror cell to kill local officials and foreigners.

December 28, 2002. *France.* Police arrested Abderazak Besseghir, 27, a Frenchman of Algerian origin who worked as a baggage handler at Charles de Gaulle airport after they found radical Islamic and pro-Palestinian documents, information regarding pilot uniforms, a pistol, five cakes of plastic explosives, two detonators, and a fuse hidden in his car. He was detained in the morning on suspicion of possessing arms and explosives after a passenger told police he was acting suspiciously at the trunk of his car. He was also questioned on possible al Qaeda ties. Police later went to his home in Bondy, a Paris suburb, and took his father, two brothers, and a male family friend into custody. Besseghir had no criminal record—except for a 1997 vandalism incident—and no known ties to Islamic militants.

On December 31, French police took into custody the retired French soldier who reported Besseghir, who had been unable to explain the arms in his vehicle. 02122801

December 29, 2002. *Ivory Coast.* Rebels said William Foster, a Lutheran missionary caught behind their lines, was safe and would soon be handed over unharmed to the Red Cross. The American had lived for the past 8 years at Toulepleu near the Liberian border. He was later reported "safe and sound" by John Mueller, director for missionary service at the Lutheran Church-Missouri Synod in St. Louis, who claimed that Foster had not been held hostage by the rebels. 02122901

December 29, 2002. *United States.* The FBI asked the public to be on the lookout for five men believed to have entered the United States illegally circa December 24, possibly from

Canada—Abid Noraiz Ali, 25; Iftikhar Khozmai Ali, 21; Mustafa Khan Owasi, 33; Adil Pervez, 19; and Akbar Jamal, 28. The Bureau's Seeking Information: War on Terrorism Web site said there was no specific information tying them to terrorist activities, but that the Bureau wanted to locate and question them. The FBI said the names and ages could be faked. The Bureau later said that they were "terror suspects" connected with a passport smuggling operation with possible ties to terrorists. The men may have lived in Pakistan and could be part of a larger group planning New Year's attacks. The *Washington Post* reported that they were part of a group of 19 who had sought fake documents to use to enter the United States. The *Toronto Sun* said that the five arrived at Toronto's Pearson International Airport two weeks earlier, lived in the Toronto area for a few days, then were smuggled into the United States. A British Columbia woman saw two of them on a Vancouver Island ferry on December 10.

Pakistani Jeweler Muhammad Asghar, 30, said that his photo was that used to identify Mustafa Khan Owasi. Asghar said he had never traveled abroad, having been stopped two months ago from traveling to the United Kingdom when United Arab Emirate police found he had a forged passport. He suggested that those who faked his passport had gone on to use his photo with this latest crop.

By January 2, 2003, the investigation into the manufacture of fake IDs had extended into Canada, Pakistan, and the United Kingdom, and the United States was considering publishing the names of 6 others, possibly 14. There was no record at the U.S. Immigration and Naturalization Service (INS) of anyone by any of those names coming into the United States.

Michael John Hamdani, who had been arrested in October in Toronto with $600,000 in fake American Express and Thomas Cook traveler's checks and passport counterfeiting equipment, was identified as the source of the information on the five men who had traveled from Pakistan to the United Kingdom to Canada and to the United States. Hamdani faced charges of fraud and possession of instruments of forgery in Canada. He told investigators that he was contacted months earlier by people offering $20,000 to $30,000 for each man who could sneak from Pakistan into the United States. He had a long history of immigrant smuggling. Using the name Michael Javed, he was arrested in Canada in 1995 with a Pakistani woman he was attempting to get into Canada and the United States. The duo was carrying faked New Jersey driver's licenses and faked U.S. passports. In 1998, he was stopped at a Brussels bank for using fraudulent traveler's checks. Pakistani authorities sentenced him to ten years in prison. In October 2002, police in Peel, a Toronto suburb, heard of a ring of artists cashing faked $100 traveler's checks that were traced to Hamdani. In his apartment, police found counterfeiting equipment, the traveler's checks, faked Pakistani driver's licenses, piles of passport photos, and faked immigration papers from several countries, along with fake Indian consul general documents. He was also wanted on a 1996 FBI warrant in New York in another counterfeiting case. He was freed on January 3, 2003, from a Canadian jail after the Canadian charges were dropped the previous day so that he could face the 1996 charges. He was represented by attorney Deepak Paradkar.

On January 9, 2003, Hamdani was ordered held without bail in New York after he pleaded not guilty to charges in a 1996 fraud case. He was charged with trafficking in fraudulent travel and ID documents. He was also accused of giving the FBI false tips on terrorism suspects. The FBI called off the hunt for the would-be terrorists on January 6, saying it was a hoax.

December 30, 2002. *Yemen.* A gunman walked into a meeting room and shot to death a U.S. missionary doctor, Martha Myers, 57, of Montgomery, Alabama, and her two U.S. colleagues, hospital administrator William Koehn, 60, of Arlington, Texas, and purchasing agent Kathleen Gariety, 53, from Wauwatosa, Wisconsin, at the Jibla Baptist mission hospital in Ebb Province,

105 miles south of San'a. The terrorist then moved to another room, where he shot a fourth American, pharmacist Donald Caswell, 49, of Levelland, Texas. (Caswell underwent surgery for removal of two bullets.) The terrorist then aimed at a Filipino hospital employee, but the gun jammed. The terrorist surrendered. Abed Abdel Razzak Kamel, 30 (or 32), was arrested as the killer. He posed as a patient, and when it became his turn to be treated, he opened fire. He said he had hoped the killings would bring him closer to God. He said he was a member of Yemen's Islamic Jihad and shot the Americans because they were preaching Christianity. Yemen said the Islamic extremist had al Qaeda ties and was a member of the Islamic opposition Islah Party. The Party said he had left their group to join Islamic Jihad because they were "too soft against the West and America." Yemen detained numerous militants and set up roadblocks. Kamel was an associate of Ali Ahmed Mohamed Jarallah, who had killed an opposition leader two days earlier. Kamel and Jarallah were trained in Afghanistan, according to local security officials. Police said that the duo had provided a list of eight targets indicating that they planned to attack other foreigners, journalists, and Yemeni political leaders. One target was a guesthouse used by Ismaili Muslims in San'a. By January 2, 2003, Yemeni authorities had detained 30 people in the case, picking up another five on that date. No charges had been filed.

The mission was affiliated with the Richmond-based Southern Baptist Convention's International Mission Board, which has run the hospital in Jibla for 35 years. Gariety had worked in Yemen for a decade. Myers worked there for a quarter of a century. Koehn had worked for the mission board for 28 years and was to retire in October.

At the opening of the trial on April 20, 2003, prosecutors called for the death penalty, which the Garietys' siblings opposed on April 25. The defendant said at the trial, "Yes, I killed them to take revenge on Christians and Americans. I am comfortable" with the attack because he acted "out of religious duty" and for revenge against "those who converted Muslims from their religion and made them unbelievers." He said he coordinated the attack with Ali al-Jarallah. The trial was held in a court in Ebb Province, 105 miles south of San'a.

On May 10, 2003, Kamel was sentenced to death. According to Kamel's attorney, Mahrous Oqba, the verdict violated Islamic law so he would appeal. Jarallah was sentenced to death in a separate trial in 2003. On December 1, 2003, a tribunal affirmed the death sentence of Kamel, who said he would appeal the decision to the Yemen Supreme Court. Court officials expected that the conviction would be upheld and passed to President Saleh, who was expected to sign off on the order to carry out the sentence. 02123001

December 30, 2002. *Puerto Rico.* Five prisoners broke out of a maximum security prison after two confederates diverted a helicopter they had rented from Caribbean Helicorp in San Juan, claiming they needed to inspect construction work in Ponce. The two hijackers forced the pilot at gunpoint to land on the roof of Las Cucharas prison during morning recreation. Orlando Valdes Cartagena, Jose A. Perez Rodriguez, Victor Gonzalez Diaz, Hector Marrero Diaz, and Jose M. Rojas Tapia boarded, flew to a remote area in the central mountains, and escaped. The five had been serving sentences in excess of 100 years for murder and other crimes. Corrections Secretary Miguel Periera said it was possible that prison guards helped the escapees. By January 3, 2003, four of the prisoners were back in custody and the two hijackers had been captured. Police were searching for the fifth prisoner, who might have been killed. 02123002

December 30, 2002. *United States.* Security was stepped up in New York harbor and pleasure craft were banned from the area after receipt of a tip that eight "diversionary attacks" would occur throughout the state before a major attack in the harbor. The Department of Homeland

Security issued the warning 36 hours before New Year's Day.

December 30, 2002. *Philippines.* A bomb went off on a Manila commuter train, killing 22 people. In May 2003, security forces arrested Saifullah Yunos (alias Muklis Yunos), a subcommander of the separatist Moro Islamic Liberation Front (MILF) in connection with the case. During his arraignment in July 2003, he entered a guilty plea for his involvement in the bombing.

December 31, 2002. *Indonesia.* Police seized a half-ton of ammonium nitrate, the same material used to make the Bali explosives, from a house in Palu, Sulawesi Island. The homeowner was being questioned.

December 31, 2002. *Worldwide.* The *Washington Post* reported that U.S. intelligence was following 15 cargo freighters that could be controlled by al Qaeda or used by the group to ferry terrorists, money, materiel, or other items or used as attack vessels.

December 31, 2002. *Philippines.* Shortly before 8:00 p.m., a 60-mm mortar shell or a grenade with a timer went off next to a fireworks stall in a market in Tacurong in Sultan Kudarat Province in Mindanao, killing at least 4 people and injuring 26. The Moro Islamic Liberation Front was suspected.

December 31, 2002. *United States.* Fox News reported that someone on a Web site threatened to unleash a supervirus against computers if the United States attacked Iraq.

2002. *Israel.* In a conference of international police officials in mid-January 2003, Israel's National Police Inspector General, Shlomo Aharonishky, announced that more than 350 Israelis died in 1,776 incidents authorities deemed terrorist attacks.

2002. *Cambodia.* On December 28, 2004, the prosecution began of Egyptian citizen Esam Mohamid Khidr Ali; Thai citizens Chiming Abdul Azi and Muhammadyalludin Mading; and Cambodian citizen Sman Esma El accused of colluding with Indonesian al Qaeda and Jemaah Islamiah terrorist Riduan Isamuddin (alias Hambali) to attack the U.K. and U.S. embassies in 2002. On December 29, 2004, the court sentenced the two Thai Muslims and the Cambodian to life. Ali, the director of an Islamic school, was found not guilty.

2003. *Peru.* Spain extradited Adolfo Hector Olaechea, a suspected Sendero Luminoso (Shining Path) official, to Peru. He was released from custody but ordered to remain in Peru while the public prosecutor prepared the case for trial.

2003. *Germany.* A court sentenced a Turkish citizen to 18 months for illegal possession of explosives and on drug charges. The prosecution failed to convict him on charges of planning a terrorist attack on the U.S. Army's European Headquarters in Heidelberg.

2003. *Yemen.* Authorities arrested al Qaeda operative Fawaz al-Rabi'l (alias Furqan) and al Qaeda associate Hadi Dulqum.

2003. *Colombia.* The government extradited Gerardo Herrera Iles to the United States. Iles was accused of kidnapping oil workers of U.S and other nationalities.

2003. *Bolivia.* Suspected National Liberation Army–Bolivia organizer Colombian Francisco Cortes and two Bolivian radical members of the Movement Towards Socialism party were arrested and charged with espionage, terrorism, and subversion after they were found with weapons and organizational materials about guerrilla networks and plans to instigate violent revolution in Bolivia.

2003. *Denmark.* The Danish government froze the assets of the Danish branch of the al-Aqsa Martyrs Brigade and arrested a Danish citizen originally from Morocco with alleged ties to al Qaeda. Weapons charges were still pending as of early 2004.

2003. *Italy.* Twenty-eight Pakistanis were exonerated of Naples police claims that they were involved in a plot with al Qaeda and the Mafia to assassinate a British admiral.

2003. *Israel.* The government arrested several Jewish extremists who were planning terrorist attacks against various Palestinian targets. Courts sentenced to prison several prominent Jewish extremists who were planning to detonate a bomb near a girls' school in East Jerusalem in 2002.

2003. *Laos.* During the year, several incidents of domestic terrorism were carried out by antigovernment groups. Some of them were ambushes against buses and private vehicles, resulting in the deaths of 34 civilians. Other attacks led to the deaths of three Lao officials. The Free Democratic People's Government of Laos claimed credit for a least one in a series of bombings in the latter half of the year that killed one person and injured several others.

January 2003. *Jordan.* A court convicted ten Jordanians of weapons charges but acquitted them of participating in a plot to target U.S. interests in Jordan.

January 2003. *Colombia.* Rebels killed Doris Gil, the former Miss Colombia, and her businessman husband on June 25, 2003, after kidnapping them six months earlier.

January 2003. *Egypt.* Police arrested 43 members of Gund Allah (Soldiers of God) for planning attacks against U.S. and Israeli interests. They were to appear before a military tribunal in 2004.

January 1, 2003. *Israel.* A police antiterrorist unit killed a Palestinian gunman who had barricaded himself in a house in Maor for three hours. He fired a shot but then his gun jammed, permitting the couple who lived there to escape.

January 1, 2003. *Israel.* A Palestinian died when explosives in his bag went off as troops fired at him as he was moving between the Yitzhar and Immanuel settlements.

January 4, 2003. *Algeria.* Islamic militants attacked a military convoy during the night, killing 43 soldiers and seriously wounding 19.

Also during the night, Islamic terrorists killed 13 people from two families in Zabana, 30 miles south of Algiers.

January 4, 2003. *Pakistan.* Karachi Airport police arrested three people, including Jack Terrence Thomas, 29, an Australian with al Qaeda ties. The Melbourne taxi driver had gone to Pakistan for Islamic study in 2001, but trained in Afghanistan.

January 5, 2003. *Israel.* At 6:30 p.m. on two parallel streets in the old bus station section and a nearby pedestrian mall in central Tel Aviv, two Palestinian suicide bombers set off 33 pounds of explosives within 30 seconds of each other. At least 23 people died and 107 were injured, 9 seriously. Of the 21 dead who were identified, 15 were Israelis, 2 were Romanians, and 1 each were from Ukraine, Bulgaria, China, and Ghana. Many of the injured were foreign workers who did not seek medical assistance because they were in the country illegally. Some 67 people remained in the hospital after the first day. The blasts destroyed plate-glass windows 300 feet away. The bombs were packed with ball bearings and metal fragments. The al-Aqsa Martyrs Brigades said it was retribution for the destruction of Palestinian homes by Israeli forces and told al-Jazeera that the bombers were Boraq Halfa and Saver al-Nouri from Nablus. Other al-Aqsa spokesmen said the duo was not on their rolls.

Among those injured was Yevgeny Shreiver, 53, a Russian immigrant who worked as a security guard, who suffered shrapnel wounds in his legs. A backpack filled with rice was shredded, but saved his life.

The bomb on the pedestrian boulevard went off within ten yards of a pub where another suicide bomber had injured 32 people the previous year. 03010501

January 5, 2003. *United States.* An acid bomb was used outside the apartment of John Reedy, a friend of an informer in the case of Palestinian American Jesse Maali, who was involved in a federal immigration and money laundering case. Maali's nephew was charged the previous week with assaulting Reedy.

January 5, 2003. *Germany.* During the afternoon, German student Franz-Stephan Strambach, 32, hijacked a single-engine plane from the small Babenhausen airfield southeast of Frankfurt. After paying for a sightseeing tour, he pulled a pistol on the assigned pilot and forced him out of the plane. The hijacker threatened to crash the Austrian-made Super Dimona motorized glider into the European Central Bank in Frankfurt's financial center. He said he did not want to harm anyone, but threatened to commit suicide when he ran out of fuel. He landed safely two hours later, under the watchful eyes of pilots in two air force jets and a police helicopter. He said he wanted to draw attention to Judith Resnik, one of seven astronauts killed on the space shuttle Challenger in January 1986. "I want to make my great idol Judith Resnik famous with this. She deserves more attention. She was the first Jewish astronaut, and maybe that's why she isn't really considered." The hijacker ran a Web site dedicated to Resnik's career. He also wanted to telephone someone in Baltimore, possibly a relative of the astronaut. Authorities had shut down the airport and Frankfurt's railway station, and evacuated high rises. 03010502

January 5, 2003. *United Kingdom.* Antiterrorist police arrested six North African men after discovering traces of ricin, a toxin, in a north London apartment in the Wood Green district. The men were in their late teens, 20s, and 30s and were arrested in locations in north and east London. A woman detained with them was later released. They were held without charge under the United Kingdom's antiterrorist laws. Police said they were following a tip from French intelligence. A seventh man was grabbed on

January 7. Some press reports said they were Algerians.

On January 11, police charged Mouloud Feddag, 18; Sidali Feddag; Samir Feddag, 26; and Mustapha Taleb, 33, with possession of articles of value to a terrorist and being concerned in the development or production of chemical weapons. Nasreddine Fekhadji was charged with forgery and counterfeiting. A sixth man was arrested for possession of drugs and immigration offenses. The six were to appear in court on January 13. A seventh man, 33, was turned over to immigration officials. Four of the North African men appeared in court for the first time on January 13. They were identified as Mouloud and Samir Feddag and Mustapha Taleb, along with a 17-year-old, whose name was withheld because of his age. They were charged with possession of articles for the "commission, preparation or instigation of an act of terrorism" and with "being concerned in the development or production of chemical weapons."

Ricin traces had been found in an Afghanistan house in 2002, that had been used by al Qaeda. There is no antidote. Police believed the suspects would kill a small number of people with the ricin to cause widespread panic. Some observers suggested that the terrorists intended to use ricin to spike food that was to be delivered to a British military base. One of the detainees worked for a firm that served food on the base. The FBI issued a warning to local police about ricin on January 10.

On February 26, British authorities charged three men with conspiring to make chemical weapons.

By April 2004, nine individuals associated with the ricin threat were charged with conspiracy to murder and other related charges. Their trials were slated for May and September 2004. 03010503

January 5, 2003. *India.* No one claimed credit for setting off a hand grenade at a bus station in Kulgam, Kashmir, that injured 36 private citizens and 4 security personnel.

January 5, 2003. *Pakistan.* Two terrorists fired on the Peshawar residence of an Afghan diplomat, injuring a guard. The diplomat was not in his home at the time. No one claimed credit. 03010501

January 6, 2003. *Egypt.* An Islamic Web site hosted by Montasser Zayat, an Egyptian lawyer who spent time in prison with Ayman Zawahiri, carried a 150-word message from the al Qaeda deputy, saying Americans should be killed and the September 11 attacks helped Islam. He told Zayat not to "stop the new Muslim souls who trust your word from taking the road of holy war, represented by killing all Americans as they are killing us all…. [After September 11] the number of young people who follow the Islamic faith has increased to an unimaginable degree and in a short time."

January 9, 2003. *Pakistan.* Pakistani authorities and FBI agents arrested three al Qaeda suspects, including two Arabs and a Pakistani (National Public Radio said three suspects; Associated Press said two) after a gun battle in Karachi in which one of the terrorists threw a grenade. Police seized rifles, grenades, street maps of Karachi, Hyderabad, and Lahore, a satellite telephone, a laptop computer, suspicious documents, literature calling for a holy war, and more than $30,000 in cash (most of it American) from the terrorists' house. Two of the detainees claimed to be Abu Hamza of Yemen and Abu Umar of Egypt. Abu Umar's wife and three children were also detained. Seven other suspects were later released. They were all family members of Sabiha Shahid, a leader of the Jamaat-e-Islami party, who lived on the first floor. Police said the duo appeared to have entered Pakistan from Afghanistan in 2002. 03010901

January 9, 2003. *Gambia.* Authorities arrested two people involved in a suspected plot against U.S. Ambassador Jackson McDonald.

January 9, 2003. *United States.* The United States designated Lajnat al-Daawa al Islamiyya a terrorist organization after France submitted the group's name to the UNSCR 1267 Sanctions Committee for worldwide asset freezing. Lajnat al-Daawa al Islamiyya is a Kuwaiti-based charity with links to al Qaeda.

January 10, 2003. *Germany.* Police working with the FBI arrested Sheik Mohammed Ali Hassan al Mouyad (variant Moayad), 54, and his assistant, Mohammed Moshen Yaya Zayed, 29, both Yemenis, at an airport hotel in Frankfurt. Mouyad was an aide to Abd al Rahim al-Nashiri, an imam at a large mosque in San'a, Yemen, and an al Qaeda financier. (Al-Nashiri was chief of al Qaeda operations in the Persian Gulf and was arrested in the United Arab Emirates in October.) The Germans believed the duo could have been transiting through Frankfurt to an undisclosed location. The Germans considered an extradition request from the United States to send him to New York to face federal charges of providing material support to a terrorist organization. Moayad was represented by attorney Achim Schlott-Kotschote.

The *Washington Post* later reported details of the sting operation. A man claiming to be a Muslim from New York named Mohammed Aansi (variant Alanssi) approached Moayad in Yemen and attempted to get him to come to the United States to meet with a financier. When Moayad balked, he suggested Germany as a safe place to meet. Moayad flew from Yemen and was met at the airport and driven in a Mercedes to the airport's Sheraton to meet a wealthy American Muslim from New York who wanted to donate to Moayad's Middle Eastern charities. The man claimed to be a U.S.–born Muslim convert, Said Sharif bin Turi. For three days, the duo met to discuss monthly $50,000 tranches, not all for charity, some for bin Laden. Moayad claimed he was one of bin Laden's spiritual advisors and had been involved in fund-raising and recruiting for al Qaeda. German police arrested him the morning of January 10. He was believed to be a major financial supporter of al Qaeda and the

Palestinian Islamic Resistance Movement (Hamas).

Yemeni diplomats said that in 1998, Moayad cofounded San'a's Al Ehsan Mosque and Community Center, which feeds 9,000 poor families each day and provides free education and medical care. He is a senior member of Islah, an Islamic opposition political party. The FBI said he had collected money for several years from individuals and a Brooklyn mosque and sent the money to al Qaeda. On January 5, 2003, a federal judge in the Eastern District of New York had issued a sealed warrant for his arrest.

On March 4, 2003, the U.S. Attorney General indicted Moayab and Zayed for fund-raising for al Qaeda in Brooklyn's al Farouq mosque and hosting a service for suicide bombers. The FBI had taped meetings with five Brooklyn residents regarding money for al Qaeda. He had bragged of delivering $20 million to bin Laden before the September 11 attacks. The United States requested extradition and was given 30 days to provide enough evidence. The duo faced possible life sentences. The al Farouq mosque had previously been used by Egyptian cleric Sheik Omar Abd-al-Rahman, who was later convicted for the 1993 World Trade Center bombing. An FBI informant said he attended a September 2002 wedding hosted by Moayad in Yemen at which a senior Hamas official said that they would read about an operation the next day. That day a suicide bomber blew up a Tel Aviv bus, killing 5 and injuring 50.

On July 21, a Frankfurt court approved extradition of the duo to the United States, which had guaranteed that they would not be tried by a military or other special court. The German government administration had the final say on whether to extradite. On November 16, 2003, the duo was extradited to the United States, arriving at John F. Kennedy International Airport. Moayad was arraigned in U.S. District Court in Brooklyn on November 18 on charges of supplying arms, recruits, and more than $20 million to al Qaeda and Hamas. Moayad faced 60 years in prison; Zayed faced 30 years. Court

papers filed on December 6, 2004, indicated that when he arrived in New York, Moayad told FBI agents that "Allah will bring storms" to the United States because of his arrest, undercutting defense claims that Moayad did not speak English. "Allah is with me. I am Mohammed al Moayad. Allah will bring storms to Germany and America."

On May 11, 2004, Judge Charles Sifton in New York ruled that Yemeni-born ice cream shop owner lfgeeh did not understand the consequences of pleading guilty in October 2003 to charges of transferring tens of thousands of dollars to bank accounts in Yemen, Switzerland, Thailand, and China. Elfgeeh had acknowledged sending money to Moayad, who had pleaded not guilty to funding terrorist groups.

On November 15, 2004, at 2:05 p.m., Yemeni-born informant Mohamed Alanssi (alias Mohamed Alhadrami), 52, of Falls Church, Virginia, asked the security detail outside the White House to deliver a message to President Bush and then set himself on fire, critically injuring himself. He had also sent a note to the *Washington Post* and to FBI agent Robert Fuller indicating that he intended to torch himself. Alanssi had acted as a translator between the FBI operative and Moayad. Alanssi was apparently distraught over his role as a witness and claimed that the FBI had mishandled his case. He claimed that he was not permitted to travel to Yemen to visit his seriously ill wife and their six children because the FBI held his passport. He also claimed he had yet to receive U.S. residency papers and a million dollars. (He said the FBI had paid him $100,000.) Two days later, he remained in serious condition at Washington Hospital Center, with burns over 30 percent of his body. The defense had claimed that Alanssi had ineptly translated comments by Moayad, making embellishments. In May 2004, Alanssi had been charged in federal court in Brooklyn, New York, with felony bank fraud for writing bad checks.

January 10, 2003. *Israel.* Palestinian gunmen killed Nathanel Ozeri, a member of the outlawed

Kach movement, as he ate Sabbath dinner with his family at their home in an illegal outpost near Hebron. He had been jailed for participating in riots during the funeral of another settler in Hebron in July.

January 12, 2003. *Pakistan.* Hyderabad police defused a bomb placed in a toilet of a Kentucky Fried Chicken restaurant. No one had claimed credit for setting off two bombs in the city in recent months, killing 4 and injuring 33, all Pakistanis.

January 12, 2003. *Malaysia.* Police arrested two more suspected members of Jemaah Islamiah, bringing the total in detention to 80.

January 12, 2003. *United Kingdom.* Police in Bournemouth arrested five men and a woman on suspicion of terrorism.

January 12, 2003. *Israel.* Zeid Baisi, 17, died when a bomb he was fabricating exploded in Gaza.

January 12, 2003. *Israel.* Soldiers shot to death a Palestinian member of Hamas who had fired on an oil delivery truck in Hebron. Palestinian sources said that Hassam Samun, 27, was not a terrorist and was merely making deliveries for his family's bakery.

January 12, 2003. *Israel.* At 7:00 p.m., two Palestinian gunmen raided Moshav Gadish, a small Israeli collective community outside the West Bank, killing an Israeli and injuring four others before Israeli security forces killed the terrorists. The terrorists shot at cars on the main road, killing a man, injuring another, and wounding three security officers during an hour-long gun battle. One gunman died in a hail of bullets; the other was run over by a security jeep.

January 12, 2003. *Israel.* Two Palestinian terrorists and an Israeli soldier died in a shoot-out near the Egyptian border. The duo was spotted approaching Israeli communities and had fired at soldiers. The duo snuck into Egypt from the

Gaza Strip, traveled south, and planned to attack small communities near Nitsana, 25 miles south of the Gaza Strip.

January 13, 2003. *France.* A Paris court sentenced to prison 13 Basque Nation and Liberty (ETA) militants and sympathizers on terrorism charges. Nine-year sentences were given to ETA members Jose Luis Turrillas Arancenta; Jesus Maria Zabala Maguira; Agurtzane Delgado Iriondo, 44, who is accused of 18 murders in Spain; explosives expert Ignacio Santesteban Goicoechea, 39; and Angel Picabea Ugalde, 44, who handled transportation of explosives. Two other ETA members received five-year sentences. Six ETA sympathizers who provided logistical support received up to a year in prison.

January 13, 2003. *Israel.* Israeli troops shot to death two Palestinians who had thrown grenades at an Israeli bus in the Gaza Strip as it left the Jewish settlement of Netzarim.

Elsewhere, an Islamic Jihad terrorist died in an explosion in the West Bank.

January 13, 2003. *Russia.* Special Forces units in Chechnya found instructions for making poisons, including ricin, in the possession of an Islamic separatist. Russian authorities said some Chechens trained with al Qaeda in using biological and chemical weapons.

January 14, 2003. *United Kingdom.* During a police arrest of suspected terrorists in Manchester, an unarmed British policeman was stabbed to death with a large kitchen knife when one of the suspects started to flee from a kitchen. Four others were injured in the raid that was linked to the January 5 ricin raid. Police expected to detain one man under antiterrorist legislation, but found two others in their 20s at the scene. 03011301

January 15, 2003. *Germany.* Authorities banned Hizb ut-Tahrir (Party of Liberation), a radical Islamic group accused of spreading violent anti-Semitism on university campuses and establishing contacts with illegal neo-Nazi groups. Police raided 25 sites, including the Duisburg home of the group's leader, Shaker Assem, seizing his computer and documents. Assem had lectured in summer 2001 at the Islamic study group founded by September 11 hijack leader Mohamad Atta at the Technical University in Hamburg. The German Interior Ministry said, "The organization supports the use of violence as a means to realize political interests. Hizb ut-Tahrir denies the right of the state of Israel to exist and calls for its destruction. The organization also spreads extremely anti-Jewish hate propaganda and calls for the killing of Jews." The group was founded in Jordan in 1953 by a Palestinian. The group calls for the overthrow of Arab governments and the creation of a single Islamic state. In Egypt, 26 members were on trial in a state security court for trying to revive the group. It is banned in several Arab countries.

January 16, 2003. *Colombia.* At 8:00 a.m., an 88-pound car bomb outside the attorney general's offices in Medellin killed 4, injured 32, and damaged buildings and cars. Among the dead were a three-year-old boy, two employees of the attorney general's office, and a cafeteria worker. Police suspected the bomb was in retaliation for the mass arrests of rebel militias earlier in the week.

January 16, 2003. *United States.* James D. Brailey, Jr., 43, of Olympia, Washington, was charged in U.S. District Court in Tacoma on a federal firearms charge as part of a plot to kill Governor Gary Locke. He reportedly made "dry runs" on the Capitol building. He was jailed at the SeaTac Federal Detention Center. The previous day, the FBI's Seattle Joint Terrorism Task Force searched his van when he returned from a meeting in Arkansas of Christian Identity members, a white supremacist group. The FBI found two handguns in his van. In March 2001, an informant told the FBI that Brailey had been planning the assassination since 1998 and

believed that he was the true governor. He also hated the Chinese American governor because of his ethnicity. Brailey was also a member of the Jural Society, an organization that believes in a "people's government" based on Christian principles and common law. The group had elected him governor of Washington in 1998.

January 16, 2003. *Madagascar.* A grenade was thrown at the home of a U.S. embassy staff member (a U.S. citizen) in Antananarivo, damaging the building but causing no injuries. The grenade was tossed over the compound's wall and may have bounced off the house before exploding in the yard. 03011601

January 17, 2003. *Israel.* Hamas gunmen killed an Israeli and injured three others in an attack in Givat Harina on the West Bank.

January 17, 2003. *United Nations.* The Security Council unanimously voted to extend sanctions against the Taliban, al Qaeda, and Osama bin Laden, imposing a travel ban and arms embargo against 150 people and 172 groups on a list compiled by a UN Security Council committee.

January 19, 2003. *United Kingdom.* The London-based *Asharq al-Awsat* newspaper published excerpts of a 26-page statement written and signed by Osama bin Laden. Journalist Mohamed Shafaie said the letter was mailed from an Islamic source in London. The letter noted, "The current situation Muslim are living in requires a deployment of all efforts to fight the Islamic battle against the crusader coalition, which has revealed its real, evil intentions.... Their target now is Islam and Muslims and not only the [Middle East] region." Bin called on Muslims to "wake from their deep sleep ... and stop [acting as] rivals and fire their arrows toward their enemies instead of themselves."

January 19, 2003. *Colombia.* Right-wing paramilitaries kidnapped U.S.–Canadian war correspondent Robert Young Pelton, a freelancer writer and television reporter from Redondo

Beach, California, and two American colleagues identified as Mark Wedeven of Bremerton, Washington, and Megan Smaker of Brentwood, California, near the border with Panama and held them "for their own safety." The kidnappers said they would free the trio on January 21. The three were freed on January 23 and handed over to a Roman Catholic priest in the remote village of Unguia, 280 miles northwest of Bogota. They said they were not mistreated by the United Self-Defense Forces of Colombia. (The State Department's updated *Patterns of Global Terrorism 2003* said that the kidnapping took place on January 14 in Darien, Panama.) 03011901

January 20, 2003. *Colombia.* Leftist terrorists ambushed a police car at a roadblock on a northern mountain pass, firing machine guns and throwing grenades. Six officers and a civilian were killed.

January 20, 2003. *Algeria.* Three unarmed young men tried to hijack a domestic Algerian flight but were overpowered by security forces when the plane landed in Algiers. No one was injured. Their motives were undisclosed. 03012001

January 21, 2003. *United Kingdom.* In a dawn raid on the North London Central Mosque run by Abu Hamza al-Masri, who praised Osama bin Laden, 150 police in body armor used battering rams and ladders to break in. They found a canister of CS tear gas, a blank-firing imitation firearm, and a stun gun. Police arrested seven men—six north Africans and one East European. The mosque is in the Finsbury Park suburb and is believed to be a center for recruiting and supporting violent Islamic extremists. A police spokeswoman said, "Police have also recovered a large quantity of documents, including passports, identity cards, and credit cards." Masri, a leader of Supporters of Sharia, said two of those arrested were security staff and the other five were volunteer cleaners.

January 21, 2003. *Colombia.* The National Liberation Army (ELN) Domingo Lain Front kidnapped British reporter Ruth Morris, a former Reuters staffer in her 30s, and U.S. photographer Scott Dalton, 34, from Conroe, Texas, as they were on a freelance assignment for the *Los Angeles Times* in Arauca Province. (Some reports gave the capture date as January 24.) Two days later, a guerrilla radio broadcast said they would release them "when the time is right" under "political and military conditions." The ELN said they had entered the area without the rebels' permission. The duo had been traveling in a taxi along a road between Saravena and Tame, which are often hit by the leftists. Driver Madiel Ariza was released by the rebels on January 22. He said the hostages were hooded and taken to a secret guerrilla camp for a meeting with a senior ELN commander. The ELN misidentified Morris as an American—she has U.S. residency status. The group complained that the Colombian army was "assaulting and indiscriminately machine-gunning" local citizens.

On January 28, the ELN said that the pair would be held until the army stopped military operations in the area. "As long as the conditions in Arauca state, the continuous bombing and indiscriminate killing by the armed forces ... don't change, the conditions won't exist to hand over the journalists," said the group in a broadcast on a clandestine radio station in Arauca.

The ELN freed the two journalists on February 1 to an International Committee of the Red Cross team in Arauca Province. The duo was in good health. 03012101

January 21, 2003. *Kuwait.* At 9:14 a.m., Michael Rene Pouliot, 46, a software engineer for Tapestry Solutions of San Diego, was killed when an AK-47 assault rifle was fired at his silver Toyota Prado SUV at a busy intersection of Highway 85 west of Kuwait City, five miles from Camp Doha. Fellow San Diegan David Caraway, 37, a senior software engineer for Tapestry, was hit by six shots in the shoulder, chest, and thigh and was in stable condition after three hours of surgery. Both were working on a contract for the U.S. Army, providing logistics planning and software support. Pouliot was the father of two children. The gunman hid behind bushes at the intersection before firing at the vehicle being driven by Caraway. The getaway car was hidden 400 yards away on a parallel dirt road. Police found 24 shell casings at the scene. Footprints suggested only one shooter, possibly aided by a getaway car driver. Authorities detained dozens of suspected militants, many of whom trained in Afghan camps. Among them were 50 people, including Kuwaitis, Egyptians, Afghans, Pakistanis, and other immigrants.

On January 23, the Kuwaiti Interior Ministry said it had in custody Sami al-Mutayri, 25, a Kuwaiti man who confessed to the attack and who supports al Qaeda. There was no evidence of an organizational link. He was arrested by Saudi border guards as he tried to get into Saudi Arabia; he was handed over to Kuwaiti authorities. He had visited Pakistan to meet with militant groups soon after September 11. He majored in social studies at Kuwait University and once worked at the Social Services Ministry. Authorities found the rifle and ammunition at his workplace. He acted alone but had assistance in planning the attack. No group claimed credit.

On June 4, 2003, a Kuwaiti court sentenced the killer to death. 03012102

January 22, 2003. *Colombia.* In Arauquita, military officials blamed either the National Liberation Army (ELN) or the Revolutionary Armed Forces of Colombia (FARC) for bombing a section of the Cano Limon–Covenas oil pipeline, causing damage. The pipeline is owned by U.S. and Colombian oil firms. 03012201

January 23, 2003. *Israel.* Three Israeli soldiers were shot to death by a Palestinian gunman who attacked their patrol on a road near the Beit Haggai Jewish settlement south of Hebron. Hamas and the al-Aqsa Martyrs Brigades claimed credit.

January 24, 2003. *United States.* The State Department warned Americans overseas to be ready to leave their residency country quickly in an emergency. U.S. citizens were told to maintain a supply of prescription medicines, up-to-date passports, and stocks of food in the event of terrorist attacks or other violent events.

January 24, 2003. *Spain.* Working on a tip from French intelligence, Catalonia police arrested 16 suspected al Qaeda members in predawn raids. They found explosives and bomb components, suspected toxic material, fake documents and credit cards, communications equipment, and manuals on chemical warfare at the 12 sites in Barcelona and elsewhere. Most of the detainees were Algerians who had trained in Afghan camps. They had been in contact with North Africans recently arrested in France and the United Kingdom. They were also in touch with Islamic radicals in Chechnya and Algeria. Police believed they were planning to contaminate food supplies at a U.K. military base.

January 24, 2003. *United States.* The United States designated as terrorists two key members of the Jemaah Islamiah, Nurjaman Riduan Isasmuddin (alias Hambali) and Mohamad Iqbal Abdurrahman (alias Abu Jibril), whose names were also listed by the UNSCR 1267 Sanctions Committee.

January 25, 2003. *Kuwait.* No one was injured when shots were fired at a U.S. military convoy near Kuwait City. 03012501

January 25, 2003. *Nepal.* Gunmen shot to death Inspector General Krishna Mohan Shrestha of the Nepal Armed Police, which was created to fight the Maoist insurgents, as he was taking a morning walk with his wife and bodyguard, both of whom also died. No one claimed credit in the attack in Kathmandu's suburbs.

January 27, 2003. *India.* A homemade bomb injured at least 27 people in a crowded street market in Bombay.

January 27, 2003. *Afghanistan.* Two security officers escorting several UN vehicles in Nangarhar were killed when terrorists attacked the convoy. No one claimed credit. 03012701

January 29, 2003. *Nepal.* Maoist rebels lead by Pushpa Kamal Dahal (alias Prachanda), announced a cease-fire and willingness to enter into peace talks with the government to end the six-year conflict. The group said the government had agreed to stop calling the rebels terrorists and to drop reward offers for the group's leaders.

January 29, 2003. *Italy.* Naples police arrested 28 Pakistanis and charged them with terrorist offenses. Police found enough explosives in their apartment in central Naples to blow up a three-story building. Police, who were conducting a nighttime raid against illegal immigrants, found 28 ounces of explosives, 230 feet of fuse, and several electronic detonators hidden behind a false wall. They also found religious texts, photos of "martyrs of the jihad," piles of false documents, maps of the Naples area, more than 100 cell phones, and addresses of contacts around the world.

On February 12, Judge Ettore Favara ordered their release, saying there was reason to believe that the Pakistanis were not aware that explosives were hidden in the apartment in which they were renting rooms. Among the defense attorneys was Gennaro Razzino.

January 30, 2003. *United States.* FBI agents interviewed and released Megan McRee, an American who was deported from Russia, accused of communicating with Islamic extremists and proposing attacks on Hollywood.

January 30, 2003. *United States.* The United States designated Lashkar-e-Jhangvi as a terrorist organization. Lashkar-e-Jhangvi was also listed by the UNSCR 1267 Sanctions Committee.

January 31, 2003. *United States.* Al Qaeda operative Mohamed Suleiman Nalfi, 40, admitted he worked for bin Laden in Sudan in the early

1990s and pleaded guilty to conspiring to destroy national defense materials, which carries a maximum ten-year sentence. He said he created a jihad group in Sudan in 1989 and helped to build businesses there that aided al Qaeda. Al Qaeda used the firms as fronts to procure explosives, chemicals, and weapons. In 1990, Nalfi and others traveled to Egypt in a camel caravan to establish an al Qaeda weapons smuggling route. Nalfi told U.S. District Judge Kevin Thomas Duffy in New York that in 1992, he attended a meeting in which al Qaeda leaders discussed how to oust U.S. and UN forces from Somalia and Saudi Arabia. Nalfi had been arrested in 2000 in a conspiracy case involving the 1998 bombings of the U.S. embassies in Tanzania and Kenya. The government agreed to a lesser charge.

January 31, 2003. *United States.* Tahir Ibrihim Aletwei, 30, a Jordanian graduate student at the University of Texas at Arlington, was arrested and charged with immigration violations, making him subject to deportation. He was ordered thrown out of the country on February 7 after he acknowledged that he considered becoming a suicide bomber if the United States invaded Iraq. He told Immigration Judge D. Anthony Rogers, "I was looking at America as my enemy. If someone would have approached me and asked me to do something against the country, I was willing to do it." He claimed he changed his views and confessed to help authorities guard against people like him. He had arrived in the United States in August 2001 as part of a Jordan-sponsored exchange program. He was three months shy of getting a Master's degree in software engineering. He had told the FBI that he was involved in terrorism.

January 31, 2003. *India.* Armed terrorists killed a local journalist when they entered his office in Srinagar, Kashmir. No one claimed credit.

January–February 2003. *Afghanistan.* During the early weeks of the year, several attacks were conducted against relief groups:

- During the night, dynamite was thrown over the back wall of the Kandahar compound of six foreigners with the French Action Against Hunger. Windows were shattered, but no one was hurt.
- Sixteen shots hit a car belonging to an aid group.
- Two foreign land mine removal specialists sustained slight injuries when their car hit a booby-trapped mine.
- Afghan workers with aid groups were tied up and robbed.
- A grenade was thrown at an Afghan relief organization's car.
- Leaflets urged attacks on foreigners and their Afghan aides.
- Several cars pulled up beside a U.S. military convoy leaving Kandahar and fired three rocket-propelled grenades, all of which missed.
- A land mine blew up a minibus on a road near Kandahar, killing eight people.

February 2003. *Northern Ireland.* The Loyalist Volunteer Force was suspected in the bombing of a Catholic home. There were no injuries.

February 2003. *Turkey.* During the first week of the month, a man tried to hijack a Turkish Airlines flight, apparently intending to divert it to Moscow for a visit with his girlfriend. Police stormed the plane. The hijacker had candles wrapped in the shape of dynamite. 03029901

February 2003. *Mexico.* Indian members of the Zapatista National Liberation Army threatened American landowners if they remained in the country. Among those receiving the handwritten notes was Glen Wersch, 49, a former Peace Corps volunteer from Idaho who bought his Nuevo Jerusalen ranch in 1993 and who, with his wife, Ellen Jones, 55, turned it into a macadamia nut and flower farm and the Rancho Esmeralda tourist lodge. On January 31, the State Department had issued a travel advisory for Chiapas State. That day, 20 men dragged Ernesto Cruz Kanter, 20, one of Wersch's employees, from a taxi and beat him in the town school. The U.K., Netherlands, German, and Canadian embassies advised their citizens to leave. 03029902

February 2003. *Algeria.* In late February, several European tourists disappeared in the Sahara Desert. By April 7, their total had grown to 29, including 15 Germans, 4 Swiss citizens, and 8 Austrians. German and Austrian police went to the region to search for them. Austrian Foreign Minister Benita Ferrero-Waldner said, "I have no information about what kind of groups might be involved here, if they are terrorist groups or purely criminal groups. Nothing can be ruled out at this point."

On April 30, an Algerian official said 32 European tourists, who had traveled in seven groups, were being held hostage by terrorist groups, and that the Algerian army had determined that they were being held in the Illizi region, 810 miles southeast of Algiers near the Libyan border. "They are alive and are being held in several groups separated geographically," said the unnamed official, according to the Associated Press. None of the tourists had a local guide. They had set off in seven separate groups on four-wheel drive vehicles or motorcycles. They included 16 Germans, 10 Austrians, 4 Swiss, 1 Dutch citizen, and 1 Swede. The official said the Algerian army planned to use force to rescue the captives, but the German government objected, fearing for its citizens' safety. On May 4, the Algerian government said it was in contact with the hostage-takers, but backtracked from that statement two days later.

On May 13, Algerian troops rescued 17 European tourists in a gun battle with the Salafist Group for Preaching (Call) and Combat (GSPC), but the other 15 kidnapped Europeans, including 10 Germans (among them Witek Mitko, who was kidnapped on March 8), a Dutchman, and 4 Swiss, remained missing. Nine terrorists died in the fight, which lasted several hours near Illizi. The 17 kidnap victims flew back to Europe the next day and were reported to be in good health. They included six Germans, ten Austrians, and the Swede. Among those freed was Melanie Simon. The terrorists are affiliated with al Qaeda. The *El Watan* newspaper said the other hostages were held several hundred miles away, near the Libyan border.

Former hostage Gerhard Wintersteller, 63, an Austrian, said the hostages were frequently marched around at night and that the kidnappers were demanding ransom so that they could purchase weapons. "We were fleeing every night, had to walk at night. Our shoes were shredded, and we were at the end of our physical strength…. They prayed every day and told us they wanted to install an Islamic state in Algeria and overthrow the government…. They wanted ransom money—no political demands, as far as I know." Wintersteller's four-car convoy stopped to talk to a carload of German tourists coming from the other direction. "The shock was enormous because, as we stopped, eight terrorists jumped out and held their Kalashnikovs in front of us. We had to throw ourselves on the ground. They ripped the car keys out of our hands."

In June, a German woman hostage died of heat stroke and was buried by the terrorists.

On August 18, the terrorists freed the remaining 14 European tourists in a negotiated release in Mali. The nine Germans, four Swiss, and one Dutch citizen were turned over to Malian officials who had negotiated the release. Some of the freed hostages arrived in Germany on August 20.

Swiss Defense Minister Samuel Schmid said that Switzerland did not pay a ransom for its four citizens. Some media reports said a $5 million ransom had been paid by Germany.

On May 24, 2004, the Movement for Democracy and Justice in Chad said that in March it had captured ten Algerian extremists, including Amari Saifi (alias Abderrazak Para), leader of the Salafist Group for Preaching (Call) and Combat, and the former Algerian paratrooper behind the kidnappings of the Europeans, after a brief firefight. They were being held in a rebel-controlled zone. The rebel spokesman said that the group had attempted to contact Algeria, France, Germany, Niger, and the United States about

handing over the terrorists. A government would have to pick them up, because the Movement did not have the means to transfer them. On October 27, 2004, Libya extradited Saifi to Algeria. 03029903

February 1, 2003. *Turkey.* A time bomb was discovered in a McDonald's restaurant in Istanbul. A cleaning man spotted the explosive device by identifying the timer and cables attached to a box hidden under a table. Police experts defused the device. No one was injured. No one claimed credit. 03020101

February 2, 2003. *Nigeria.* An explosion at a bank in Lagos killed at least 40 people. The blast destroyed the bank and dozens of apartments above it. Police were investigating the possibility that it was a bank heist. Hundreds of looters grabbed fistfuls of cash.

February 2, 2003. *Indonesia.* During a 7:15 a.m. roll call, a bomb went off at the Indonesian police headquarters compound in Jakarta, damaging two cars and a social hall but causing no injuries. Someone found a black bag with cables and what appeared to be an explosive. Bomb technicians were unable to arrive before the low-explosive bomb went off.

February 2, 2003. *Indonesia.* Authorities arrested Singaporean Mas Selamat Kastari, chief of operations for the Jamaat Islamiya (JI), on the Indonesian island of Batam, near Singapore. Police had been tipped off by Singaporean authorities. He was alleged to have planned to hijack a plane and crash it into Singapore's Changi Airport.

February 4, 2003. *United States.* At 9:40 p.m., Virginia state trooper H. A. Chambers, 32, was wounded in the arm and another man killed during a raid on a trailer home on Kellam Drive in rural Accomack County. Ipolito Campos had threatened to poison the state's drinking water. Campos was arrested on fraud charges for using a false social security number and a fake alien registration number. An informant had told the Accomack Sheriff's Office on January 18 that a man known as Polo from an "Arabian" country had been sent to poison the water. An FBI affidavit said, "Polo further stated that if he did not poison the water, somebody would kill him." Campos had been fired in December from the Eastern Shore Seafood Products firm when he failed a random drug test. Prosecutors said Campos was an illegal immigrant from Mexico who lived with two men named Falco and Carlos (alias Richard Guillen).

February 5, 2003. *United Nations.* U.S. Secretary of State Colin Powell outlined to the UN Security Council the U.S. case against Iraq, noting Iraq's attempts to develop nuclear, chemical, and biological weapons, create missile delivery systems, and establish relations with al Qaeda.

February 5, 2003. *Saudi Arabia.* Three gunmen fired on a British citizen as he was traveling from work to home in Riyadh. Five bullets were fired at the vehicle, but the British Airways employee sustained only superficial wounds from flying glass. No one claimed credit. 03020501

February 6, 2003. *United States.* The State Department issued a "worldwide caution," warning U.S. citizens of a growing threat of terrorist attacks with chemical or biological weapons.

February 6, 2003. *United States.* A passenger on an American Trans Air plane leaving Ronald Reagan National Airport for Chicago sent the pilot a note that read, "fast. neat. average." Air Force Academy cadets use the phrase (often used in mess hall surveys) as a request to visit the cockpit. The plane returned to the gate. The note writer, who is not an Academy grad (nor was the pilot), was detained for questioning.

February 6, 2003. *United States.* Three passengers were removed from a Northwest Airlines flight to Baltimore after engaging in suspicious behavior, walking around the interior and speaking in a foreign language. After the pilot radioed

the ground, two F-16 fighters were scrambled from Andrews Air Force Base and escorted the plane to Baltimore-Washington International Airport. The trio were quizzed for three hours before being released.

February 6, 2003. *Germany.* Police arrested three men in raids on Islamic centers in Muenster, Minden, and four other sites in a search for terrorists planning an attack on a U.S. target in Germany and individuals suspected of having ties to the Hamburg September 11 cell. Two of the men were suspected of planning attacks in Germany in late 2001 to early 2002 including an attack "on an American installation in the Frankfurt metropolitan area." The third individual was suspected of supporting the Hamburg cell.

February 6, 2003. *United Kingdom.* Lothian and Borders Police in Scotland conducted raids in Glasgow and Edinburgh, while other police were conducting raids in London and Manchester against suspected terrorists. Four people were picked up in Scotland; another three in England. The six men and one woman were held under the Terrorism Act of 2000. The Act bans two dozen international terrorist groups and makes it illegal to belong to or support the groups.

February 6, 2003. *Colombia.* Military officials in Arauquita blamed either the Revolutionary Armed Forces of Colombia (FARC) or National Liberation Army (ELN) for bombing the Cano Limon–Covenas oil pipeline, causing damage. The pipeline is owned by U.S. and local firms. 03020601

February 7, 2003. *Sri Lanka.* Three Liberation Tigers of Tamil Eelam suicide bombers blew up their boat when they were found trying to smuggle an antiaircraft gun and hundreds of rounds of ammunition into Sri Lanka. Two European peace monitors had boarded the boat and were unharmed after the terrorists asked them to jump overboard. The monitors had found an antiaircraft gun, spare parts, two boxes of ammunition, three hand grenades, and a radio communication set.

February 7, 2003. *Colombia.* At 8:00 p.m., At least 34 people were killed and 168 were injured when a 440-pound car bomb exploded at the exclusive Club El Nogal in northern Bogota. The Revolutionary Armed Forces of Colombia (FARC) was suspected, particularly when it said on its Web site, resistencia.org, that right-wing paramilitaries frequented the club. The U.S. ambassador's residence is behind the club. The explosion probably came from inside the parking garage. The blast destroyed several of the building's ten floors. Among those killed were newly-wed Luisa Solarte, a Coca-Cola executive, and cook Marco Tulio Hernandez. At least six children were killed, including Juan Sebastian Carrillo, a second grader at Colegio Anglo–Colombiano in Bogota. (The school is affiliated with the U.K. Embassy.) His body was found with a cell phone against his ear; he apparently was trying to reach his father, who lay injured nearby. Rescuers pulled an injured Maria Camila Garcia, 12, from the rubble; her parents and four-year-old sister were found dead at their restaurant table. Students at the American school Colegio Nuevo Granada lost two fathers and a mother. Ana Maria Arango, a seventh-grader at Colegio Buckingham, died, as did her mother, father, and younger sister.

Police said on March 14 that the chief suspect may have been tracking the youngest son of President Alvaro Uribe. 03020701

February 7, 2003. *United States.* Attorney General John D. Ashcroft announced that the government had raised the terrorist threat index to its second-highest Orange (high risk) for only the second time in the brief history of the five-tiered system. Officials were particularly concerned with the use of chemical, biological, or radiological weapons, including ricin, cyanide, and dirty bombs. Al Qaeda and other terrorists could conduct attacks coinciding with the hajj pilgrimage to Mecca. Citizens were encouraged to use duct tape and plastic sheeting to seal their homes and places of business against chemical and biological attacks, set up a safe room in their homes, and stock up with provisions for several days. Washington, New York, and sites of Jewish importance were cited as likely targets; Saudi Arabia was later added to the list.

February 7, 2003. *United States.* The FBI announced it was seeking Mohammed Sher Mohammad Khan, a Pakistani wanted for questioning in connection with terrorist threats against the United States and who may have entered the United States illegally after September 11. The FBI said his name and birth date could be fictitious.

February 7, 2003. *Saudi Arabia.* Eight gunmen fired on police in Riyadh, killing a Kuwaiti and wounding three other people, including two police officers. 03020702

February 11, 2003. *United Kingdom.* The *Guardian* reported that London police had gone to high alert after receiving high quality intelligence that Islamic extremists had smuggled SAM-7 antiair missiles into the United Kingdom. Heathrow Airport was ringed with 450 troops.

February 11, 2003. *Qatar.* Al-Jazeera ran a 16-minute audiotape of Osama bin Laden, who called on Iraqis to conduct suicide attacks against Americans. He said:

We stress the importance of martyrdom operations against the enemy, these attacks that have scared Americans and Israelis like never before....

We are following with utmost concern the Crusaders' preparations to occupy the former capital of Islam [Baghdad], loot the fortunes of the Muslims and install a puppet regime on you that follows its masters in Washington and Tel Aviv like the rest of the treacherous puppet Arab governments as a prelude to the formation of Greater Israel....

How can the evil powers defeat the Islamic nation? Don't worry about American lies and their smart bombs and laser ones; they can't see but the obvious targets ... take the earth as a shelter.... We advise about the importance of drawing the enemy into long, close and exhausting fighting, taking advantage of camouflaged positions in plains, farms, mountains and cities.... The enemy fears town fights and streets fights.... The most effective means to devoid the aerial forces of its content is by digging large numbers of trenches and camouflaging them.

Anyone who helps America, from the Iraqi hypocrites or Arab rulers ... whoever fights with them or offer them bases or administrative assistance, or any kind of support or help, even if only with words, to kill Muslims in Iraq, should know that he is an apostate and that [shedding] his blood and money is permissible [in Islam] ...

Oh God, who sent down the Book, who ran the clouds, who defeated the parties, defeat them and grant us the triumph over them.... Fighting should be for Allah only, not to support nationalism or pagan regimes in all the Arab countries, including Iraq.... True Muslims should act, incite and mobilize the nation in such great events ... in order to break free from the slavery of these tyrannic and apostate regimes, which is enslaved by America, in order to establish the rule of Allah on Earth. Among regions ready for liberation are Jordan, Morocco, Nigeria, the country of the two shrines [Saudi Arabia], Yemen, and Pakistan.... This war concerns the Muslims, regardless of whether the socialist party and Saddam remain or go."

Bin Laden described his holing up during the battle in Tora Bora, saying his survival proves U.S. "cowardice and fear and lies." He claimed he and 300 mujaheddin dug 100 trenches in which to hide in the battle:

that great fight in which the power of belief overcame the material power of evil. The Pentagon ... was devoted with all its allied forces to blow up this tiny spot and annihilate it. So the airplanes poured fire over us, especially after they ended their mission in Afghanistan.... We managed to confront all their attacks, thanks be to Allah, and we forced them back each time defeated, carrying their dead and injured.

He said the United States wants to "reoccupy the ancient capital of Islam" and achieve "the Zionist dream of establishing a Greater Israel."

U.S. Secretary of State Colin Powell told the Senate Budget Committee that the tape shows bin Laden is "in partnership with Iraq."

February 11, 2003. *Philippines.* Foreign Secretary Blas Ople told Iraqi diplomats that an intelligence report linked a senior Iraqi embassy diplomat to the Abu Sayyaf group. The Iraqi diplomat had phone contact with Abu Sayyaf guerrillas in October, shortly after a bombing that killed a U.S. soldier.

February 13, 2003. *United Kingdom.* Gatwick Airport authorities and Sussex police arrested a Venezuelan man of Bangladeshi origin, 37, for hiding a hand grenade in his luggage. The North Terminal was closed for hours and flights were suspended. He had arrived on British Airways flight 2048 that originated in Caracas with stops in Bogota, Colombia, and Barbados. He was charged with possession of explosives, and possession of materials that could damage an aircraft under the Terrorism Act. 03021301

February 13, 2003. *United Kingdom.* Hounslow authorities arrested two men outside Heathrow Airport.

February 13, 2003. *Colombia.* At 9:30 a.m., a U.S. government Cessna 208 plane carrying four Americans and a Colombian working on an anti-drug program crashed after its engine failed in guerrilla-controlled territory between Puerto Rico and Florencia in Caqueta Province. The aircraft was photographing southern coca fields. The American employees of the Reston, Virginia-based DynCorp and California Microwave Systems, Inc., of Sunnyvale, California, a communications service subsidiary of Northrop Grumman, were working on a contract with the Office of Regional Administration in the U.S. Embassy in Bogota and U.S. Southern Command. Colombian FARC rebels shot to death one American—Thomas J. Janis, 56, a pilot and decorated army veteran—and Colombian army intelligence Sgt. Luis Alcides Cruz before government troops arrived at 10:00 a.m. and found the bodies. One man was shot in the head; the other in the chest. The terrorists apparently kidnapped the three survivors. Colombia scrambled five UH-60 Black Hawk and UH-1N Huey transport helicopters in a search-and-rescue mission. Within two days, four soldiers were injured when mines exploded in the search area. Authorities believed FARC's 14th and 15th Fronts were the likeliest kidnappers.

On February 22, the FARC said that the trio it was holding were CIA agents, echoing an erroneous report in Western media, and observed, "We can only guarantee the life and well-being of the three gringo officers in our power if the Colombian army immediately calls off the military operations and over-flights." The guerrillas claimed to have shot down the helicopter. A witness said that the plane had ten bullet holes in it.

On March 25 at 7:30 p.m., three Americans working for the Pentagon died when their Cessna 208 crashed into a mountain face behind El Paujil, 15 miles from the Colombian army post of Larandia, 240 miles south of Bogota. They were searching for the kidnapped Americans.

The Pentagon offered $300,000 and a U.S. visa for information leading to the rescue of the hostages.

On April 22, the Colombian attorney general's office identified the hostages as Keith Donald Stansell of Georgia, and Marco Gonzalves (variant Marc Gonsalves) and Thomas Howes, 50, both from Florida. Home towns were not released.

On August 28, rebels permitted a journalist to videotape the three hostages, showing them to be in good health. Gonzalves sent a message to his family. The rebels labeled the hostages "gringo CIA agents" and "prisoners of war" and demanded the release of guerrillas held in Colombian jails.

Thomas Howes warned against a rescue attempt, saying, "This isn't the movies. If you come to rescue us, we will die." He was quoted in *Cromos* magazine dated September 13. Colombian journalist Jorge Enrique Botero photographed the three hostages in a wooden hut. The trio looked healthy and clean but grim. Guerrillas armed with assault rifles stood guard. The hostages told Botero (the interview was scheduled to run on *60 Minutes II* on October 8) that authorities should negotiate rather than risk a rescue attempt. The interview was taped in July. Botero and U.S. journalists Victoria Bruce and Karin Hayes produced a documentary called *Held Hostage in Colombia*, portions of which aired on the History Channel on October 9.

On October 19, Colombian troops killed Edgar Gustavo Navarro, second in command of an elite FARC unit, and ten other rebels in a gunfight near San Vicente del Caguan. He was behind the capture of the Americans.

As of June 18, 2004, the trio were still being held hostage.

On August 23, 2004, the FARC criticized a government proposal to trade jailed terrorists for kidnapped politicians, soldiers, and the American trio. FARC said freed rebels should be permitted to return to the FARC.

In a FARC communique dated September 14, 2004, the group called for the government to pull troops from two southern towns as a condition for a prisoner exchange that would include the kidnapped trio. FARC said it required a neutral area for the swap of 50 guerrillas for 72 FARC hostages. The government rejected the demand.

On December 17, 2004, President Alvaro Uribe signed extradition orders for Ricardo Palmera (alias Simon Trinidad), 54, a FARC commander and former banker, after obtaining Supreme Court approval to send him to New York to face cocaine trafficking charges. President

Uribe said he would revoke the decision if the FARC released 63 hostages, including the three Americans and a German, before December 30, 2004. FARC did not make the deadline, and on December 31, 2004, Palmera was sent to the United States to face drug and kidnapping charges. 03021302

February 14, 2003. *Colombia.* A bomb exploded just before dawn in Neiva during a police raid on a hideout of the Revolutionary Armed Forces of Colombia (FARC), killing 15 people and injuring 30 others, as the police foiled a plot to kill President Alvaro Uribe, who was to visit Neiva the next day. The dead included eight police officers; one was the provincial head of criminal investigations and one was a government prosecutor. The bomb's chemical components resembled those used in the February 7 Club El Nogal car bomb.

February 15, 2003. *Colombia.* Military authorities in Saravena said either the Revolutionary Armed Forces of Colombia (FARC) or National Liberation Army (ELN) bombed the Cano Limon–Covenas oil pipeline, which is owned by local and U.S. firms. 03021501

February 15, 2003. *Bahrain.* Authorities arrested five Bahraini men for planning terrorist attacks against Americans in Bahrain, which hosts the headquarters of the U.S. Navy's Fifth Fleet. Two detainees were members of the country's military. The Bahrain news agency said that "security forces arrested a cell which was planning terrorist attacks after receiving information on their movement which targeted national interests in the kingdom and the lives of innocent nationals." Police seized ammunition and weapons. In May, the government released three of the five, claiming to have insufficient evidence to support a trial. In June and July, the other two were convicted—one by a civilian criminal court and one by court martial—for illegal gun possession. In December, the king reduced the sentenced of the civilian from three years to two.

February 18, 2003. *Saudi Arabia.* Interior Minister Prince Nayef announced that the government would try 90 Saudis for membership in al Qaeda. Another 250 people were being interrogated; another 150 were released after questioning.

February 18, 2003. *Philippines.* Following a gun battle with government troops, Abu Sayyaf faction leader Mujib Susukan died of his wounds. His capture or death carried a $92,500 bounty. He was shot at his hideout outside Talipao, on Jolo Island.

February 18, 2003. *South Korea.* At 9:55 a.m., Kim Dae Han, 56, who has a history of depression and angry threats set fire to a flammable liquid inside a subway car in Taegu. The resulting fire spread from the train at Joongang Station to an arriving train and killed at least 182 people and injured 146; another 388 were unaccounted for by February 20. Kim Dae Han, a former taxi driver, was treated for minor injuries.

February 19, 2003. *Philippines.* Heavily armed gunmen fired on a farming village in Zamboanga del Norte Province and torched homes, killing 14 people in a nighttime raid. Three residents were wounded and another three missing. Five homes were hit with grenades and M-60 machine-gun fire.

A separate bomb attack in an open market in Kabacan, in North Cotabato Province, killed the suspected bomber.

The Moro Islamic Liberation Front was blamed for both attacks.

February 19, 2003. *United States.* The United States froze the U.S. assets of former Afghan Prime Minister Gulbuddin Hekmatyar because he had taken part in "terrorist acts" by al Qaeda and the Taliban. He was named a Specially Designated Global Terrorist under the authority of Executive Order 13224.

February 20, 2003. *United States.* The United States designated Ansar al-Islam, a terrorist group operating in northeastern Iraq with close links to and support from al Qaeda. The UNSCR 1267 Sanctions Committee listed the group on February 24.

February 20, 2003. *Saudi Arabia.* Robert Dent, a British Aerospace Engineering (BAE) Systems employee, was shot dead in his car while waiting at a Riyadh traffic light. Dent, in his 30s, was a commercial officer at BAE's Riyadh headquarters. He was married. Police arrested the assailant minutes later. He was identified as Saud bin Ali bin Nasser, 30, a naturalized Saudi of Yemeni origin who worked at a car dealership. He had recently traveled to Pakistan and named his youngest son Osama. No group claimed credit.

Two weeks earlier, another Briton working for BAE was attacked in his car by gunmen and sustained minor injuries. 03022001, 03029903

February 20, 2003. *United States.* The Justice Department forwarded a 50-count, 120-page indictment in Tampa, Florida, accusing former University of South Florida computer engineering Prof. Sami Amin al-Arian, 45, and seven other people of conspiracy to commit murder via suicide attacks in Israel and the Palestinian territories, operating a criminal racketeering enterprise since 1984 that supports the Palestine Islamic Jihad (PIJ) terrorist organization, conspiracy to kill and maim people abroad, conspiracy to provide material support to the group, extortion, visa fraud, perjury, money laundering, and other charges. The seven other people included three Muslim activists arrested that day and several Islamic Jihad officials. Authorities arrested the Kuwait-born al-Arian at his suburban Tampa home and said he had been a top PIJ leader, serving as secretary of its Shura Council (top governing body) for several years. He faced life in prison if convicted. He was represented by attorney Nicholas Matassini. The government cited numerous faxes and phone calls and documents seized at al-Arian's offices to show that he had managed PIJ's worldwide finances and relayed messages between its leaders. He

allegedly raised and sent money to the families of PIJ suicide bombers. Al-Arian ran the World and Islamic Studies Enterprise and the Islamic Committee for Palestine. Police searching their offices found the wills of three PIJ members who died committing terrorist acts.

Al-Arian's brother-in-law, Mazen al-Najjar, was jailed for three years on evidence not made available to him or his attorney. Al-Najjar was deported to Lebanon in 2002.

Also charged were Ramadan Abdullah Shallah, a close associate of al-Arianin Tampa during the 1990s who now heads PIJ from Damascus, Syria; and Abd-al-Aziz Awda, a founder and spiritual leader of PIJ.

Khaled Batsh, a PIJ leader in the Gaza Strip, said that of the eight who were indicted, only Ramadan Abdullah Shallah was an active PIJ member.

On February 26, the University of South Florida fired the tenured al-Arian because he had abused his position. University President Judy Genshaft said, "He has misused the university's name, reputation, resources and personnel. He has violated the policies of this university."

On December 9, 2003, it was announced that Florida court workers had erroneously destroyed 1995 search warrants used to collect evidence against al-Arian.

February 20, 2003. *India.* A land mine planted near a busy marketplace in Varmul, Kashmir, exploded, killing six and wounding three. No one claimed credit.

February 20, 2003. *Algeria.* Four Swiss tourists were kidnapped by the Salafist Group for Preaching (Call) and Combat (GSPC) when they were visiting the Sahara Desert in a small group without a guide. From then until mid-May, the GSPC kidnapped 32 European tourists in eight separate incidents. On May 13, Algerian Special Forces rescued 17 hostages. One hostage, a German woman, died of heatstroke on July 28 while in captivity. On August 18, the remaining 14 hostages were released in northern Mali. Press reports claimed a ransom of 4.6 million euros was paid to the GSPC in return for the hostages. 03022002

February 21, 2003. *Philippines.* A car bomb went off next to a military airfield in Cotobato, on the southern island of Mindanao.

February 22, 2003. *Pakistan.* Gunmen fired automatic weapons inside a Shi'ite mosque in the south, killing nine worshipers and injuring another nine during evening prayers before speeding off on motorcycles. Sunni Muslims were suspected.

February 22, 2003. *Turkey.* Two people threw a bomb into a British Airways office in Istanbul, shattering windows but causing no casualties. No one claimed credit. 03022201

February 22, 2003. *Algeria.* Four German tourists were kidnapped in the Sahara Desert by the Salafist Group for Preaching (Call) and Combat. From late February until mid-May, the GSPC kidnapped 32 European tourists in eight separate incidents. On May 13, Algerian Special Forces rescued 17 hostages. One hostage, a German woman, died of heatstroke on July 28 while in captivity. On August 18, the remaining 14 hostages were released in northern Mali. Press reports claimed a ransom of 4.6 million euros was paid to the GSPC in return for the hostages. 03022202

February 24, 2003. *Kuwait.* Authorities arrested three Kuwaiti Islamic radicals and supporters of bin Laden for planning attacks against U.S. forces. Police seized arms and ammunition during the arrests of the individuals, who were planning to ambush a U.S. military convoy. The men had been under surveillance for some time. They were identified as Ahmad Mutlaq Mutairi, 29; his brother, Abdullah Mutlaq Nasser Mutairi, 32; and Mussaed Hawran Shbeib Enizi, 28. Ahmad had traveled in 2001 to Afghanistan. 03022401

February 25, 2003. *Venezuela.* Two bombs exploded minutes apart at the Spanish Embassy and Colombian Consulate in Caracas, injuring four people—one Colombian and three Venezuelans—and damaging both buildings. Leaflets in support of President Hugo Chavez were found outside the Spanish Embassy, although no one claimed credit. Two days earlier, Chavez had warned Colombia and Spain not to meddle in Venezuela's domestic affairs. Both countries had expressed concern over the previous week's arrest of opposition leader Carlos Fernandez, one of the leaders of the two-month general strike. On February 28, Venezuela announced that it had identified suspects in the bombings. 03022501, 03022503

February 25, 2003. *Saudi Arabia.* An incendiary bomb was thrown at a McDonald's restaurant in al-Dammam. Two people drove up to the site in a car, and the passenger got out and threw the bomb. The bomb did not explode. The passenger failed to reignite the canister before fleeing. Police arrested a person whose clothes contained the same substances as in the bomb and who was later identified by witnesses. No one claimed credit. 03022502

February 25, 2003. *People's Republic of China.* Two bombs exploded in cafeterias at China's major universities, injuring nine people. Homemade charcoal gunpowder went off at 11:55 a.m. during lunch at Tsinghua University, injuring five professors and a student. Ninety minutes later, a bomb blew out a dining hall's windows and a door at Beijing University, injuring three. U.S. Secretary of State Colin Powell had visited the country the day before. Uighur separatists were suspected.

February 26, 2003. *United States.* Federal officials indicted five men connected to the Islamic Assembly of North America (IANA), a Saudi charity that operates out of Ann Arbor, Michigan, in connection with two money-raising and distribution efforts.

Sami Omar al-Hussayen, 34, a Saudi doctoral candidate at the University of Idaho, was accused of raising and distributing $300,000 through Web sites that promote terrorism and violence against the United States. The money went to pay a top IANA official and went to individuals and organizations in Jordan, Saudi Arabia, Pakistan, Egypt, and Canada. One of the sites published a fatwa by a radical sheik in June 2001 that advocated suicide attacks. Al-Hussayen was charged with 11 counts of visa fraud and making false statements on documents by misrepresenting to the Immigration and Naturalization Service (INS) that he was in the United States solely to attend school. He allegedly supplied expertise to a Web site that stated, "The mujahid must kill himself if he knows that this will lead to killing a great number of the enemies. In the new era, this can be accomplished with the modern means of bombing or bringing down an airplane on an important location that will cause the enemy great losses." He had been studying in the United States since 1994, first at Southern Methodist in Dallas and Ball State in Muncie, Indiana, where he received a Master's degree in computer science. He joined Idaho's doctoral program in computer science in 1999, specializing in computer security and intrusion techniques. He received a monthly living stipend and tuition aid from the Saudi government. The Saudi Embassy terminated the scholarship on March 11. He pleaded guilty to an 11-count federal indictment. He was represented by defense attorney David Nevin. Magistrate Mikel Williams gave al-Hussayen house arrest until his April 15 trial. The defendant was to wear a monitoring device, permit police to listen to his phone calls, and agree to unannounced searches of his residence.

Four Arab men living near Syracuse were accused of conspiracy to evade U.S. sanctions against Iraq by raising $2.7 million for individuals in Baghdad through the Help the Needy charity (an IANA affiliate). The funds were placed in New York banks, then laundered through an account at the Jordan Islamic Bank in Amman

before they were distributed to people in Baghdad. Those indicted included Iraqi-born U.S. citizen Rafil Dhafir, 55, an oncologist in Fayetteville, New York; Maher Zagha, 34, a Jordanian who attended college in New York; Ayman Jarwan, 33, of Syracuse, a Jordanian citizen born in Saudi Arabia who worked as the Executive Director of Help the Needy; and Osameh al-Wahaidy, 41, of Fayetteville, a Jordanian employed as a spiritual leader at the Auburn Correctional Facility and as a math instructor at the State University of New York at Oswego. They were charged with conspiracy and violation of the International Emergency Economic Powers Act, which makes it illegal to send money to Iraq. Two of the men could face 265 years in prison and fines of more than $14 million. The other two faced five years in prison and a $250,000 fine.

On March 11, the FBI announced that it had found before- and after-September 11 photographs of the World Trade Center on al-Hussayen's computer. Prosecutors asked the court in Boise to withhold bond, saying he had ties to two radical sheiks who support anti-U.S. violence—Saudi sheiks Salman al-Ouda and Safar al-Hawali. FBI agent Michael Gneckow said he found thousands of photographs of planes hitting buildings, plane crashes, the Pentagon, and the Empire State Building. He said al-Hussayen had access to some classified information.

On March 16, federal officials said former Idaho student Bassem K. Khafagi, an Egyptian who was arrested in January near New York's LaGuardia Airport to face bank fraud charges in Michigan, was connected to the IANA investigation. He was a founding member of the assembly. He was held for investigation of violating U.S. immigration laws. Investigators decided not release the name of a former University of Idaho student who lives in Detroit as an associate of IANA. Ismail Diab, a former Washington State University student, was held as a material witness.

On April 25, 2003, Judge Anna Ho ruled that al-Hussayen had violated the terms of his student visa by accepting pay to create the Internet pages and could legally be deported. He was to remain in custody pending a possible appeal. His IANA case was slated to go to trial on January 20, 2004. The Saudi government, which sponsored his U.S. studies, provided money for his legal defense and sought his release.

On January 9, 2004, a federal grand jury in Idaho issued a 12-count indictment that charged al-Hussayen with conspiring to help terrorist organizations wage jihad by using the Internet to raise funds, field recruits, and locate prospective U.S. military and civilian targets in the Middle East. The Web site and e-mail group disseminated messages from him and two radical Saudi clerics that supported jihad. The indictment said that he "knew and intended that the material support he provided were to be used in preparation for, and to commit, violations of federal law involving murder, maiming, kidnapping and the destruction of property" and that he sought to conceal his work. He was charged with conspiracy to provide material support to terrorists through his control of the Web sites, his financial support to IANA, and by signing contracts and doing Internet work for the al-Haramain Islamic Foundation, a Saudi-based charity whose Bosnia and Somalia branches have been designated terrorist organizations by the Treasury Department. His Web sites solicited for Hamas. In February 2003, he had sent e-mail that issued an "urgent appeal" to Muslims in the military to identify locations of U.S. military bases in the Middle East, residences of civilian base workers, storage facilities for weapons and ammunition, facilities of U.S. oil companies, and routes followed by oil tankers, as possible terrorist targets. The e-mail also called for an attack on a senior U.S. military officer. He faced 15 years in prison. On January 13, 2003, he pleaded not guilty to the additional charge of supporting terrorism. He had already been held for nearly a year on visa fraud charges.

On March 4, 2004, federal prosecutors expanded the charges against al-Hussayen and said he ran more than a dozen Web sites to recruit and raise money for Islamic terrorists in Israel, Chechnya, and elsewhere. The new charges from the Idaho federal grand jury accused him of providing and concealing material support to terrorists.

On April 13, his trial began in Boise, Idaho, before a jury of eight women and four men. His defense attorneys, David Nevin and Joshua Dratel (who had represented former bin Laden aide Wadih al-Hage), said his Internet activities constituted free speech while the prosecution said it was material support for terrorists. The prosecution was expected to call as witnesses five men convicted on terrorism-related cases in Portland, Oregon, Lackawanna, New York, and Northern Virginia, who would testify that they watched videotapes on an Islamway.com Web server that showed mujaheddin in Chechnya killing Russian soldiers. U.S. District Judge Edward J. Lodge rejected pretrial defense motions for dismissal.

On April 26, 2004, the judge ruled that the jury could not see Web pages or e-mail if the prosecution could not prove that the defendant created them. However, on May 19, the judge said prosecutors could show the jury the Internet pages because they had established the foundation to show a possible conspiracy existed between Hussayen and unindicted coconspirators associated with the Islamic Assembly of North America, which had created Web sites supporting suicide attacks in Israel and Chechnya and asking Muslims to contract money to terrorists. Judge Lodge was to rule on May 24 whether the jury could hear testimony from two American men, one of whom pleaded guilty to training with the Virginia jihad network. The duo was Khwaja Mahmood Hasan of Fairfax, Virginia, and Yahya Goba of Buffalo. Hasan was serving 11 years after admitting practicing military tactics while playing paintball in Virginia. Goba trained at an al Qaeda camp in Afghanistan in May 2001.

On June 10, 2004, a day after the jury reportedly was stalemated, the jury acquitted Hussayen on three counts of providing material support to terrorism. The jury acquitted him on 3 of 11 counts of false statements and visa fraud, and deadlocked on the 8 others. Hussayen remained in jail pending deportation hearings. On June 30, 2004, the government agreed to drop the remaining charges in return for his dropping his appeal of his deportation order.

In mid-October 2004, Rafil Dhafir's trial began. More than 85 federal agents had been involved in his arrest and the search of his home. A federal prosecutor had suggested that an Arab engineer who was Dhafir's friend might be proficient at making "dirty bombs." A federal magistrate denied bail to Dhafir, who sat in jail for 19 months. Dhafir had emigrated to the United States from Iraq 32 years earlier and obtained U.S. citizenship. He was charged with defrauding his charity, violating U.S. sanctions by sending millions of dollars to feed children and build mosques in Saddam-era Iraq, Medicare fraud, and tax evasion. He faced at least ten years in prison and millions of dollars in fines. He was represented by attorney Deveraux L. Cannick. Dhafir was denied bond five times. He is a member of the Salafist sect of Islam.

February 27, 2003. *United States.* The Bush administration lowered the terrorist threat index to Yellow (significant risk), although some jurisdictions chose to remain at Orange (high risk).

February 28, 2003. *United States.* The State Department listed three Chechen rebel groups as terrorist organizations whose U.S. assets were to be frozen. The United States believed the three groups took part in the mass hostage situation at the Moscow's Dubrovka Theater in October 2002. The State Department also said Riyadus-Salikhn Reconnaissance and Sabotage Battalion of Chechen Martyrs (a 200-strong group led by Shamil Basayev, responsible for the theater attack), the Special Purpose Islamic Regiment (led by Movsar Barayev, who led the hostage-takers and died at the scene) , and the Islamic International Brigade (led by Basayev until a few months ago) had contacts with the Taliban

and al Qaeda. The State Department said Basayev and rebel commander Khattab asked bin Laden for assistance in October 1999. Bin Laden promised money and several hundred fighters. In turn, Khattab sent fighters to Afghanistan in October 2001 to help the Taliban. Khattab was killed by Russian troops a year ago. Basayev was believed to be hiding in the southern Chechnya mountains.

February 28, 2003. *Pakistan.* One or two Islamic gunmen attacked a police post outside the U.S. Consulate in Karachi, killing two police officers and wounding five policemen and a civilian. No Americans were hurt. Pakistani Zulfigar Ali, 30 (initial reports said 25), was arrested by police after a chase in a nearby park. He screamed at them to kill him. Police found a note in his pocket saying, "I am going to kill the police officers who are protecting the infidels. This is my religious obligation." Ali said he acted alone, firing from a motorbike. He was carrying two pistols and several rounds of ammunition. Police said Ali was involved with a local Islamic jihadi group. Police believed other gunmen were involved, noting that witnesses said that two gunmen firing a submachine gun and a pistol fired on the police, who were having lunch inside the police post. Karachi Police Chief Asad Ashraf Malik said that "the automatic weapon used in the incident was snatched from a policeman who was returning to the post from the men's room in the nearby park." However, Ali claimed that he had been given two loaded pistols just before the shooting, along with the promise of a getaway car. Pakistani authorities said that the Karachi factory worker was hired by an Arab and a Pakistani religious militant at a local mosque to conduct the attack. 03022801

March 2003. *Spain.* The Supreme Court banned Basque Nation and Liberty's (ETA) political wing, Batasuna.

March 2003. *Spain.* The Reconstituted Communist Party of Spain (PCE/R), the political wing of the terrorist group First of October

Antifascist Resistance Group (GRAPO), was outlawed, the first time in the organization's 28-year history that the Spanish judicial system ruled that the GRAPO and the PCE/R comprised a single organization.

March 2003. *United States.* In late March, prosecutors indicted six Denver-area residents on charges of harboring an illegal immigrant from Pakistan. A federal magistrate released five of them on bail, but ordered the jailing of Pakistani citizen Haroon Rashid, 32, pending trial. On March 31, FBI agent Michael Castro told a U.S. magistrate at a bail hearing that Rashid had been trained at a terrorist camp in Pakistan shortly after September 11 and wanted to take part in a jihad against the United States. A pawn shop owner said that Rashid had shopped for a rifle with a scope equipped for night firing. Rashid had been convicted of murder in Pakistan, but was freed on appeal. The FBI said that three of the Denver-area men had been trained in terrorist techniques and posed a danger to the community. Rashid was represented by attorney Anthony Joseph. U.S. Magistrate Michael Watanabe ordered Rashid held without bail on the immigration charge. Irfan Kamran and Sajjad Nasser were due to appear for an April 4 bail hearing. Prosecutors opposed their release on the same grounds and that they were flight risks. Prosecutors had appealed their initial release, and the duo was jailed pending the hearing. The other three were Abdul Qayyum, Rashid's wife Saima Saima, and Chris Marie Warren, who were free on $10,000 bail.

On April 8, U.S. District Judge Lewis T. Babcock ruled that "the government has failed to establish" that Kamran and Naseer posed any danger and ordered them released. Kamran had already posted his $30,000 bail. Naseer was released on $100,000 bail, but was detained by the Bureau of Immigration and Customs Enforcement on a separate charge. Federal prosecutors said they still believed the duo was dangerous and that they might appeal the release. The FBI had reported that Naseer had gone to a camp in Pakistan in the summer of 2001. The camp was run by the Army of Mohammed, which the United States lists as a terrorist organization. Naseer said he left after four or five days because he did not like the strenuous physical training. The FBI said that Naseer "also attended rallies in support of al Qaeda and Osama bin Laden," which amounts "to providing material support for a foreign terrorist organization."

March 2003. *Kyrgyzstan.* An attack on a bus traveling between Kyrgyzstan and China killed 21 people, including 19 Chinese citizens. As of April 2004, the incident was under investigation as to whether it was terrorism or crime related.

March 2003. *Chile.* An individual protesting the war in Iraq threw a Molotov cocktail at the perimeter wall of the U.S. Embassy. Carabineros guarding the embassy quickly arrested the perpetrator. 04039901

March 2003. *Chile.* Small bombs exploded at a BellSouth office in Concepcion. 04039902

March 2, 2003. *Italy.* Police shot to death Mario Galesi, 37, a Red Brigades terrorist wanted for the 1999 slaying of a labor reform adviser to the Italian government, after he fired on police on a train, killing one officer and wounding another. His female companion, also a Red Brigades member, was arrested. She refused to answer questions.

March 2, 2003. *Venezuela.* At 5:00 a.m., a C-4 semtex car bomb exploded in Maracaibo, damaging several buildings, including the local office of the U.S. oil firm Chevron Texaco. The bomb was similar to those that exploded the previous week at the Spanish and Colombian embassies. The bomb went off outside the home of Antonio Melian, a controversial cattle livestock producer and a leading activist in Zulia State. He had been the center of opposition-government debate in the wake of a two-month nationwide labor-management stoppage that failed to bring down the government of President

Hugo Chavez Frias. No one claimed credit. 03030201

March 3, 2003. *Greece.* Greece began the trial of 19 members of the 17 November terrorist group. A three-judge panel ordered the removal of a bulletproof security enclosure around the defendants.

March 4, 2003. *United States.* In testimony before the Senate Judiciary Committee, U.S. Attorney General John Ashcroft announced the unsealing of a federal complaint that al Qaeda financiers raised money at the Masjid al-Farouq mosque in Brooklyn, New York. The FBI said that worshipers donated $10,000 to a representative of Mohammed Ali Hassan Moayad, a Yemeni cleric and an al Qaeda member, on December 29, 1999. The FBI said he had raised $20 million in various countries, including the United States. The mosque had in the 1990s been the base for Omar Abd-al-Rahman, the Egyptian cleric jailed for life in connection with the 1993 World Trade Center bombing and associated terrorist plots.

March 4, 2003. *United States.* Security was increased at the Hindu Temple of St. Louis, which was firebombed twice during the week. No one was injured. On March 24, Paul Laird and Nathaniel Conner, both 17, were charged in Clayton, Missouri, with second-degree arson and criminal possession of a weapon in the attacks.

March 4, 2003. *Philippines.* Moro Islamic Liberation Front (MILF) member Montasher Sudang, 23, from North Cotabato, planted a backpack bomb 50 yards from the main terminal of Davao Airport. The bomb exploded prematurely at 5:20 p.m., killing him, an American missionary— Reverend William P. Hyde, a resident of Davao —and 19 other people, and wounded at last 149, including 3 Americans. Hyde had come to pick up an American missionary family. Three members of his family—Barbara Wallis Stevens, 33, her 10-month-old son, Nathan, and daughter Sarah, 4—were treated for injuries at the Davao Doctors Hospital. The bomb had been placed in an open air shelter where a crowd was welcoming arriving passengers from a Cebu Pacific Air flight from Manila. Davao Mayor Rodrigo Duterte said the government would charge MILF chairman Hashim Salamat, spokesman Eid Kabalu, political chief Ghazali Jaafar, and military chief Al Haj Murad. MILF denied credit. The next day, authorities announced the detention of five MILF terrorists. Police said the attack appeared to be in retaliation for a week-long military offensive against a Moro compound in which 40 rebels and 5 soldiers died. The military downplayed an Abu Sayyaf claim of responsibility, saying that the group has an agreement with MILF to claim credit for MILF attacks. Some authorities blamed the Balik Islam leader, an Abu Sayyaf commander named Hamsiraji Sali who works with the MILF. Sali claimed to be receiving Iraqi financing.

On March 9, prosecutors announced charges against the leaders of the MILF. 03030401

March 5, 2003. *Colombia.* A bomb exploded in an underground parking garage at a Cucuta shopping mall near the Venezuelan border, killing 7 people and injuring 68 others. Parked cars caught fire. Authorities blamed the National Liberation Army (ELN).

March 5, 2003. *Israel.* At 2:15 p.m., a Hamas suicide bomber set off a backpack bomb on Number 37 Egged bus in Haifa, killing himself, 14 Israelis, and 1 American. The American was Abigail Litle, 14, a U.S.–born teen who had spent most of her life in Israel, where her father, Philip Litle, 43, a Missouri native, works for a Baptist ministry. Most of the victims were teenagers. Two of the victims were a boy and girl, both aged 13; nine schoolchildren died, including Yuval Mendelevich, 13. Also killed was Mitel Katav, 20, who had finished her mandatory military service a month earlier and was on her way home from her new job at a gas station. Among the 40 people who were injured was Sol Tzur, nanny Odette Elezra, 51, and bus driver Marwan

Damouni, 31, an Israeli Arab. The bomb was packed with shards of metal, nuts, and bolts. The bus had arrived at a kiosk on Moriya Boulevard in the neighborhood of Carmelia. An ID card identified the bomber as Mahmoud Amdan Salim Kawasme, 20, of Hebron. Police found a letter in Arabic near his body praising "the terror attacks on the twin towers on September 11." The letter claimed that the Koran foretold that the World Trade Center towers and the people near Ground Zero would collapse into hell. The letter included a prayer to protect the bomber from capture prior to detonation. Soldiers detained his father and two brothers on suspicion of involvement in the attack. 03030501

March 7, 2003. *Germany.* Sabine Callsen, a suspected member of the disbanded Red Army Faction (Baader-Meinhof Gang), surrendered at the Frankfurt Airport after returning from a 2-year exile in the Middle East.

March 7, 2003. *United Kingdom.* Judge Peter Beaumont in London sentenced to nine years in prison Abdullah el-Faisal, a Jamaican-born convert to Islam, for urging his followers to kill Hindus, Jews, and Americans and for stirring up racial hatred. The judge made the sentences consecutive to emphasize the United Kingdom's "abhorrence of the views you expressed." He will have to serve at least half his sentence before becoming eligible for parole. The judge also recommended possible extradition to Jamaica.

March 7, 2003. *Israel.* Two Palestinian Islamic Resistance Movement (Hamas) gunmen, disguised as Jewish seminary students, walked into a Kiryat Arba home during Sabbath dinner and shot to death two U.S. citizens—a husband and wife, Rabbi Elnatan Eli Horowitz and Debra Ruth Horowitz—and injured six people. Soldiers shot the terrorists to death. One of the terrorists had an explosives belt taped to his body; the explosives did not detonate. 03030701

March 7, 2003. *Israel.* Three Palestine Islamic Jihad gunmen were shot to death after firing at a convoy of Jewish settlers in Gaza.

March 7, 2003. *Israel.* Soldiers shot and killed two Palestinian gunmen trying to infiltrate the Negohot settlement. One terrorist had an explosives belt which blew up. There were no Israeli casualties.

March 9, 2003. *India.* Terrorists kidnapped and murdered a private citizen in Doda District, Kashmir. No one claimed credit.

March 9, 2003. *India.* A bomb injured a student in Sogam, Kashmir. No one claimed credit.

March 10, 2003. *Sri Lanka.* The navy conducted a gun battle with an Liberation Tigers of Tamil Eelam (LTTE) boat off the northeastern coast, 195 miles from the island nation, sinking the rebels' vessel and probably killing all ten on board. Four sailors were injured. LTTE claimed their vessel was in international waters. The government said it was in Sri Lankan waters; the government claims a 200-mile limit.

March 11, 2003. *India.* A bomb exploded in a candy store in Rajouri, Kashmir, killing two and injuring four people. No one claimed credit.

March 12, 2003. *Serbia.* Snipers shot to death Prime Minister Zoran Djindjic, 50, outside the door to Belgrade's main government building. He was a key figure in the overthrow of Slobodan Milosevic in the October 2000 democratic revolution. Police blamed a criminal gang led by Milorad Lukovic (alias Legija), the former head of the Red Berets, an elite paramilitary police unit. He was a key U.S. ally. He was hit in the abdomen and back by two bullets from high-powered rifles as he walked using crutches from his armored automobile to the door. Another bullet hit his car. He died in the hospital at 1:30 p.m.

Three weeks earlier, a gangster tried to swerve a truck into his car.

On March 14, the government bulldozed a four-story shopping complex belonging to

Dusan Spasojevic, one of the alleged assassins, in Zemun.

On March 16, Djindjic's party proposed Zivan Zivkovic, 42, as premier. Zivkovic pledged to crack down on organized crime, which he deemed responsible for the murder of his ally. As of March 20, the government had arrested one thousand members of criminal organizations. Among the detainees was Deputy State Prosecutor Milan Sarajlic, who admitted to being on the payroll of the criminal gangs. The government also forced the retirement of 35 judges who did not prosecute those behind the assassination.

On March 25, police arrested Zvezdan Jovanovic, a former deputy commander of a special unit of police troops under former Yugoslav President Slobodan Milosevic. Police seized a German-made sniper rifle suspected of being the murder weapon. Police also arrested Sasa Pejakovic for aiding the sniper.

On March 27, police shot and killed Dusan Spasojevic and Milan Lukovic, leaders of the Zemun group and chief suspects, as they resisted arrest. Police announced the arrest of Milica Gajic, daughter-in-law of Milosevic. Her husband, Marko Milosevic, fled the country shortly after the overthrow of his father. He was suspected to have criminal ties.

On April 8, investigators said the killing was orchestrated by The Hague Brotherhood—a gang that wanted to replace Djindjic with allies of Milosevic. The group opposed the UN war crimes tribunal in The Hague. The group planned to stage a coup after the assassination. Police believed the paramilitary United for Special Operations, formed under Milosevic's rule, was part of the plot. Its deputy commander was Zvezdan Jovanovic, who said he killed Djindjic because he was told his unit would be handed over to the war crimes tribunal.

On April 9, Serbian police arrested former Yugoslav President Vojislav Kostunica's security adviser, Rade Bulatovic, and the former head of army intelligence, Gen. Aca Tomic, on suspicion of having connections to the plotters. As of that date, police had detained more than 2,500 people in the case.

On August 21, prosecutors charged 44 people, including Milorad Lukovic, in the assassination. Lukovic and 15 others were charged with murder. The other 28 were charged with conspiracy to commit murder.

On November 5, the *Washington Post* identified the shooter as Zvezdan Jovanovic, a former member of the elite combat unit the Red Berets. Jovanovic fired a Winchester .308 caliber bullet into Djindjic as he was getting his crutches out of the car. Two dozen defendants were scheduled for trial in December.

On December 6, Rotterdam police arrested Ninoslav Kostantinovic and his brother, Sladjan, in connection with the assassination.

On December 22, the trial of 36 suspects—15 of them still at large—began. The indictment said they formed a "criminal enterprise" aimed at overthrowing the government. Still at large was mastermind Milorad Lukovic. The defendants faced 40-year terms for conspiracy against the state, terrorism, and first degree murder.

On December 25, the judge read a statement to police by accused triggerman Zvezdan Jovanovic, who said that "I personally liquidated Zoran Djindjic. I'm not a criminal. I would never do this for money." He said he waited for three days in an apartment near government headquarters, and shot the prime minister to stop suspects from being handed over to the UN war crimes tribunal in The Hague. "For me, this is a political killing to prevent further sending of warriors to The Hague. I think the Hague is the biggest disgrace."

On May 2, 2004, at 9:00 p.m., Milorad Lukovic, 39, surrendered in Belgrade. He had led a paramilitary group during the 1990s wars in Croatia, Bosnia, and Kosovo, led a Belgrade criminal gang, and remained the chief suspect in the assassination.

On June 14, Lukovic denied involvement in the killing in court and claimed that former members of Djindjic's government had sanctioned sales of 1500 pounds of heroin from police vaults to drug dealers in Western Europe.

On July 16, 2004, suspect Dejan Milenkovic, 34, was captured in Thessaloniki, Greece.

March 13, 2003. *India.* At 8:45 p.m., a bomb exploded on a crowded commuter train in Bombay as it was leaving Victoria Terminus in suburban Mulund station, killing 11 people and wounding more than 60. The roof of the coach was blown off. The bomb was hidden near the women's compartment of the train. The bomb went off a day after the tenth anniversary of several bombings in Bombay that killed 250 people. Police suspected the banned Students' Islamic Movement of India.

March 13, 2003. *India.* A bomb exploded on a bus parked at a terminal in Rajouri, Kashmir, killing four people. No one claimed credit.

March 15, 2003. *Pakistan.* Lahore police arrested Yassir Yasiri, a second-tier al Qaeda operative and associate of Khalid Sheik Mohammed and Osama bin Laden lieutenants.

March 16, 2003. *India.* Terrorists attacked a police installation in Indh, Kashmir, killing nine police officers and two civilians and wounding eight police officers and one civilian. No one claimed credit.

March 17, 2003. *United States.* Dwight W. Watson, 50, a down-on-his-luck North Carolina tobacco farmer, drove his John Deere tractor into a shallow pond at Constitution Gardens near the Vietnam Veterans Memorial off Constitution Avenue in Washington, D.C. He threatened to damage the Mall and demanded that Washington be evacuated in 82 hours. He claimed that he had rigged organic phosphates (fertilizers) to explode at three other locations and said he would set them off if police approached him. He tied up traffic for days. Several federal buildings were closed; others were open only to pedestrian traffic.

On March 19 at 11:35 a.m., he was led away in handcuffs after surrendering 47 hours after he began his siege, just before the opening of the war in Iraq. Many observers wondered if Washington was prepared for possible terrorist attacks associated with the war if a lone nut could tie up the city. All police found in the tractor was a toy hand grenade. No devices were found at the sites the 82nd Airborne veteran mentioned: a billboard for a tobacco company on Interstate 96 in Richmond, on Columbia Island in Washington, and behind the Marine Corps Museum in Washington. He was charged with one count of making false threats about an explosive and destroying government property. His tractor caused $27,000 worth of damage.

On June 25, 2003, U.S. District Judge Thomas Penfield Jackson ruled at a detention hearing that he was not convinced that Watson did not represent a danger to the community and ordered him held in prison until his September 16 trial. Jackson noted that he had made threats and made an outburst during a previous court appearance. Watson was represented by public defenders A. J. Kramer and Erica J. Hashimoto. Judge Jackson ruled on the opening day of the trial against Watson's request to call as witnesses former President Bill Clinton, former Minnesota Governor Jesse Ventura, former Mississippi Attorney General Mike Moore, and former Food and Drug Administrator David Kessler among others. Watson, facing ten years, defended himself at the trial. Watson said he preferred a jury trial, even though the judge warned that it would be hard to find 12 individuals who weren't resentful of his actions.

On September 26, 2003, a federal jury needed 45 minutes to find Watson guilty of seizing the corner of the Mall and destroying federal property. He faced six years in prison. Sentencing was scheduled for December 16.

On June 23, 2004, Watson was sentenced to six years by Judge Thomas Penfield Jackson. But on June 30, his sentenced was reduced to 16 months after a Supreme Court decision (*Blakely v. Washington*) raised issues about sentencing guidelines. The Court said juries, not judges, were to decide on facts used to increase sentences beyond maximum ranges. Watson was freed on July 1.

March 17, 2003. *France.* Police found two flasks containing traces of the ricin toxin in a luggage locker at the Gare de Lyon rail station in Paris. Interior Minister Nicolas Sarkozy said a link might be established between the toxin and arrests made near Paris in late 2002 of Islamic militants who were planning an attack in Paris. The amount of ricin was a "nonlethal quantity."

March 18, 2003. *Yemen.* A Yemeni gunman shot to death three oil workers, including an American, and wounded a fourth before killing himself. The gunman first shot to death an American supervising drilling operations for Hunt Oil Company, then shot two Canadians, one of whom survived, and a Yemeni citizen working for Hunt in the oil-rich northern province of Marib. The Westerners were working in the oil field. 03031801

March 18, 2003. *France.* Police in the Oise region northwest of Paris detained two people with links to a network supporting Chechen rebels planning chemical weapons attacks on Russian targets. The arrests added to the nine people arrested in December 2002, when police discovered the anti-Russian plot. Three had traveled to training camps in Afghanistan and to Georgia. 03031802

March 19, 2003. *Cuba.* At 7:45 p.m., six knife-wielding Cubans hijacked a Cuban Aero Taxi DC-3 en route from the Isle of Youth to Havana and diverted it to Key West, Florida. The group broke down the cockpit door and tied up four crew members with tape and rope. Five of the hijackers had knives. The U.S. military scrambled jet fighters and a U.S. Customs Department Black Hawk helicopter to escort the plane. No injuries were reported. The plane landed at Key West International Airport at 8:06 p.m., where the hijackers surrendered. The six were arraigned on air piracy charges and faced 20 years to life in prison if convicted. The 25 passengers and 6 crew were held at an immigration detention center near Miami. On March 22, 16 of the passengers returned to Cuba; the others opted to stay in the United States. Cuba demanded the return of the plane, its crew, and all of the passengers, saying it was an "act of terrorism." Cuba later said U.S. prosecution would be acceptable. Reports were unclear on the nationality of the passengers. One report said no passengers were Cuban and that one was Italian.

The hijackers were identified as Alvenis Arias Isquierdo, 24; Alexis Normiella Morales, 31; Eduardo Javier Mejias Morales, 26; Neudis Infante Hernandez, 31; Yainer Olivares Samon, 21; and Maikel Guerra Morales, 31.

On August 7, 2003, U.S. Magistrate Judge John O'Sullivan said confessions by Neudis Infantes Hernandez and Yainer Olivares Samon should not be used at trial because the FBI did not give them their Miranda warnings immediately. Edited summaries of the confessions of their four colleagues could be used in the September trial. Prosecutors were given ten days to respond to his ruling. Infantes was represented by attorney Martin Feigenbaum.

On December 11, 2003, the six Cuban defendants were convicted after jurors were not persuaded that it as a "freedom flight" undertaken with the crew's cooperation. Conviction entails a mandatory 20 years, with a possible life sentence. On April 21, 2004, four hijackers were sentenced to 20 years in prison; the plot's leader and his brother received 24 years. 03031901

March 19, 2003. *Somalia.* Militiamen handed a wounded Yemeni al Qaeda suspect over to the FBI (or to Kenyan authorities, according to other reports). The Yemeni was captured by a militia at a hospital north of the capital. Somali officials said the Yemeni had been wounded in a gun battle as police attempted to rescue him from the militia. A Kenyan government official said that he was a senior al Qaeda operative who was involved in recent terrorist activities in east Africa.

March 20, 2003. *United States.* The FBI announced that it was searching for Adnan G. El Shukrijumah, 27, a suspected Saudi al Qaeda member, who it said was planning terrorist attacks. A law enforcement spokesman said that he could be an organizer similar to Mohamad Atta, the September 11 orchestrator. Shukrijumah's name came up often in interrogations of Khalid Sheik Mohammed, the operations chief of al Qaeda. He was believed to have a connection to Jose Padilla, who was arrested in May 2002 on suspicion of planning to set off a radiological bomb in the United States. His alias was also linked to the Oklahoma flight school where Zacarias Moussaoui studied aviation. The suspect could be traveling on passports from Guyana, Trinidad, Canada, or Saudi Arabia. He last entered the United States before September 11 and left later in 2001. Some authorities believed he was in Morocco or had reentered the United States illegally. The family had moved to Miramar, north of Miami, Florida, in 1995. His father is a prominent Muslim leader in that suburb and leads a prayer center, Masjid al Hijrah, next door to his home, which was searched by FBI agents. One of the suspect's addresses was a house in Pembroke Pines, Florida, where Padilla attended a mosque. The FBI said he had taken the battle name Ja'far al-Tayar (Ja'far the Pilot), used the alias Abu Arif, and had conferred with Ramzi Binalshibh, a September 11 coordinator; field commander Abu Zubayda; and Khalid Sheik Mohammed, al Qaeda operations chief. He attended an al Qaeda explosives training camp in 2000, according to investigators. His name was also connected to Norman, Oklahoma, where Zacarias Moussaoui received flight training.

Adnan G. El Shukrijumah was the eldest of five children. He was born in 1975 in Saudi Arabia to a Guyanese father and Saudi mother. His father was the first Westerner to graduate from Medina's Islamic University. His father worked as a missionary in Trinidad and New York, leaving the family in Saudi Arabia.

The FBI rescinded a February alert issued against Mohammed Sher Mohammed Khan, an alias of Shukrijumah.

On March 25, the FBI's Baltimore office said it wanted to question a Pakistani couple, Aafia Siddiqui, 31, and her husband, Mohammed Khan, 33, about possible terrorist activities and their ties to Shukrijumah. She resided in the Boston area and had visited Gaithersburg, Maryland, in late December or January. She has a doctorate in neurological science and has studied at MIT and Brandeis University, as well as in Houston, Texas. She listed her home as in Karachi. At MIT, she wrote a paper on how to set up a Muslim student organization. The duo are officers of the Institute of Islamic Research and Teaching, Inc., of Roxbury, Massachusetts.

Within the week of the worldwide alert, Shukrijumah's father lost his job as spiritual leader of the Masjid al Hijrah next door to his home. He had testified as a character witness for Clement Hampton-el, a member of his New York mosque who was sentenced to 35 years in prison for plotting an "urban terror war" along with the men accused of bombing the World Trade Center in 1993.

Shukrijumah had also been a suspect in a plot by Imran Mandhai, currently serving 11 years after pleading guilty to conspiracy on charges of planning a "jihad cell" of 30 men that would target electrical substations, an armory, Jewish institutions, and Mount Rushmore. An FBI informant bugged Mandhai, who was heard naming Shukrijumah as an accomplice.

In spring 2001, Shukrijumah refused to be an FBI informant. He left the country in May 2001.

March 20, 2003. *Germany.* Police detained five suspected Islamic militants who "possibly would use the beginning of the war in Iraq as an opportunity to carry out an attack." Police searched six Berlin buildings, including the Al-Nur mosque and offices of an Islamic community group.

March 20, 2003. *Germany.* On May 4, 2004, Ihsan Garnaoui, 33, a Tunisian, was charged in Berlin with planning to bomb Jewish and U.S. targets in Germany during the U.S.–led invasion of Iraq. The indictment said he entered Germany illegally in January 2003 to plan the attacks, for which he had trained at an al Qaeda camp beginning in July 2001. According to the charge sheet, "There the accused first learned battle training and how to produce and handle explosives and weapons. After that he was active as a trainer for al Qaeda. During this time he made the personal acquaintance of Osama bin Laden." He was represented by attorneys Michael Rosenthal and Margarete von Galen. Six other plotters were not charged. As of May 30, 2004, security officials had refused to permit two confidential informants to testify and a key police report had gone missing. The prosecution had been unable to specify what attacks Garnaoui was planning.

At the trial on June 1, Ben Slimane, 37, a Tunisian imam at a Berlin mosque, implicated Mohammed Fakihi, a Saudi diplomat who serves as director of Islamic Affairs at the embassy, as a member of an al Qaeda cell. On March 22, 2003, Germany had ordered Fakihi to leave the country.

Garnaoui had been arrested at 5:00 p.m. after he left the apartment of Abdel-Karim Jahha. 03032002

March 20, 2003. *Malaysia.* Police broke up a plot by an al Qaeda affiliated group to target U.S. and other Western embassies in Singapore. Police confiscated four tons of ammonium nitrate (a fertilizer that can be used in explosives) that Jemaah Islamiah (JI) planned to use. The cache was found buried at a plantation near Muar, where police had detained a JI suspect on March 14. The chemical had been purchased in September 2000 by ex-army captain and scientist Yazid Sufaat, who in early 2004 was under ISA detention for involvement in JI activities. The chemicals were to be used by JI in Singapore to make truck bombs to attack foreign embassies and other Western targets. 03032001

March 20, 2003. *United States.* Federal agents in the Operation Green Quest terrorist financing task force arrested nine people and executed nine search warrants.

On March 20, the FBI and Bureau of Immigration and Customs Enforcement arrested four people and seized $71,000 in an investigation of Pakistani money remittance business in New York. The Manhattan Foreign Exchange had illegally moved more than $33 million to Pakistan in three years. Much of the money came from the sale of faked U.S., U.K., Pakistani, and Canadian passports. An undercover federal agent claiming to be a drug money launderer told Shaheen Butt, owner of the Exchange, that drugs were the source of $200,000 he gave Butt. An aide of Butt told the agent that he could obtain a fake driver's license, photo ID card, immigration green card, and social security card for $21,000. Butt was charged with money laundering, immigration fraud, and other counts.

Green Quest agents in Los Angeles arrested Mahmoud Harkous and executed search warrants on his tobacco shop. He was accused of illegally structuring financial deals to evade IRS reporting requirements. Agents intercepted more than 270 money orders worth $135,000 that were smuggled from California to residents in Beirut via private express parcels.

Minneapolis agents arrested four people on charges of structuring illegal financial deals worth $2 million, mostly involving unpaid tobacco taxes. The investigators searched five tobacco shops. The four were charged with smuggling hundreds of thousands of dollars in financial instruments to Jordan and Lebanon. Agents found $156,925 in cashier's checks sewn into the lining of a handbag on a flight in Beirut.

Customs agents in Newark seized $48,000 from two bank accounts that involved numerous transactions entailing sending bulk currency by private express parcel to Yemen.

Two Iraqi brothers in Denver were arrested for operating an unlicensed money transferring business that sent more than $7 million to Iraq in two and a half years. They were identified as

Maitham Abdulla Jaber Samar, 39, and Qassim Abdulla Jaber Samar. Maitham Samar does business as Alrafden Transactions.

March 20, 2003. *Peru.* A Peruvian court announced the life sentence of Abimael Guzman, founder of the Maoist Shining Path terrorist group, because his treason conviction was handed down by an unconstitutional secret military court. The courts granted new trials to 2,000 Shining Path guerrillas, who could go free.

March 20, 2003. *Norway.* Police arrested Mullah Krekar, an Iraqi Kurdish founder of the Islamic militant group Ansar al-Islam. He had refugee status in Norway since 1991. A lower court ruled that police could keep him jailed for a month. However, on April 2, an appeals court freed him.

During his February address to the UN Security Council, U.S. Secretary of State Colin Powell noted that Ansar al-Islam had sheltered al Qaeda members, including a senior Baghdad agent of the network.

March 20, 2003. *Greece.* Terrorists placed four gas canisters at the entrance to the Citibank branch in Kholargos, setting them on fire. Minor damage was reported. No one claimed credit. 03032003

March 20, 2003. *Lebanon.* A bomb containing two kilograms of TNT exploded on the first floor stairs of a Sidon apartment building, killing two and wounding nine people. The likely target was a Dutch woman who lived on that floor with her Lebanese husband. Three apartments were damaged and several cars were set on fire. No one claimed credit. 03032004

March 21, 2003. *Sri Lanka.* A Tamil Tiger (LTTE) rebel boat attacked and sank a vessel carrying Chinese fishermen off eastern Sri Lanka, killing 17 people on board. The Chinese government said it was "extremely concerned" by the apparent case of mistaken identity. 03032101

March 21, 2003. *United States.* CNN reported that the FBI was seeking a female al Qaeda member in the United States.

March 21, 2003. *Norway.* Antiwar protestors threw a Molotov cocktail into a McDonald's restaurant in Oslo before opening time, causing limited damage and no injuries. 03032102

March 22, 2003. *Greece.* A makeshift incendiary device exploded in an ATM outside a Citibank branch in Koropi, causing severe damage to the ATM. No one claimed credit. 03032201

March 22, 2003. *Iraq.* Sayed Sadiq, an Australian journalist and cameraman, died instantly when a taxi drove up next to him and exploded. His colleague, also an Australian journalist on assignment for the Australian Broadcasting Corporation, sustained shrapnel wounds. Eight others were injured in the bombing. Ansar al-Islam was believed responsible. 03032202

March 23, 2003. *Indonesia.* CNN quoted the State Department as warning that it had credible information that terrorists would attack in retaliation for the war in Iraq.

March 23, 2003. *India.* Masked gunmen shot to death Abdul Majid Dar, 47, former chief commander of Hizb ul-Mujaheddin, the largest guerrilla group in Kashmir, who had favored dialogue in the region. He was killed when the gunmen fired on his car near his brother's home in Sopore, 30 miles south of Srinagar. His sister and mother were injured. Two separatist groups claimed credit.

March 23, 2003. *Ecuador.* A bomb exploded at the British Consulate in Guayaquil, leaving a hole in the ground, destroying two windows and a bathroom, and damaging the building's electrical control board. No injuries were reported. The People's Revolutionary Militias (MRP) sent an e-mail claiming credit. 03032301

March 24, 2003. *India.* Muslim militants wearing military uniforms were blamed for shooting to death 24 people in Nadimarg, a Hindu village 30 miles south of Srinagar, the summer capital of Jammu and Kashmir. Two small boys and 11 women were among the dead. The victims had been lined up and shot. No one claimed credit.

March 24, 2003. *Bahrain.* In April, Bahrain expelled an Iraqi diplomat for involvement in setting off an explosive device near the entrance of the headquarters of the U.S. Navy Fifth Fleet on March 24. The government arrested the bomber—a major in the Iraqi Intelligence Service—tried him in open court, and sentenced him to three years in prison. 04032401

March 25, 2003. *Lebanon.* A 400-gram explosive device went off on the U.S. Embassy wall in Beirut, causing light damage and no casualties. No one claimed credit. 03032503

March 25, 2003. *Serbia.* Four bombings were carried out against the UN Interim Administration Mission in Kosovo (UNMIK) police stations. Police suspected the founder and commander of a local mujaheddin unit. 03032505-08

March 25–26, 2003. *Italy.* Terrorists firebombed three cars belonging to U.S. service members. The Anti-Imperialist Territorial Nuclei (NTA), believed to be close to the new Red Brigades, claimed credit. 03032501-02, 03032604

March 26, 2003. *Yemen.* Authorities raided a San'a house during the night and arrested a small group of Iraqis. Police seized a small cache of explosives to be used against the U.S. and U.K. embassies. 03032601

March 26, 2003. *Jordan.* Authorities raided an Amman site and arrested a group of Iraqis. Police seized explosives to be used to bomb a hotel frequented by Westerners. 03032602

March 26, 2003. *Afghanistan.* A gunman fatally shot Ricardo Munguia, 39, a Salvadoran-Swiss water engineer working for the International Committee of the Red Cross, on a road in southern Helmand Province. (Some reports said March 27, 2003, and 60 gunmen.) The gunman stopped a two or three-vehicle convoy in the Shah Wali Kot district of Kandahar, then phoned Dadullah, a former Taliban commander. Dadullah ordered the murder. The gunman fired two bullets from a Kalashnikov rifle into the victim. Munguia, the first foreign aid worker to die since the ouster of the Taliban, was developing water wells for the town of Tirin Kot in Uruzgan Province. The Taliban was blamed for the murder. Interior Minister Ali Ahmad Jalali said the killers pulled out Munguia, the only Westerner in the convoy, to make a political statement. The Red Cross suspended field operations.

On April 21, U.S. Special Forces captured the assassin in a nighttime raid during which the gunman opened fire on them. 03032603

March 26, 2003. *India.* A bomb placed inside of the engine of an empty oil tanker parked outside a fuel storage area in Narwal, Kashmir, exploded and caught fire, killing one person and injuring six others. No one claimed credit.

March 27, 2003. *Burma.* A bomb was found in a park in front of the U.S. Embassy in Rangoon. Another bomb exploded outside a state telecommunications office, killing one person and wounding three during Armed Forces Day. No one claimed credit. 03032701

March 27, 2003. *Chile.* Antiwar protestors set off a small bomb at a branch of the Bank of Boston in Santiago, smashing windows, destroying an ATM, and causing minor damage to two neighboring stores. Police found a pamphlet at the site that said "death to the empire," which they took as a reference to the United States. No one claimed credit. 03032703

March 28, 2003. *Turkey.* Ozgur Gencarslan, 20, hijacked a Turkish Airlines airbus A310 that took off from Istanbul at 10:00 p.m. en route to Ankara and diverted it to Athens, Greece, where he surrendered after a three hour standoff. The hijacker, who was sitting in business class, apparently was upset about family problems. He rushed into the cockpit when the cabin door opened 25 minutes after takeoff. He claimed to have explosives and wanted refueling in Athens before departing for Berlin. Several Turkish legislators and government officials were among the 194 passengers and 9 crew members on the flight. During negotiations on the runway of Eleftherios Venizelos International Airport, Turhan Comez, a legislator with the governing Justice and Development Party, called Prime Minister Recep Tayyip Erdogan and handed his cell phone to the hijacker. Several passengers called Turkish television stations on their cell phones. One woman reported, "The hijacker made a statement to the passengers and said his family was arrested in Germany and he had no intention of harming us. He said nothing would happen to us."

On March 31, Gencarslan was arraigned and ordered to undergo a psychiatric evaluation. He faced three charges. He said he was emotionally distraught because of family problems. Prosecutors said he used razor blades and candles disguised as dynamite in the hijacking. 03032801

March 28, 2003. *Worldwide.* The U.S. State Department warned ten countries that small groups of Iraqi intelligence agents were planning attacks against Americans and other Westerners. The United States had learned that bombings had been planned in the United Kingdom, Pakistan, Turkey, and Syria.

March 28, 2003. *Italy.* Radicals firebombed a Ford–Jaguar dealership in Rome. The two brands were taken as symbols of the U.S.–U.K.-led coalition fighting in Iraq. A dozen Fords were burned and another ten damaged. A five-pointed star—symbol of the Red Brigades, who were not known to plan firebomb attacks—was found at the site. No one claimed credit. 03032802

March 28, 2003. *Afghanistan.* Gunmen in Tirin Kot shot to death a Salvadoran Red Cross worker who was traveling with Afghan colleagues to check on water supplies. The group was captured. The kidnap leader was told via phone to kill the only Westerner in the group. No one claimed credit. 03032803

March 29, 2003. *Greece.* At 1:20 a.m., someone threw a British "mills" hand grenade at a McDonald's restaurant in Athens, causing significant material damage. No one claimed credit. 03032901

March 30, 2003. *Israel.* At 1:00 p.m., a Palestine Islamic Jihad (PIJ) suicide bomber injured 38 people, including 10 soldiers, at a mall in Netanya when he was stopped from entering the London Café. His 6.5-pound bomb was laden with nails and shrapnel. Among the injured was Levona Mazaltim, 51, who suffered a leg wound; and Saul Eviatar's infant son, who was treated for shock. PJO leader Abdullah Shami said the bombing was in retaliation for the deaths of Palestinians and a "sign of support for the Iraqi people and to encourage them to remain steadfast." It was the first suicide bombing in the area since the start of the war in Iraq.

March 30, 2003. *Bosnia/Herzegovina.* Islamic terrorists placed a hand grenade with an anti-U.S. message near a local Coca-Cola company in Sarajevo. No one claimed credit. 03033001

March 30, 2003. *India.* A bomb exploded in a field where a cricket match was being played in Punch (variant Poonch), Kashmir, killing one person and injuring two others. No one claimed credit.

March 31, 2003. *Cuba.* Adermis Wilson Gonzalez, 33, claiming to have two grenades, hijacked a Cuban Airlines plane flying 32 people (reports differ as to the number of people originally on the plane, but included 7 crew serving 12 men, 9 women, and 4 children) from the Isle of Youth and forced the pilot to refuel in Havana. The next day, more than 20 passengers left the aircraft unharmed. The plane sat on the runway for 12 hours and later flew to Key West, where he surrendered and was led away in handcuffs. Some

25 passengers were still on board. He was traveling with his wife and 3-year-old son. Gonzalez was wearing a red windbreaker with the word America stitched in white on the back. Two fake grenades were found. U.S. officials said he would be prosecuted and denied asylum. Cuba blamed the United States for lax treatment of earlier hijackers. 03033101

March 31, 2003. *United States.* Federal authorities detained as a material witness Pakistani citizen Uzair Paracha, 23, in the offices of a New York clothing import firm owned by his father. He had ties to the shipping industry and senior al Qaeda leaders. Investigators said the family business might have been used to smuggled al Qaeda terrorists or weapons into the United States. His father owns a Pakistani textile company that shipped large containers of clothes and other goods into Newark. He was arrested by Karachi police while trying to board an airplane in Karachi in July; he was held incommunicado. Uzair Paracha was fingered by Khalid Sheik Mohammed, a senior jailed al Qaeda member. Uzair Paracha was also linked to Ohio truck driver Iyman Faris, who pleaded guilty on May 1 to providing material support to a terrorist organization.

On August 8, federal authorities in Manhattan filed terrorism charges against Paracha, including conspiracy to provide material support to terrorists, which entails a 15-year sentence. The indictment said that for a $200,000 business investment, the younger Paracha agreed to pose as an unnamed al Qaeda associate while in the United States to secure immigration documents for him. During a March interview with the FBI and New York Police Department, Paracha admitted to possession of a Maryland driver's license, an ATM card, a key to a post office box, and documents linked to the al Qaeda member. Prosecutors had earlier said that he could also be charged with helping to obtain weapons of mass destruction and with conspiracy. His attorney, Anthony Ricco of New York, denied the allegations.

March 31, 2003. *Italy.* IBM employees in Bologna found an explosive device in a large bag and notified the police. The bomb squad said it was a "dangerous, though rudimentary" bomb. Investigators said the modus operandi of this incident was similar to an earlier bombing in July 2001 in Bologna. No one claimed credit. 03033102

March 31, 2003. *Cyprus.* A 26-year-old man threw a Molotov cocktail against the outside wall of the U.S. Embassy in Nicosia. No damage was reported. The man was arrested. 03033103

March–April 2003. *Chile.* The Chilean American Binational Centers were subject to violent protests, some vandalism, and bomb threats by Chileans opposed to U.S. policy in Iraq.

April 2003. *United States.* Stewards on a cruise ship found threatening notes in two bathrooms. One threatened to "kill all Americanos abord [sic]" if the liner stopped in Hawaii. The other read, "Give this warning to El Caption to save all lives. Do take this serious he sent me from far away land for mission I will complete if port on American soil [sic]." The ship dropped anchor off Oahu while 100 federal and local agents and 40 bomb-sniffing dogs traveled on a Coast Guard cutter to get to the ship. They interrogated most of the 1,700 passengers and 700 crew. The search cost $300,000. Kelley Ferguson said she had seen someone plant the notes in the bathroom.

On May 15, Kelley Marie Ferguson, 20, pleaded guilty in U.S. District Court in Honolulu to making false threats. She had hoped that the ship would return to Mexico and she could get back to Orange County and her boyfriend, whom her parents disliked. (He had been arrested on drug and theft charges.) She was represented by federal public defender Loretta Faymonville. Her parents said they would not post bail even if the judge granted it. She faced 20 years and a $25,000 fine on two felony counts of issuing false threats to kill passengers on a vehicle of mass transportation. Prosecutors dropped one count as part of her plea. She was ordered freed on $5,000 bail and placed under house arrest in her parents' custody, with no contact with her boyfriend. She also announced she was pregnant.

April 2003. *Japan.* The Revolutionary Workers Association, a group of leftists protesting the Iraq War, fired projectiles at the Atsugi Naval Air Facility, a U.S. military base south of Tokyo, during the first week of April. No injuries were reported. The group claimed credit on April 7. 03049901

April 2003. *Indonesia.* Bombs went off at Jakarta's international airport and near the UN headquarters. No deaths were reported.

April 2003. *Iraq.* Coalition forces arrested Muhammad Abbas (alias Abu Abbas), the leader of the Palestine Liberation Front. He died in custody of natural causes in March 2004.

April 2003. *Solomon Islands.* Nathaniel Sado, an Anglican missionary, disappeared and was believed to have been killed. Later in the month, another six missionaries serving in Melanesian Brotherhood set off to look for him but were kidnapped by warlord Harold Keke. On August 15, 2003, Richard Carter, chaplain to the Brotherhood, announced that the six had been murdered. Keke apparently used the group as human shields, and they were killed by one of his lieutenants. 03049902-03

April 1, 2003. *Yemen.* Authorities arrested 11 people with suspected al Qaeda links, including two of the government's Most Wanted suspects. Security was increased around the U.S., U.K., and Kuwaiti embassies.

April 1, 2003. *Italy.* Authorities arrested six men, including an imam, after newspapers reported that some of them were preparing to leave for Iraq.

April 1, 2003. *Jordan.* The government arrested six Iraqis suspected of plotting to poison a water tank near the Iraqi border that serves hundreds of U.S. troops at a base in Khao, 17 miles northeast of Amman.

Police were investigating a plot by four Iraqis to bomb an apartment complex at the Grand Hyatt Hotel in Amman. Western journalists, executives, and aid workers stay at the hotel.

The previous week, Jordan expelled five Iraqi diplomats on security grounds, saying that they intended to "undermine Jordan's internal security."

April 1, 2003. *India.* The Hmar People's Convention attacked several villages in the remote northeast of Assam State's Cachar District during the night, burning huts and taking 28 hostages. Police searching the mountain jungles found the bodies of 22 kidnapped farmers who had been shot to death. The Convention is fighting for the rights of the Hmar ethnic group in southern Assam, which borders Bangladesh.

April 2, 2003. *Cuba.* At 1:30 a.m., eight to ten Cuban hijackers took over the Baragua, a 50-foot ferry, in Havana harbor and sailed it to sea until it ran out of fuel. The hijackers claimed by radio to be armed with three pistols and a knife, and threatened to throw the 50 passengers overboard unless they were given another boat to reach the United States, about 40 miles away. The ferry is part of a small flotilla that shuttles Cubans from one side of Havana Bay to the other. The FBI sent a hostage negotiation team. The Coast Guard dispatched two cutters. Cuba also sent two ships from the Frontier Guards and threatened to use force to free the hostages. The hijackers freed three ill adults. The hijackers agreed to let the ferry be towed to Mariel, west of Havana. On the afternoon of April 3, authorities rescued the hostages and arrested the hijackers. The hostages, including one Frenchman, had begun jumping overboard at a signal from Cuban officers. Military divers helped the hostages swim to safety. Some hijackers jumped overboard, but were captured.

On April 11, despite the protests of human rights groups, Cuban firing squads executed three of the hijackers at dawn after convicting them on terrorism charges. They were identified as Lorenzo Enrique Copello Castillo, Barbaro Leodan Sevilla Garcia, and Jorge Luis Martinez Isaac. They had been given three days to appeal. The death sentences were upheld by Cuba's Supreme Tribunal and by the ruling Council of State. Four other hijackers received life sentences. 03040201

April 2, 2003. *Philippines.* A bomb exploded during the night in a row of food stands at a ferry terminal in Davao, killing 16 and wounding 55. The blast went off after a ferry from Manila docked. The explosion shattered car windows and sprayed blood and body parts on the pavement. No one claimed credit, but police suspected the Moro Islamic Liberation Front (MILF). MILF spokesman Eid Kavalu said, "The MILF has never been involved in such kind of bombings, where civilians are a target. We consider it a heinous crime against humanity." Among the dead was Pablita Espera, 60, and a young boy holding a toy. A young woman was decapitated. Sister Dulce de Guzman, a Franciscan nun and peace activist from Zamboanga, also died.

On April 8, the head of Philippine police intelligence said that a regional terrorist group, Jemaah Islamiah (JI), with links to al Qaeda, may have been involved. Two Indonesian members of the group were suspected. Authorities arrested two Philippine men in connection with the attack. They were identified as Ismael Acmad (alias Toto), the alleged planner, and accomplice Tahome Urong (alias Sermin Tohami). They belong to the Special Operations Group of the MILF. MILF spokesman Eid Kabalu said the duo was not MILF members, but pump boat operators forced into confessing MILF affiliation. Army spokesman Maj. Julieto Ando said the duo also said they were involved in the March bombing of Davao airport that killed 22 people, including a U.S. missionary. The ammonium nitrate explosive used in the attack is similar to that purchased by a JI Indonesian operative Fathur Rohman al-Ghozi and seized by police

in January 2002 following his arrest. The Philippine president said that several JI Indonesian members had been sighted in "terrorist training camps" in Mindanao. 03040201

April 3, 2003. *Turkey.* Bombs exploded within a few hours of each other at the British Consulate and outside a branch of the United Parcel Service (UPS) in Istanbul, causing damage but no injuries. At the Consulate, an individual threw a bomb around 12:50 a.m., shattering windows and damaging a gate and walls of the building, and leaving a Turkish hotel guest next door with minor cuts. The UPS bomb blew out windows of two nearby shops—a pharmacy and an olive-seller's shop. No one claimed credit, but the Marxist-Leninist Communist Party (MLK-P) was suspected. Turkish police believe that the bomb at the consulate was a resonant device (sound bomb) of relatively crude construction. 03040301-03040302

April 3, 2003. *Lebanon.* The U.S. Embassy advised Americans to consider leaving the country, citing terrorist threats and antiwar demonstrations.

April 3, 2003. *Russia.* Talgat Tadzhuddin, who claims to speak for 29 of the country's 48 muftis, declared a jihad against the United States and called on Russia's 20 million Muslims to support the people of Iraq. He said his group would "raise donations for a fund and use the money to buy weapons for fighting America and food for the people of Iraq." Muslims comprise 13 percent of Russia's population.

April 3, 2003. *Algeria.* Eight Austrian tourists were kidnapped by the Salafist Group for Preaching (Call) and Combat (GSPC) in the Sahara Desert. From late March until mid-May, the GSPC kidnapped 32 European tourists in eight separate incidents. On May 13, Algerian Special Forces rescued 17 hostages. One hostage, a German woman, died of heatstroke on July 28 while in captivity. On August 18, the remaining 14 hostages were released in northern Mali. Press reports claimed a ransom of 4.6 million euros was paid to the GSPC in return for the hostages. 03040303

April 4, 2003. *Algeria.* During the week, the Salafist Group for Preaching (Call) and Combat (GSPC) kidnapped 11 German tourists traveling in small groups without guides in the Sahara Desert. This brought the total of Germans abducted in this kidnapping spree to 15. From late March until mid-May, the GSPC kidnapped 32 European tourists in eight separate incidents. On May 13, Algerian Special Forces rescued 17 hostages. One hostage, a German woman, died of heatstroke on July 28 while in captivity. On August 18, the remaining 14 hostages were released in northern Mali. Press reports claimed a ransom of 4.6 million euros was paid to the GSPC in return for the hostages. 03040401

April 5, 2003. *Lebanon.* At 4:40 p.m., a 500-gram TNT bomb exploded in a trash can in a men's restroom in a McDonald's in Dowra, near Beirut, wounding ten, including a small child, and causing considerable damage. Five to ten seconds later, a minor explosion went off in a vehicle adjacent to the building. Police later found a car in the parking lot that contained 120 pounds of TNT, C-4, and three gas-filled containers. The detonator had malfunctioned and the explosives were dismantled. The bomb was a three-stage device that had three timers. Police believed that the first blast was intended to lure people to the scene, where the second bomb would kill more. No one claimed credit, but anti-Iraq War protestors were suspected.

On April 12, the government announced that it was holding 18 people, including 2 army draftees, in the case. The government said people behind the bomb also organized attacks on six other U.S.–style food outlets and planned attacks on Western embassies. Police seized a rocket, hand grenades, pistols, machine guns, and silencers from one of the detainees.

On May 4, Lebanon's army arrested the leader of the network responsible for the series of attacks on fast food restaurants and other Western targets. By that date, the government had charged more than 30 people with belonging to a terrorist group. The State Department's *Patterns in International Terrorism 2003* attributed the attack to 'Asbat al-Ansar. In October, Lebanese security forces arrested Ibn al-Shahid, who is believed to be associated with the group and charged him with masterminding the bombing of three fast food restaurants in 2003 and the Mac attack in April 2003.

On May 8, Syria handed over to Lebanon a Lebanese man suspected of being one of the bombers. Lebanon said the gang members planned to kill U.S. Ambassador Vincent Battle in Tripoli, Lebanon. The individual handed over by Syria had no direct links to that plot. His brother, an army draftee, was also arrested for the restaurant attacks.

In July, Lebanese security forces began a series of arrests in connection with the bombing. 03040501

April 5, 2003. *Israel.* Israeli troops shot and killed a Palestinian gunman who fired shots at a security guard outside the Kiryat Arba Jewish settlement.

April 7, 2003. *Worldwide.* In an audiotape purportedly recorded by Osama bin Laden, the al Qaeda leader called for suicide attacks against the United States and United Kingdom to "avenge the innocent children … assassinated in Iraq."

April 8, 2003. *Jordan.* At 10:45 a.m., a U.S. diplomat was slightly wounded when terrorists fired at him as he left his Amman hotel to use his cell phone. Three people fired a shot from a passing car, leaving a superficial wound. No one claimed credit. 03040801

April 8, 2003. *Turkey.* Concussion hand grenades exploded in front of the Bornova Court, Citibank, and the British Consulate in Izmir, causing material damage but no injuries. The MLK-P was suspected. 03040802-03

April 8, 2003. *Algeria.* The Salafist Group for Preaching (Call) and Combat (GSPC) kidnapped a Swede and a Dutch citizen. From late March until mid-May, the GSPC kidnapped 32 European tourists in eight separate incidents. On May 13, Algerian Special Forces rescued 17 hostages. One hostage, a German woman, died of heatstroke on July 28 while in captivity. On August 18, the remaining 14 hostages were released in northern Mali. Press reports claimed a ransom of 4.6 million euros was paid to the GSPC in return for the hostages. 03040804

April 10, 2003. *Germany.* At 6:00 a.m., police raided more than 80 buildings in 11 states across the country in a crackdown on members of the 50-year-old Hizb ut-Tahrir organization, which had been banned in January for promoting anti-Jewish sentiments in universities and elsewhere. Police seized computers, bank account details, and documents. The organization denies the right of Israel to exist and promotes the use of violence, including the killing of Jews and their expulsion from Israel.

April 10, 2003. *Israel.* Two Palestinian gunmen used wire cutters to get through a security fence at the Israeli military's largest base in the northern Jordan Valley at dawn. They opened fire, killing two guards and wounding nine others, some of whom were inside their tents. Soldiers fired back, killing the intruders. The Popular Front for the Liberation of Palestine (PFLP) and the al-Aqsa Martyrs Brigades claimed credit jointly.

April 10, 2003. *Cuba.* Authorities claimed to have foiled a planned hijacking with the arrest of four armed men outside the airport on the Isle of Youth, 85 miles south of Havana. On May 17, they sentenced four men to life in prison for terrorism in planning to hijack the plane to the United States with stolen rifles and knives. Three accomplices received 20 to 30 year terms.

April 10, 2003. *India.* A bomb exploded in the Mughal Garden, causing no damage. No one claimed credit.

April 10, 2003. *Germany.* Unknown individuals torched a party bus for children in the parking lot of a McDonald's restaurant in Hamburg, then set fire to a McDonald's billboard. Fliers for a leftist extremist group were found at both sites. 03041001-02

April 11, 2003. *Afghanistan.* Orfeo Bartolini, 51, was found shot to death in Zabul Province on the road from Kabul to Kandahar. Police investigated whether it was robbery or anti-Western terrorism. He had been riding a motorbike to India on a dangerous stretch of road in the south where bandits and remnants of the Taliban are active. Some of Bartolini's belongings were left at the scene, suggesting terrorism. 03041101

April 11, 2003. *Colombia.* Defense lawyers produced a videotape to indicate that one of three Irish Republican Army suspects charged with training Colombian leftist terrorists in bomb making was in Belfast at the time he was alleged to have been in the Colombian jungles.

April 11, 2003. *Algeria.* Two Austrian mountaineers were kidnapped in the Sahara Desert by the Salafist Group for Preaching (Call) and Combat (GSPC), bringing the tally of kidnapped Austrians to ten. From late March until mid-May, the GSPC kidnapped 32 European tourists in eight separate incidents. On May 13, Algerian Special Forces rescued 17 hostages. One hostage, a German woman, died of heatstroke on July 28 while in captivity. On August 18, the remaining 14 hostages were released in northern Mali. Press reports claimed a ransom of 4.6 million euros was paid to the GSPC in return for the hostages. 03041102

April 12, 2003. *Afghanistan.* Unidentified attackers threw two hand grenades—one did not detonate—at Italian troops on patrol near the eastern city of Khost. No one was injured. Italian troops detained one person. 03041201

April 12, 2003. *Venezuela.* A C-4 bomb exploded in the Caracas office of the

Organization of American States, significantly damaging the basement but causing no injuries. No one claimed credit. 03041202

April 12, 2003. *India.* Terrorists threw a hand grenade at a Kulgam police patrol, but missed, injuring two private citizens standing nearby. No one claimed credit.

April 12, 2003. *India.* Terrorists threw a hand grenade into a bus station in Qazigund-Anantnag, Kashmir, killing 1 person and injuring 20. No one claimed credit. Meanwhile, militants threw a grenade at an army patrol in Anantnag, wounding 21 civilians and 2 soldiers.

April 12, 2003. *Serbia/Montenegro/Kosovo.* Kosovo's UN governor German diplomat Michael Steiner announced that the Albanian National Army (ANA) is a terrorist group whose members can be jailed for up to 40 years. The group had claimed credit for setting off a bomb on a railway in a Serbian part of the province. The ANA wants to unite ethnic Albanian soil in the Balkans. In a statement on its Web site, it said its attack was aimed at cutting the railway that links "Serbian-occupied" parts of Kosovo with Belgrade. Steiner said the aim of the attack aimed was killing "a large number of innocent civilians and damaging public property." Police found the remains of two people by a bridge that was damaged by the nighttime explosion near Avecan in northern Kosovo. 03041202

April 13, 2003. *Afghanistan.* A taxi rigged with explosives blew up 200 yards from a U.S. airfield in the east near Khost, killing a Yemeni man, two Pakistanis, and Zarat Khan, an Afghan who was a former Taliban intelligence officer with ties to al Qaeda. They were probably planning a terrorist attack as they were testing a remotely controlled device when the explosion occurred. Authorities arrested some members of Khan's family and turned them over to U.S.–led coalition forces for questioning. The group had driven the taxi across the Pakistani border. They parked the car at Khan's home near Khost. The bomb destroyed

his two-story home and injured a woman nearby. Khan was believed to be involved in firing rockets at a U.S. base in the area. 03041301

April 13, 2003. *Philippines.* Terrorists in Siasi kidnapped a Filipino–Chinese businesswoman on her way to the local mosque. She was last seen being taken to Jolo, an island stronghold of the Abu Sayyaf Group. 03041302

April 13, 2003. *Pakistan.* Terrorists shot and killed two relatives of the governor of Kandahar, Afghanistan, and wounded another as they were traveling by car to a bazaar in Charman. An attacker was later caught and identified as a member of Fazlur Rahman's Jui (Jamiat Ulema-e Islami). 03041303

April 14, 2003. *Brazil.* Armed thugs in two cars fired machine guns at the historic landmark Hotel Gloria in Rio de Janeiro. The gang members escaped into hillside *favelas* (slums) nearby. No one was hurt. Police spokesman Frederico Caldas said, "This is the strategy of the (drug) dealer, to attack well-known places to draw attention. We're looking to who was responsible for this episode."

April 14, 2003. *Afghanistan.* A missile fired at the U.S. Embassy landed four kilometers away in Yakatut and failed to explode, causing no damage or injuries. No one claimed credit.

April 14, 2003. *France.* Terrorists torched a car parked outside the rear entrance of a McDonald's restaurant in Sergy, partially destroying the restaurant. No one claimed credit. 03041401

April 15, 2003. *Turkey.* A bomb damaged a McDonald's restaurant in Istanbul's Sirkeci section, shattering windows and damaging walls, but causing no injuries. Another bomb caused extensive damage to a government-run hotel for judges and civil servants in Istanbul, again causing no injuries. A third bomb went off in another McDonald's in Istanbul, injuring a pedestrian when a wall collapsed. The Revolutionary People's

Liberation Party/Front (DHKP/C) claimed credit. 03041501-02

April 15, 2003. *Israel.* At 4:00 a.m., a Palestinian shot to death Lt. Daniel Mandel, a newly trained 24-year old commander of an Israeli military reconnaissance team, as Mandel was arresting him in Nablus. The helicopter-supported unit was responding to a tip that three Hamas militants were in an apartment. Two surrendered. The third fired on the native of Canada who moved to Israel as a child. Other soldiers killed the Hamas gunman.

An 18-year-old Hamas terrorist died while planting a homemade mine in the rocky sand in the southern Gaza Strip near the Egyptian border. Soldiers fired five rockets at him, according to witnesses. The armed forces said he was killed by machine-gun fire.

At noon, Mohammad Yunis, 18, fired a rifle at and threw hand grenades inside a commercial trucking terminal at the Karni (variant Qarni) border crossing between Israel and the Gaza Strip. In the shoot-out, the gunman and two Israelis died, one perhaps from friendly fire. The dead Israelis were truck driver Ahmed Kra, 20, and forklift operator Zachar Chankayev. Another nine were injured. Hamas claimed credit, saying it was retaliating for the helicopter gunship attack that killed local Hamas leader Saed Arabeed and six other Palestinians the previous week.

April 15, 2003. *France.* The government said it would deport any immigrant Muslim leaders espousing violence or anti-Semitism.

April 15, 2003. *Russia.* Sixteen civilians died when a bomb exploded on a bus near Khankala.

April 16, 2003. *United States.* Homeland Security Secretary Tom Ridge lowered the national threat level to Yellow (significant risk).

April 16, 2003. *Nigeria.* Circa 100 striking oil workers took 97 foreigners hostage, including 17 Americans, 35 Britons, and 170 Nigerian oil workers, on four off-shore oil rigs owned by Houston-based Transocean, Inc. The strikers threatened to blow up the rigs. Talks dragged on for two weeks before the first group of hostages was freed on May 3 in Port Harcourt. A helicopter flew Briton Paul Baker, 25, six Nigerian hostages, and two Nigerian hostage-takers from one rig.

April 16, 2003. *Afghanistan.* A bomb destroyed the UNICEF building in Jalalabad. No one claimed credit. 03041601

April 21, 2003. *Laos.* Gunmen fired on a bus in the north, killing 12 and injuring 30. Hmong rebels were suspected.

April 21, 2003. *United States.* Detroit police detained two men who had a tiny amount of dynamite, a collapsible baton, and shotgun shells in their car when they were spotted by authorities videotaping the Ambassador Bridge to Windsor, Canada. They were released on April 22 after being questioned by the FBI.

April 22, 2003. *United States.* Some 100 people in a U.S. Postal Service center in Tacoma, Washington, were evacuated after an initial test suggested that a white powder found among some envelopes might be toxic. Samples were sent to the Centers for Disease Control and Prevention. Follow-up tests indicated no threat.

Six USPS workers in Fort Myers, Florida, were taken to the hospital after exposure to an unknown white powder when they opened a mail container unloaded from a FedEx plane from Memphis. One individual complained of a burning sensation in his nose. The powder was tested.

April 22, 2003. *India.* A bomb exploded in a dairy yard in Gulshanpora Batagund, Kashmir, killing 6 people and injuring 12 others. Several cows also died. No one claimed credit.

April 22, 2003. *Argentina.* A homemade bomb exploded in front of a McDonald's restaurant on Mitre Avenue and Berutti Street in Avellaneda, shattering windows but causing no interior damage or injuries. Police found evidence of gunpowder. No one claimed credit. 03042201

April 24, 2003. *Israel.* An 18-year-old from a Nablus suburb got off a bus in a Kfar (variant Kefar) Saba train station, but was prevented from entering by a dual Israeli–Russian nationality security guard. The terrorist set off a ten-pound nail bomb. The terrorist and the guard were killed; 12 people were wounded, including a second guard. Al-Aqsa said a breakaway faction was responsible. 03042401

April 25, 2003. *Germany.* A Lebanese man, 17, armed with a pistol loaded with blanks hijacked a bus with 16 passengers in Bremen and demanded the release of 4 people, including Ramzi Binalshibh, one of the Hamburg-based September 11 plotters who is in U.S. custody. He had been seated behind the driver and pointed the gun at the driver's back. He released three elderly women in Bremen. He forced the driver to take the bus onto the autobahn, where he led police on a long-distance highway chase during the seven-hour episode. He claimed a bag he was carrying was packed with explosives. Two hours into the chase, he stopped near Hanover and began negotiating with police over the telephone. He asked for water, a cell phone, and another driver. He demanded to talk to Bremen Mayor Hennig Scherf. The hijacker freed seven more passengers; another man escaped. No shots were fired when police stormed the bus to free the driver and four others shortly after 4:00 p.m. No one was injured. The hijacker had left a letter for his parents on April 24 in which he praised the September 11 hijackers. 03042501

April 25, 2003. *India.* A bomb exploded on the lawn of a courthouse in Patan, Kashmir, killing 3 and injuring 34 others. No one claimed credit.

April 26, 2003. *India.* In a car bombing and gun battle, three Islamic militants and two Indian soldiers died at the offices of the state-run radio and television station in Srinagar, Kashmir. One terrorist died in the blast; the other two were killed in the firefight. Three members of the paramilitary Central Reserve Police Force were wounded. Soldiers found explosives strapped to the bodies of two dead attackers. Two Pakistan-based Islamic rebel groups claimed credit. The Al Madina group said three Kashmiris carried out the bombing and noted, "We are not against a dialogue with India, but it should accept Kashmir as a disputed territory." The Harkat ul-Mujaheddin (Movement of Holy Strugglers) group in Muzaffarabad also claimed credit for a "suicide car bombing attack." Spokesman Abu Samayia said five Indian soldiers were killed.

Hours later, two more attacks occurred in Kashmir. In one attack, terrorists attempted to assassinate the state's finance minister, Muzaffar Hussain Beig, by setting off a remotely detonated device in Baramulla, 34 miles north of Srinagar. Beig was inaugurating a branch of a government bank. The bomb wounded 11 civilians.

In another attack, five soldiers were wounded when a remotely detonated bomb went off in Sumriyal, a village close to the disputed border with Pakistan. 03042601

April 26, 2003. *Indonesia.* Just as the State Department announced that U.S. Embassy staffers' families could return to the country, a bomb went off near a fast-food restaurant at Jakarta's main airport, wounding three people. 03042602

April 27, 2003. *United States.* Walter Reid Morrill, 78, an usher and caretaker at the Gustaf Adolph Lutheran Church in New Sweden, Maine, died and 15 people were hospitalized after drinking arsenic-laced coffee at a church reception. As of May 6, three victims were in critical condition and four others were in serious condition at a Bangor hospital. Five others were in stable condition in a Caribou hospital. As of May 17, two people remained hospitalized. Among those who drank the coffee were Lois Anderson, Janet Erickson, Shirley Erickson, 63, Bob Bengtson, his mother Peggy, June Greenier, and Erich Margeson, 30. Investigators said

Daniel Bondeson, 53, a farmer who died of a self-inflicted gunshot wound on May 2, was linked to the case. His farm is a few miles from the church; he was not among the 40 people who attended services on April 27. His suicide note said he was involved in the poisonings and may not have acted alone. The motive for the attack was unclear, but the killer(s) may have been trying to poison the church's 12-member council over a policy dispute. The council planned to merge the church with neighboring congregations.

On May 20, investigators said two congregants were probably involved, and narrowed the list of suspects to six to ten parishioners. Police determined that the brewed coffee, not the coffee beans, were poisoned.

April 29, 2003. *Pakistan.* Authorities in Karachi conducted two simultaneous raids and arrested six members of an al Qaeda cell, including Waleed Muhammad bin Attash (alias Khalid al-Attash, alias Walid ba Attash, alias Tawfiq bin Attash, alias Tawfiq Attash Khallad), a Yemeni believed involved in the October 12, 2000, bombing of the USS *Cole* and the August 1998 bombings of the U.S. embassies in Tanzania and Kenya; and Ali Abd Aziz (alias Ammar Baluchi), in his mid-20s, a nephew of al Qaeda's third-ranking leader, Khalid Sheik Muhammad. Authorities seized 330 pounds of high explosives, a large quantity of arms and ammunition, detonators, transmitters, and timer switches. Police said they were tipped off during the interrogation of Khalid Sheik Muhammad, who had been picked up on March 1. U.S. authorities said that bin Attash and Ramzi Binhalshibh trained a group that plotted suicide attacks in 2002 in the Strait of Gibraltar. Bin Attash was at a meeting in January 2000 in Malaysia that also included September 11 hijackers Khalid Almihdhar and Nawaf Alhazmi. CNN said bin Attash was a Saudi citizen of Yemeni descent. *Time* magazine reported that Aziz sent $120,000 to September 11 leader Mohamad Atta. Police said five of those arrested were Pakistanis who worked "hand in glove with al Qaeda." Police found grenades, assault rifles, and detonators hidden in several different caches. Police said the group members told them that they had planned to fill a small fixed-wing plane or a helicopter with explosives and crash it into the U.S. Consulate. They had not yet obtained the plane. 03042902

April 29–30, 2003. *Israel.* About 30 minutes after midnight and just five hours after Mahmoud Abbas (variant Abu Mazen), 68, was elected Palestinian prime minister, two suicide bombers tried to enter Mike's Place restaurant in Tel Aviv, a beachfront bar popular with Europeans and Americans, but were stopped by the guard. One of the two bombers, Pakistani-born Assif Muhammad Hanif, 21, a British citizen who grew up in Hounslow, a blue-collar London suburb, set off the bomb at the door, killing himself, a waitress, and two musicians (other reports said one was a guard). The other bomber, Omar Khan Sharif, 27, of Derby, United Kingdom, fled the scene when his bomb failed to detonate. Sixty-four people were injured, including two tourists, one French and one American. Hamas and al-Aqsa said that they jointly planned the attack. This was the first suicide bombing by a foreigner in the 31-month-old Palestinian intifada against Israeli occupation. The restaurant's owner, Gal Ganzman, told the Associated Press, "One of the waitresses lost an arm but she's still alive." The bar is located next door to the U.S. Embassy and about 500 yards from the Hayarkon 48 Hostel, where the duo stayed.

Hanif was the third of four brothers. He studied business at Cranford Community College, then pursued a science degree at Kingston University, dropping out after several months. He had a religious awakening and traveled in the Arab world.

After fleeing, Sharif got rid of his coat and the explosives. He remained at large as of May 9. However, the State Department reported later that his body was found washed up on a Tel Aviv beach. He was born in Derby to an immigrant from Mirpur in the Pakistani-controlled section of Kashmir. His late father had opened Derby's first kebab stand and later owned launderettes and amusement arcades. The youngest of six children, Sharif boarded for two years at the $18,000 per year prep school Foremarke Hall. He attended Kingston University in London, where he became a Muslim fundamentalist. He dropped out after a few months and married a woman who spoke little English and wore a *burqa*. They moved into a cheap row house in Derby near a radical mosque. They had two daughters, now aged 3 and 7. He attended religious classes by Sheikh Omar Bakri Muhammed, Syrian-born leader of al-Muhajiroun (the Emigrants), a radical Islamic group.

The duo traveled to Damascus in 2003, where Hanif attended an Arabic course at Damascus University. Sharif told friends he was going to study religion there. Hanif and Sharif had visited the International Solidarity Movement (ISM) in the West Bank on April 25, 2003. ISM provides "human shields" to protect Palestinians.

The duo may have used plastic explosives which they smuggled into Israel hidden in a Koran. They entered Israel at the Allenby Bridge border crossing from Jordan. Most of the injuries were blast injuries, rather than cuts from shrapnel.

On May 2, British antiterror police, using a special terrorism law, arrested two men and two women in Derbyshire and one woman in Nottinghamshire in central England in connection with the bombing.

As of May 9, three of Sharif's relatives were in custody: his brother, Zahid Hussain Sharif, 46; his sister, Paveen Akthor Sharif, 35; and his wife, Tahari Shad Tabassum , 27, all of Derby. They were held for failing to disclose information about acts of terrorism. Hussain was also charged with aiding and abetting acts of terrorism overseas. 03042901

April 30, 2003. *United Kingdom.* At 2:00 a.m., gunmen fired at a house in Bolton, near Manchester, where the family of Johnny Adair, Northern Ireland's most famous Protestant guerrilla, was believed to be living. The shots went through the window, causing no injuries. It was not clear whether anyone was home at the time.

April 30, 2003. *United States.* The State Department put Hizb ul-Mujaheddin, a Kashmiri nationalist group, on its list of "other terrorist organizations." The group, founded in 1990, has its political headquarters in Pakistan.

May 2003. *Iraq.* Early in the month, U.S. military units in Baghdad arrested Abu Muaz, an aide to Abu Musab Zarqawi, a Jordanian who ran al Qaeda's relations with Saddam Hussein.

May 2003. *Turkey.* A Revolutionary People's Liberation Party (DHKP/C) female suicide bomber prematurely detonated her explosives belt in Istanbul, killing herself and wounding another person.

May 2003. *Kyrgyzstan.* On February 16, 2004, the Uzbekistan Supreme Court convicted and sentenced to death Azizbek Karimov, 25, who has ties to al Qaeda, for the bombing of a market in Bishkek, Kyrgyzstan, in December 2002 and a Western Union office in Osh, Kyrgyzstan, in May 2003. The attacks killed eight people. The Islamic Movement of Uzbekistan (IMU) was responsible for the attack in Osh. 03059901

May 2003. *Lebanon.* A military tribunal convicted eight people of attempting to establish an al Qaeda cell in Lebanon.

May 2003. *Sudan.* Authorities raided a probable terrorist training camp in Kurdufan State, arresting more than a dozen extremists and seizing illegal weapons. The majority of the trainees captured were Saudis and were extradited to Saudi Arabia to face charges in accordance with a bilateral agreement.

May 1, 2003. *Jordan.* A bag exploded near the luggage screening area of Queen Alia International Airport in Amman, killing a security guard and injuring three people. The suspected owner of the bag, Hiroki Gomi, a Japanese photojournalist for *Mainichi Shimbun*, who had just arrived from Baghdad, told authorities he did not know a bomb was in his possession. The official Petra news agency called the attack "a remnant from the war in Iraq."

On June 1, Gomi was sentenced to 18 months in prison. He told the court he took the item from Iraq as a souvenir. When the cluster bomb was detected in an x-ray machine, a guard searched his bag, setting off the detonator. Gomi was talking on his cell phone several feet away when the bomb went off. 03050101

May 1, 2003. *Iraq.* At 1:00 a.m., several men approached the compound of the 82nd Airborne in Fallujah, 35 miles west of Baghdad. Individuals believed to be hostile Iraqis threw two grenades, wounding seven soldiers. None of the injuries were life-threatening. The soldiers fired back, but apparently no one was hit. The town had been the scene of recent anti-U.S. protests apparently orchestrated by die-hard Saddam Hussein loyalists. 03050102

May 1, 2003. *Saudi Arabia.* An American civilian working as a contractor at the King Abdul Aziz naval base in Jubail was shot three times in the abdomen by an individual in a Saudi naval uniform. He was expected to recover. The attacker fled. 03050103

May 2, 2003. *Saudi Arabia.* The State Department warned Americans to avoid travel to Saudi Arabia, citing information indicating al Qaeda planned to conduct terrorist attacks against American targets there.

May 3, 2003. *Iraq.* Iraqi American Aban Elias, 41, was kidnapped. As of September 18, 2004, he was still being held. 04050301

May 4, 2003. *Turkey.* Five sound bombs exploded during the night in Adana at a United Postal Service (UPS) office, a Tommy Hilfiger store, a Turkish bank, the U.S. Consulate, and the Nationalist Turkish Political party headquarters, causing minor material damage, but no injuries. No one claimed credit. 03050401-03

May 5, 2003. *Philippines.* The government offered a $960,000 reward for information leading to the arrest of key Moro Islamic Liberation Front leaders.

May 5, 2003. *Colombia.* In a failed hostage rescue effort by government forces, Revolutionary Armed Forces of Colombia (FARC) kidnappers killed ten hostages, including Governor of Antioquia State Guillermo Gaviria and former Defense Minister Gilberto Echeverri. The duo was kidnapped on April 21, 2002, as they led hundreds of peace marchers from Medellin to Caicedo to meet with FARC commanders. One hostage escaped unharmed and two others were wounded. The government said that "a guerrilla known as The Paisa gave the order to murder the hostages." Ten bodies were discovered in a common grave near Urrao, 30 miles west of Medellin. One survivor, Cpl. Antinor Hernandez, said the guerrillas fired on the prisoners as soon as they heard government helicopters flying overhead. The guerrillas fled; the army arrived 20 minutes later.

May 5, 2003. *Saudi Arabia.* The U.S. Embassy Web site warned, "The U.S. Government remains deeply concerned about the security of U.S. citizens overseas. U.S. citizens are encouraged to maintain a high level of vigilance and to take appropriate steps to increase their security awareness. Credible information has indicated terrorist groups may be planning attacks against U.S. interests in the Middle East."

May 5, 2003. *India.* A bomb exploded at a bus stand in Doda, Kashmir, killing 1 person and injuring 25. No one claimed credit.

May 5, 2003. *India.* Terrorists threw a hand grenade at a National Conference leader's car in Duderhama, Kashmir, injuring him. No one claimed credit.

May 6, 2003. *Saudi Arabia.* Local television showed the faces of 19 men—17 Saudis, 1 Yemeni, and 1 Iraqi (who held Kuwaiti and Canadian citizenship)—being sought following the discovery of a large arms cache in Riyadh. Authorities said the terrorists planned attacks in the kingdom. After a gunfight with police in which the getaway car was damaged, the suspects stole vehicles and fled into a densely populated section of the city. In the car and an apartment in Riyadh's Ashbiliya district, police found that some of the men had stored five suitcases of explosives weighing more than 830 pounds, AK-47 assault rifles, 2,545 bullets of different calibers, 55 hand grenades, computers, communications equipment, travel documents, $80,000 in U.S. and Saudi currency, and disguise gear. The government also found identity papers for Khaled Jehani. The government later said the terrorists planned attacks on the royal family and received their orders directly from Osama bin Laden. A senior Saudi security official said terrorists were targeting Interior Minister Prince Nayef and his brother, Defense Minister Prince Sultan.

The government offered a reward of $80,000 for information leading to the cell and $10,000 for information about the terrorists.

Among those sought was Abdul Kareem Yazijy, 35, who might have been one of the 9 suicide bombers who killed 25 people on May 12 in Riyadh. Also sought was Khaled Jehani, 29, a Saudi who succeeded the arrested Abd-al-Rahim al-Nashiri as head of al Qaeda's Persian Gulf operations. Jehani is part of the Harbi tribe in western Saudi Arabia. His group had planned several terrorist attacks, including one on an expatriate residential community in Jiddah. He had recorded a martyrdom videotape that was recovered from an Afghan compound. He had been on the FBI's Most Wanted Al Qaeda list since January 2002.

On May 18, Saudi authorities were investigating reports that al Qaeda had purchased arms from the national guard. The seized arms were traced to national guard stockpiles.

May 6, 2003. *United States.* Upon arriving in Los Angeles from Frankfurt, Saudi consular official Fahad al Thumairy, 31, was informed that his visa had been revoked in March. He was barred from returning to the United States for five years and put on an international flight two days later. He was suspected of having links to a terrorist group. He had been at the Saudi Consulate in Los Angeles since 1996, working in the Islamic and cultural affairs section.

May 8, 2003. *Israel.* At a military checkpoint during the evening, a suicide bomber died when he crashed his explosives-packed car into an Israeli tank near the Jewish settlement of Kfar Darom in central Gaza. The terrorist died, but the tank was undamaged and the soldiers were not injured.

May 9, 2003. *Israel.* Hamas fired six rockets at the Sderot (variant Sederot) kibbutz settlement, injuring two people.

May 9, 2003. *Russia.* A Victory Day bombing at the Dynamo Stadium in Groznyy, the Chechen capital, injured three people.

May 11, 2003. *United Kingdom.* The British media reported that Freddy Scappaticci was "Stakeknife," a British army informer inside the Irish Republican Army (IRA), who had supplied information that foiled several IRA operations. He denied the reports that he was a senior IRA official who walked into a British army base outside Belfast in 1978 and joined the payroll of the Force Research Unit, a military intelligence bureau. The press said that he was paid $130,000 annually and that his information led to British Special Forces shooting down three unarmed IRA members in Gibraltar in 1988. Stakeknife allegedly was involved in the 1991 shooting of Irish farmer Thomas Oliver, who was allegedly an informer, and the 1992 torture and murder of Aidan Starrs, Gregory Burns, and John Dignam, who were accused by the IRA of killing a young Catholic woman and of working for U.K. intelligence.

May 12, 2003. *Saudi Arabia.* At 11:25 a.m., suicide bombers set off three truck bombs in a residential complex in Riyadh, killing 34 people, including 8 Americans, 2 Britons, 7 Saudis, 2 Jordanians, 2 Filipinos, a Lebanese, a Swiss, and 9 terrorists. Another 190 people were injured. The facilities were identified as the Cordoval, Gedawal (variant Jedawal), and Hamra residences. The terrorists first fired at the sentries before pushing a button that opened the gates and permitted them to drive deep into the compounds. A member of the Saudi national guard was killed in a gun battle. Two Filipino employees of Vinnell were also killed and several employees were injured, two critically. Jordanian children Zeina Abassi, 10, and her brother Yazan, 5, were killed. A ninth American died on June 1.

The dead Americans included:

- Jason Eric Bentley
- James Lee Carpenter, II
- Herman Diaz
- Alex Jackson
- Quincy Lee Knox
- Clifford J. Lawson, 46, of Snellville, Georgia, retired as a staff sergeant in 1997, when he joined Vinnell. He was a missile specialist during his 20-year army career. He left behind a wife and son.
- Todd Michael Blair, 37, had retired from the army in 2002. His United Kingdom-born wife, Samantha, and their two sons, aged 8 and 11, lived in the United Kingdom. He specialized in logistics and transportation.
- Mawa Sadek's husband, who served as a manager for Cisco Systems, Inc. A glass sliding door blew into their home in Al Hamra, and he died instantly. She will return home to southern Lebanon with their daughter.
- Obadiah Yusuf Abdullah, who had converted to Islam. The former army sergeant had served in the military for 11 years before joining Vinnell. He was a fire control specialist. In January, he completed the Hajj. He left behind a wife and daughter in Colorado Springs.

The 2-week-old niece of Jim Young, 41, an entrepreneur from Dalton, Georgia, was badly injured in the face. Also injured was Erika Warrington, 15, from the United Kingdom.

In Vinnell (some reports incorrectly identified it as Cordoba, another compound), the terrorists fired at guards, detonated the bomb, then escaped. The compound houses several Britons; a British school is on the grounds. The terrorists worked their way through three levels of security, including the Saudi national guard. The Dodge Ram truck contained 400 pounds of plastic explosives and damaged every building in the compound. The terrorists also drove a white Ford Crown Victoria, which they left outside; it was impaled on the gate in the explosion. Two attackers died; three escaped on foot.

At Al Hamra, two cars, including a car bomb, drove up to the main entrance at 11:30 p.m. The terrorists shot the security guards. As one car drove toward the recreation area, the terrorists continued firing, wounding or killing several people on the street. The car bomb went off outside a pool area where a barbecue party was underway. The car landed in the pool. At least ten people died and dozens were wounded. Saudi officials worried that some of the attackers were still on the grounds hours later. The press reported that gunfire could be heard in the early morning in Riyadh. Injured were Saudis Berkel, husband Jelal, and their 3-year-old son; two little girls from Jordan—their father was in a coma—and a Lebanese man. Al Hamra and Jedawal are home to workers from Turkey, Lebanon, the United States, and United Kingdom. Two attackers died; three escaped on foot. Mohammed Atef al Kayyaly was killed.

The Gedawal facility housed Americans working for a local subsidiary of the Fairfax, Virginia-based Vinnell Corporation, a subsidiary of Northrop Grumman Corporation. The firm is jointly owned by U.S. and Saudi interests and trains the Saudi national guard. U.S. Ambassador Robert W. Jordan had asked the Saudi Interior Ministry for more security on April 29 and May 7, and on May 10, specifically requested more security for Gedawal. (The house raided on May 6 is just across the street from Gedawal.)

The compound's elaborate security system mini-mized the effect of the bombing of the 408 six-bedroom, two-story villas in the complex. At 11:25 p.m., a guard posted at one of the four towers at the corners of the facility went to a small room below to have tea with other guards. Shortly thereafter, a General Motors Corporation pickup and a Ford sedan drove up to that gate. The terrorists shot to death two guards and wounded two other guards and another employ-ee. They raised a gate by hand. Guards at a near-by interior gate heard shooting and keyed in a security code that prevented the metal gate from opening. The car and truck stopped outside the second gate. The three men in the Ford left the car, while the duo in the truck set off the truck bomb, killing them and the other three terrorists, who had grenades strapped to their waists. No residents died. The blast destroyed the gates, sew-age tanks, and the terrorists' vehicles.

At least some of the attackers wore Saudi Ara-bian national guard uniforms and drove vehicles commonly used by residents and guards. When the sentries requested ID, the terrorists opened fire.

Ali al-Khudair and two other new-generation radicals called on Saudis not to cooperate in the investigation. They were rebuffed and forced to retract their statements.

President Bush vowed "American justice" would be given the terrorists.

The Saudis said the 50 to 60 member al Qaeda cell attacked on May 6 was responsible. It was led by Khaled Jehani, 29, who had left the country at age 18 and fought in Bosnia and Chechnya. He served in Afghan camps. After the November 2002 capture of Abd-al-Rahim al-Nashiri, he moved up in the organization.

The bombings came hours before U.S. Secre-tary of State Colin Powell was due to arrive in Riyadh.

Only three dead terrorists were positively identified via DNA. Possibly among the dead was Abdul Kareem Yazijy, 35, who was suspected of membership in the terrorist cell. His younger brother, Abdullah, called on him to turn himself in and noted that he had disappeared 18 months

earlier. He had a long history of "emotional insta-bility," according to Abdullah. His brother went to Afghanistan for a few months in 1990 and lat-er worked for two years in Sarajevo for the Saudi charity Supreme Committee for the Collection of Donations for Bosnia–Herzegovnia, which was raided in 2002 for al Qaeda ties.

Saudi officials said three al Qaeda cells, with 50 operatives, were operating in the country before the bombings. The cells were set up by Abd-al-Rahim al-Nashiri, the former head of operations for al Qaeda in the Persian Gulf. He was captured in November and is in U.S. cus-tody. He was involved in the USS *Cole* attack in October 2000 and had planned other attacks on U.S. and Western ships. He was succeeded by Khaled Jehani, 29, a Saudi-Afghan War veteran, who was in charge of planning the attack. The bombing team leader was Mishal Dandani, another Saudi-Afghan War veteran who remained at large.

Saudi officials suggested that all of the dead terrorists came from the list of 19 who were sought in the May 6 case.

On May 14, the Saudis said they were holding a suspect who turned himself in to authorities the day of the bombings.

On May 18, Saudi Interior Minister Prince Nayef said that four al Qaeda suspects detained in the last three days knew in advance of the attacks.

On May 24, the Bush administration sus-pended contacts with Iran over reports that an al Qaeda cell in Iran was involved in the bomb-ings. Saif Adel, an Egyptian serving as the group's military commander, was believed to have given the order to attack. He was believed hiding in Iran along with Abu Mohammed Masri, the group's training chief, Saad bin Laden, Osama's son, and Abu Musab Zarqawi, who had been in Baghdad. Iranian Foreign Ministry spokesman Hamid Reza Asefi told IRNA that Tehran had arrested several al Qaeda members, "but we don't know who these people are to be able to say whether they are senior or not. They need to be identified and interrogated." Iran claimed it had deported 500 al Qaeda members in the past year. Saudi Foreign Minister Prince Saud said the kingdom will seek to extradite anyone who had a role in the bombings.

A second command group was believed to be on the Pakistan-Afghan border.

Saudi oil and security analyst Nawaf Obaid wrote in the May 18 *Washington Post* that a captured senior member of the cell said they rushed the attack because the May 6 group feared it was about to be wrapped up by the authorities. He noted that two leaders of the cell and most of the explosives had come through Yemen.

On May 20, Saudi officials said that some al Qaeda members fled the country to the United States before the attacks.

Saudi officials arrested Ali Ambdulrahman Gamdi, 29, a key figure in the bombings in Riyadh on May 27. The Saudi had attended al Qaeda camps in Afghanistan. He was picked up with two other Saudis after they left an Internet café; authorities said the trio were planning an attack on a major hotel and commercial center in Riyadh. Authorities confiscated the computers they were using.

Saudi authorities announced on May 28 that they had captured nine al Qaeda suspects in Medina during the previous 24 hours, along with Ali Khudair and Ahmed Khalidi, two clerics who had called on their followers not to cooperate with the investigation. The London-based Movement for Islamic Reform in Arabia said that the two clerics were shot dead in Medina. A third cleric, Nasser Fahd, remained at large. Those detained included three Moroccans, including a woman stopped at a checkpoint. Saudi Special Forces had also surrounded two groups of seven extremists in Medina. Police found explosives and bomb-making equipment at one of the Medina buildings.

In a gun battle on May 31, Saudi authorities killed Youssef Saleh Eiery, a Saudi national who belonged to the 19-member gang, and arrested another after the duo threw hand grenades at a police patrol, killing two policemen.

The United States asked the Saudis to arrest Ahmed Abu-Ali in the case. His family's residence in Falls Church, Virginia, was searched by the FBI. He was represented by attorney Ashraf Nubani, who also represented some of the defendants in the June 25, 2003, arrests in northern Virginia against Lashkar-i-Taiba.

Saudi media reported on June 26 the arrest of Ali Aburahman Gamdi, 30, a key figure in the bombing who was in contact with bin Laden at Tora Bora. He and two others were picked up at an Internet café in Medina, where they were planning an attack on a major hotel and commercial center in Riyadh. He was the first of the 19 people Saudi officials said were involved in the bombing. As of that date, Saudi officials had arrested 44 people, including 4 women picked up in Mecca.

On July 3, following a five-hour standoff, Saudi police killed Turki Mishal Dandani and three associates when the terrorists ran out of ammunition in a shoot-out in a house in Suweir in the north.

On September 23, 2003, Saudi forces killed three terrorists, including Zubayr Rimi, a suspected al Qaeda militant believed involved in the attack who was named in an FBI terror alert on September 5. The gun battle occurred at a housing complex in Jizan, near the Yemen border. One security officer died. Two suspects were arrested.

On January 8, 2004, 100 Swiss police officers raided homes throughout the country and arrested 8 foreigners suspected of being al Qaeda supporters who aided the attacks. They questioned 20 other people in five states. The detainees were held on suspicion of providing logistical support to a criminal organization, but were not formally charged.

As of April 2004, Saudi security forces had arrested more than 600 individuals on counterterrorism charges. 03051201-03

May 12, 2003. *Algeria.* The Salafist Group for Preaching (Call) and Combat kidnapped a German tourist in the Sahara Desert, bringing the tally of kidnapped Germans to 16. From mid-February until mid-May, the GSPC kidnapped 32 European tourists in eight separate incidents. On May 13, Algerian Special Forces rescued 17 hostages. One hostage, a German woman, died of heatstroke on July 28 while in captivity. On August 18, the remaining 14 hostages were released in northern Mali. Press reports claimed a ransom of 4.6 million euros was paid to the GSPC in return for the hostages. 03051204

May 13, 2003. *Saudi Arabia.* A few hours after the Riyadh blasts, a bomb went off at the headquarters of the Saudi Maintenance Company (variant Siyanco), a jointly owned venture of Frank E. Basil, Inc., of Washington, and local Saudi partners. No one was injured. 03051301

May 13, 2003. *Russia.* A truck bomb exploded at a government compound in Znamenskoye, northern Chechnya, killing 60 people and seriously wounding more than 270. The bomb destroyed Russian offices, apartment buildings, and homes, and left a crater 30 feet wide and 12 feet deep. Three government buildings, including the local police and security headquarters, were leveled. Two members of the Federal Security Service were killed, as were six children. At least 23 survivors were pulled out of the rubble. Chechen rebels were blamed for ramming the military-style truck against a steel barrier. Russian officials later blamed local Arab militants, led by Abu Walid, a Saudi. Police said two women and a man were responsible.

May 14, 2003. *Kenya.* Al Qaeda planner Fazul Abdullah Mohammed, a Comoran, was reported to be in the country. He was wanted for the 1998 bombings of the U.S. embassies in Kenya and Tanzania and with the attacks on Mombasa, Kenya, on November 28, 2002. Mohammed was seen in Mogadishu after the bombing of the Paradise Hotel in Mombasa.

On May 15, the United Kingdom suspended flights to and from Kenya. The U.K. government warned of a "clear terrorist threat" in Uganda, Ethiopia, Tanzania, Somalia, Eritrea, and Djibouti. On May 16, U.S. and U.K. Marines searched the borders with Somalia and Sudan during heightened fears of an al Qaeda attack.

May 14, 2003. *Russia.* Police initially believed that Shakida Baimuradova, a female Chechen in her late 40s or early 50s, blew herself up at an Islamic prayer meeting in Iliskhan-Yurt, a village outside Gudermes, killing 18 people and injuring between 45 and 150. She was within six feet of Akhmad Kadryov, the Moscow-appointed head of the Chechen government. He was unharmed, but several of his bodyguards died or sustained serious injuries in the afternoon attack outside a mosque. The terrorist had ties to a rebel unit led by Shamil Basayev, a Chechen rebel commander. She had a pound of TNT hidden on her body or in her video camera. A second female terrorist, also carrying explosives, died when the first bomb went off. Baimuradova's husband died in 1999; investigators found his death certificate on her body.

Six weeks later, investigators determined that the terrorist was actually Larisa Musalayeva and that the other dead women were victims. Musalayeva sought revenge for her dead brother who killed himself when pro-Moscow Chechens attempted to arrest him.

On May 17, President Vladimir Putin and local Chechen leader Akhmad Kadyrov pledged to provide rapid compensation to local residents affected by the two suicide bombings.

In a May 19 posting to a rebel Web site, Chechen rebel leader Shamil Basayev claimed credit for both bombings, saying that "our martyrs' two sabotage attacks are only a small part of the operations we have planned for this year."

May 15, 2003. *Pakistan.* Explosions went off outside 19 Shell gas stations in Karachi, slightly injuring four employees. Two men on a motorcycle went to each station before dawn and hid small explosive devices in garbage cans. Bombs also hit three Caltex gasoline stations in southern Karachi, injuring seven people. The small bombs were firecrackers fitted with timing devices and were packed into boxes placed in garbage bins. The Muslim United Army claimed credit in a fax sent to the newspaper *Dawn*. 03051501-18, 20-23

May 15, 2003. *Lebanon.* The government arrested nine people for plotting to attack the U.S. Embassy and kidnap officials to force the release of Islamic militant prisoners. The Lebanese army said that Syrian military intelligence assisted in detaining a cell planning "sabotage and attacks on various targets, the most important being the embassy of a major Western state, security and military outposts, and kidnappings of officials." The military targets were Lebanese and Syrian installations. The terrorists also planned to kidnap Lebanese officials to obtain the release of men jailed during an Islamic uprising in Dinniyeh in northern Lebanon on January 1, 2000. The detainees included two Palestinians and seven Lebanese. 03051519

May 15, 2003. *Romania.* The local intelligence service said that before the Iraq War, Iraqi operatives had planned "to organize terrorist attacks on Israeli and Western targets," including the U.S. and Israeli embassies. The Romanians declared persona non grata 10 Iraqi diplomats and 31 other people.

May 15, 2003. *Russia.* President Vladimir Putin proposed legislation granting amnesty to Chechen rebels who disarmed between August 1, 1993 and August 1, 2003. Some 2,000 rebels could be eligible. The amnesty did not apply to foreigners or Russians who were guilty of murder, kidnapping, rape, or other serious crimes. By a vote of 354 to 18, the lower house of the Russian Parliament gave the legislation initial approval on May 21. Two follow-up votes are required.

May 15, 2003. *Philippines.* Police arrested Mokhlis Yunos (alias Saifullah Mokhlis Yunos), special operations chief of the Philippine Moro Islamic Liberation Front. Police learned that he would be flying Philippine Airlines flight 182

from Cagayan de Oro in the southern Philippines to Manila. Yunos was disguised in head-to-toe bandages; his traveling companion, Dia Mahmoud Gabri, a Middle Eastern-looking man, said that "Alex Soriano" had been in a car accident. Yunos was accused of bombing electric power stations in Mindanao in 2003 and of collaboration with Jemaah Islamiah. He had trained with Riduan Isamuddin (alias Hambali), JI operations chief, in the artillery division of the al Qaeda camp in Saddah, Afghanistan, from 1987 to 1989. Police believed he assisted Isamuddin and JI operative Fathur Rahman al-Ghozi in carrying out a bombing in Manila that killed 22 and injured more than 100.

May 16, 2003. *Morocco.* At 10:00 p.m., suicide bombers killed 45 people, including 13 terrorists, in five attacks in Casablanca, the country's commercial capital. More than 100 people were injured. The sites were the Casa de Espana, the empty Cercle de l'Alliance Israelite Jewish community center, the Arab-owned five star Hotel Safir (other reports identified it as the Kuwaiti goverment-owned Farah Hotel) in the city center, a Jewish cemetery, and either the five-story Belgian Consulate or the Jewish-owned Positano Italian restaurant across the street. Eight people died at the Hotel Safir. The bomb at the Belgian Consulate killed two policemen and a security guard. At the Casa de Espana, a popular private club and restaurant, the security guard's head was nearly detached. Burned cars and body parts were found at the scenes. Among the dead were 22 Moroccans (including Hamid Mahraz, 33), 3 French nationals, 4 Spaniards, and an Italian.

A security guard saw three young men approaching the consulate. When a security guard moved to confront them, the trio set off the explosives strapped to their bodies, killing themselves and the guard. Forensics examiners determined that the restaurant guard suffered stab wounds before the bombs went off. A security guard inside the consulate was injured by the blast. Blood spattered 20 feet up onto the Positano's sign.

At the hotel, a suicide bomber got as far as the circular cement entryway before killing himself, a bellman, and a guard whom he slashed with a knife. The guard noticed two men, aged between 18 and 20, whose basketball shoes and sports clothes did not match the hotel guests' upscale attire. When he tried to stop them, one of them pulled a knife on him. The bellman ran to help and grabbed an attacker, but the explosives belt blew up, killing the terrorist, the bellman, and the already seriously injured guard. The second attacker fled but was captured by police. He was carrying a satchel packed with explosives. By nightfall, police had detained more than two dozen people for questioning.

On May 18, police had identified 8 of the 14 attackers as Moroccans in their late teens and early 20s. (The government later said they were between 21 and 32.). By May 19, police had detained scores of suspected Islamic militants from local slums. Many of the suicide bombers had lived in Sidi Moumen, a Casablanca slum. Among those arrested was a Moroccan chemistry graduate student who might have been in contact with al Qaeda. Police found his safe house filled with explosives. Newspapers said two foreigners, including an Egyptian, were questioned. Some of the bombers had recently visited an unnamed foreign country.

Authorities believed foreign organizers were behind the attacks. The government blamed Assirat al-Moustaquim (The Righteous Path), a small, ultraconservative Islamic group. The group is led by Youssef Fikri, who in mid-April sent a letter to a local paper saying his group was responsible for killing suspected atheists in the slums. He was arrested before the bombings. His group is an offshoot of the Salafia Jihdia led by imam Abu Hafs, 28, who was also in custody. Hafs is an al Qaeda admirer.

In January, the media had reported that terrorists were suspected in the theft of arms from a military base.

On May 25, tens of thousands of demonstrators in Casablanca chanted, "No to terrorism."

On May 28, Moroccan authorities announced that a key planner of the suicide bombings, a 30-year-old cobbler from Fez, had died in custody of liver, heart, and kidney failure.

On June 2 at 9:30 a.m., Moroccan authorities reported that the plot was prepared by Mohamed Omari, 24, a parking lot attendant who gave five teams a Casio watch to ensure simultaneous explosions. Authorities said the attacks were ordered by Jordanian Abu Musab Zarqawi, who obtained $50,000 to $70,000 from al Qaeda for the attacks. Zarqawi leads Tawhid, which either has links to or is a part of al Qaeda. He had hidden in Iraq, but could have moved to Iran. Police said they had arrested 33 other would-be suicide bombers from the slums. None of the bombers were previously known to the police. They included Mohamed Mheni, 25; Youssef Kaoutari, 31; and Adel Tahir, 23. Omari's compatriot set off the explosions early, killing himself and another terrorist and injuring Omari, who attempted to flee.

On June 3, Moroccan police in Tangier arrested Robert Richard Antoine-Pierre (alias Lhaj, alias Abu Abderrahmane), a Frenchman suspected of involvement.

On August 18, 2003, a Moroccan court sentenced four men to death for the premeditated murder of the victims. Two of those sentenced were among the 14-member suicide team, but survived. Another 83 got ten years to life for membership in the Salafist Jihad. A mosque preacher received a life term; three other clerics received 30 years.

On May 1, 2004, security forces arrested three men armed with sabers; the trio were injured during an overnight gun battle in Casablanca's southern suburbs. Abdelmalek Bouzgarene, 27, was believed to be a top planner of the coordinated attacks. The other two were Mohamed el Jarmouni, 27, and Mourad el Mnaouar, 24.

On October 14, 2004, the *Washington Post* reported that one of the suicide bombers was Abel Fattah Boulikdane, 27, who had lived in a two-room shack with his mother in the Carriere Thomas section on the outskirts of Casablanca.

He wore an explosives belt that he set off on the other side of town. His mother said he was not particularly religious and gave no warning of what was to come. 03051601-05

May 16, 2003. *Thailand.* Bangkok authorities arrested Arifin bin Ali (alias John Wong Ah Hung), 42, a Singaporean member of Jemaah Islamiah. His arrest was announced on June 10, when Thai authorities arrested three of his Thai colleagues who were planning attacks on five Western embassies, including the U.S. Embassy, and tourist locales. He was transferred to Singapore a day later. He was a senior JI member, responsible for providing arms training to Muslim radicals. He worked closely with Riduan Isamuddin (alias Hambali), an at-large Indonesia who was JI's operations chief. Bin Ali left Singapore in December 2001 during a government crackdown on Islamic militants. He initially went to Malaysia, where the Singapore head of JI asked him to help other fugitives. He then went to ground in Thailand in January 2002. He told police he was planning to bomb embassies in Bangkok during the Asia–Pacific Economic Cooperation (APEC) summit that President Bush was scheduled to attend in October. The Chinese president, Japanese prime minister, and other regional leaders planned to attend as well. 03051606

May 17, 2003. *Israel.* A Palestinian suicide bomber, 19, killed an Israeli man and his pregnant wife during the night near a Jewish settlement near Hebron. The bomber was disguised as a religious Jewish settler. Soldiers challenged him in Arabic, and he ran a few steps before setting off the bomb. Hamas claimed credit on its Web site.

May 18, 2003. *Philippines.* The air force bombed Moro Islamic Liberation Front (MILF) bases in Mindanao, killing 60 guerrillas. President Gloria Macapagal Arroyo, who began a state visit to the United States, gave the MILF a June 1 deadline to renounce violence or be declared a terrorist organization.

May 18, 2003. *Israel.* At 6:00 a.m., a 20-year-old electrical engineering student killed himself and seven people on an Egged Number 6 commuter bus in northeast Jerusalem's French Hill area when he set off his explosives vest. Another 26 were wounded, including a U.S. citizen. The terrorist's belt was filled with metal balls and bullets that served as shrapnel. Six of the dead were from the same neighborhood in Pisgat Zeev. The Izz al-Din al-Qassam Brigades, the military wing of Hamas, claimed credit on its Web site.

U.S.–born Steve Averbach, 37, tried to pull a gun on the terrorist when he noticed that the last person to get on the bus, a man dressed as a religious Jew, was an Arab, but the terrorist had already hit the detonator. Averbach was hit by a ball bearing in the spinal cord; the ball stayed in the back of his neck. By January 2004, Averbach could only wiggle his toes, flex his left foot, and move his left thumb and index finger. Averbach had moved from New Jersey to Israel at age 18. 03051801

May 18, 2003. *Israel.* A suicide bomber blew himself up near the site of the Egged Number 6 bus bombing 30 minutes later. No one else was hurt. Hamas claimed credit for the three recent bombings, saying that the trio were friends from the West Bank and that two were students at the Palestine Polytechnic University. The trio were disguised as Jews by wearing skullcaps, white shirts, and black trousers.

May 18, 2003. *Israel.* A bomb went off at a road junction a few miles away from the Jerusalem bus blast, but caused no injuries.

May 18, 2003. *Israel.* A Palestinian gunman snuck into the Jewish settlement of Shaare Tikva, 12 miles east of Tel Aviv and 2 miles inside the West Bank, and shot and injured two Israelis.

May 19, 2003. *Saudi Arabia.* Two Moroccans suspected of al Qaeda membership were arrested at Jiddah Airport in connection with a plot to hijack an airplane and crash it into a building in the city. The duo was boarding a plane to

Khartoum, Sudan. A third man was being sought. The trio were tied to the al Qaeda cell responsible for the May 12 suicide bombings in Riyadh. One Saudi official said one of the targets was the National Commercial Bank, Jiddah's tallest building. 03051901

May 19, 2003. *United States.* At 11:30 a.m., a car carrying two people drove up next to an 18-wheel tractor trailer and told the driver that explosives hidden in his truck would go off if he stopped. Driver Joseph Reed, 24, phoned police, parked in an evacuated area on the George Washington Memorial Parkway in northern Virginia outside Washington, D.C., and ran from the truck. Bomb squad investigators and a robot determined that there were no explosives in the truck. After three hours, the parkway was reopened.

May 19, 2003. *Israel.* In the morning, a man on a bicycle set off a bomb near the Kfar Darom settlement, killing himself and injuring three Israel soldiers near an Israeli army jeep.

May 19, 2003. *Israel.* In the afternoon, a Palestinian suicide bomber set off explosives at the entrance of a shopping mall in Afula, killing the terrorist and three other people. Guards prevented him from entering after a metal detecting wand beeped whenever it was near the man. At least 52 people were injured, 13 seriously. Among those injured was Pvt. Maor Suissa, 19, whose face was burned and who had metal fragments throughout his body. The bodies of a man and a woman were so ripped apart by the bomb that police had difficulty identifying them and determining who carried the bomb. Islamic Jihad and the al-Aqsa Martyrs Brigades claimed credit. The Brigades said the bomber was Hiba Azem Daraghmeh, 19, a freshman at an Al-Quds Open University campus in Jenin in the West Bank, ten miles south of Afula.

May 19, 2003. *India.* Terrorists fired into a private residence in Rajauri (variant Rajouri), Kashmir, killing six people. No one claimed credit.

May 19, 2003. *India.* Two bombs exploded at Kashmir's busiest bus terminal in Srinagar, injuring 14 people in Srinagar. No one claimed credit.

May 20, 2003. *United States.* The Bush administration raised the terrorist threat level to Orange (high risk). Homeland Security Secretary Tom Ridge said, "The U.S. Intelligence Community believes that al Qaeda has entered an operational period worldwide, and this may include attacks in the U.S." The press reported that the government had intercepted al Qaeda communications suggesting that it was planning attacks overseas.

May 20, 2003. *Saudi Arabia.* The U.S., U.K., Italian, and German governments ordered their embassies and consulates temporarily closed. On May 24, the U.K., German, and Italian embassies reopened. The next day, the U.S. Embassy and the consulates in Jiddah and Dhahran reopened.

May 21, 2003. *United States.* At 5:00 p.m., a bomb exploded in a first-floor classroom at Yale Law School, causing no injuries but damaging the classroom and an adjacent lounge. FBI agents showed students a sketch of a man seen leaving an empty classroom just before the explosion. The school said there was no indication that international terrorists were involved. Police said the explosion was being treated as a crime. On May 22, investigators found guns and ammunition in a student's dorm room. The law student was taken into custody and polygraphed.

May 21, 2003. *Saudi Arabia.* Al-Jazeera television broadcast an audiotape apparently recorded by al Qaeda deputy Ayman Zawahiri, in which he called on Muslims to attack Western facilities around the world and kill Western civilians and Jews. The voice says, "The crusaders and the Jews only understand the language of murder and bloodshed and are only convinced by coffins, destroyed interests, burning towers, and a shattered economy.... Be strong, O Muslims, and attack the missions of the United States, the United Kingdom, Australia, and Norway, and their interests, companies, and employees. Turn the ground beneath their feet into an inferno and kick them out of your countries." The tape might have been recorded during the war in Iraq. The spokesperson says, "O Iraqi people, we have defeated those crusaders several times before and kicked them out of our countries and sanctities. Know that you are not alone in this battle. The next few days will reveal to you news that will gladden your hearts, God willing." The speaker also condemned Arab nations for supporting the U.S. war effort, citing Saudi Arabia, Kuwait, Qatar, Egypt, Yemen, and Jordan. He belittled nonviolence, saying that "protests, demonstrations and conferences are of no use to you. The only thing that will benefit you is carrying arms and spiting your enemies, the Americans and Jews."

May 21, 2003. *Canada.* Montreal police arrested Adil Charkaoui, a Moroccan deemed a threat to national security. He had lived in the country since 1995. Reportedly, Charkaoui had ties to Ahmed Ressam, an Algerian who lived in Montreal in the 1990s and who was convicted in the United States in April 2001 of plotting to bomb Los Angeles International Airport during millennium celebrations. Canadian authorities sought federal court approval to deport him. He was held at least through December 2004 for having trained at an al Qaeda camp in Afghanistan. He was held without formal charge on a security certificate, a procedure that was deemed constitutional by an Ottawa federal appeals court on December 10, 2004.

May 22, 2003. *United States.* The FBI arrested Sayed Abdul Malike, 43, a New York cabdriver who allegedly attempted to buy enough explosives "to blow up a mountain." He allegedly surveilled bridges and cruise ships in Miami and lied to the FBI about his activities. U.S. Magistrate Judge Roanne L. Mann ordered him held without bail after Assistant U.S. Attorney Catherine Friesen said he could be a terrorist and that she

would prove that he tried to buy explosives in Queens. She warned that he might not have acted alone and was expecting Pakistani-based financing. Malike is a U.S. resident from Afghanistan. He was held on charges of unlawful possession of Valium and lying to law enforcement officers.

May 22, 2003. *Israel.* Israel seized a boat off its Mediterranean coast carrying equipment for "terror attacks." Eight arms smugglers, including two Lebanese Hizballah guerrillas, were arrested. The gear was bound for Palestinian militants in the Gaza Strip, according to the foreign minister. Yasir Arafat's Fatah movement denied Israeli charges that the gear was destined for Gaza.

May 24, 2003. *Afghanistan.* Three people working for a nongovernmental organization were injured when their vehicle hit a remotely controlled land mine in Haska Meyna. No one claimed credit.

May 27, 2003. *Colombia.* The National Liberation Army (ELN) and Revolutionary Armed Forces of Colombia (FARC) were blamed for bombing a section of the Cano Limon–Covenas oil pipeline, spilling 7,000 barrels of crude oil into the Cimitarra creek, a major source of drinking water for more than 5,000 people and causing extensive damage. The pipeline is owned by Colombian and U.S. oil firms. 03052701

May 29, 2003. *Cambodia.* The government ordered the expulsion of 50 Muslims, including 28 teachers, and their family members, including women and children, from Sudan, Egypt, and Thailand for raising money for Jemaah Islamiah (JI). Authorities arrested two Muslims from southern Thailand at an Islamic religious school south of Phnom Penh. The government said the duo had planned a JI terrorist attack somewhere in southeast Asia in June. They later picked up an Egyptian and accused him and the two Thais of acts of international terrorism and links to JI. On June 11, Cambodia arrested and charged a fourth man, a Cambodian Muslim, with belonging to JI. The school was run by the Saudi Arabia–based nongovernmental organization Umm al-Qura. The school allegedly was used as a front for channeling al Qaeda money into Cambodia from Saudi Arabia. The government closed down two branches of the school.

May 29, 2003. *Australia.* A man stabbed two flight attendants and injured two passengers with sharpened sticks as he tried to enter the cockpit of a Qantas domestic flight en route to Tasmania. He shouted that he wanted to crash the plane. He was taken into custody. 03052901

May 29, 2003. *United States.* The Treasury Department declared the al-Aqsa Foundation a terrorist financing organization, having determined that the charity funnels money to Hamas. The German-based group's assets were frozen and financial institutions must block any deals involving the group. The head of the group's Yemen office, Sheik Mohammed Ali Hassan Moayad, was arrested in January by the Germans on charges of supporting terrorists. He claims to have ties to Osama bin Laden.

May 30, 2003. *Spain.* The Basque Nation and Liberty (ETA) was blamed for setting off a car bomb in the early afternoon in Sanguesa in Navarra Province that killed two police officers, severely injured a third police officer, and slightly injured a man who was standing near their car.

May 30, 2003. *United States.* The government reduced the terrorist threat level to Yellow (significant risk).

May 30, 2003. *Colombia.* Terrorists in Guamalito attacked a section of the Cano Limon–Covenas oil pipeline, spilling another 7,000 barrels of crude oil and leaving 4,700 families without drinking water. The pipeline is owned by Ecopetrol of Colombia and a consortium of West European and U.S. firms. No one claimed credit, but the Revolutionary Armed Forces of Colombia (FARC) and National Liberation Army (ELN) were suspected. 03053001

May 31, 2003. *United States.* Sometime after midnight, an employee called to three scuba divers he saw near the NRG Electric Generating Plant at Somerset, Massachusetts. The trio ran off without their scuba gear. No explosives were found. Some authorities suggested it was a drug operation.

May 31, 2003. *Democratic Republic of the Congo.* The Party for the Unity and Safeguarding of the Integrity of Congo on June 2 claimed that the rival Lendu fighters were responsible for "killing 352 civilians, men, women, and children, 37 of whom were at the Tchomia hospital" in a weekend raid near Bunia.

May 31, 2003. *Georgia.* Tedo Mokeliya (variant Makeria), 33, a taxi driver, was detained by police after they discovered nerve gas and two containers of radioactive cesium-137 and strontium in his cab. The two are likely ingredients for a "dirty bomb." A third container had a vial of brown liquid that is a precursor for mustard gas. Police believed the buyer was in Turkey or Iran. He was on his way to Tbilisi's main rail station. His cab was stuffed with lead-lined boxes that made his springs sag. He was serving as a courier for a criminal gang. The containers were given to him by Giorgi Samkhakiuli, 29, a Georgian acquaintance of his father-in-law. Samkhakiuli had a history of drug offenses. Makeria was to bring the boxes by train to Adzharia Province on the southwestern frontier. Other couriers would then take the containers across the border to an unidentified buyer. The cesium was manufactured in the USSR in the 1970s for industrial use.

May 31, 2003. *India.* A hand grenade exploded in Khudwani, Kashmir, injuring 11 civilians and 2 police officers. No one claimed credit.

June 2003. *Pakistan.* Police arrested Adil Jazeeri, an Algerian and suspected longtime aide to Osama bin Laden, in Hayatabad, Peshawar. Police also arrested Abu Naseem, a Tunisian who was believed to be an al Qaeda member, near

Peshawar. On July 13, Jazeeri was handed over to U.S. authorities, who flew him out of the country from Peshawar airport. The Associated Press said he might have been brought to Bagram, Afghanistan, for questioning.

June 2003. *Solomon Islands.* Rebels led by Harold Keke kidnapped two Melanesian Brotherhood Anglican missionaries and five novices. By August 15, they had been released. 03069901

June 2003. *Turkey.* Members of the Revolutionary People's Liberation Party (DHKP/C) set off a remotely detonated bomb under a bus carrying Turkish prosecutors in Istanbul.

June 2003. *Sudan.* The government detained several individuals linked to the publication of a hit list attributed to al-Takfir wa al-Hijra. The list called for killing 11 prominent Sudanese Christian and leftist politicians, jurists, journalists, and others.

June 1, 2003. *France.* Police at Charles de Gaulle Airport arrested Karim Mehdi, 34, a Moroccan who had arrived from Germany and planned to leave for Reunion Island. He was allegedly planning a terrorist attack against a Reunion tourist complex. He also was suspected of having ties to the al Qaeda cell in Hamburg whose members aided the September 11 hijackers. He was a resident of Germany. 03060101

June 1, 2003. *India.* Terrorists set fire to a private residence in Jammu, Kashmir, then engaged in a gun battle with police, killing two civilians and wounding two others in the crossfire before escaping. No one claimed credit.

June 1, 2003. *Afghanistan.* A bomb exploded at the office of the German nongovernmental organization Deutsche Fuer Technische Zusammenarbeit in Kandahar, causing minor damage to the building, which was closed for the weekend. No injuries were reported. Al Qaeda was suspected. 03060101

June 2, 2003. *France.* Police at Charles de Gaulle Airport arrested German citizen Christian Ganczarski, believed to be a senior al Qaeda recruiter who was linked to the April 11, 2002, bombing of a Tunisian synagogue that killed 21 people, including 14 German tourists.

June 4, 2003. *Belgium.* Police in Deinze detained an Iraqi man, 45, after ten envelopes containing phenarsazine chloride (adamsite), an arsenic derivative used in nerve gas, were sent to the prime minister's office; the Oostende airport; the Antwerp port authority; the U.S., Saudi, and U.K. embassies; and a court trying al Qaeda suspects. Twenty people, including five police and two postal workers, went to the hospital after exposure to the brownish-yellow powder. Three people in Oostende were hospitalized. Police suspected a 45-year-old Iraqi political refugee opposed to the war in Iraq. On June 5, police searched his residence and confiscated a document and a plastic bag containing some powder. The antiterrorism investigators also suffered skin irritation, eye irritation, and breathing difficulty. The Iraqi was charged with premeditated assault. 03060401-10

June 5, 2003. *Russia.* At 7:30 a.m., after a woman failed to stop a bus carrying Russian soldiers to an air base near Chechnya, she set off a belt bomb, killing herself and 18 other people and wounding 15 more, 8 critically. Many of them were Russian air force technicians. The bombing took place near Mozdok in North Ossetia, 80 miles northwest of Grozny. Witnesses said the bomber had cased the area several times, asking about the bus schedule. She appeared to be in her late 20s. A man who had been seen with her drove off shortly before the attack.

The suicide terrorist was later identified as Samara resident Lidiya Khaldykhoroyeva.

June 5, 2003. *Georgia.* Gunmen kidnapped three UN observers on routine patrol in the remote Kodori Gorge. The trio were identified as Klaus Ott and Herbert Bauer of Germany and Henrik Soerensen of Denmark. Also taken hostage was Lasha Chikashua, their Georgian interpreter. The group was part of the 100 UN monitors on the border with Abkhazia. On June 8, a $3 million ransom was demanded. The four were freed on June 10. 03060501

June 7, 2003. *Afghanistan.* A car bomb exploded next to a bus filled with German peacekeepers of the International Security Assistance Force in the business district of east Kabul, killing 5 German peacekeepers and injuring 31. The peacekeepers were one their way to catch a flight to Germany. No civilians were injured. The U.S.–funded police school 300 feet down the street lost 13 windows. Apparently only one person was in the taxi-bomb. Al Qaeda and the Taliban were suspected. Afghan President Hamid Karzai blamed foreign-based terrorists. "I tell you with a guarantee that the person who had a suicide attack the day before yesterday you'll find out was not from Afghanistan.... The problem is mostly foreign in our case. I'm not worried about a resurgence of the Taliban. There will not be one. The Taliban movement as a movement is finished, gone." 03060701

June 8, 2003. *Pakistan.* Two gunmen on motorcycles fired machine guns on a pickup truck carrying policemen near Quetta, killing 11 and wounding 9. Most of the policemen were Shi'ites on their way to a training school. The gunmen escaped.

June 8, 2003. *Israel.* Three Palestinian gunmen dressed in Israeli army uniforms conducted a dawn raid at the Erez Crossing between the Gaza Strip and Israel, killing four Israeli soldiers and injuring another four before they were killed at an army post near an industrial zone after a 20-minute gun battle. In a joint statement, the Islamic Resistance Movement (Hamas), al-Aqsa Martyrs Brigades, and Islamic Jihad said that they had conducted a joint attack, with one member of each group participating. "This joint operation was committed to confirm our people's united choice of holy war and resistance until the end of occupation over our land

and holy places." Israel shut down the border crossing.

Later that day, Palestinian gunmen twice attacked Israeli soldiers in Hebron, killing one and wounding another before they were killed. On June 9, Palestinian Prime Minister Mahmoud Abbas condemned the attacks.

June 8, 2003. *Somalia.* An armed militia group fired on a car carrying a U.S. freelance journalist, his driver, and his interpreter in Mogadishu, slightly wounding the journalist. No one claimed credit. 03060801

June 9, 2003. *Gaza Strip.* Israeli soldiers shot to death two Palestinian gunmen trying to infiltrate the Netzarim Jewish settlement.

June 10, 2003. *Peru.* Six members of the Sendero Luminoso (Shining Path) kidnapped 3 police guards and 68 oil pipeline workers working for the Techint Group, an Argentine firm building a Camisea natural gas pipeline in Tocate in Ayacucho Province. The hostages included 64 Peruvians, 4 Colombians, 2 Argentines, and a Chilean. Police freed the hostages in a raid later that day, but the kidnappers escaped. It was unclear whether a ransom had been paid. 03061001

June 10, 2003. *Russia.* The Federal Security Service (FSB) announced the arrest of 55 leaders and members of the Moscow branch of Hizb ut-Tahrir (Party of Liberation), banned the previous February for terrorist connections. They were accused of plotting against the government. The FSB found plastic explosives, hand grenades, dynamite, and detonator cords in raids. FSB spokesman Sergei Ignatchenko said, "They were preparing fighters to send to Chechnya" and planning attacks in Moscow. Ignatchenko said they were "Muslim brothers" of al Qaeda. Most of those arrested were from Uzbekistan and Tajikistan, and included Alisher Musayev, head of the Moscow branch of the group, and Akram Dzhalolov, a leading activist.

June 10, 2003. *Thailand.* Thai authorities announced the arrests of four Jemaah Islamiah (JI) terrorists—one Singaporean and three Thais—who were planning attacks on five Western embassies, including those of the U.S., Singapore, United Kingdom, and Australia, and Thai beach resorts popular with Western tourists, including Pattaya and Phuket. The Thais were arrested in Narathiwat Province near the Malaysian border. One of the Thais was Zubair, a JI and al Qaeda member suspected of laundering al Qaeda funds through front companies, non-profit organizations, and orphanages.

June 11, 2003. *Israel.* During the 5:00 p.m. rush hour, Abdel Muati Shaban, 18, a Palestinian suicide bomber disguised as an ultraorthodox Jew, set off his bomb in the middle of Bus 14 in downtown Jerusalem, killing 16 people, including the driver and 3 passers-by, and wounding more than 70. Hamas claimed credit for the Jaffa Road attack near the Klal Center, saying it was retaliating for Israel's attempted assassination of senior Hamas leader Abdel Aziz Rantisi in Gaza City on June 10. The attack occurred at the stop at Mahane Yehuda, an open-air market near Klal Center.

Among the dead were Yaftha and Yehuda Malin, who had been married for 42 years; U.S. citizen Bertin Joseph Tita; and Alan Bier (or Beer), 47, originally from Cleveland, who had immigrated to Israeli four years earlier. The injured included Rawan Dalol, 3, and her mother, and American citizen Sari Zinger, daughter of U.S. Representative Robert Zinger. 03061101

June 11, 2003. *Turkey.* Cumali Kizilgoca, 33, a Turk, threw two grenades at a U.S. consulate garden, shattering windows but causing no injuries. One of the grenades did not explode and was later detonated by police. Kizilgoca was arrested. He said he was retaliating for the recent assassination attempt by Israel on a Hamas leader. 03061102

June 12, 2003. *Greece.* Individuals entered the front lobby of the U.S.–owned Citibank in Thessalonika, doused the ATM in a flammable liquid, placed a gas canister in it, and set it on fire. The explosion destroyed the ATM and caused extensive damage to the lobby and office equipment. 03061201

June 13, 2003. *Yemen.* San'a police defused a bomb outside the Hadda Hotel minutes before it was to explode.

June 13, 2003. *Italy.* The imam of Rome's main mosque, Mahmoud Ibrahim Moussa, was suspended from the national Muslim league after he praised Palestinian suicide bombers at Friday prayers, calling on Allah to "annihilate the enemies of Islam."

June 13, 2003. *Thailand.* Police acting on a tip from the U.S. Customs Service arrested Narong Penanam, 47, a Thai who was attempting to smuggle 66 pounds of radioactive cesium-137 from Laos. The arrest took place in a Bangkok hotel parking lot. Police believed the cesium originated in Russia and may have been destined for use in Muslim militant attacks. Penanam was charged with illegal possession of a radioactive substance. He was asking $240,000 for the goods. As of November 2003, authorities were still searching for his accomplices and additional caches of cesium.

June 14, 2003. *Saudi Arabia.* Police killed five al Qaeda terrorists in nighttime gun battles against militants planning a terrorist attack. Two police officers died in the shoot-out at a checkpoint. Five security agents and four bystanders were wounded. The next day, Mecca police raided an apartment in the Khalidiya district filled with booby-trapped bombs. Several people were arrested for links to the suicide bombings in May.

June 15, 2003. *Lebanon.* Terrorists fired two rockets into Prime Minister Rafiq Hariri's Future TV building, causing extensive damage to a news studio. The previously unknown Partisans of God (Ansar Allah) threatened more attacks against "anyone, no matter how influential he is, who directs his poisonous arrows at the heart of the resistance and jihad and mujaheddin." Interior Minister Elias Murr said the attackers were also responsible for recent attacks against U.S. fast food restaurants in Lebanon.

June 17, 2003. *France.* French police raided the compound and 12 other sites of the Iranian oppositionist Mujaheddin-e Khalq. They arrested 159 people on suspicion of plotting terrorist attacks in France and building a support base for operations abroad. Among those arrested was Maryam Rajavi, wife of Iraq-based leader Massoud Rajavi, and his brother, Saleh. Police seized $1.3 million in U.S. currency, mostly in $100 bills, plus computers and satellite telecommunications equipment from the walled compound in Auvers-Sur-Ooise, north of Paris. The head of French intelligence said that the group was planning to attack Iranian diplomatic missions in Europe and elsewhere. An individual in London set himself on fire outside the French Embassy in protest. German police arrested 50 demonstrators after they broke into the Iranian consulate in Hamburg. On June 18, three Iranians set themselves on fire to protest the arrests. As of June 20, nine people had self-immolated; one died. On July 2, a Paris court ordered the release of Maryam Rajavi.

June 17, 2003. *Kenya.* Police arrested Salmin Mohammed Khamis, believed involved in the November 2002 al Qaeda bombing of a hotel north of Mombasa. On October 24, 2003, the press reported that he had told investigators that al Qaeda was going to destroy the U.S. Embassy in Nairobi in June with a truck bomb and an explosives-laden hijacked plane. The embassy was closed June 20 to June 24. Kenya had banned flights to and from Somalia from June 20 to July 8. Khamis mentioned a coded e-mail from Saleh Ali Saleh Nabhan, an at-large suspect in the hotel bombing, who invited Khamis to participate in "al Qaeda activities." Khamis attended a meeting of al Qaeda terrorists in May in Malindi, a coastal venue,

where he met with Nabhan, two Somalis, and an Arab.

June 17, 2003. *Italy.* A bomb exploded in front of the Liceo Cervantes (Spanish School Cervantes) in Rome, damaging the school and a few cars within a 20-meter radius. Police believed the device contained 500 grams of chlorite- and nitrate-based explosives. The roof of the school is the terrace of the Spanish ambassador's residence. No one claimed credit, but police said the bombers were experienced with explosives and were probably connected to an Italian anarchist group aligned with the Basque Nation and Liberty (ETA). Similar devices had been used in earlier attacks and had been linked to Italian anarchists supporting ETA. 03061701

June 17, 2003. *India.* A bomb exploded outside a store selling chickens in Shopian, Kashmir, injuring five people. No one claimed credit.

June 17, 2003. *India.* Terrorists entered a private residence in Kashmir, killing the son of a Muslim politician. No one claimed credit.

June 18, 2003. *Corsica.* The Corsican National Liberation Front set off bombs during the early morning in Yvelines, seriously damaging two French villas and a British housing company. The homes were unoccupied and no injuries were reported. 03061801

June 19, 2003. *Israel.* At 6:00 a.m., a suicide bomber walked into a grocery store in Sde Trumot and set off his explosives, killing himself and the owner, Avener Mordechai, 63. The town is in northern Israel near the border of the West Bank and Jordan. Police believed that the bomb went off prematurely and that the terrorist planned to set off the bomb in a bus. Islamic Jihad claimed credit.

June 19, 2003. *United States.* Alexandria federal court papers were unsealed regarding Columbus, Ohio, trucker Iyman Faris (alias Mohammad Rauf), 34, a Kashmiri-born naturalized U.S. citizen, who pleaded guilty on May 1 to plotting to take down the Brooklyn Bridge and launch a simultaneous attack in Washington, D.C., to derail trains. Faris had met with bin Laden, Khalid Sheik Mohammed, and other senior al Qaeda officials in Afghanistan and Pakistan during the plot. He carried cash for al Qaeda, provided information about ultralight aircraft as getaway vehicles, and scouted equipment for sabotaging railroad tracks and cutting suspension bridge cables. He ordered 2,000 light-weight sleeping bags for al Qaeda, obtained extensions for six airline tickets for al Qaeda members traveling to Yemen, and delivered cash and cell phones to Khalid Sheik Mohammed, who later fingered him to police. After researching cutting torches to use against the Brooklyn Bridge, he determined that the plan would not work, and reported that "the weather is too hot." Faris faced a 20-year sentence and a $500,000 fine after pleading guilty to conspiracy to provide material support to terrorists and providing material support for terrorism. As part of his plea agreement, he agreed to cooperate with ongoing federal investigations of al Qaeda. He was represented by attorney J. Frederick Sinclair.

Faris had a contact in the United States who sent coded messages for him to a senior al Qaeda member in Pakistan between April 2002 and March 2003. Faris entered the United States in 1994 on a student visa and obtained citizenship in 1999. He had married Geneva Bowling when he worked at H&M Auto in Columbus, Ohio, and later divorced amicably in April 2000.

On July 24, 2003, U.S. District Judge Leonie M. Brinkema delayed sentencing after the defense requested a hearing to determine mental competence. Sentencing was rescheduled for September 26.

On October 28, 2003, he was sentenced to 20 years in prison after Judge Brinkema rejected his attempt to withdraw his guilty plea. Faris claimed he was trying to fool the FBI in the process of gathering material for a book.

June 20, 2003. *Kenya.* The U.S. Embassy was closed after the United States received a "serious terrorist threat" that al Qaeda operatives were planning an attack, possibly involving a truck bomb or light aircraft. The embassy was reopened on June 25.

On June 29, the government arrested a Kenyaborn Pakistani, a teacher at the Young Muslim Association, in Garissa near the Somali border shortly after he returned from Somalia. The previous week, police detained dozens for questioning.

June 20, 2003. *Israel.* Hamas gunmen fired on a car carrying Americans driving from the Jewish settlement of Eli (other reports said Ofra), three miles northeast of Ramallah, killing U.S. citizen Zvi Goldstein (variant Howard Craig Goldstein), 47, a resident of Eli (or Ofra), and injuring his visiting parents, Gene and Lorraine Goldstein, both 73, of Plainview, New York, and his wife, Michal. 03062001

June 20, 2003. *Israel.* During the week, Palestinian gunmen fired on the car of an Israeli family on a major Israeli highway near the West Bank border, killing a 7-year-old girl.

June 20, 2003. *India.* A bomb exploded at a crowded market in Srinagar, Kashmir, injuring 16 people. No one claimed credit.

June 20, 2003. *India.* A hand grenade was thrown at a police station in Charar-i-Sharif, Kashmir, injuring two officers inside. No one claimed credit.

June 20, 2003. *Russia.* A man and a woman set off a truck bomb near the Ministry of the Interior building in Groznyy, killing themselves and wounding 36.

June 21, 2003. *Malawi.* The Malawi National Intelligence Bureau and immigration authorities in Blantyre detained five suspected members of al Qaeda two weeks before President Bush was scheduled to visit Africa. Malawian officials said the group was sending money to al Qaeda and that they were flown to Botswana on an Air Malawi plane by U.S. officials the next day, despite a court order preventing their deportation. Two were identified as Mahmud Sardar Issa, a Sudanese who heads the Islamic Zakat Fund Trust in Blantyre, and Saudi citizen Fahad Ral Bahli, director of the Malawi branch of Registered Trustees of the Prince Sultan Bin Abdul Aziz Special Committee on Relief.

On July 25, they were released in Sudan after being cleared of suspicion of al Qaeda membership. The two Turks, a Saudi, a Kenyan, and a Sudanese were to be sent to their respective countries.

June 21, 2003. *Yemen.* Authorities blamed the outlawed Aden-Abyan Islamic Army, formed by Yemenis and other Arabs who fought in the anti-Soviet Afghan war, for attacking a military medical convoy in the south and wounding seven Yemeni soldiers. On June 27, security forces arrested four members of the al Qaeda linked group.

June 22, 2003. *United Kingdom.* Two men stabbed and wounded in the leg Saad al-Fagih, head of the London-based Movement for Islamic Reform in Arabia and a critic of the Saudi royal family, at his London home during the evening. The duo, claiming to be plumbers, sprayed him with something that made him drowsy. He nonetheless fought back, grabbing a table to defend himself. A colleague, Mohammed al-Masari, said that "as they were going away, they said, 'Take that as a message from the Saudi government.'" 03062201

June 23, 2003. *India.* A hand grenade was thrown at a military vehicle in Pulwama, Kashmir. The grenade missed its intended target but killed 2 people and wounded 48 civilians standing near by. No one claimed credit.

June 25, 2003. *Pakistan.* Authorities arrested Haris bin Asim, an Egyptian member of al Qaeda, in a raid on a Peshawar house, where police found a video cassette of bin Laden warning of attacks against U.S. interests in Saudi Arabia.

June 25, 2003. *Yemen.* Troops attacked a mountain hideout of the Aden-Abyan Islamic Army, which has al Qaeda ties, killing at least 6 militants and arresting 11 others. One army officer died; five soldiers were injured. The Central Security Forces also seized a large amount of explosives and weapons. Negotiations lasted for days but finally broke down. The terrorists had earlier attacked a military medical convoy, wounding seven soldiers.

June 25, 2003. *United States.* In a 42-count indictment that was unsealed on June 27, federal prosecutors charged 11 members of a "Virginia jihad network" with training to work with Muslim terrorists overseas. The U.S. District Court in Alexandria, Virginia, was told that the men trained and fought for Lashkar-i-Taiba, a group trying to get India out of Kashmir and named a terrorist group by the U.S. government. In raids on June 27, federal agents arrested six men in the Washington, D.C., suburbs and Pennsylvania. Two were already in custody as part of the investigation, which began in 2000. Three others were in Saudi Arabia. The nine U.S. citizens and two foreigners faced weapons counts and violating the Neutrality Act. While there was no evidence that they intended attacks within the United States, defendant Masoud Ahmad Khan, 31, of Gaithersburg, Maryland, had downloaded an Internet photo of FBI headquarters. Other defendants were Ibrahim Ahmed al-Hamdi, 26, of Alexandria, Virginia; Mohammed Aatique; Khwaja Mahmood Hasan, 27; Sabri Benkhala; Caliph Basha Ibn Abdur-Raheem, 29; Randall Todd Royer, 30, of Falls Church, Virginia; Yong Ki Kwon, 27; Hammad Abdur-Raheem, 35, a Gulf War veteran; Donald Thomas Surratt, 30, and Seifullah Chapman. The latter three were accused of instructing the others in combat tactics based upon their U.S. military experience. An unindicted coconspirator had told them that fighting U.S. troops in Afghanistan was "a valid jihad for Muslims." Authorities found pistols and rifles in the homes of some of the defendants. The indictment said they had trained at private and military firearms ranges in northern Virginia to ready themselves for attacks in Chechnya, the Philippines, Kashmir, and other locations. They practiced small-unit tactics on private property in Spotsylvania County, using paintball games as a cover. Royer and another defendant were alleged to have fired at Indian positions in Kashmir after training at a Lashkar-i-Taiba camp in Pakistan.

On June 30, U.S. Magistrate Judge T. Rawles Jones, Jr., ordered the release of Khan at a bail hearing, but ordered him to be electronically monitored. Prosecutors said they would appeal to U.S. District Court. Khan was represented by attorney Danny C. Onorato. Jones later ordered the release of the two Abdur-Raheems, Royer, and Surratt, but ordered them to be electronically monitored. The prosecution did not challenge the release of Surratt and Caliph Abdur-Raheem, but appealed the release of Khan, Hammad Abdur-Raheem, and Royer. On July 1, U.S. District Judge Leonie M. Brinkema (who was also hearing the Moussaoui case) ordered the release delayed and set a hearing for July 2. Al-Hamdi and Kwon were held on other charges.

On July 2, Judge Brinkema upheld the release of Caliph Abdur-Raheem and ordered the release of Hammad Abdur-Raheem on a $25,000 unsecured bond. (Hammad Abdur-Raheem was represented by attorney Pleasant S. Brodnax.) However, she agreed that Khan is a "danger to the community" and ordered him detained, along with Aatique. Royer's appeal was set for July 8. She set a November 17 trial date for eight of the suspects, who pleaded not guilty. On July 11, Judge Brinkema ruled that Royer should remain in jail, saying she was not satisfied with his explanation of why he had an AK-47-style rifle and more than 200 rounds of ammunition in his car two weeks after September 11. Royer was represented by attorneys Ashraf Nubani and Stanley Cohen.

On July 19, a law enforcement spokesman announced the arrest of the last three of the 11 suspects—Seifullah Chapman, Khawaja

Mahmood Hasan, and Sabri Benkhala (variant Benkahla)—who had been living in Saudi Arabia. They were scheduled to attend bail hearings the next day. Trial of the original eight was scheduled for November 17.

On July 25, prosecutors told Judge Brinkema that Benkhala's phone number was found in a cell phone directory of an admitted member of al Qaeda, Ahmed Abu Ali, who was picked up by the Saudis on suspicion of involvement in the May 12 bombings. She nonetheless ordered him freed before the trial. Benkhala was represented by attorney John A. Boneta.

Judge Brinkema refused to release Kwon in a hearing on August 1. His brother claimed that he was cooperating with the FBI.

On August 1, Assistant U.S. Attorney Gordon D. Kromberg told Judge Brinkema that the government was considering filing a superseding indictment against the defendants, noting that the group intended "to fight American soldiers" and not just do battle against Indian troops.

By August 25, Kwon, Hasan, and Surratt had pleaded guilty to conspiracy and gun charges. The previous week, Hasan pleaded guilty to one count of conspiracy and to discharging a firearm in relation to a crime of violence. On August 22, Surratt pleaded guilty to conspiracy and illegal transportation of a firearm in interstate commerce. On August 25, Kwon pleaded guilty to conspiracy, transfer of a firearm for use in a crime of violence, and discharge of a firearm in relation to a crime of violence. He admitted to training with firearms in Northern Virginia to prepare for a jihad abroad, and to training in Pakistan at a Lashkar-i-Taiba camp. He said he fired machine guns and rocket-propelled grenades. Kwon and Hasan faced a life sentence, although they were likely to serve less than 20 years. Surratt faced 15 years. Sentencing was scheduled for November 7. The other eight pleaded not guilty and readied for a November trial. Hasan was represented by attorney Thomas Abbenante.

On September 22, 2003, Aatique pleaded guilty to preparing to fight for Muslim causes abroad, and that his coconspirators might have taken up arms against the United States if they had not been arrested. Sentencing was scheduled for December 12.

On September 25, 2003, a new indictment was issued against seven defendants. Royer and Khan were charged with conspiracy to provide material support to al Qaeda and the Taliban. Benkhala was accused of supplying services to the Taliban. Three others faced increased charges of conspiring to support Lashkar-i-Taiba. Arraignment was scheduled for September 29 in the U.S. District Court in Alexandria, Virginia.

On November 7, 2003, Kwon was sentenced to 11 years 6 months for his larger role in the conspiracy. Hasan received 11 years and three months. Surratt received less than four years.

On December 17, Aatique was sentenced to more than ten years on a gun charge. Judge Brinkema said that she was hamstrung by sentencing guidelines. Prosecutors had praised his cooperation in the case. Brinkema gave him six months for aiding and abetting. He was represented by attorney Alan Dexter Bowman.

On January 16, 2004, Royer pleaded guilty to one count of using and discharging a firearm during and in relation to a crime of violence and to carrying an explosive during the commission of a felony, but denied he intended to harm Americans. He said he and his colleagues intended to fight in Muslim causes abroad. Sentencing was set for April 9. The government had dropped charges that he conspired to provide material support to the Taliban and al Qaeda. Al-Hamdi also pleaded guilty to possession of a firearm during and in relation to a crime of violence and to carrying an explosive during the commission of a felony. He faced at least 15 years in prison. As part of the plea agreement the duo was to cooperate with federal investigators. Four defendants were scheduled for trial in February; another was to be tried in March. The other four who pleaded guilty were cooperating with authorities.

On January 27, 2004, four defendants waived their right to a jury trial, claiming that a Northern Virginia jury could not be impartial in considering terrorism charges against Muslim men.

Chapman (represented by John K. Zwerling), Hammad Abdur-Raheem (represented by William B. Cummings), Caliph Abdur-Raheem (represented by Christopher Amolsch), and Khan (represented by Bernard Grimm and Jonathan Shapiro, who had also defended now-convicted Washington area sniper John Allen Muhammad) were scheduled for a February 9 bench trial in front of Judge Brinkema. Defendant Benkahla did not waive his right and was on the March docket.

On February 9, 2004, the trial opened in U.S. District Court in Alexandria, Virginia.

On February 20, 2004, Judge Brinkema threw out the case against Caliph Abdur-Raheem, saying that prosecutors had failed to present any evidence that he was involved in a conspiracy to train for jihadist combat abroad. She noted that he had fallen asleep at one of the meetings of the alleged coconspirators. She also dismissed various counts against the other three defendants, but refused to drop the most serious charges. The prosecutors rested their case.

On March 4, 2004, Judge Brinkema found the trio guilty of conspiring to aid Lashkar-i-Taiba and on weapons charges. She rejected the charge against Khan that he conspired to provide material support to al Qaeda. Defense attorneys were considering an appeal. Sentencing was scheduled for June. Khan was the only defendant convicted of conspiracy to wage war against the United States and assist the Taliban. He faced more than 100 years. Chapman was convicted of conspiring to support Lashkar-i-Taiba and using arms in connection with a crime of violence. He faced 60 years. Hammad Abdur-Raheem was guilty of weapons charges and supporting Lashkar-i-Taiba. He did not attend the training camp but was accused of helping train his friends in the United States. On June 15, 2004, Judge Brinkema imposed an 85-year sentence on Chapman, a life sentence on Khan, and a 97-month sentence on Hammad Abdur-Raheem.

On March 9, 2004, after a one-day trial, Judge Brinkema acquitted Benkhala of the charges, saying that although the prosecution had shown that he was "very interested in violent jihad," they had not proved that he had fought for the Taliban.

On April 9, 2004, Royer was sentenced to 20 years in prison (two consecutive 10-year sentences); Al-Hamdi received 15 years. Judge Brinkema said the latter would likely be deported at the end of his sentence. The duo pleaded guilty and did not go to trial. The three convicted at trial faced more than 100 years in prison.

On September 23, 2004, Ali al-Timimi, 40, an Islamic spiritual leader, was indicted on charges that his preaching inspired the group to train for violent jihad overseas. The Fairfax County residence was a frequent lecturer at the Center for Islamic Information and Education (Dar all-Arqam) in Falls Church, Virginia. Al-Timimi was represented by attorney Martin F. McMahon. The grand jury in U.S. District Court in Alexandria, Virginia, charged that on September 16, 2001, al-Timimi told his followers at a Fairfax meeting that "the time had come" to join the violent jihad in Afghanistan and that U.S. troops were legitimate targets. Earlier, Al-Timimi had been an unindicted coconspirator in the case. This time, he faced a life sentence. Al-Timimi was five weeks from receiving his Ph.D. in cancer gene research at George Mason University. Arraignment was scheduled for October 1. He was to be charged with conspiracy and attempting to contribute services to the Taliban, and on firearms and explosives counts. He was not accused of firing weapons but of inciting others who illegally fired guns and RPGs at the terrorist training camp.

June 25, 2003. *United States.* The FBI's Denver office warned law enforcement agencies after a detained al Qaeda member said three or four members of a group were planning to start forest fires in Colorado, Montana, Utah, and Wyoming using timed detonators.

June 26, 2003. *Russia.* The UN Security Council named former Chechen President Zelimkhan Yandarbiyev a supporter of bin Laden. He lives in exile in Doha, Qatar. The Russian government was seeking his extradition, saying he helped orchestrate the 1999 incursion into Dagestan by Chechen rebels. UN members must bar him from traveling to their countries, freeze his assets, and prevent him from transporting weapons.

June 26, 2003. *Georgia.* Border guards using U.S.–supplied radiation detectors seized more than a pound of uranium at the Georgia-Armenia border. The material may have originated in Russia, for resale in Iran.

June 27, 2003. *Kenya.* Terrorists in Mandera threw hand grenades, killing one person and seriously injuring four others, including a doctor from the Netherlands working with Doctors Without Frontiers. No one claimed credit. 03062701

June 28, 2003. *Gaza Strip.* Several bombs went off near a U.S. Embassy car in Bayt Lahiyah. The bombs apparently were aimed at a diplomatic-plated vehicle belonging to the U.S. Consulate, because the Israeli Defense Forces were not operating in the area. 03062801

June 30, 2003. *Israel.* The al-Aqsa Martyrs Brigades fired on a truck in Yabed, northern Israel, killing a Bulgarian construction worker. 03063001

July 2003. *Kyrgyzstan.* The Interior Ministry seized a cache of weapons hidden in the Batken region.

July 1, 2003. *Israel.* Troops shot and killed a man who ran toward a military checkpoint near Tulkarm, firing his AK-47 assault rifle. No group claimed credit.

July 2, 2003. *Saudi Arabia.* The FBI reported that al Qaeda had obtained stolen unissued Saudi passports from the E-series.

July 3, 2003. *Colombia.* The Revolutionary Armed Forces of Colombia (FARC) kidnapped five people, including a Swiss citizen working for the nongovernmental organization Hands of Colombia Foundation. 03070301

July 3, 2003. *Iraq.* Terrorists killed a British journalist outside the Iraq National Museum in Baghdad. No one claimed credit. 03070301

July 4, 2003. *Russia.* Three armed men kidnapped Ali Astamirov, a Chechen journalist working for *Agence France-Presse* in Nazran, Ingushetia. The trio did not kidnap his colleagues, one working for Reuters and one for Radio Liberty, but did steal their mobile phones. 03070401

July 4, 2003. *Pakistan.* At least three suicide bombers killed 47 people and wounded at least 50 at a Shi'ite mosque in Quetta. Information Minister Sheikh Rashid Ahmed blamed "sectarian elements," referring to outlawed Sunni extremists. Two thousand people were in the mosque when the bomb went off. Some observers said a fourth bomber was arrested. Two died in the mosque; a third died in a shoot-out with guards outside. Zulfiquar Ali, a survivor who was slightly wounded, said, "First they killed security guards outside the mosque. Then they moved inside the mosque and started firing on the people." After a security guard killed an attacker, "the other attacker blew himself up." Hours later, police found two bombs hidden in tin canisters near the mosque's main wall. Shi'ite youths torched a hospital where victims were being treated.

July 4, 2003. *Corsica.* Police arrested Yvan Colonna, a Corsican separatist leader, on a sheep farm. They believe he shot to death Corsica's most senior French official, Prefect Claude Enrignac, on February 6, 1998, in an Ajaccio street. Colonna had added weight and grew long hair and a beard in an effort to throw off his pursuers.

July 4, 2003. *India.* Terrorists killed a school teacher and a private citizen and wounded 20 others, including the rural development minister of Jammu-Kashmir, 2 government officials, 2

police officers, and 15 others when they fired on and threw several hand grenades into a meeting between the minister and health officials in Larnu, Kashmir. No one claimed credit.

July 5, 2003. *Russia.* At 2:45 p.m. and 3:00 p.m., two female suicide bombers killed 16 and hospitalized at least 60 at an afternoon outdoor rock concert at Moscow's Tushino Airfield. Eleven victims died at the scene; two others in the hospital. Authorities said the casualty figures would have been higher if the terrorists had gotten past guards and into the festival, where 40,000 were in attendance. One of the attackers was Zalikhan Elikhadzhiyeva, 20, a Chechen from Kurchaloi, whose passport was found at the scene. She had left home six months earlier. Her brother is a Wahhabist leader and her husband is an American. The duo had worn belts with TNT and metal fragments. The first terrorist's belt didn't completely explode, and she remained alive for a time. Among the victims was Anna Popkova, 21. A spokesman for Chechen rebel leader Aslan Maskhadov denied involvement. The Wings concert continued until after 8:00 p.m.

July 7, 2003. *Corsica.* Bombs exploded in the empty vacation homes of mainlanders the day after Corsican voters rejected greater autonomy. No casualties were reported.

July 7, 2003. *Israel.* During the night, Ahmad Fathi Yihia, 22, an Islamic Jihad (IJ) member from Kufeirat, near Jenin, set off a bomb that killed Mazal Afari, 65, in the living room of her Kfar Yavetz home. Yihia died when the roof collapsed. Three of Afari's grandchildren were slightly injured. An IJ spokesman said the bombing was not sanctioned by the leadership, which had agreed to a three-month truce.

July 8, 2003. *Afghanistan.* Terrorists attacked the Pakistani Embassy in Kabul, destroying computers and telephones. No one claimed credit. 03070801

July 9, 2003. *India.* Terrorists threw a hand grenade at a security patrol in Aram Mohalla Shopian, Kashmir, but missed. The bomb exploded on the roadside, injuring three people. No one claimed credit.

July 10, 2003. *Russia.* Police detained a woman who intended to enter a Moscow restaurant on Tverskaya Street with a pound of military-issue explosives in a bag. Zarima Muzhikhoyeva, 22, was led away in handcuffs from a table in the Mon café. Federal Security Service (FSB) bomb technician Georgi Trofimov, 29, died when trying to dismantle the bomb. He had defused part of an explosives belt at the rock concert days earlier. Police reported that she was a widow from the Ingush ethnic group who lived in a Chechen village. Her husband died fighting against the Russians. Her bomb was similar to those used in the rock concert blasts. On April 5, 2004, a jury found her guilty of terrorism. On April 8, a Moscow court sentenced her to 20 years in prison.

July 11, 2003. *Indonesia.* Police arrested seven suspected members of Jemaah Islamiah, one of whom committed suicide during questioning. In a raid on a bomb-making factory, police found explosives more powerful than those used in the Bali bombing. They also found three books containing schedules of Christian church services in Indonesia.

July 11, 2003. *Israel.* Authorities believed that a missing Israeli taxi driver, Eliyahu Goral, 61, was kidnapped by militants. Palestinian prisoners called for his release. The possible kidnapping threatened the truce between Israel and Palestinian terrorists.

On July 14, shortly before midnight, the taxi driver was rescued from a house in Beitunia, a Ramallah suburb. He was bound but uninjured. Police said the kidnappers might have been robbers who botched the attempt and did not appear to have terrorist ties. The *Washington Post* quoted an Israeli security source as saying, "When the kidnappers understood they were in over their heads, they tried to pass him on to [militants], but no one wanted to take him."

July 11, 2003. *Greece.* Bomb technicians dismantled a bomb in an Athens office building near a branch of the American Life Insurance Company. The device resembled those used by the Revolutionary Nuclei and Revolutionary People's Struggle (ELA). 03071101

July 13, 2003. *Spain.* Following a phoned warning by Basque Nation and Liberty (ETA), police defused an 8-pound bomb in the basement of the crowded Maisonnave tourist hotel during the Pamplona festival. The bomb was found in a women's restroom bin. The hotel was evacuated. The call came before the annual running of the bulls.

July 13, 2003. *Philippines.* Salamat Hashim, who had agreed to resume peace talks and renounced terrorism on behalf of the Moro Islamic Liberation Front (MILF), died of a heart ailment and an ulcer and was buried in Butig in Lanao del Sur Province. The MILF central committee named military chief of staff Al Haj Murad as his successor.

July 13, 2003. *Greece.* Three Molotov cocktails were thrown at an Athens branch office of Eurobank, causing minor damage. No one claimed credit. 03071301

July 14, 2003. *Indonesia.* A bomb went off at the Parliament in Jakarta, spewing nails around the area. No one was hurt and damage was minor.

July 14, 2003. *Israel.* At 1:30 a.m., a Palestinian attempted to entered a restaurant in Tel Aviv on the southern waterfront, but was stopped by a security guard. The Palestinian stabbed the guard in the neck, then ran down the wide walkway. The restaurant's owner and the guard chased the terrorist, who meanwhile stabbed two more people, killing Amir Simon, 24, and seriously wounding a woman. An Israeli man shot the terrorist in the leg. The terrorist was a 23-year-old Palestinian from East Jerusalem. It was the first attack by a Palestinian in an Israeli city since the beginning of the cease-fire. The al-Aqsa Martyrs Brigades claimed credit.

July 14, 2003. *Afghanistan.* A bomb exploded near the Jalalabad offices of the UN Human Rights Commission (UNHRC), causing minor damage to two buildings. No one claimed credit. 03071401

July 16, 2003. *United States.* Rabih Haddad, 43, cofounder of a Muslim charity leader accused of having al Qaeda links, was deported from Detroit to Lebanon. In November, an Immigration Court judge had ruled that he and his family should be deported because he was a security threat. He had spent 19 months in custody without being charged with a terrorist crime.

July 16, 2003. *Colombia.* In La Pesquera, military officials reported that either the National Liberation Army (ELN) or Revolutionary Armed Forces of Colombia (FARC) bombed a section of the Cano Limo–Covenas oil pipeline at the KM 71 and 26 W intersection, as well as at the KM 07 and 02N intersection, causing damage. The pipeline is owned by U.S. and Colombian oil firms. 03071601-02

July 17, 2003. *Russia.* At 10:00 a.m., a bomb attached to a parked motorcycle or scooter exploded near a Khasavyurt, Dagestan, police station, killing 3 people, including a police officer, a pregnant woman, and a 5-year-old girl, and injuring 18 others.

July 18, 2003. *Mexico.* The Federal Investigative Agency arrested six Spaniards and three Mexicans at several locations on charges that they had ties to the Basque Nation and Liberty (ETA). Mexican officials said they were laundering money for ETA and forging documents to support ETA members.

July 20, 2003. *Corsica/France.* During the weekend, several bombs exploded in Nice and the island of Corsica. On July 21, a caller to I-Television in Ajaccio, Corsica, claimed credit for the Corsican National Liberation Front's bombing of an airport office and an earlier bombing at Nice government offices that injured 16 people.

July 21, 2003. *Saudi Arabia.* The government announced the arrest of 16 individuals linked to al Qaeda. Tractors dug up an underground cache of 20 tons of bomb-making chemicals, detonators, rocket-propelled grenades, and rifles. Police also found night-vision goggles, surveillance cameras, bulletproof vests, passports, and forged identity cards.

July 21, 2003. *India.* Two hand grenades exploded at a crowded community kitchen in Jammu, Kashmir, killing 7 and wounding 42. No one claimed credit.

July 21, 2003. *India.* The Lashkar-i-Taiba and the Students Islamic Movement of India were the chief suspects in the bombing of a Hindu temple in Katra that killed six people and caused extensive damage to the building.

July 22, 2003. *Spain.* Bombs exploded ten minutes apart in two hotels in Mediterranean resorts located about 25 miles apart, wounding 13 people, including 7 foreigners. The bomb in Benidorm wounded four policemen and a civilian. Eight people were injured in Alicante; among them was a Dutch man who underwent surgery for a head injury. A German man was also seriously wounded. The Basque Nation and Liberty (ETA) gave advance warning in a call to a Basque newspaper, but the bombs exploded 10 to 20 minutes early. Interior Ministry officials deemed the bombs "booby traps." 03072201

July 23, 2003. *Iran.* The government acknowledged press reports that it had arrested several senior al Qaeda members. *ABC News* said they included spokesman Sulaiman Abu Ghaith (whose citizenship was revoked by Kuwaiti authorities) and security chief Saif Adel, an Egyptian. The *Washington Post* added the names of Saad bin Laden (son of Osama), 23, heir apparent, and Abu Musab Zarqawi, a Jordanian who ran the chemical weapons program and who had escaped from Iraq. The interior minister said some would be tried, some deported, some extradited. As of August 11, Tehran was accused of dragging its feet in extraditing the 15 terrorists to Arab countries.

July 23, 2003. *Sri Lanka.* Terrorists stoned a vehicle carrying two Scandinavians working as truce monitors in Valanchchenai. The duo was not injured, but the car was damaged. No one claimed credit.

July 26, 2003. *United States.* The Transportation Security Administration warned U.S. airline services that terrorists working in teams of five could be plotting suicide hijack missions on the East Coast, Europe, or Australia during the summer, using "common items carried by travelers, such as cameras, modified as weapons …. The plan may involve the use of five-man teams, each of which would attempt to seize control of a commercial aircraft either shortly after takeoff or shortly before landing at a chosen airport. This type of operation would preclude the need for flight-trained hijackers." The *Washington Post* reported on August 2 that the information came from captive al Qaeda member Ali Abd al-Rahman al-Faqasi al-Ghamdi (alias Abu Bakr), who appeared to have been with bin Laden at Tora Bora, Afghanistan. He was arrested by Saudi authorities in June.

July 27, 2003. *Spain.* A car bomb exploded in a parking lot of Santander Airport after a warning call from the Basque Nation and Liberty (ETA). The bomb destroyed 12 cars and wrecked the front of the terminal but caused no casualties.

July 27, 2003. *Russia.* A female suicide bomber killed herself near a Russian base commanded by Ramzan Kadyrov, a son of Chechnya's administration chief, wounding another woman.

July 28, 2003. *Saudi Arabia.* In a firefight at a Qassim Province farm, six Muslim militants and two police officers died and another eight police officers were wounded. Police had asked the terrorists to surrender but were met with gunfire and hand grenades.

July 29, 2003. *Sierra Leone.* Foday Sankoh, 65, leader of the Revolutionary United Front, died in a Freetown hospital following a stroke. His terrorists specialized in cutting off the hands, legs, ears, and lips of their victims. He had been indicted by the UN Special Court for Sierra Leone on charges of mass murder, rape, abduction, use of child soldiers, and sexual slavery.

July 29, 2003. *Russia.* A bomb exploded under a two-vehicle Russian troop convoy during the evening near Galashki, Ingushetia, killing four soldiers immediately. A fifth died of his injuries on July 30.

Another explosive went off under a military truck southeast of Grozny, Chechnya, wounding a soldier.

August 2003. *Ecuador.* Police broke up an arms smuggling operation supplying Colombian narcoterrorists.

August 2003. *Paraguay.* A court sentenced Ali Nizar Dahroug, a prominent Hizballah fundraiser, to a long prison term.

August 1, 2003. *Morocco.* Authorities detained British citizens Anthony Perry Jensen, 37, and businessman Abdellatif Merroun, 42, on suspicion of having ties to the Salafia Jihadia, a group of underground Islamic extremists involved in the May 16 suicide bombings in Casablanca. The group has ties to al Qaeda. The duo was not suspected of involvement in the attacks. In June, authorities had arrested a French citizen in the investigation of the group.

August 1, 2003. *Kenya.* A man arrested as an Islamic militant set off a hand grenade in the back of a police car, killing himself and a policeman in Mombasa and letting a confederate escape. Police had arrested another man in what they deemed "marked a major breakthrough by Kenyan police in their fight against terrorism."

August 1, 2003. *Turkey.* CNN ran footage of the deaths of a dozen people as a bomb technician attempted to defuse an explosive left by a left-wing terrorist. The bomb went off on a crowded street.

August 1, 2003. *Russia.* At 7:00 p.m., a truck filled with explosives drove through the gates of a military compound in Mozdok, North Ossetia, and exploded outside a hospital, killing 52 patients and medical personnel and wounding 82 people. Chechen militants were blamed, but a spokesman for Chechen leader Aslan Maskhadov denounced the attack.

Hours earlier, authorities killed nine Chechen rebels in Argun at a training base for suicide bombers. Twenty Russian soldiers and police officers died in the gun battle.

August 1, 2003. *United States.* A banner reading, "If you build it, we will burn it, ELF" was left at the site of an arson at the five-story San Diego University Town Centre apartment complex under construction. The fire caused $50 million in damage. The Earth Liberation Front claims to be "an international underground organization that uses direct action in the form of economic sabotage to stop the destruction of the natural environment." The group did not claim credit on its Web site. No one was injured.

August 2, 2003. *Lebanon.* Ali Hussein Saleh, a Hizballah member who worked as a driver for the Iranian Embassy in Beirut, and his passenger were killed by a car bomb. 03080201

August 3, 2003. *Dubai.* Al-Arabiya broadcast an audiotape from al Qaeda deputy Ayman Zawahiri, who said, "America has announced it will start putting on trial in front of military tribunals the Muslim detainees at Guantanamo and might sentence them to death.... I swear in the name of God that the crusader America will pay a dear price for any harm it inflicts on any

of the Muslim detainees. We tell America only one thing: what you have suffered until now is only the initial skirmishes. The real battle has not started yet."

August 3, 2003. *Israel.* Palestinian terrorists shot and seriously wounded an Israeli mother, moderately wounded her nine-year-old daughter, and slightly injured her two other children in an attack on their car on the road connecting the Har Gilo settlement to Jerusalem. The terrorists escaped.

August 3, 2003. *Serbia/Montenegro.* Satish Menon, 43, an Indian working as a UN police officer, was shot to death with a semiautomatic rifle in his car in Mitrovica in northern Kosovo. The killers had created a road hazard with boulders to slow down the car. The British policeman who was driving jumped from the red and white Toyota, which had UN markings and escaped unharmed. Eight bullets hit the car. 03080301

August 4, 2003. *Laos.* Without warning, a time bomb exploded in Vientiane, wounding ten people.

August 4, 2003. *India.* Terrorists shot to death an educator attending a wedding in Mahore Tehsil, Kashmir. No one claimed credit.

August 5, 2003. *Indonesia.* The Jemaat Islamiah (JI) was suspected of setting off a metallic blue Toyota Kijang minivan bomb (some reports said a taxi bomb or truck bomb) at the entrance of Jakarta's Marriott Hotel, killing at least 16 people and injuring 149, including 2 Americans and 1 Australian. No guests were killed; several taxi drivers died. One of the dead was a security guard directing traffic. A guard who approached the suspicious van was among those killed. Four jerrycans of gasoline were wrapped around the bomb. Among the injured were three hotel guests (out of the 230) and eight employees (out of the 642). Observers said the hotel had been viewed as relatively safe because the entrance is at the back of the building and the Australian prime minister often stays there. The hotel was 80 percent occupied at the time of the 12:45 p.m. lunchtime blast. Its 33 floors have 333 rooms. Windows 21 floors up were broken; windows in neighboring buildings were also shattered. The nearby Mutiara Plaza high-rise lost all windows on the side facing the hotel. At least eight cars and limos were destroyed by fire. The hotel is managed by the Bethesda, Maryland-based Marriott International firm for Tan Kian, a Chinese–Indonesian businessman. Marriott stock dropped 78 cents to $40.04.

Most of those injured were Indonesians. The hotel's ground-floor restaurant was occupied by 250 customers at the time of the explosion. Irna Fahrianti, 19, who was training to be a waitress, was hit in the leg. Waiter Gede Susriawawan, 27, had a forehead gash from flying glass. Hospital emergency rooms listed names: Astrid Wikastri; Agus; USA; Oscar, 24; and Pieter, 37.

The explosion went off on the day that JI spiritual leader Abubakar Baasyir was testifying at his treason trial. On August 10, he told Muslims to not worry about being labeled terrorists. Officials at a school he founded confirmed that the suicide bomber, Asnar Latin Sani, 28, had graduated from the school in 1994.

Indonesian police reported that they had found documents the previous month in a raid in Semarang in central Java that listed the hotel's district as a possible terrorist target. Authorities arrested eight JI members and seized 2,000 pounds of potassium chlorate, a fertilizer compound that can be used in explosives. U.S. officials and Marriott employees said they had not been warned. Officials from the nearby Park Lane Jakarta and Sahid Jaya hotels, and from the Jakarta Convention Center also had not been warned.

Police released a sketch of Asnar, the man who bought the van for $3,000 a fortnight earlier, which some officials believed was detonated with a cell phone. Other reports said it was a suicide attack and that the killer's head was found nearby; parts of his body were found on the third floor. Police were searching for DNA samples of

the suspect to match those of a severed hand found nearby.

The Jakarta bureau of Singapore's *Straits Times* newspaper received a call from JI saying the bombing was a "bloody warning" to the president to stop the crackdown on Islamic militants.

The defense minister claimed that the perpetrators had trained with al Qaeda in Afghanistan and Pakistan.

On October 28, 2003, Indonesian police, including members of Special Detachment 88, arrested key bombing suspects and alleged JI members in a resort town. The suspects included Tohir, purported JI field commander, and Ismail, the purchaser of the vehicle used in the bombing.

On June 23, 2004, a Jakarta court sentenced Malikul Zurkoni, a Muslim extremist, to three years in prison for storing the explosives used in the blast. He gave TNT and detonators to JI's chief bomb maker, known as Dr. Azahari, who remained at large.

In late June 2004, prosecutors opened the case against Rusman Gunawan (alias Gun Gun), 27, arrested September 22, 2003, in Pakistan. Gunawan is the younger brother of JI leader Riduan Isamuddi (alias Hambali). Prosecutors charged him with providing $50,000 to the terrorists behind the attack. Gunawan had been living as a student in Pakistan when his brother asked him to send the money from Amar Baluchi to the planners of the attack via various intermediaries. Gunawan allegedly led al Ghuraba, a group of militant Indonesian and Malaysian students living in Karachi; several received weapons training. Gunawan was detained in late 2003 after his brother was captured in Thailand. Pakistan turned him over to Indonesian authorities with five other students. Three faced terrorism charges in Indonesia; two were released for lack of evidence.

On October 15, 2004, Indonesian prosecutors charged militant Muslim cleric Abubakar Baasyir, 66, under a new antiterror law, accusing him of leading the JI and encouraging terrorist acts, including the Marriott bombing. His lawyers noted that the constitutional court had ruled that the 2003 law could not be applied retroactively and much of the state's evidence predated the law. 03080501

August 5, 2003. *Iraq.* At 11:30 a.m., a remotely controlled antitank mine exploded under the car of Fred Bryant, an American civilian defense contractor delivering mail to U.S. troops, killing him. He was the first American civilian killed in a spate of attacks that had previously targeted American soldiers. He worked for the Houston-based Kellogg Brown and Root, a subsidiary of Halliburton Company. The bomb exploded as he was driving to the Tikrit North Airfield. Two soldiers from the 720th Military Police Battalion, who were part of the military police convoy escorting him, were injured. He was part of a team supporting the army project called Material Company Logcap III.

August 5, 2003. *India.* Two people were injured by mortar shelling in Dhar Galoon, Kashmir. No one claimed credit.

August 5, 2003. *India.* Terrorists shot to death one person in Katjidhok, Kashmir. No one claimed credit.

August 7, 2003. *Iraq.* At 11:00 a.m., a car (or green minivan, or truck) bomb exploded at the Jordanian Embassy in Baghdad's upscale Mansour district, killing 19 people and injuring more than 50. Many of those injured were waiting for visas. A compact car landed on the roof of a neighboring three-story building. The dead included Mohammed Obeid. Among the injured was Utba Thakafy, a driver for the UN World Health Organization (WHO), who was inside the building delivering a letter when his leg was hit by debris. A fellow WHO driver was pulled out of a demolished car. Four Iraqi police guarding the embassy were killed. No Americans were at the scene. The embassy had received a written threat the previous day. A mob of Iraqis ripped up photos of the Jordanian king and his late father but were quickly dispersed. 03080701

August 7, 2003. *Afghanistan.* At 4:00 a.m., 40 suspected Taliban members in four vehicles fired assault rifles at a government office in the south, killing 6 Afghan soldiers and a driver for Mercy Corps, a U.S. aid organization located in Deshu district.

August 7, 2003. *Colombia.* Police seized three and a half tons of explosives in a rural area 15 miles south of Bogota and arrested four members of the Revolutionary Armed Forces of Colombia (FARC) suspected of planning an attack on President Alvaro Uribe during his first anniversary in office.

August 7, 2003. *Russia.* Chechen rebels shot down a Russian military helicopter with a shoulder-fired missile in the Chechen mountains, killing three crew members.

August 9, 2003. *United States.* Seattle-Tacoma International Airport authorities arrested two Pakistani men who were on the antiterrorist "no fly" list. They were held on immigration charges. One suspect, 36, paid cash for a one-way ticket to New York. He attempted to walk away leaving his ticket on the counter. The ticket agent summoned help in detaining the man, who had a British Columbia, Canada, driver's license. The second man, 29, who also paid cash, had a New York driver's license.

August 10, 2003. *Eritrea.* Terrorists attacked a vehicle in Adobha carrying Eritreans working for the U.S. charity Mercy Corps, killing two people and injuring three. No one claimed credit; Eritrean authorities blamed the Eritrean Islamic Jihad. 03081001

August 12, 2003. *Israel.* At 9:10 a.m., a Palestinian suicide bomber killed Yehezkel Yeketieli, 43, a construction worker as he shopped for breakfast for his wife and two children in eastern Rosh Haayin, a Tel Aviv suburb. Fourteen people were injured. The al-Aqsa Martyrs Brigades claimed credit. Khamis Jarwan, 18, from the Askar refugee camp outside Nablus, wearing an explosives-packed knapsack, walked past a Russian-born security guard at the Half Price supermarket in a shopping mall.

At 10:00 a.m., 14 miles to the east, another Nablus suicide bomber killed Erez Hershkovitz, 21, a recent high school graduate and resident of Elon Moreh settlement, and injured three other hitchhikers at a small bus kiosk at the highway intersection near the Ariel settlement. The bombing injured six people. Hamas claimed credit. Islam Yousef Qafisha wore a green shirt and an explosives belt.

Prime Minister Ariel Sharon stopped the planned release of 76 Palestinian prisoners. The next day, Israeli troops leveled the West Bank refugee camp family home of one of the suicide bombers, described as a 17-year-old street vendor.

August 12, 2003. *United States.* Federal officials in Newark, New Jersey, arrested British citizen and arms dealer Hemant Lakhani, 68, charging him with selling Russian shoulder-fired SA-18 missiles to agents posing as al Qaeda terrorists planning to take down U.S. planes on U.S. soil. Police in New York arrested Muslim and Malaysian resident Moinuddeen Ahmed Hameed and Orthodox Jew and Manhattan jewelry dealer Yehuda Abraham, 76, who ran a *hawala* that wired Lakhani, who is of Indian descent, the funds overseas for the Grouse/Igla missiles. Lakhani had approached Russian criminals for an SA-18 as part of what would have been a longer-term deal for 50 more for $5 million and a separate deal for tons of C-4 plastique. The Russian Federal Security Service (FSB) alerted the United States of the purchase attempt and provided an inert SA-18 for the sting operation. The trio were initially held without bail, although on August 15, a judge set Abraham's bail at $10 million. Abraham posted the bond on August 20. Lakhani was charged with providing material support to terrorists and illegal weapons dealing. The FBI taped 150 conversations Lakhani had with their undercover agents, include his praise of bin Laden and the

September 11 attacks. In January 2002, when an FBI informant claiming to be part of a Somali group seeking antiaircraft guns and missiles talked to Lakhani, the arms dealer said bin Laden "straightened them all out" and "did a good thing." In April 2002, when the informant said he represented a buyer who needed missiles for jihad against planes, Lakhani observed, "The Americans are bastards." Abraham was arraigned on charges of arranging a $30,000 payment for the first missile; the FBI eventually paid $86,500 for it. Hameed, charged with operating an unlicensed money-transmitting business, was brought into the deal a week before the arrests to handle a payment of $500,000 for the additional missiles. was charged with conspiracy to operate an unlicensed money transmitting business.

On September 4, Lakhani's bail hearing was postponed to September 11 so that prosecutors could present a witness to bolster its case.

On December 18, prosecutors said Lakhani also offered to deliver tanks, antiaircraft guns, and a radioactive "dirty bomb." He was represented by attorney Henry E. Klingeman, who said his client was not a terrorist and had no history of illegal arms trafficking.

On March 30, 2004, Abraham pleaded guilty to unwittingly handling a $30,000 payment for the smugglers. He could be fined $250,000 and sentenced to five years in prison.

August 12, 2003. *Thailand.* At 11:00 p.m., a dozen Thai antiterrorist agents, working with the CIA, broke into Number 601 at an apartment building in Ayutthaya and arrested Nurjaman Riduan Isamuddin (alias Hambali), 39, an Indonesian. Isamuddin is al Qaeda's top strategist in Southeast Asia and leader of Jemaah Islamiah. The sleeping Isamuddin did not have time to awake and fire his handgun. He was with his Malaysian wife, Noralwizah Lee, in a $75 per month apartment. Authorities also arrested two Malaysian lieutenants with him in Ayutthaya, 60 miles north of Bangkok. Isamuddin was fingered by Muslim Thais and by a phone intercept.

He had moved between Thailand, Malaysia, Cambodia, and Burma.

Isamuddin was brought to an unnamed country for questioning on:

- plans to bomb the U.S. embassies in Manila and Singapore
- mid-1990s abortive plot to blow up 11 U.S. planes over the Pacific
- August 2000 car bombing of the Philippine ambassador's house in Jakarta, with the assistance of the Moro Islamic Liberation Front (MILF)
- plans to bomb 11 sites in Indonesia on Christmas Eve, 2000
- plans for car bombings on the U.S. and Israeli embassies in Singapore in the summer of 2001
- September 11 attacks. He had been videotaped at a January 2000 meeting in Malaysia with two of the hijackers. He had also arranged for flying lessons for Zacarias Moussaoui, and obtained a letter of accreditation for him to a U.S. flying school.
- October 2002 bombings in Bali that killed 202 people
- August 2003 bombing of the J. W. Marriott Hotel in Indonesia that killed ten people
- his interest in recruiting pilots for terrorist operations

August 13, 2003. *Saudi Arabia.* British Airways canceled all flights to and from Saudi Arabia after receiving information about a terrorist threat.

August 13, 2003. *India.* A bomb attached to a bicycle exploded outside the State Bank of India branch in Bandipora, Kashmir, injuring 31 people. No one claimed credit.

August 14, 2003. *Canada.* Canadian officials arrested 19 men between the ages of 18 and 33 who followed "a pattern of suspicious behavior," including one man who took multiengine commercial pilot flying lessons over the Pickering Nuclear Power Plant. Instructors said he was an "unmotivated student" who had taken the lessons for three years; the normal course is one year. Police found two of the men outside the gates

of the plant at 4:15 a.m. one day in April 2002. The duo asked that "they be allowed to enter the perimeter in order to go for a walk on the beach." Some of their associates had access to nuclear gauges which could be used to make a dirty bomb. One of their associates who lived with a suspect worked for the Global Relief Foundation, which supports al Qaeda. Some of the men lived in two apartments that had unexplained fires. The group faced immigration charges and were held as possible threats to national security. All but one had connections to the Punjab Province of Pakistan. Two of the men were represented by attorney Mohammed Syed.

On August 27, immigration officials said that they should be detained indefinitely. They were in Canada before September 5, 2001. The Project Thread investigators said 18 suspects were Pakistani; the other was an Indian.

On September 8, Immigration and Refugee Board adjudicator Ilze Decarlo ruled that Manzoor Qadar Joyia should remain in jail while police continued to investigate. "More than two and a half years after he arrived, what he was up to remains a mystery." He had applied in Ontario to marry a woman who lived in Pensacola, Florida, but there was no evidence that they had married. A tenant in his apartment building told the superintendent that he saw men from the apartment throw paper bags out the window to a man in a waiting taxi. The tenant claimed there were passports and other ID documents in a bag. Joyia was represented by attorney Tariq Shah.

August 15, 2003. *United States.* Two Washington, D.C., offices of the Iranian National Council of Resistance of Iran (variant Mujahedeen Khalq, MEK, and National Council of Resistance) were ordered closed and had their assets frozen.

August 15, 2003. *India.* A hand grenade was thrown at a police patrol in Pakheropa, Kashmir, but missed, landed in a crowd of bystanders, and injured 18 people. No one claimed credit.

August 16, 2003. *Saudi Arabia.* Police in southern Jizan Province arrested between 11 and 21 Saudi and Bangladeshi militants and seized a large cache of weapons, including rockets and explosive chemicals. The raid took place in a village near Yemen.

August 16, 2003. *United Kingdom.* London police arrested Muslim leader Abdurahman Alamoudi, 51, when they found $340,000 in undeclared cash in his luggage as he was preparing to travel to Damascus, Syria. He was freed after forfeiting the cash. He said an unidentified Libyan official gave him the money in a London hotel room.

On September 28, 2003, U.S. authorities arrested Alamoudi as he attempted to enter the United States. On October 23, 2003, he was indicted on charges of money laundering and fraud. The 18-count indictment said he assisted al Qaeda, Hamas, and other terrorists, and that he took hundreds of thousands of dollars from Libya and attempted to hide its origin and purpose. He was held without bond. One of the charities he sent $160,000 to was implicated in the foiled December 2000 millennium plot by al Qaeda to bomb Los Angeles International Airport and the Seattle Space Needle. The government said he had been in contact with eight known terrorists. He was represented by attorneys Stanley L. Cohen and James P. McLoughlin, Jr. Alamoudi, a naturalized U.S. citizen born in Eritrea, is director of the American Muslim Foundation in Alexandria, Virginia. A bail hearing was set for October 29. His trial was later set for August 2004. Charges included taking money from a nation designated as a terrorist patron, attempting to launder money, and lying to officials when he denied Hamas ties.

In mid-June 2004, the *Washington Post* and *New York Times* reported that Alamoudi, who was being held in an Alexandria jail on 34 counts of money smuggling, had claimed that Libyan leader Moammar Qadhafi intended to use the money to finance the assassination of Saudi government leader Crown Prince Abdullah. The *Post*

said his story was corroborated by Libyan intelligence Col. Mohamed Ismael, who was in Saudi custody. Alamoudi said he met twice with Qadhafi in May and June of 2003 regarding the plot. The plot was to involve the use of small arms or rocket-propelled grenades. Ismael then traveled to Egypt, where he was arrested. On November 27, 2003, Saudi authorities arrested Ismael's confederates at a Mecca hotel as they awaited cash payments from their Libyan handlers.

U.S. officials were quoted as believing that Saad Faqih, a radical Saudi dissident in London, was involved. He admitted he had known Alamoudi for years.

On July 30, 2004, Alamoudi pleaded guilty to illegally moving cash from Libya and admitted involvement in the assassination plot, working with two Saudi dissidents—Mohammad Massari and Saad Faqih. He said he obtained nearly $1 million from Libya. Two other guilty pleas covered charges of tax violations and lying on his immigration form. He faced 23 years in prison; he faced life without the plea bargain. The Eritrean-born Alamoudi lost his U.S. citizenship with the plea and has signed a deportation order. On October 15, U.S. District Judge Claude M. Hilton sentenced Alamoudi to the maximum 23-year prison term.

August 18, 2003. *Pakistan.* Al-Arabiya television aired an audiotape by Abdur Rahman Najdi, a Saudi-born al Qaeda terrorist sought by the United States. Najdi called on Muslims to join the fight in Iraq against the U.S.–led occupation and to overthrow the Saudi royal family, whom he termed U.S. puppets.

August 18, 2003. *United States.* Two packages containing wires and propane canisters were placed outside a home belonging to Charles Schwab, 66, and a Carmel office of the brokerage he founded. The Santa Cruz bomb squad blew up the packages. No one was hurt; no note was found; no one was charged. The Carmel device was found at 7:15 a.m. The other device was found in Schwab's driveway and blown up at 4:15 p.m.

August 19, 2003. *Algeria.* A 55-year-old man from Boumerdes, which had been leveled by an earthquake on May 21, attempted to hijack an Air Algerie jet, threatening the crew with what he claimed was a grenade. He said that he had lost everything and no longer wanted to live in Algeria. The quake killed 2,300 people. He surrendered to security officials. 03081901

August 19, 2003. *Israel.* At 9:10 p.m., Raed Abdul Hamid Misk, 29, a cleric at the Mosque of the Arches, became another Hamas suicide bomber from Hebron when he set off a 12-pound bomb loaded with ball bearings and other metal objects in a double-cabin Egged Number 2 bus in an ultra-Orthodox Jewish neighborhood in Jerusalem. He killed 21 people, including 5 Americans and 6 children, and injured more than 140 people, including 40 children. The blast went off across from the Synagogue of the Jews of the Caucasus on Shmuel Hanavi Street in the Beit Israel neighborhood north of the Old City. Three of the dead children were U.S. citizens: Itzak Reinitz, 9, whose father, Mordechai, 49, also was killed; Thillia Nathanson, 3; and Eli Zarkowski, 3 months, whose mother, Goldie, 43, also died. The dead included Shmuel Zargari, 11 months; his wounded parents were in intensive care. American Yessucher Dov Reinitz and two other boys aged 12 and 15 also died. Among those injured was Tzvi Weiss, 18, a Brooklyn, New York, native. Shira Cohen, 18 months, lost an eye. Her mother, Ora Cohen, 42, and her one-month-old son, Elchanan, were also injured. Yaakov Porus, 21, a student at a religious school and son of an Israeli parliamentarian, was hit in the eyes by shrapnel. Hamas and the Islamic Jihad claimed credit. Israeli authorities blew up the bomber's family home.

By January 2004, bus driver Hasser Hirbawi, 40, an Israeli Arab who lives in Jerusalem, was still unable to work. When the bomb went off, he was thrown down the front steps of the bus and a mounted television set hit him in the head and back. He sustained a slipped disc and half hearing loss in each ear. He has a wife and six children. 03081902

August 19, 2003. *Iraq.* At 4:30 p.m., an East European-built Kamaz flat-bed cement truck crashed into a security wall under construction at the UN headquarters in Baghdad's Canal Hotel and set off more than 1,000 pounds of Soviet-made explosives. The explosion killed the driver and 23 others, including 19 UN staff members, and injured 160 people. Among those killed was Sergio Vieira de Mello, 55, a Brazilian citizen who led UN efforts in Baghdad and whom many suggested would become the next UN Secretary General. Also killed were:

- Saad Hermiz, who worked in the UN coffee shop
- Martha Teas, a U.S. citizen
- Arthur C. Helton, a prominent New York immigration lawyer and senior fellow at the Council on Foreign Relations who was an authority on refugees and humanitarian issues
- Nadia Younes, 57, Vieira de Mello's chief of staff, an Egyptian who had been deputy spokeswoman for UN Secretary General Javier Perez de Cuellar from 1988-1993
- Gillian Clark, 47, a Canadian aid worker who worked for the Christian Children's Fund, an American nongovernmental organization
- Richard "Rick" Hooper, special assistant to Vieira de Mello and a 1990 Georgetown Master of Science in Foreign Studies specializing in Arab Studies (he was the first Georgetown MSFS graduate to be killed in the line of duty)
- Christopher Klein-Beekman, a Canadian who served as UNICEF program coordinator in Iraq

Among the injured were:

- UN employee Jean-Jacques Frere, a senior public health specialist, who was hit by shrapnel in his left arm
- Hameed Hassoun, 51, who was at the neurological hospital to visit his son, Majid Hameed, 16

- Majid Kadhim, 39, who was hit while being driven home in a car
- Ahmed Nima, 47, an Iraqi policeman.

The blast left a 15-foot-wide crater and damaged the neighboring National Spinal Cord Injury Center hospital and a tourism training institute. Various groups—Saddam loyalists, al Qaeda, Ansar al-Islam—were suspected. Several Islamic groups outside Iraq, including the previously unknown Armed Vanguards of the Second Muhammad Army, claimed credit. Israeli officials said the truck came from Syria.

On August 26, the UN Security Council unanimously approved a resolution that declared attacks on UN and other humanitarian workers in armed conflicts a war crime. The resolution called for the prosecution of anyone who attempts to harm them. The sponsors dropped an initial reference to the International Criminal Court after the United States objected.

On October 10, U.S. military forces announced that in September they had arrested one or two suspected foreign terrorists linked to the UN and Jordanian embassy bombings. The duo was arrested in a raid on a house in Ramadi, west of Baghdad. In the firefight, two soldiers died and seven were injured.

On March 29, 2004, UN Secretary General Kofi Annan accepted the resignation of Tun Myat of Myanmar, the UN's security coordinator, who was deemed "oblivious" to the worsening security situation in Baghdad weeks before the attack. Annan demoted Ramiro Lopes da Silva of Portugal, who had been the UN's senior humanitarian coordinator in Iraq. He was to return to his former job at the UN World Food Program. UN security official Robert Adolph, also reassigned, and da Silva were barred from taking assignments involving security of UN staffers. Paul Aghadjanian of Jordan, chief of the UN Office of Humanitarian Coordination in Iraq, and Pa Momodou Sinyan, a Gambian who is the UN agency's building manager, were charged with misconduct; Annan initiated disciplinary proceedings. A panel headed by retired UN official Gerald Walzer said the 15-member steering group, led by UN Deputy Secretary General Louise Frechette of Canada, failed to exercise "due care of diligence" in assessing the security situation in Iraq. Annan rejected Frechette's resignation. 03081903

August 19, 2003. *United States.* The government alleged in an affidavit in federal court in Virginia that Muslim charities gave $3.7 million to BMI, Inc., an Islamic investment company in New Jersey that passed the money to terrorist groups. Some $10 million from unnamed donors in Jiddah, Saudi Arabia, comprised the group's endowment. The affidavit said that BMI founder Soliman S. Biheiri, an Egyptian, who had been indicted two weeks earlier for making false statements to obtain U.S. residence and other immigration charges, did business with other designated terrorist financiers. One of BMI's chief investors was Saudi businessman Yasin Qadi, whom the United States and UN named a "specially designated global terrorist" in October 2001 for his support of al Qaeda and Hamas. Another BMI investor was Hamas leader Mousa Abu Marzook. Biheiri's laptop computer also had contact information on UN and U.S.–listed terrorists Ghaled Himmat and Youssef Nada, members of the Muslim Brotherhood.

On January 12, 2004, U.S. District Judge T. S. Ellis, III, sentenced Biheiri to a year in prison; Biheiri had been convicted in October for lying under oath to obtain U.S. citizenship, a charge that usually carries a six-month sentence. Prosecutors had sought ten years, saying that he had business dealings with Marzook, including funneling hundreds of thousands of dollars to him. Judge Ellis said the government had failed to prove that Biheiri had "intended to support a crime of terrorism" by obtaining U.S. citizenship. Biheiri was represented by attorney Jim Clark. Judge Ellis also ruled that Biheiri must return to Egypt, where he hadn't lived for 30 years. Biheiri had earlier forfeited his U.S. citizenship.

On May 10, 2004, Biheiri was indicted for lying to federal agents about his business and personal connections with Hamas leader Marzook and Sami al-Arian, a former Florida professor charged with being a leader of Palestine Islamic Jihad (PIJ). He was also charged with illegally possessing and using a U.S. passport. The charges carried a minimum 20-year sentence. The al-Arian charge was dismissed in late September or early October 2004.

On October 6, 2004, in U.S. District Court in Alexandria, Biheiri pleaded guilty to illegally possessing and using a U.S. passport to enter the United States in 2003. After his plea, he went on trial on a separate charge of lying to federal agents about his ties to terrorists. Biheiri was represented by attorney Danny C. Onorato.

August 19, 2003. *Serbia.* Two hand grenades were thrown into the courtyard of a Bujanova house belonging to Ramiz Ramizi, an ethnic Albanian, wounding his 8-year-old grandson and four other family members. No one claimed credit.

August 20, 2003. *Yemen.* The U.S. State Department advised Americans to avoid travel to Yemen, saying that al Qaeda was trying to regroup there and could target Americans.

August 20, 2003. *Iraq.* The British Embassy was evacuated after receiving a bomb threat. 03082001

August 21, 2003. *United States.* Shortly before 5:00 a.m., arson destroyed 20 and damaged another 20 Hummer H2s and several Chevrolet Tahoe SUVs and destroyed the warehouse at Clippinger Chevrolet in West Covina, an eastern suburb of Los Angeles, causing at least $2.3 million damage. Several vehicles had been sprayed "ELF," "Fat, Lazy Americans," "Greedy Little Pig," and "I ♥ pollution." In three separate attacks at dealerships in neighboring Monrovia, Arcadia, and Duarte, dozens of other vehicles were painted with antipollution graffiti. The Earth Liberation Front Web site said that while the attacks were "ELF actions," they had not heard from the perpetrators. No injuries were reported.

An individual later identified as William Jensen Cottrell used an alias to send an e-mail to the *Los Angeles Times* in September to claim credit for the ELF. In a January 2004 interview with the FBI, Cottrell denied involvement.

On September 12, federal agents arrested Joshua Thomas Connole, 25, at his Pomona, California, home.

On March 17, 2004, William Jensen Cottrell, 23, a second year graduate student in physics at the California Institute of Technology, was indicted on nine counts of arson and conspiracy in connection with the firebombing and vandalizing of 125 SUVs. He had been arrested the previous week in the Pasadena apartment of his girlfriend, miles from the attacks. He faced a mandatory 35-year sentence. U.S. Magistrate Judge Carolyn Turchin denied bond, saying other targets of the investigation had fled and it was doubtful that his father, a North Carolina physician, could ensure his appearance in court. Cottrell pleaded not guilty. The trial was set for October 2004. On August 21, 2004, Cottrell was linked to one SUV dealership by DNA taken from a hair found at the scene.

August 21, 2003. *Israel.* The government retaliated for the suicide bombing two days earlier by firing a missile at a car that killed Ismail Abu Shanab, a political leader of Hamas, and two people riding in his car and injured 30 bystanders.

August 22, 2003. *United States.* President Bush froze the assets of six leaders of the Islamic Resistance Movement (Hamas) and called on allies to join him by cutting off European sources of donations. The individuals were:

- Sheik Ahmed Yassin, the leader of Hamas in Gaza
- Imad Khalil al-Alami, a member of the Hamas Political Bureau in Damascus, Syria
- Usama Hamdan, a senior Hamas leader in Lebanon
- Khalid Mishaal, head of the Hamas Political Bureau and Executive Committee in Damascus

- Mousa Abu Marzook, deputy chief of the Hamas Political Bureau in Syria
- Abdel Aziz Rantisi, a Hamas leader in Gaza, reporting to Sheik Yassin

The president also banned U.S. financial transactions with five charities based in Austria, the United Kingdom, France, Lebanon, and Switzerland that accept donations for Hamas and support violence. They were identified as:

- Commite de Bienfaisance et de Secours aux Palestiniens, of France
- Association de Secours Palestinien, of Switzerland
- Palestinian Relief and Development Fund (Interpal), headquartered in the United Kingdom
- Palestinian Association, in Austria
- Sanibil Association for Relief and Development, based in Lebanon

August 24, 2003. *Colombia.* A bomb exploded in the hands of a passenger getting off a boat in Puerto Rico village, killing her and five other people, including a child, and wounding more than two dozen. The boat was carrying 56 passengers on the Ariari River. Government troops in the area had taken fire from the Revolutionary Armed Forces of Colombia (FARC).

August 25, 2003. *India.* Two taxi bombs went off within 15 minutes of each other in parking lots in Bombay, the country's financial capital, killing 53 people and injuring another 160. One bomb went off at the Gateway of India tourist area and another in a jewelry market in the Zaveri Bazaar. Police blamed the Students Islamic Movement of India (SIMI) and the Lashkar-i-Taiba. Among those killed was a Muslim, Abdul Mullah, who worked at a shoe shop.

Several hours later, authorities found nine detonators on train tracks 75 miles north of Bombay.

In early September, police arrested a Bombay motorized-rickshaw driver, his wife, and teenage daughter for planting the bomb in a taxi near the Gateway of India.

On September 12, police shot to death Naseer, believed to be the mastermind, and another man in a gunfight in central Bombay. The duo was fleeing in a car containing hidden detonators, explosives, and guns.

August 25, 2003. *Colombia.* Rebels were suspected of firing at a U.S. drug-spraying plane piloted by a U.S. contractor, forcing him to make a crash landing 220 miles north of Bogota. The pilot was injured. 03082501

August 25, 2003. *Russia.* Three bombs exploded simultaneously in Krasnodar, killing 4 and injuring more than 20.

August 27, 2003. *Russia.* Magomedsalikh Gusayev, a Russian official in Dagestan who opposed radical Islamic ideology, was killed by a car bomb in Makhachkala, the Dagestani capital. He had led a crackdown against Wahhabis.

August 27, 2003. *France.* Suspected mercenaries told investigators that they had plotted to assassinate Ivory Coast President Laurent Bagbo. Former Army Sgt. Ibrahim Coulibaly, the leading suspect, denied the charges.

August 27, 2003. *Nepal.* Maoist rebels ended the seven-month cease-fire and said they would withdraw from the peace talks.

August 28, 2003. *United States.* Two homemade bombs went off at the Chiron Corporation's headquarters in San Francisco, California. The Americans for Medical Progress said the explosions could have been the work of animal rights activists. Police had no suspects.

August 28, 2003. *Israel.* Hamas fired a Qassam rocket into the outskirts of Ashkelon, six miles north of the Gaza Strip. No damage was reported.

August 29, 2003. *Israel.* A al-Aqsa Martyrs Brigades gunman shot to death Shalom Harmelech, 25, a Jewish settler, in his car in the West Bank. The car overturned east of Ramallah. Limor, his pregnant wife, was wounded. She delivered a healthy baby girl by Caesarian section.

August 29, 2003. *Israel.* Palestinian gunmen fired on Israeli soldiers. No injuries were reported by either side.

August 29, 2003. *Iraq.* A car bomb exploded in Najaf next to the holy shrine of Imam Ali, Iraq's most sacred Shi'ite shrine. The explosion killed at least 125 people, including Ayatollah Mohammed Bakir Hakim, 64, son of the leader of the Supreme Council for the Islamic Revolution in Iraq (SCIRI). He had supported the U.S. occupation. Suspects included rivals in the SCIRI, al Qaeda, and other Shi'ites, Wahhabis, or Saddam loyalists. Hussein's agents assassinated one of Hakim's brothers in 1988. Among the 200 injured were Mazdi Mehamin, a Shi'ite pilgrim from Iran; Ghalib Abed, a fabric store worker who was cut on his arms, legs, and shoulder by flying glass; peanut vendor Qassim Jabr; and Yusuf Ali, a young cloth salesman whose stomach was torn apart. Mustafa Hassan, 14, had a severed nerve in his right calf and no feeling in his lower leg. Casualties included Iraqis, Iranians, and pilgrims from India. Said Ali Rada of Gujarat, India, had injuries to his head and body. The 12-year-old son of Saed Hussein Hammami needed ten stitches for a cut in his scalp. Other casualties included Aida Ali Abbas; Mohammed Nasser; Abbas Hussein Ali; Ali Abbas, 20; Zahra Hussein Ali Yusuf; and Hussein Abed Jawad.

U.S. investigators said it appeared that the car bomb had been parked for 24 hours on a curbside and was remotely detonated. Investigators said it was either an SUV or a BMW. The explosives were believed to be the same as those used in the August 19 bombing of the UN headquarters and the Jordanian Embassy on August 7.

Five or six Iraqis were taken into custody by nightfall.

On September 1, a new audiotape purporting to be by Saddam Hussein denied involvement in the attack. 03082901

August 30, 2003. *India.* Police killed two members of Jaish-i-Muhammad in a New Delhi park hours after explosives were confiscated during the arrest of three people. Police said that they had prevented a spectacular attack.

September 2003. *Peru.* Four Chilean defendants were retried and convicted of membership in the Tupac Amaru Revolutionary Movement (MRTA) and participation in an attack on the Peru-North American Cultural Institute and a kidnap and murder in 1993.

September 2003. *Egypt.* Interior Minister Habib Adli told *al Mussawar* that the government had arrested 23 men and was seeking 2 more on charges of belonging to a terrorist group. They included 19 Egyptians, 3 Bangladeshis, a Turk, an Indonesian, and a Malaysian who were planning to fight U.S. forces in Iraq.

September 2003. *Iraq.* Coalition forces arrested Ansar al-Islam members in Kirkuk who were transporting 1,200 kilograms of TNT.

September 2003. *Sudan.* A court convicted a Syrian engineer and two Sudanese of training a group of Saudis, Palestinians, and others to carry out attacks in Iraq, Eritrea, Sudan, and Israel. The court said the Syrian was training others to carry out attacks against U.S. forces in Iraq.

September 2003. *Ecuador.* An army captain was arrested and accused of providing operational information to the Revolutionary Armed Forces of Colombia (FARC).

September 2003. *Yemen.* Late in the month, authorities arrested several members of an al Qaeda affiliated cell planning attacks against a variety of targets in the country.

September 2003. *Poland.* Police arrested six people for plotting to sell more than a pound of radioactive cesium for $153,000. Police seized large quantities of guns and explosives.

September 2003. *Poland.* Authorities arrested an Algerian wanted in Algeria on terrorist charges.

September 2003. *Azerbaijan.* U.S. and Georgian officials tracked down Abu Ayat, a one-legged al Qaeda commander, and two dozen guards in Baku.

September 2003. *Lebanon.* Military tribunals began hearing the cases of more than 40 individuals charged with planning or executing a series of attacks on U.S. restaurants and planning to assassinate the U.S. ambassador to Lebanon and bomb the U.S. Embassy in Beirut.

September 1, 2003. *Morocco.* Members of the POLISARIO Front rebel group seeking independence for the Western Sahara finally released 243 Moroccan prisoners, some of whom they had held for three decades. The International Committee of the Red Cross flew the former hostages from Polisario camps in southwest Algeria to a military base near Agadir, Morocco.

September 2, 2003. *Israel.* Soldiers at a checkpoint near Jenin shot to death a Palestinian man who got out of his car pointing a gun at them. He was a student leader, 21, of Islamic Jihad.

September 2, 2003. *Turkey.* KADEK (PKK) rebels announced the end of their five-year cease-fire with the government because Ankara had not lived up to its part of the truce.

September 3, 2003. *Russia.* Two bombs exploded simultaneously on a rail bed, destroying an early morning commuter train carrying 700 passengers in the Stavropol region bordering Chechnya. At least 6 people died and 92 were injured, a dozen seriously. Most of the dead were students going to class. The train was going from Kislovodsk to Mineralniye Vody and was near the Northern Caucasus spa town of Pyatigorsk. Criminal gangs were suspected.

September 3, 2003. *Iran.* Six shots were fired from a passing motorbike at the British Embassy, hitting first and second floor windows and walls

but causing no injuries. The British closed its embassy. Tehran recalled Morteza Sarmadi, its ambassador to London, during a period of tension over the British arrest of former Iranian Ambassador to Argentina Hadi Soleimanpour. Soleimanpour was held after Argentina requested his extradition for the 1994 bombing of the Jewish community center in Buenos Aires. 03090301

September 4, 2003. *United States.* The Department of Homeland Security warned that al Qaeda was considering new types of attacks in the United States using car bombs, men dressed as women, and hijacking planes from nearby countries and crashing them into U.S. targets.

September 5, 2003. *United States.* Abelhaleem Ashqar, 45, a former Howard University professor and Hamas activist, turned himself in to authorities in Chicago and was jailed for the second time in five years for refusing to address a grand jury investigating the group's finances and activities. He had been granted immunity in an earlier case and was held in contempt. He was represented by attorney Zuhair Nubani.

On October 10, Ashqar was indicted on criminal contempt charges for refusing to testify despite a grant of immunity. He had been held for civil contempt; the charge was upgraded to a criminal charge. Ashqar was on a hunger strike and was being fed intravenously.

On November 3, he was released on $1 million bail.

September 5, 2003. *Spain.* Authorities detained for questioning Syrian-born al-Jazeera journalist Tayssir Alouni, 48, a Spanish citizen. He had interviewed bin Laden shortly after September 11. He was taken into custody in Alfacar, a suburb of Granada. Judge Baltasar Garzon questioned him about his ties with Osama bin Laden. Al-Jazeera Brussels Bureau Chief Ahmad Kamel said, "Al-Jazeera condemns this arrest, and we ask for the liberation of our colleague immediately because he is a journalist, just a journalist. He is not a member of al Qaeda for sure, for sure." He was suspected of relaying messages and funds to al Qaeda cells in Europe.

On September 11, Judge Garzon charged Alouni with membership in an armed group and ordered him jailed in Soto del Real prison. Garzon said that "removed from his work as a journalist but taking advantage of it, he carries out support, financing and coordination, which are the characteristics of a qualified militant of the organization." Alouni's name appeared in an indictment against Osama bin Laden and 34 other terrorist suspects. Judge Garzon freed Alouni on $7,000 bail on October 23 after his lawyers complained that the reporter had heart trouble.

On November 30, the Francisca Mateos Foundation awarded Alouni a peace prize for his coverage of the wars in Iraq and Afghanistan. The Spanish nongovernmental organization is dedicated to international cooperation and social work within Spain.

September 5, 2003. *United States.* The FBI put out a worldwide alert for Adnan El Shukrijumah, Abderraouf Jdey, Zubayr Al-Rimi, and Karim El Mejjati, who were believed to be engaged in planning for terrorist attacks. The information was provided by Khalid Sheik Mohammed, al Qaeda's operations chief. The first two individuals were the subjects of earlier FBI lookouts. The FBI provided the following information:

- Shukrijumah, 28, was Saudi-born, but carried passports issued in Guyana, Trinidad, Canada, and Saudi Arabia, a U.S. social security card, and a Florida driver's license. He was initially mentioned by Khalid Sheik Muhammad in March. He had earlier lived in south Florida, where his family resides. The FBI noted that "he is a pilot, speaks English, has false documents, and knows the country." U.S. authorities had linked an alias he had used to an Oklahoma flight school where Zacarias Moussaoui had received flight training. He apparently did not train in the United States. He was believed connected to Jose Padilla, the would-be "dirty bomber" arrested in May 2002. Police suspected he could be in Morocco.

- Jdey, 38, born in Tunisia, had lived in Montreal, Canada, where he obtained his passport. He had been sought by the United States since January 2002 when his face was seen on an al Qaeda videotape with four others who said they would conduct suicide attacks.

- El Mejjati, 35, was born in Morocco and held a Moroccan ID card. He entered the United States in 1997 and 1999. Several passports were issued for him in France. He was suspected in the May bombings in Casablanca that killed 30 people and 12 terrorists.

- Al Rimi was born in Saudi Arabia and married a Moroccan woman. Saudi authorities said he was a member of the al Qaeda cell that set off bombs on May 12 in Riyadh that killed 25 people plus 9 terrorists. His wife was arrested in June raids.

September 6, 2003. *India.* A bomb exploded in a busy marketplace in Srinagar, Kashmir, killing 6 people and injuring 37 others, including an Indian army officer. Police believed the target was the army officer. No one claimed credit.

September 7, 2003. *Dubai.* In an audiotape dated September 3 but played on September 7 on al-Arabiya Arabic television, a person claiming to be al Qaeda spokesman Abu Abdel-Rahman Najdi said, "We announce there will be new attacks inside and outside, which would make America forget the attacks of September 11…. We assure the Muslims that al Qaeda ranks have doubled…. Our coming martyrdom operations will prove to you what we are saying." The broadcast included a photo of a bearded man in a *kaffiyeh*. The speaker denied involvement in the Najaf car bombing in Iraq in August. "We strongly deny that al Qaeda had any hand in this bombing that killed Mohammed Bakir Hakim, violated the sanctity of one of God's houses and killed innocent people." The tape suggested Israeli and U.S. involvement because of Hakim's Iranian ties.

September 8, 2003. *Afghanistan.* Four Danish aid workers were jumped, tied together, and shot to death as they were coming back from installing water pumps in a southeastern village in Ghazni Province. A fifth worker who survived, but sustained bullet wounds in his legs, said the killers said, "We warned you not to work" for foreign aid groups. The five were employees of the Danish Committee for Aid to Afghan Refugees. Danish officials said at least two of the nine attackers, who were riding motorbikes, were members of the Taliban. The dead included a 23-year-old engineer who had joined DACAAR in August, a pump mechanic, a driver, and a drilling contractor. 03090801

September 8, 2003. *Spain.* Madrid authorities defused a parcel bomb hidden in a book sent to the Greek Consulate. Authorities suspected an anarchist group. 03090802

September 9, 2003. *Iraq.* A car bomb exploded outside an office used by U.S. soldiers in Irbil, killing an Iraqi and wounding 41 Iraqis, among them children from nearby houses and Iraqi Kurdish guards, and 6 U.S. Defense Department personnel. 03090901

September 9, 2003. *Israel.* At 5:55 p.m., a Hamas suicide bomber set off explosives at a hitchhiking and bus stop 150 feet from Tzrifin military base, one of the country's largest military bases, located 12 miles south of Tel Aviv near Rishon Letzion. The explosion killed 7 Israeli soldiers, 3 of them women, and wounded 15 others. The bomber was Ihad Abed Qader Abu Salim, a 19-year-old Palestinian from Rantis on the West Bank. His mother, Itaf Mirshed, 46, said, "He has taken revenge for the Palestinian people." The terrorist was a journalist student at Bir Zeit University.

At 11:19 p.m., a second Hamas suicide bomber, Ramez Simi Izzedin Abu Salim, 22, a friend and distant cousin of the first bomber, walked past sidewalk tables and set off his bombs when a guard tried to stop him inside the entrance of Café Hillel on Emek Refaim Street in an affluent Jerusalem neighborhood. There were about 50 customers at the café at the time. The explosion killed 7 people and injured 30. Among the injured was Annie Portal, 23. Naava Applebaum, 20, and her father, Detroit native Dr. David Applebaum, 50, chief of the emergency room and trauma services of Jerusalem's Shaare Zedek Medical Center, were chatting about her planned wedding the next day, when they were killed. They were buried side by side. She had just completed her national service. Her fiancé, Chanan Yaacov Sand, 20, placed a small box containing her wedding band into the grave. Two days earlier, Dr. Applebaum had addressed a seminar in New York on mass casualty medicine. He left behind a wife, Debra, and five other children. He had moved to Israel 20 years ago. He earned his medical degree at the Medical College of Ohio in Toledo. He was also an Orthodox rabbi. The terrorist was studying Islamic law at Al-Quds Open University. The attack took place near the Asaf Harofe Hospital.

Hamas did not directly claim credit, but its military wing told al-Jazeera that "the time has come for paying the bill of the daily Israeli crimes. It's no longer time for words, but time for retaliation."

The two bombers had been arrested in December 25, 2002, on suspicion of being Hamas operatives and had spent three months in prison. 03090902

September 9, 2003. *India.* Terrorists shot at a former state forest minister in Sopat, Kashmir, injuring him and killing a security officer. No one claimed credit.

September 9, 2003. *Iran.* Terrorists fired three or four shots at the British Embassy in Tehran, causing no damage or injuries. No one claimed credit. 03090903

September 10, 2003. *Qatar.* Al-Jazeera broadcast a videotape of Osama bin Laden and Ayman Zawahiri walking in rocky woods in an unidentified mountain range. The television station said the tape was probably filmed in late April or early May. The CIA verified a section of the audio as being Zawahiri's voice, but it was unclear whether bin Laden's voice was on the tape. On the tape, Zawahiri calls on his followers to "rely on God, and pounce on the Americans just as the lions pounce on their prey. Bury them in Iraq's graveyard.... We advise the mothers of the crusade soldiers, if they hope to see their sons, to quickly ask their governments to return them before they return to them in coffins." Referring to the Palestinians, Zawahiri counsels against the U.S. proposal, deeming it the "road map to hell.... Palestine will only be liberated with jihad." The bin Laden voice praised September 11's "great damage to the enemy. These persons learned from the traditions of our prophet Mohammed."

September 10, 2003. *Sweden.* Foreign Minister Anna Lindh, 46, was stabbed ten times in the arm, stomach, and chest while shopping in a Stockholm department store, dying of her wounds the next morning at Karolinska Hospital after nine hours of surgery. Police were unable to get fingerprints from the knife. Her attacker—a tall "Swedish-looking" man with shoulder-length hair and acne—dropped his knife and camouflage jacket and escaped. His image was found on a department store surveillance videotape. Police said there was no evidence that the attack was related to international terrorism or her campaign to move Sweden into the euro zone. On September 16, police detained a Swedish male drifter, 35, near a restaurant in Solna, a northwest Stockholm suburb. Two other men who had been questioned were no longer considered suspects. Prosecutors obtained a court order holding the man for another week as investigators gathered more evidence. On September 24, police arrested a new suspect and freed the previous one.

On January 6, 2004, Mijailo Mijailovic, 25, confessed during police questioning. Defense attorney Peter Althin said the killing was random. Mijailovic's DNA was found on the murder knife. Mijailovic said voices in his head told him to kill her. He faced ten years to life in prison. He was sentenced to life in prison on March 23, 2004. On July 8, 2004, the Svea Court of Appeals ruled 5 to 0 to throw out the life sentence, ruling that Mijailovic should receive treatment for his "significant psychiatric problems" that included "borderline personality disorder."

September 10, 2003. *Colombia.* A bomb attached to a horse exploded in the village of Chita in Boyaca Province, killing 8 and wounding 20. The Revolutionary Armed Forces of Colombia (FARC) was blamed.

September 11, 2003. *United States.* The U.S. State Department issued a worldwide alert for possible terrorist attacks against where Americans congregate, including places of worship, restaurants, hotels, beaches, and resorts. Chemical weapons attacks could be launched in Western Europe, according to interrogation of a captured al Qaeda operative and intercepted cell phone conversations. The cautionary bulletin said, "The U.S. government remains deeply concerned about the security of U.S. citizens overseas.... We are seeing increasing indications that al Qaeda is preparing to strike U.S. interests abroad.... We expect al Qaeda will strive for new attacks that will be more devastating than the September 11 attack, possibly involving nonconventional weapons such as chemical or biological weapons.... We also cannot rule out the potential for al Qaeda to attempt a second catastrophic attack within the U.S.... Terrorists do not distinguish between official and civilian targets. These may include facilities where American citizens and other foreigners congregate or visit."

September 11, 2003. *India.* A hand grenade thrown at a military bunker house in Srinagar, Kashmir, missed its target and killed a private citizen. Fourteen others standing nearby were injured. No one claimed credit.

September 12, 2003. *Colombia.* Eight foreign tourists—four Israelis, two Britons, a German, and a Spaniard—were kidnapped early in the morning from cabins in the Ciudad Perdida (Lost City) ruins in the Sierra Nevada de Santa

Marta mountains (some reports said September 14. The Revolutionary Armed Forces of Colombia (FARC) denied involvement, blaming the military. On September 22, Matthew Scott, 19, of London, jumped off a cliff to escape (some reports said September 25). He was found by Indians on September 23. One of his rescuers said, "He was dizzy and vomiting. Since he barely spoke Spanish, he didn't tell me what was wrong with him." On September 29, the National Liberation Army (ELN) claimed credit, saying it was open to negotiations to "find a solution." The ELN warned that President Alvaro Uribe would be to blame if the hostages were harmed.

On November 22, a humanitarian mission, consisting of representatives of the UN, the Roman Catholic Church, and local human rights officials, arrived into northern Colombia to look into human rights abuses, thereby meeting a key demand of the kidnappers.

On November 24, the kidnappers freed the Spaniard and the German. A humanitarian mission helicoptered them from the mountains. The duo stood for photos with their erstwhile captors. Reinhilt Weigel posed with an AK-47 under her arm. The Spaniard was identified as Asier Huegen Echeverria. The duo said they were not mistreated by the rebels. The terrorists said it wanted to raise awareness about the hardships imposed by right-wing paramilitaries and the army on the Indian inhabitants of the Sierra Nevada.

On December 21, the four Israelis and one British citizen began their trek to a location in the Sierra Nevada mountains, where they were expected to be released within the week, according to Cesar Velasquez, a member of the negotiating team. The State Department's *Patterns of International Terrorism 2003* reported that all had escaped or been released. 03091201

September 12, 2003. *Germany.* German police foiled a right-wing plot to bomb a Jewish center in Munich. The plot was set for November 9 on the 65th anniversary of Kristallnacht, the Nazi pogrom that killed dozens of Jews and destroyed thousands of synagogues and Jewish shops. Police arrested several people and seized explosives, weapons, and far right literature.

September 12, 2003. *United States.* The State Department reissued its warning that Americans were at risk of terrorist attack in Kenya and elsewhere in East Africa, citing possible attacks at seaports or against planes by terrorists using shoulder-fired missiles.

September 15, 2003. *Russia.* Two suicide bombers drove a truck bomb into a government security building in the capital of Ingushetia, Magas, killing three people and injuring at least 25. No one claimed credit.

September 15, 2003. *Jordan.* The Central Bank froze the bank accounts of six Hamas leaders and five charities that send money to the group. The next day, the bank reversed itself, saying the freezing was "for banking purposes only" and had no "political dimensions."

September 15, 2003. *Iran.* Shots were again fired at the British Embassy, causing no injuries. No one claimed credit. 03091501

September 15, 2003. *Somalia.* Islamic militants were believed responsible for killing a Kenyan aid worker in the Gedo region of southwestern Somalia. No one claimed credit. 03091502

September 19, 2003. *United States.* U.S. District Court Chief Judge Robert Holmes sentenced to nine years in prison Randy Jay Bertram, 39, a former supermarket employee, who poisoned 111 people by mixing insecticide into 250 pounds of ground beef. The victims including 40 children, a pregnant women, and a man, 67, who had an artificial heart valve.

September 19, 2003. *Venezuela.* A bomb was thrown from a vehicle at the Miraflores Presidential Palace, shattering windows and damaging a guard shack but causing no injuries.

September 19, 2003. *Afghanistan.* Four rockets were fired at a facility in Ghazni that housed Turkish road workers and equipment, causing no injuries or damage. The Taliban was suspected. 03091901

September 19, 2003. *United States.* The United States designated Abu Musa'ab al-Zarqawi, a terrorist with ties to al Qaeda, Asbat al-Ansar, Ansar al-Islam, and Hizballah. Al-Zarqawi provided financial and material support for the assassination of a U.S. diplomat and was cited as a suspect in the bombing of the Jordanian Embassy in Baghdad. Germany and the United States jointly submitted his name to the UNSCR 1267 Sanctions Committee.

September 21, 2003. *India.* A bomb in a video recorder went off in a busy market in Kashmir, killing 3 and wounding 28 people, 7 critically. No one claimed credit.

September 22, 2003. *Pakistan.* Police captured Rusman Gunawan, an Indonesian, the younger brother of Riduan Isamuddin (alias Hambali), the Jemaah Islamiah leader. Gunawan and 16 other students were captured in raids on three Islamic schools in Karachi. The Foreign Ministry said they were "suspected terrorists or have links with terrorists."

September 22, 2003. *Iraq.* At 8:00 a.m., a suicide bomber set off his small grey Opel sedan outside the UN headquarters in Baghdad, killing himself and an Iraqi guard and injuring 19 people, including 2 Iraqi UN employees. The driver was directed away from the compound and told to park on the perimeter, 250 yards from the buildings. A guard had asked the driver to open the hood, whereupon the terrorist set off the explosives. No Americans were hurt. Among those injured was guard Mohammed Moussa, 30, who had lacerations on his face, arms, and back. The facility had been truck bombed on August 19. 03092201

September 25, 2003. *Iraq.* At 7:00 a.m., a small bomb went off near Baghdad's Aike Hotel that houses NBC News staffers. The explosion killed Oweis Jaber, a Somali guard, and injured an Iraqi guard and David Moodie, 44, a Canadian soundman for NBC. 03092501

September 26, 2003. *Israel.* A Palestinian gunman armed with an M-16 assault rifle snuck into the Negohot Jewish settlement five miles southwest of Hebron. He knocked on a door and when the occupants opened it, he began firing. He killed two people, including the man who opened the door and a 2-month-old girl, and injured the girl's parents before being shot to death by Israeli soldiers.

September 27, 2003. *Afghanistan.* Islamic insurgents torched the single-story Shaga Primary School for girls in Nangahar Province in the east. No injuries were reported. The government blamed the Taliban.

September 28, 2003. *United Arab Emirates.* Al-Jazeera and al-Arabiya ran an audiotape by al Qaeda deputy Ayman Zawahiri, who called for Pakistanis to overthrow President Pervez Musharraf for "betraying" Islam. He called for Muslims to fight the "Christian-Zionist Crusade ... aimed at eradicating Islam and Muslims." He said Musharraf had aided in overthrowing the Taliban and claimed he was planning to send Muslim troops to Iraq "to be killed instead of American soldiers."

September 28, 2003. *India.* Muslim rebels were suspected in the shooting death of a policeman and his two children in Indian-controlled Kashmir.

September 28, 2003. *Turkey.* A Turkish soldier died in a gun battle with Kurdish rebels in the southeast on the border of Tunceli and Bingol provinces.

September 28, 2003. *Colombia.* At 3:00 a.m., a ten-pound remotely detonated bomb attached to a motorcycle exploded in front of a Florencia nightclub, killing at least 10 and wounding 50. Leftist rebels were believed responsible. Among the dead were two children, aged 11 and 12, and two police officers.

September 30, 2003. *United Kingdom.* British police arrested 11 Algerian men in their 30s in early morning raids in north, south, and east London and in Manchester. Officers from the Anti-Terrorist Branch interrogated them.

September 30, 2003. *India.* A hand grenade was thrown at a police patrol in Gagran, Kashmir, injuring 6 police officers and 14 civilians. No one claimed credit.

October 2003. *Yemen.* On October 16, police announced that Yemeni militants arrested during the previous month had confessed to planning attacks on the U.S. and U.K. embassies and had ties to al Qaeda. Police found ammunition and bomb-making equipment in the lair of 20 suspects from Yemen, Saudi Arabia, and Syria. The group used the name Unitarian Brigade and received their orders from Afghanistan.

October 2003. *Italy.* Police arrested six members of the New Red Brigades–Communist Combatant Party (BR-PCC).

October 2003. *Pakistan.* Pakistani soldiers killed Hassan Makhsum, the leader of the Eastern Turkistan Islamic Movement (ETIM) during raids on al Qaeda associated compounds in western Pakistan. ETIM is a small Islamic extremist group based in China's western Xinjiang Province and a militant ethnic Uighur separatist group.

October 2003. *Colombia.* The government released National Liberation Army (ELN) leader Felipe Torres from prison in hopes of spurring the ELN to accept government demands to declare a cease-fire and come back to the negotiating table. As of January 2004, peace talks had not resumed.

October 2003. *Yemen.* Despite repeated statements that Aden-Abyan Islamic Army (AAIA) leader Khalid Abd-al-Nabi was dead, Yemeni officials revealed that he was not killed in the confrontations between the hardline Islamic group and a Yemeni Army antiterrorism unit. Instead, he surrendered to Yemeni authorities, was released from custody, and as of April 2004 was not facing charges for any of his activities.

October 2003. *Lebanon.* The government arrested 3 men and indicted 18 others *in absentia* on charges of preparing to carry out terrorist attacks and forging documents and passports.

October 2003. *France.* A Paris court sentenced presumed Basque Nation and Liberty (ETA) militant Alberto Rey-Domecq to six and a half years in prison for participating in a criminal association with terrorist aims.

October 2003. *India.* The People's War Group—a Maoist Naxalite organization—claimed credit for a car bomb that seriously injured Chandrababu Naidu, chief minister of Andhra Pradesh.

October 2003. *Sudan.* In mid-month, nine Sudanese who worked for the U.S. Agency for International Development were killed while transferring aid to displaced Sudanese in camps in the western Darfur region. It was unclear who killed them. It appeared they were caught in the middle of tribal clashes.

October 2003. *Egypt.* Police arrested 12 members of al-Takfir wa al-Hijrah.

October 2003. *Philippines.* Police arrested Taufek Refke, a Jemaah Islamiah (JI) operative, at a JI safe house in Cotabato City on the southern island of Mindanao. Police recovered manuals on bomb making and chemical-biological warfare.

October 2, 2003. *Pakistan.* Pakistani soldiers killed 12 suspected al Qaeda members and arrested 8 others in a raid on an al Qaeda hideout in Angore Adda. They all appeared to be foreigners.

October 2, 2003. *Pakistan.* Gunmen on motorcycles fired on a bus carrying 20 Shi'ite Muslim employees of the country's space agency in Karachi, killing six and wounding six, two critically, before escaping. No one claimed credit, but Sunni Muslim extremists were suspected.

October 2, 2003. *United States.* Ballou High School in Washington, D.C., was closed after students stole mercury from a lab and spread it among five classrooms and the cafeteria. No one was injured by the potentially poisonous liquid.

October 2, 2003. *Malaysia.* Terrorists kidnapped three Indonesians, two Filipinos, and a Malaysian from a Sabah resort. One escaped. Five were found executed on October 29 in Languyan, Philippines. No one claimed credit, but the Abu Sayyaf Group was suspected. 03100201

October 4, 2003. *Israel.* At 2:20 p.m., Hanadi Tayseer Jaradat, 29, a female Palestinian suicide bomber from Jenin in the West Bank, killed 19 people, including a U.S. citizen, and injured another 60 when she set off a 22-pound bomb in the Maxim restaurant during lunch in Haifa. The restaurant is run by Arab and Jewish families. Among the dead was a 2-month-old and three children aged 1, 5, and 6, along with a newlywed couple and four Arab Israelis. The attack came just before the Jewish holy day of Yom Kippur. Islamic Jihad (IJ) said the bomber had recently graduated from a law school in Jordan. She had watched Israeli troops shoot and kill her brother, Fadi Jaradat, 23, and cousin Salah Jaradat, both IJ supporters, in their family home in June. Among the injured was Gideon Zilberstein, 63, an accountant treated at Carmel Medical Center for pain in his ears and stomach. Five members of one family died: Bruria Zer-Aviv, 54; Bezalel Zer-Aviv, 30; Keren Zer-Aviv, 29; Libran Zer-Aviv, 4; and Noya Zer-Aviv, 1, from Kibbutz Yagur, near Haifa. Three generations of the Almog family, including the former

commander of Israel's Naval Academy, had been sitting at a table; five family members died: Zeev Almog, 71, former submarine commander who headed the Academy in the 1990s; wife Ruth, 70; son Moshe, 43; Moshe's son, Tomer, 9; and another grandchild, Asaf Shtayer, 11. Moshe's wife and their other children, and Asaf's mother, were wounded. Nir Regeb, 25, the son of the current head of Israel's Naval Academy, Comdr. Eli Regev, also died. Israeli authorities demolished the terrorist's family home.

On January 16, 2004, Israeli Ambassador Zvi Mazel ripped out cords to floodlights and threw one of the lights into a pool that consisted of Jaradat's picture on a small ship floating in a pool of red water. The exhibit was by Israeli-born Jewish artist Dror Feiler and Swedish artist Gunilla Skold, who said the piece calls attention to how weak, lonely people are capable of horrible things. The ambassador told Feiler that the piece glorified suicide bombers and legitimized genocide. Israel demanded that it be removed. On January 18, Israeli Prime Minister Ariel Sharon praised Mazel's actions, saying the "entire government stands behind him" for vandalizing the exhibit in Stockholm's Museum of National Antiquities.

October 5, 2003. *Saudi Arabia.* In a shoot-out with suspected terrorists, Saudi security forces arrested four terrorists, but three escaped. The agents arrested members of two terrorist cells. One cell was in al-Qassim, 220 miles northwest of Riyadh. He said three colleagues were at a nearby farm, which was raided. In an ensuing car chase, two security officers were injured. Agents at the farm discovered arms and chemicals to be used in bomb making.

Earlier, officials arrested three people in a desert east of Riyadh.

October 5, 2003. *Somalia.* At 8:00 p.m., a gunman fired two rounds from a pistol into the forehead of Annalena Tonelli, 60, an Italian aid worker/missionary who had provided medical help to Somalis for 33 years. The attack occurred outside the hospital in Boorama she founded to treat tuberculosis. The gunman escaped. She had also created awareness programs regarding AIDS and the harmful effects of female circumcision. No one claimed credit.

October 5, 2003. *Afghanistan.* A bomb exploded next to the Kabul offices of the international aid agencies Oxfam and Save the Children. There were no casualties. No one claimed credit. 03100501

October 6, 2003. *Pakistan.* Gunmen shot to death Azam Tariq, former leader of the outlawed Sunni group Sipah-i-Sahaba (Guardians of the Friends of the Prophet) and a member of Parliament. Tariq's driver and three bodyguards also died as they drove near the outskirts of Islamabad. His group had strong ties to the Taliban.

October 6, 2003. *Israel.* At 4:30 p.m., masked men fired on a military patrol near Metula, on the border with Lebanon, killing an Israeli soldier. They were believed to be members of Hizballah who fired a few dozen yards inside Lebanon.

October 7, 2003. *Philippines.* Early in the morning, Buyungan Bongkak, a detained Islamic rebel, grabbed a guard's rifle and opened fire in Manila's police headquarters, killing three officers and wounding three others before being shot to death. He was one of five Abu Sayyaf suspects arrested for a 2002 bomb attack in southern Zamboanga City.

October 8, 2003. *Spain/France.* Police arrested 33 people in raids against the Basque Nation and Liberty (ETA). Spanish police in the northern Basque and Navarre regions arrested 28 suspected ETA members for recruiting for the organization. French police arrested four men and a woman connected to the banned Basque youth group Segi in Bayonne.

October 8, 2003. *Colombia.* A car bomb hidden in a jeep in the San Andresito black market shopping area in Bogota went off when two police

officers approached it on a tip from suspicious residents. Both officers were killed, along with four civilians. The blast injured 12 people. Right-wing criminals trying to muscle in on the local contraband market were suspected. Among the dead was the mother of Maria de Jesus Beltran.

October 9, 2003. *Israel.* A female suicide bomber set off a bomb at an Israeli army office near Tulkarm, West Bank, killing the attacker and seriously wounding an Israeli. Another Israeli and a Palestinian were slightly wounded.

October 9, 2003. *Iraq.* At 7:45 a.m., a gunman shot to death Spanish military attaché Jose Antonio Bernal Gomez outside his Baghdad home in the Mansour district. The Spanish Foreign Ministry said he was an air force sergeant attached to the country's National Intelligence Center. Three men in an Opel sedan with foreign plates arrived a few minutes after an armed sentry had left. Gomez's guards, Ahmed Ismail, 26, and Awad Edan, said that the Western-garbed assassin chased his victim down the street in his underwear; an accomplice dressed as a Shi'ite cleric had rung the diplomat's doorbell. The third man jumped out of the car and fired his 9-mm handgun four times, missing Gomez. Unfortunately, Gomez fell and the initial gunman caught up to him, put the pistol behind his ear, and fired. The terrorists threatened the guards, then escaped in the car. The guards had neither guns nor radios. 03100901

October 9, 2003. *Iraq.* At 8:45 a.m., a bearded man wrapped in electrical wire drove an Oldsmobile station wagon car bomb through a gate at a police station at the edge of Sadr City in Baghdad, killing five Iraqi civilians and three police officers. Seventy Iraqi police officers were lining up for their monthly $120 salaries. Several dozen Iraqis were wounded. They included Haitham Hadi Hassan, 28, and Juma Khalaf Badr, 57, a 32-year police veteran. A local Shi'ite cleric had threatened the station because former Baathists were still working there.

October 12, 2003. *Iraq.* At 1:00 p.m., a suicide bomber set off his car bomb at the Baghdad Hotel, which was frequented by Iraqi officials and U.S. contractors, killing himself and seven Iraqis (including four Iraqi security guards and two civilians). The blast injured 45, including 3 Americans and Mowaffak Rubaie, a member of Iraq's Governing Council. Ten people were in critical condition. Body parts were found on nearby roofs. Only one dead body was fully intact. Iraqi guards had shot at the driver before he managed to get his white Toyota around concrete barriers and set off the explosives. Among the injured was Ali Adel, one of the guards who fired at the driver. Investigators said the driver of a second car, also killed in the blast, was a possible decoy.

On October 13, several suspects were arrested. 03101201

October 13, 2003. *Lebanon.* Security officers arrested Moammar Abdullah Awamah (alias Ibn Shaheed or Son of the Martyr), 29, a Yemeni male member of al Qaeda who was engineering bombings of Western targets in Lebanon. He was detained on the outskirts of the Ain Helweh Palestinian refugee camp near Sidon. He was among 35 people indicted by state prosecutors for bombing U.S. and U.K. targets in Lebanon between May 2002 and April 2003.

October 14, 2003. *Iraq.* Shortly before 3:00 p.m., a Volkswagen Passat crashed into a concrete barrier and exploded outside the Turkish Embassy, killing the terrorist and injuring two embassy staff members, a Turk and an Iraqi. The embassy said there were other victims, including two Iraqi policemen and an embassy employee. No one claimed credit. 03101401

October 15, 2003. *Colombia.* The Revolutionary Armed Forces of Colombia (FARC) was blamed for firing a shoulder-held rocket at Jorge Visbal, president of the National Livestock Federation and a close ally of President Alvaro Uribe. At 9:00 a.m., Visbal was getting out of his car and walking into the organization's Bogota

building when the rocket was fired from a passing car. It missed his vehicle and hit the building, causing little damage. Police detained two of three suspects and recovered the rocket launcher from a vehicle. One suspect, a woman, was wounded in a shoot-out.

October 15, 2003. *Gaza Strip.* At 10:15 a.m., a remotely detonated 200-pound bomb exploded under a van of security guards escorting a three-vehicle U.S. diplomatic convoy through the northern Gaza Strip on Saladin Street, killing three Americans and injuring one. The armor-plated vehicle was overturned. The dead were John Branchizio, 36; Mark T. Parson, 31; and John Martin Linde, Jr., 30. All were employees of Reston, Virginia-based DynCorp, a government contractor that provides security services to the U.S. Embassy in Tel Aviv. The attack came five hours after the United States vetoed a UN Security Council resolution that condemned Israel for building a fence around the West Bank. Hamas and Islamic Jihad denied responsibility. The Palestinian Revolutionary Committee initially claimed credit but later withdrew the claim.

The U.S. Embassy suspended official travel to the Gaza Strip. Palestinian security officials arrested seven members of the Popular Resistance Committee for questioning. The Popular Resistance Committee is a group of militants from other Palestinian groups, including the al-Aqsa Martyrs Brigades. Naim Abu Foul, 42, and Bashir Abu Laban, 41, were arrested on the day of the blast and were members of the Popular Resistance Committee. Mohammed Hamad, 21, and Ahmed Safi, 23, were arrested in December.

On February 7, 2004, a Palestinian military tribunal at the Saraya Prison and security compound in central Gaza City charged Palestinians Safi, Hamad, Laban, and Foul in connection with the case. Charges included possessing explosives and weapons and planting mines in the area where the attack occurred. They were not directly charged with the murders. Chief Judge Khalid Hamad adjourned the trial until February 29 to permit the defendants to obtain counsel.

When the Gaza City military tribunal began in February, the group were charged with possessing explosives and weapons and of planting mines in the general vicinity of where the Americans died. The prosecutor said the group were planting mines to take out Israeli tanks.

On March 14, 2004, a Palestinian court ruled that there was insufficient evidence against the defendants and ordered them released. Their release was delayed pending an official directive to do so by Yasir Arafat. Arafat advisor Bassam Abu Sharif said the trio "were found innocent and because they arrested three other guys who are under investigation and interrogation."

The United States had offered a $5 million reward for the arrest and prosecution of those responsible. As of April 2004, the Palestinian Authority had not brought the killers to justice. 03101501

October 15, 2003. *India.* A land mine was triggered by rebels in a forested area in Lolab, Kashmir, injuring nine people. No one claimed credit.

October 16, 2003. *United States.* Box cutters, matches, bleach, and a claylike substance were found by a New Orleans airline worker in a Southwest Airlines plane, along with a note that questioned the security procedures of U.S. carriers. Similar material was found on a Southwest plane in Houston. The FBI questioned Nathaniel T. Heatwole, 20, of Damascus, Maryland. The government ordered all planes to be searched. On October 20, the United States indicted Heatwole for carrying concealed weapons on an aircraft. The government said that Heatwole had also placed dangerous items on two other Southwest flights in February, but the items were not found until April. His hearing was set for November 10 in U.S. District Court in Baltimore. On June 24, 2004, he was given probation and sentenced to 100 hours of community service.

October 16, 2003. *United States.* A vial of ricin was found in an envelope at a Greenville, South Carolina post office. The Department of Homeland Security said it was probably a criminal case. A letter inside the envelope mentioned congressional legislation involving truckers and included an extortion threat against the government. None of the ricin had escaped.

October 17, 2003. *Saudi Arabia.* Police claimed to have broken up a cell of al Qaeda sympathizers who worked for Aramco Oil in 2002. The cell included an American who was among seven to ten people captured during the summer of 2002.

October 18, 2003. *Qatar.* Al-Jazeera broadcast an audiotape in which bin Laden vowed suicide attacks "inside and outside" the United States. He warned Iraqis against cooperation with the United States and called on youths in neighboring countries to attack Americans. "We reserve the right to respond at the appropriate time and place against all the countries participating in this unjust war, particularly Britain, Spain, Australia, Poland, Japan, and Italy," and there will be "no exception for those participating from the countries of the Islamic world and the Gulf, especially Kuwait. I tell the American people we will continue fighting you, and we will continue martyrdom operations inside and outside the United States until you stop your injustice, and you end your foolishness." The speaker referred to the government of Palestine Prime Minister Mahmoud Abbas, who resigned on September 6.

October 19, 2003. *Israel.* At 6:45 p.m., three Palestinian gunmen fired on Israeli soldiers on foot patrol in a desert area between the Palestinian village of Ein Yabroud and the Jewish settlement of Ofra, 11 miles north of Jerusalem. Three Israeli soldiers died and a fourth was injured. The al-Aqsa Martyrs Brigades terrorists got into their car and escaped.

Palestinians fired eight Qassam rockets from the northern Gaza Strip toward Sderot, causing no injuries or damage.

October 20, 2003. *Somaliland.* Richard G. Eyeington, 62, and wife Enid, 61, two British teachers working for SOS-Kinderdorf (SOS Children's

Villages), an Austrian children's organization, were found shot to death in their apartment in Sheikh, in the autonomous region of northern Somalia. Somaliland authorities suspected Islamic militants and arrested several people by year's end. 03102001

October 20, 2003. *India.* Terrorists shot to death two people in Doda, Kashmir. No one claimed credit.

October 20, 2003. *India.* A grenade was thrown at a police security patrol in Battamaloo, Kashmir, but missed and exploded at a busy bus stop, killing 1 person and wounding 53. No one claimed credit.

October 20, 2003. *India.* A hand grenade thrown at a security patrol missed its target and exploded in a busy market in Anantnag, Kashmir, killing one person and injuring seven others. No one claimed credit.

October 24, 2003. *United States.* The Treasury Department listed Mokhtar Belmokhtar of Ghardaia, Algeria; Mustapha Nasri Ait El Hadi of Tunis; and Djamel Lounici of Algiers as financiers of the Algerian terrorist organization Salafist Group for Preaching (Call) and Combat. Treasury also listed Al-Bakoun ala al-Ahd Organization (Faithful to the Oath), another Salafist supporter, as a terrorist financier group.

October 24, 2003. *Gaza Strip.* At 4:20 a.m., a Palestinian gunman sneaked into a military compound inside the heavily guarded Netzarim Jewish settlement and fired on sleeping soldiers, killing Sgt. Sarit Sheneor and Sgt. Adi Osman, both 19-year-old women, and S.Sgt. Alon Avrahami, 20. Soldiers returned fire, killing the terrorist. Hamas and Islamic Jihad identified the gunman as Samir Fodah, 22, a resident of the Jabalya refugee camp, and said it was a joint operation.

October 25, 2003. *Iraq.* During the afternoon, gunmen attacked a U.S. civilian convoy near Habbaniya, 50 miles west of Baghdad, killing

an American man, a British woman, and three Iraqis and injuring American David Rasmussen and Iraqi security guard Laith Yousef. A roadside bomb hit three vehicles, which were then fired on with rocket-propelled grenades and small arms. The vehicles belonged to the United Kingdom-based European Landmine Solutions. There was some dispute as to whether the convoy was caught in a crossfire between terrorists and U.S. troops.

October 25, 2003. *Iraq.* At 6:10 a.m., eight to ten rockets were fired from a blue vehicle at the 462-room al-Rashid Hotel in Baghdad, where Deputy Secretary of Defense Paul D. Wolfowitz was staying. He was uninjured. Lt. Col. Charles H. Buehring was killed. At least 17 people were injured. The rocket launcher was disguised as a power generator. The United States abandoned the hotel. Among the injured was Bret A. Flinn, a Defense Department employee, who was cut on the arms, legs, and face and underwent surgery. The jury-rigged device included Russian and French missiles. No one claimed credit. 03102501

October 26, 2003. *India.* Terrorists dressed in army uniforms hijacked a car in Gagal, Kashmir, killing two of the occupants and injuring four others. No one claimed credit.

October 26, 2003. *India.* A bomb exploded in the restroom of a coach car of a train in Samba, Kashmir, causing no injuries but derailing five cars. No one claimed credit.

October 26, 2003. *India.* A hand grenade was thrown at a military convoy in Bijbehara, Kashmir. It missed its target and exploded on the road, injuring 14 people, including a police officer and a person who worked in the office of the Indo–Tibetan border police. No one claimed credit.

October 27, 2003. *Iraq.* Foreign terrorists were blamed for setting off four car bombs in Baghdad outside the headquarters of the International

Committee of the Red Cross (ICRC) and three police stations (Bayaa, Shaab, and Khadra) between 8:45 and 9:30 a.m. A fifth terrorist was stopped before the terrorist could get the New Baghdad police station. The bombs killed 35 people, including a U.S. soldier at a police station, and wounded more than 230, including 8 U.S. soldiers. A dozen people died at the ICRC facility; 23 died at the police stations. One police official said 8 police officers were killed and 65 wounded; the rest were civilians. Among the dead were Police Officer Haidar Hadi and ICRC guard Jumaa Thamed. The injured included Mohammed Arsan Zubeidi, 23, who lost an ear. He had graduated from the police academy two months earlier. Several of those killed were children on their way to school. On November 8, the ICRC announced that it was closing its offices in Baghdad and Basra. 03102701-04

October 27, 2003. *Afghanistan.* U.S. government contract workers William Carlson and Christopher Glenn Mueller were killed in an ambush by the Taliban in Shkin. 03102705

October 28, 2003. *India.* A bomb exploded at the customer billing counter in a telegraph office building in Lal Chowk, Kashmir, injuring 36 people. No one claimed credit.

October 29, 2003. *India.* A hand grenade thrown at a police patrol in Anantnag, Kashmir, missed its target and exploded in a busy market, injuring 13 people. No one claimed credit.

October 30, 2003. *Afghanistan.* Insurgents kidnapped Hasan Onal, 45, a Turkish engineer working on a U.S.–funded road project, and his Afghan driver. The gunmen intercepted their vehicle, then blindfolded the duo and drove them away. The kidnappers freed the driver with a note demanding the release of six Taliban prisoners being held by U.S. forces in the southern province of Ghazni. Onal had worked since June on a contract to repair part of the 300-mile highway between Kabul and Kandahar. The kidnappers demanded their release within two days.

Kurtulus Ergin, the Kabul-based manager of the construction firm, said that he contacted the kidnappers on Onal's satellite phone. They claimed to be members of al Qaeda. Turkish officials blamed the Taliban. The project is managed by the Louis Berger Group of East Orange, New Jersey.

On November 6, Afghan Interior Minister Ali Ahmad Jalali said that Afghanistan would not hand over the prisoners, despite threats to kill Onal. "Afghanistan does not make deals with terrorists."

Mullah Roazi, who claimed to be the senior Taliban official in Zabol Province, said on November 29 that the kidnappers had released the Turkish engineers to tribal elders, who would hand him over to his Turkish company on the morning of November 30. Onal appeared before journalists on November 30, thanking the tribal elders who negotiated his release "without conditions." The negotiators included Ghazni Province Governor Asadullah Khan Khalid, Islamic religious leaders, and an anti-Soviet guerrilla leader nicknamed Mullah Rockety. The Taliban claimed that he was released before the government freed several other Taliban prisoners for the Muslim holiday of Eid al-Fitr. The company said Onal had not been harmed. He had attempted to escape but was recaptured by the kidnappers, who were led by Rozi Khan, a Taliban official. 03103001

November 2003. *Kyrgyzstan.* Authorities captured three male Islamic extremists planning to bomb a U.S. military base outside Bishkek. 03119901

November 2003. *Afghanistan.* A bomb went off near Save the Children USA's offices in Kabul. The agency had provided education, health, and economic assistance to children and families in the country for more than two decades. 03119902

November 2003. *Afghanistan.* Two Romanians were fatally shot in an ambush. 03119903

November 2003. *Pakistan.* An antiterrorism court in Karachi handed down death sentences to three members of the banned Lashkar-e-Jhangvi for planning and committing sectarian murders.

November 2003. *Saudi Arabia.* Authorities seized a truck bomb at an al Qaeda safe house in Riyadh.

November 2003. *Iraq.* Coalition forces killed two senior members of Ansar al-Islam during a raid on a terrorist hideout in Baghdad.

November 2003. *Ecuador.* A Drug Enforcement Administration (DEA)-trained counter-drug policeman apprehended an Italian citizen trying to board a Continental Airlines flight in Quito with explosives and a firearm.

November 2003. *Yemen.* Authorities arrested Muhammad Hamdi al-Ahdal (alias Abu Asim al-Makki), the senior-most extremist in Yemen, who had supported mujahedin and terrorist operations throughout the Middle East and Chechnya.

November 2003. *Cambodia.* Cambodian authorities arrested seven members of the antigovernment Cambodian Freedom Fighters, who were planning a terrorist attack in the southwestern town of Koh Kong.

November 2003. *Italy.* The minister of the Interior for the first time exercised ministerial authority to expel seven terrorist suspects who he assessed posed a serious threat to Italy's national security. The government declared that while there may have been insufficient evidence to arrest them, lengthy investigation had compiled compelling evidence that the seven were Islamic extremists who posed a threat to national security.

November 1, 2003. *Gaza Strip.* Israeli authorities arrested Jamal Akkal, 24, a Gaza-born Canadian citizen, and charged him with conspiring to commit manslaughter. On November 24, 2004, he pleaded guilty to planning attacks on Israelis in North America and was sentenced by a military court to four years in prison. He planned to attack Israeli officials traveling in the United States and to bomb Jewish targets in North America.

November 2, 2003. *Iraq.* A homemade bomb exploded during the morning as the SUV of two U.S. contractors working for the Knoxville, Tennessee-based EOD Technology, Inc., drove past outside Fallujah. The duo, David "Butch" Dyess, 53, of Havelock, North Carolina, and Roy Buckmaster, 47, were helping the Army Corps of Engineers defuse bombs and destroy munitions of the Saddam regime. They were air force veterans. Another contractor, E. Frank Johnson, 51, was hit in the eyes with shrapnel and rendered unconscious. 03110201

November 3, 2003. *Northern Ireland.* Abbas Boutrab, 25, an Algerian man, was arrested at Maghaberry prison near Belfast on suspicion of terrorist offenses and links with al Qaeda. He was scheduled for a court appearance on November 10. He had been held at the prison near Belfast for six months as a suspected illegal immigrant. He was charged with "receiving instructions in the use of explosives, possession of items of use to terrorists, and possession of documents also of use to terrorists." A police lawyer told the Belfast high court that a search of his home revealed computer disks containing "a terrorist training manual."

November 3, 2003. *Saudi Arabia.* Authorities broke up a terrorist cell that was planning an attack against Muslims in Mecca during Ramadan. Two terrorists were shot dead and a police officer was wounded. Six suspects were arrested. Police seized a large number of weapons. Police believed they were planning a Ramadan attack in Mecca.

November 4, 2003. *France.* Police arrested five French nationals in Brittany and Normandy suspected of supporting the Real Irish

Republican Army (Real IRA). Police also found a cache of arms.

November 4/12, 2003. *United States.* Four threatening letters, each containing a powdery substance, arrived at The *Washington Post*, a Denver radio station, the Centers for Disease Control and Prevention in Atlanta, and News 12, a Long Island television station in Woodbury, New York. They were all postmarked, had postage from, or had a return address from Pakistan. The identical letters had a message: "Death to Americans … Penicillin won't help you … Long live jihad … Long live Islam." The powder did not contain biologically hazardous matter. The CDC and Denver letters arrived on November 4. The News 12 and *Post* letters arrived on November 12.

November 6, 2003. *Saudi Arabia.* An al Qaeda suspect was killed in a gun battle with security forces in Riyadh.

November 6, 2003. *Saudi Arabia.* Two suspected al Qaeda terrorists blew themselves up in Mecca to avoid arrest.

November 7, 2003. *Saudi Arabia.* Police raided a house in a Riyadh suburb, touching off a gun battle. Several terrorists escaped, but police arrested a 17-year-old who said that he and the others had been planning to bomb a residential compound in Riyadh.

November 7, 2003. *Middle East.* The United States closed the U.S. Embassy and two consulates in Saudi Arabia as part of its issuance of a new terrorist alert in the Persian Gulf and Afghanistan based on "highly credible and specific information." The U.S. Embassy in Kabul warned journalists that Taliban rebels were searching for U.S. journalists to take hostage "to use as leverage for the release of Taliban currently under U.S. control."

November 7, 2003. *United States.* The FBI and Department of Homeland Security warned that al Qaeda operatives were considering hijacking cargo jets in Canada, Mexico, or the Caribbean

to crash into nuclear plants and other critical infrastructure, including bridges and dams.

November 8, 2003. *Philippines.* Early in the day, a former aviation chief and a navy officer seized the control tower of Manila Airport and held it for three hours. In a gun battle with police, Panfilo Villaruel, a former chief of the Air Transport Office, yelled in Tagalog over the radio, "They are killing us here! We surrender," at about 3:00 a.m. Villaruel and former Navy officer Ricardo Cachillar had fired on a police special operations team that stormed the building. The duo was shot and killed. Police found a stick of dynamite, a hand grenade, tear gas, a .45-caliber handgun and a 9-mm handgun. Villaruel said he wanted to tell his countrymen to "stand up and tell their leaders to wake up." He apparently was protesting corruption.

November 8, 2003. *Saudi Arabia.* Shortly after midnight, a powerful al Qaeda car bomb exploded at Riyadh's Muhaya residential complex, killing 17, including 5 children, and wounding 132, including 4 Americans who were treated for minor wounds and released from the hospital. The terrorists, disguised as security forces, shot their way into the compound and then set off the bomb. Attackers in police uniforms drove to the compound's gates in vehicles painted to resembled police vehicles, in an attempt to deceive the guards. Observers believed al Qaeda mistakenly thought that the compound housed Americans, which was the case until the late 1990s. The compound houses mostly Arab foreigners. The compound is near the diplomatic quarter. 03110801

November 10, 2003. *Burundi.* Hutu rebels fired rockets into Bujumbura, killing five people, destroying part of the Chinese Embassy, and hitting the home of a U.S. military attaché. 03111001

November 10, 2003. *Iraq.* A bomb was remotely detonated against a convoy in Samarra, injuring three Fijians working for a

British security firm. No one claimed credit. 03111002

November 11, 2003. *Afghanistan.* A car bomb exploded outside the UN Assistance Mission in Afghanistan (UNAMA) office in Kandahar, killing one person, wounding a student, and breaking windows and doors of the UN buildings. The Taliban and al Qaeda were suspected. 03111101

November 11, 2003. *Greece.* Authorities neutralized a bomb found outside the Athens Citibank branch. A person phoned an Athens newspaper to warn that the bomb was going to explode. The Organization Khristos Kassimis was suspected. 03111102

November 12, 2003. *Iraq.* At 10:50 a.m., a truck bomb killed 29 people (eventually 31), including 18 Italians (among them 12 carabinieri, 4 soldiers, and 2 civilians) and 11 Iraqis, and wounded another 100, including 12 Italians and 83 Iraqis. The bomb went off at the Italian Carabinieri Corps' Multinational Specialized Unit base in the former chamber of commerce in Nasiriya, which had been devoid of violence since the end of formal hostilities. The two civilians were a producer who was working with the four soldiers on a documentary film and an Italian aid worker. Most of those killed were due to leave Iraq in two days. The explosion set alight many cars, some with people still in them, for hundreds of yards. Some 300 Italians and 100 Romanians were in the facility at the time of the attack. It was the Italian military's single largest loss of life since World War II. Among the injured was Fadhil Abbas, a guard at a relief agency across the street, and Abbas Ali, 32, a lawyer cut by flying glass from a nearby courthouse. The dead included four girls and a taxi driver.

Two vehicles were involved. A blue truck pulling a tank trailer crashed through the base entrance, followed by a car, which then exploded. Some witnesses said the truck had the explosives. A passenger in the truck fired a pistol at the Italian guards. The driver then opened the door and an explosion was heard.

On November 15, the toll reached 19 Italians, when Pietro Petrucci, 22, a soldier who was pronounced brain-dead, died in Kuwait after life support was ended.

On November 16, in an e-mail to the London *al-Majalla* weekly, Abu Muhammad Ablay said al Qaeda was responsible for the November 15 synagogue bombings and the November 12 bombing in Nasiriyah that killed 19 Italians and 12 Iraqis.

On November 17, approximately 300,000 Italians walked past the 19 coffins before a state funeral in a Rome basilica.

On December 8, the *Washington Post* reported that Italian intelligence had warned three times of an imminent attack on the Italian contingent. The warnings came on October 6, 8, and 9. On October 8, Italian intelligence said that two of the conspirators were former Iraqi army officers: Moustapha Hamid Lafta and Majid Kassem. The October 9 warning said that two other Iraqi Fedayeen fighters involved in the plotting were Jaseem Kahtan Omar from Balad and Abdullah Aboud Mahmoud from a village near Baghdad. Following the bombing, Italian intelligence said another Fedayeen plotter was Majed Jameel. Also in the plot were Mohammed Fahd and Suleiman Hardouchi—Saudis carrying false Iraqi IDs—and Mohammed Rashid, an Iraqi member of Ansar al-Islam. A theology professor at Baghdad University may have financed the bombing. Also believed involved was Mohammed Majid (alias Mullah Fouad), an Iraqi Kurd and key Ansar organizer in Parma, Italy, who fled to Syria a year earlier. 03111201

November 12, 2003. *Iraq.* A bomb exploded at the Catholic Relief Services site in Nasiriyah. 03111202

November 14, 2003. *Czech Republic.* Undercover police officers in the Voronez Hotel in Brno, 125 miles southeast of Prague, arrested two Slovaks who tried to sell them nearly seven pounds of radioactive material for $700,000. Tests of the four parcels found traces of thorium and uranium. The duo, from the eastern Slovak town of Presov, faced 15 years if convicted of illegal production and possession of radioactive material and a highly dangerous substance.

November 14, 2003. *India.* Militants fired on a Christian school and one of the school's buses in Pulwama, Kashmir, but caused no injuries. No one claimed credit.

November 15, 2003. *France.* The annex of a Jewish school north of Paris was firebombed.

November 15, 2003. *Afghanistan.* Authorities arrested two suspects believed to be Taliban militia who shot to death Bettina Goislard, 29, a French woman working for the UN High Commissioner for Refugees in Ghazni. Two men on a motorcycle fired on her vehicle with a pistol. Her Afghan driver sustained gunshot wounds. Goislard had been in Ghazni since June 2002. She had also worked for the UN in Rwanda and Guinea. She was the first foreign UN worker to be killed in Afghanistan since the fall of the Taliban in November 2001.

On February 10, 2004, a Kabul court convicted Abdul Nabi and Zia Ahmad of murdering Goislard and sentenced them to death. The duo appealed. 03111501

November 15, 2003. *Turkey.* Between 9:15 and 9:20 a.m., two Turkish suicide bombers set off Isuzu truck bombs packed with 800 pounds of compressed fuel oil, nitrate, and ammonium sulfate blocks apart at two Istanbul synagogues—the Beth Israel Synagogue in Sisli and the Neve Shalom Synagogue in the city's historic district—killing 25 people, including an Istanbul policeman, and injuring 303 (a woman died of her injuries two days later). Six of the dead and 60 of the injured were Jews; the majority of the dead and injured were Muslims passing by. Nearby shops were heavily damaged; 20 buildings might require demolition near the Neve Shalom synagogue because of severe structural damage.

Police found the bodies of the terrorists with wire cables attached to them.

Among the dead was Sisli synagogue security guard Mehmet Ates, 27, who left a wife of two years and a one-year-old daughter, and another security guard, Metin Bostanoglu. A third guard, Hasan Ozsoy, 42, and his son Hamza, 13, underwent surgery for broken bones and hip and head injuries.

Also killed was Anet Rubinstein, 8 (other reports identified her as Anette Rubinstein Talu, 9) and her grandmother, Anna, whose body was not found for two days. Berta Ozdogan, a Jew, and her husband Ahmet, a Muslim, also died. Berta was five months pregnant.

Police discounted the claim of credit by the domestic Islamic Great East Raiders Front.

Al Qaeda and its affiliate, the Abu-Hafs al-Masri Brigades, claimed credit in an e-mail to the *al-Quds al-Arabi* newspaper. The note said, "We tell the criminal Bush and his Arab and Western tails—especially Britain, Italy, Australia and Japan—that cars of death will not stop at Baghdad, Riyadh, Istanbul, Nasiriyah, Jakarta, etc., until you see them with your own eyes in the middle of the capital of this era's tyrant, America." The group believed that Mossad agents were inside the synagogues. The group also cited Israel's occupation of the Palestinian territories as a reason for attacking Jews worldwide. The group, which had claimed credit for the car bombing at UN Headquarters in Baghdad in August in which 23 people died, said, "The remaining operations are coming, God willing, and by God, Jews around the world will regret that their ancestors even thought about occupying the land of Muslims." The group is named after Muhammad Atef (alias Abu Hafs), a senior al Qaeda leader who died in November 2001 in Afghanistan during the U.S.–led coalition campaign. The group also said—incorrectly—that it caused the August 14 power blackout across Canada and the northeastern United States.

A second e-mail to the London *al-Majalla* weekly said al Qaeda was responsible for these bombings and the November 12 bombing in Nasiriyah that killed 19 Italians and 12 Iraqis. The note was signed by Abu Mohammed Ablaj, an al Qaeda operative.

Gokhan Elaltuntas, 22, who had recently moved to Istanbul, drove the truck at the Neve Shalom synagogue. A family member owns an Internet café in Bingol in which the two suicide bombers and colleague Azad Ekinci often met. Elaltuntas, who managed the Bingol Internet Merkezi Café, was engaged to be married later that month to a woman he met on the Internet. Members of his extended family were tied to Turkish Hizballah.

Police found the passport of Mesut Cabuk, 29, in the wreckage; he was identified as the driver at the Beth Israel synagogue. Azad Ekinci, a suspected accomplice, had gone to Pakistan and Iran with Cabuk. Police believed Ekinci used his brother Metin's ID card to purchase one of the trucks. Cabuk was detained and released by Turkish authorities in 1995 in connection with investigations of the Islamic Great East Raiders Front. Police used DNA to identify the terrorists. Three of the four suspects came from Bingol, Turkey, a town in the eastern mountains. The fourth suspect was from Istanbul. They had traveled to Pakistan and Iran for "religious training." Police said Azad had been to Iran six times and was training in bomb making. He also had been detained for questioning regarding the Islamic Great East Raiders Front. Police said Cabuk was a member of the Islamic Movement.

Metin Ekinci said he had lost his ID card during last summer's earthquake in the area.

Police found two falsified registration documents for the trucks.

Police questioned Ahmet Ugurlu from Eskisehir, whose name appeared on the registration papers for one of the trucks. He said that his son, Feridun, had stolen his ID card and had not been in contact with his family for several months. Ahmet had studied in Pakistan.

On November 22, another victim died of her wounds, raising the death toll to 26, in addition to the bombers.

On November 24, a Turkish court charged nine suspected accomplices with aiding or belonging to an illegal organization, which carries a five-year sentence. One individual was charged with aiding and abetting; the eight others, with membership. Four other detainees were released, apparently for lack of evidence. Three other suspects were released, according to defense attorney Selhahattin Karahan.

There are only 19 synagogues in Turkey.

Neve Shalom was the site of the 1986 attack by Abu Nidal terrorists who fired machine guns and threw grenades inside the locked synagogue, killing 22 people.

On November 29, police announced that they had arrested a man believed to have been the planner and leader of the bombing attacks. He was grabbed on November 25 while trying to sneak into Iran at the Gurbulak crossing in eastern Agri Province. He was charged with trying to overthrow Turkey's constitutional order by force.

On November 29, a Turkish court charged Yusuf Polat, an alleged accomplice in the bombings; he was captured trying to cross into Iran. He told police he had surveilled the Beth Israel synagogue for its weakest point. He told police he and the two bombers were "followers of Osama bin Laden." He told the truck's driver, Mesut Cabuk, that the rear entrance was easier and "you can come now. May your campaign for Islam be blessed." Police found Polat using Cabuk's prepaid cell phone card that was found in the debris. Polat had fought in Chechnya.

On December 14, a Turkish court charged Fevzi Yitiz, a Turk who confessed to recruiting the suicide bombers and preparing the truck bombs. He was detained on December 10 in southeastern Turkey near the Iranian and Iraqi borders. He was carrying a forged passport and attempting to flee. He rented an Istanbul workshop where the bombs were made. Police believed he helped rig the trucks used in the November 15 and 20 bombings. He named Adnan Ersoz as one of the leaders of the al Qaeda cell.

On December 23, Turkish authorities arrested Mehmet Kus and charged him with "aiding and abetting an illegal organization" after 12 bags of a substance used for making explosives were found at his home. Kus blamed a relative for storing the potassium nitrate, which was used in the Istanbul bombings.

On May 31, 2004, a state security court postponed the trial of 69 suspected members of an al Qaeda cell accused in the suicide bombings when it ruled that it did not have authority to hear the case. In May, the Turkish Parliament had abolished this type of court, although the order was not to take effect for another month. The reform was part of Turkey's bid to join the European Union. 03111502-03

November 16, 2003. *Colombia.* Rebels threw grenades at two Bogota bars frequented by Americans, killing a Colombian woman and injuring 72 other people, including an American Airlines pilot and 4 other Americans, along with a German citizen. Eighteen were in critical condition. Police said the Revolutionary Armed Forces of Colombia (FARC) was responsible for the attack in the Zona Rosa neighborhood. After the first attack on the Bogota Beer Garden Company, the terrorist ran to the Palos de Moguer bar and threw another grenade. One suspect was arrested.

On November 29, Raul Reyes, a Revolutionary Armed Forces of Colombia (FARC) commander, warned that U.S. military personnel assisting the government's troops would face attack. In an interview on the Web site of the New Colombia news agency, he said, "The invasive foreign troops are a military target for the FARC." He said he did not know whether FARC was responsible for the bar attacks.

On September 7, 2004, the U.S. government indicted Colombian citizen Arturo Montano, 26, and unidentified accomplices with trying to kill Americans in the attacks, which were to retaliate for the death of a FARC deputy commander, Edgar Gustavo Navarro (alias El Mocho), at the hands of the Colombian armed forces in October 2003. Montano was charged with attempted

murder of U.S. nationals, conspiracy, and use of a weapon of mass destruction. 03111601-02

November 17, 2003. *Brazil/Paraguay.* Brazil extradited to Paraguay Assad Ahmad Barakat, 35, a Lebanese-born businessman accused of leading and fund-raising for Hizballah.

November 18, 2003. *Israel.* At 6:00 a.m., a terrorist who had hidden an AK-47 assault rifle under a prayer mat shot to death Sgt. Maj. Shlomi Belsky, 23, and Staff Sgt. Shaul Lahav, 20. The gunman escaped, apparently into a waiting car near the first checkpoint south of Jerusalem on southbound Route 60. The gunman might have fled to El Khader, a small Palestinian community west of Bethlehem. The next day, Palestinian police arrested suspect Jaber Atrash, a member of the Palestinian National Security Forces.

November 19, 2003. *Israel.* At 10:30 a.m., a gunman shot at a large group of tourists at the Arava crossing on the Israel-Jordan border, killing an Ecuadoran woman in her 30s and wounding four others, two seriously. Airport Authority guards shot to death the gunman at the Yitzhak Rabin terminal of Israel's southernmost border crossing with Jordan, just north of Eilat. The gunman apparently had emerged from a truck. The Jordanian government said the attacker was a truck driver from Az-Zarqa, 12 miles northeast of Amman. 03111901

November 19, 2003. *United States.* A federal grand jury indicted attorney Lynne Stewart and an Arabic translator, Mohammed Yousry, for their roles in a conspiracy led by imprisoned Egyptian cleric Omar Abd-al-Rahman to kill and kidnap people overseas. The duo was accused of helping Abd-al-Rahman issue fatwas and other messages to Ahmed Abdel Sattar, a State Island postal worker, who then circulated the messages around the world. Sattar was indicted for conspiring with Rahman and others to kill and kidnap people abroad; he posted on the Internet the "Fatwah Mandating the Killing of Israelis Everywhere." Stewart and Yousry were freed on bond; Sattar remained in custody.

On July 22, 2003, U.S. District Judge John G. Koeltl had dismissed similar charges against Stewart and Yousry. The new charges provided more details and cited a different legal statute.

On October 13, 2004, testimony was postponed until October 18 amid reports that Sattar had suffered a mild heart attack and was hospitalized.

November 20, 2003. *Turkey.* Turkish suicide bombers set off truck bombs at a British bank headquarters and the British Consulate killing at least 30 people and wounding 450. All but three of the dead were Turkish Muslims. The attack came while President Bush was meeting with British Prime Minister Tony Blair. The bombing also destroyed the Evin Restaurant owned by Veysel Demirtas, 52.

The first bomb went off at 10:55 a.m. at the Turkish headquarters of the London-based Hong Kong–Singapore Bank (HSBC) in the Levent commercial center, seriously damaging the 20-story building. Body parts were found two blocks away. HSBC is the fifth-largest private bank in Turkey. It shut down its 150 plus branches across the country.

Five minutes later, the second truck bomb went off three and a half miles away. The pickup truck had a catering company logo on its side. It crashed into the front gate of the British Consulate in Taksim, Istanbul's most popular business and shopping district.

Among the dead from the bomb at the bank was Kerem Yilmazer, 58, one of the country's famed theater actors, who was walking past the bank at the time. Also dead was Suleyman Aydogan. As of November 21, some 54 people remained hospitalized; 3 more people died on November 21.

Among the dead at the Consulate was U.K. Consul General Roger Short, 58, his aide, and Ahmet Dama, 22. The injured at the Consulate included Muradiye Demir, 38, who worked in a household appliance store nearby. She sustained major damage to her left hand and face. Also injured was Yasemin Silivrili, 47, who worked for an ad agency across the street. She sustained cuts on her face and hands.

Two policemen died in the attacks.

On November 21, police announced the arrest of several people for the attacks. Investigators focused on 1,050 Turkish men who fought or trained with Islamic guerrillas in Afghanistan, Chechnya, or Bosnia. The bombers were tentatively identified as Azad Ekinci, 27, and Feridun Ugurlu. They had earlier been named as suspected accomplices of the synagogue bombers. Istanbul Police Chief Celalettin Cerrah said that the duo had avoided capture because of Turkish media publicity about the terrorists' identities. Police later said that the HSBC bank bomber was Illyas Kuncak, 47, of Ankara.

By November 22, the tally in the November 15 synagogue bombings and the November 20 British bombings stood at 58 dead, 750 injured.

Al Qaeda and affiliated groups claimed credit. The Abu Hafs al-Masri Brigades claimed credit on the al-Mujahidoun Web site, saying the bombs were to "shatter the peace of Britain … which battles Islam." The bank was hit to "let Britain and its people know that its alliance with America will not bring it prosperity or security." The group said it specifically targeted U.K. Consul General Roger Short, who had entered the walled compound's gates two minutes before the green Isuzu truck exploded. The group said it regretted the large number of civilian casualties, caused by an improperly positioned "car of death."

On November 25, a Turkish court charged nine accomplices. Another seven were held as suspected accomplices. One was a Swedish citizen.

On November 26, a Turkish court charged two more women and a man with belonging to and aiding an illegal organization, which carries a five-year term. The trio were believed to be accomplices in the attacks.

On November 30, Syria extradited 22 Turks wanted for questioning in the bombings. Two detainees—Hilmi Tuglaoglu and his wife, Leyla —were believed linked to Azad Ekinci, 27, who police said bought two of the Isuzu trucks used in the bombings and who was believed to have masterminded the attacks. One of those returned was Aykut Ekinci.

On December 7, a Turkish court charged three more men with "membership in an illegal organization and aiding and abetting the organization," plus involvement in the bombings, which now included 30 suspects. They faced five years in prison. Four other people were released after questioning in court. Some 160 people had been questioned.

On December 14, Selahattin Yildirim, 31, died from his injuries from the bank bombing.

On December 19, Adnan Eroz was charged with treason and with helping to organize the series of bombings. He was believed to be a senior member of al Qaeda in Turkey. On December 20, Ersoz said al Qaeda provided $150,000 for the attacks. He said an Iranian sent him $50,000 by courier. He later contacted Habip Aktas, al Qaeda's chief in Turkey, for another $100,000. Ersoz denied advance knowledge of the attacks or that he had received orders from bin Laden. He received military training in Afghanistan. 03112001-02

November 21, 2003. *Iraq.* At 7:20 a.m., missiles were fired from donkey carts at the Palestine Hotel, Sheraton Hotel, and Oil Ministry in Baghdad. Two people, including a U.S. contractor, were injured in the attack. The rockets heavily damaged five floors of the Palestine Hotel and slightly damaged the 16th and 18th floors of the Sheraton. Authorities later found a makeshift multiple rocket launcher with 30 unfired rockets in its tubes close to the Italian Embassy. No one claimed credit. 03112101

November 22, 2003. *Israel.* Gunmen shot to death two Israeli security guards at a construction site for the security fence being erected along the West Bank frontier.

November 22, 2003. *Iraq.* The wing of a DHL parcel service cargo plane caught on fire over Baghdad when it was struck by a SAM-7 man-portable surface-to-air missile. The plane landed safely. No one claimed credit. 03112201

November 23, 2003. *Afghanistan.* A rocket was fired at Kabul's Intercontinental Hotel, which was crowded with guests, including foreign diplomats, journalists, and UN aid workers. No one was injured and minimal damage was reported. No one claimed credit, although the Taliban and al Qaeda were suspected. 03112301

November 25, 2003. *Saudi Arabia.* CNN reported that Saudi authorities had arrested individuals in a truck loaded with explosives on their way to a suicide bombing site.

November 27, 2003. *United Kingdom.* Police in Gloucester arrested a 24-year-old man after police evacuated 119 neighboring homes and cordoned off three roads out of concern that he had explosives. Police recovered a "relatively small amount of explosive material."

Manchester police arrested a 39-year-old man on suspicion of terrorist offenses.

Birmingham police arrested a man, 33, on suspicion of involvement in terrorism. They were searching three homes and firms for weapons and explosives.

One was believed to have links with Richard C. Reid, the al Qaeda shoe bomber.

Police did not release the suspects' nationalities or the charges against them.

November 27, 2003. *Algeria.* A well-known poet and member of the Saudi Royal family was killed and four others were injured in an apparent terrorist attack in Messad. No one claimed credit, but the Salafist Group for Preaching (Call) and Combat were suspected. 03112701

November 28, 2003. *Italy/Germany.* Rome police arrested two individuals suspected of recruiting suicide bombers against coalition forces. Police in Hamburg arrested their Algerian ringleader. Two other terrorists—an Iraqi man and a Tunisian woman—remained at large. The five were charged with association with the aim of international terrorism.

On March 19, 2004, Germany extradited Algerian citizen Abderrazak Mahdjoub to Italy.

November 29, 2003. *United Kingdom.* Akhmad Zakayev, 44, a Chechen leader wanted in Russia on charges of terrorism and murder, was granted refugee status. A British judge had turned down an extradition request, saying he would have been tortured if he was returned to Russia. He had fought against Russian forces between October 1995 and December 2000.

November 29, 2003. *Iraq.* More than a dozen gunmen fired from two moving SUVs and from behind a concrete wall, shooting to death seven Spanish intelligence officers on a highway near Latifiya, south of Baghdad. Saddam loyalists were blamed for firing automatic rifles and rocket-propelled grenades, forcing the lead Spanish vehicle off the road and into a muddy field. A waiting group of killers then fired from behind the concrete wall. Some of the Spaniards returned fire during a 20-minute gun battle. A fire caused by one of the rocket-propelled grenades destroyed the first car. Two badly burned bodies were dragged from the vehicle and placed in the median. Two other bodies were trapped in the front seats of the vehicle. One of the Spaniards in the second car was able to escape and was rescued by a passing motorist. A witness said one of the gunman said, "By the name of Saddam, we kill you." Rampaging youths kicked three of the bodies.

The next day, Spanish Prime Minister Jose Maria Aznar said Spain would remain in Iraq. He said the agents were "professionals who worked for our liberty and security. They wanted to fight a terrorism that threatens us here and there…. Fanaticism has decided to hit us as many times as it can, whether it be in New York, Istanbul, Casablanca or Baghdad. There are no borders in the fight against terrorism because the fanatics don't want there to be any." 03112901

November 29, 2003. *Iraq.* Two Japanese diplomats were killed in an ambush near Tikrit. An organization believed to have been al Qaeda had stated in mid-October and mid-November that Japan and other countries helping the United States would be targeted. 03112902

November 29, 2003. *Iraq.* A Colombian civilian contractor was killed when Iraqi insurgents fired light weapons on his vehicles 45 miles north of Baghdad near Balad. Two of his colleagues were wounded. He worked for the U.S. defense contractor Kellogg Brown and Root, a subsidiary of Halliburton Company. 03112903

November 30, 2003. *Iraq.* Two South Korean engineers were killed and two other South Koreans were wounded in a 1:30 p.m. attack on a highway outside Tikrit. Kyung Hae Kwak, Mansoo Kim, and their Iraqi driver, Luay Harby, were dead. Soldiers found Jae Suk Lim and Sang Won Lee bleeding in the back seat of a car that had belonged to Saddam Hussein. Lim had a gunshot wound in the leg. Lee was hit three times in the leg and twice in the hip and buttocks. They were evacuated to a U.S. hospital in Germany.

On December 7, the remaining 60 South Korean contract engineers and technicians working for the U.S. government on a project to fix electrical power lines north of Baghdad decided to leave the country. The Koreans were employees of Ohmoo (variant OMU) Electric Company of Korea, a subcontractor of the Shiloh Company of the Philippines. Shiloh Company is a subcontractor for the Washington Group International, Inc., a Boise, Idaho-based construction firm that has a $110 million contract with the Army Corps of Engineers. 03113001

December 2003. *Afghanistan.* Early in the month, two Indians working on a U.S.–funded road project on the Kabul-Kandahar highway were kidnapped in the southern province of Zabol. Government officials dismissed a Taliban claim of responsibility. The duo was freed on December 24 and said that they had been treated well by their captors. 03129901

December 2003. *France.* During the month, French police arrested top leaders of Basque Nation and Liberty's (ETA) military wing who were allegedly planning attacks in Spain to coincide with the Christmas season.

December 2003. *Lebanon.* Late in the month, a military tribunal sentenced 25 members of a terrorist group accused of targeting U.S. official and commercial targets to prison terms ranging from six months to life.

December 2003. *Spain.* Authorities arrested three members of the First of October Antifascist Resistance Group (GRAPO).

December 2003. *Kuwait.* On June 28, 2004, a criminal court sentenced Kuwaiti soldier Ali Nasser Ajmi, 30, to 15 years in jail for shooting at U.S. servicemen and expatriate workers in December. His attorney planned an appeal. Ajmi attacked two U.S. military convoys outside Kuwait City, slightly injuring four soldiers, and fired on a bus carrying Asian and Arab workers near Shuaiba port, wounding five people. 03129902-04

December 2, 2003. *Kenya.* The Barclays Bank building and a Barclays branch office in downtown Nairobi were evacuated after receiving a bomb threat. No explosives were found. The Barclays Bank building had housed the U.S. Embassy's public affairs office until it was moved earlier in the year. 03120201-02

December 2, 2003. *Kenya.* The U.S. Embassy warned Americans to stay out of downtown Nairobi after receiving information about a potential terrorist attack on two popular hotels—the Stanley Hotel and the Hilton—"within the next several days."

December 2, 2003. *Saudi Arabia.* The U.S. Embassy warned Americans that compounds, including the Seder Village in Riyadh, housing Westerners had been under terrorist surveillance. Saudi intelligence had discovered a surveillance videotape of the Seder Village and a list of other compounds.

December 2, 2003. *United Kingdom.* British police arrested 14 people on suspicion of terrorist offenses in raids in London and other cities. The detainees' names and nationalities were not released.

On December 3, Noureddinne Mouleff, an Algerian, was charged with terrorism and fraud offenses. 03120203

December 2, 2003. *Germany/Netherlands.* Munich authorities arrested an Iraqi planning to send militants to Iraq for suicide attacks against U.S. forces. He was charged with smuggling Iraqis into Germany. He was believed to be a member of Ansar al-Islam, which is linked to al Qaeda.

On the evening of December 6, Dutch security officials at Amsterdam's Schiphol Airport arrested another Iraqi male, age 32, who was attempting to board a plane to Turkey. The German warrant for his arrest said he was charged with forming a criminal organization. Germany requested extradition. He was to appear before a judge at the Haarlem District Court on December 9. 03120204

December 2, 2003. *India.* Militants threw a grenade at the district police headquarters in Kashmir, injuring 18 policemen. No one claimed credit.

December 3, 2003. *Afghanistan.* Two Americans were injured when an attacker threw a grenade at their vehicle in Kandahar. No one claimed credit. 03120301

December 3, 2003. *United States.* The Department of Homeland Security warned that al Qaeda might be planning to use personal items to blow up a plane. British authorities in Gloucester, United Kingdom, found a pair of socks with traces of explosives in them during the arrest of Sajid Badat on November 20. He was charged with conspiracy in the Richard Reid shoe bomber case.

December 4, 2003. *France.* Police arrested Ibon Fernandez Iradi, a suspected Basque Nation and Liberty (ETA) military commander who had escaped from custody a year earlier, in Mont-de-Marsan with two other ETA suspects, including a woman.

December 5, 2003. *Russia.* At 7:40 a.m., a male suicide bomber set off more than 20 pounds of explosives on commuter train Number 6309 some 500 yards away from the station at Yassentuki in the Stavropol region, between Mineralnyye Vody and Kislovodsk near Chechnya. The explosion occurred two days before the national elections. The bomber killed 47 people and injured 155 (20 had serious head wounds). The explosion destroyed the second car of an electric train, throwing passengers and shrapnel through the air. Chechen separatist leader Aslan Maskhadov denied charges that his group was responsible. The terrorist had grenades strapped to his legs; the grenades did not go off. Authorities said he may have had three female accomplices, one of whom was critically injured. The other two jumped from the moving train moments before the explosion.

December 6, 2003. *Iraq.* Terrorists set off a roadside bomb alongside the convoy of L. Paul Bremer, chief U.S. civilian administrator in Iraq, then fired on the vehicles near Baghdad's international airport. The attack was apparently on a target of convenience, rather than a specific assassination attempt. No injuries were reported. 03120601

December 7, 2003. *Saudi Arabia.* The United States issued a warning about the threat of terrorist attacks in the Saudi Kingdom.

December 8, 2003. *Iran.* Two Germans and an Irish tourist who were cycling were kidnapped on the Ram-Zahedan road in Sistan-Baluchestan Province, close to the Pakistani border, an area used by drug smugglers.

December 8, 2003. *Saudi Arabia.* Security forces raided a gas station and killed Ibrahim Mohammed Abdullah Rayes, a Saudi on the list of the country's 26 Most Wanted, all of whom were connected to recent suicide bombings in Riyadh. A second terrorist was also killed in the raid in Riyadh's Sweidi neighborhood.

December 8, 2003. *Venezuela.* French tourist Stephanie Minana, 25, was kidnapped by masked, armed men while visiting her brother in Valera, 240 miles west of Caracas. She was freed by Venezuelan and French police from a jungle camp in the mountains of Trujillo State in the Andrean region of western Venezuela on January 23, 2004, when raiders killed one of her kidnappers and captured two others. Police blamed common criminals.

December 9, 2003. *Iraq.* A suicide car bomber set off his explosives outside a 101st Airborne U.S. Army base in Tall Afar in the north, wounding 58 soldiers and three Iraqis. The bomber killed only himself, apparently because he detonated the explosives prematurely when troops fired on him as he rushed the gate.

December 9, 2003. *Russia.* At 11:00 a.m., a female suicide bomber killed herself and 5 others and wounded 14, including a Chinese citizen, in front of the historic National Hotel in central Moscow opposite the Kremlin and Red Square, and near Parliament. An accomplice apparently escaped. Police evacuated a train station after a bomb scare. She was well-dressed in a tan coat. She said, "Where is the Duma?" and may have set off the 2-pound dynamite bomb accidentally before getting to the Duma. Hotel windows were shattered and a Mercedes Benz was destroyed. Other explosives found near the hotel were destroyed. An undetonated explosive was found on the woman's body. Chechen rebels were suspected. 03120901

December 9, 2003. *Bangladesh.* The State Department warned that it had received terrorist threat information against the U.S. Embassy in Dhaka and warned Americans to be vigilant in places frequented by foreigners.

December 9, 2003. *France.* Police arrested Gorka Palacios Alday, 29, a Basque Nation and Liberty (ETA) military commander wanted for a series of bombings. Three others were arrested with him in a dawn raid in Lons, a small village near the southwestern town of Pau.

December 9, 2003. *United States.* Mohammed Abdullah Warsame (alias Abu Maryam), 30, a Canadian citizen of Somali descent, was arrested as a material witness in Minneapolis. He said he knew Zacarias Moussaoui, the "20th September 11 hijacker." Warsame was under investigation for other possible links to al Qaeda. He attended an al Qaeda training camp in Afghanistan with Moussaoui and lived with him. Warsame is studying computer programming at Minneapolis Community Technical College.

A similar name—Mohamed Warsama—was on a Kenyan business card seized in 1997 from Wadih el-Hage, a Lebanese and naturalized U.S. citizen who worked for several years as bin Laden's private secretary. El-Hage was convicted in 2001 in New York for his role in the August 7, 1998, bombings of U.S. embassies in Kenya and Nairobi.

Warsame was scheduled to have a hearing on December 16 regarding an extradition request from the Southern District of New York. The Warsame case has been sealed.

On January 21, 2004, Warsame was accused in an unsealed federal indictment in Minnesota of one count of conspiring to provide material support to al Qaeda from March 2000 until his arrest. He was represented by the public defender's office. On February 9, he was ordered held without bail after prosecutors said he was a flight risk. He pleaded not guilty to a charge of providing support to a terrorist organization. An FBI affidavit said that he trained in martial arts and with weapons, and taught English to al Qaeda members.

December 10, 2003. *Lebanon.* Authorities prevented a bomb attack against the U.S. Embassy, arresting two men outside the compound. One individual was lugging more than two pounds of explosives. Abed Mreish, a Lebanese man in his 30s, was attempting to enter the embassy when he was stopped at an army checkpoint 500 yards from the complex. He was carrying a bag containing TNT, nitroglycerin, and a detonator. A Palestinian taxi driver was arrested as a possible accomplice.

On December 12, police arrested Mehdi Hasan, a Lebanese man, after he was fingered by the duo as having ordered the bombing. 03121001

December 10, 2003. *Iraq.* A terrorist threw a bomb into a U.S. Army Humvee carrying several U.S. journalists and two U.S. soldiers. Michael Weisskopf, 57, Washington-based senior correspondent for *Time Magazine*, threw the grenade from the vehicle before it exploded, likely saving everyone's lives. Weisskopf was seriously wounded, losing his right hand. He was taken to the local hospital for surgery. Also wounded was James Nachtwey, 55, a *Time* contributing photographer, who was hit by shrapnel. The two soldiers from the 1st Armored Division were also injured. The two journalists were transferred to a U.S. military hospital in Landstuhl, Germany.

December 10, 2003. *India.* Two terrorists threw grenades and open fired at a Kashmir bus stop, killing a policeman and a civilian and wounding six other people. No one claimed credit.

December 12, 2003. *Russia.* Rebels shot to death four Russian soldiers and two police officers.

December 12, 2003. *Iraq.* Terrorists fired on a Beyci restaurant, killing two Turkish truck drivers. No one claimed credit. 03121201

December 13, 2003. *Philippines.* Police arrested American brothers Michael Ray Stubbs and James Stubbs (alias Jamil Daud Mujahid) for possible links to the Moro Islamic Liberation Front (MILF) and the Abu Sayyaf. James is on a U.S. watch list for al Qaeda links. Michael worked as a heating and air conditioning technician at Lawrence Livermore National Laboratory (LLNL) near San Francisco for ten years until 2000. LLNL is a state-run, high-security nuclear and biological research facility. The Islamic men are of Middle Eastern origin and are married to Filipinas. On December 30, the government said it would deport the duo to the United States. Immigration Commissioner Andrea Domingo said that James had met with members of Abu Sayyaf and the MILF. The duo arrived on tourist visas, but their documents indicated they were soliciting funds for the construction of mosques and Muslim schools. James had left his job as a teacher in California to study Arabic in Sudan. He met in May with charity groups that are believed to be al Qaeda fronts.

December 14, 2003. *Pakistan.* Would-be assassins failed to kill Pakistani President General Pervez Musharraf when a remotely detonated C-4 plastique bomb exploded seconds after his motorcade passed over the Lai bridge in Rawalpindi. The limousine's electronic jamming system delayed the trigger. Authorities blamed al Qaeda and the Taliban. No one was hurt. Police later determined that more than a dozen low-ranking air force technicians were involved, placing large quantities of explosives under the bridge.

On March 15, 2004, Musharraf said that a Libyan member of al Qaeda was behind two attempts to kill him. He claimed a Libyan terrorist had paid between $26,100 and $34,000 to a Pakistani to recruit local Islamic radicals to set off the bombs.

On May 27, 2004, three senior Pakistani officials said that Amjad Farooqi, a Pakistani Jaish-i-Mohammed militant with al Qaeda links who was involved in the two failed assassination attempts on December 14 and 25 was also central to the January 2002 kidnap and murder of *Wall Street Journal* reporter Danny Pearl. He helped force Pearl into the kidnap vehicle and was present at the beheading. He was one of seven Pakistanis indicted in the Pearl case; as of May 27, 2004, four had been convicted. The government said that some of the plotters were not motivated by religion, but simply by money. Farroqi recruited the air force technicians from Chaklala Air Base in Rawalpindi with the help of other Islamists, including three clerics. He provided them with the plastique from an al Qaeda supply in Afghanistan.

On August 20, 2004, the *Los Angeles Times* reported that Pakistani officials had offered $350,000 for the arrest of a Libyan al Qaeda leader, Abu Faraj Farj (alias Abu Faraj Libbi, alias Dr. Taufeeq), as the man who gave instructions for the two failed assassination attempts. He was in contact with al Qaeda computer expert Mohammed Naeem Noor Khan, who was captured on July 13. Officials were also offering $85,000 for five Pakistanis and $350,000 for Pakistani suspected Amjad Hussain (alias Amjad Farooqi), believed to have been a leader in the kidnap and murder of Daniel Pearl.

On August 29, 2004, authorities arrested Omar Rehman and two of his relatives in his village home in the North West Frontier Province.

On December 24, 2004, a Pakistani soldier was sentenced to death and another soldier was given ten years in prison in the case. 03121401

December 14, 2003. *Italy.* Police announced the closure of the main road leading to the Vatican every night during the Christmas holidays after warnings of a possible terrorist attack against Christian sites.

December 15, 2003. *Persian Gulf.* The guided-missile destroyer USS *Decatur* stopped a four-foot boat near the Strait of Hormuz and seized two tons of hashish in what was believed to be an al Qaeda smuggling operation.

December 15, 2003. *People's Republic of China.* The Ministry of Public Security issued a list of East Turkestan groups and individuals that the government considers to be terrorist entities: East Turkestan Islamic Movement (ETIM), East Turkestan Liberation Organization (SHAT), World Uighur Youth Congress, and East Turkestan Information Center.

December 17, 2003. *Saudi Arabia.* The United States issued a warning about the threat of terrorist attacks in the Saudi Kingdom, ten days after an initial warning.

December 18, 2003. *Singapore/Malaysia/Indonesia.* Authorities in these three countries announced the arrests of 11 Islamic militants being groomed as the next leaders of Jemaah Islamiah. They were connected to a cell in Pakistan called al Ghuraba (The Foreigners) established in 1999 by Hambali. The Indonesians and Malaysians were among 19 Southeast Asians arrested in September in a sweep by Pakistanis. The Singaporeans were part of a separate group. Most of the detainees studied at Abu Bakar Islamic University or another institution in Karachi.

Singapore said that in October it had arrested al Ghuraba members Muhammad Arif bin Naharudin, 20, and Muhammad Amin bin Mohamed Yunos, 21. The duo had undergone military training in Afghanistan or with a Pakistani militant group.

Indonesian police said they would charge four of the militants, including Rusman Gunawan, the younger brother of al Qaeda and Jemaah Islamiah leader Riduan Isamuddin (alias Hambali) with facilitating terrorism. The group helped Isamuddin in unspecified ways. Gunawan and three others were deported in mid-December from Pakistan to Indonesia. Pakistan had accused the foursome of having links to Jemaah Islamiah. Gunawan allegedly was the leader of al Ghuraba.

Malaysia held five Islamic students connected to Gunawan's cell. The five underwent weapons and explosives training in Afghanistan and in Pakistan and some met Osama bin Laden before the coalition war against Afghanistan began in 2001, according to Malaysian police.

Arif, a Singaporean, trained with Lashkar-i-Taiba, a Pakistan-based group, from 2000 to 2001. His father is a member of the Philippine Moro Islamic Liberation Front. Amin trained in Kandahar, Afganistan. Gunawan learned bomb making and weapons use in Kandahar. His father is a member of Jemaah Islamiah. Indonesian detainee Muhammad Saifuddin received eight months of training in Afghanistan. Three of the five Malaysians are sons of Jemaah Islamiah members. Two of the suspects were released within days of their repatriation to Indonesia.

December 19, 2003. *Syria.* Syria arrested six Arab couriers with links to al Qaeda and seized $23.5 million.

December 19, 2003. *United Arab Emirates.* Al-Jazeera aired an audiotape from Ayman Zawahiri, who said, "America has been defeated (by) our fighters in Afghanistan despite all its military might, its weaponry…. With God's help we are still chasing Americans and their allies everywhere, including their homeland." He issued a warning to Americans, saying, "How can we excuse you after all the warnings that we gave you? You reap what you sow." The CIA said that an audiotape that aired the next day was bin Laden's voice, but was a rerun from a previous broadcast. The CIA also said the Zawahiri broadcast "most likely" was authentic.

December 19, 2003. *Iraq.* Three gunmen in a car fired on a UN building, causing no casualties. No one claimed credit. 03121901

December 21, 2003. *United States.* The Department of Homeland Security raised the threat level to Orange (high risk) after receiving intelligence that al Qaeda was plotting multiple catastrophic attacks in the United States. One plan was to hijack commercial or cargo flights originating overseas.

December 21, 2003. *Italy.* Two small bombs exploded near the Bologna home of Romano Prodi, president of the European Commission. The bombs were made with a cooking pot, gas cylinder, and a timer, and were hidden in trash bins a few feet from his home, which was empty when they went off. The Informal Anarchic Federation (FAI) claimed credit, saying he represented the repressive "new European order."

December 22, 2003. *United Nations.* At U.S. and Saudi request, the Bosnian charity Vazir, a front for the Saudi-based charity al Haramain; its director, Safet Durguti; and Hochburg AG based in Vaduz, Liechtenstein, were added to the UN's list of terrorist financiers whose assets could be frozen. Al Haramain was designated a terrorist financier in March 2002. Terrorist supporter Yousef Nada has a controlling interest in Hochburg AG. Individuals on the list are under an international travel ban.

December 24, 2003. *Spain.* Police arrested two Basque Nation and Liberty (ETA) terrorists planning to set off two powerful bombs on a train at a Madrid station. The duo was arrested in towns in the Basque region. One was picked up in San Sebastian, carrying a 55-pound bomb in a suitcase. Police then found a second suspect who had placed another 55-pound bomb on a train traveling from San Sebastian to Madrid. The train was stopped in northern Burgos. After the train was evacuated, police defused the bomb, which was set to exploded at 4:00 p.m., when Madrid's Chamartin Station would have been packed with travelers. On December 25, police said that the suspects also planned to attack a rail line in Zaragoza Province in northeastern Spain on Christmas Eve. The explosion occurred a day too early and caused limited damage without disrupting rail traffic.

The duo was identified as Gorka Loran, 25, and Garikoitz Arruarte, 24.

December 24, 2003. *France.* Air France canceled three round-trip flights from Paris to Los Angeles based on intelligence indicating terrorist plans to hijack a plane and crash it into a facility in California, Las Vegas, New York, or Washington, D.C. Paris police questioned 13 people who had checked in for two of the Air France flights but released them for lack of evidence.

On December 25, U.S. government officials said some of the no-shows on three of the canceled flights might have intended to hijack the plane and crash it into Las Vegas. American officials gave French authorities a list of names of suspect travelers. Of particular concern was Air France flight 68 from Charles De Gaulle Airport; one of the no-shows was a trained pilot. Police questioned seven police, including four Americans, a German, a Belgian, and a French citizen. Six people on flight 70 were questioned.

Air France resumed flights on December 26.

December 24, 2003. *United States.* U.S. officials ordered the emergency installation in California of more Biowatch sensors that could detect airborne biological pathogens.

Los Angeles International Airport banned curbside dropoffs and pickups for the next two weeks.

December 25, 2003. *Afghanistan.* A bomb exploded outside a Kabul house for UN staffers, destroying a wall around the property and shattering nearby windows. No injuries were reported. 03122501

December 25, 2003. *Thailand/Vietnam.* Judge Pairath Noonprade of the Rayong Provincial Court in Rayong, Thailand, reduced the sentenced of Ly Tong, a Vietnamese American pilot, to 7 years and 4 months from 11 years for hijacking a small plane in Thailand and flying illegally over Vietnam to scatter anticommunist leaflets. The judge said he was rewarding the cooperation of the former bomber pilot in South Vietnam's air force.

December 25, 2003. *Pakistan.* Three pickup truck-driving suicide bombers killed 15 people and wounded 46 in a failed attempt to assassinate Pakistani President General Pervez Musharraf,

60. The duo drove their Suzuki pickups into his motorcade in Rawalpindi. Among the dead were four military policemen. Apparently the trucks could not keep up with the 80 mph motorcade and crashed into the rear of it without getting near Musharraf's Mercedes. The attack occurred 500 yards from the bridge where a bomb had been remotely detonated on December 14, seconds after Musharraf's motorcycle passed by. Witnesses said two clean-shaven Pakistani men in their mid-20s waited at separate gas stations on the limousine's route from Islamabad to Musharraf's Rawalpindi residence. Both trucks contained 75 pounds of C-4 plastic explosive, the same type as that used on December 14.

On December 26, officials said that one of three suicide terrorists was a foreigner—either an Afghan or an Arab—based upon the discovery of part of an attacker's face found in the rubble. Police retrieved an ID card that showed the terrorist grew up in Pakistani-held Kashmir; he was once associated with Harkat ul-Ansar and later a Jaish-i-Muhammad faction. He trained in Afghanistan during the 1990s and joined with the Taliban against U.S. forces in late 2001. Afghan troops arrested and imprisoned him near Kabul, but he was eventually returned to Pakistan, where he was freed in September 2003.

On January 3, 2004, in an early morning raid on a Lahore mosque, Pakistani security officials arrested six members of Jaish-i-Muhammad in connection with the two attacks in Musharraf. By January 13, investigators using call records from a memory chip found in the debris further linked Jaish-i-Muhammad and Lashkar-e-Jhangvi to the attacks, leading to the arrests of 40 people, including members of the two groups. On May 27, 2004, the government said that the terrorists were tipped off on the movements of Musharraf's motorcade by a police official assigned to Rawalpindi's Civil Lines police station. 03122502

December 25, 2003. *Israel.* At 6:20 p.m., a Palestinian suicide bomber killed himself and 4 Israelis, including 3 uniformed soldiers and a civilian, and injured at least 15, including 1 Palestinian, at a bus stop in Bnei Brak, a Tel Aviv suburb. The terrorist walked up to a group of people at one of several bus stops at a major highway interchange. He was carrying a small bag and wearing a dark coat. The bomb included metal fragments. The Popular Front for the Liberation of Palestine (PFLP) claimed credit, saying it was retaliating for Israeli military forces killing two PFLP members in Nablus earlier in the week. The group said the bomber was Saed Hanani, 18, who had lived in Nablus. Police said he was related to one of the dead PFLP members.

December 25, 2003. *Israel.* Israeli helicopter gunships fired on a car in the Saftawi neighborhood of Gaza City, killing six people, including Mokled Humaid, Islamic Jihad's military leader, who was planning a massive attack in Israel.

December 27, 2003. *Italy.* A letterbomb exploded when it was opened by Romano Prodi, president of the European Commission, at his Bologna home. The package contained a book packed with explosive powder and burst into flame, burning furniture and carpet. He was not harmed. The book was *The Pleasure,* a novel by Gabriele D'Annunzio, a Fascist who died in 1938. The Informal Anarchic Federation (FAI) was suspected. The package was addressed to his wife. The return address was a nonexistent location in Bologna. He lives in Brussels, but was spending Christmas in his home town of Bologna.

December 27, 2003. *Iraq.* Four coordinated suicide car bombings in Karbala killed 6 soldiers from Bulgaria and Thailand and 7 Iraqis and injured more than 100 people. At least 80 Iraqis were among the injured, including Karbala Mayor Akram Yassiri. Five American soldiers were also injured. Soldiers fired on the trucks before they could get closer to the base. A Polish military spokesman said 25 troops were injured, but U.S. Army Brig. Gen. Mark Kimmitt said it was 37.

December 29, 2003. *Netherlands.* Police intercepted and defused a letter bomb sent to the director of Europol, an international police agency based in The Hague. No one was injured. Police believed it was linked to the earlier letter bomb attack in Bologna against Romano Prodi, president of the European Commission. 03122901

December 29, 2003. *Germany.* An explosive was sent to the Frankfurt office of the European Central Bank president, Jean-Claude Trichet. The letter was postmarked from Bologna, scene of earlier letter bombs. 03122902

December 29, 2003. *Burundi.* Local officials blamed the National Liberation Forces, a Hutu rebel group, for shooting to death papal nuncio Archbishop Michael Courtney, 58, in an attack near Minago, 25 miles south of Bujumbura. The Irish priest was shot three times—behind the right ear, in the thorax, and in the right leg—and died while undergoing surgery. He was traveling in a diplomatic car that flew the Vatican flag. The Burundian occupants of the vehicle were not harmed. He had been returning from a funeral for a priest in Minago. He had lived in the country for three years and was scheduled to leave for Cuba within the month. The group denied responsibility. 03122903

December 29, 2003. *Saudi Arabia.* A bomb went off, apparently intended to kill a senior official of the Interior Ministry's Mabahith branch. No one was injured in the Riyadh blast.

December 29, 2003. *Iraq.* Gunmen fired on a vehicle in Baghdad's Mahmudia neighborhood, killing a British engineer and two Iraqi sentries. No one claimed credit. 03122904

December 30, 2003. *Saudi Arabia.* Mansour Mohammed Ahmed Faqih, a terrorist suspect, surrendered to authorities. He was 14th on a list of 26 wanted terrorists.

December 30, 2003. *Germany.* German officials sealed a 300-bed military hospital in Hamburg that had treated U.S. soldiers after receiving a tip from U.S. intelligence that Ansar al-Islam was planning a car bomb attack.

December 30, 2003. *Netherlands.* A parcel bomb was found at The Hague headquarters of Eurojust, a European Union law enforcement agency that coordinates investigations of organized crime. The book-size package contained explosives. A Dutch bomb squad deactivated it. 03123001

December 30, 2003. *Colombia.* More than 500 members of the Revolutionary Armed Forces of Colombia (FARC) and the National Liberation Army (ELN) attacked the village of Pozo Azul, in Bolivar State, firing homemade mortars and burning vehicles. The village was controlled by outlawed paramilitary forces. Some 39 militia fighters and a female villager were killed in the battle. The rebels also attacked the villages of Monterrey and Pueblo; no deaths were initially reported. The two sides were competing for control of the local drug trade.

December 30, 2003. *India.* Hizbul-Mujahedin claimed credit for setting off a bomb against a bus carrying Indian troops, killing 4 people and injuring 33 soldiers and 1 woman.

December 31, 2003. *Iraq.* A car bomber left his vehicle outside Nabil's Restaurant in Baghdad's upscale Arasat neighborhood and set it off remotely (or perhaps with a timer), killing 8 people and injuring 35 Iraqis and Westerners celebrating New Year's Eve. Among them were three American journalists who worked for the *Los Angeles Times*—Chris Kraul, Tracy Wilkinson, and Ann M. Simmons—hit by flying glass. Also hurt was Mohammed Arrawi, technical director of the *Los Angeles Times* bureau in Baghdad. Authorities speculated that the attackers could have been Islamic fundamentalists offended by the serving of alcohol at the restaurant. No one claimed credit. 03123101